Jaime Hernandez

The GIRL from H.O.P.P.E.R.S.

A LOVE AND ROCKETS BOOK

FANTAGRAPHICS BOOKS

The GIRL from H.O.P.P.E.R.S.

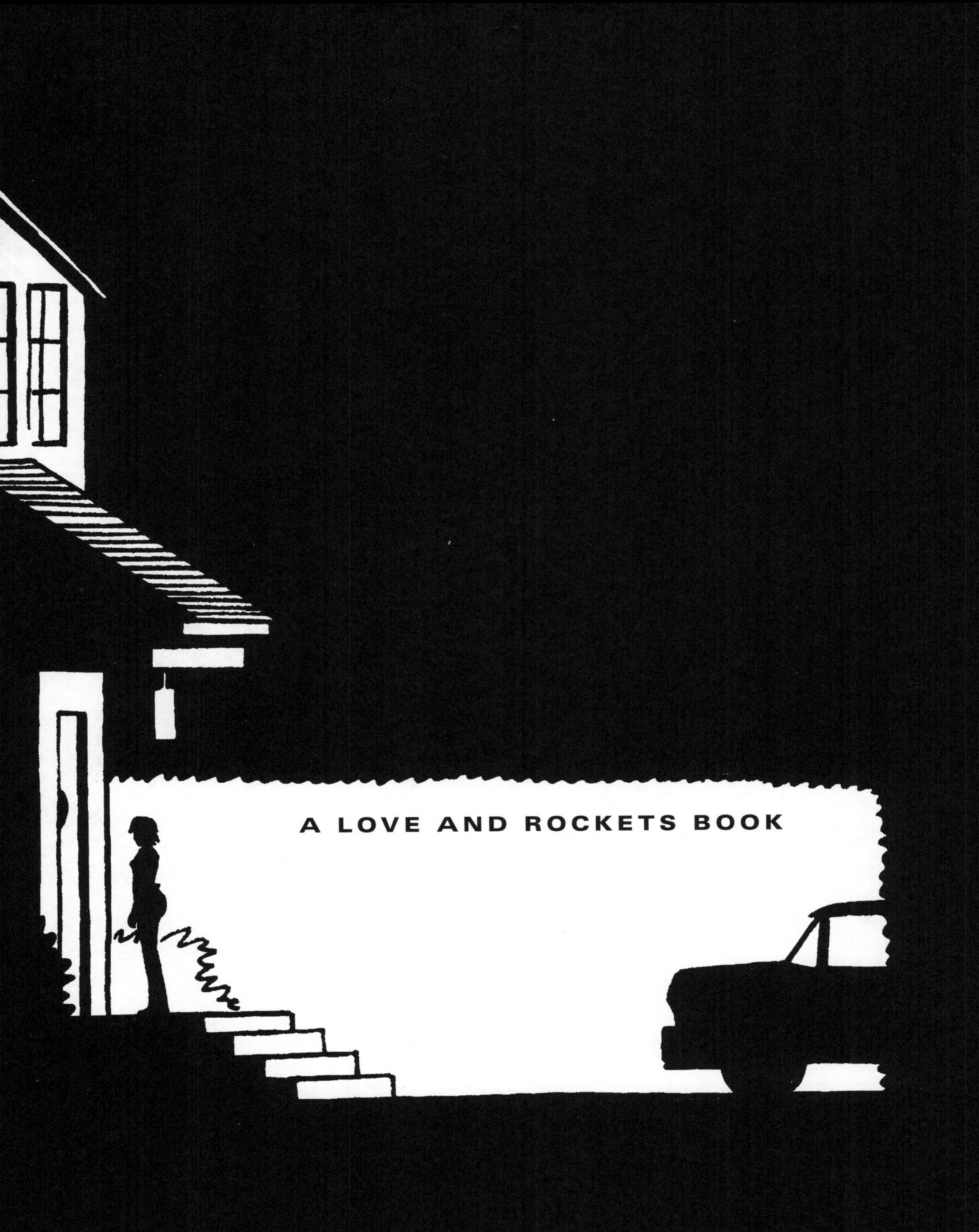
A LOVE AND ROCKETS BOOK

THE GIRL FROM H.O.P.P.E.R.S.

THE LOVE AND ROCKETS LIBRARY VOL. 3

Fantagraphics Books

7563 Lake City Way NE

Seattle WA 98115

Visit the Fantagraphics website

at www.fantagraphics.com

Edited by Kim Thompson

Original series edited by Gary Groth

Design and art direction by Jacob Covey

Production by Paul Baresh

Associate Publisher: Eric Reynolds

Publisher: Gary Groth

First edition: July 2007

Second edition: April 2012

Third edition: August 2014

Fourth edition: September 2018

Fifth edition: December 2020

ISBN: 978-1-56097-851-0

Printed in China

These stories were originally published in *Love and Rockets*

Vol. 1 #13–32 and *The Complete Love and Rockets Vol. 5:*

House of Raging Women.

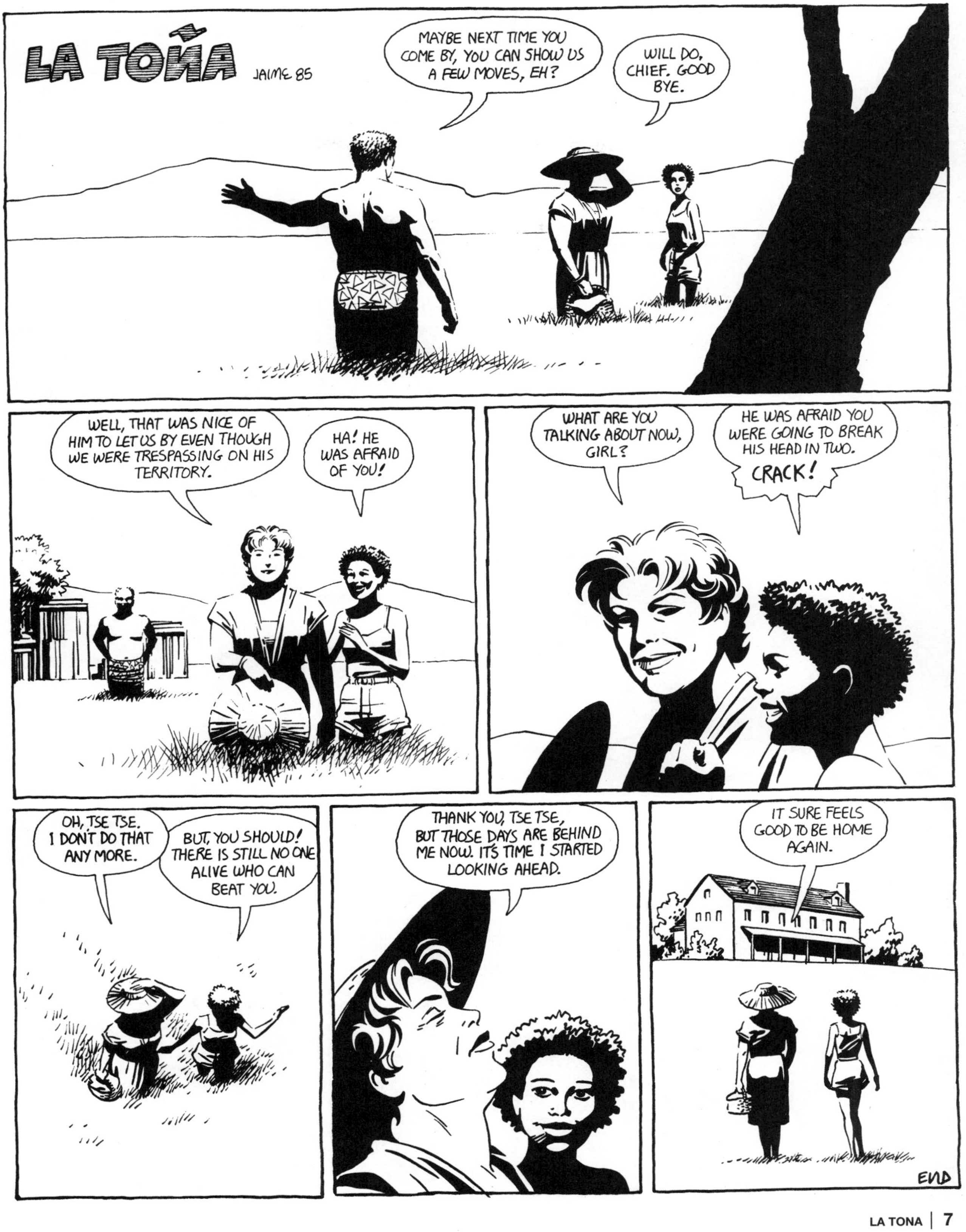

LA TOÑA
JAIME 85
MAYBE NEXT TIME YOU COME BY, YOU CAN SHOW US A FEW MOVES, EH?
WILL DO, CHIEF. GOOD BYE.
WELL, THAT WAS NICE OF HIM TO LET US BY EVEN THOUGH WE WERE TRESPASSING ON HIS TERRITORY.
HA! HE WAS AFRAID OF YOU!
WHAT ARE YOU TALKING ABOUT NOW, GIRL?
HE WAS AFRAID YOU WERE GOING TO BREAK HIS HEAD IN TWO.
CRACK!
OH, TSE TSE. I DON'T DO THAT ANY MORE.
BUT, YOU SHOULD! THERE IS STILL NO ONE ALIVE WHO CAN BEAT YOU.
THANK YOU, TSE TSE, BUT THOSE DAYS ARE BEHIND ME NOW. IT'S TIME I STARTED LOOKING AHEAD.
IT SURE FEELS GOOD TO BE HOME AGAIN.
END

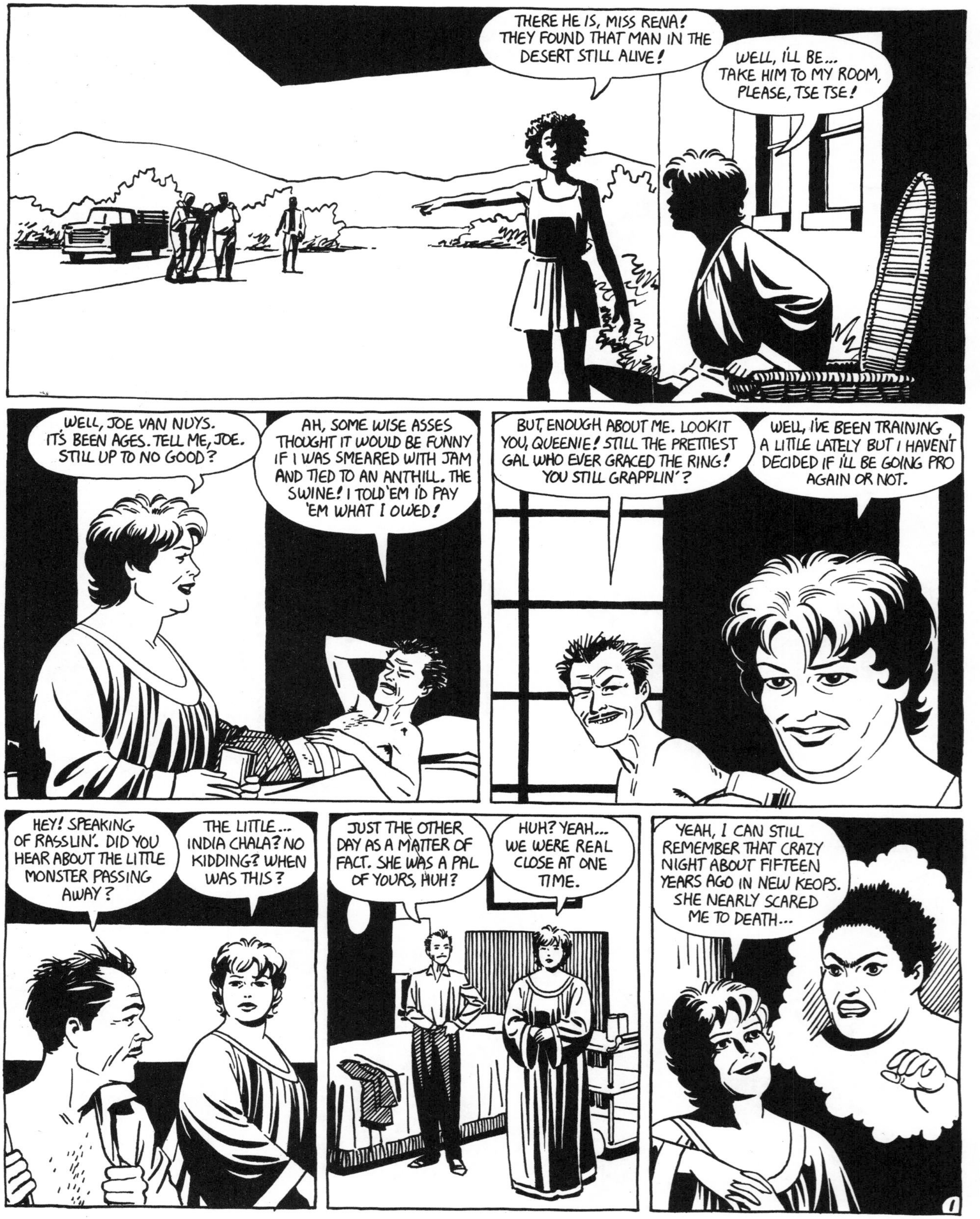
THERE HE IS, MISS RENA! THEY FOUND THAT MAN IN THE DESERT STILL ALIVE!
WELL, I'LL BE... TAKE HIM TO MY ROOM, PLEASE, TSE TSE!
WELL, JOE VAN NUYS. IT'S BEEN AGES. TELL ME, JOE. STILL UP TO NO GOOD?
AH, SOME WISE ASSES THOUGHT IT WOULD BE FUNNY IF I WAS SMEARED WITH JAM AND TIED TO AN ANTHILL. THE SWINE! I TOLD 'EM I'D PAY 'EM WHAT I OWED!
BUT, ENOUGH ABOUT ME. LOOKIT YOU, QUEENIE! STILL THE PRETTIEST GAL WHO EVER GRACED THE RING! YOU STILL GRAPPLIN'?
WELL, I'VE BEEN TRAINING A LITTLE LATELY BUT I HAVEN'T DECIDED IF I'LL BE GOING PRO AGAIN OR NOT.
HEY! SPEAKING OF RASSLIN'. DID YOU HEAR ABOUT THE LITTLE MONSTER PASSING AWAY?
THE LITTLE... INDIA CHALA? NO KIDDING? WHEN WAS THIS?
JUST THE OTHER DAY AS A MATTER OF FACT. SHE WAS A PAL OF YOURS, HUH?
HUH? YEAH... WE WERE REAL CLOSE AT ONE TIME.
YEAH, I CAN STILL REMEMBER THAT CRAZY NIGHT ABOUT FIFTEEN YEARS AGO IN NEW KEOPS. SHE NEARLY SCARED ME TO DEATH...
1

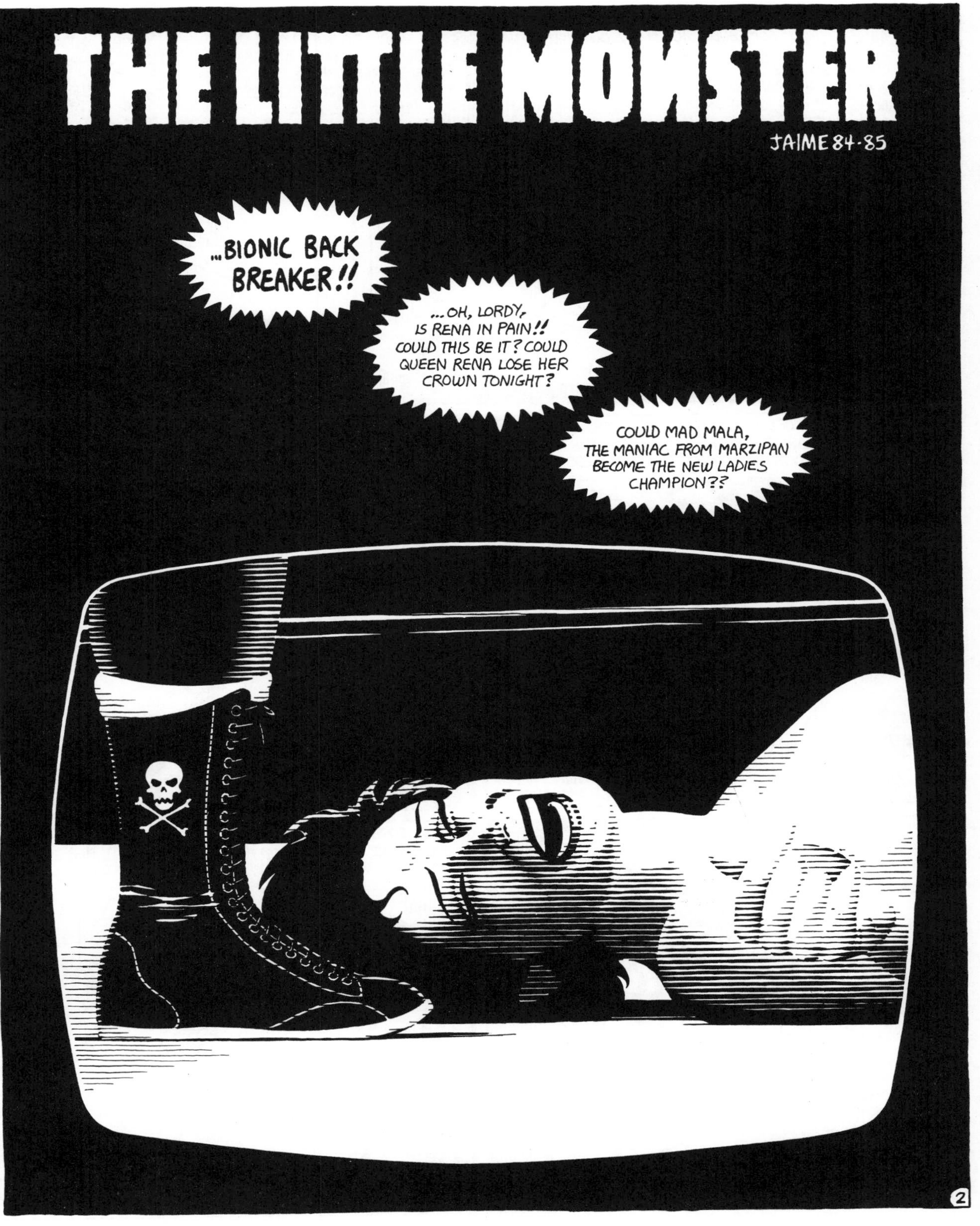
THE LITTLE MONSTER
JAIME 84-85
...BIONIC BACK BREAKER!!
...OH, LORDY, IS RENA IN PAIN!! COULD THIS BE IT? COULD QUEEN RENA LOSE HER CROWN TONIGHT?
COULD MAD MALA, THE MANIAC FROM MARZIPAN BECOME THE NEW LADIES CHAMPION??
2

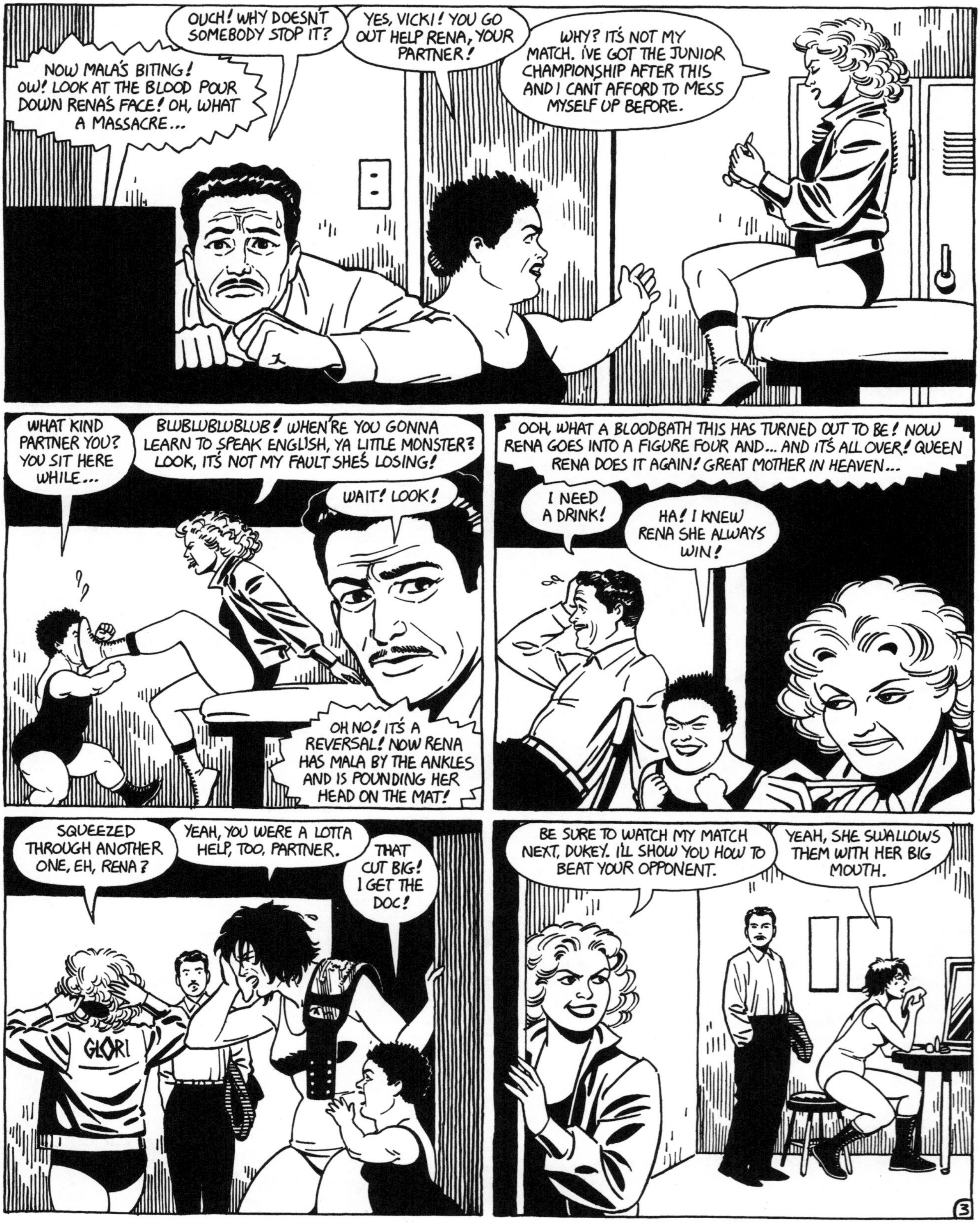
NOW MALA'S BITING! OW! LOOK AT THE BLOOD POUR DOWN RENA'S FACE! OH, WHAT A MASSACRE...
OUCH! WHY DOESN'T SOMEBODY STOP IT?
YES, VICKI! YOU GO OUT HELP RENA, YOUR PARTNER!
WHY? IT'S NOT MY MATCH. I'VE GOT THE JUNIOR CHAMPIONSHIP AFTER THIS AND I CAN'T AFFORD TO MESS MYSELF UP BEFORE.
WHAT KIND PARTNER YOU? YOU SIT HERE WHILE...
BLUBLUBLUBLUB! WHEN'RE YOU GONNA LEARN TO SPEAK ENGLISH, YA LITTLE MONSTER? LOOK, IT'S NOT MY FAULT SHE'S LOSING!
WAIT! LOOK!
OH NO! IT'S A REVERSAL! NOW RENA HAS MALA BY THE ANKLES AND IS POUNDING HER HEAD ON THE MAT!
OOH, WHAT A BLOODBATH THIS HAS TURNED OUT TO BE! NOW RENA GOES INTO A FIGURE FOUR AND... AND IT'S ALL OVER! QUEEN RENA DOES IT AGAIN! GREAT MOTHER IN HEAVEN...
I NEED A DRINK!
HA! I KNEW RENA SHE ALWAYS WIN!
SQUEEZED THROUGH ANOTHER ONE, EH, RENA?
YEAH, YOU WERE A LOTTA HELP, TOO, PARTNER.
THAT CUT BIG! I GET THE DOC!
GLORI
BE SURE TO WATCH MY MATCH NEXT, DUKEY. I'LL SHOW YOU HOW TO BEAT YOUR OPPONENT.
YEAH, SHE SWALLOWS THEM WITH HER BIG MOUTH.
3

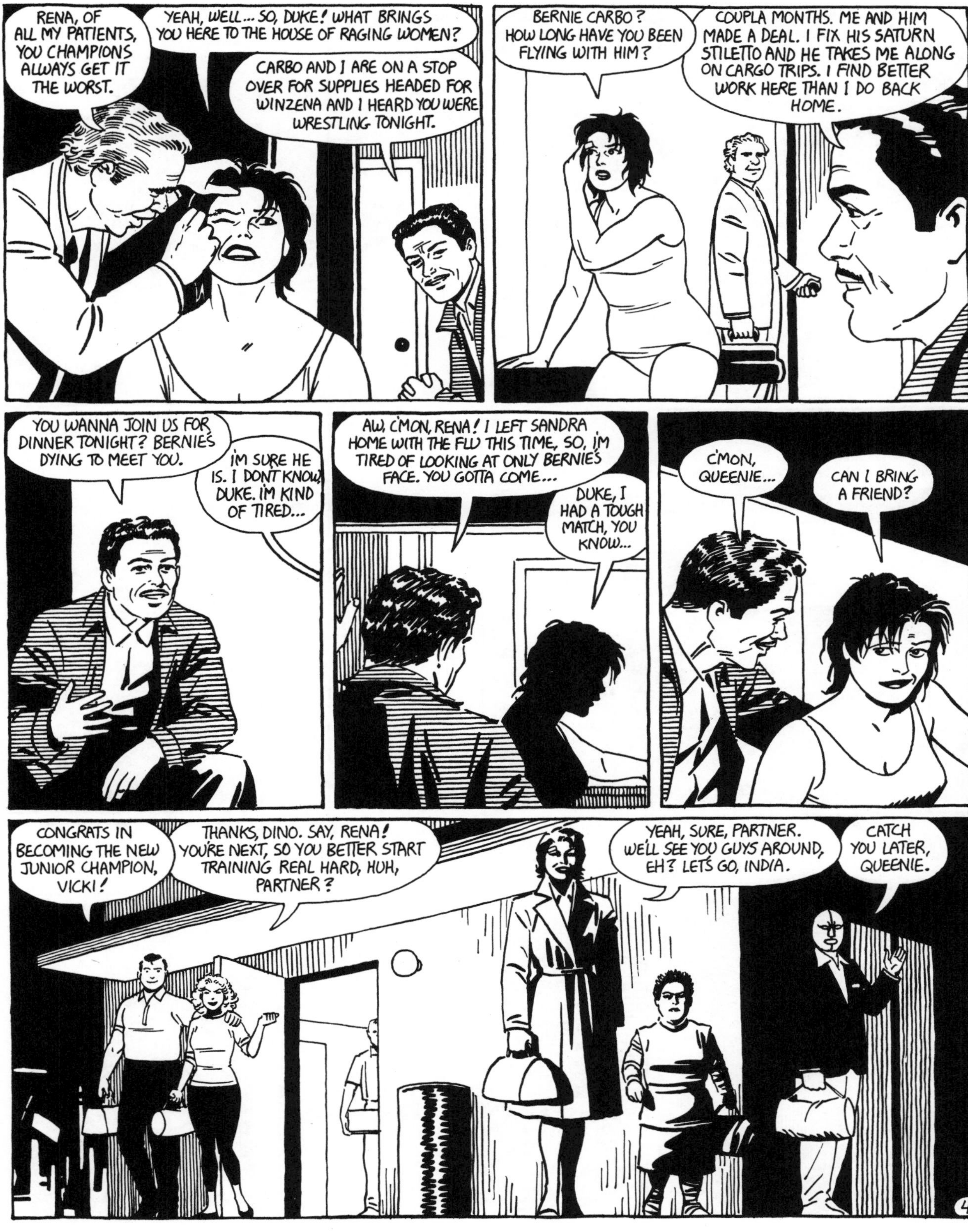
RENA, OF ALL MY PATIENTS, YOU CHAMPIONS ALWAYS GET IT THE WORST.
YEAH, WELL... SO, DUKE! WHAT BRINGS YOU HERE TO THE HOUSE OF RAGING WOMEN?
CARBO AND I ARE ON A STOP OVER FOR SUPPLIES HEADED FOR WINZENA AND I HEARD YOU WERE WRESTLING TONIGHT.
BERNIE CARBO? HOW LONG HAVE YOU BEEN FLYING WITH HIM?
COUPLA MONTHS. ME AND HIM MADE A DEAL. I FIX HIS SATURN STILETTO AND HE TAKES ME ALONG ON CARGO TRIPS. I FIND BETTER WORK HERE THAN I DO BACK HOME.
YOU WANNA JOIN US FOR DINNER TONIGHT? BERNIE'S DYING TO MEET YOU.
I'M SURE HE IS. I DON'T KNOW, DUKE. I'M KIND OF TIRED...
AW, C'MON, RENA! I LEFT SANDRA HOME WITH THE FLU THIS TIME, SO, I'M TIRED OF LOOKING AT ONLY BERNIE'S FACE. YOU GOTTA COME...
DUKE, I HAD A TOUGH MATCH, YOU KNOW...
C'MON, QUEENIE...
CAN I BRING A FRIEND?
CONGRATS IN BECOMING THE NEW JUNIOR CHAMPION, VICKI!
THANKS, DINO. SAY, RENA! YOU'RE NEXT, SO YOU BETTER START TRAINING REAL HARD, HUH, PARTNER?
YEAH, SURE, PARTNER. WE'LL SEE YOU GUYS AROUND, EH? LET'S GO, INDIA.
CATCH YOU LATER, QUEENIE.
4

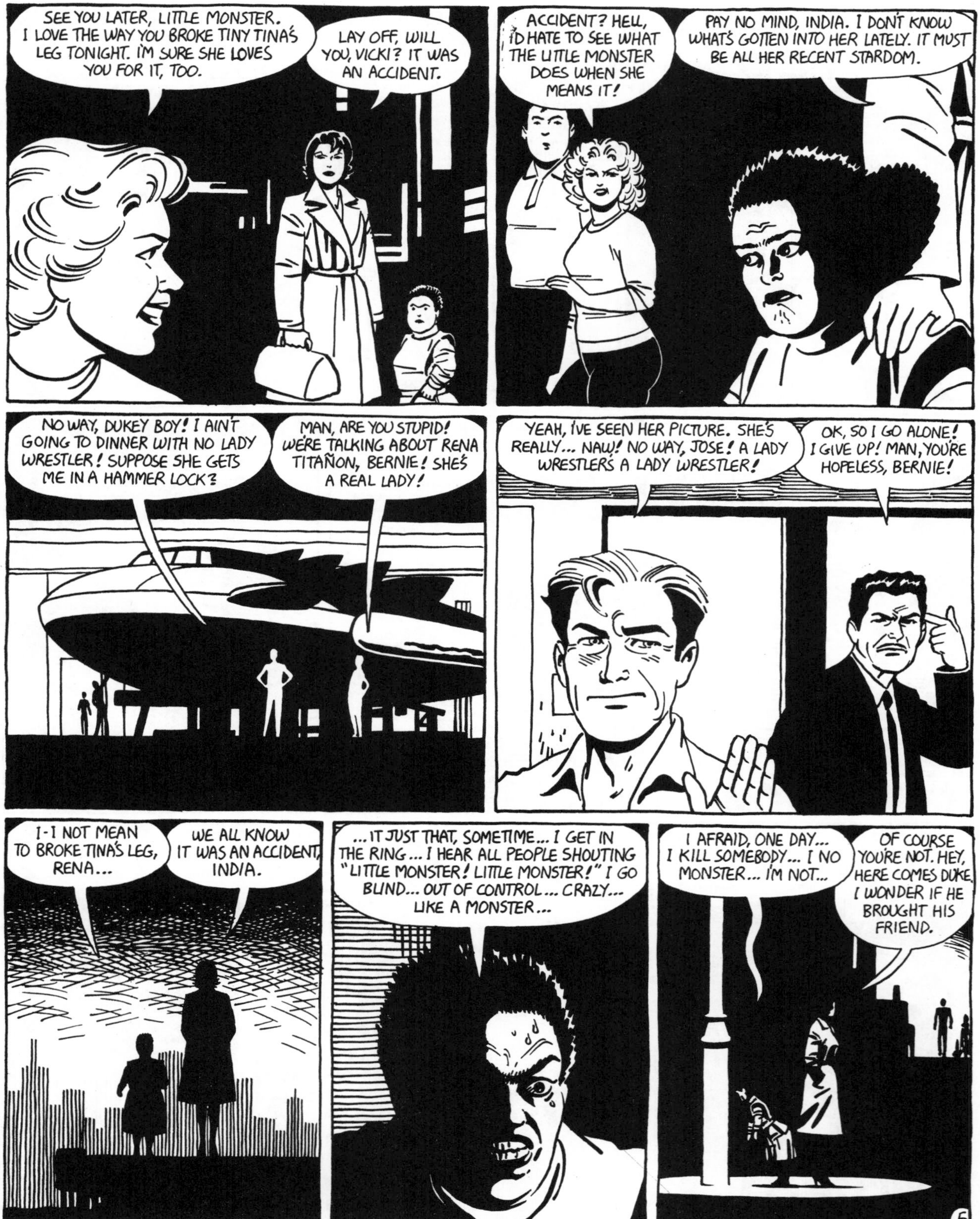
SEE YOU LATER, LITTLE MONSTER. I LOVE THE WAY YOU BROKE TINY TINA'S LEG TONIGHT. I'M SURE SHE LOVES YOU FOR IT, TOO.
LAY OFF, WILL YOU, VICKI? IT WAS AN ACCIDENT.
ACCIDENT? HELL, I'D HATE TO SEE WHAT THE LITTLE MONSTER DOES WHEN SHE MEANS IT!
PAY NO MIND, INDIA. I DON'T KNOW WHAT'S GOTTEN INTO HER LATELY. IT MUST BE ALL HER RECENT STARDOM.
NO WAY, DUKEY BOY! I AIN'T GOING TO DINNER WITH NO LADY WRESTLER! SUPPOSE SHE GETS ME IN A HAMMER LOCK?
MAN, ARE YOU STUPID! WE'RE TALKING ABOUT RENA TITAÑON, BERNIE! SHE'S A REAL LADY!
YEAH, I'VE SEEN HER PICTURE. SHE'S REALLY... NAW! NO WAY, JOSE! A LADY WRESTLER'S A LADY WRESTLER!
OK, SO I GO ALONE! I GIVE UP! MAN, YOU'RE HOPELESS, BERNIE!
I-I NOT MEAN TO BROKE TINA'S LEG, RENA...
WE ALL KNOW IT WAS AN ACCIDENT, INDIA.
...IT JUST THAT, SOMETIME... I GET IN THE RING... I HEAR ALL PEOPLE SHOUTING "LITTLE MONSTER! LITTLE MONSTER!" I GO BLIND... OUT OF CONTROL... CRAZY... LIKE A MONSTER...
I AFRAID, ONE DAY... I KILL SOMEBODY... I NO MONSTER... I'M NOT...
OF COURSE YOU'RE NOT. HEY, HERE COMES DUKE. I WONDER IF HE BROUGHT HIS FRIEND.
5

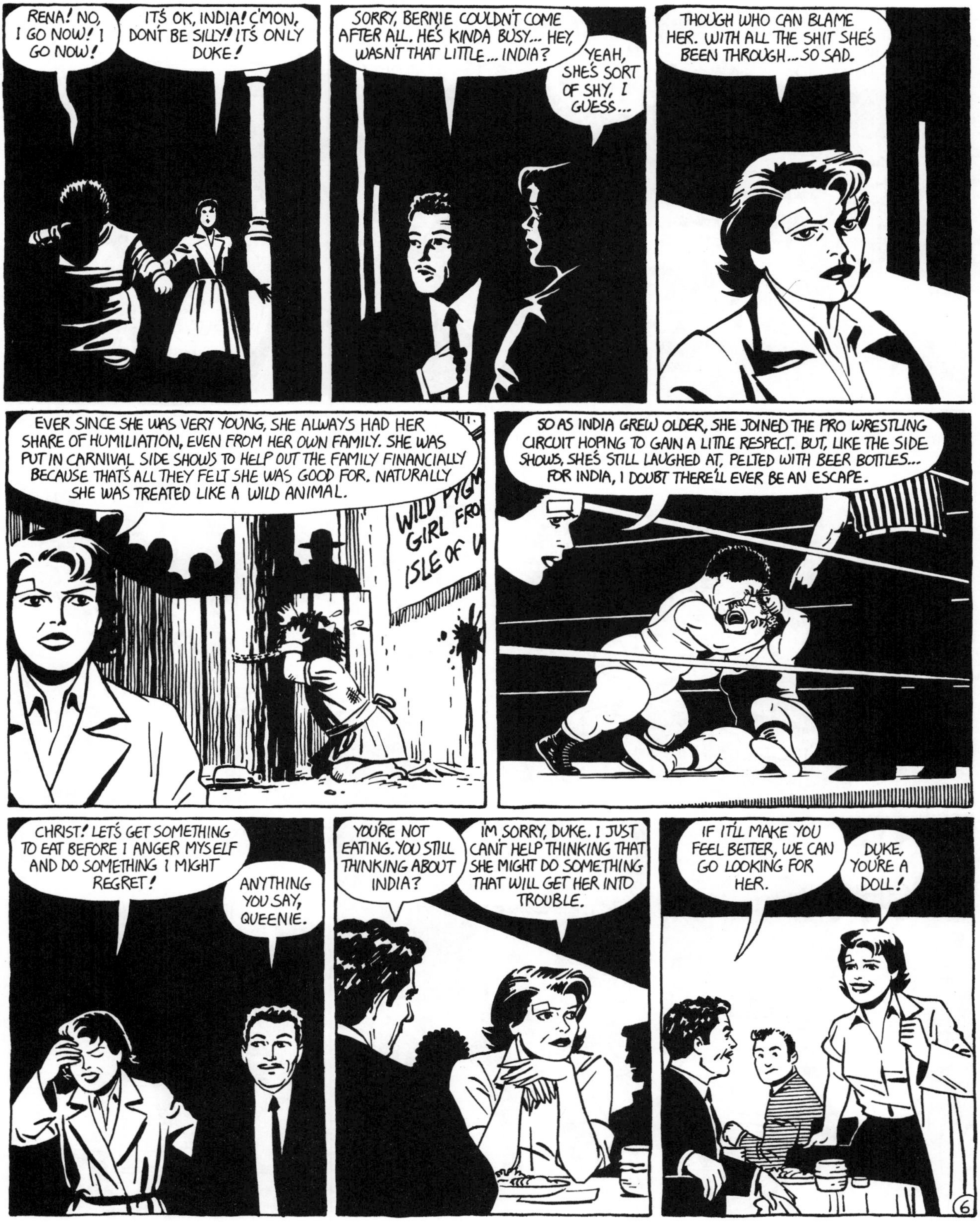
RENA! NO, I GO NOW! I GO NOW!
IT'S OK, INDIA! C'MON, DON'T BE SILLY! IT'S ONLY DUKE!
SORRY, BERNIE COULDN'T COME AFTER ALL. HE'S KINDA BUSY... HEY, WASN'T THAT LITTLE... INDIA?
YEAH, SHE'S SORT OF SHY, I GUESS...
THOUGH WHO CAN BLAME HER. WITH ALL THE SHIT SHE'S BEEN THROUGH... SO SAD.
EVER SINCE SHE WAS VERY YOUNG, SHE ALWAYS HAD HER SHARE OF HUMILIATION, EVEN FROM HER OWN FAMILY. SHE WAS PUT IN CARNIVAL SIDE SHOWS TO HELP OUT THE FAMILY FINANCIALLY BECAUSE THAT'S ALL THEY FELT SHE WAS GOOD FOR. NATURALLY SHE WAS TREATED LIKE A WILD ANIMAL.
WILD PYGM
GIRL FRO
ISLE OF
SO AS INDIA GREW OLDER, SHE JOINED THE PRO WRESTLING CIRCUIT HOPING TO GAIN A LITTLE RESPECT. BUT, LIKE THE SIDE SHOWS, SHE'S STILL LAUGHED AT, PELTED WITH BEER BOTTLES... FOR INDIA, I DOUBT THERE'LL EVER BE AN ESCAPE.
CHRIST! LET'S GET SOMETHING TO EAT BEFORE I ANGER MYSELF AND DO SOMETHING I MIGHT REGRET!
ANYTHING YOU SAY, QUEENIE.
YOU'RE NOT EATING. YOU STILL THINKING ABOUT INDIA?
I'M SORRY, DUKE. I JUST CAN'T HELP THINKING THAT SHE MIGHT DO SOMETHING THAT WILL GET HER INTO TROUBLE.
IF IT'LL MAKE YOU FEEL BETTER, WE CAN GO LOOKING FOR HER.
DUKE, YOU'RE A DOLL!
6

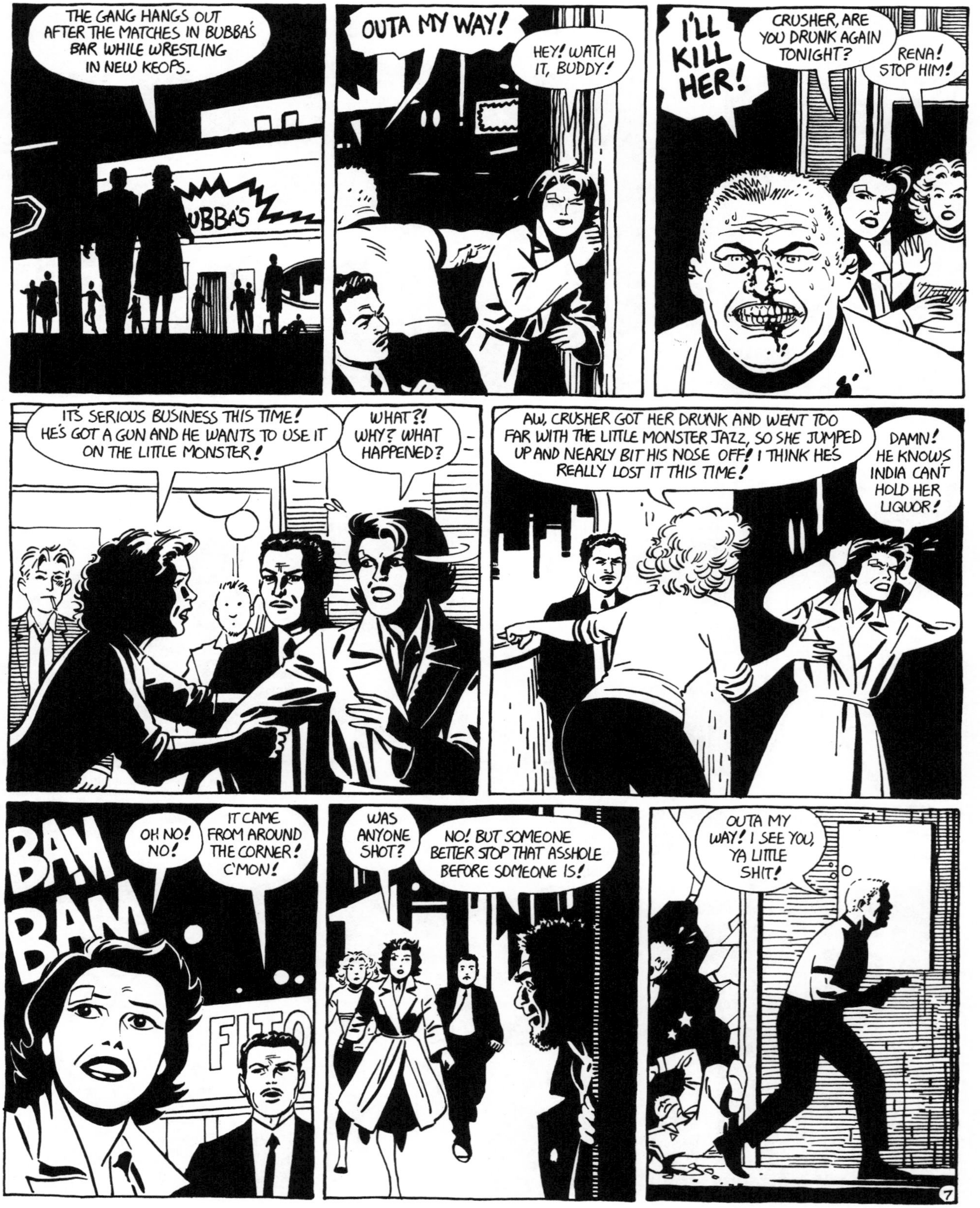
THE GANG HANGS OUT AFTER THE MATCHES IN BUBBA'S BAR WHILE WRESTLING IN NEW KEOPS.
UBBA'S
OUTA MY WAY!
HEY! WATCH IT, BUDDY!
I'LL KILL HER!
CRUSHER, ARE YOU DRUNK AGAIN TONIGHT?
RENA! STOP HIM!
IT'S SERIOUS BUSINESS THIS TIME! HE'S GOT A GUN AND HE WANTS TO USE IT ON THE LITTLE MONSTER!
WHAT?! WHY? WHAT HAPPENED?
AW, CRUSHER GOT HER DRUNK AND WENT TOO FAR WITH THE LITTLE MONSTER JAZZ, SO SHE JUMPED UP AND NEARLY BIT HIS NOSE OFF! I THINK HE'S REALLY LOST IT THIS TIME!
DAMN! HE KNOWS INDIA CAN'T HOLD HER LIQUOR!
BAM BAM
OH NO! NO!
IT CAME FROM AROUND THE CORNER! C'MON!
FITO
WAS ANYONE SHOT?
NO! BUT SOMEONE BETTER STOP THAT ASSHOLE BEFORE SOMEONE IS!
OUTA MY WAY! I SEE YOU, YA LITTLE SHIT!
7

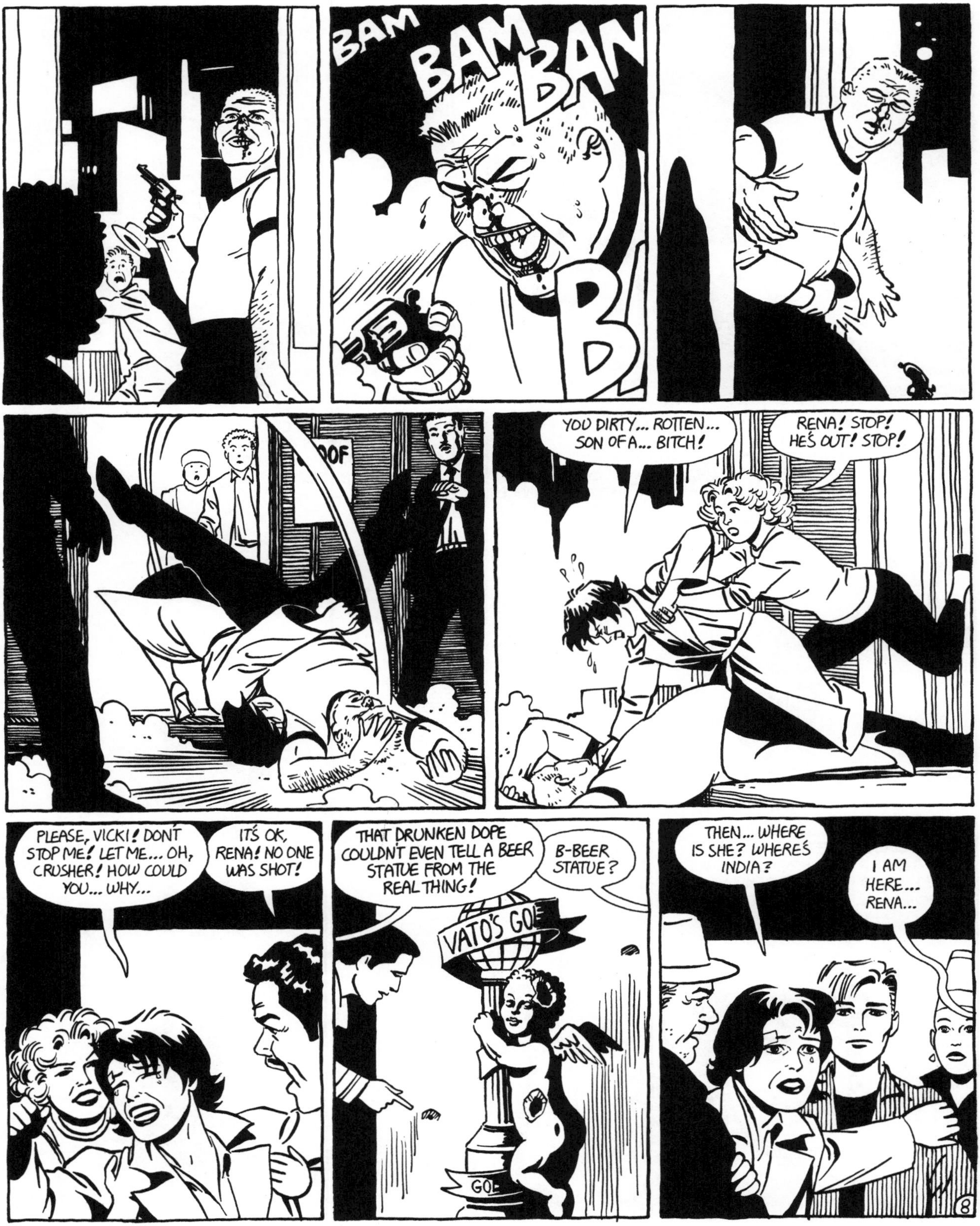
BAM
BAM
BAN
B
OOF
YOU DIRTY... ROTTEN... SON OF A... BITCH!
RENA! STOP! HE'S OUT! STOP!
PLEASE, VICKI! DON'T STOP ME! LET ME... OH, CRUSHER! HOW COULD YOU... WHY...
IT'S OK, RENA! NO ONE WAS SHOT!
THAT DRUNKEN DOPE COULDN'T EVEN TELL A BEER STATUE FROM THE REAL THING!
B-BEER STATUE?
VATO'S GO
GO
THEN... WHERE IS SHE? WHERE'S INDIA?
I AM HERE... RENA...
8

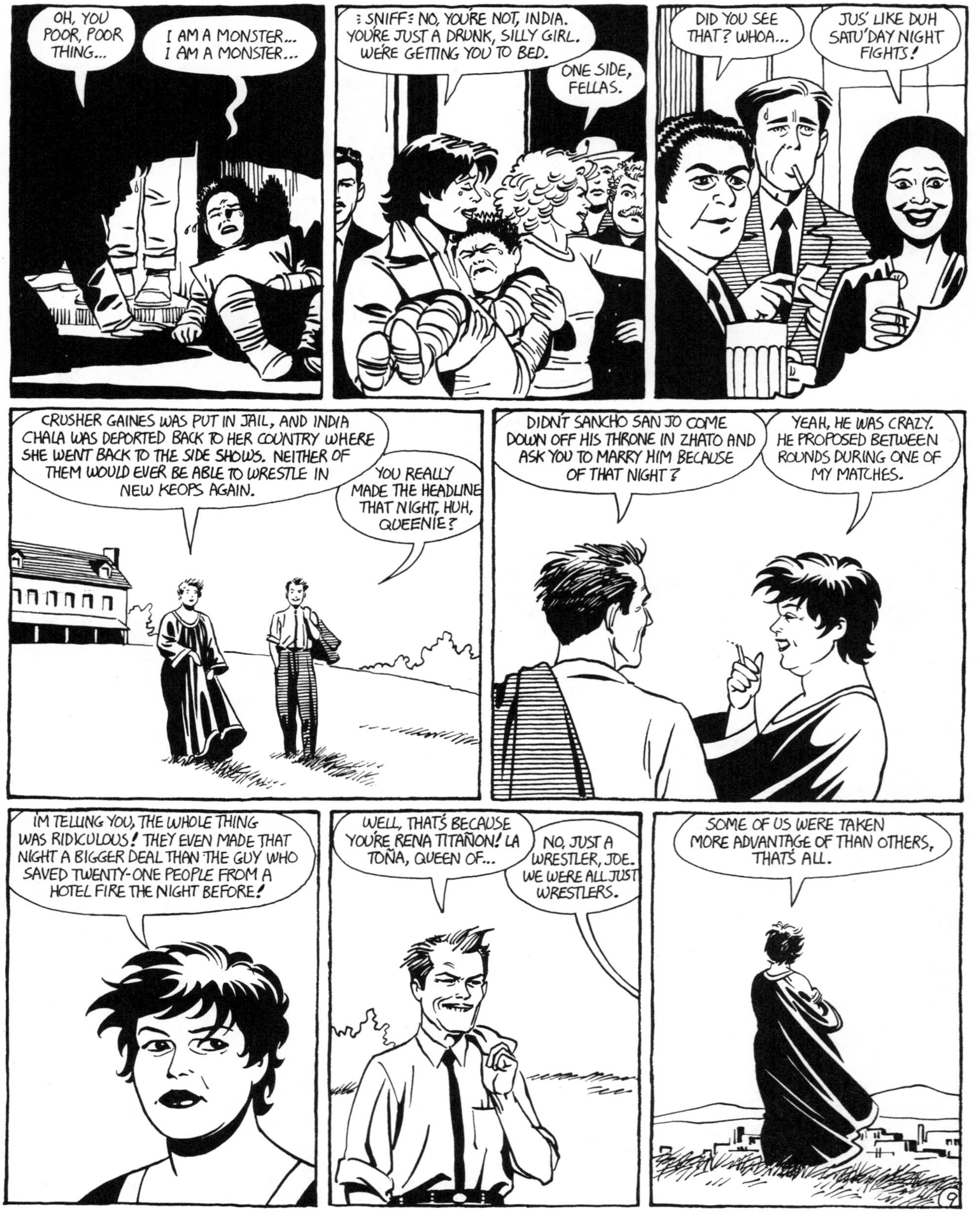
OH, YOU POOR, POOR THING...
I AM A MONSTER... I AM A MONSTER...
:SNIFF: NO, YOU'RE NOT, INDIA. YOU'RE JUST A DRUNK, SILLY GIRL. WE'RE GETTING YOU TO BED.
ONE SIDE, FELLAS.
DID YOU SEE THAT? WHOA...
JUS' LIKE DUH SATU'DAY NIGHT FIGHTS!
CRUSHER GAINES WAS PUT IN JAIL, AND INDIA CHALA WAS DEPORTED BACK TO HER COUNTRY WHERE SHE WENT BACK TO THE SIDE SHOWS. NEITHER OF THEM WOULD EVER BE ABLE TO WRESTLE IN NEW KEOPS AGAIN.
YOU REALLY MADE THE HEADLINE THAT NIGHT, HUH, QUEENIE?
DIDN'T SANCHO SAN JO COME DOWN OFF HIS THRONE IN ZHATO AND ASK YOU TO MARRY HIM BECAUSE OF THAT NIGHT?
YEAH, HE WAS CRAZY. HE PROPOSED BETWEEN ROUNDS DURING ONE OF MY MATCHES.
I'M TELLING YOU, THE WHOLE THING WAS RIDICULOUS! THEY EVEN MADE THAT NIGHT A BIGGER DEAL THAN THE GUY WHO SAVED TWENTY-ONE PEOPLE FROM A HOTEL FIRE THE NIGHT BEFORE!
WELL, THAT'S BECAUSE YOU'RE RENA TITAÑON! LA TOÑA, QUEEN OF...
NO, JUST A WRESTLER, JOE. WE WERE ALL JUST WRESTLERS.
SOME OF US WERE TAKEN MORE ADVANTAGE OF THAN OTHERS, THAT'S ALL.
9

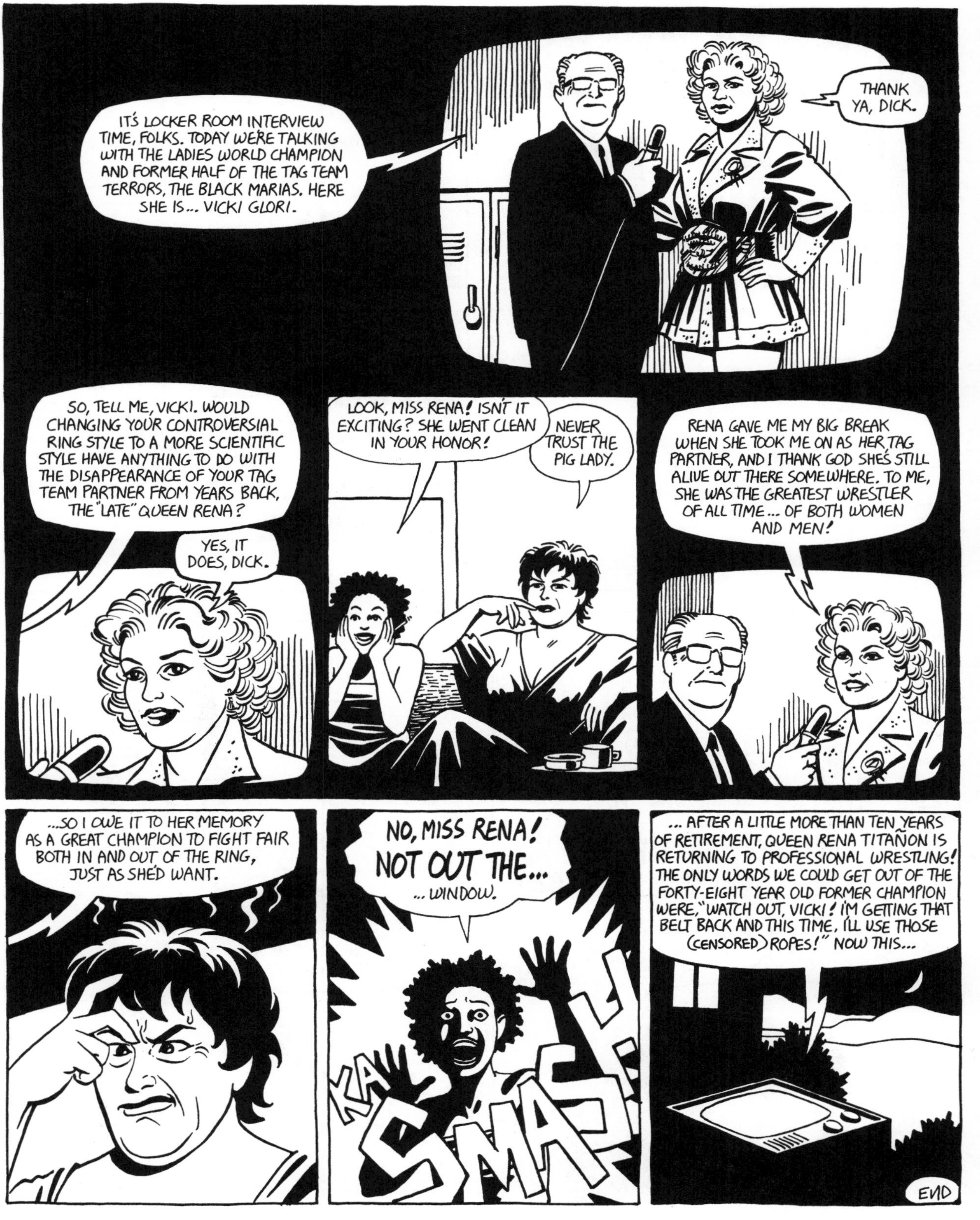
IT'S LOCKER ROOM INTERVIEW TIME, FOLKS. TODAY WE'RE TALKING WITH THE LADIES WORLD CHAMPION AND FORMER HALF OF THE TAG TEAM TERRORS, THE BLACK MARIAS. HERE SHE IS... VICKI GLORI.
THANK YA, DICK.
SO, TELL ME, VICKI. WOULD CHANGING YOUR CONTROVERSIAL RING STYLE TO A MORE SCIENTIFIC STYLE HAVE ANYTHING TO DO WITH THE DISAPPEARANCE OF YOUR TAG TEAM PARTNER FROM YEARS BACK, THE "LATE" QUEEN RENA?
YES, IT DOES, DICK.
LOOK, MISS RENA! ISN'T IT EXCITING? SHE WENT CLEAN IN YOUR HONOR!
NEVER TRUST THE PIG LADY.
RENA GAVE ME MY BIG BREAK WHEN SHE TOOK ME ON AS HER TAG PARTNER, AND I THANK GOD SHE'S STILL ALIVE OUT THERE SOMEWHERE. TO ME, SHE WAS THE GREATEST WRESTLER OF ALL TIME... OF BOTH WOMEN AND MEN!
...SO I OWE IT TO HER MEMORY AS A GREAT CHAMPION TO FIGHT FAIR BOTH IN AND OUT OF THE RING, JUST AS SHE'D WANT.
NO, MISS RENA! NOT OUT THE...
...WINDOW.
KA-SMASH!
... AFTER A LITTLE MORE THAN TEN YEARS OF RETIREMENT, QUEEN RENA TITAÑON IS RETURNING TO PROFESSIONAL WRESTLING! THE ONLY WORDS WE COULD GET OUT OF THE FORTY-EIGHT YEAR OLD FORMER CHAMPION WERE, "WATCH OUT, VICKI! I'M GETTING THAT BELT BACK AND THIS TIME, I'LL USE THOSE (CENSORED) ROPES!" NOW THIS...
END

QUEEN RENA
LIFE AT 34

STILL WOMEN'S WORLD WRESTLING CHAMPION
NOW RIVAL AND FORMER TAG-TEAM PARTNER OF VICKI GLORI
STILL AVOIDING BERNIE CARBO

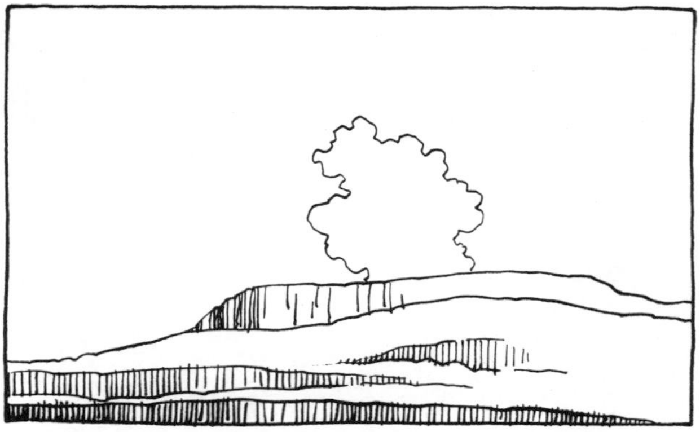

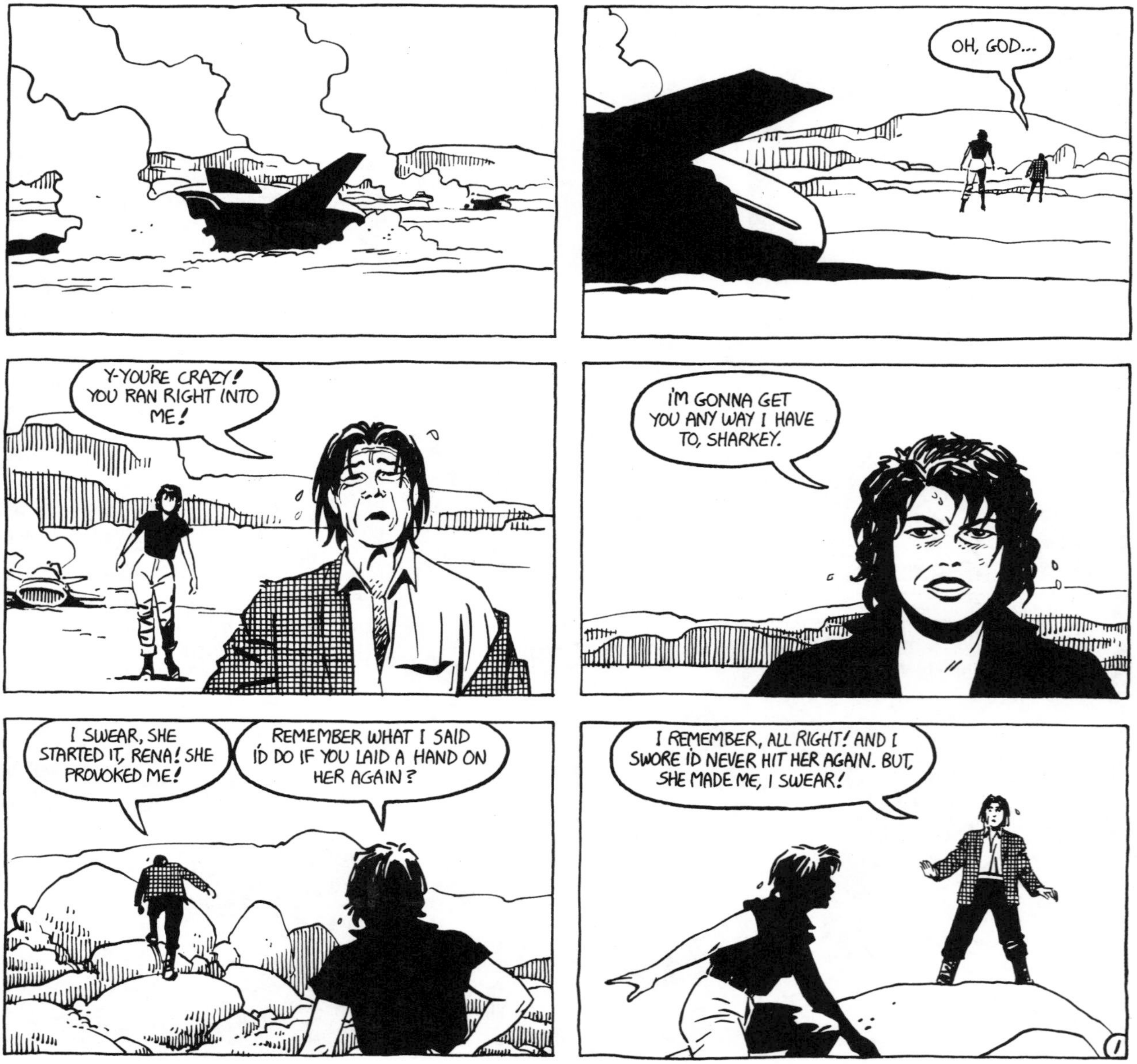
OH, GOD...
Y-YOU'RE CRAZY! YOU RAN RIGHT INTO ME!
I'M GONNA GET YOU ANY WAY I HAVE TO, SHARKEY.
I SWEAR, SHE STARTED IT, RENA! SHE PROVOKED ME!
REMEMBER WHAT I SAID I'D DO IF YOU LAID A HAND ON HER AGAIN?
I REMEMBER, ALL RIGHT! AND I SWORE I'D NEVER HIT HER AGAIN. BUT, SHE MADE ME, I SWEAR!
1

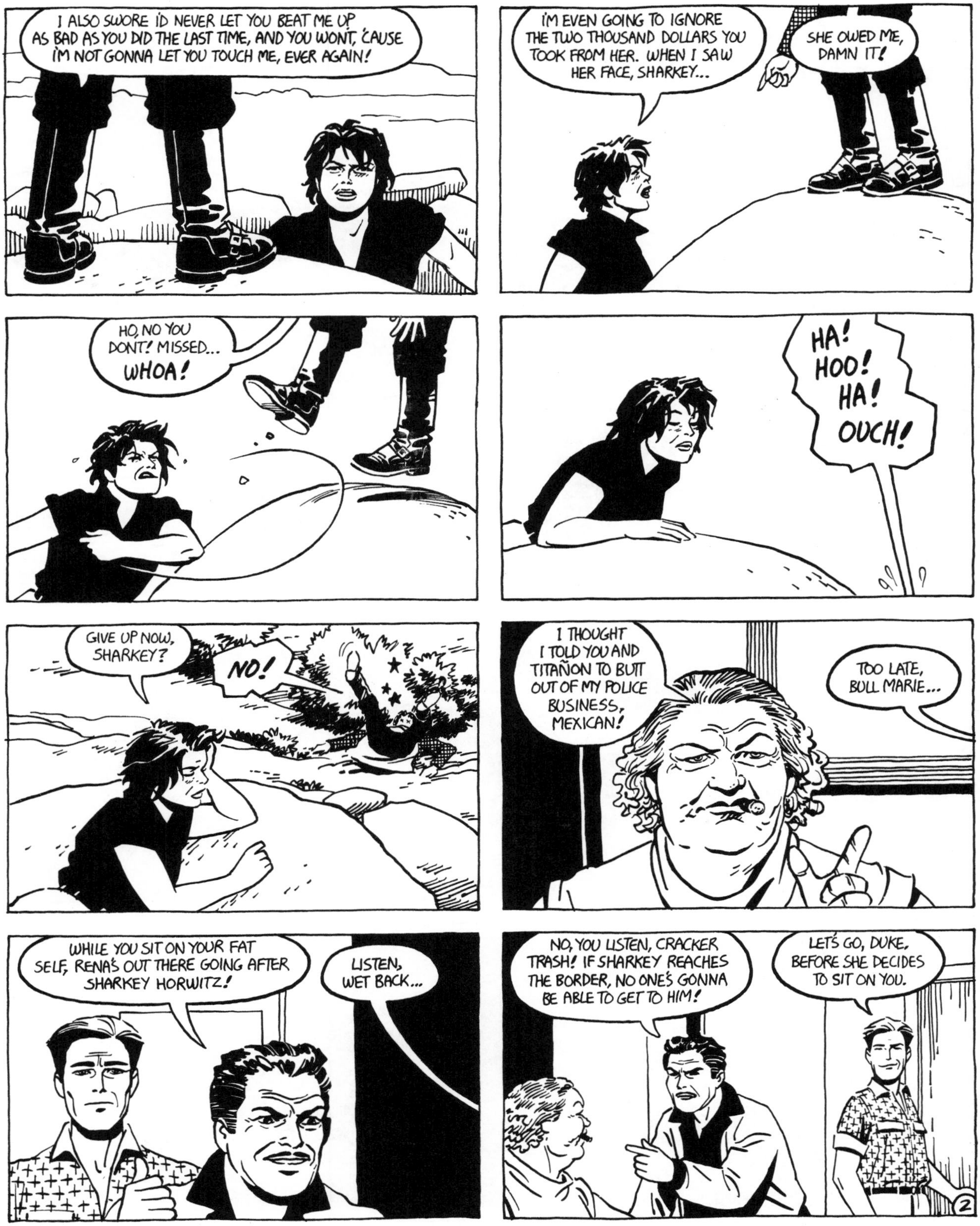
I ALSO SWORE I'D NEVER LET YOU BEAT ME UP AS BAD AS YOU DID THE LAST TIME, AND YOU WON'T, 'CAUSE I'M NOT GONNA LET YOU TOUCH ME, EVER AGAIN!
I'M EVEN GOING TO IGNORE THE TWO THOUSAND DOLLARS YOU TOOK FROM HER. WHEN I SAW HER FACE, SHARKEY...
SHE OWED ME, DAMN IT!
HO, NO YOU DON'T! MISSED... WHOA!
HA! HOO! HA! OUCH!
GIVE UP NOW, SHARKEY?
NO!
I THOUGHT I TOLD YOU AND TITAÑON TO BUTT OUT OF MY POLICE BUSINESS, MEXICAN!
TOO LATE, BULL MARIE...
WHILE YOU SIT ON YOUR FAT SELF, RENA'S OUT THERE GOING AFTER SHARKEY HORWITZ!
LISTEN, WET BACK...
NO, YOU LISTEN, CRACKER TRASH! IF SHARKEY REACHES THE BORDER, NO ONE'S GONNA BE ABLE TO GET TO HIM!
LET'S GO, DUKE, BEFORE SHE DECIDES TO SIT ON YOU.
2

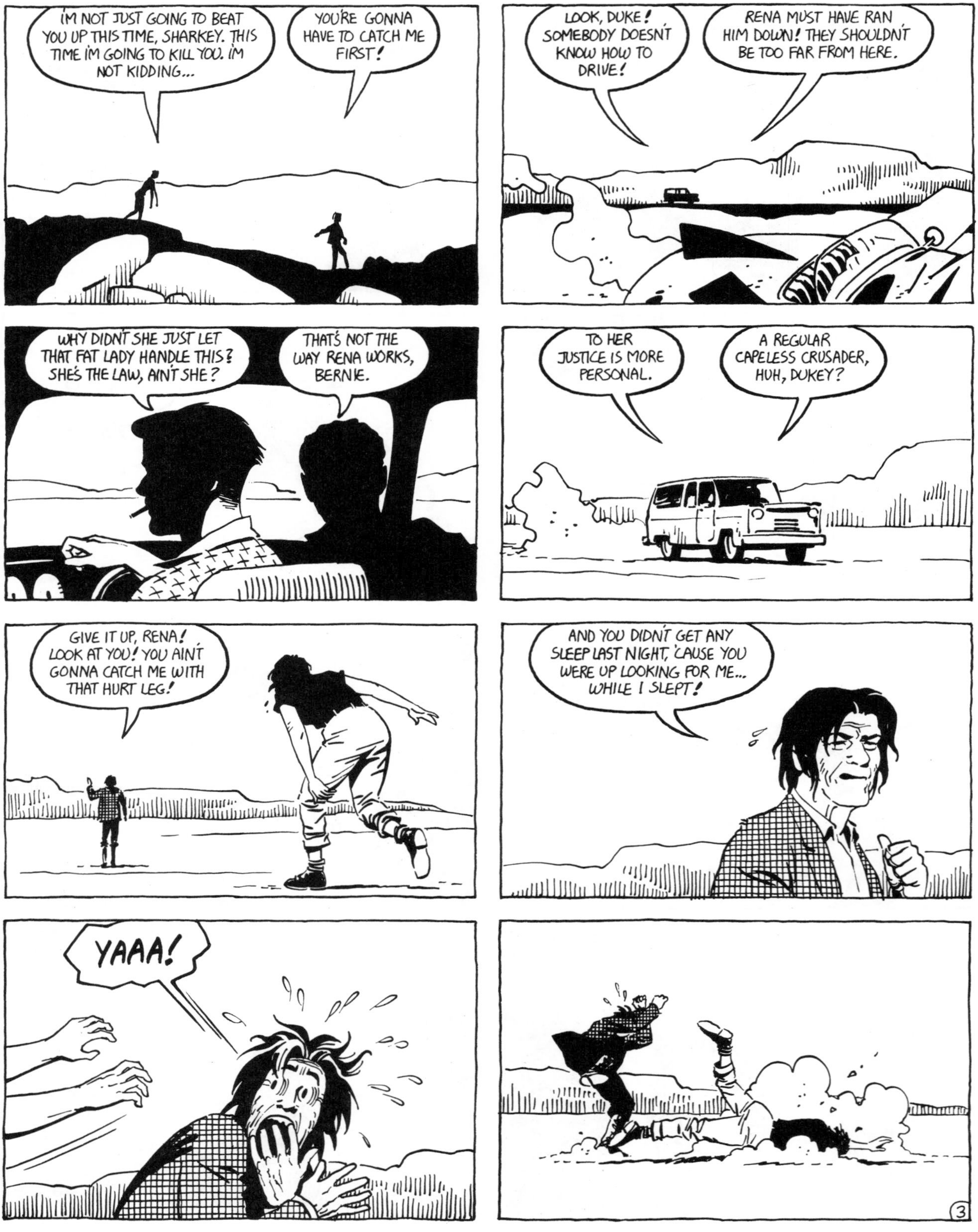
I'M NOT JUST GOING TO BEAT YOU UP THIS TIME, SHARKEY. THIS TIME I'M GOING TO KILL YOU. I'M NOT KIDDING...
YOU'RE GONNA HAVE TO CATCH ME FIRST!
LOOK, DUKE! SOMEBODY DOESN'T KNOW HOW TO DRIVE!
RENA MUST HAVE RAN HIM DOWN! THEY SHOULDN'T BE TOO FAR FROM HERE.
WHY DIDN'T SHE JUST LET THAT FAT LADY HANDLE THIS? SHE'S THE LAW, AIN'T SHE?
THAT'S NOT THE WAY RENA WORKS, BERNIE.
TO HER JUSTICE IS MORE PERSONAL.
A REGULAR CAPELESS CRUSADER, HUH, DUKEY?
GIVE IT UP, RENA! LOOK AT YOU! YOU AIN'T GONNA CATCH ME WITH THAT HURT LEG!
AND YOU DIDN'T GET ANY SLEEP LAST NIGHT, 'CAUSE YOU WERE UP LOOKING FOR ME... WHILE I SLEPT!
YAAA!
3

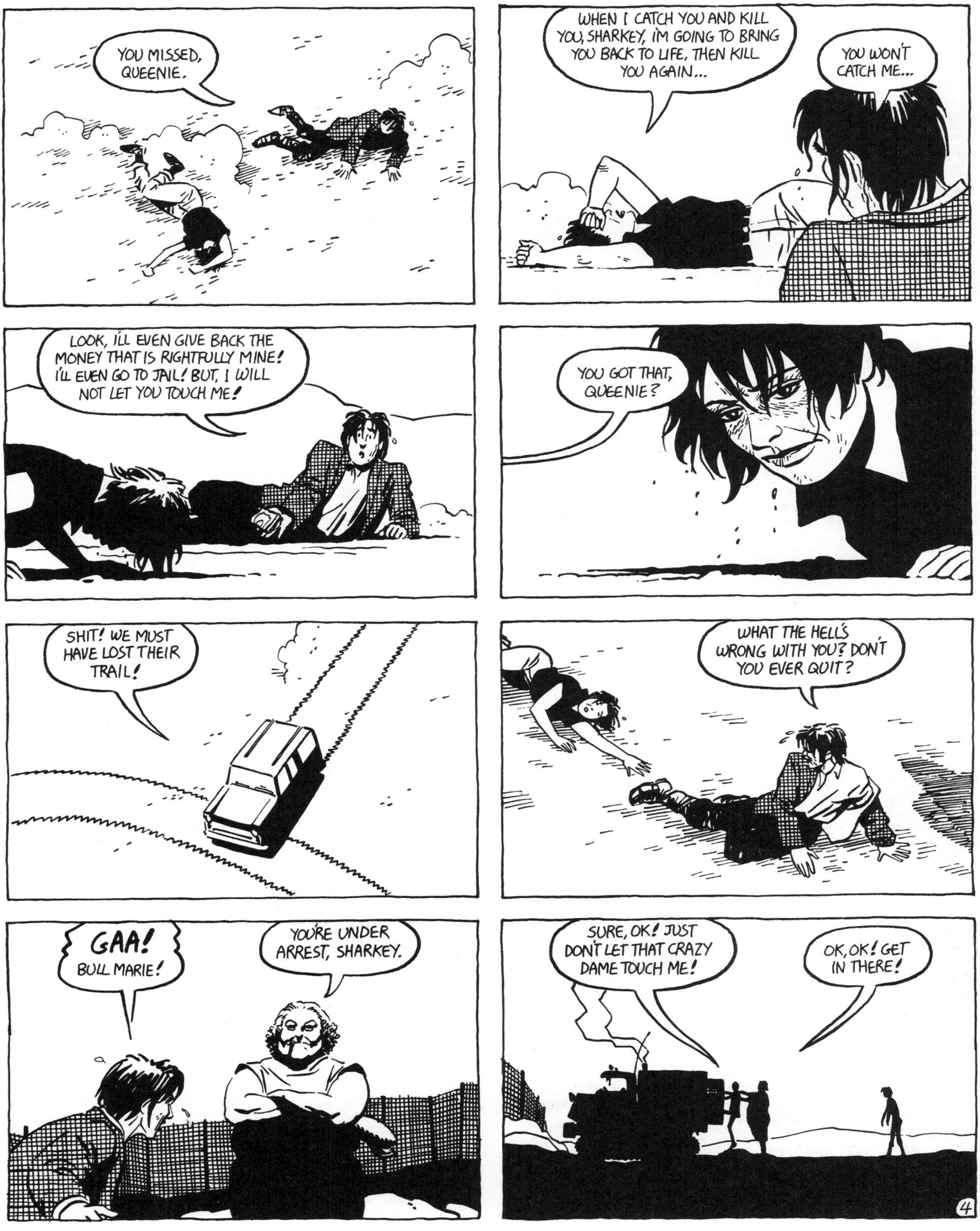
YOU MISSED, QUEENIE.
WHEN I CATCH YOU AND KILL YOU, SHARKEY, I'M GOING TO BRING YOU BACK TO LIFE, THEN KILL YOU AGAIN...
YOU WON'T CATCH ME...
LOOK, I'LL EVEN GIVE BACK THE MONEY THAT IS RIGHTFULLY MINE! I'LL EVEN GO TO JAIL! BUT, I WILL NOT LET YOU TOUCH ME!
YOU GOT THAT, QUEENIE?
SHIT! WE MUST HAVE LOST THEIR TRAIL!
WHAT THE HELL'S WRONG WITH YOU? DON'T YOU EVER QUIT?
GAA! BULL MARIE!
YOU'RE UNDER ARREST, SHARKEY.
SURE, OK! JUST DON'T LET THAT CRAZY DAME TOUCH ME!
OK, OK! GET IN THERE!
4

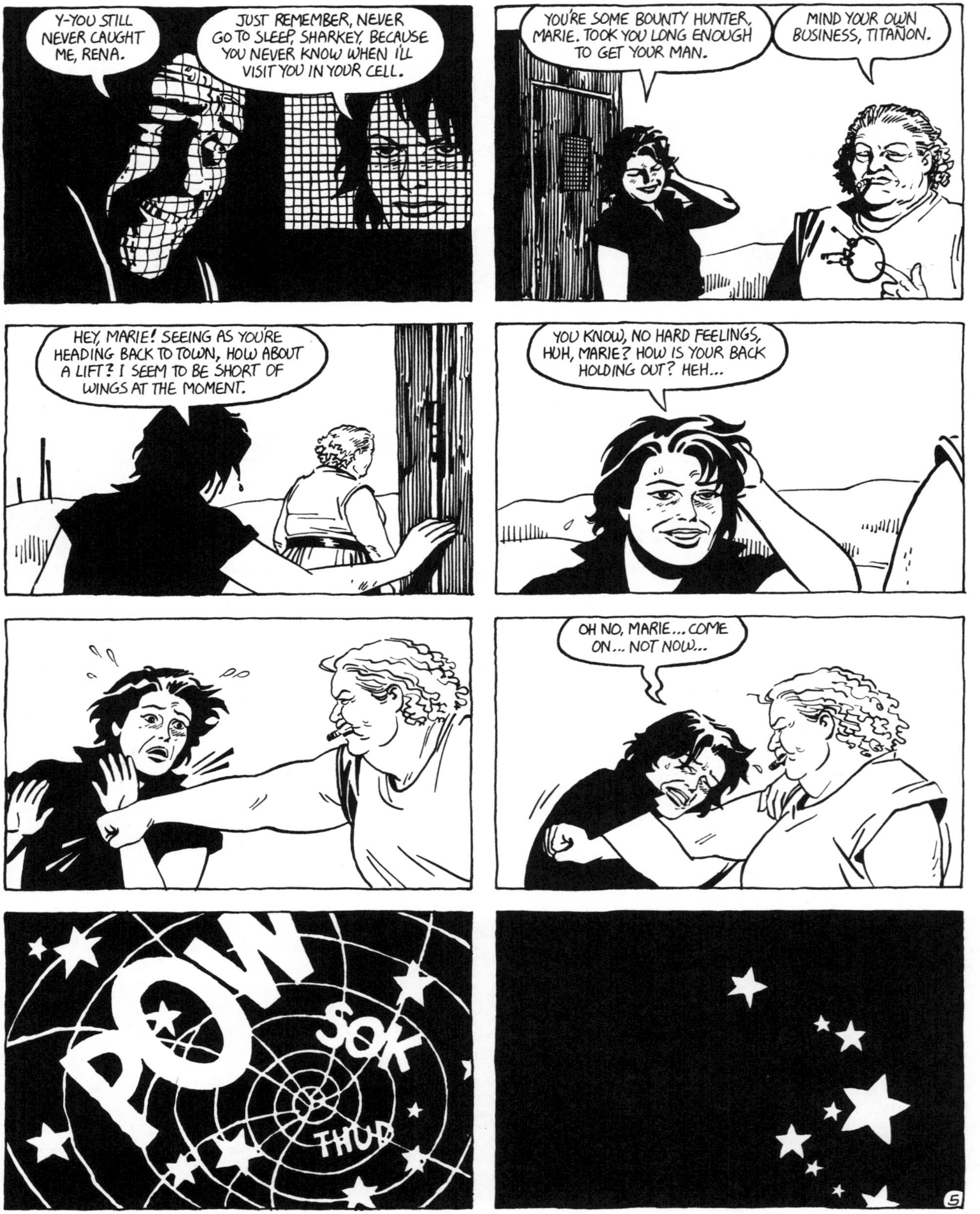
Y-YOU STILL NEVER CAUGHT ME, RENA.
JUST REMEMBER, NEVER GO TO SLEEP, SHARKEY, BECAUSE YOU NEVER KNOW WHEN I'LL VISIT YOU IN YOUR CELL.
YOU'RE SOME BOUNTY HUNTER, MARIE. TOOK YOU LONG ENOUGH TO GET YOUR MAN.
MIND YOUR OWN BUSINESS, TITAÑON.
HEY, MARIE! SEEING AS YOU'RE HEADING BACK TO TOWN, HOW ABOUT A LIFT? I SEEM TO BE SHORT OF WINGS AT THE MOMENT.
YOU KNOW, NO HARD FEELINGS, HUH, MARIE? HOW IS YOUR BACK HOLDING OUT? HEH...
OH NO, MARIE... COME ON... NOT NOW...
POW
SOK
THUD
5

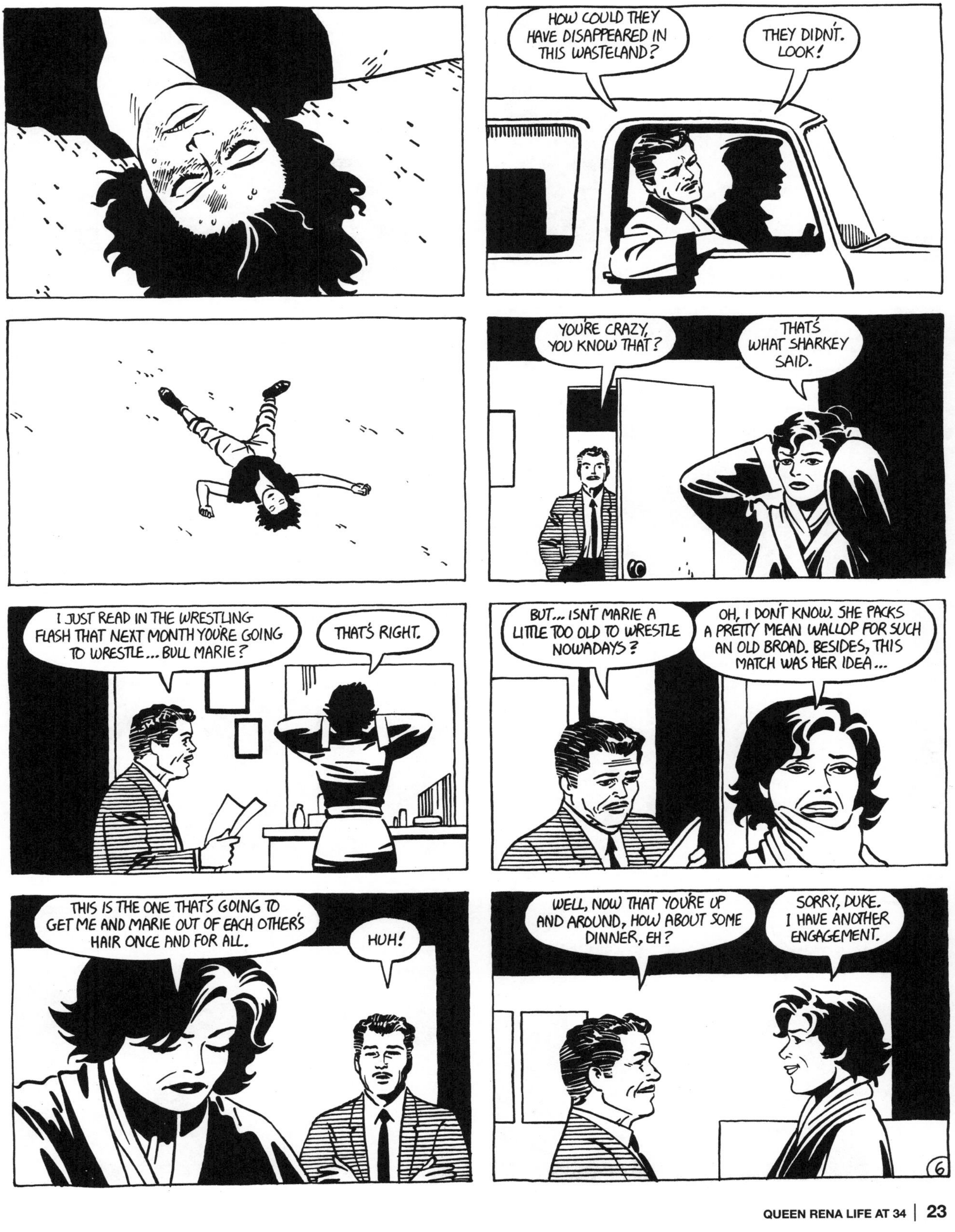
HOW COULD THEY HAVE DISAPPEARED IN THIS WASTELAND?
THEY DIDN'T. LOOK!
YOU'RE CRAZY, YOU KNOW THAT?
THAT'S WHAT SHARKEY SAID.
I JUST READ IN THE WRESTLING FLASH THAT NEXT MONTH YOU'RE GOING TO WRESTLE... BULL MARIE?
THAT'S RIGHT.
BUT... ISN'T MARIE A LITTLE TOO OLD TO WRESTLE NOWADAYS?
OH, I DON'T KNOW. SHE PACKS A PRETTY MEAN WALLOP FOR SUCH AN OLD BROAD. BESIDES, THIS MATCH WAS HER IDEA...
THIS IS THE ONE THAT'S GOING TO GET ME AND MARIE OUT OF EACH OTHER'S HAIR ONCE AND FOR ALL.
HUH!
WELL, NOW THAT YOU'RE UP AND AROUND, HOW ABOUT SOME DINNER, EH?
SORRY, DUKE. I HAVE ANOTHER ENGAGEMENT.
6

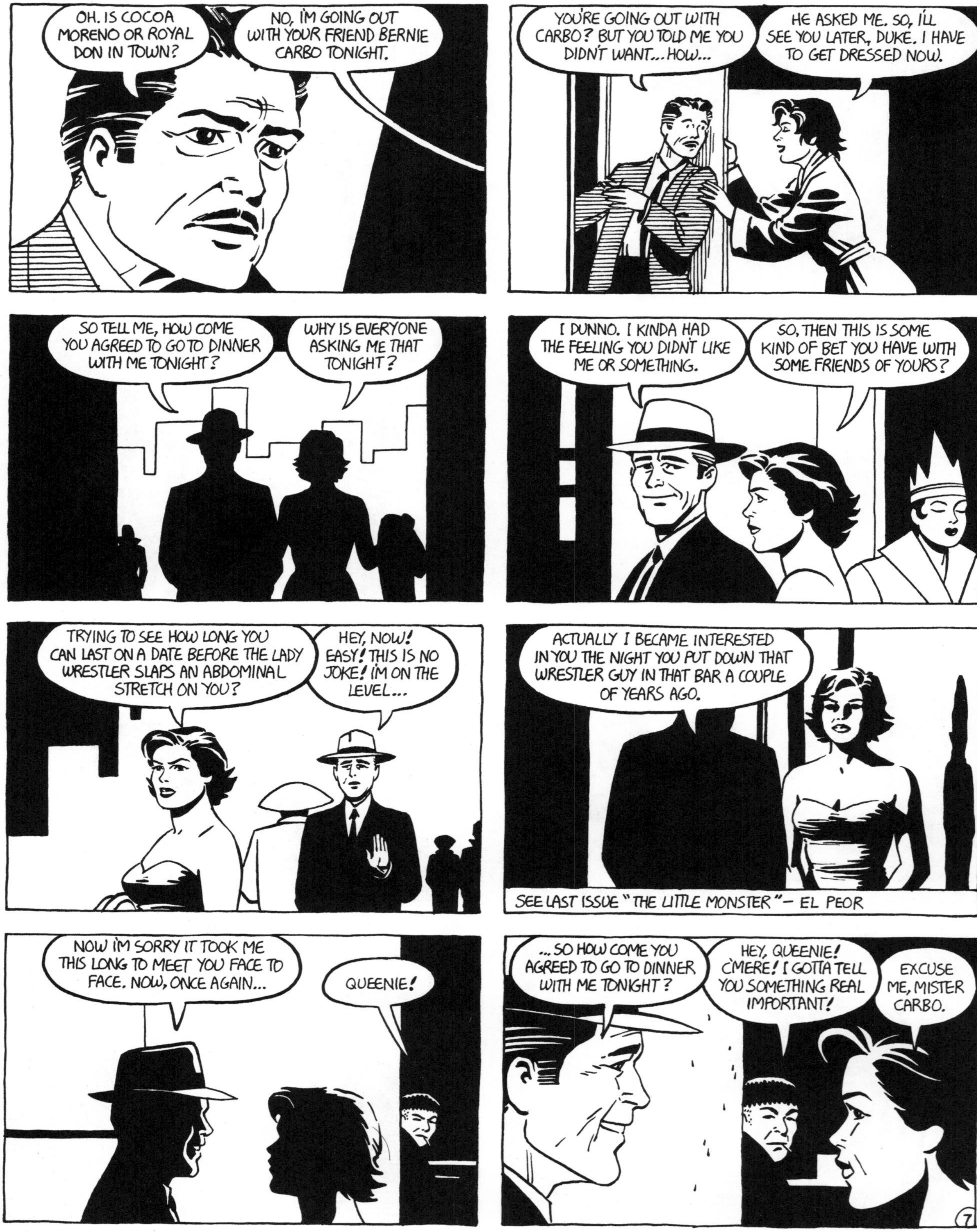
OH. IS COCOA MORENO OR ROYAL DON IN TOWN?
NO, I'M GOING OUT WITH YOUR FRIEND BERNIE CARBO TONIGHT.
YOU'RE GOING OUT WITH CARBO? BUT YOU TOLD ME YOU DIDN'T WANT... HOW...
HE ASKED ME. SO, I'LL SEE YOU LATER, DUKE. I HAVE TO GET DRESSED NOW.
SO TELL ME, HOW COME YOU AGREED TO GO TO DINNER WITH ME TONIGHT?
WHY IS EVERYONE ASKING ME THAT TONIGHT?
I DUNNO. I KINDA HAD THE FEELING YOU DIDN'T LIKE ME OR SOMETHING.
SO, THEN THIS IS SOME KIND OF BET YOU HAVE WITH SOME FRIENDS OF YOURS?
TRYING TO SEE HOW LONG YOU CAN LAST ON A DATE BEFORE THE LADY WRESTLER SLAPS AN ABDOMINAL STRETCH ON YOU?
HEY, NOW! EASY! THIS IS NO JOKE! I'M ON THE LEVEL...
ACTUALLY I BECAME INTERESTED IN YOU THE NIGHT YOU PUT DOWN THAT WRESTLER GUY IN THAT BAR A COUPLE OF YEARS AGO.
SEE LAST ISSUE "THE LITTLE MONSTER" — EL PEOR
NOW I'M SORRY IT TOOK ME THIS LONG TO MEET YOU FACE TO FACE. NOW, ONCE AGAIN...
QUEENIE!
...SO HOW COME YOU AGREED TO GO TO DINNER WITH ME TONIGHT?
HEY, QUEENIE! C'MERE! I GOTTA TELL YOU SOMETHING REAL IMPORTANT!
EXCUSE ME, MISTER CARBO.
7

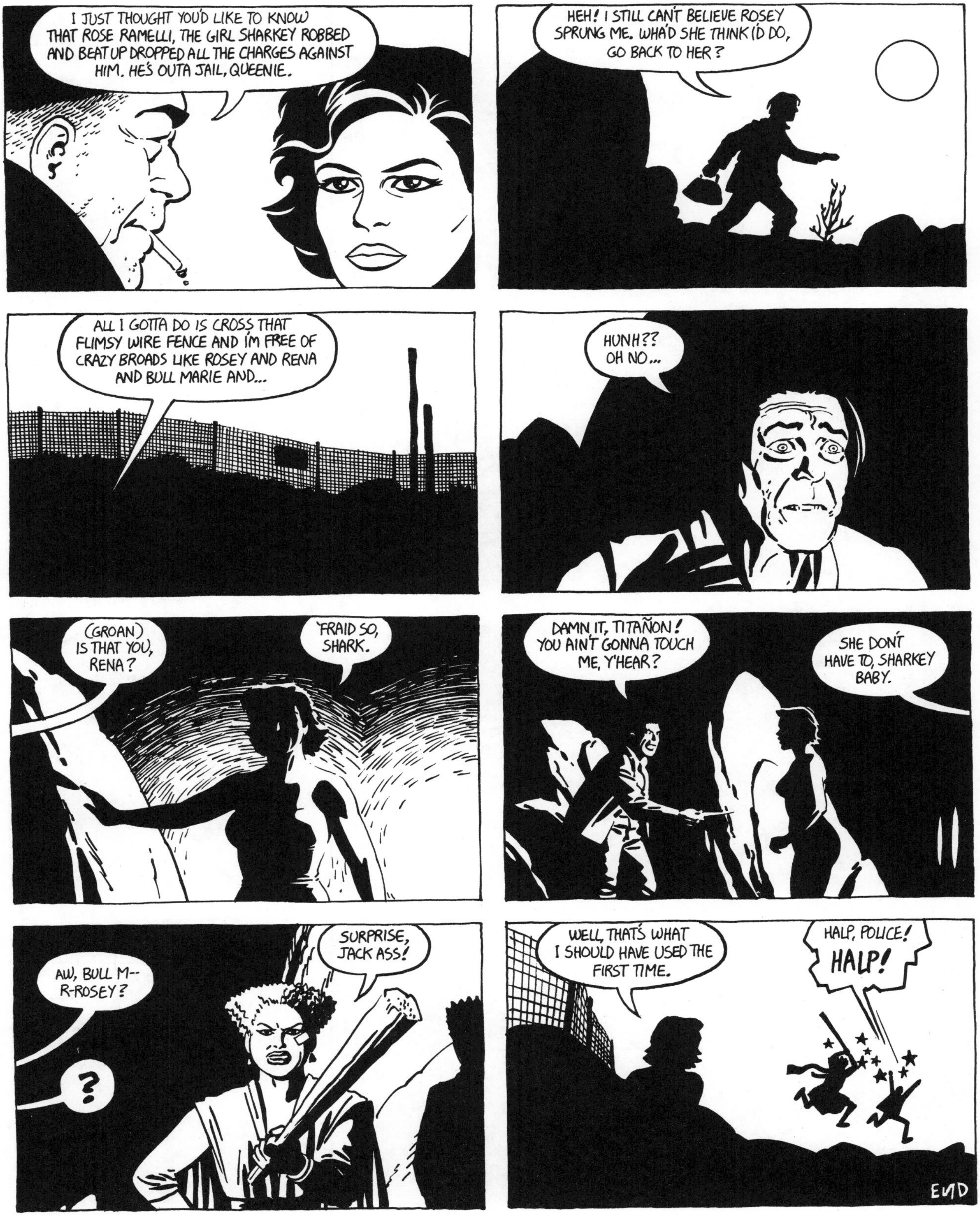
I JUST THOUGHT YOU'D LIKE TO KNOW THAT ROSE RAMELLI, THE GIRL SHARKEY ROBBED AND BEAT UP DROPPED ALL THE CHARGES AGAINST HIM. HE'S OUTA JAIL, QUEENIE.
HEH! I STILL CAN'T BELIEVE ROSEY SPRUNG ME. WHA'D SHE THINK I'D DO, GO BACK TO HER?
ALL I GOTTA DO IS CROSS THAT FLIMSY WIRE FENCE AND I'M FREE OF CRAZY BROADS LIKE ROSEY AND RENA AND BULL MARIE AND...
HUNH?? OH NO...
(GROAN) IS THAT YOU, RENA?
'FRAID SO, SHARK.
DAMN IT, TITAÑON! YOU AIN'T GONNA TOUCH ME, Y'HEAR?
SHE DON'T HAVE TO, SHARKEY BABY.
AW, BULL M-- R-ROSEY?
SURPRISE, JACK ASS!
?
WELL, THAT'S WHAT I SHOULD HAVE USED THE FIRST TIME.
HALP, POLICE!
HALP!
END

TITAÑON TO INVADE U.S.
ON NOV. 10 THE FORMER LADIES WORLD WRESTLING CHAMPION RENA TITANON WILL BE APPEARING AT THE OLYMPIA ARENA WHERE SHE AND HER NEWEST TAG TEAM PARTNER THE PUERTO RICAN JUNIOR CHAMPION PEPPER MARTINEZ WILL BE CHALLENGING THE WORLD CHAMPION SUGAR TWINS.
JUST A FEW MONTHS AGO TITANON CAME OUT OF OVER TEN YEARS RETIREMENT AND HAS BEEN TEARING UP THE CIRCUITS OVERSEAS.
IT HAS BEEN THIRTEEN YEARS SINCE TITANON HAS
IN THE U.S. SINCE
house of RAGING WOMEN
SLOB 84-86
SO SLAM HER ALREADY, YOU COW!
SHUT UP BEFORE I GO OUT THERE AND USE YOU AS THE MAT, PICKLE HEAD!
GO RENA! FINISH IT OFF, BABE!
MOO!
MOO
PEPPER AND RENA DARK HOGS
TOÑA
TWINS
MOO
DARK ANGELS GO HOME
RENA IS STILL CHAMP
1

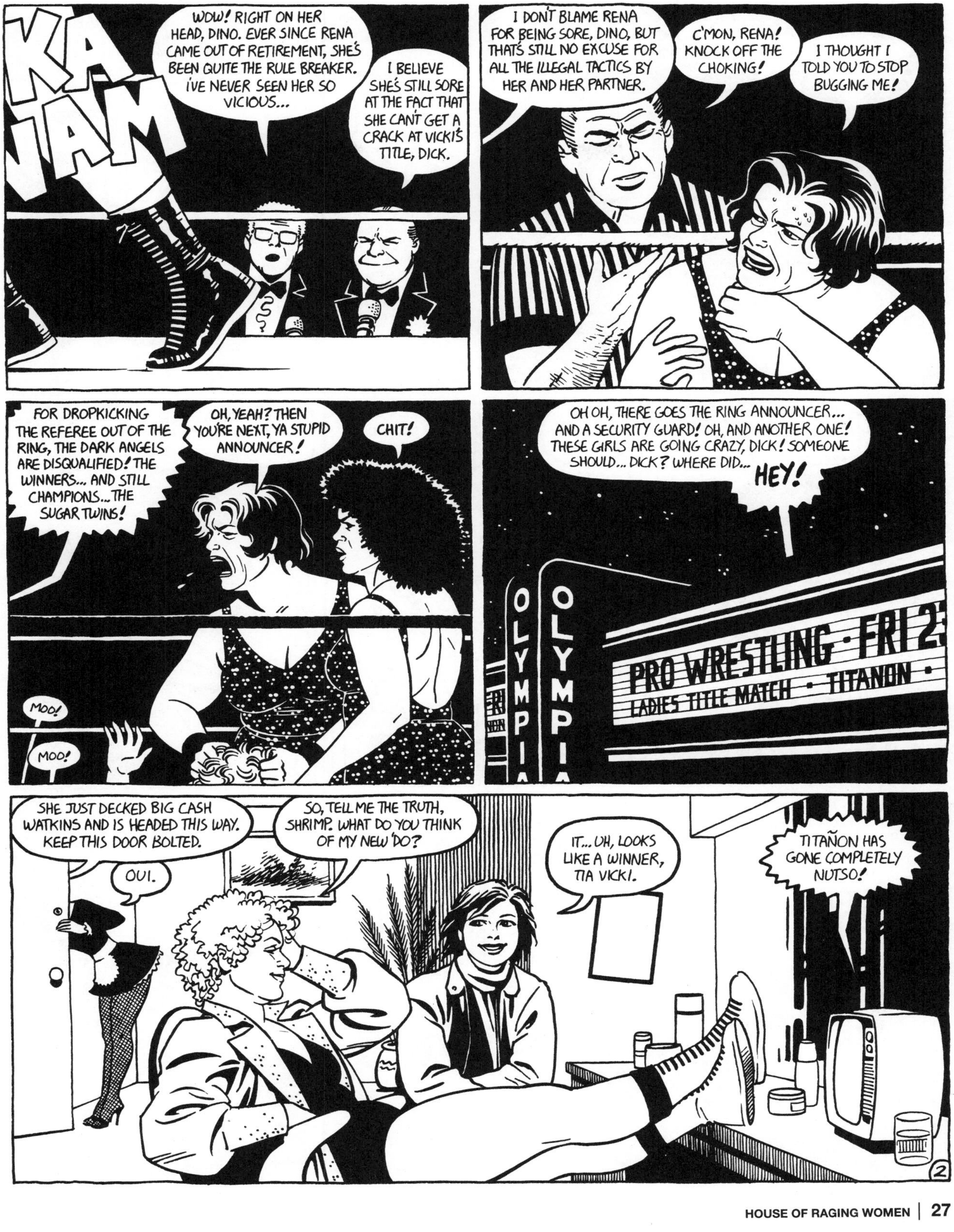

KA JAM
WOW! RIGHT ON HER HEAD, DINO. EVER SINCE RENA CAME OUT OF RETIREMENT, SHE'S BEEN QUITE THE RULE BREAKER. I'VE NEVER SEEN HER SO VICIOUS...
I BELIEVE SHE'S STILL SORE AT THE FACT THAT SHE CAN'T GET A CRACK AT VICKI'S TITLE, DICK.
I DON'T BLAME RENA FOR BEING SORE, DINO, BUT THAT'S STILL NO EXCUSE FOR ALL THE ILLEGAL TACTICS BY HER AND HER PARTNER.
C'MON, RENA! KNOCK OFF THE CHOKING!
I THOUGHT I TOLD YOU TO STOP BUGGING ME!
FOR DROPKICKING THE REFEREE OUT OF THE RING, THE DARK ANGELS ARE DISQUALIFIED! THE WINNERS... AND STILL CHAMPIONS... THE SUGAR TWINS!
OH, YEAH? THEN YOU'RE NEXT, YA STUPID ANNOUNCER!
CHIT!
MOO!
MOO!
OH OH, THERE GOES THE RING ANNOUNCER... AND A SECURITY GUARD! OH, AND ANOTHER ONE! THESE GIRLS ARE GOING CRAZY, DICK! SOMEONE SHOULD... DICK? WHERE DID... HEY!
OLYMPIA
OLYMPIA
PRO WRESTLING · FRI 2
LADIES TITLE MATCH · TITANON ·
SHE JUST DECKED BIG CASH WATKINS AND IS HEADED THIS WAY. KEEP THIS DOOR BOLTED.
OUI.
SO, TELL ME THE TRUTH, SHRIMP. WHAT DO YOU THINK OF MY NEW 'DO?
IT... UH, LOOKS LIKE A WINNER, TIA VICKI.
TITAÑON HAS GONE COMPLETELY NUTSO!
2

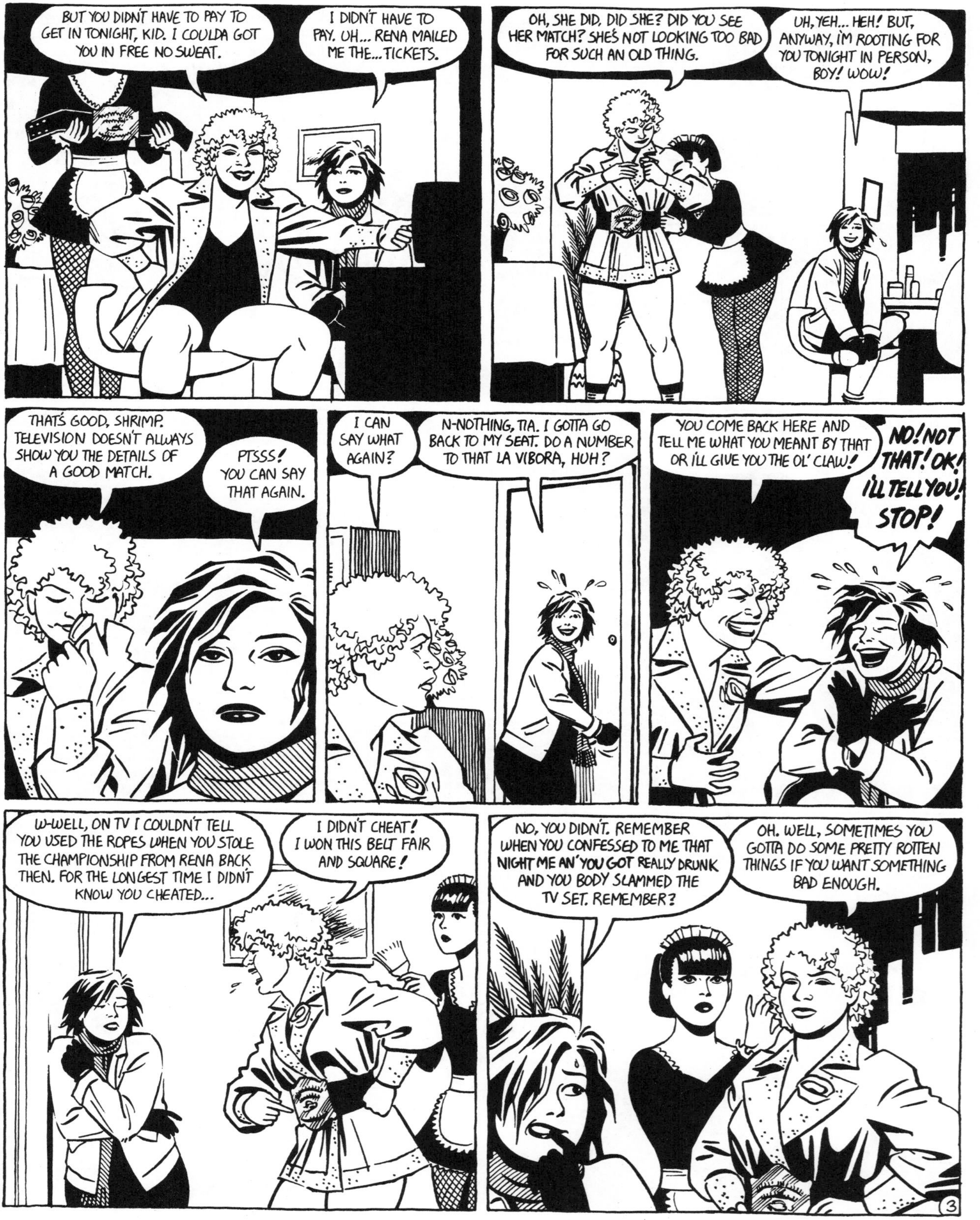

BUT YOU DIDN'T HAVE TO PAY TO GET IN TONIGHT, KID. I COULDA GOT YOU IN FREE NO SWEAT.
I DIDN'T HAVE TO PAY. UH... RENA MAILED ME THE... TICKETS.
OH, SHE DID, DID SHE? DID YOU SEE HER MATCH? SHE'S NOT LOOKING TOO BAD FOR SUCH AN OLD THING.
UH, YEH... HEH! BUT, ANYWAY, I'M ROOTING FOR YOU TONIGHT IN PERSON, BOY! WOW!
THAT'S GOOD, SHRIMP. TELEVISION DOESN'T ALWAYS SHOW YOU THE DETAILS OF A GOOD MATCH.
PTSSS! YOU CAN SAY THAT AGAIN.
I CAN SAY WHAT AGAIN?
N-NOTHING, TIA. I GOTTA GO BACK TO MY SEAT. DO A NUMBER TO THAT LA VIBORA, HUH?
YOU COME BACK HERE AND TELL ME WHAT YOU MEANT BY THAT OR I'LL GIVE YOU THE OL' CLAW!
NO! NOT THAT! OK! I'LL TELL YOU! STOP!
W-WELL, ON TV I COULDN'T TELL YOU USED THE ROPES WHEN YOU STOLE THE CHAMPIONSHIP FROM RENA BACK THEN. FOR THE LONGEST TIME I DIDN'T KNOW YOU CHEATED...
I DIDN'T CHEAT! I WON THIS BELT FAIR AND SQUARE!
NO, YOU DIDN'T. REMEMBER WHEN YOU CONFESSED TO ME THAT NIGHT ME AN' YOU GOT REALLY DRUNK AND YOU BODY SLAMMED THE TV SET. REMEMBER?
OH. WELL, SOMETIMES YOU GOTTA DO SOME PRETTY ROTTEN THINGS IF YOU WANT SOMETHING BAD ENOUGH.
3

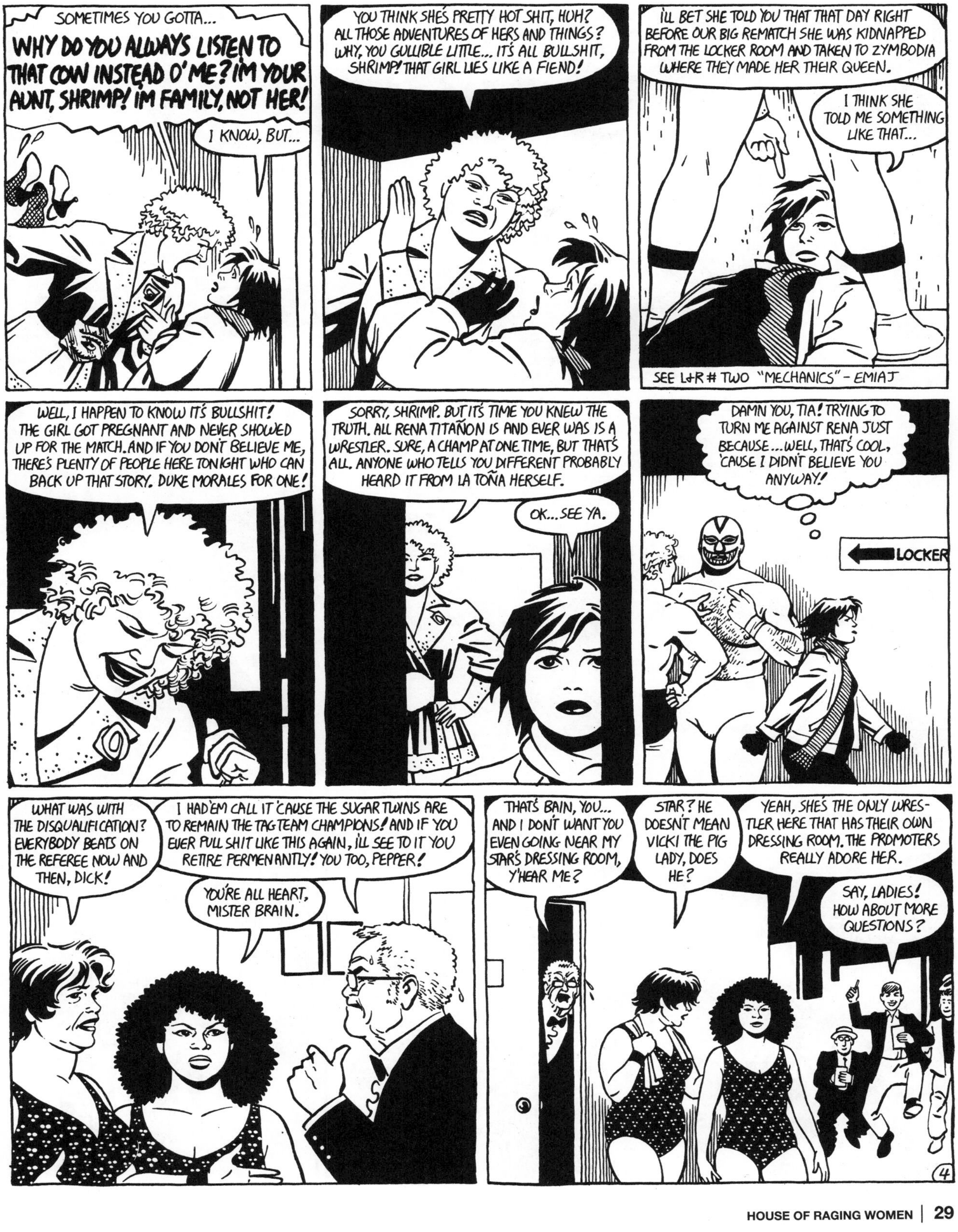
SOMETIMES YOU GOTTA...
WHY DO YOU ALWAYS LISTEN TO THAT COW INSTEAD O' ME? I'M YOUR AUNT, SHRIMP! I'M FAMILY, NOT HER!
I KNOW, BUT...
YOU THINK SHE'S PRETTY HOT SHIT, HUH? ALL THOSE ADVENTURES OF HERS AND THINGS? WHY, YOU GULLIBLE LITTLE... IT'S ALL BULLSHIT, SHRIMP! THAT GIRL LIES LIKE A FIEND!
I'LL BET SHE TOLD YOU THAT THAT DAY RIGHT BEFORE OUR BIG REMATCH SHE WAS KIDNAPPED FROM THE LOCKER ROOM AND TAKEN TO ZYMBODIA WHERE THEY MADE HER THEIR QUEEN.
I THINK SHE TOLD ME SOMETHING LIKE THAT...
SEE L&R # TWO "MECHANICS" - EMIAJ
WELL, I HAPPEN TO KNOW IT'S BULLSHIT! THE GIRL GOT PREGNANT AND NEVER SHOWED UP FOR THE MATCH. AND IF YOU DON'T BELIEVE ME, THERE'S PLENTY OF PEOPLE HERE TONIGHT WHO CAN BACK UP THAT STORY. DUKE MORALES FOR ONE!
SORRY, SHRIMP. BUT IT'S TIME YOU KNEW THE TRUTH. ALL RENA TITAÑON IS AND EVER WAS IS A WRESTLER. SURE, A CHAMP AT ONE TIME, BUT THAT'S ALL. ANYONE WHO TELLS YOU DIFFERENT PROBABLY HEARD IT FROM LA TOÑA HERSELF.
OK... SEE YA.
DAMN YOU, TIA! TRYING TO TURN ME AGAINST RENA JUST BECAUSE... WELL, THAT'S COOL, 'CAUSE I DIDN'T BELIEVE YOU ANYWAY!
LOCKER
WHAT WAS WITH THE DISQUALIFICATION? EVERYBODY BEATS ON THE REFEREE NOW AND THEN, DICK!
I HAD 'EM CALL IT 'CAUSE THE SUGAR TWINS ARE TO REMAIN THE TAG TEAM CHAMPIONS! AND IF YOU EVER PULL SHIT LIKE THIS AGAIN, I'LL SEE TO IT YOU RETIRE PERMENANTLY! YOU TOO, PEPPER!
YOU'RE ALL HEART, MISTER BRAIN.
THAT'S BAIN, YOU... AND I DON'T WANT YOU EVEN GOING NEAR MY STAR'S DRESSING ROOM, Y'HEAR ME?
STAR? HE DOESN'T MEAN VICKI THE PIG LADY, DOES HE?
YEAH, SHE'S THE ONLY WRESTLER HERE THAT HAS THEIR OWN DRESSING ROOM. THE PROMOTERS REALLY ADORE HER.
SAY, LADIES! HOW ABOUT MORE QUESTIONS?
4

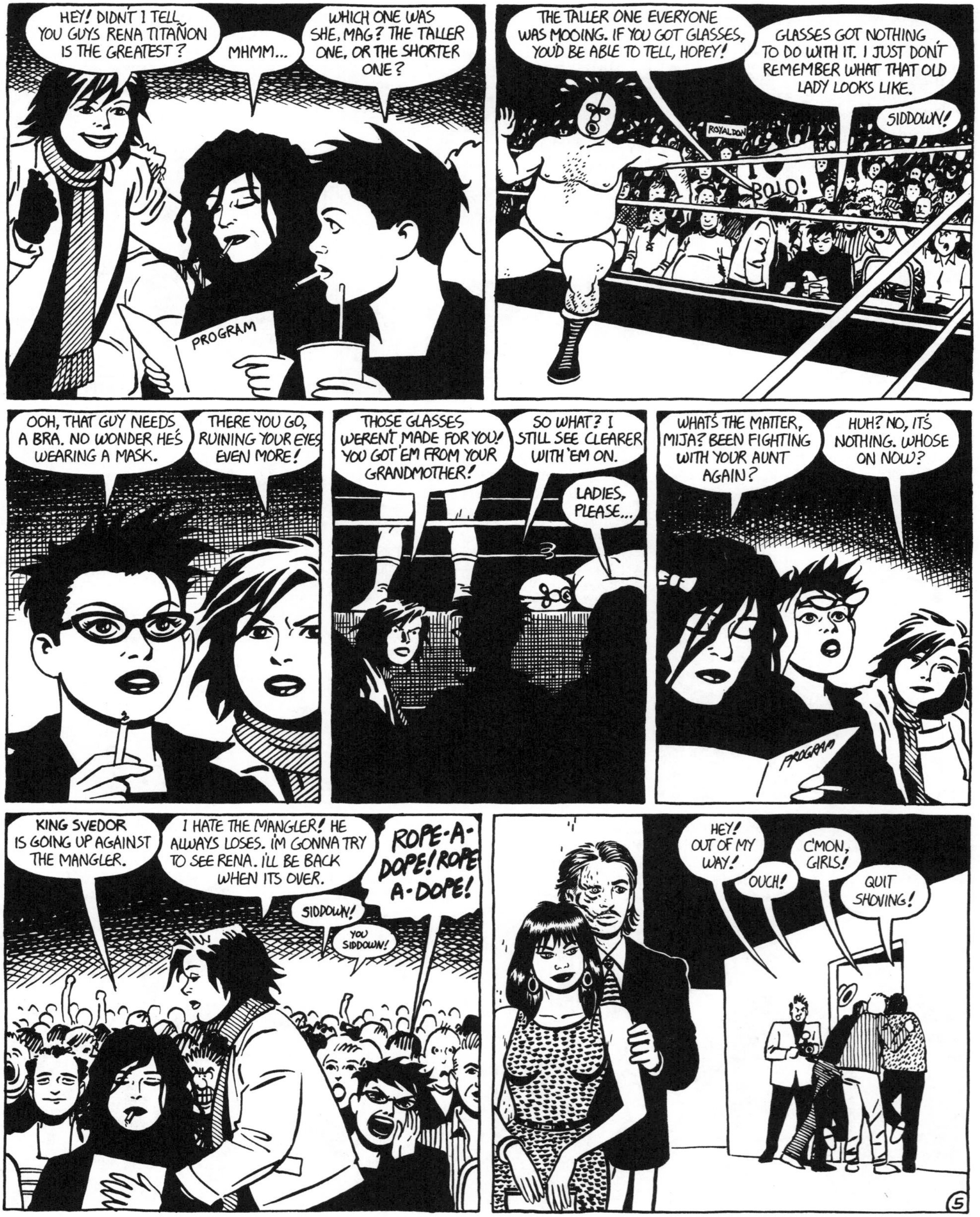
HEY! DIDN'T I TELL YOU GUYS RENA TITAÑON IS THE GREATEST?
MHMM...
WHICH ONE WAS SHE, MAG? THE TALLER ONE, OR THE SHORTER ONE?
PROGRAM
THE TALLER ONE EVERYONE WAS MOOING. IF YOU GOT GLASSES, YOU'D BE ABLE TO TELL, HOPEY!
GLASSES GOT NOTHING TO DO WITH IT. I JUST DON'T REMEMBER WHAT THAT OLD LADY LOOKS LIKE.
SIDDOWN!
ROYALDON
BOLO!
OOH, THAT GUY NEEDS A BRA. NO WONDER HE'S WEARING A MASK.
THERE YOU GO, RUINING YOUR EYES EVEN MORE!
THOSE GLASSES WEREN'T MADE FOR YOU! YOU GOT 'EM FROM YOUR GRANDMOTHER!
SO WHAT? I STILL SEE CLEARER WITH 'EM ON.
LADIES, PLEASE...
WHAT'S THE MATTER, MIJA? BEEN FIGHTING WITH YOUR AUNT AGAIN?
HUH? NO, IT'S NOTHING. WHOSE ON NOW?
PROGRAM
KING SVEDOR IS GOING UP AGAINST THE MANGLER.
I HATE THE MANGLER! HE ALWAYS LOSES. I'M GONNA TRY TO SEE RENA. I'LL BE BACK WHEN ITS OVER.
ROPE-A-DOPE! ROPE-A-DOPE!
SIDDOWN!
YOU SIDDOWN!
HEY! OUT OF MY WAY!
OUCH!
C'MON, GIRLS!
QUIT SHOVING!
5

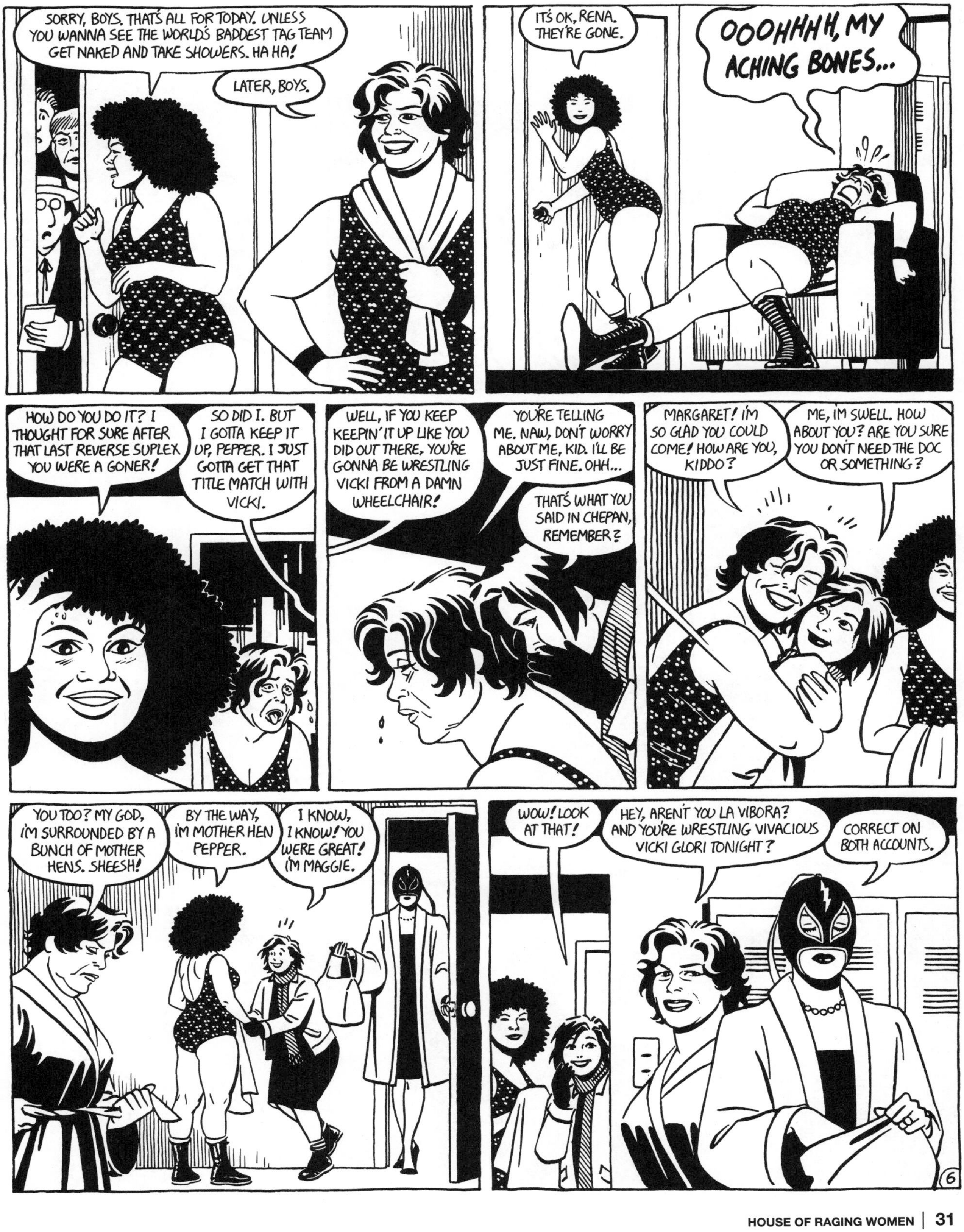
SORRY, BOYS. THAT'S ALL FOR TODAY. UNLESS YOU WANNA SEE THE WORLD'S BADDEST TAG TEAM GET NAKED AND TAKE SHOWERS. HA HA!
LATER, BOYS.
IT'S OK, RENA. THEY'RE GONE.
OOOHHHH, MY ACHING BONES...
HOW DO YOU DO IT? I THOUGHT FOR SURE AFTER THAT LAST REVERSE SUPLEX YOU WERE A GONER!
SO DID I. BUT I GOTTA KEEP IT UP, PEPPER. I JUST GOTTA GET THAT TITLE MATCH WITH VICKI.
WELL, IF YOU KEEP KEEPIN' IT UP LIKE YOU DID OUT THERE, YOU'RE GONNA BE WRESTLING VICKI FROM A DAMN WHEELCHAIR!
YOU'RE TELLING ME. NAW, DON'T WORRY ABOUT ME, KID. I'LL BE JUST FINE. OHH...
THAT'S WHAT YOU SAID IN CHEPAN, REMEMBER?
MARGARET! I'M SO GLAD YOU COULD COME! HOW ARE YOU, KIDDO?
ME, I'M SWELL. HOW ABOUT YOU? ARE YOU SURE YOU DON'T NEED THE DOC OR SOMETHING?
YOU TOO? MY GOD, I'M SURROUNDED BY A BUNCH OF MOTHER HENS. SHEESH!
BY THE WAY, I'M MOTHER HEN PEPPER.
I KNOW, I KNOW! YOU WERE GREAT! I'M MAGGIE.
WOW! LOOK AT THAT!
HEY, AREN'T YOU LA VIBORA? AND YOU'RE WRESTLING VIVACIOUS VICKI GLORI TONIGHT?
CORRECT ON BOTH ACCOUNTS.
6

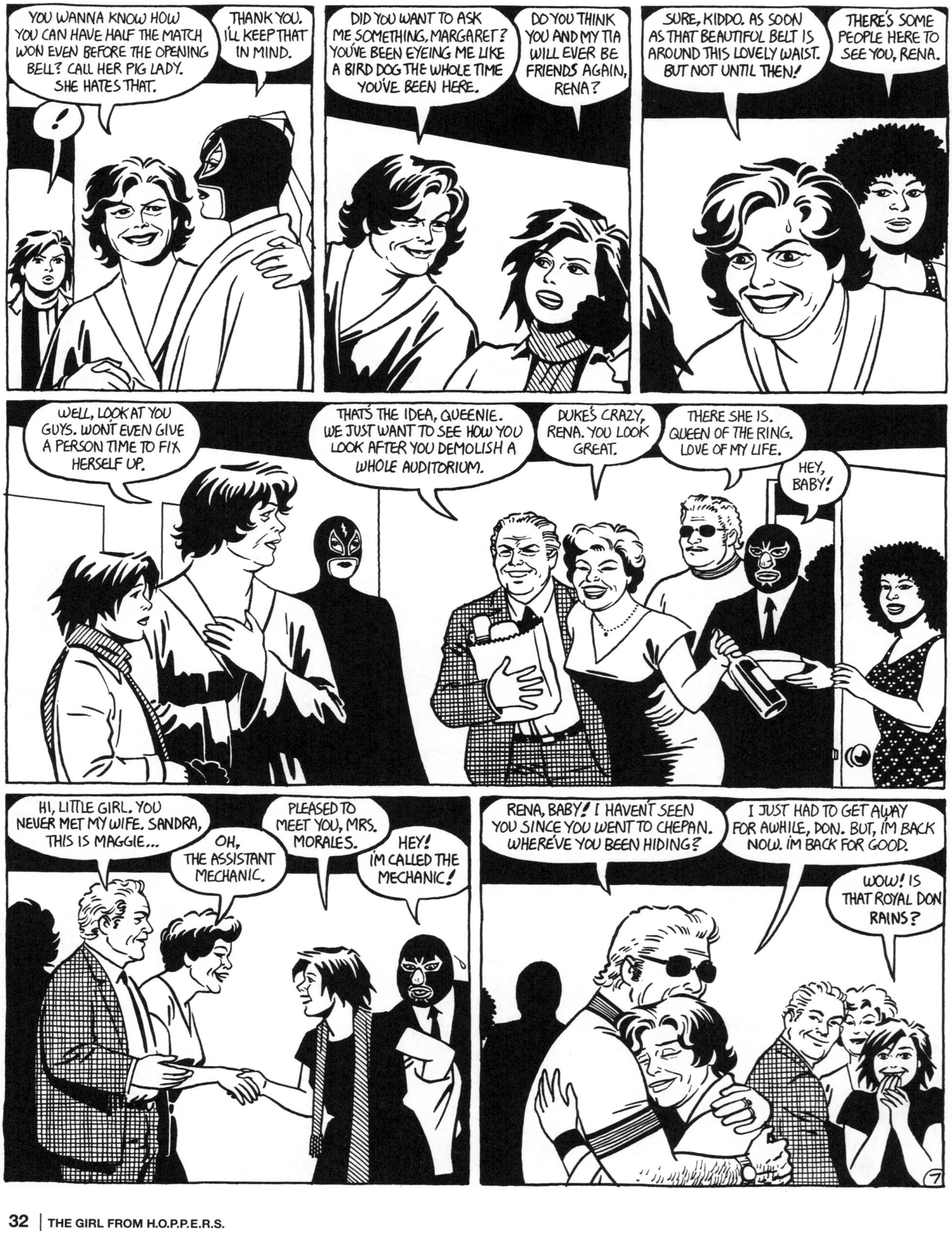
YOU WANNA KNOW HOW YOU CAN HAVE HALF THE MATCH WON EVEN BEFORE THE OPENING BELL? CALL HER PIG LADY. SHE HATES THAT.
!
THANK YOU. I'LL KEEP THAT IN MIND.
DID YOU WANT TO ASK ME SOMETHING, MARGARET? YOU'VE BEEN EYEING ME LIKE A BIRD DOG THE WHOLE TIME YOU'VE BEEN HERE.
DO YOU THINK YOU AND MY TIA WILL EVER BE FRIENDS AGAIN, RENA?
SURE, KIDDO. AS SOON AS THAT BEAUTIFUL BELT IS AROUND THIS LOVELY WAIST. BUT NOT UNTIL THEN!
THERE'S SOME PEOPLE HERE TO SEE YOU, RENA.
WELL, LOOK AT YOU GUYS. WON'T EVEN GIVE A PERSON TIME TO FIX HERSELF UP.
THAT'S THE IDEA, QUEENIE. WE JUST WANT TO SEE HOW YOU LOOK AFTER YOU DEMOLISH A WHOLE AUDITORIUM.
DUKE'S CRAZY, RENA. YOU LOOK GREAT.
THERE SHE IS. QUEEN OF THE RING. LOVE OF MY LIFE.
HEY, BABY!
HI, LITTLE GIRL. YOU NEVER MET MY WIFE. SANDRA, THIS IS MAGGIE...
OH, THE ASSISTANT MECHANIC.
PLEASED TO MEET YOU, MRS. MORALES.
HEY! I'M CALLED THE MECHANIC!
RENA, BABY! I HAVEN'T SEEN YOU SINCE YOU WENT TO CHEPAN. WHERE'VE YOU BEEN HIDING?
I JUST HAD TO GET AWAY FOR AWHILE, DON. BUT, I'M BACK NOW. I'M BACK FOR GOOD.
WOW! IS THAT ROYAL DON RAINS?
7

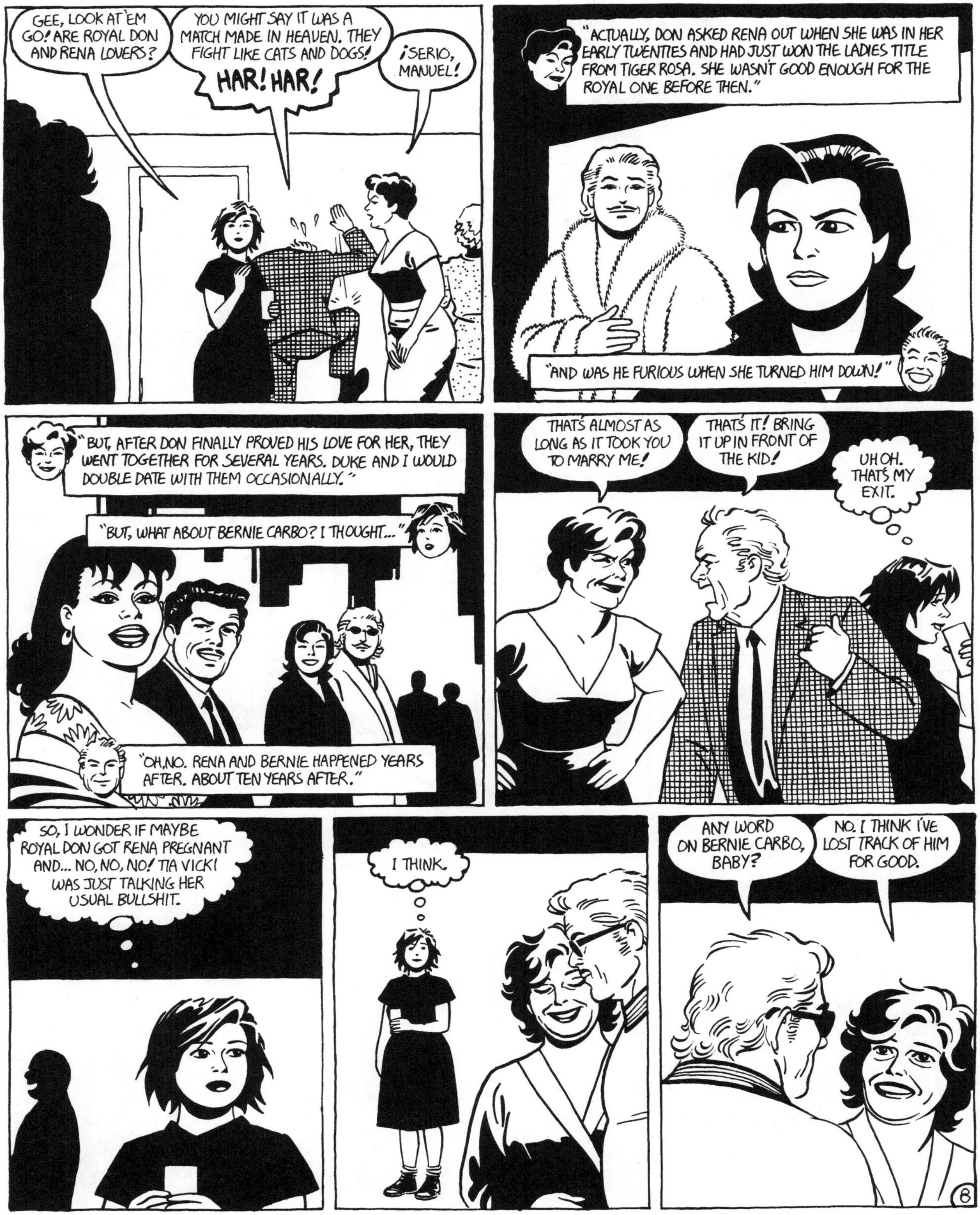
GEE, LOOK AT 'EM GO! ARE ROYAL DON AND RENA LOVERS?
YOU MIGHT SAY IT WAS A MATCH MADE IN HEAVEN. THEY FIGHT LIKE CATS AND DOGS! HAR! HAR!
¡SERIO, MANUEL!
"ACTUALLY, DON ASKED RENA OUT WHEN SHE WAS IN HER EARLY TWENTIES AND HAD JUST WON THE LADIES TITLE FROM TIGER ROSA. SHE WASN'T GOOD ENOUGH FOR THE ROYAL ONE BEFORE THEN."
"AND WAS HE FURIOUS WHEN SHE TURNED HIM DOWN!"
"BUT, AFTER DON FINALLY PROVED HIS LOVE FOR HER, THEY WENT TOGETHER FOR SEVERAL YEARS. DUKE AND I WOULD DOUBLE DATE WITH THEM OCCASIONALLY."
"BUT, WHAT ABOUT BERNIE CARBO? I THOUGHT..."
"OH, NO. RENA AND BERNIE HAPPENED YEARS AFTER. ABOUT TEN YEARS AFTER."
THAT'S ALMOST AS LONG AS IT TOOK YOU TO MARRY ME!
THAT'S IT! BRING IT UP IN FRONT OF THE KID!
UH OH. THAT'S MY EXIT.
SO, I WONDER IF MAYBE ROYAL DON GOT RENA PREGNANT AND... NO, NO, NO! TIA VICKI WAS JUST TALKING HER USUAL BULLSHIT.
I THINK.
ANY WORD ON BERNIE CARBO, BABY?
NO. I THINK I'VE LOST TRACK OF HIM FOR GOOD.
8

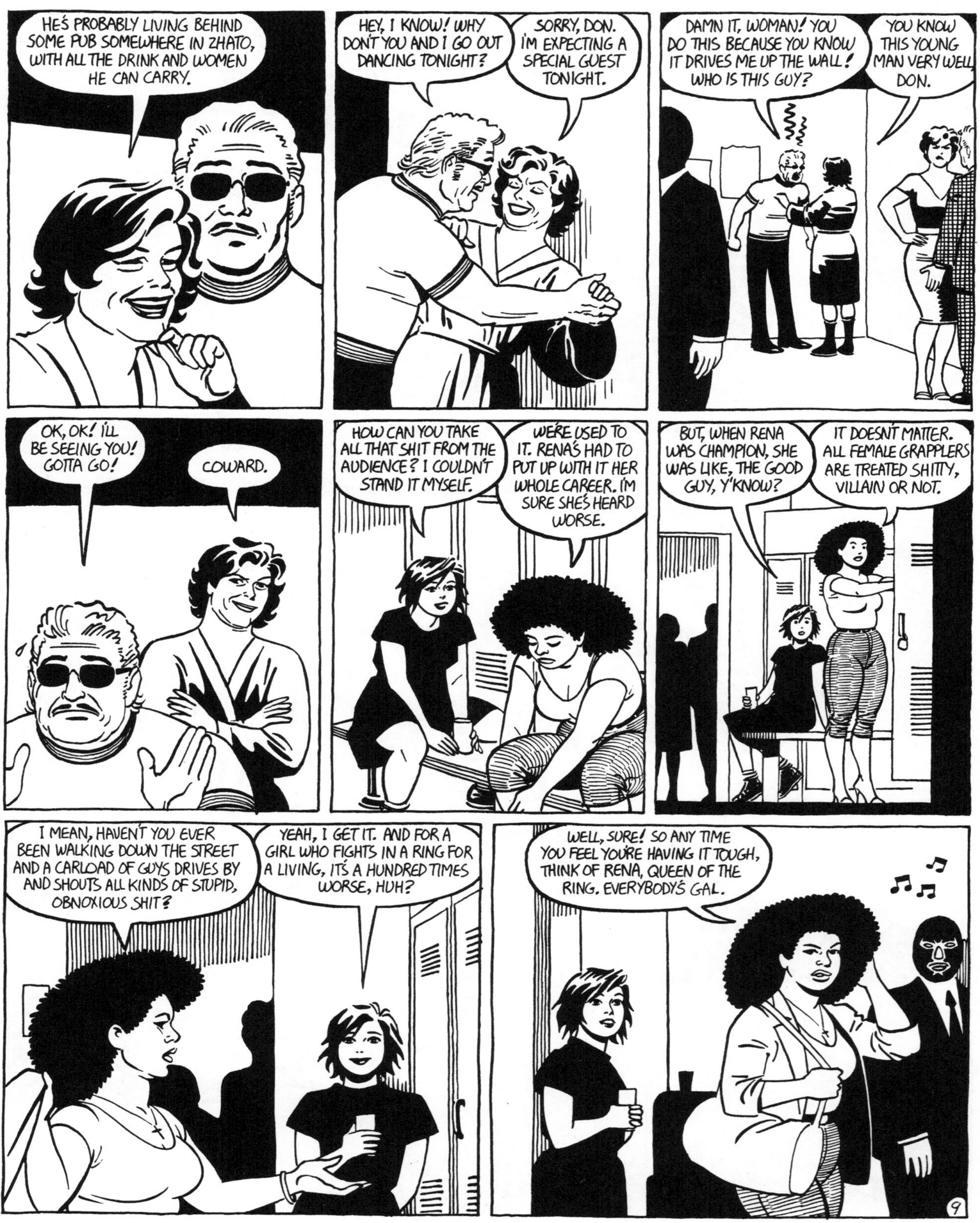
HE'S PROBABLY LIVING BEHIND SOME PUB SOMEWHERE IN ZHATO, WITH ALL THE DRINK AND WOMEN HE CAN CARRY.
HEY, I KNOW! WHY DON'T YOU AND I GO OUT DANCING TONIGHT?
SORRY, DON. I'M EXPECTING A SPECIAL GUEST TONIGHT.
DAMN IT, WOMAN! YOU DO THIS BECAUSE YOU KNOW IT DRIVES ME UP THE WALL! WHO IS THIS GUY?
YOU KNOW THIS YOUNG MAN VERY WELL, DON.
OK, OK! I'LL BE SEEING YOU! GOTTA GO!
COWARD.
HOW CAN YOU TAKE ALL THAT SHIT FROM THE AUDIENCE? I COULDN'T STAND IT MYSELF.
WE'RE USED TO IT. RENA'S HAD TO PUT UP WITH IT HER WHOLE CAREER. I'M SURE SHE'S HEARD WORSE.
BUT, WHEN RENA WAS CHAMPION, SHE WAS LIKE, THE GOOD GUY, Y'KNOW?
IT DOESN'T MATTER. ALL FEMALE GRAPPLERS ARE TREATED SHITTY, VILLAIN OR NOT.
I MEAN, HAVEN'T YOU EVER BEEN WALKING DOWN THE STREET AND A CARLOAD OF GUYS DRIVES BY AND SHOUTS ALL KINDS OF STUPID, OBNOXIOUS SHIT?
YEAH, I GET IT. AND FOR A GIRL WHO FIGHTS IN A RING FOR A LIVING, IT'S A HUNDRED TIMES WORSE, HUH?
WELL, SURE! SO ANY TIME YOU FEEL YOU'RE HAVING IT TOUGH, THINK OF RENA, QUEEN OF THE RING. EVERYBODY'S GAL.
9

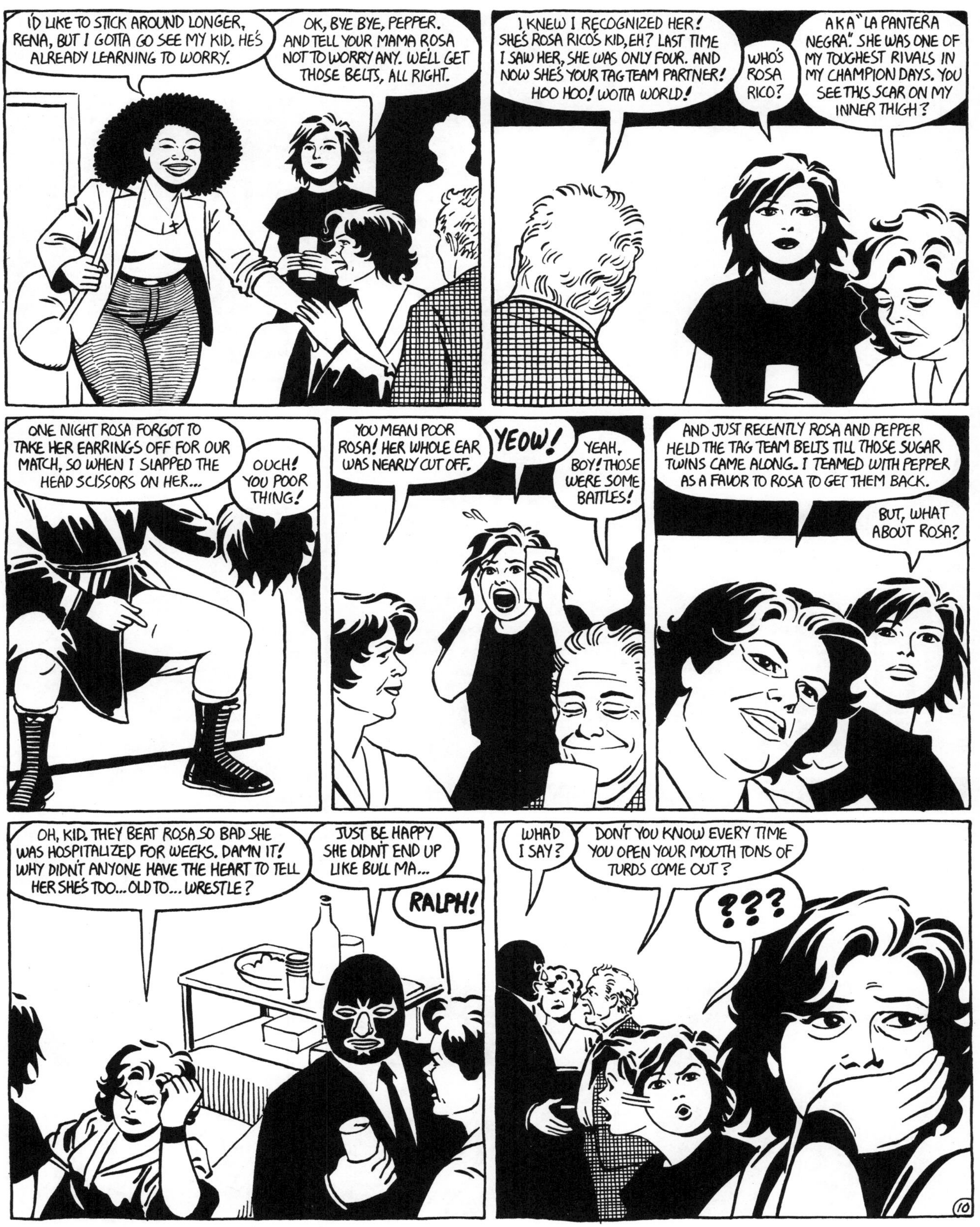
I'D LIKE TO STICK AROUND LONGER, RENA, BUT I GOTTA GO SEE MY KID. HE'S ALREADY LEARNING TO WORRY.
OK, BYE BYE, PEPPER. AND TELL YOUR MAMA ROSA NOT TO WORRY ANY. WE'LL GET THOSE BELTS, ALL RIGHT.
I KNEW I RECOGNIZED HER! SHE'S ROSA RICO'S KID, EH? LAST TIME I SAW HER, SHE WAS ONLY FOUR. AND NOW SHE'S YOUR TAG TEAM PARTNER! HOO HOO! WOTTA WORLD!
WHO'S ROSA RICO?
A K A "LA PANTERA NEGRA". SHE WAS ONE OF MY TOUGHEST RIVALS IN MY CHAMPION DAYS. YOU SEE THIS SCAR ON MY INNER THIGH?
ONE NIGHT ROSA FORGOT TO TAKE HER EARRINGS OFF FOR OUR MATCH, SO WHEN I SLAPPED THE HEAD SCISSORS ON HER...
OUCH! YOU POOR THING!
YOU MEAN POOR ROSA! HER WHOLE EAR WAS NEARLY CUT OFF.
YEOW!
YEAH, BOY! THOSE WERE SOME BATTLES!
AND JUST RECENTLY ROSA AND PEPPER HELD THE TAG TEAM BELTS TILL THOSE SUGAR TWINS CAME ALONG. I TEAMED WITH PEPPER AS A FAVOR TO ROSA TO GET THEM BACK.
BUT, WHAT ABOUT ROSA?
OH, KID. THEY BEAT ROSA SO BAD SHE WAS HOSPITALIZED FOR WEEKS. DAMN IT! WHY DIDN'T ANYONE HAVE THE HEART TO TELL HER SHE'S TOO...OLD TO... WRESTLE?
JUST BE HAPPY SHE DIDN'T END UP LIKE BULL MA...
RALPH!
WHA'D I SAY?
DON'T YOU KNOW EVERY TIME YOU OPEN YOUR MOUTH TONS OF TURDS COME OUT?
???
10

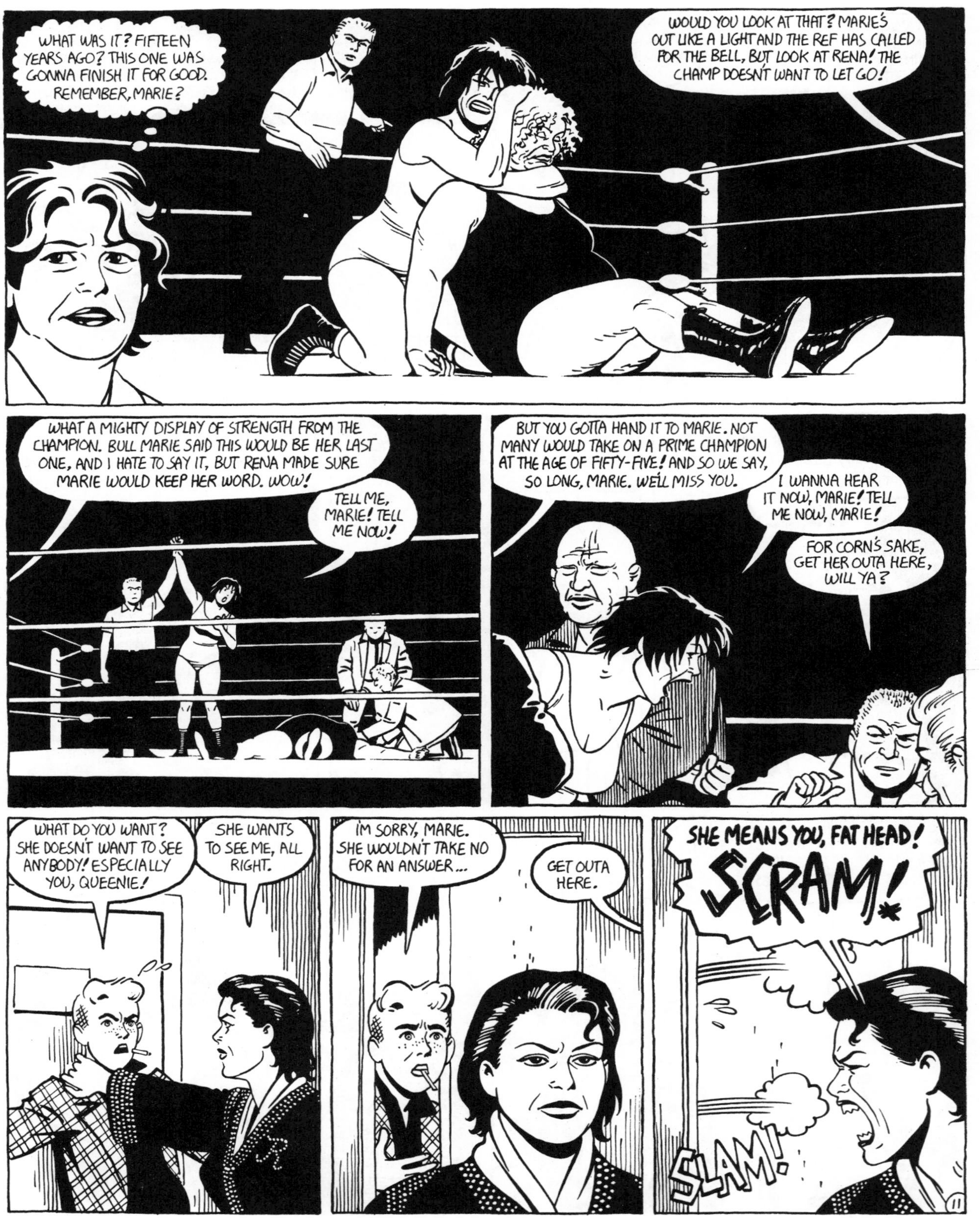
WHAT WAS IT? FIFTEEN YEARS AGO? THIS ONE WAS GONNA FINISH IT FOR GOOD. REMEMBER, MARIE?
WOULD YOU LOOK AT THAT? MARIE'S OUT LIKE A LIGHT AND THE REF HAS CALLED FOR THE BELL, BUT LOOK AT RENA! THE CHAMP DOESN'T WANT TO LET GO!
WHAT A MIGHTY DISPLAY OF STRENGTH FROM THE CHAMPION. BULL MARIE SAID THIS WOULD BE HER LAST ONE, AND I HATE TO SAY IT, BUT RENA MADE SURE MARIE WOULD KEEP HER WORD. WOW!
TELL ME, MARIE! TELL ME NOW!
BUT YOU GOTTA HAND IT TO MARIE. NOT MANY WOULD TAKE ON A PRIME CHAMPION AT THE AGE OF FIFTY-FIVE! AND SO WE SAY, SO LONG, MARIE. WE'LL MISS YOU.
I WANNA HEAR IT NOW, MARIE! TELL ME NOW, MARIE!
FOR CORN'S SAKE, GET HER OUTA HERE, WILL YA?
WHAT DO YOU WANT? SHE DOESN'T WANT TO SEE ANYBODY! ESPECIALLY YOU, QUEENIE!
SHE WANTS TO SEE ME, ALL RIGHT.
I'M SORRY, MARIE. SHE WOULDN'T TAKE NO FOR AN ANSWER...
GET OUTA HERE.
SHE MEANS YOU, FAT HEAD!
SCRAM!
SLAM!
11

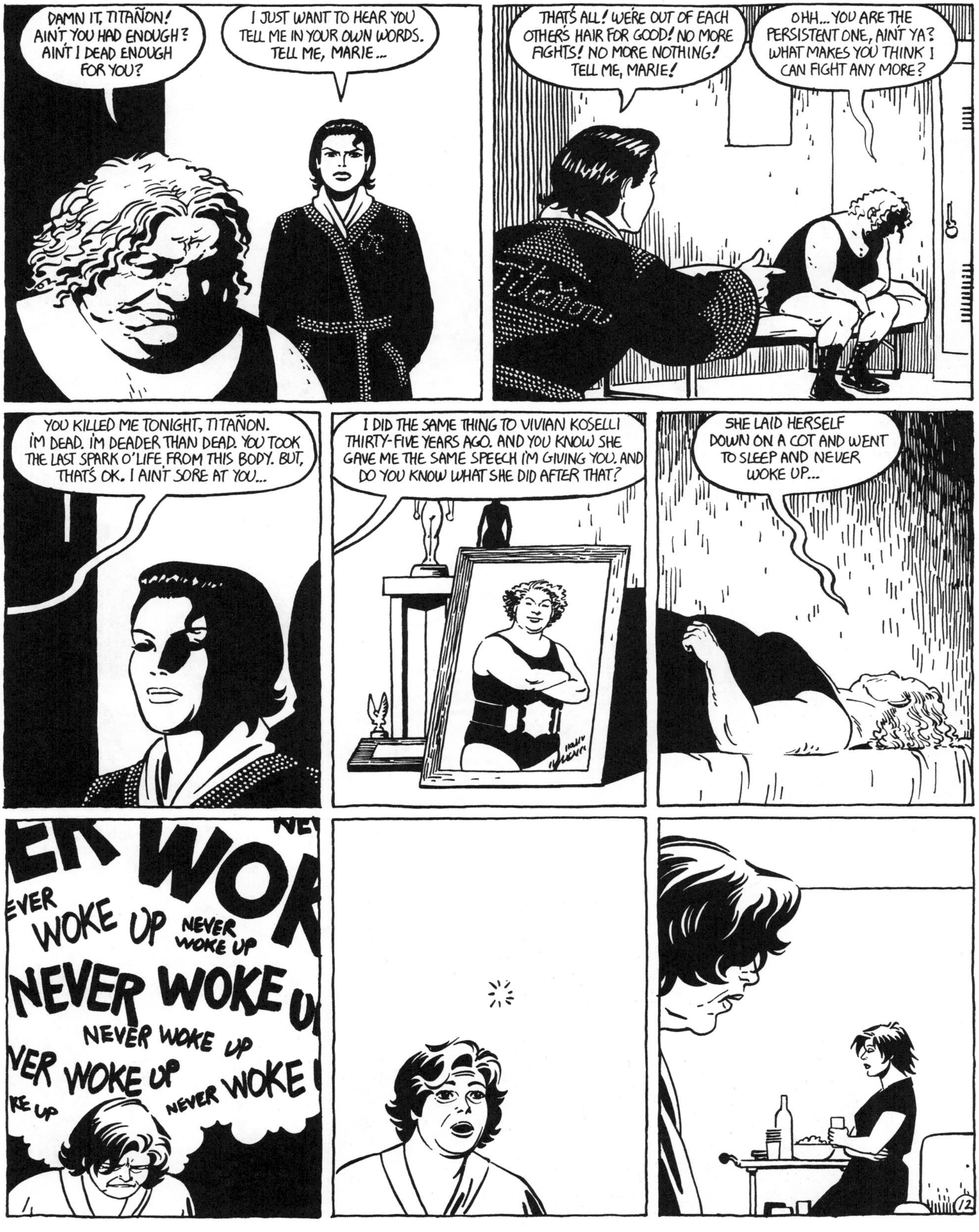
DAMN IT, TITAÑON! AIN'T YOU HAD ENOUGH? AIN'T I DEAD ENOUGH FOR YOU?
I JUST WANT TO HEAR YOU TELL ME IN YOUR OWN WORDS. TELL ME, MARIE...
THAT'S ALL! WE'RE OUT OF EACH OTHER'S HAIR FOR GOOD! NO MORE FIGHTS! NO MORE NOTHING! TELL ME, MARIE!
OHH... YOU ARE THE PERSISTENT ONE, AIN'T YA? WHAT MAKES YOU THINK I CAN FIGHT ANY MORE?
Titañon
YOU KILLED ME TONIGHT, TITAÑON. I'M DEAD. I'M DEADER THAN DEAD. YOU TOOK THE LAST SPARK O' LIFE FROM THIS BODY. BUT, THAT'S OK. I AIN'T SORE AT YOU...
I DID THE SAME THING TO VIVIAN KOSELLI THIRTY-FIVE YEARS AGO. AND YOU KNOW SHE GAVE ME THE SAME SPEECH I'M GIVING YOU. AND DO YOU KNOW WHAT SHE DID AFTER THAT?
SHE LAID HERSELF DOWN ON A COT AND WENT TO SLEEP AND NEVER WOKE UP...
NEVER WOKE UP NEVER WOKE UP
NEVER WOKE
NEVER WOKE UP
NEVER WOKE UP
NEVER WOKE
12

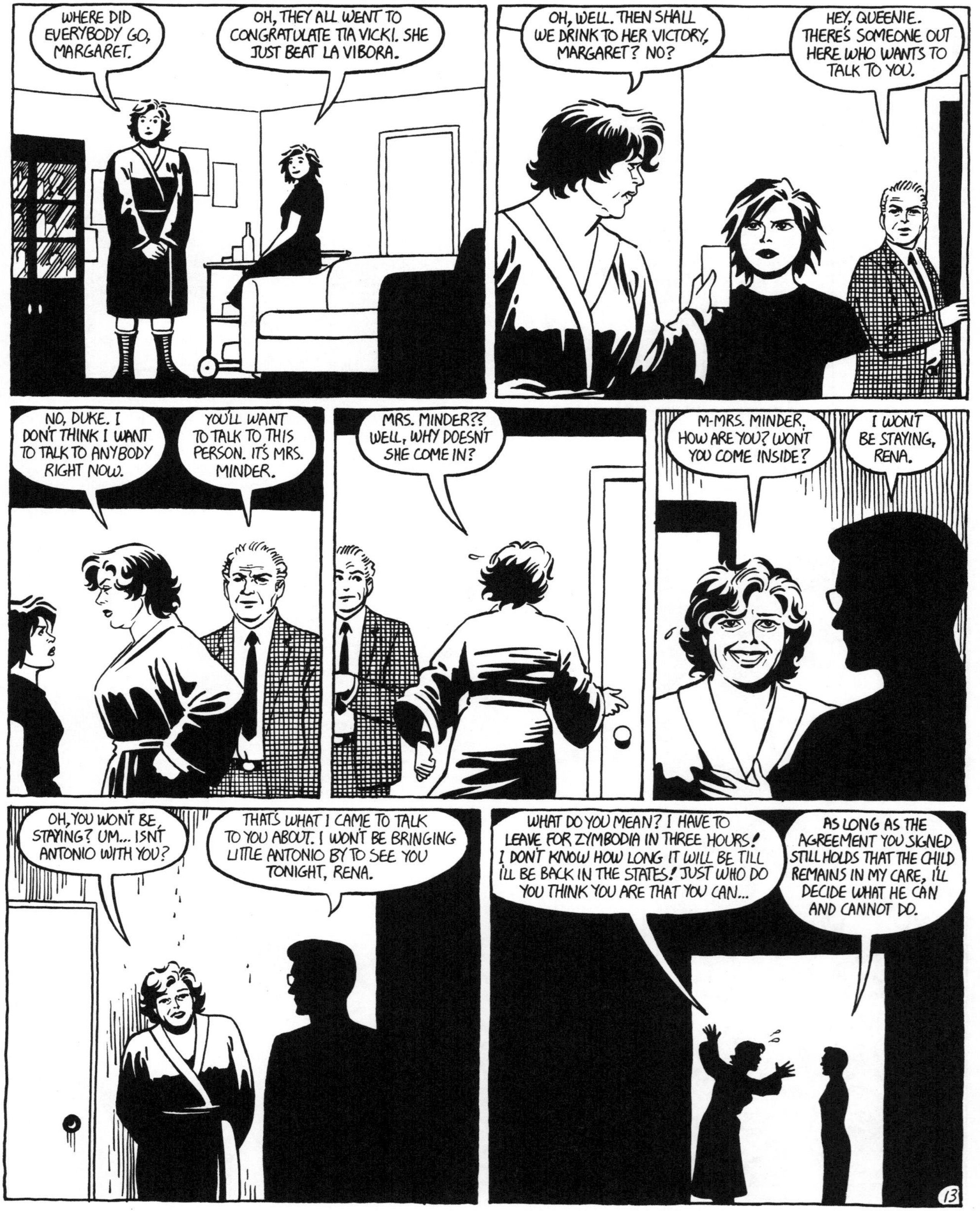
WHERE DID EVERYBODY GO, MARGARET.
OH, THEY ALL WENT TO CONGRATULATE TIA VICKI. SHE JUST BEAT LA VIBORA.
OH, WELL. THEN SHALL WE DRINK TO HER VICTORY, MARGARET? NO?
HEY, QUEENIE. THERE'S SOMEONE OUT HERE WHO WANTS TO TALK TO YOU.
NO, DUKE. I DON'T THINK I WANT TO TALK TO ANYBODY RIGHT NOW.
YOU'LL WANT TO TALK TO THIS PERSON. IT'S MRS. MINDER.
MRS. MINDER?? WELL, WHY DOESN'T SHE COME IN?
M-MRS. MINDER, HOW ARE YOU? WON'T YOU COME INSIDE?
I WON'T BE STAYING, RENA.
OH, YOU WON'T BE STAYING? UM... ISN'T ANTONIO WITH YOU?
THAT'S WHAT I CAME TO TALK TO YOU ABOUT. I WON'T BE BRINGING LITTLE ANTONIO BY TO SEE YOU TONIGHT, RENA.
WHAT DO YOU MEAN? I HAVE TO LEAVE FOR ZYMBODIA IN THREE HOURS! I DON'T KNOW HOW LONG IT WILL BE TILL I'LL BE BACK IN THE STATES! JUST WHO DO YOU THINK YOU ARE THAT YOU CAN...
AS LONG AS THE AGREEMENT YOU SIGNED STILL HOLDS THAT THE CHILD REMAINS IN MY CARE, I'LL DECIDE WHAT HE CAN AND CANNOT DO.
13

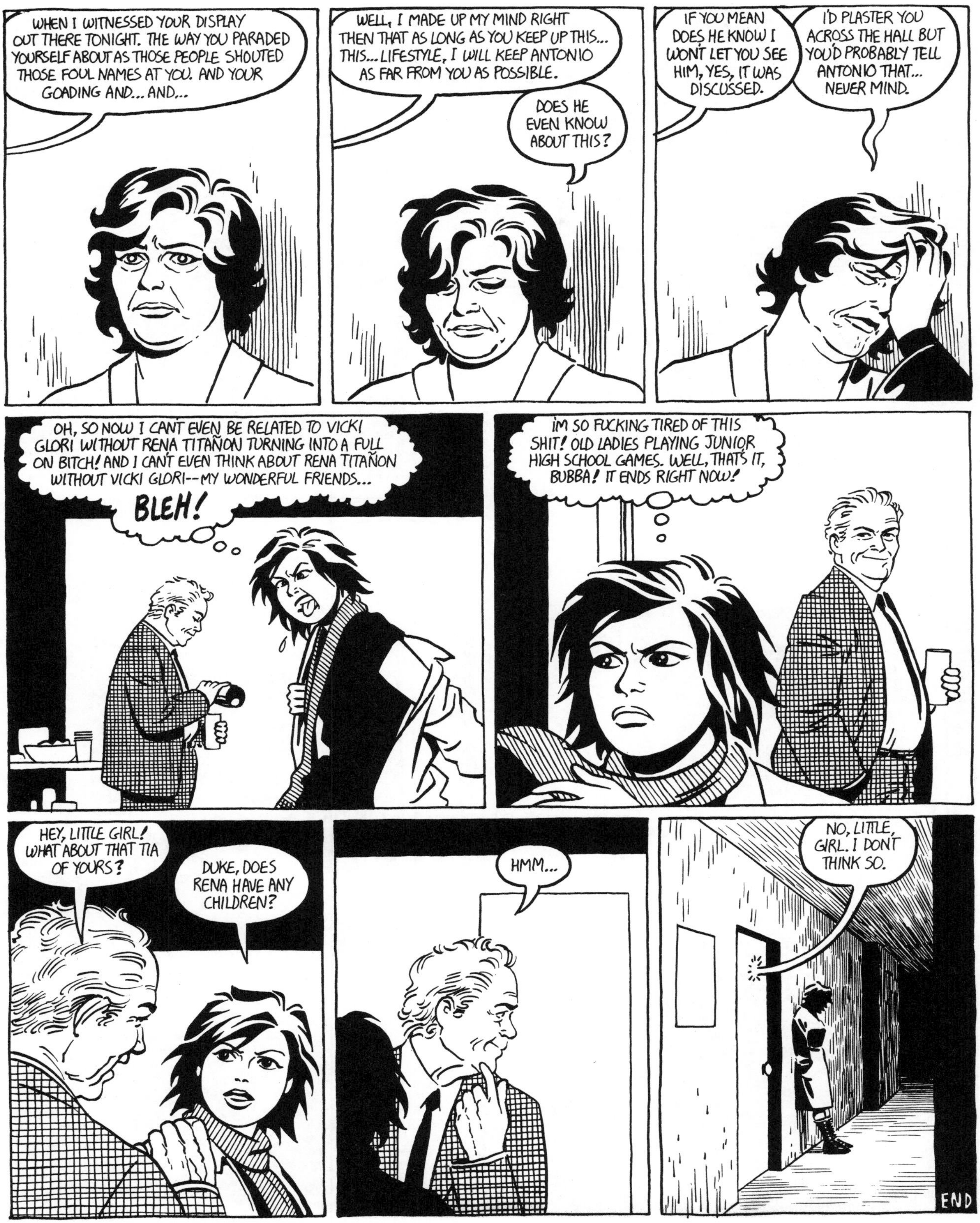
WHEN I WITNESSED YOUR DISPLAY OUT THERE TONIGHT. THE WAY YOU PARADED YOURSELF ABOUT AS THOSE PEOPLE SHOUTED THOSE FOUL NAMES AT YOU. AND YOUR GOADING AND... AND...
WELL, I MADE UP MY MIND RIGHT THEN THAT AS LONG AS YOU KEEP UP THIS... THIS... LIFESTYLE, I WILL KEEP ANTONIO AS FAR FROM YOU AS POSSIBLE.
DOES HE EVEN KNOW ABOUT THIS?
IF YOU MEAN DOES HE KNOW I WON'T LET YOU SEE HIM, YES, IT WAS DISCUSSED.
I'D PLASTER YOU ACROSS THE HALL BUT YOU'D PROBABLY TELL ANTONIO THAT... NEVER MIND.
OH, SO NOW I CAN'T EVEN BE RELATED TO VICKI GLORI WITHOUT RENA TITAÑON TURNING INTO A FULL ON BITCH! AND I CAN'T EVEN THINK ABOUT RENA TITAÑON WITHOUT VICKI GLORI--MY WONDERFUL FRIENDS...
BLEH!
I'M SO FUCKING TIRED OF THIS SHIT! OLD LADIES PLAYING JUNIOR HIGH SCHOOL GAMES. WELL, THAT'S IT, BUBBA! IT ENDS RIGHT NOW!
HEY, LITTLE GIRL! WHAT ABOUT THAT TIA OF YOURS?
DUKE, DOES RENA HAVE ANY CHILDREN?
HMM...
NO, LITTLE GIRL. I DON'T THINK SO.
END

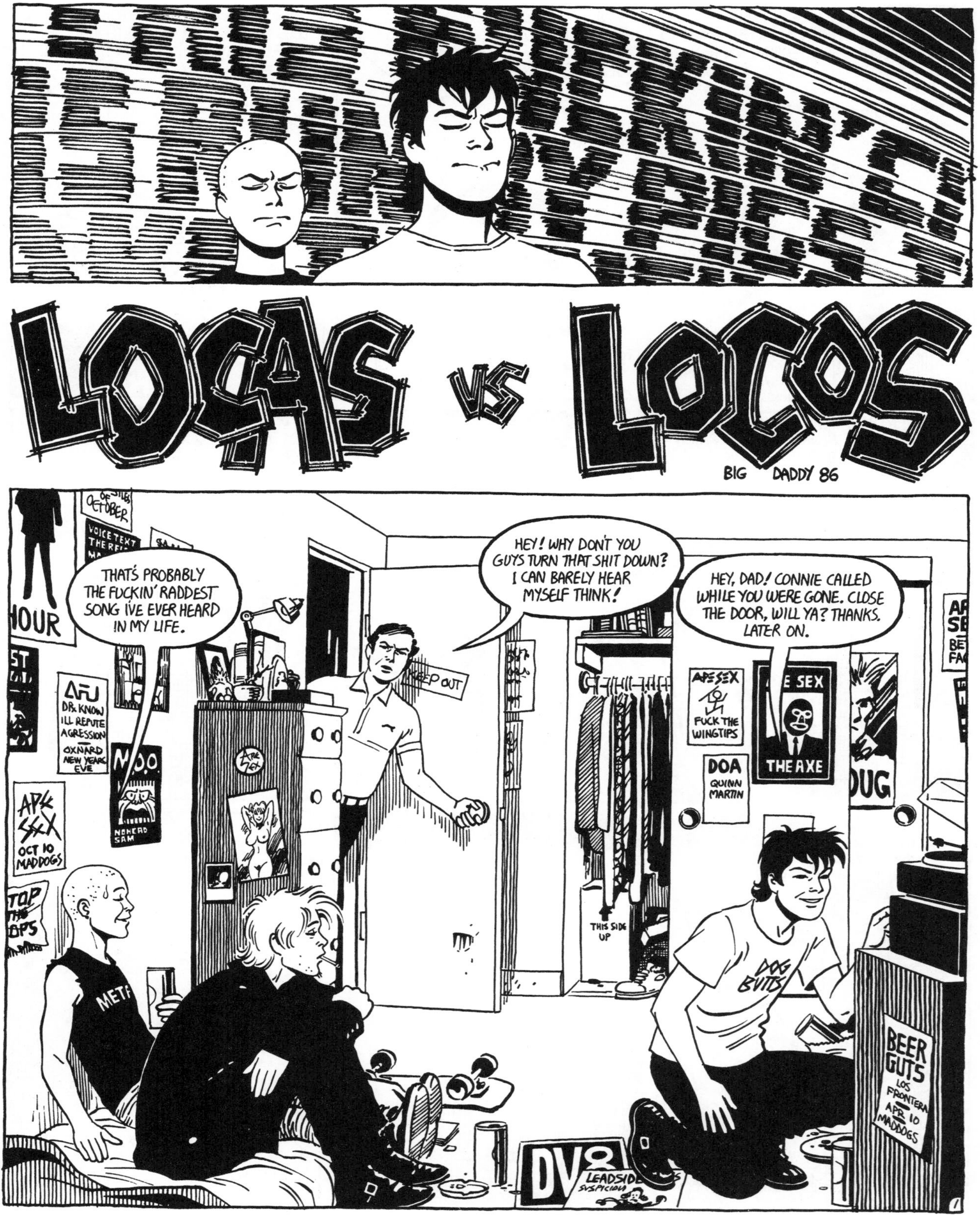
LOCAS vs LOCOS
BIG DADDY 86
THAT'S PROBABLY THE FUCKIN' RADDEST SONG I'VE EVER HEARD IN MY LIFE.
HEY! WHY DON'T YOU GUYS TURN THAT SHIT DOWN? I CAN BARELY HEAR MYSELF THINK!
HEY, DAD! CONNIE CALLED WHILE YOU WERE GONE. CLOSE THE DOOR, WILL YA? THANKS. LATER ON.
KEEP OUT
DR. KNOW ILL REPUTE AGRESSION OXNARD NEW YEARS EVE
APE SEX OCT 10 MADDOGS
APE SEX FUCK THE WINGTIPS
THE AXE
DOA QUINN MARTIN
THIS SIDE UP
DOG GUTS
BEER GUTS LOS FRONTERA APR 10 MADDOGS
DV8
LEADSIDE
1

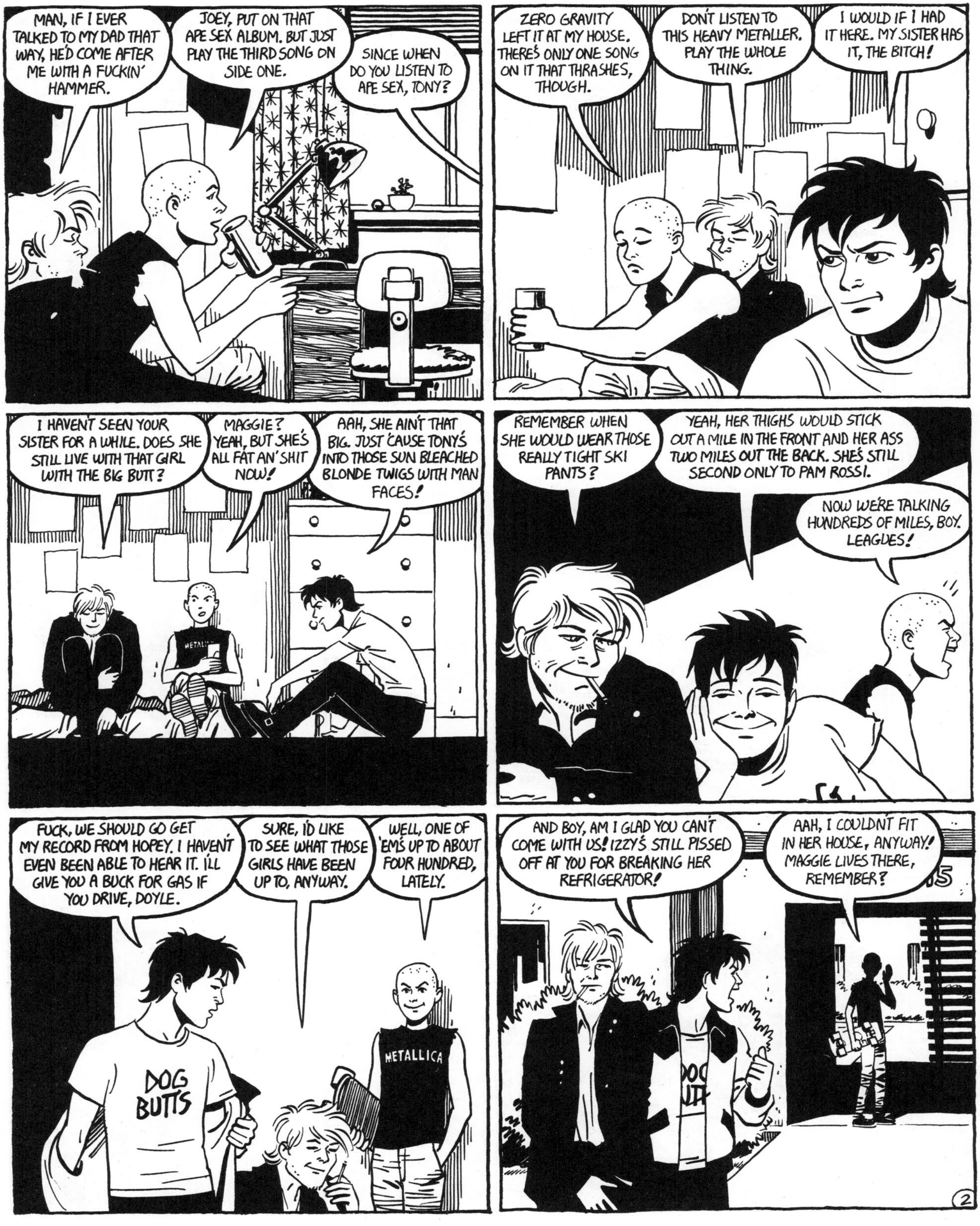

MAN, IF I EVER TALKED TO MY DAD THAT WAY, HE'D COME AFTER ME WITH A FUCKIN' HAMMER.
JOEY, PUT ON THAT APE SEX ALBUM. BUT JUST PLAY THE THIRD SONG ON SIDE ONE.
SINCE WHEN DO YOU LISTEN TO APE SEX, TONY?
ZERO GRAVITY LEFT IT AT MY HOUSE. THERE'S ONLY ONE SONG ON IT THAT THRASHES, THOUGH.
DON'T LISTEN TO THIS HEAVY METALLER. PLAY THE WHOLE THING.
I WOULD IF I HAD IT HERE. MY SISTER HAS IT, THE BITCH!
I HAVEN'T SEEN YOUR SISTER FOR A WHILE. DOES SHE STILL LIVE WITH THAT GIRL WITH THE BIG BUTT?
MAGGIE? YEAH, BUT SHE'S ALL FAT AN' SHIT NOW!
AAH, SHE AIN'T THAT BIG. JUST 'CAUSE TONY'S INTO THOSE SUN BLEACHED BLONDE TWIGS WITH MAN FACES!
METALLICA
REMEMBER WHEN SHE WOULD WEAR THOSE REALLY TIGHT SKI PANTS?
YEAH, HER THIGHS WOULD STICK OUT A MILE IN THE FRONT AND HER ASS TWO MILES OUT THE BACK. SHE'S STILL SECOND ONLY TO PAM ROSSI.
NOW WE'RE TALKING HUNDREDS OF MILES, BOY. LEAGUES!
FUCK, WE SHOULD GO GET MY RECORD FROM HOPEY. I HAVEN'T EVEN BEEN ABLE TO HEAR IT. I'LL GIVE YOU A BUCK FOR GAS IF YOU DRIVE, DOYLE.
SURE, I'D LIKE TO SEE WHAT THOSE GIRLS HAVE BEEN UP TO, ANYWAY.
WELL, ONE OF 'EM'S UP TO ABOUT FOUR HUNDRED, LATELY.
DOG BUTTS
METALLICA
AND BOY, AM I GLAD YOU CAN'T COME WITH US! IZZY'S STILL PISSED OFF AT YOU FOR BREAKING HER REFRIGERATOR!
AAH, I COULDN'T FIT IN HER HOUSE, ANYWAY! MAGGIE LIVES THERE, REMEMBER?
2

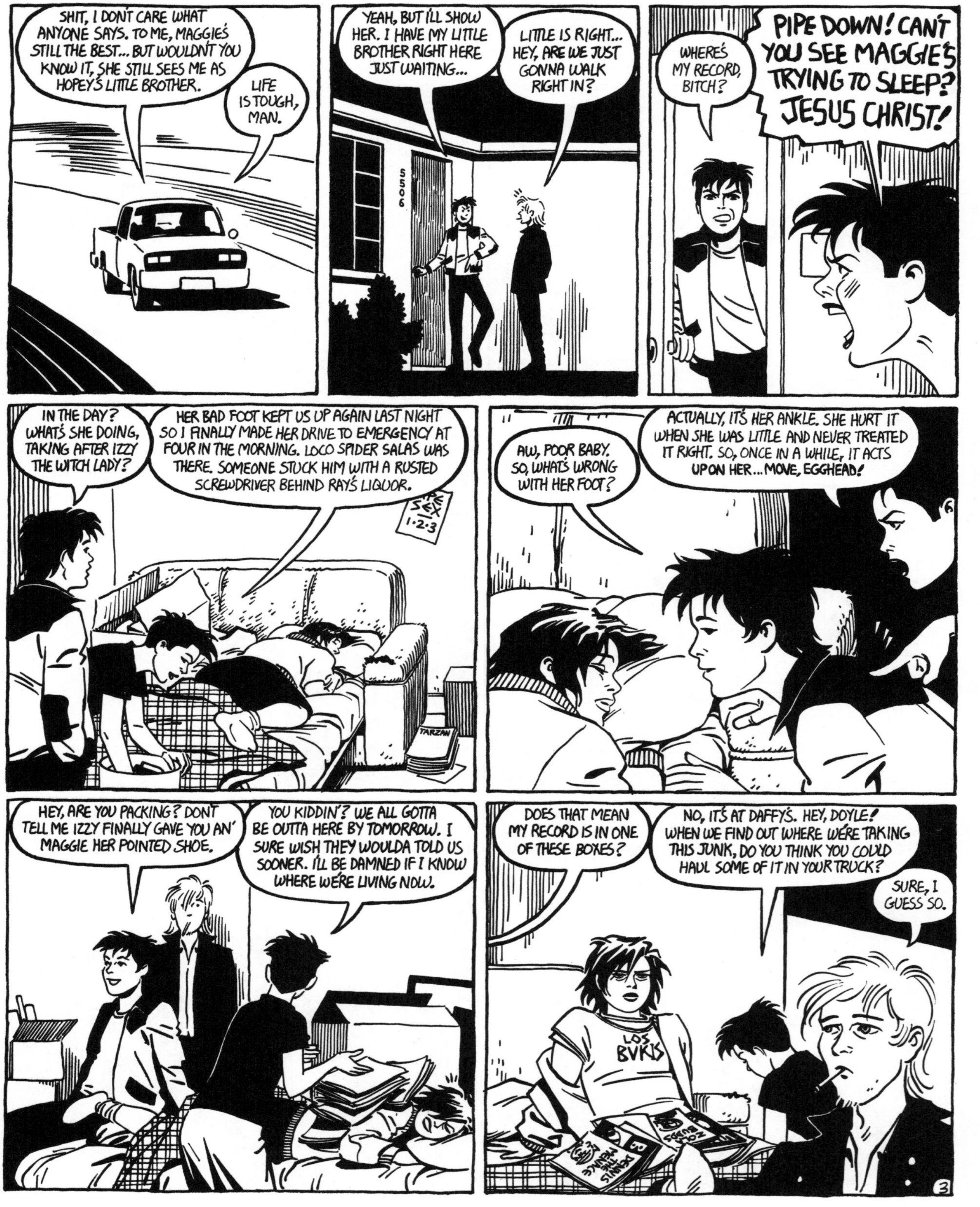
SHIT, I DON'T CARE WHAT ANYONE SAYS. TO ME, MAGGIE'S STILL THE BEST... BUT WOULDN'T YOU KNOW IT, SHE STILL SEES ME AS HOPEY'S LITTLE BROTHER.
LIFE IS TOUGH, MAN.
YEAH, BUT I'LL SHOW HER. I HAVE MY LITTLE BROTHER RIGHT HERE JUST WAITING...
LITTLE IS RIGHT... HEY, ARE WE JUST GONNA WALK RIGHT IN?
5506
WHERE'S MY RECORD, BITCH?
PIPE DOWN! CAN'T YOU SEE MAGGIE'S TRYING TO SLEEP? JESUS CHRIST!
IN THE DAY? WHAT'S SHE DOING, TAKING AFTER IZZY THE WITCH LADY?
HER BAD FOOT KEPT US UP AGAIN LAST NIGHT SO I FINALLY MADE HER DRIVE TO EMERGENCY AT FOUR IN THE MORNING. LOCO SPIDER SALAS WAS THERE. SOMEONE STUCK HIM WITH A RUSTED SCREWDRIVER BEHIND RAY'S LIQUOR.
SEX 1·2·3
TARZAN
AW, POOR BABY. SO, WHAT'S WRONG WITH HER FOOT?
ACTUALLY, IT'S HER ANKLE. SHE HURT IT WHEN SHE WAS LITTLE AND NEVER TREATED IT RIGHT. SO, ONCE IN A WHILE, IT ACTS UP ON HER... MOVE, EGGHEAD!
HEY, ARE YOU PACKING? DON'T TELL ME IZZY FINALLY GAVE YOU AN' MAGGIE HER POINTED SHOE.
YOU KIDDIN'? WE ALL GOTTA BE OUTTA HERE BY TOMORROW. I SURE WISH THEY WOULDA TOLD US SOONER. I'LL BE DAMNED IF I KNOW WHERE WE'RE LIVING NOW.
DOES THAT MEAN MY RECORD IS IN ONE OF THESE BOXES?
NO, IT'S AT DAFFY'S. HEY, DOYLE! WHEN WE FIND OUT WHERE WE'RE TAKING THIS JUNK, DO YOU THINK YOU COULD HAUL SOME OF IT IN YOUR TRUCK?
SURE, I GUESS SO.
LOS BVKIS
DENNIS THE MENACE
3

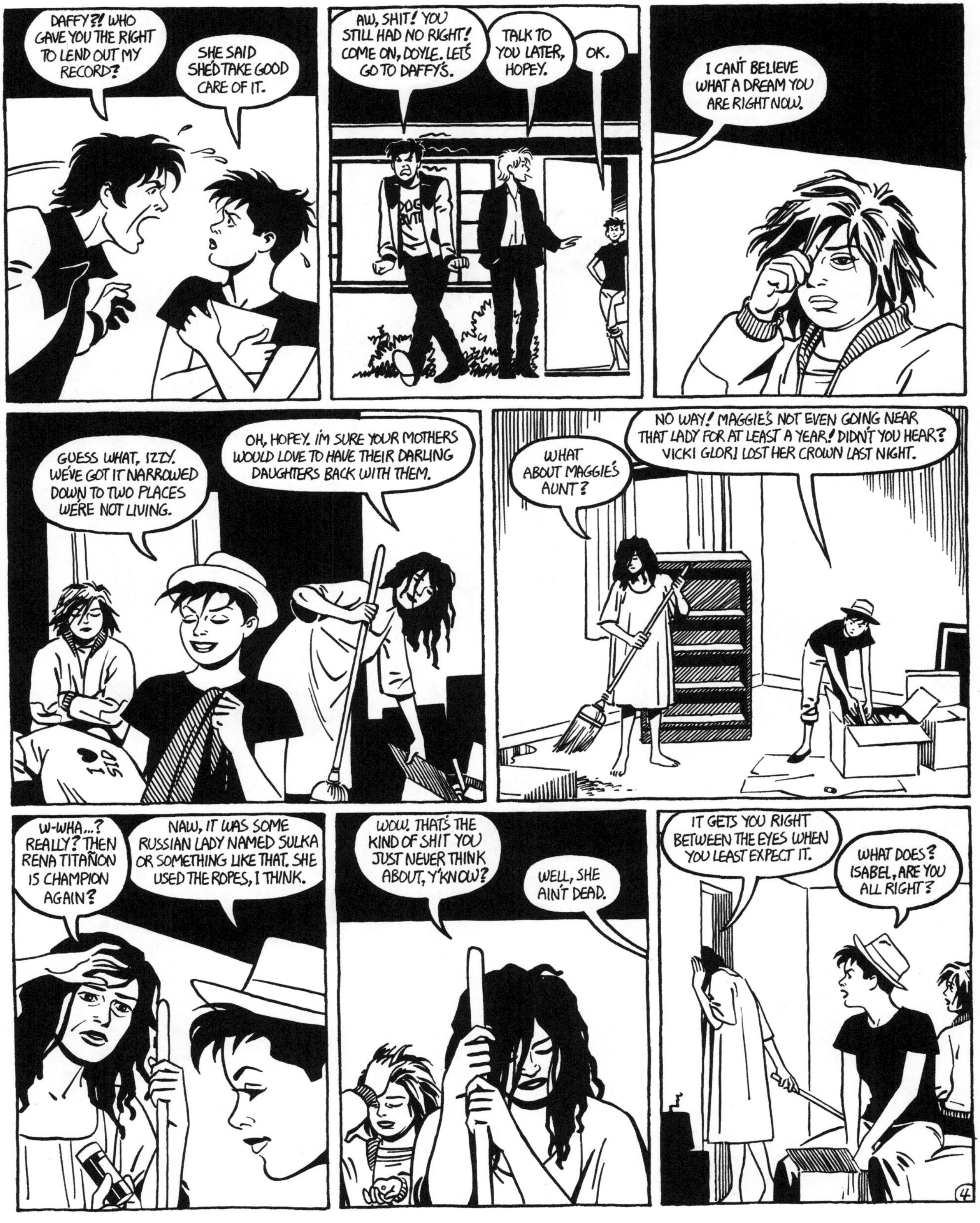
DAFFY?! WHO GAVE YOU THE RIGHT TO LEND OUT MY RECORD?
SHE SAID SHE'D TAKE GOOD CARE OF IT.
AW, SHIT! YOU STILL HAD NO RIGHT! COME ON, DOYLE. LET'S GO TO DAFFY'S.
TALK TO YOU LATER, HOPEY.
OK.
I CAN'T BELIEVE WHAT A DREAM YOU ARE RIGHT NOW.
GUESS WHAT, IZZY. WE'VE GOT IT NARROWED DOWN TO TWO PLACES WE'RE NOT LIVING.
OH, HOPEY. I'M SURE YOUR MOTHERS WOULD LOVE TO HAVE THEIR DARLING DAUGHTERS BACK WITH THEM.
WHAT ABOUT MAGGIE'S AUNT?
NO WAY! MAGGIE'S NOT EVEN GOING NEAR THAT LADY FOR AT LEAST A YEAR! DIDN'T YOU HEAR? VICKI GLORI LOST HER CROWN LAST NIGHT.
W-WHA...? REALLY? THEN RENA TITAÑON IS CHAMPION AGAIN?
NAW, IT WAS SOME RUSSIAN LADY NAMED SULKA OR SOMETHING LIKE THAT. SHE USED THE ROPES, I THINK.
WOW. THAT'S THE KIND OF SHIT YOU JUST NEVER THINK ABOUT, Y'KNOW?
WELL, SHE AIN'T DEAD.
IT GETS YOU RIGHT BETWEEN THE EYES WHEN YOU LEAST EXPECT IT.
WHAT DOES? ISABEL, ARE YOU ALL RIGHT?
4

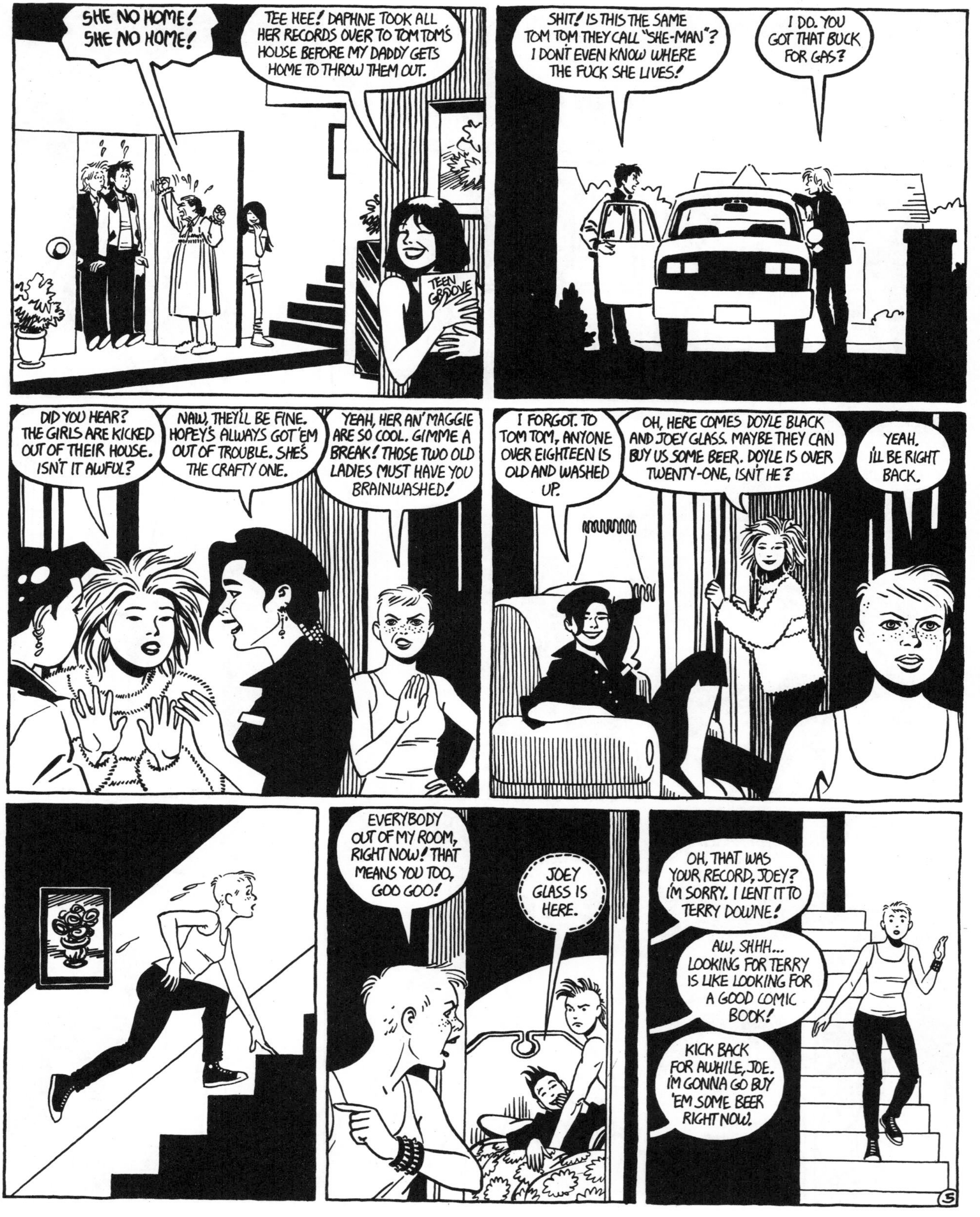
SHE NO HOME! SHE NO HOME!
TEE HEE! DAPHNE TOOK ALL HER RECORDS OVER TO TOM TOM'S HOUSE BEFORE MY DADDY GETS HOME TO THROW THEM OUT.
TEEN GROOVE
SHIT! IS THIS THE SAME TOM TOM THEY CALL "SHE-MAN"? I DON'T EVEN KNOW WHERE THE FUCK SHE LIVES!
I DO. YOU GOT THAT BUCK FOR GAS?
DID YOU HEAR? THE GIRLS ARE KICKED OUT OF THEIR HOUSE. ISN'T IT AWFUL?
NAW, THEY'LL BE FINE. HOPEY'S ALWAYS GOT 'EM OUT OF TROUBLE. SHE'S THE CRAFTY ONE.
YEAH, HER AN' MAGGIE ARE SO COOL. GIMME A BREAK! THOSE TWO OLD LADIES MUST HAVE YOU BRAINWASHED!
I FORGOT. TO TOM TOM, ANYONE OVER EIGHTEEN IS OLD AND WASHED UP.
OH, HERE COMES DOYLE BLACK AND JOEY GLASS. MAYBE THEY CAN BUY US SOME BEER. DOYLE IS OVER TWENTY-ONE, ISN'T HE?
YEAH. I'LL BE RIGHT BACK.
EVERYBODY OUT OF MY ROOM, RIGHT NOW! THAT MEANS YOU TOO, GOO GOO!
JOEY GLASS IS HERE.
OH, THAT WAS YOUR RECORD, JOEY? I'M SORRY. I LENT IT TO TERRY DOWNE!
AW, SHHH... LOOKING FOR TERRY IS LIKE LOOKING FOR A GOOD COMIC BOOK!
KICK BACK FOR AWHILE, JOE. I'M GONNA GO BUY 'EM SOME BEER RIGHT NOW.
5

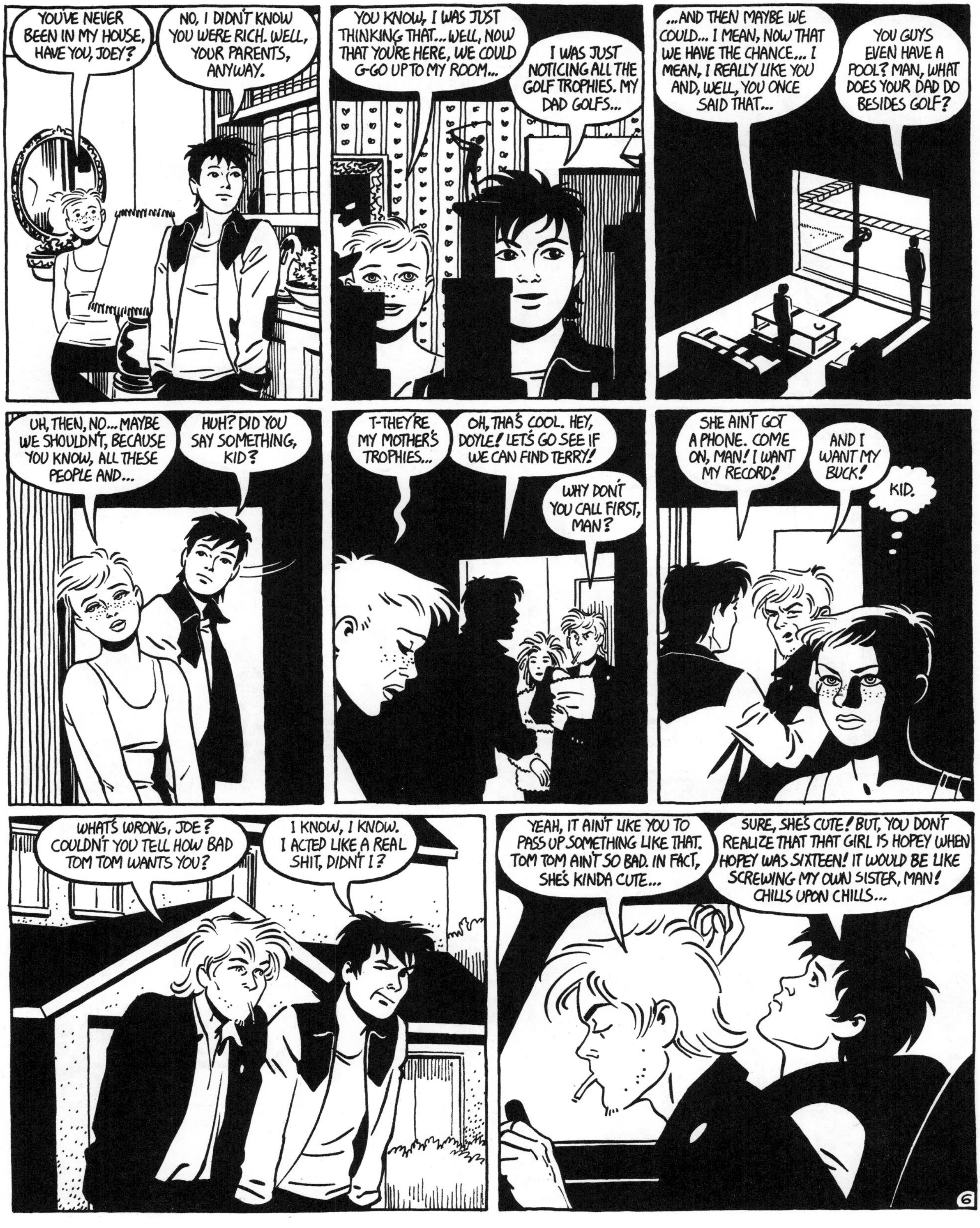
YOU'VE NEVER BEEN IN MY HOUSE, HAVE YOU, JOEY?
NO, I DIDN'T KNOW YOU WERE RICH. WELL, YOUR PARENTS, ANYWAY.
YOU KNOW, I WAS JUST THINKING THAT... WELL, NOW THAT YOU'RE HERE, WE COULD G-GO UP TO MY ROOM...
I WAS JUST NOTICING ALL THE GOLF TROPHIES. MY DAD GOLFS...
...AND THEN MAYBE WE COULD... I MEAN, NOW THAT WE HAVE THE CHANCE... I MEAN, I REALLY LIKE YOU AND, WELL, YOU ONCE SAID THAT...
YOU GUYS EVEN HAVE A POOL? MAN, WHAT DOES YOUR DAD DO BESIDES GOLF?
UH, THEN, NO... MAYBE WE SHOULDN'T, BECAUSE YOU KNOW, ALL THESE PEOPLE AND...
HUH? DID YOU SAY SOMETHING, KID?
T-THEY'RE MY MOTHER'S TROPHIES...
OH, THA'S COOL. HEY, DOYLE! LET'S GO SEE IF WE CAN FIND TERRY!
WHY DON'T YOU CALL FIRST, MAN?
SHE AIN'T GOT A PHONE. COME ON, MAN! I WANT MY RECORD!
AND I WANT MY BUCK!
KID.
WHAT'S WRONG, JOE? COULDN'T YOU TELL HOW BAD TOM TOM WANTS YOU?
I KNOW, I KNOW. I ACTED LIKE A REAL SHIT, DIDN'T I?
YEAH, IT AIN'T LIKE YOU TO PASS UP SOMETHING LIKE THAT. TOM TOM AIN'T SO BAD. IN FACT, SHE'S KINDA CUTE...
SURE, SHE'S CUTE! BUT, YOU DON'T REALIZE THAT THAT GIRL IS HOPEY WHEN HOPEY WAS SIXTEEN! IT WOULD BE LIKE SCREWING MY OWN SISTER, MAN! CHILLS UPON CHILLS...
6

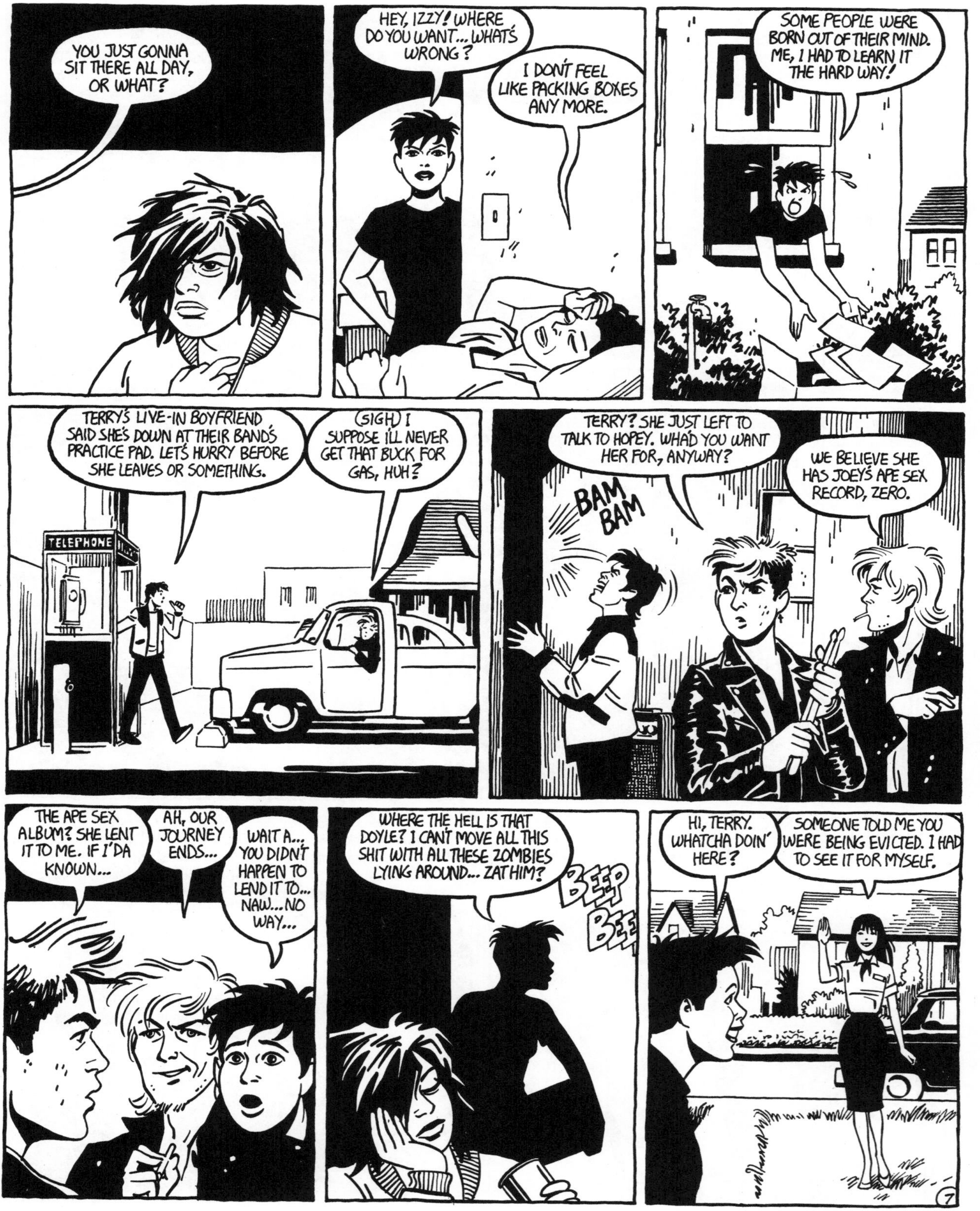
YOU JUST GONNA SIT THERE ALL DAY, OR WHAT?
HEY, IZZY! WHERE DO YOU WANT... WHAT'S WRONG?
I DON'T FEEL LIKE PACKING BOXES ANY MORE.
SOME PEOPLE WERE BORN OUT OF THEIR MIND. ME, I HAD TO LEARN IT THE HARD WAY!
TERRY'S LIVE-IN BOYFRIEND SAID SHE'S DOWN AT THEIR BAND'S PRACTICE PAD. LET'S HURRY BEFORE SHE LEAVES OR SOMETHING.
(SIGH) I SUPPOSE I'LL NEVER GET THAT BUCK FOR GAS, HUH?
TELEPHONE
TERRY? SHE JUST LEFT TO TALK TO HOPEY. WHA'D YOU WANT HER FOR, ANYWAY?
BAM BAM
WE BELIEVE SHE HAS JOEY'S APE SEX RECORD, ZERO.
THE APE SEX ALBUM? SHE LENT IT TO ME. IF I'DA KNOWN...
AH, OUR JOURNEY ENDS...
WAIT A... YOU DIDN'T HAPPEN TO LEND IT TO... NAW... NO WAY...
WHERE THE HELL IS THAT DOYLE? I CAN'T MOVE ALL THIS SHIT WITH ALL THESE ZOMBIES LYING AROUND... ZAT HIM?
BEEP BEE
HI, TERRY. WHATCHA DOIN' HERE?
SOMEONE TOLD ME YOU WERE BEING EVICTED. I HAD TO SEE IT FOR MYSELF.
7

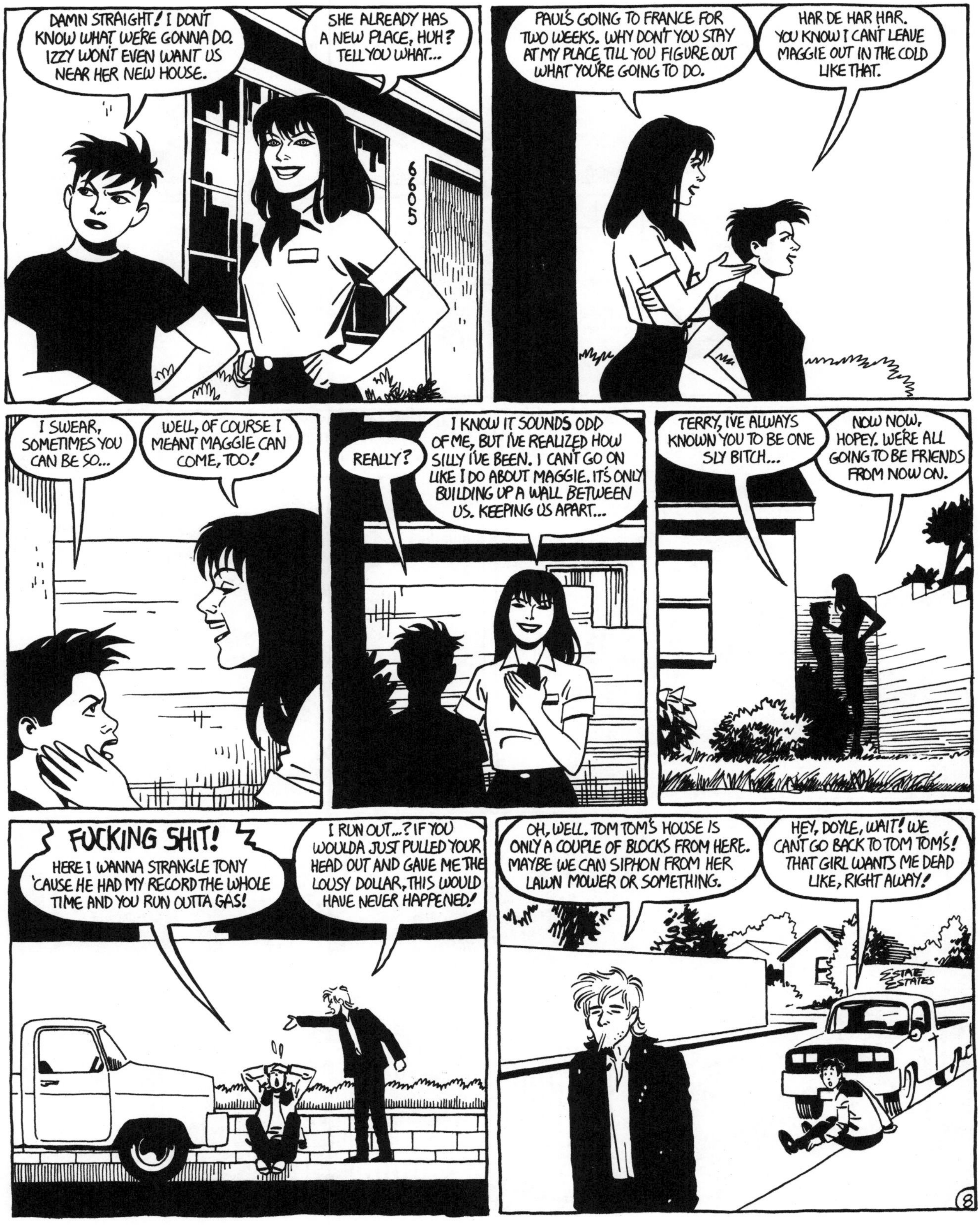
DAMN STRAIGHT! I DON'T KNOW WHAT WE'RE GONNA DO. IZZY WON'T EVEN WANT US NEAR HER NEW HOUSE.
SHE ALREADY HAS A NEW PLACE, HUH? TELL YOU WHAT...
6605
PAUL'S GOING TO FRANCE FOR TWO WEEKS. WHY DON'T YOU STAY AT MY PLACE TILL YOU FIGURE OUT WHAT YOU'RE GOING TO DO.
HAR DE HAR HAR. YOU KNOW I CAN'T LEAVE MAGGIE OUT IN THE COLD LIKE THAT.
I SWEAR, SOMETIMES YOU CAN BE SO...
WELL, OF COURSE I MEANT MAGGIE CAN COME, TOO!
REALLY?
I KNOW IT SOUNDS ODD OF ME, BUT I'VE REALIZED HOW SILLY I'VE BEEN. I CAN'T GO ON LIKE I DO ABOUT MAGGIE. IT'S ONLY BUILDING UP A WALL BETWEEN US. KEEPING US APART...
TERRY, I'VE ALWAYS KNOWN YOU TO BE ONE SLY BITCH...
NOW NOW, HOPEY. WE'RE ALL GOING TO BE FRIENDS FROM NOW ON.
FUCKING SHIT! HERE I WANNA STRANGLE TONY 'CAUSE HE HAD MY RECORD THE WHOLE TIME AND YOU RUN OUTTA GAS!
I RUN OUT...? IF YOU WOULDA JUST PULLED YOUR HEAD OUT AND GAVE ME THE LOUSY DOLLAR, THIS WOULD HAVE NEVER HAPPENED!
OH, WELL. TOM TOM'S HOUSE IS ONLY A COUPLE OF BLOCKS FROM HERE. MAYBE WE CAN SIPHON FROM HER LAWN MOWER OR SOMETHING.
HEY, DOYLE, WAIT! WE CAN'T GO BACK TO TOM TOM'S! THAT GIRL WANTS ME DEAD LIKE, RIGHT AWAY!
ESTATE ESTATES
8

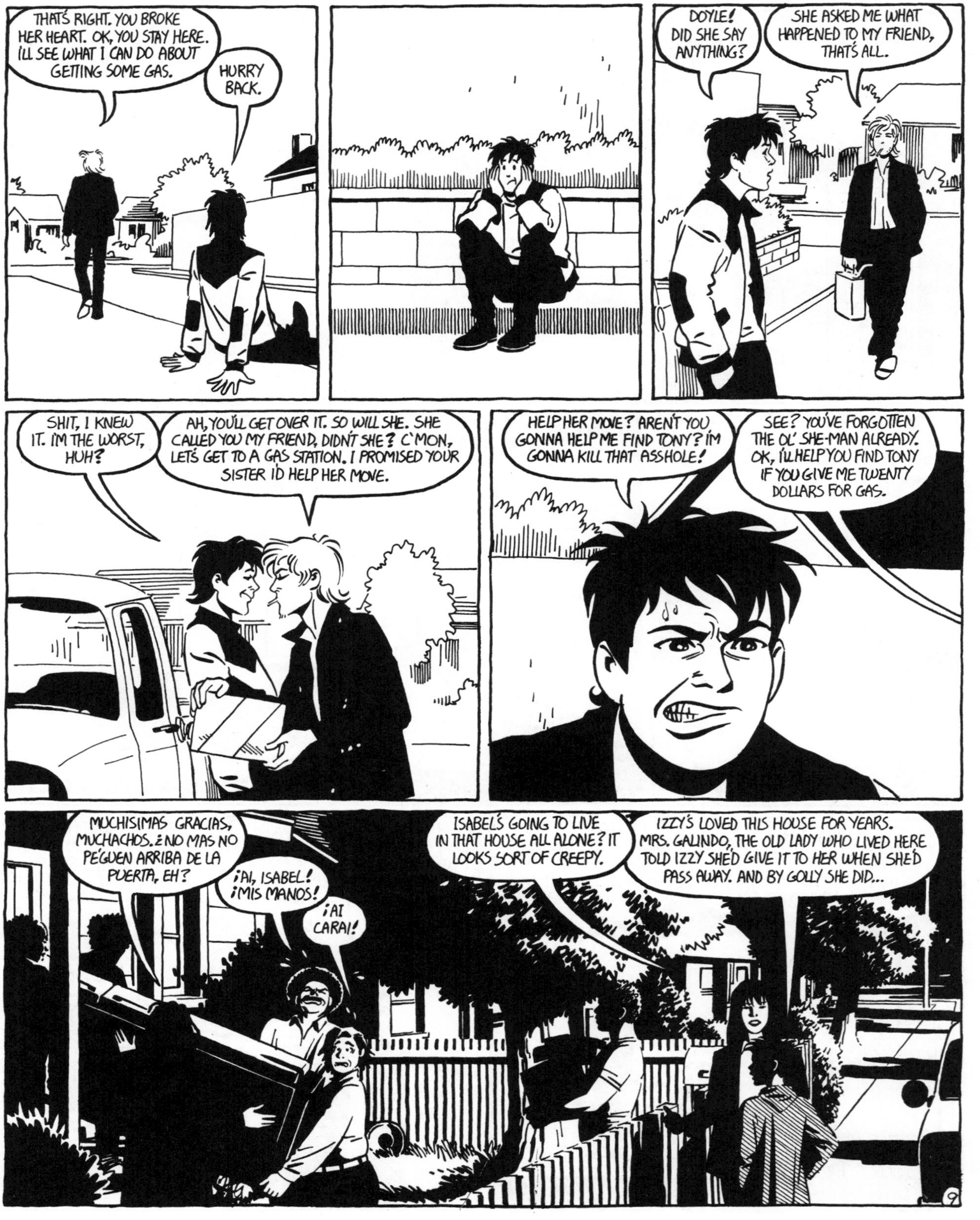
THAT'S RIGHT. YOU BROKE HER HEART. OK, YOU STAY HERE. I'LL SEE WHAT I CAN DO ABOUT GETTING SOME GAS.
HURRY BACK.
DOYLE! DID SHE SAY ANYTHING?
SHE ASKED ME WHAT HAPPENED TO MY FRIEND, THAT'S ALL.
SHIT, I KNEW IT. I'M THE WORST, HUH?
AH, YOU'LL GET OVER IT. SO WILL SHE. SHE CALLED YOU MY FRIEND, DIDN'T SHE? C'MON, LET'S GET TO A GAS STATION. I PROMISED YOUR SISTER I'D HELP HER MOVE.
HELP HER MOVE? AREN'T YOU GONNA HELP ME FIND TONY? I'M GONNA KILL THAT ASSHOLE!
SEE? YOU'VE FORGOTTEN THE OL' SHE-MAN ALREADY. OK, I'LL HELP YOU FIND TONY IF YOU GIVE ME TWENTY DOLLARS FOR GAS.
MUCHISIMAS GRACIAS, MUCHACHOS. ¿NO MAS NO PE'GUEN ARRIBA DE LA PUERTA, EH?
¡AI, ISABEL! ¡MIS MANOS!
¡AI CARAI!
ISABEL'S GOING TO LIVE IN THAT HOUSE ALL ALONE? IT LOOKS SORT OF CREEPY.
IZZY'S LOVED THIS HOUSE FOR YEARS. MRS. GALINDO, THE OLD LADY WHO LIVED HERE TOLD IZZY SHE'D GIVE IT TO HER WHEN SHE'D PASS AWAY. AND BY GOLLY SHE DID...
9

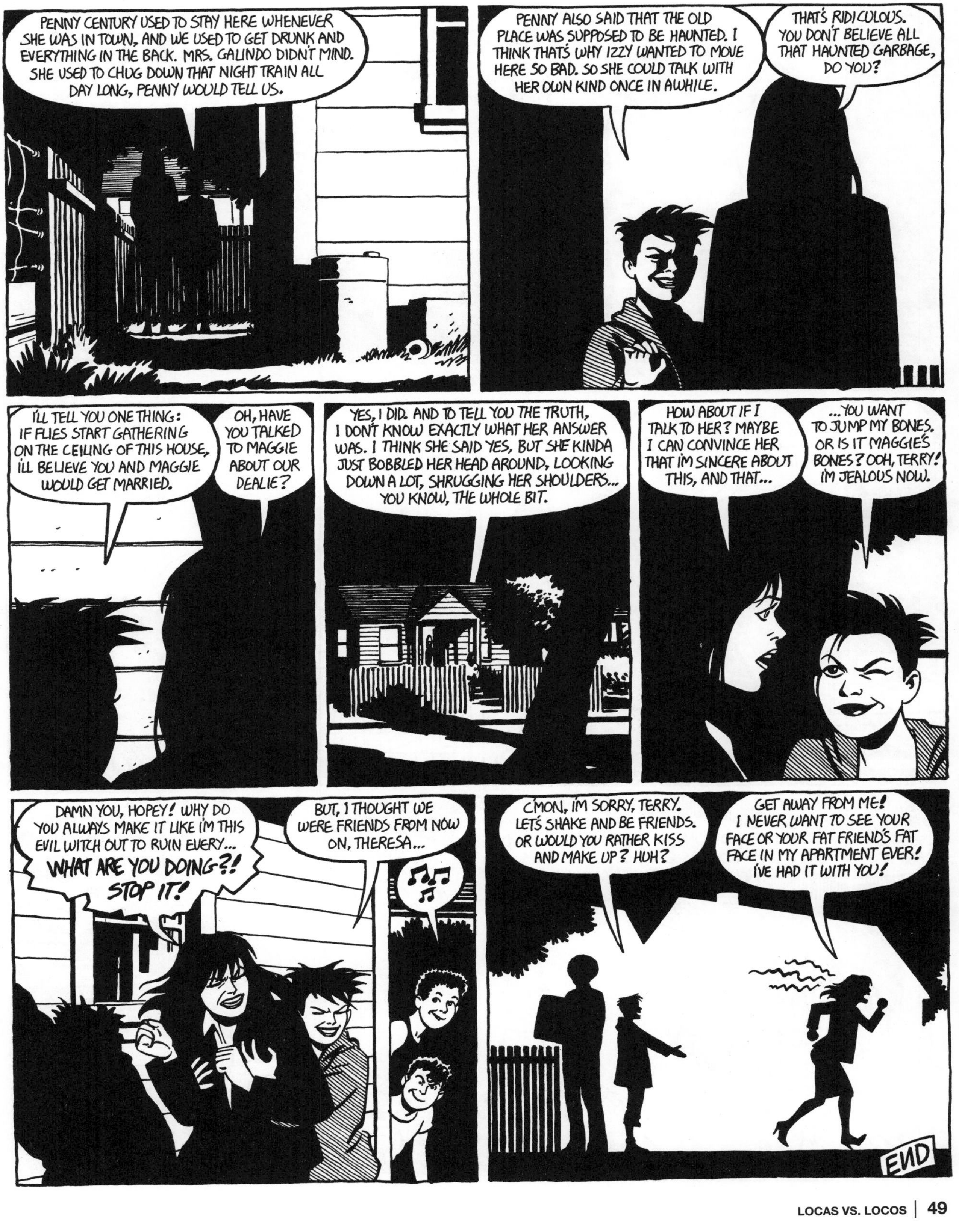
PENNY CENTURY USED TO STAY HERE WHENEVER SHE WAS IN TOWN, AND WE USED TO GET DRUNK AND EVERYTHING IN THE BACK. MRS. GALINDO DIDN'T MIND. SHE USED TO CHUG DOWN THAT NIGHT TRAIN ALL DAY LONG, PENNY WOULD TELL US.
PENNY ALSO SAID THAT THE OLD PLACE WAS SUPPOSED TO BE HAUNTED. I THINK THAT'S WHY IZZY WANTED TO MOVE HERE SO BAD. SO SHE COULD TALK WITH HER OWN KIND ONCE IN AWHILE.
THAT'S RIDICULOUS. YOU DON'T BELIEVE ALL THAT HAUNTED GARBAGE, DO YOU?
I'LL TELL YOU ONE THING: IF FLIES START GATHERING ON THE CEILING OF THIS HOUSE, I'LL BELIEVE YOU AND MAGGIE WOULD GET MARRIED.
OH, HAVE YOU TALKED TO MAGGIE ABOUT OUR DEALIE?
YES, I DID. AND TO TELL YOU THE TRUTH, I DON'T KNOW EXACTLY WHAT HER ANSWER WAS. I THINK SHE SAID YES, BUT SHE KINDA JUST BOBBLED HER HEAD AROUND, LOOKING DOWN A LOT, SHRUGGING HER SHOULDERS... YOU KNOW, THE WHOLE BIT.
HOW ABOUT IF I TALK TO HER? MAYBE I CAN CONVINCE HER THAT I'M SINCERE ABOUT THIS, AND THAT...
...YOU WANT TO JUMP MY BONES. OR IS IT MAGGIE'S BONES? OOH, TERRY! I'M JEALOUS NOW.
DAMN YOU, HOPEY! WHY DO YOU ALWAYS MAKE IT LIKE I'M THIS EVIL WITCH OUT TO RUIN EVERY... WHAT ARE YOU DOING?! STOP IT!
BUT, I THOUGHT WE WERE FRIENDS FROM NOW ON, THERESA...
C'MON, I'M SORRY, TERRY. LET'S SHAKE AND BE FRIENDS. OR WOULD YOU RATHER KISS AND MAKE UP? HUH?
GET AWAY FROM ME! I NEVER WANT TO SEE YOUR FACE OR YOUR FAT FRIEND'S FAT FACE IN MY APARTMENT EVER! I'VE HAD IT WITH YOU!
END

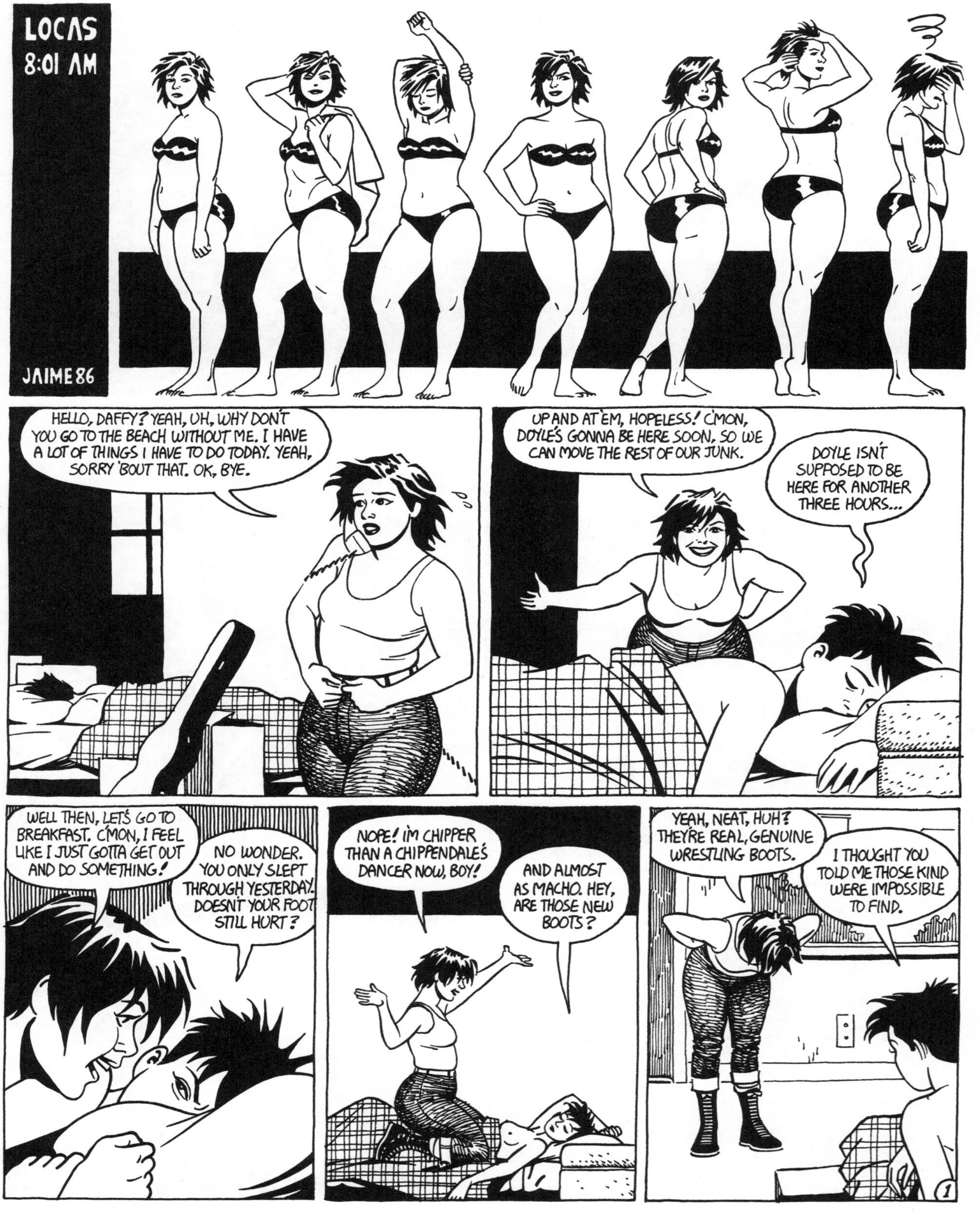
LOCAS
8:01 AM
JAIME 86
HELLO, DAFFY? YEAH, UH, WHY DON'T YOU GO TO THE BEACH WITHOUT ME. I HAVE A LOT OF THINGS I HAVE TO DO TODAY. YEAH, SORRY 'BOUT THAT. OK, BYE.
UP AND AT 'EM, HOPELESS! C'MON, DOYLE'S GONNA BE HERE SOON, SO WE CAN MOVE THE REST OF OUR JUNK.
DOYLE ISN'T SUPPOSED TO BE HERE FOR ANOTHER THREE HOURS...
WELL THEN, LET'S GO TO BREAKFAST. C'MON, I FEEL LIKE I JUST GOTTA GET OUT AND DO SOMETHING!
NO WONDER. YOU ONLY SLEPT THROUGH YESTERDAY. DOESN'T YOUR FOOT STILL HURT?
NOPE! I'M CHIPPER THAN A CHIPPENDALE'S DANCER NOW, BOY!
AND ALMOST AS MACHO. HEY, ARE THOSE NEW BOOTS?
YEAH, NEAT, HUH? THEY'RE REAL, GENUINE WRESTLING BOOTS.
I THOUGHT YOU TOLD ME THOSE KIND WERE IMPOSSIBLE TO FIND.
1

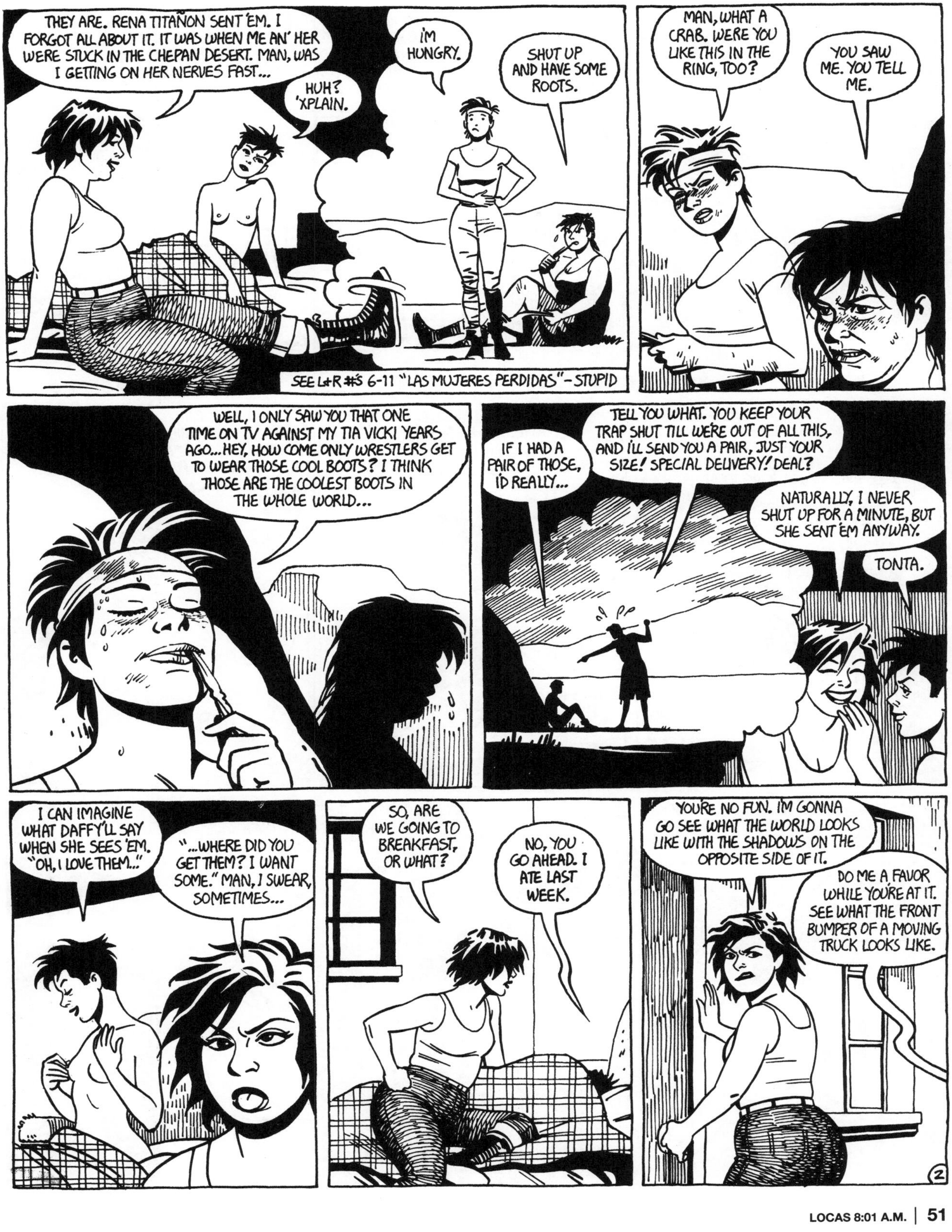
THEY ARE. RENA TITAÑON SENT 'EM. I FORGOT ALL ABOUT IT. IT WAS WHEN ME AN' HER WERE STUCK IN THE CHEPAN DESERT. MAN, WAS I GETTING ON HER NERVES FAST...
HUH? 'XPLAIN.
I'M HUNGRY.
SHUT UP AND HAVE SOME ROOTS.
SEE L&R #'S 6-11 "LAS MUJERES PERDIDAS" - STUPID
MAN, WHAT A CRAB. WERE YOU LIKE THIS IN THE RING, TOO?
YOU SAW ME. YOU TELL ME.
WELL, I ONLY SAW YOU THAT ONE TIME ON TV AGAINST MY TIA VICKI YEARS AGO... HEY, HOW COME ONLY WRESTLERS GET TO WEAR THOSE COOL BOOTS? I THINK THOSE ARE THE COOLEST BOOTS IN THE WHOLE WORLD...
IF I HAD A PAIR OF THOSE, I'D REALLY...
TELL YOU WHAT. YOU KEEP YOUR TRAP SHUT TILL WE'RE OUT OF ALL THIS, AND I'LL SEND YOU A PAIR, JUST YOUR SIZE! SPECIAL DELIVERY! DEAL?
NATURALLY, I NEVER SHUT UP FOR A MINUTE, BUT SHE SENT 'EM ANYWAY.
TONTA.
I CAN IMAGINE WHAT DAFFY'LL SAY WHEN SHE SEES 'EM. "OH, I LOVE THEM..."
"...WHERE DID YOU GET THEM? I WANT SOME." MAN, I SWEAR, SOMETIMES...
SO, ARE WE GOING TO BREAKFAST, OR WHAT?
NO, YOU GO AHEAD. I ATE LAST WEEK.
YOU'RE NO FUN. I'M GONNA GO SEE WHAT THE WORLD LOOKS LIKE WITH THE SHADOWS ON THE OPPOSITE SIDE OF IT.
DO ME A FAVOR WHILE YOU'RE AT IT. SEE WHAT THE FRONT BUMPER OF A MOVING TRUCK LOOKS LIKE.
2

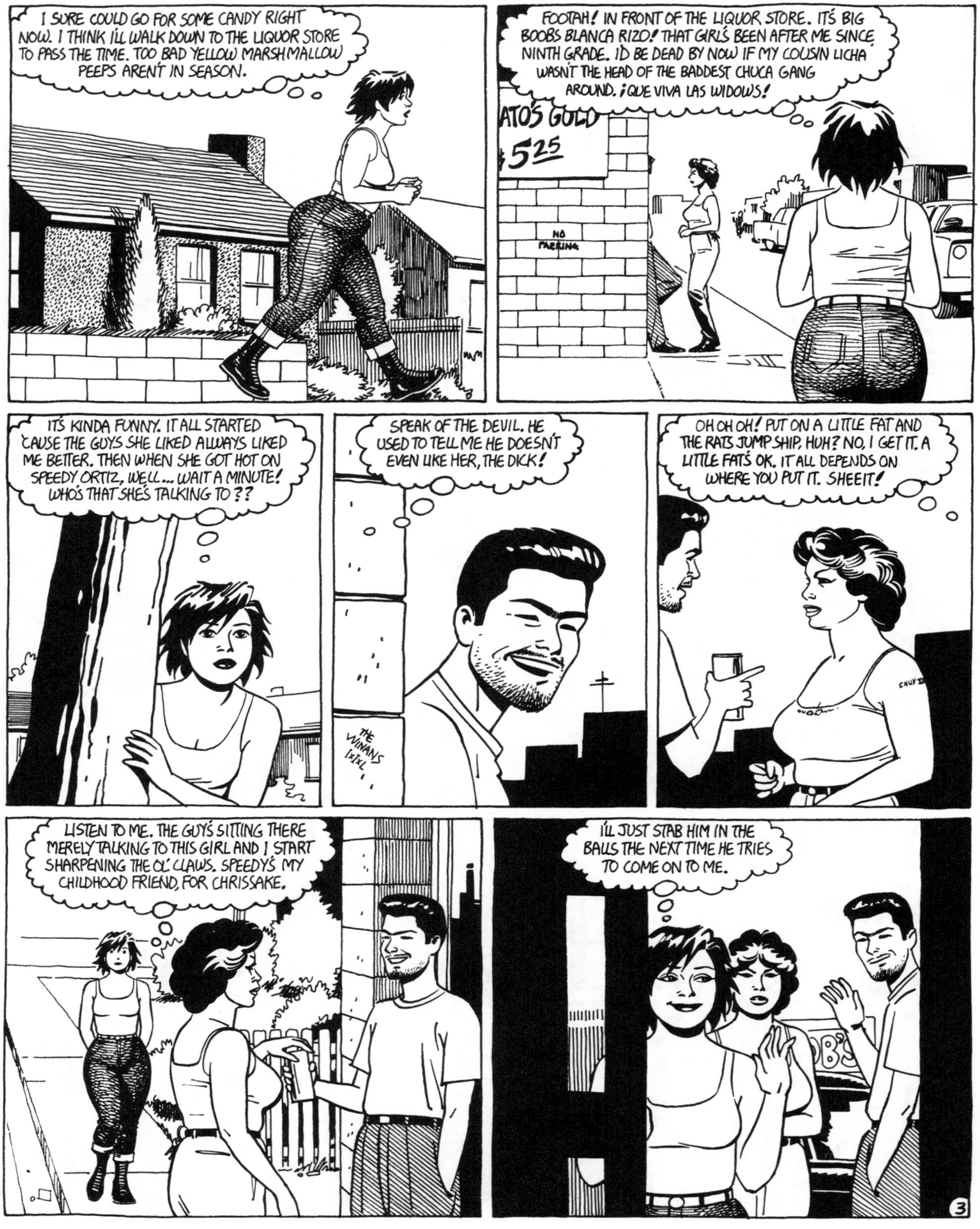
I SURE COULD GO FOR SOME CANDY RIGHT NOW. I THINK I'LL WALK DOWN TO THE LIQUOR STORE TO PASS THE TIME. TOO BAD YELLOW MARSHMALLOW PEEPS AREN'T IN SEASON.
FOOTAH! IN FRONT OF THE LIQUOR STORE. IT'S BIG BOOBS BLANCA RIZO! THAT GIRL'S BEEN AFTER ME SINCE NINTH GRADE. I'D BE DEAD BY NOW IF MY COUSIN LICHA WASN'T THE HEAD OF THE BADDEST CHUCA GANG AROUND. ¡QUE VIVA LAS WIDOWS!
ATO'S GOLD
$5.25
NO PARKING
IT'S KINDA FUNNY. IT ALL STARTED 'CAUSE THE GUYS SHE LIKED ALWAYS LIKED ME BETTER. THEN WHEN SHE GOT HOT ON SPEEDY ORTIZ, WELL... WAIT A MINUTE! WHO'S THAT SHE'S TALKING TO??
SPEAK OF THE DEVIL. HE USED TO TELL ME HE DOESN'T EVEN LIKE HER, THE DICK!
THE WINANS
OH OH OH! PUT ON A LITTLE FAT AND THE RATS JUMP SHIP, HUH? NO, I GET IT. A LITTLE FAT'S OK. IT ALL DEPENDS ON WHERE YOU PUT IT. SHEEIT!
LISTEN TO ME. THE GUY'S SITTING THERE MERELY TALKING TO THIS GIRL AND I START SHARPENING THE OL' CLAWS. SPEEDY'S MY CHILDHOOD FRIEND, FOR CHRISSAKE.
I'LL JUST STAB HIM IN THE BALLS THE NEXT TIME HE TRIES TO COME ON TO ME.
3

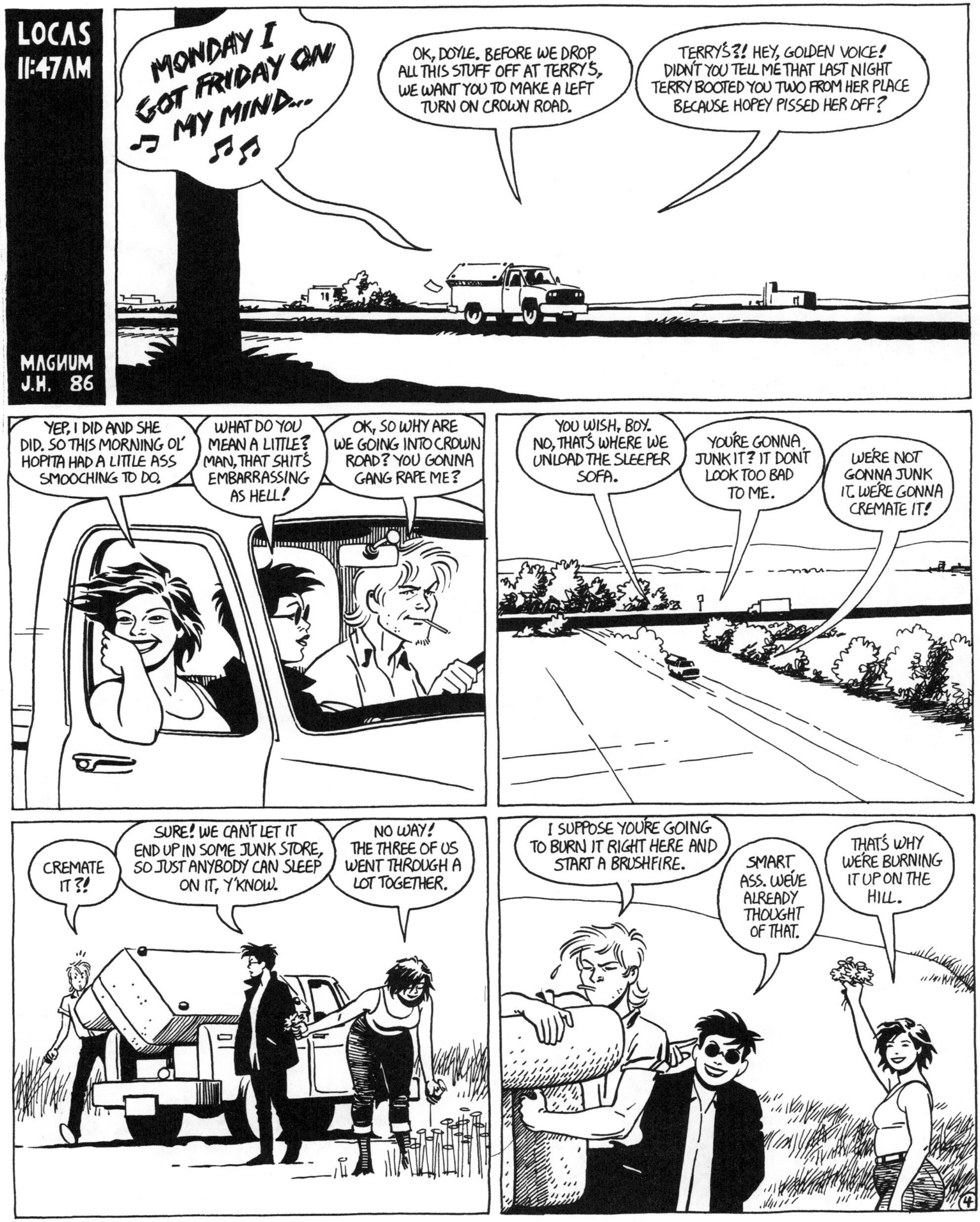
LOCAS
11:47AM
MONDAY I GOT FRIDAY ON MY MIND...
OK, DOYLE. BEFORE WE DROP ALL THIS STUFF OFF AT TERRY'S, WE WANT YOU TO MAKE A LEFT TURN ON CROWN ROAD.
TERRY'S?! HEY, GOLDEN VOICE! DIDN'T YOU TELL ME THAT LAST NIGHT TERRY BOOTED YOU TWO FROM HER PLACE BECAUSE HOPEY PISSED HER OFF?
MAGNUM
J.H. 86
YEP, I DID AND SHE DID. SO THIS MORNING OL' HOPITA HAD A LITTLE ASS SMOOCHING TO DO.
WHAT DO YOU MEAN A LITTLE? MAN, THAT SHIT'S EMBARRASSING AS HELL!
OK, SO WHY ARE WE GOING INTO CROWN ROAD? YOU GONNA GANG RAPE ME?
YOU WISH, BOY. NO, THAT'S WHERE WE UNLOAD THE SLEEPER SOFA.
YOU'RE GONNA JUNK IT? IT DON'T LOOK TOO BAD TO ME.
WE'RE NOT GONNA JUNK IT. WE'RE GONNA CREMATE IT!
CREMATE IT?!
SURE! WE CAN'T LET IT END UP IN SOME JUNK STORE, SO JUST ANYBODY CAN SLEEP ON IT, Y'KNOW.
NO WAY! THE THREE OF US WENT THROUGH A LOT TOGETHER.
I SUPPOSE YOU'RE GOING TO BURN IT RIGHT HERE AND START A BRUSHFIRE.
SMART ASS. WE'VE ALREADY THOUGHT OF THAT.
THAT'S WHY WE'RE BURNING IT UP ON THE HILL.
4

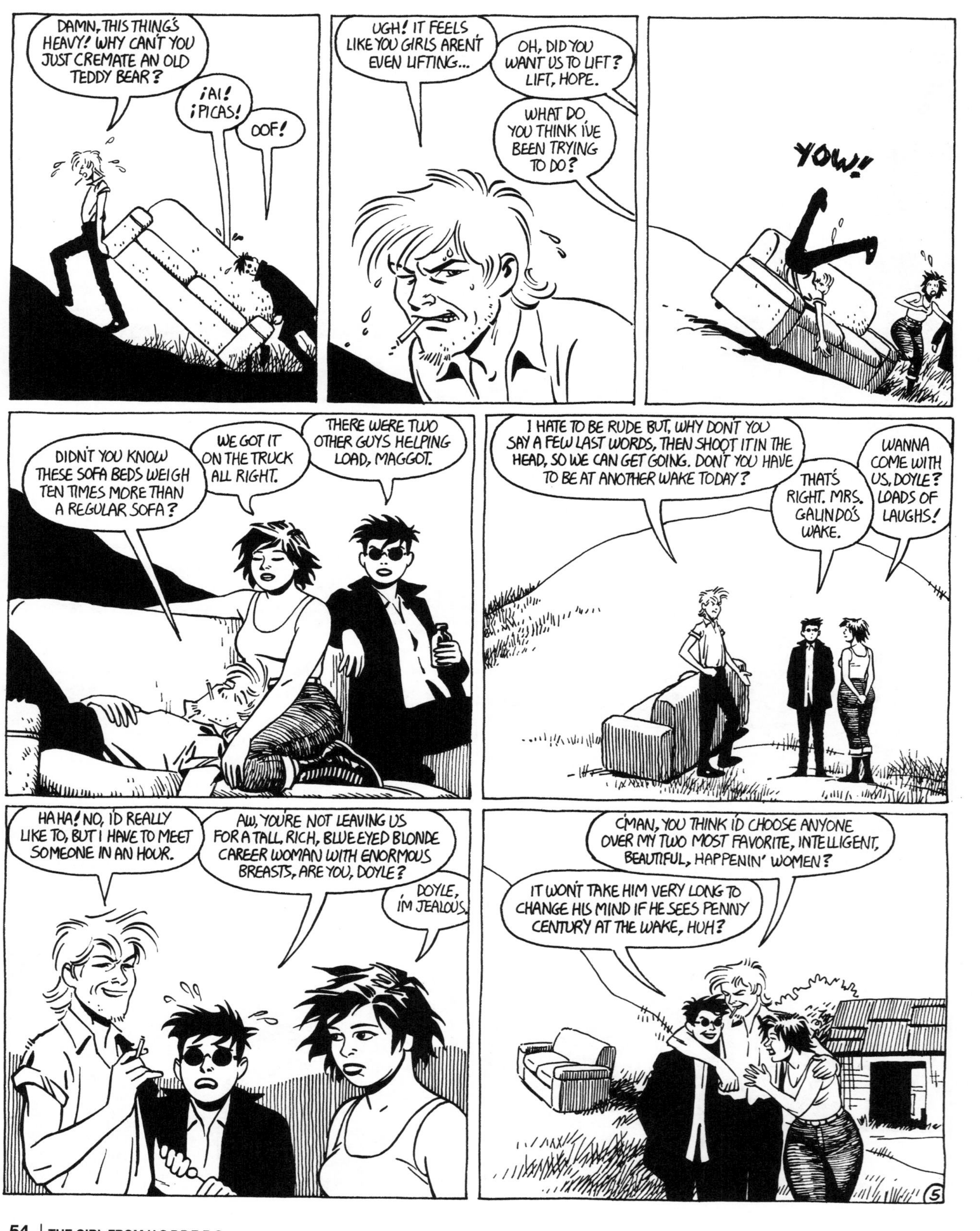
DAMN, THIS THING'S HEAVY! WHY CAN'T YOU JUST CREMATE AN OLD TEDDY BEAR?
¡AI! ¡PICAS!
OOF!
UGH! IT FEELS LIKE YOU GIRLS AREN'T EVEN LIFTING...
OH, DID YOU WANT US TO LIFT? LIFT, HOPE.
WHAT DO YOU THINK I'VE BEEN TRYING TO DO?
YOW!
DIDN'T YOU KNOW THESE SOFA BEDS WEIGH TEN TIMES MORE THAN A REGULAR SOFA?
WE GOT IT ON THE TRUCK ALL RIGHT.
THERE WERE TWO OTHER GUYS HELPING LOAD, MAGGOT.
I HATE TO BE RUDE BUT, WHY DON'T YOU SAY A FEW LAST WORDS, THEN SHOOT IT IN THE HEAD, SO WE CAN GET GOING. DON'T YOU HAVE TO BE AT ANOTHER WAKE TODAY?
THAT'S RIGHT. MRS. GALINDO'S WAKE.
WANNA COME WITH US, DOYLE? LOADS OF LAUGHS!
HA HA! NO, I'D REALLY LIKE TO, BUT I HAVE TO MEET SOMEONE IN AN HOUR.
AW, YOU'RE NOT LEAVING US FOR A TALL, RICH, BLUE EYED BLONDE CAREER WOMAN WITH ENORMOUS BREASTS, ARE YOU, DOYLE?
DOYLE, I'M JEALOUS.
C'MAN, YOU THINK I'D CHOOSE ANYONE OVER MY TWO MOST FAVORITE, INTELLIGENT, BEAUTIFUL, HAPPENIN' WOMEN?
IT WON'T TAKE HIM VERY LONG TO CHANGE HIS MIND IF HE SEES PENNY CENTURY AT THE WAKE, HUH?
5

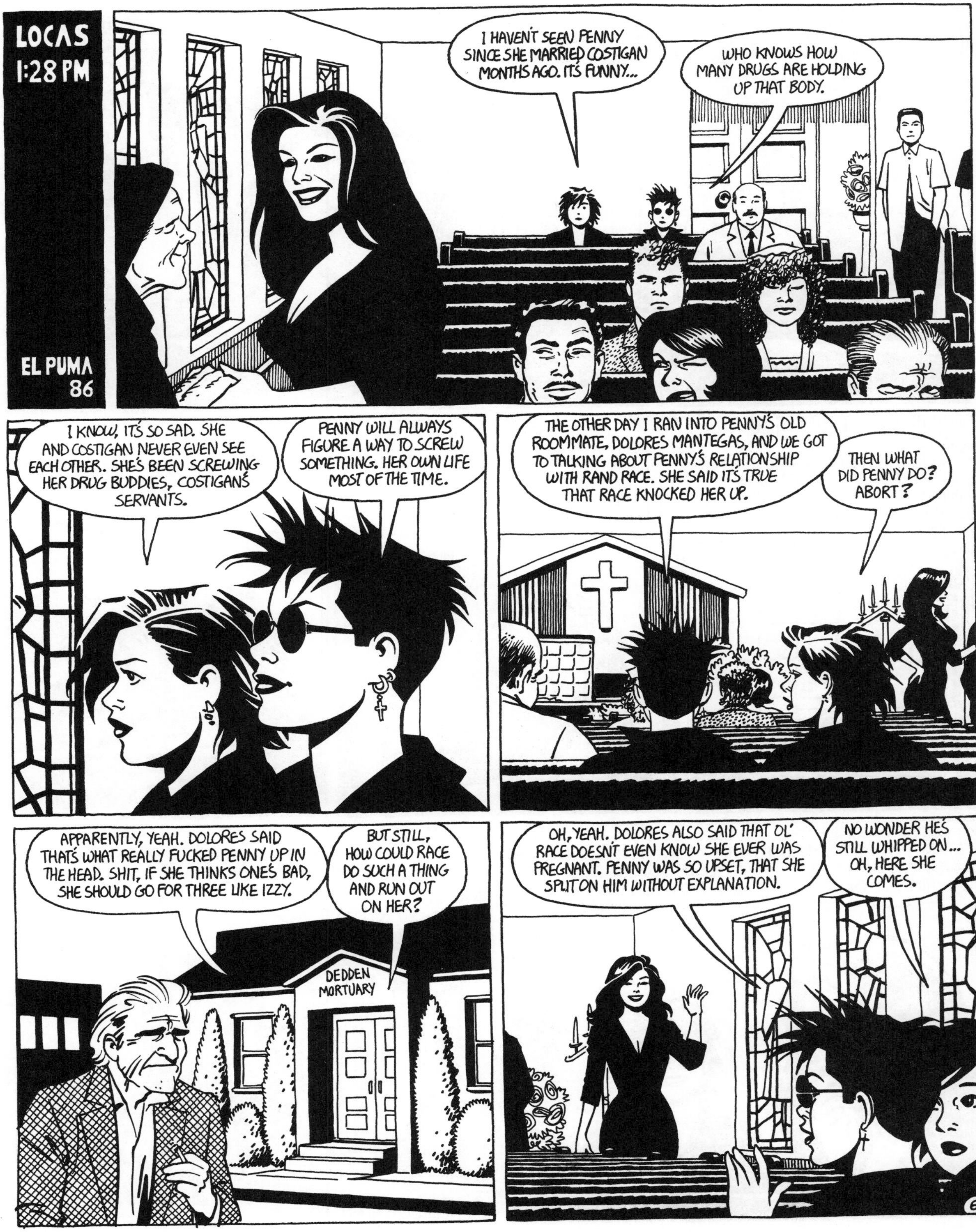

LOCAS 1:28 PM
EL PUMA 86
I HAVEN'T SEEN PENNY SINCE SHE MARRIED COSTIGAN MONTHS AGO. IT'S FUNNY...
WHO KNOWS HOW MANY DRUGS ARE HOLDING UP THAT BODY.
I KNOW, IT'S SO SAD. SHE AND COSTIGAN NEVER EVEN SEE EACH OTHER. SHE'S BEEN SCREWING HER DRUG BUDDIES, COSTIGAN'S SERVANTS.
PENNY WILL ALWAYS FIGURE A WAY TO SCREW SOMETHING. HER OWN LIFE MOST OF THE TIME.
THE OTHER DAY I RAN INTO PENNY'S OLD ROOMMATE, DOLORES MANTEGAS, AND WE GOT TO TALKING ABOUT PENNY'S RELATIONSHIP WITH RAND RACE. SHE SAID IT'S TRUE THAT RACE KNOCKED HER UP.
THEN WHAT DID PENNY DO? ABORT?
APPARENTLY, YEAH. DOLORES SAID THAT'S WHAT REALLY FUCKED PENNY UP IN THE HEAD. SHIT, IF SHE THINKS ONE'S BAD, SHE SHOULD GO FOR THREE LIKE IZZY.
BUT STILL, HOW COULD RACE DO SUCH A THING AND RUN OUT ON HER?
DEDDEN MORTUARY
OH, YEAH. DOLORES ALSO SAID THAT OL' RACE DOESN'T EVEN KNOW SHE EVER WAS PREGNANT. PENNY WAS SO UPSET, THAT SHE SPLIT ON HIM WITHOUT EXPLANATION.
NO WONDER HE'S STILL WHIPPED ON... OH, HERE SHE COMES.
6

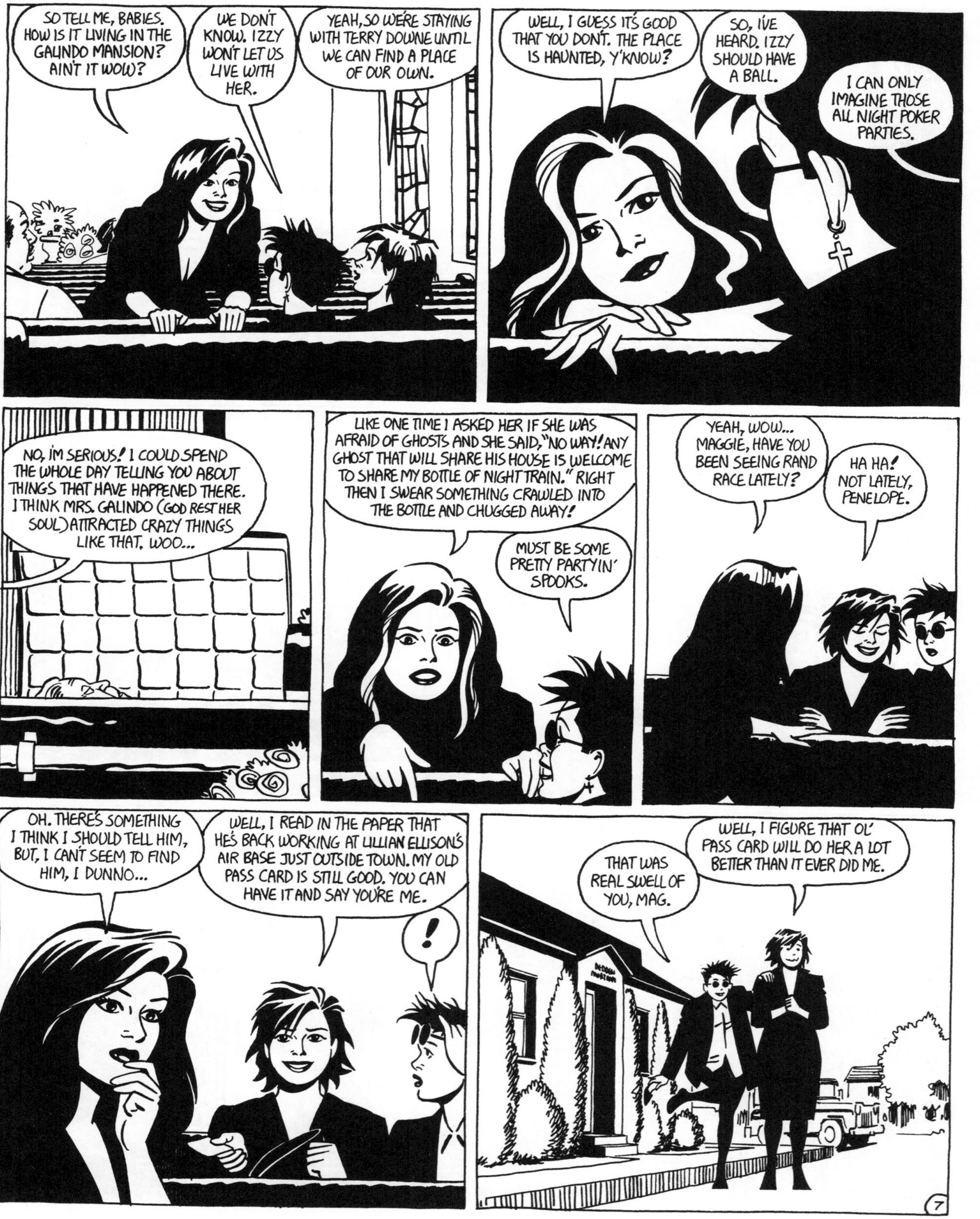
SO TELL ME, BABIES. HOW IS IT LIVING IN THE GALINDO MANSION? AIN'T IT WOW?
WE DON'T KNOW. IZZY WON'T LET US LIVE WITH HER.
YEAH, SO WE'RE STAYING WITH TERRY DOWNE UNTIL WE CAN FIND A PLACE OF OUR OWN.
WELL, I GUESS IT'S GOOD THAT YOU DON'T. THE PLACE IS HAUNTED, Y'KNOW?
SO, I'VE HEARD. IZZY SHOULD HAVE A BALL.
I CAN ONLY IMAGINE THOSE ALL NIGHT POKER PARTIES.
NO, I'M SERIOUS! I COULD SPEND THE WHOLE DAY TELLING YOU ABOUT THINGS THAT HAVE HAPPENED THERE. I THINK MRS. GALINDO (GOD REST HER SOUL) ATTRACTED CRAZY THINGS LIKE THAT. WOO...
LIKE ONE TIME I ASKED HER IF SHE WAS AFRAID OF GHOSTS AND SHE SAID, "NO WAY! ANY GHOST THAT WILL SHARE HIS HOUSE IS WELCOME TO SHARE MY BOTTLE OF NIGHT TRAIN." RIGHT THEN I SWEAR SOMETHING CRAWLED INTO THE BOTTLE AND CHUGGED AWAY!
MUST BE SOME PRETTY PARTYIN' SPOOKS.
YEAH, WOW... MAGGIE, HAVE YOU BEEN SEEING RAND RACE LATELY?
HA HA! NOT LATELY, PENELOPE.
OH. THERE'S SOMETHING I THINK I SHOULD TELL HIM, BUT, I CAN'T SEEM TO FIND HIM, I DUNNO...
WELL, I READ IN THE PAPER THAT HE'S BACK WORKING AT LILLIAN ELLISON'S AIR BASE JUST OUTSIDE TOWN. MY OLD PASS CARD IS STILL GOOD. YOU CAN HAVE IT AND SAY YOU'RE ME.
!
THAT WAS REAL SWELL OF YOU, MAG.
WELL, I FIGURE THAT OL' PASS CARD WILL DO HER A LOT BETTER THAN IT EVER DID ME.
7

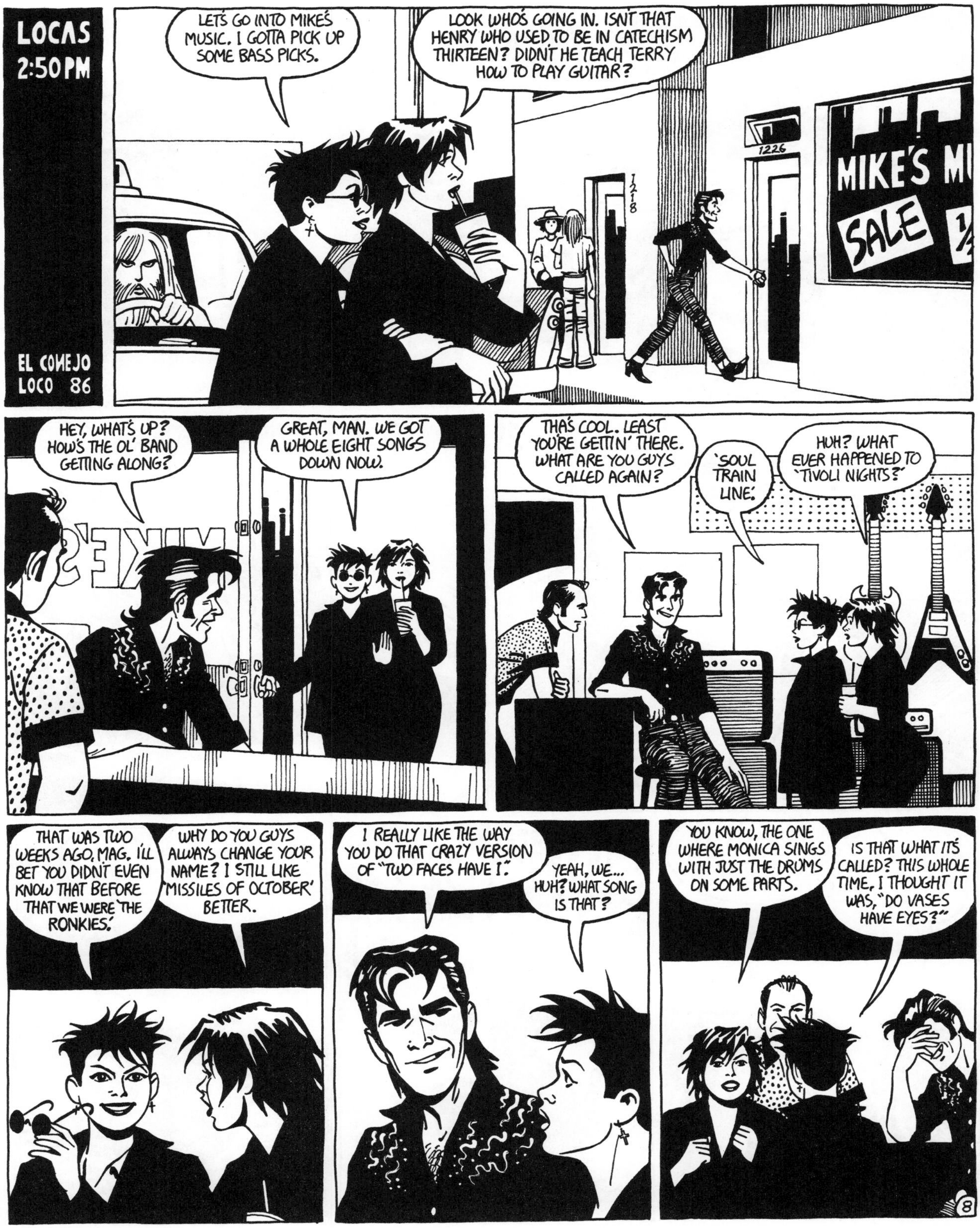
LOCAS
2:50 PM
EL COMEJO LOCO 86
LET'S GO INTO MIKE'S MUSIC. I GOTTA PICK UP SOME BASS PICKS.
LOOK WHO'S GOING IN. ISN'T THAT HENRY WHO USED TO BE IN CATECHISM THIRTEEN? DIDN'T HE TEACH TERRY HOW TO PLAY GUITAR?
1218
1226
MIKE'S MU
SALE
HEY, WHAT'S UP? HOW'S THE OL' BAND GETTING ALONG?
GREAT, MAN. WE GOT A WHOLE EIGHT SONGS DOWN NOW.
THA'S COOL. LEAST YOU'RE GETTIN' THERE. WHAT ARE YOU GUYS CALLED AGAIN?
'SOUL TRAIN LINE.'
HUH? WHAT EVER HAPPENED TO 'TIVOLI NIGHTS?'
THAT WAS TWO WEEKS AGO, MAG. I'LL BET YOU DIDN'T EVEN KNOW THAT BEFORE THAT WE WERE 'THE RONKIES.'
WHY DO YOU GUYS ALWAYS CHANGE YOUR NAME? I STILL LIKE 'MISSILES OF OCTOBER' BETTER.
I REALLY LIKE THE WAY YOU DO THAT CRAZY VERSION OF "TWO FACES HAVE I."
YEAH, WE... HUH? WHAT SONG IS THAT?
YOU KNOW, THE ONE WHERE MONICA SINGS WITH JUST THE DRUMS ON SOME PARTS.
IS THAT WHAT IT'S CALLED? THIS WHOLE TIME, I THOUGHT IT WAS, "DO VASES HAVE EYES?"
8

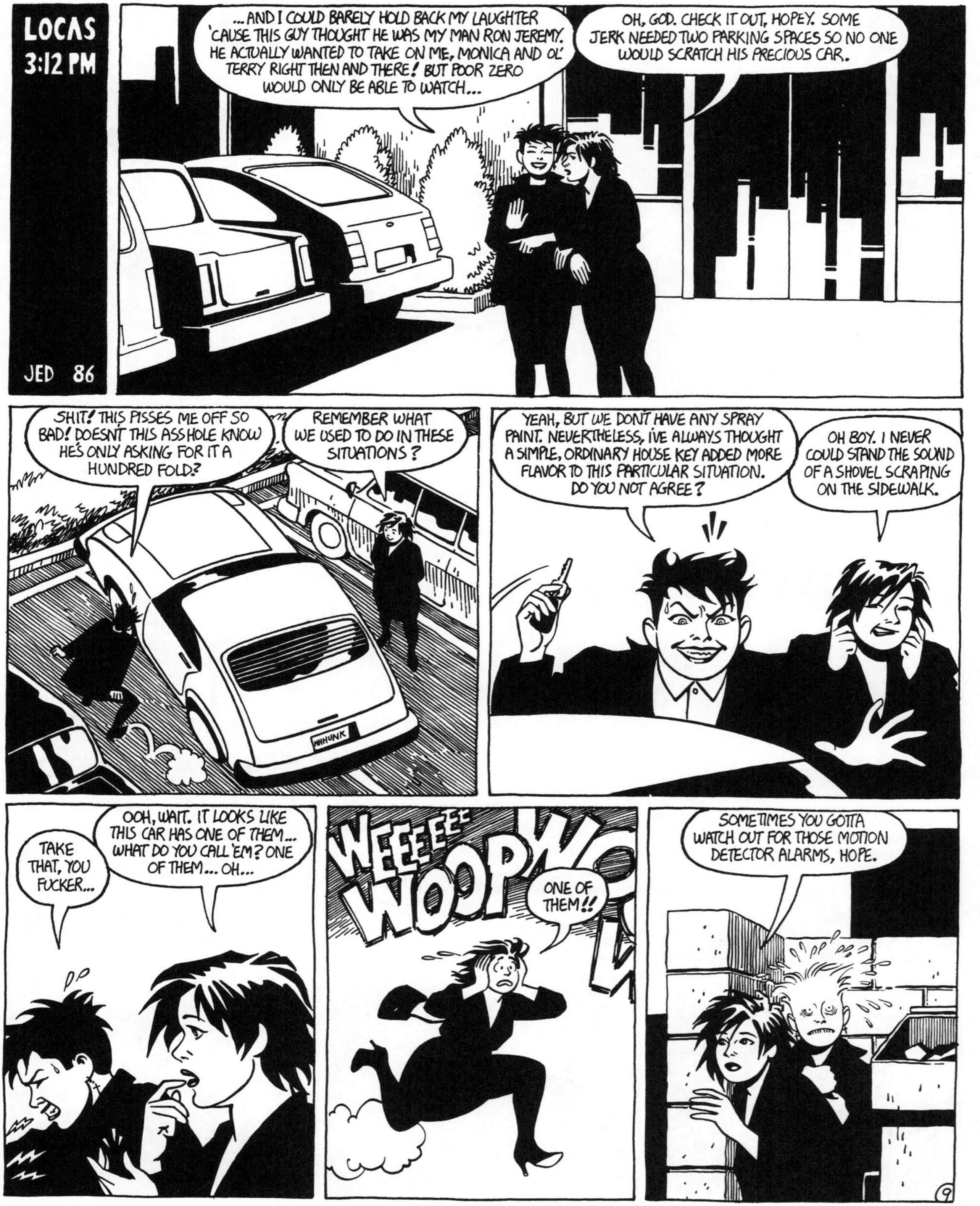
LOCAS
3:12 PM
JED 86
...AND I COULD BARELY HOLD BACK MY LAUGHTER 'CAUSE THIS GUY THOUGHT HE WAS MY MAN RON JEREMY. HE ACTUALLY WANTED TO TAKE ON ME, MONICA AND OL' TERRY RIGHT THEN AND THERE! BUT POOR ZERO WOULD ONLY BE ABLE TO WATCH...
OH, GOD. CHECK IT OUT, HOPEY. SOME JERK NEEDED TWO PARKING SPACES SO NO ONE WOULD SCRATCH HIS PRECIOUS CAR.
SHIT! THIS PISSES ME OFF SO BAD! DOESN'T THIS ASSHOLE KNOW HE'S ONLY ASKING FOR IT A HUNDRED FOLD?
REMEMBER WHAT WE USED TO DO IN THESE SITUATIONS?
HHHUNK
YEAH, BUT WE DON'T HAVE ANY SPRAY PAINT. NEVERTHELESS, I'VE ALWAYS THOUGHT A SIMPLE, ORDINARY HOUSE KEY ADDED MORE FLAVOR TO THIS PARTICULAR SITUATION. DO YOU NOT AGREE?
OH BOY. I NEVER COULD STAND THE SOUND OF A SHOVEL SCRAPING ON THE SIDEWALK.
TAKE THAT, YOU FUCKER...
OOH, WAIT. IT LOOKS LIKE THIS CAR HAS ONE OF THEM... WHAT DO YOU CALL 'EM? ONE OF THEM... OH...
WEEEEEE WOOP
ONE OF THEM!!
SOMETIMES YOU GOTTA WATCH OUT FOR THOSE MOTION DETECTOR ALARMS, HOPE.
9

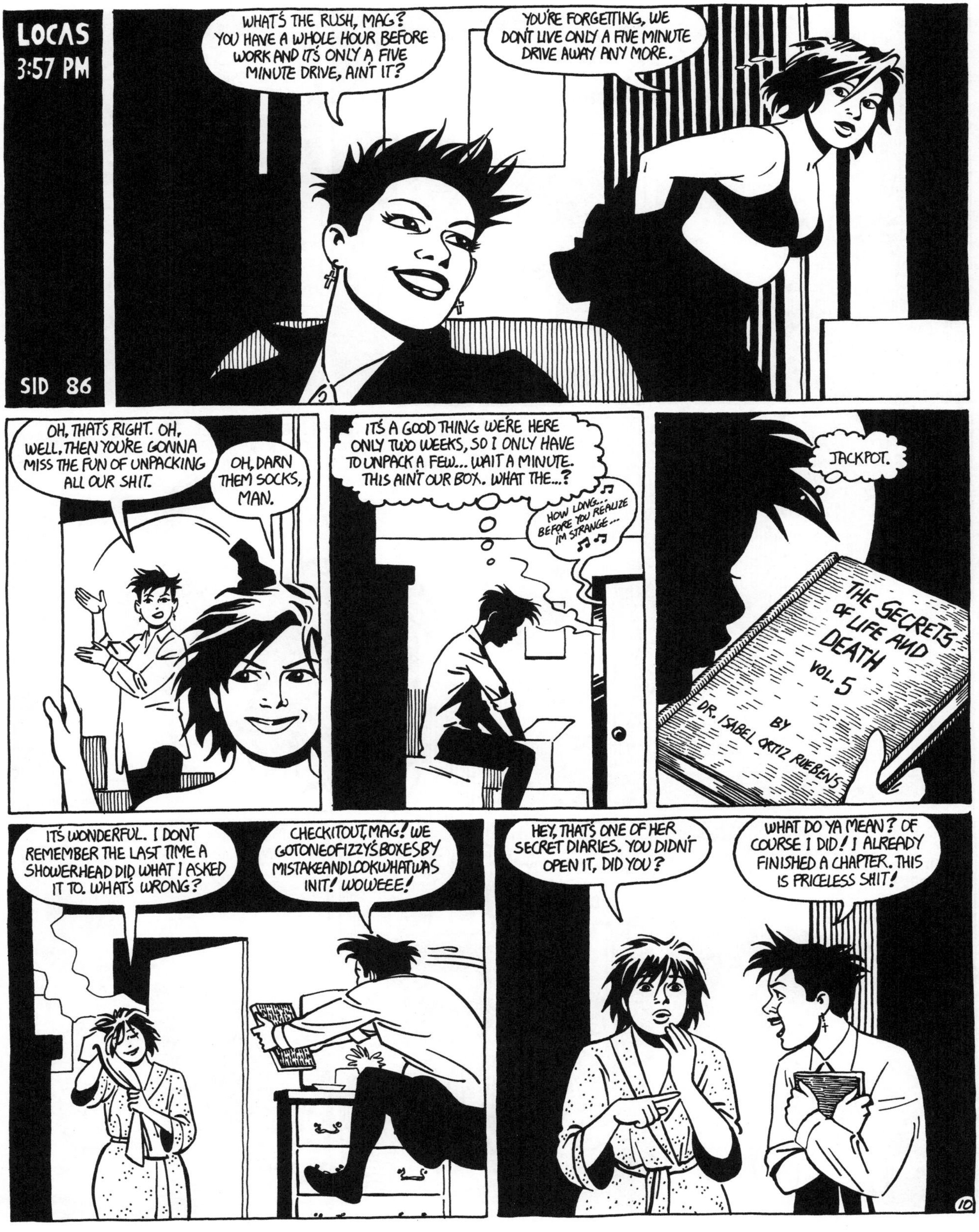
LOCAS
3:57 PM
SID 86
WHAT'S THE RUSH, MAG? YOU HAVE A WHOLE HOUR BEFORE WORK AND IT'S ONLY A FIVE MINUTE DRIVE, AINT IT?
YOU'RE FORGETTING, WE DON'T LIVE ONLY A FIVE MINUTE DRIVE AWAY ANY MORE.
OH, THAT'S RIGHT. OH, WELL, THEN YOU'RE GONNA MISS THE FUN OF UNPACKING ALL OUR SHIT.
OH, DARN THEM SOCKS, MAN.
IT'S A GOOD THING WE'RE HERE ONLY TWO WEEKS, SO I ONLY HAVE TO UNPACK A FEW... WAIT A MINUTE. THIS AIN'T OUR BOX. WHAT THE...?
HOW LONG... BEFORE YOU REALIZE I'M STRANGE...
JACKPOT.
THE SECRETS OF LIFE AND DEATH VOL. 5 BY DR. ISABEL ORTIZ RUEBENS
IT'S WONDERFUL. I DON'T REMEMBER THE LAST TIME A SHOWERHEAD DID WHAT I ASKED IT TO. WHAT'S WRONG?
CHECKITOUT, MAG! WE GOTONEOFIZZY'S BOXES BY MISTAKEANDLOOKWHATWAS INIT! WOWEEE!
HEY, THAT'S ONE OF HER SECRET DIARIES. YOU DIDN'T OPEN IT, DID YOU?
WHAT DO YA MEAN? OF COURSE I DID! I ALREADY FINISHED A CHAPTER. THIS IS PRICELESS SHIT!
10

HEY, WHERE YOU GOING? AREN'T YOU GONNA READ ME SOME?

I THOUGHT YOU HAD TO GO TO WORK?

AW, COME ON HOPEY! DON'T FUCK AROUND!

YOU GOTTA KISS MY BUTT FIRST.

OK OK! OUCH! HEY, WHERE'D YOU GET MUSCLES?

MAKIN' THEM FRENCH FRIES AIN'T NO SISSY SHIT, CHICK!

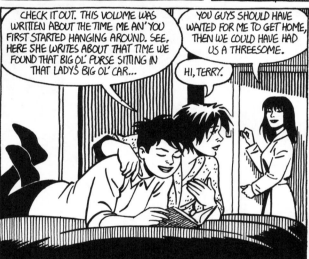

CHECK IT OUT. THIS VOLUME WAS WRITTEN ABOUT THE TIME ME AN' YOU FIRST STARTED HANGING AROUND. SEE, HERE SHE WRITES ABOUT THAT TIME WE FOUND THAT BIG OL' PURSE SITTING IN THAT LADY'S BIG OL' CAR...

YOU GUYS SHOULD HAVE WAITED FOR ME TO GET HOME, THEN WE COULD HAVE HAD US A THREESOME.

HI, TERRY.

OH, MAGGIE. BEFORE I FORGET, ISABEL TOLD ME TO TELL YOU THAT YOUR AUNT VICKI WANTS TO SEE YOU AT HER HOME AS SOON AS YOU CAN.

VICKI GLORI? SHIT!

YOU'VE HAD IT NOW, MAG...

NO, THIS IS SERIOUS SHIT. SHE'S REALLY CRAZY. AND SHE JUST LOST HER WRESTLING TITLE THE OTHER DAY. WHO KNOWS WHAT KIND OF CONDITION SHE'S IN RIGHT NOW...

IT'S TRUE, Y'KNOW...

ONE TIME SHE CHASED ME AN' DEL CHIMNEY OUT OF HER HOUSE AND DOWN THE STREET WHEN MAGGIE USED TO LIVE WITH HER.

I'LL GO AND SEE HER AFTER WORK. SHOOT, MAN...

IT'S BEEN NICE KNOWING YOU, GIRLS.

REMEMBER, MAG. IF SHE TRIES ANYTHING, RAKE THE EYES.

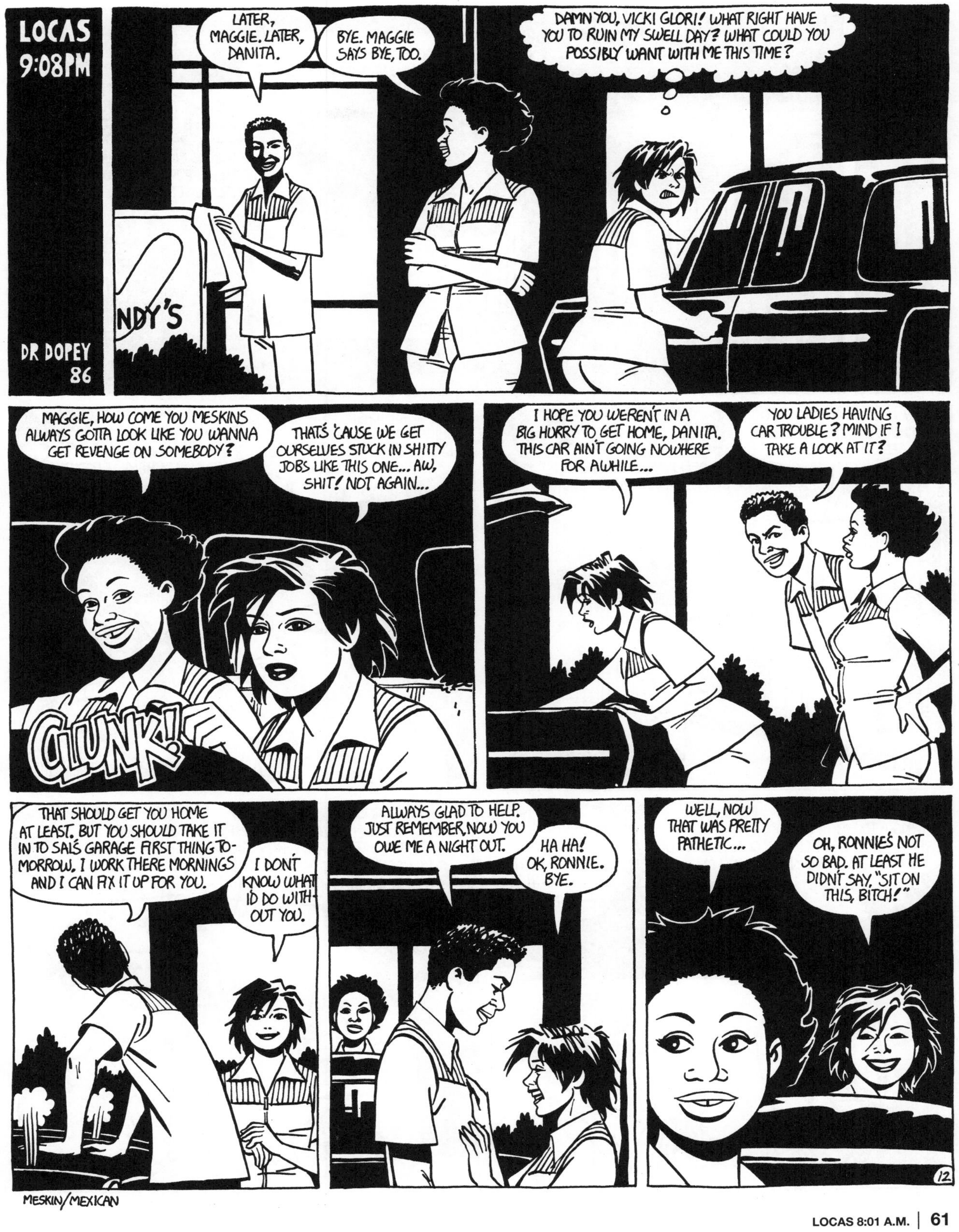
LOCAS
9:08PM
DR DOPEY
86
LATER, MAGGIE. LATER, DANITA.
BYE. MAGGIE SAYS BYE, TOO.
DAMN YOU, VICKI GLORI! WHAT RIGHT HAVE YOU TO RUIN MY SWELL DAY? WHAT COULD YOU POSSIBLY WANT WITH ME THIS TIME?
NDY'S
MAGGIE, HOW COME YOU MESKINS ALWAYS GOTTA LOOK LIKE YOU WANNA GET REVENGE ON SOMEBODY?
THAT'S 'CAUSE WE GET OURSELVES STUCK IN SHITTY JOBS LIKE THIS ONE... AW, SHIT! NOT AGAIN...
CLUNK!
I HOPE YOU WEREN'T IN A BIG HURRY TO GET HOME, DANITA. THIS CAR AIN'T GOING NOWHERE FOR AWHILE...
YOU LADIES HAVING CAR TROUBLE? MIND IF I TAKE A LOOK AT IT?
THAT SHOULD GET YOU HOME AT LEAST. BUT YOU SHOULD TAKE IT IN TO SAL'S GARAGE FIRST THING TO-MORROW. I WORK THERE MORNINGS AND I CAN FIX IT UP FOR YOU.
I DON'T KNOW WHAT I'D DO WITH-OUT YOU.
ALWAYS GLAD TO HELP. JUST REMEMBER, NOW YOU OWE ME A NIGHT OUT.
HA HA! OK, RONNIE. BYE.
WELL, NOW THAT WAS PRETTY PATHETIC...
OH, RONNIE'S NOT SO BAD. AT LEAST HE DIDN'T SAY, "SIT ON THIS, BITCH!"
12

MESKIN/MEXICAN

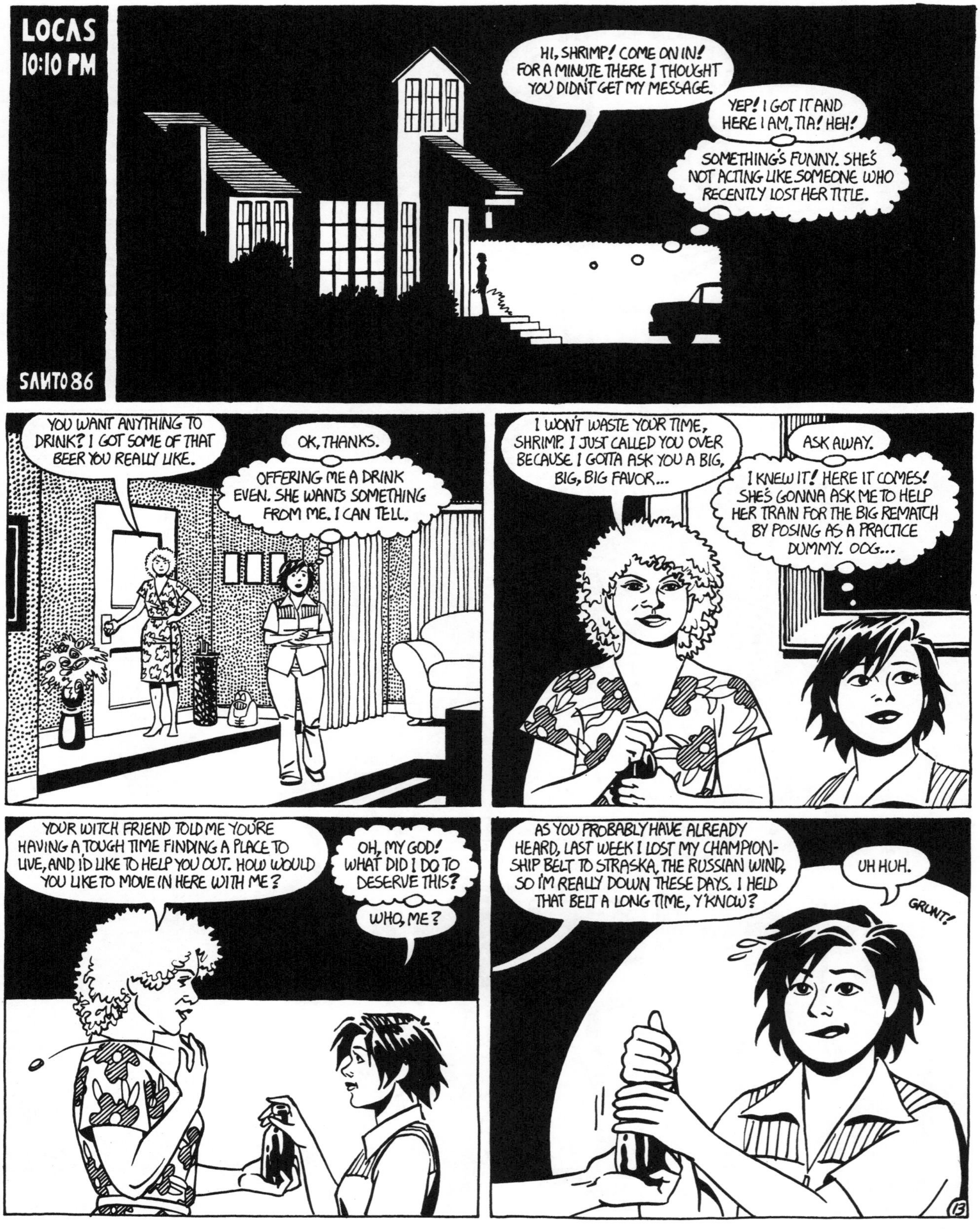
LOCAS
10:10 PM
SANTO 86
HI, SHRIMP! COME ON IN! FOR A MINUTE THERE I THOUGHT YOU DIDN'T GET MY MESSAGE.
YEP! I GOT IT AND HERE I AM, TIA! HEH!
SOMETHING'S FUNNY. SHE'S NOT ACTING LIKE SOMEONE WHO RECENTLY LOST HER TITLE.
YOU WANT ANYTHING TO DRINK? I GOT SOME OF THAT BEER YOU REALLY LIKE.
OK, THANKS.
OFFERING ME A DRINK EVEN. SHE WANTS SOMETHING FROM ME. I CAN TELL.
I WON'T WASTE YOUR TIME, SHRIMP. I JUST CALLED YOU OVER BECAUSE I GOTTA ASK YOU A BIG, BIG, BIG FAVOR...
ASK AWAY.
I KNEW IT! HERE IT COMES! SHE'S GONNA ASK ME TO HELP HER TRAIN FOR THE BIG REMATCH BY POSING AS A PRACTICE DUMMY. OOG...
YOUR WITCH FRIEND TOLD ME YOU'RE HAVING A TOUGH TIME FINDING A PLACE TO LIVE, AND I'D LIKE TO HELP YOU OUT. HOW WOULD YOU LIKE TO MOVE IN HERE WITH ME?
OH, MY GOD! WHAT DID I DO TO DESERVE THIS?
WHO, ME?
AS YOU PROBABLY HAVE ALREADY HEARD, LAST WEEK I LOST MY CHAMPIONSHIP BELT TO STRASKA, THE RUSSIAN WIND, SO I'M REALLY DOWN THESE DAYS. I HELD THAT BELT A LONG TIME, Y'KNOW?
UH HUH.
GRUNT!
13

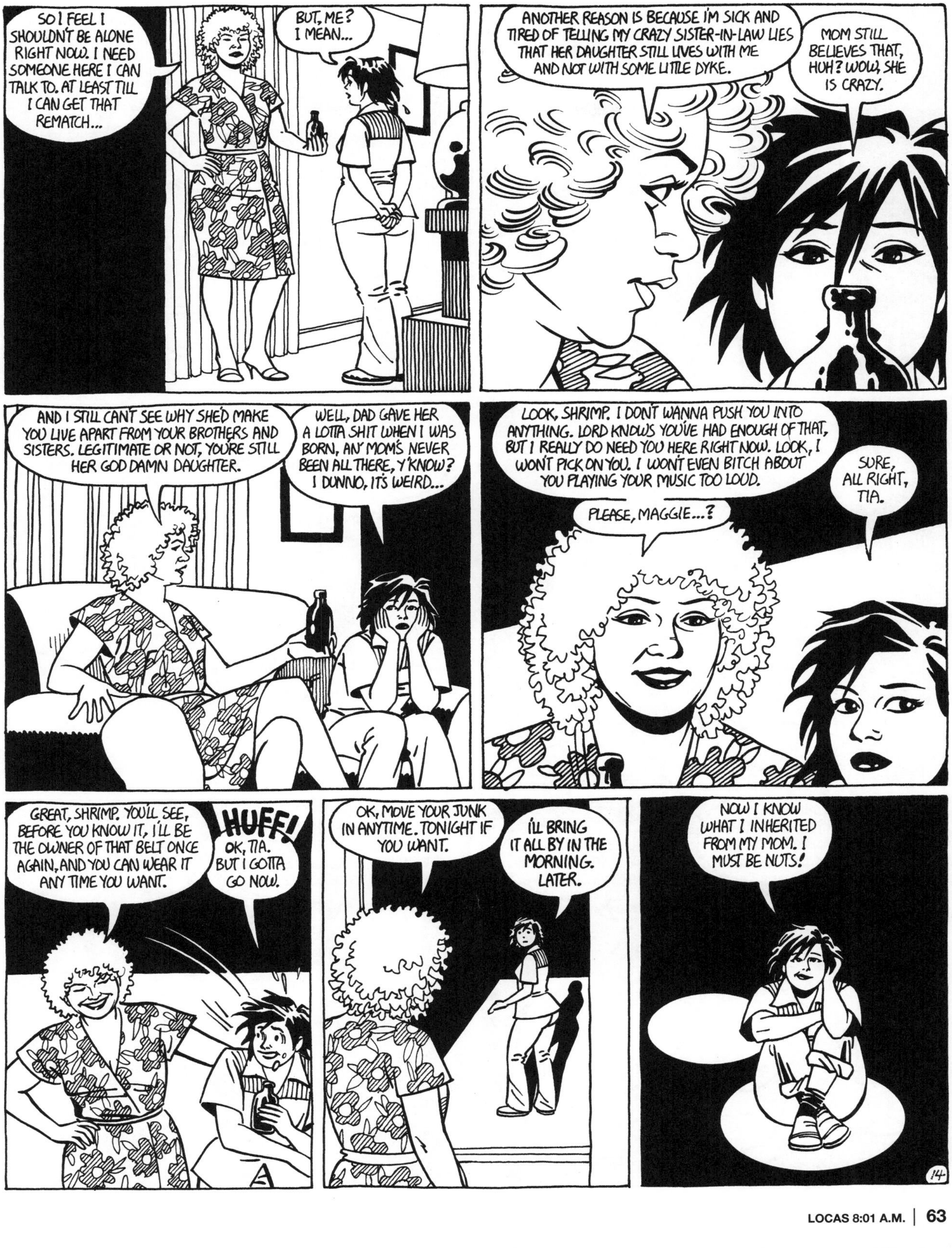
SO I FEEL I SHOULDN'T BE ALONE RIGHT NOW. I NEED SOMEONE HERE I CAN TALK TO. AT LEAST TILL I CAN GET THAT REMATCH...
BUT, ME? I MEAN...
ANOTHER REASON IS BECAUSE I'M SICK AND TIRED OF TELLING MY CRAZY SISTER-IN-LAW LIES THAT HER DAUGHTER STILL LIVES WITH ME AND NOT WITH SOME LITTLE DYKE.
MOM STILL BELIEVES THAT, HUH? WOW, SHE IS CRAZY.
AND I STILL CAN'T SEE WHY SHE'D MAKE YOU LIVE APART FROM YOUR BROTHERS AND SISTERS. LEGITIMATE OR NOT, YOU'RE STILL HER GOD DAMN DAUGHTER.
WELL, DAD GAVE HER A LOTTA SHIT WHEN I WAS BORN, AN' MOM'S NEVER BEEN ALL THERE, Y'KNOW? I DUNNO, IT'S WEIRD...
LOOK, SHRIMP. I DON'T WANNA PUSH YOU INTO ANYTHING. LORD KNOWS YOU'VE HAD ENOUGH OF THAT, BUT I REALLY DO NEED YOU HERE RIGHT NOW. LOOK, I WON'T PICK ON YOU. I WON'T EVEN BITCH ABOUT YOU PLAYING YOUR MUSIC TOO LOUD.
PLEASE, MAGGIE...?
SURE, ALL RIGHT, TIA.
GREAT, SHRIMP. YOU'LL SEE, BEFORE YOU KNOW IT, I'LL BE THE OWNER OF THAT BELT ONCE AGAIN, AND YOU CAN WEAR IT ANY TIME YOU WANT.
HUFF!
OK, TIA. BUT I GOTTA GO NOW.
OK, MOVE YOUR JUNK IN ANYTIME. TONIGHT IF YOU WANT.
I'LL BRING IT ALL BY IN THE MORNING. LATER.
NOW I KNOW WHAT I INHERITED FROM MY MOM. I MUST BE NUTS!
14

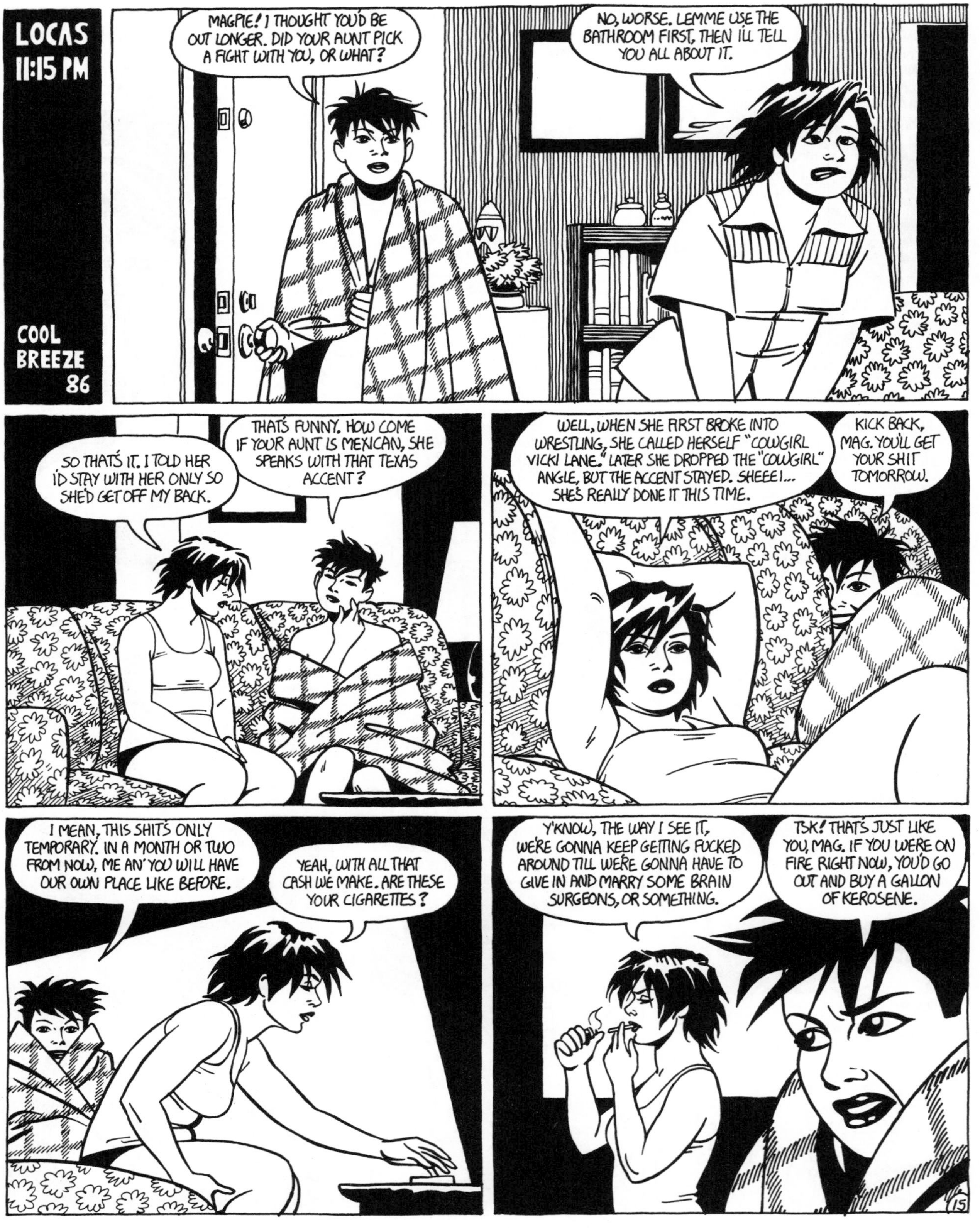
LOCAS
11:15 PM
COOL
BREEZE
86
MAGPIE! I THOUGHT YOU'D BE OUT LONGER. DID YOUR AUNT PICK A FIGHT WITH YOU, OR WHAT?
NO, WORSE. LEMME USE THE BATHROOM FIRST, THEN I'LL TELL YOU ALL ABOUT IT.
SO THAT'S IT. I TOLD HER I'D STAY WITH HER ONLY SO SHE'D GET OFF MY BACK.
THAT'S FUNNY. HOW COME IF YOUR AUNT IS MEXICAN, SHE SPEAKS WITH THAT TEXAS ACCENT?
WELL, WHEN SHE FIRST BROKE INTO WRESTLING, SHE CALLED HERSELF "COWGIRL VICKI LANE." LATER SHE DROPPED THE "COWGIRL" ANGLE, BUT THE ACCENT STAYED. SHEEEI... SHE'S REALLY DONE IT THIS TIME.
KICK BACK, MAG. YOU'LL GET YOUR SHIT TOMORROW.
I MEAN, THIS SHIT'S ONLY TEMPORARY. IN A MONTH OR TWO FROM NOW, ME AN' YOU WILL HAVE OUR OWN PLACE LIKE BEFORE.
YEAH, WITH ALL THAT CASH WE MAKE. ARE THESE YOUR CIGARETTES?
Y'KNOW, THE WAY I SEE IT, WE'RE GONNA KEEP GETTING FUCKED AROUND TILL WE'RE GONNA HAVE TO GIVE IN AND MARRY SOME BRAIN SURGEONS, OR SOMETHING.
TSK! THAT'S JUST LIKE YOU, MAG. IF YOU WERE ON FIRE RIGHT NOW, YOU'D GO OUT AND BUY A GALLON OF KEROSENE.
15

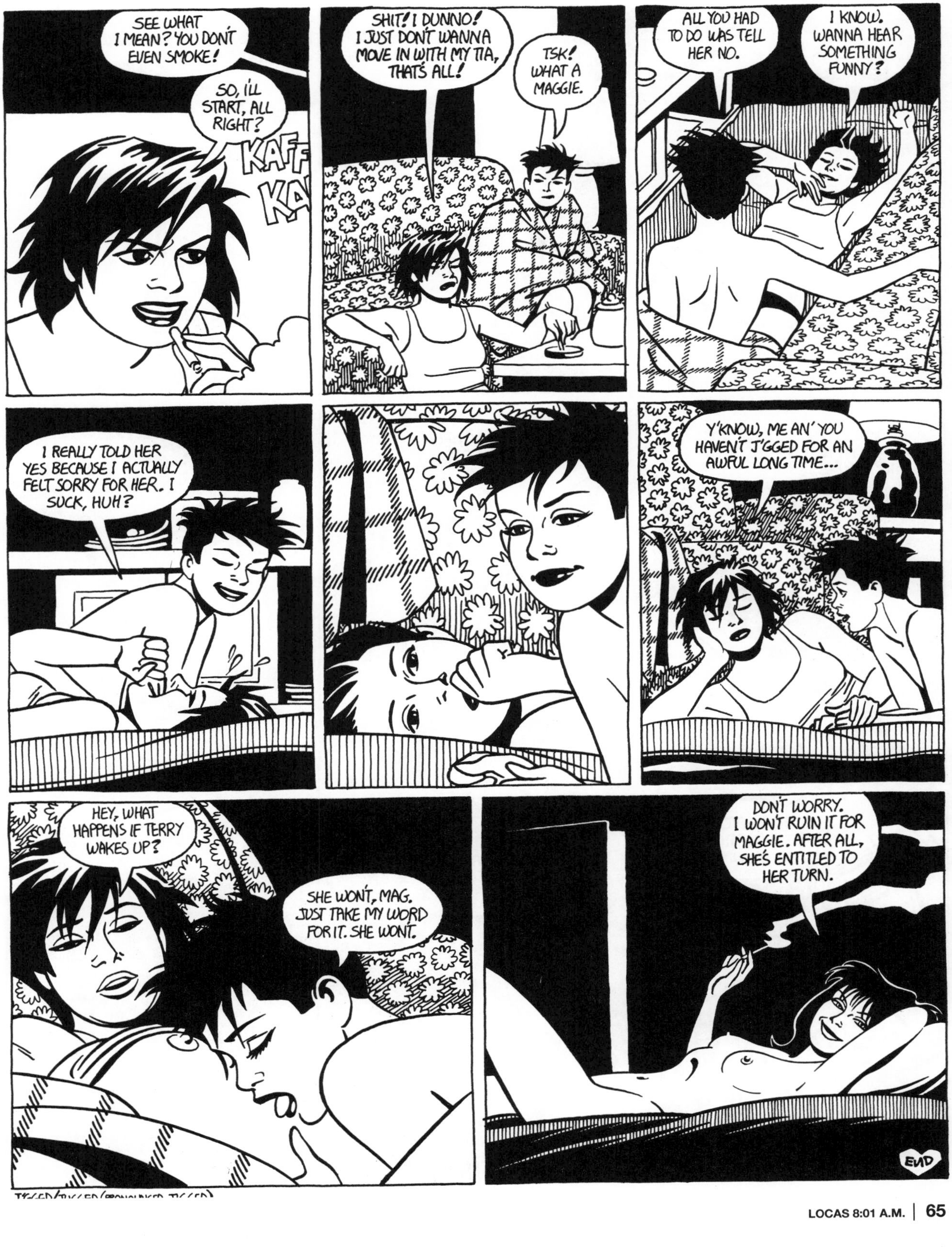
SEE WHAT I MEAN? YOU DON'T EVEN SMOKE!
SO, I'LL START, ALL RIGHT?
KAFF KA
SHIT! I DUNNO! I JUST DON'T WANNA MOVE IN WITH MY TIA, THAT'S ALL!
TSK! WHAT A MAGGIE.
ALL YOU HAD TO DO WAS TELL HER NO.
I KNOW. WANNA HEAR SOMETHING FUNNY?
I REALLY TOLD HER YES BECAUSE I ACTUALLY FELT SORRY FOR HER. I SUCK, HUH?
Y'KNOW, ME AN' YOU HAVEN'T J'GGED FOR AN AWFUL LONG TIME...
HEY, WHAT HAPPENS IF TERRY WAKES UP?
SHE WON'T, MAG. JUST TAKE MY WORD FOR IT. SHE WON'T.
DON'T WORRY. I WON'T RUIN IT FOR MAGGIE. AFTER ALL, SHE'S ENTITLED TO HER TURN.
END

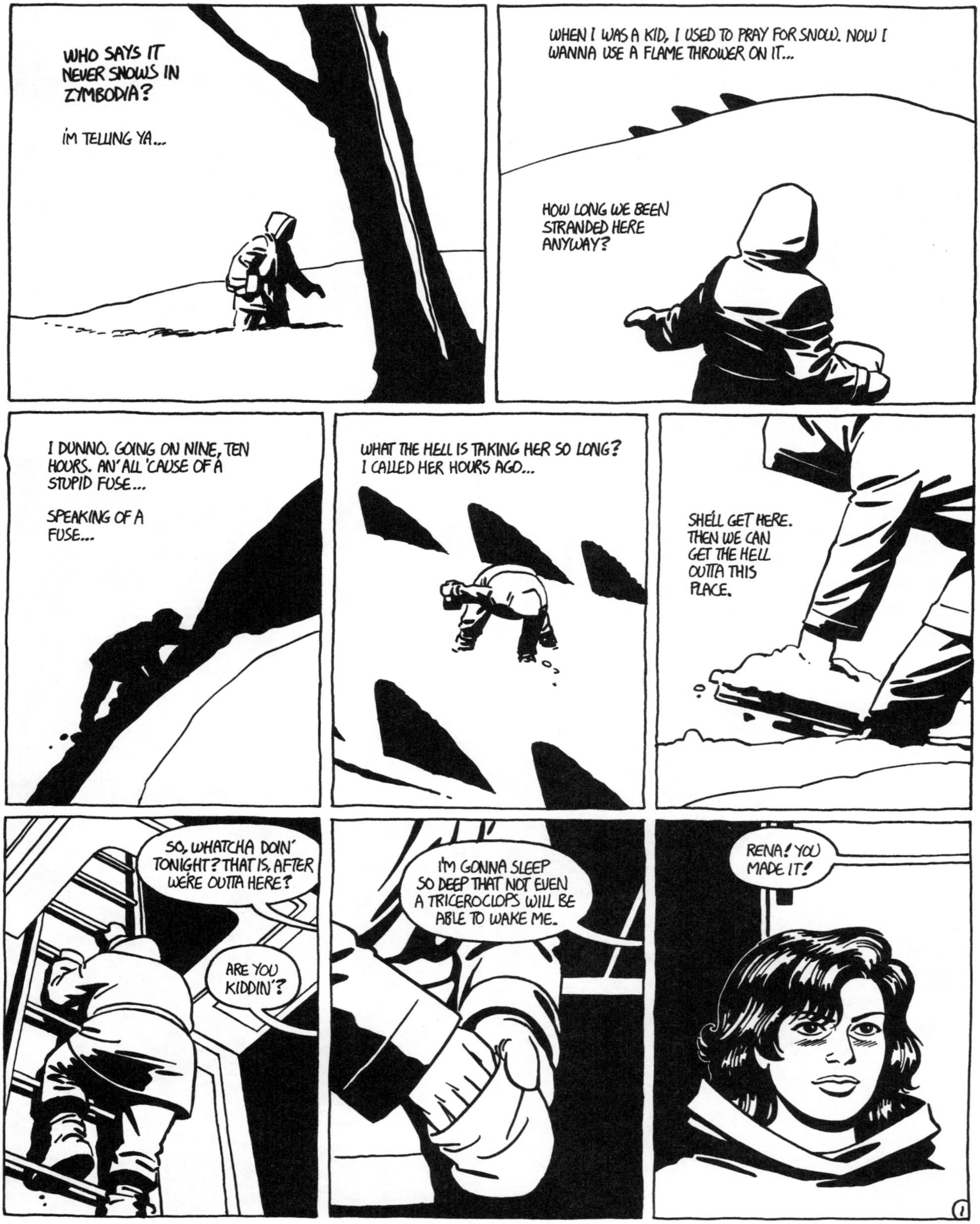
WHO SAYS IT NEVER SNOWS IN ZYMBODIA?
I'M TELLING YA...
WHEN I WAS A KID, I USED TO PRAY FOR SNOW. NOW I WANNA USE A FLAME THROWER ON IT...
HOW LONG WE BEEN STRANDED HERE ANYWAY?
I DUNNO. GOING ON NINE, TEN HOURS. AN' ALL 'CAUSE OF A STUPID FUSE...
SPEAKING OF A FUSE...
WHAT THE HELL IS TAKING HER SO LONG? I CALLED HER HOURS AGO...
SHE'LL GET HERE. THEN WE CAN GET THE HELL OUTTA THIS PLACE.
SO, WHATCHA DOIN' TONIGHT? THAT IS, AFTER WE'RE OUTTA HERE?
ARE YOU KIDDIN'?
I'M GONNA SLEEP SO DEEP THAT NOT EVEN A TRICEROCLOPS WILL BE ABLE TO WAKE ME.
RENA! YOU MADE IT!
1

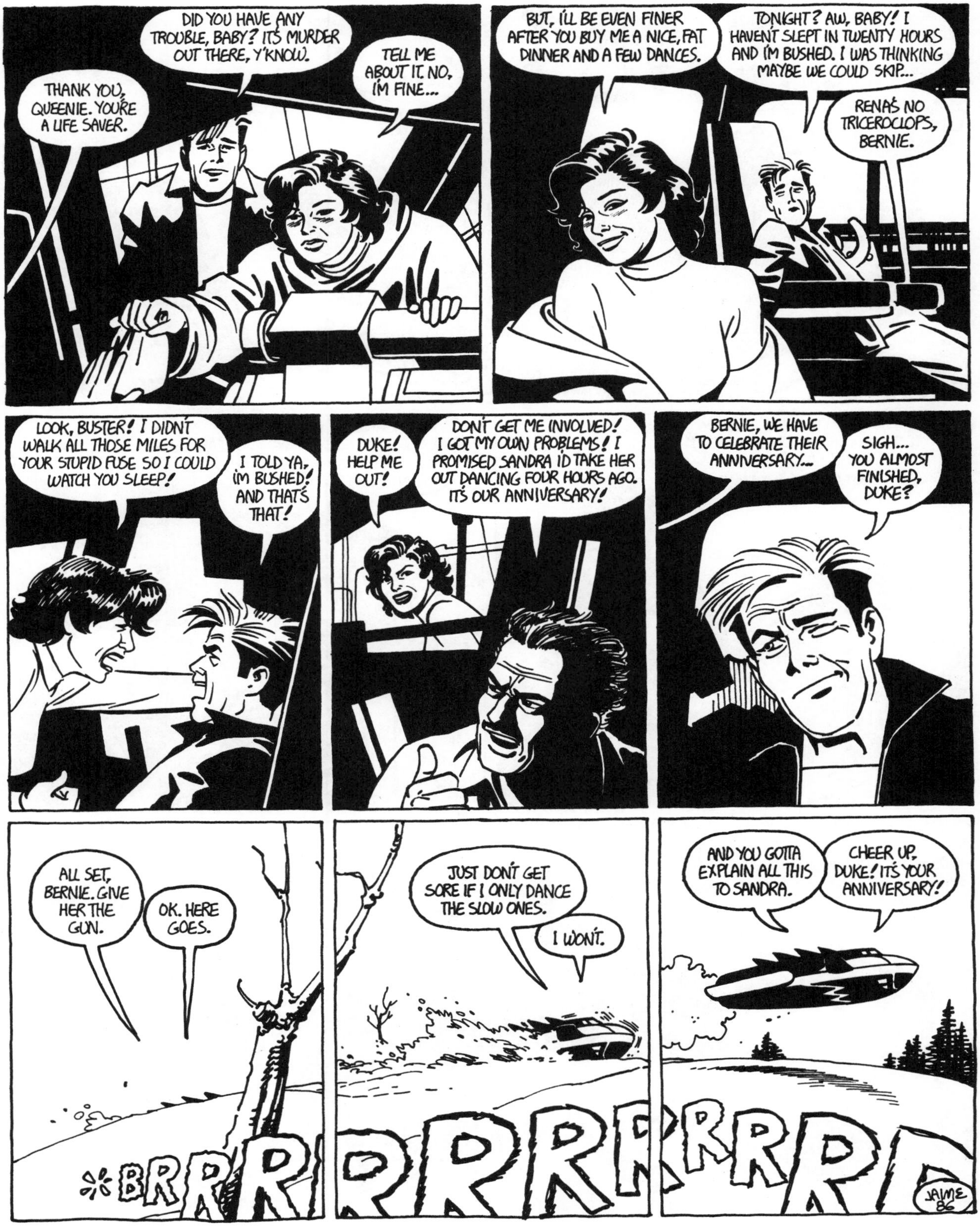
THANK YOU, QUEENIE. YOU'RE A LIFE SAVER.
DID YOU HAVE ANY TROUBLE, BABY? IT'S MURDER OUT THERE, Y'KNOW.
TELL ME ABOUT IT. NO, I'M FINE...
BUT, I'LL BE EVEN FINER AFTER YOU BUY ME A NICE, FAT DINNER AND A FEW DANCES.
TONIGHT? AW, BABY! I HAVEN'T SLEPT IN TWENTY HOURS AND I'M BUSHED. I WAS THINKING MAYBE WE COULD SKIP...
RENA'S NO TRICEROCLOPS, BERNIE.
LOOK, BUSTER! I DIDN'T WALK ALL THOSE MILES FOR YOUR STUPID FUSE SO I COULD WATCH YOU SLEEP!
I TOLD YA, I'M BUSHED! AND THAT'S THAT!
DUKE! HELP ME OUT!
DON'T GET ME INVOLVED! I GOT MY OWN PROBLEMS! I PROMISED SANDRA I'D TAKE HER OUT DANCING FOUR HOURS AGO. IT'S OUR ANNIVERSARY!
BERNIE, WE HAVE TO CELEBRATE THEIR ANNIVERSARY...
SIGH... YOU ALMOST FINISHED, DUKE?
ALL SET, BERNIE. GIVE HER THE GUN.
OK. HERE GOES.
JUST DON'T GET SORE IF I ONLY DANCE THE SLOW ONES.
I WON'T.
AND YOU GOTTA EXPLAIN ALL THIS TO SANDRA.
CHEER UP, DUKE! IT'S YOUR ANNIVERSARY!
BRRRRRRRRRRRR
JAIME 86

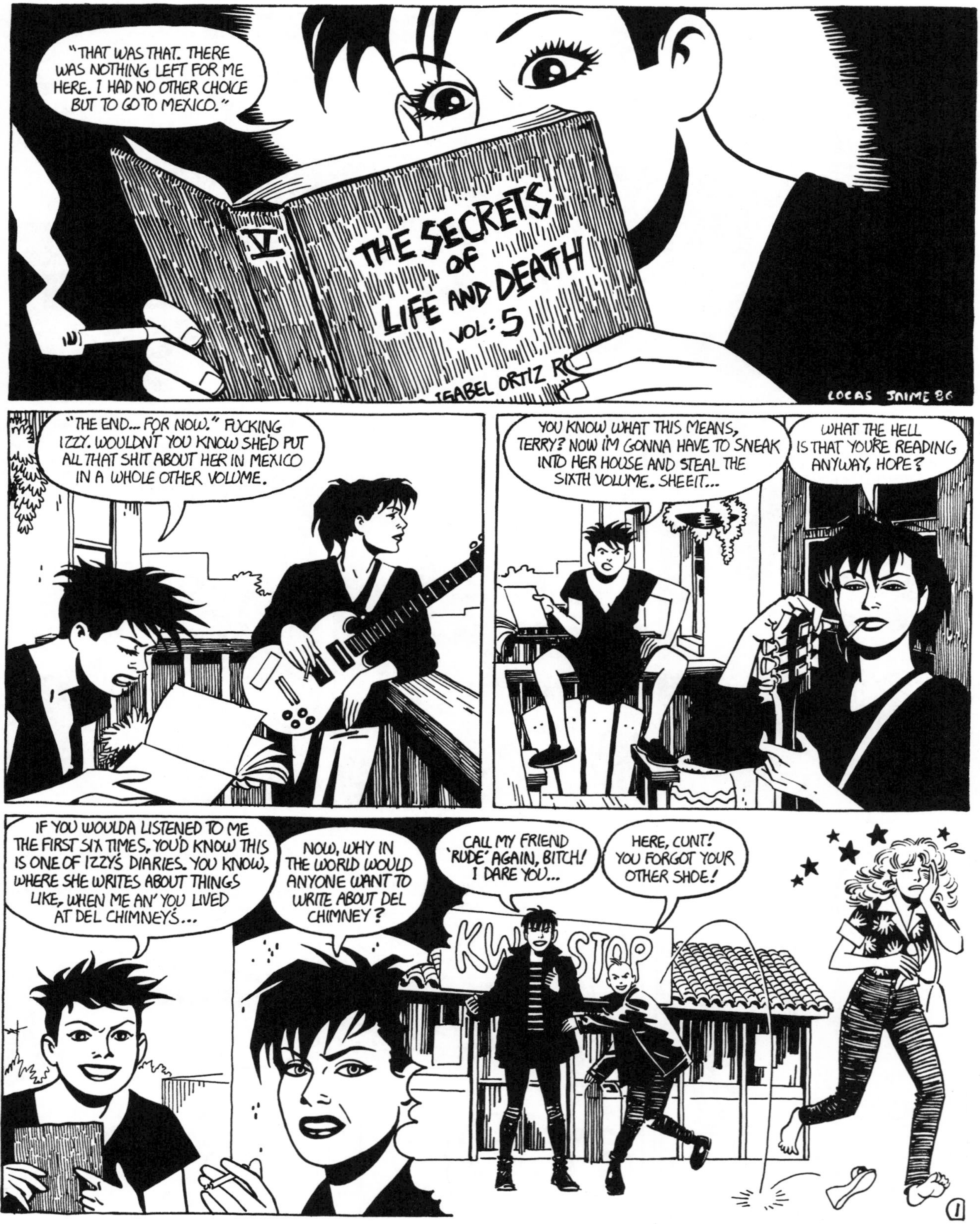
"THAT WAS THAT. THERE WAS NOTHING LEFT FOR ME HERE. I HAD NO OTHER CHOICE BUT TO GO TO MEXICO."
V
THE SECRETS OF LIFE AND DEATH VOL: 5
ISABEL ORTIZ R
LOCAS JAIME 86
"THE END... FOR NOW." FUCKING IZZY. WOULDN'T YOU KNOW SHE'D PUT ALL THAT SHIT ABOUT HER IN MEXICO IN A WHOLE OTHER VOLUME.
YOU KNOW WHAT THIS MEANS, TERRY? NOW I'M GONNA HAVE TO SNEAK INTO HER HOUSE AND STEAL THE SIXTH VOLUME. SHEEIT...
WHAT THE HELL IS THAT YOU'RE READING ANYWAY, HOPE?
IF YOU WOULDA LISTENED TO ME THE FIRST SIX TIMES, YOU'D KNOW THIS IS ONE OF IZZY'S DIARIES. YOU KNOW, WHERE SHE WRITES ABOUT THINGS LIKE, WHEN ME AN' YOU LIVED AT DEL CHIMNEY'S...
NOW, WHY IN THE WORLD WOULD ANYONE WANT TO WRITE ABOUT DEL CHIMNEY?
CALL MY FRIEND 'RUDE' AGAIN, BITCH! I DARE YOU...
HERE, CUNT! YOU FORGOT YOUR OTHER SHOE!
1

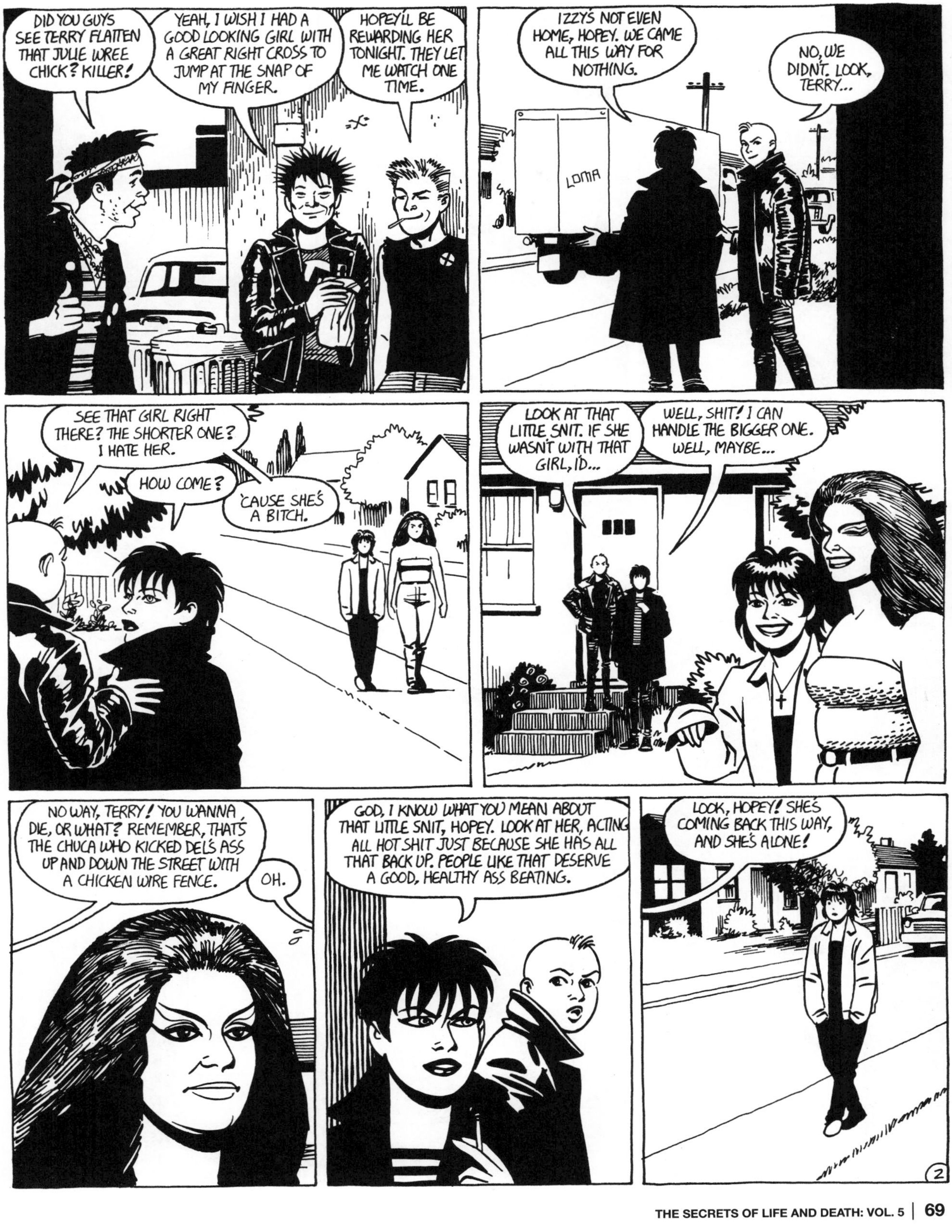
DID YOU GUYS SEE TERRY FLATTEN THAT JULIE WREE CHICK? KILLER!
YEAH, I WISH I HAD A GOOD LOOKING GIRL WITH A GREAT RIGHT CROSS TO JUMP AT THE SNAP OF MY FINGER.
HOPEY'LL BE REWARDING HER TONIGHT. THEY LET ME WATCH ONE TIME.
IZZY'S NOT EVEN HOME, HOPEY. WE CAME ALL THIS WAY FOR NOTHING.
NO, WE DIDN'T. LOOK, TERRY...
LOMA
SEE THAT GIRL RIGHT THERE? THE SHORTER ONE? I HATE HER.
HOW COME?
'CAUSE SHE'S A BITCH.
LOOK AT THAT LITTLE SNIT. IF SHE WASN'T WITH THAT GIRL, I'D...
WELL, SHIT! I CAN HANDLE THE BIGGER ONE. WELL, MAYBE...
NO WAY, TERRY! YOU WANNA DIE, OR WHAT? REMEMBER, THAT'S THE CHUCA WHO KICKED DEL'S ASS UP AND DOWN THE STREET WITH A CHICKEN WIRE FENCE.
OH.
GOD, I KNOW WHAT YOU MEAN ABOUT THAT LITTLE SNIT, HOPEY. LOOK AT HER, ACTING ALL HOT SHIT JUST BECAUSE SHE HAS ALL THAT BACK UP. PEOPLE LIKE THAT DESERVE A GOOD, HEALTHY ASS BEATING.
LOOK, HOPEY! SHE'S COMING BACK THIS WAY, AND SHE'S ALONE!
2

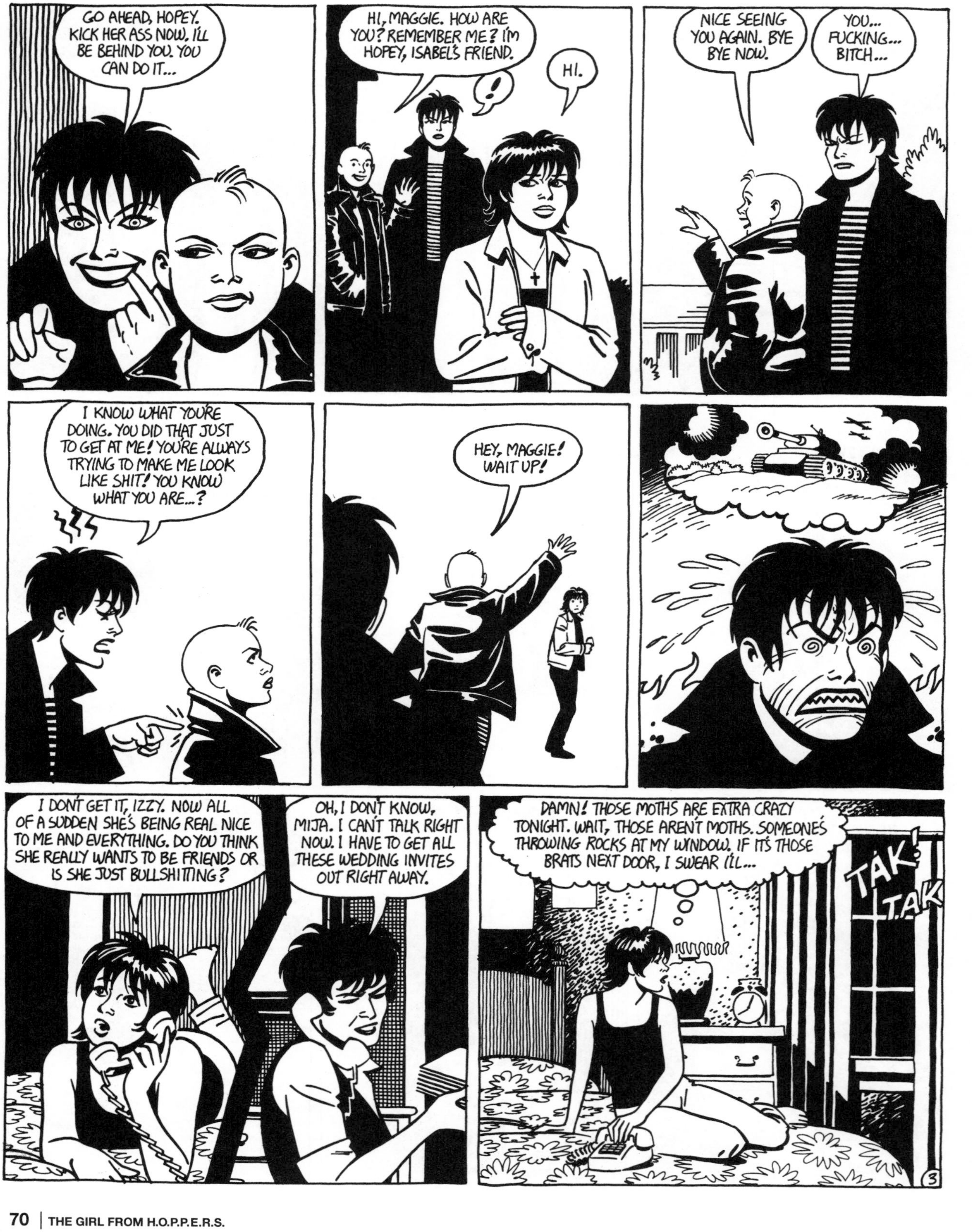
GO AHEAD, HOPEY. KICK HER ASS NOW. I'LL BE BEHIND YOU. YOU CAN DO IT...
HI, MAGGIE. HOW ARE YOU? REMEMBER ME? I'M HOPEY, ISABEL'S FRIEND.
!
HI.
NICE SEEING YOU AGAIN. BYE BYE NOW.
YOU... FUCKING... BITCH...
I KNOW WHAT YOU'RE DOING. YOU DID THAT JUST TO GET AT ME! YOU'RE ALWAYS TRYING TO MAKE ME LOOK LIKE SHIT! YOU KNOW WHAT YOU ARE...?
HEY, MAGGIE! WAIT UP!
I DON'T GET IT, IZZY. NOW ALL OF A SUDDEN SHE'S BEING REAL NICE TO ME AND EVERYTHING. DO YOU THINK SHE REALLY WANTS TO BE FRIENDS OR IS SHE JUST BULLSHITTING?
OH, I DON'T KNOW, MIJA. I CAN'T TALK RIGHT NOW. I HAVE TO GET ALL THESE WEDDING INVITES OUT RIGHT AWAY.
DAMN! THOSE MOTHS ARE EXTRA CRAZY TONIGHT. WAIT, THOSE AREN'T MOTHS. SOMEONE'S THROWING ROCKS AT MY WINDOW. IF IT'S THOSE BRATS NEXT DOOR, I SWEAR I'LL...
TAK! TAK
3

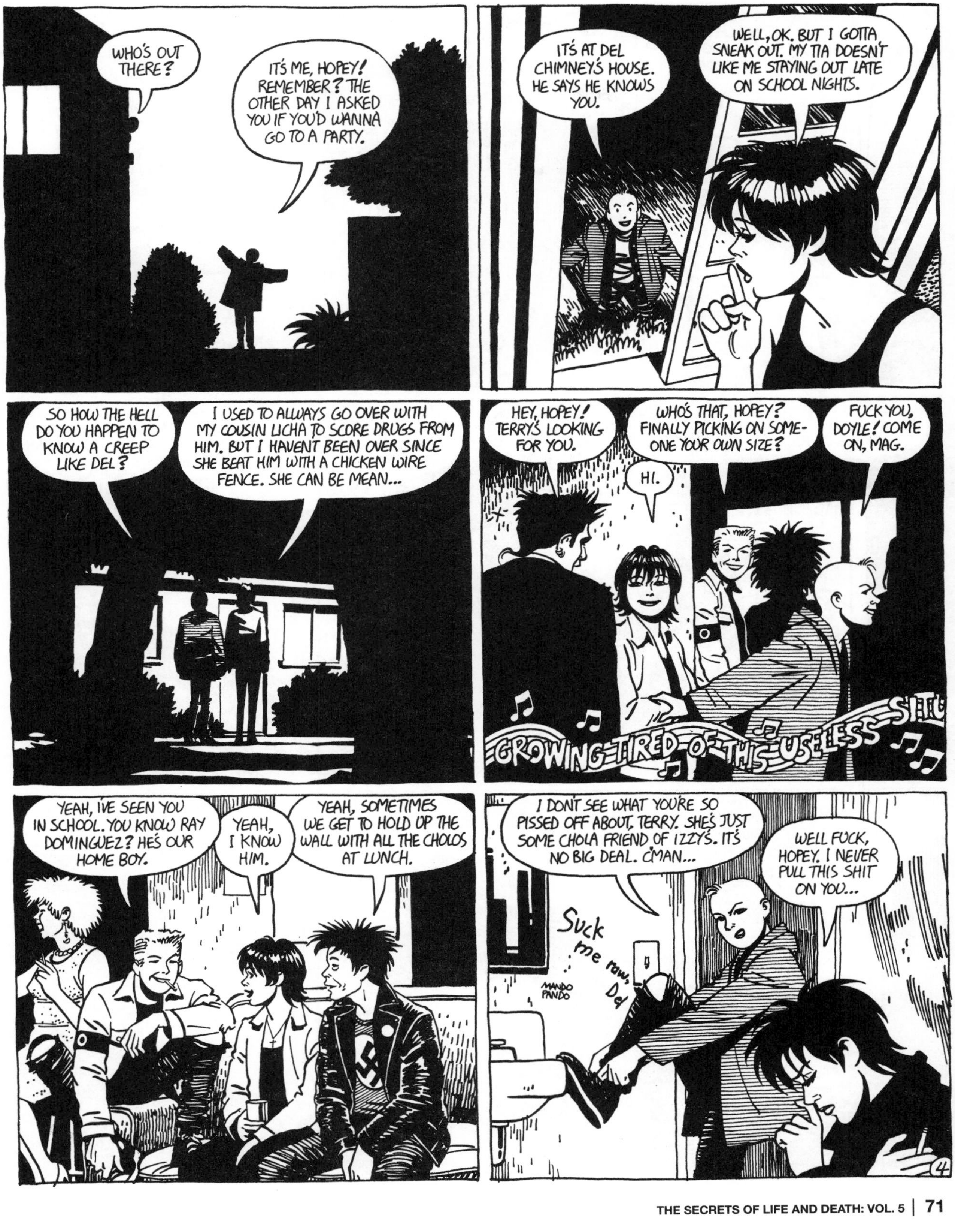
WHO'S OUT THERE?
IT'S ME, HOPEY! REMEMBER? THE OTHER DAY I ASKED YOU IF YOU'D WANNA GO TO A PARTY.
IT'S AT DEL CHIMNEY'S HOUSE. HE SAYS HE KNOWS YOU.
WELL, OK. BUT I GOTTA SNEAK OUT. MY TIA DOESN'T LIKE ME STAYING OUT LATE ON SCHOOL NIGHTS.
SO HOW THE HELL DO YOU HAPPEN TO KNOW A CREEP LIKE DEL?
I USED TO ALWAYS GO OVER WITH MY COUSIN LICHA TO SCORE DRUGS FROM HIM. BUT I HAVEN'T BEEN OVER SINCE SHE BEAT HIM WITH A CHICKEN WIRE FENCE. SHE CAN BE MEAN...
HEY, HOPEY! TERRY'S LOOKING FOR YOU.
HI.
WHO'S THAT, HOPEY? FINALLY PICKING ON SOME-ONE YOUR OWN SIZE?
FUCK YOU, DOYLE! COME ON, MAG.
GROWING TIRED OF THIS USELESS SITU
YEAH, I'VE SEEN YOU IN SCHOOL. YOU KNOW RAY DOMINGUEZ? HE'S OUR HOME BOY.
YEAH, I KNOW HIM.
YEAH, SOMETIMES WE GET TO HOLD UP THE WALL WITH ALL THE CHOLOS AT LUNCH.
I DON'T SEE WHAT YOU'RE SO PISSED OFF ABOUT, TERRY. SHE'S JUST SOME CHOLA FRIEND OF IZZY'S. IT'S NO BIG DEAL. C'MAN...
WELL FUCK, HOPEY. I NEVER PULL THIS SHIT ON YOU...
Suck me raw, Del
MANDO PANDO
4

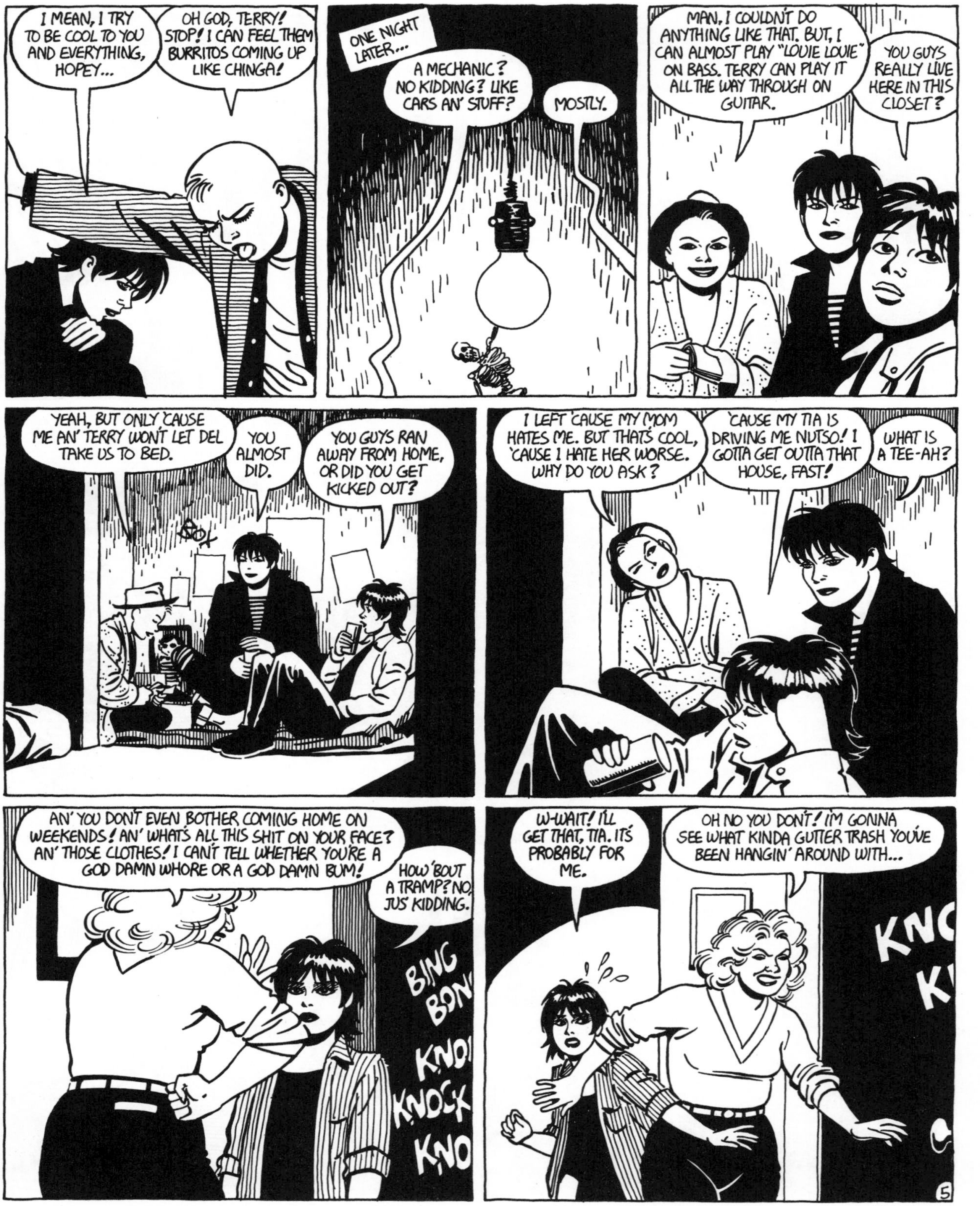
I MEAN, I TRY TO BE COOL TO YOU AND EVERYTHING, HOPEY...
OH GOD, TERRY! STOP! I CAN FEEL THEM BURRITOS COMING UP LIKE CHINGA!
ONE NIGHT LATER...
A MECHANIC? NO KIDDING? LIKE CARS AN' STUFF?
MOSTLY.
MAN, I COULDN'T DO ANYTHING LIKE THAT. BUT, I CAN ALMOST PLAY "LOUIE LOUIE" ON BASS. TERRY CAN PLAY IT ALL THE WAY THROUGH ON GUITAR.
YOU GUYS REALLY LIVE HERE IN THIS CLOSET?
YEAH, BUT ONLY 'CAUSE ME AN' TERRY WON'T LET DEL TAKE US TO BED.
YOU ALMOST DID.
YOU GUYS RAN AWAY FROM HOME, OR DID YOU GET KICKED OUT?
I LEFT 'CAUSE MY MOM HATES ME. BUT THAT'S COOL, 'CAUSE I HATE HER WORSE. WHY DO YOU ASK?
'CAUSE MY TIA IS DRIVING ME NUTSO! I GOTTA GET OUTTA THAT HOUSE, FAST!
WHAT IS A TEE-AH?
AN' YOU DON'T EVEN BOTHER COMING HOME ON WEEKENDS! AN' WHAT'S ALL THIS SHIT ON YOUR FACE? AN' THOSE CLOTHES! I CAN'T TELL WHETHER YOU'RE A GOD DAMN WHORE OR A GOD DAMN BUM!
HOW 'BOUT A TRAMP? NO, JUS' KIDDING.
BING BON
KNO KNOCK KNO
W-WAIT! I'LL GET THAT, TIA. IT'S PROBABLY FOR ME.
OH NO YOU DON'T! I'M GONNA SEE WHAT KINDA GUTTER TRASH YOU'VE BEEN HANGIN' AROUND WITH...
KNO
K
5

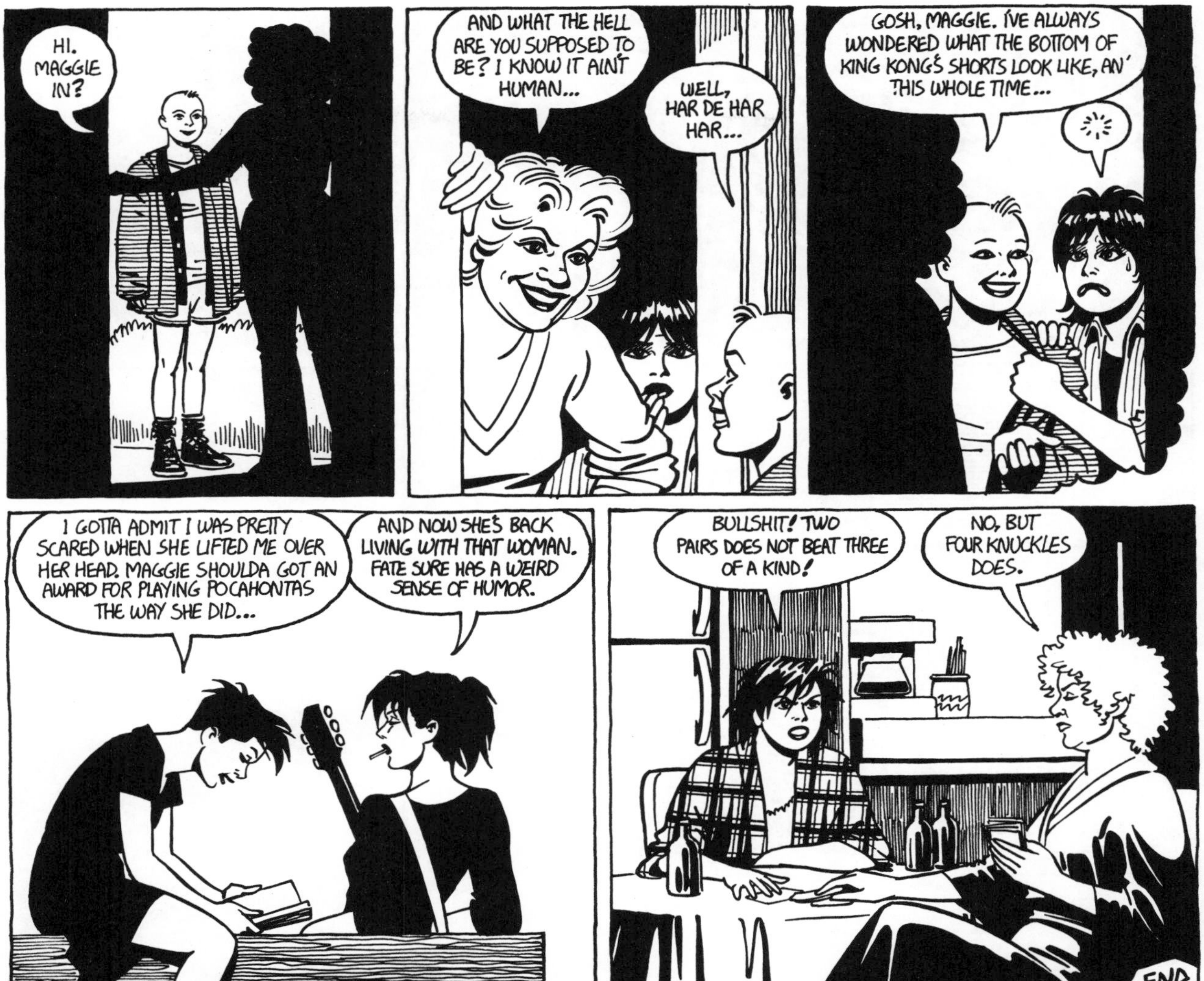
HI. MAGGIE IN?
AND WHAT THE HELL ARE YOU SUPPOSED TO BE? I KNOW IT AIN'T HUMAN...
WELL, HAR DE HAR HAR...
GOSH, MAGGIE. I'VE ALWAYS WONDERED WHAT THE BOTTOM OF KING KONG'S SHORTS LOOK LIKE, AN' THIS WHOLE TIME...
I GOTTA ADMIT I WAS PRETTY SCARED WHEN SHE LIFTED ME OVER HER HEAD. MAGGIE SHOULDA GOT AN AWARD FOR PLAYING POCAHONTAS THE WAY SHE DID...
AND NOW SHE'S BACK LIVING WITH THAT WOMAN. FATE SURE HAS A WEIRD SENSE OF HUMOR.
BULLSHIT! TWO PAIRS DOES NOT BEAT THREE OF A KIND!
NO, BUT FOUR KNUCKLES DOES.
END

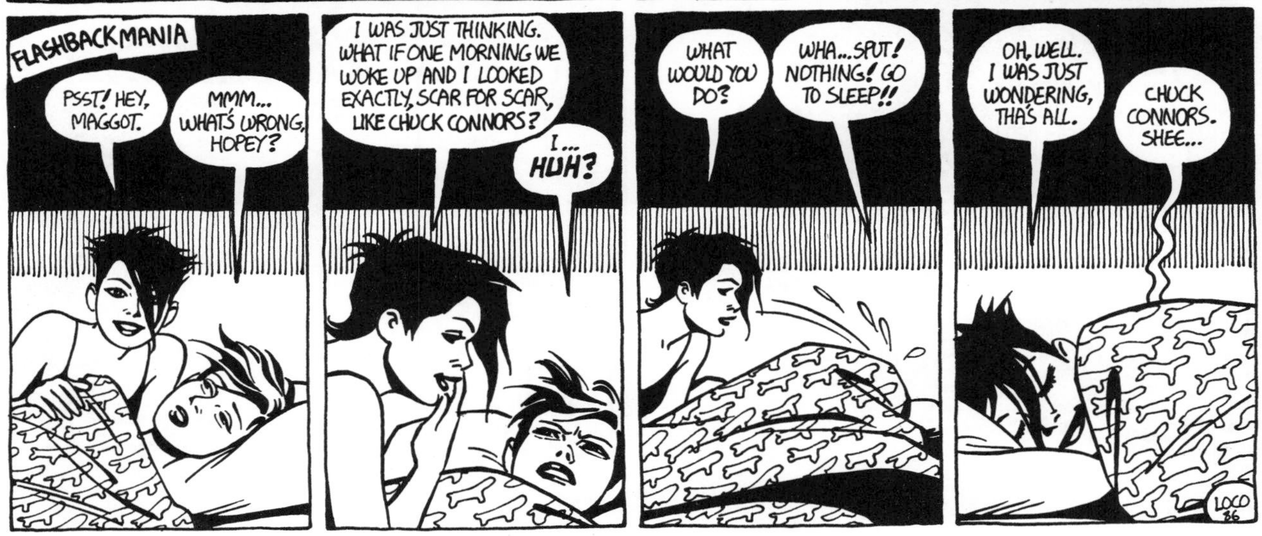
FLASHBACKMANIA
PSST! HEY, MAGGOT.
MMM... WHAT'S WRONG, HOPEY?
I WAS JUST THINKING. WHAT IF ONE MORNING WE WOKE UP AND I LOOKED EXACTLY, SCAR FOR SCAR, LIKE CHUCK CONNORS?
I... HUH?
WHAT WOULD YOU DO?
WHA...SPUT! NOTHING! GO TO SLEEP!!
OH, WELL. I WAS JUST WONDERING, THA'S ALL.
CHUCK CONNORS. SHEE...
LOCO 86

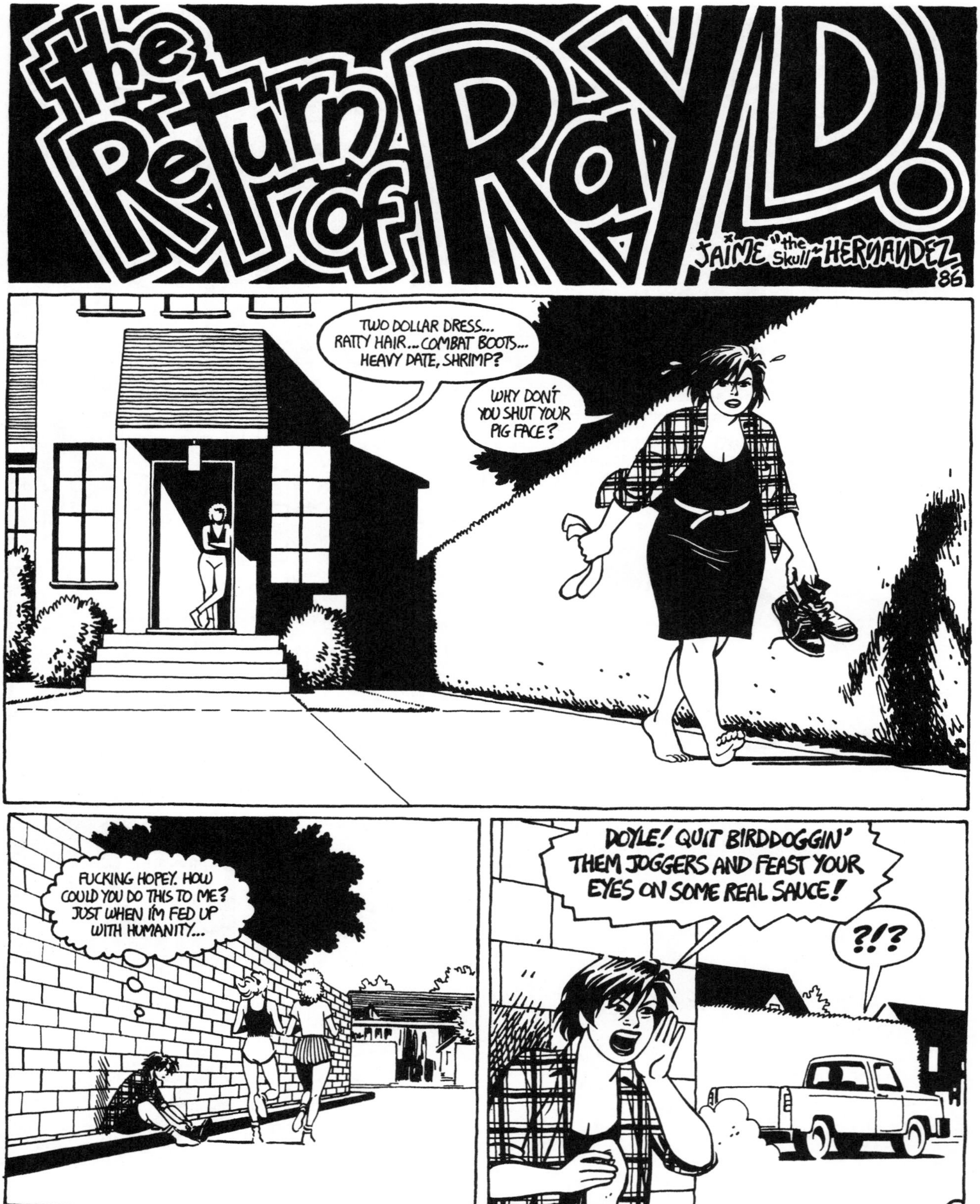
the Return of Ray D.
JAIME "the Skull" HERNANDEZ 86
TWO DOLLAR DRESS... RATTY HAIR... COMBAT BOOTS... HEAVY DATE, SHRIMP?
WHY DON'T YOU SHUT YOUR PIG FACE?
FUCKING HOPEY. HOW COULD YOU DO THIS TO ME? JUST WHEN I'M FED UP WITH HUMANITY...
DOYLE! QUIT BIRDDOGGIN' THEM JOGGERS AND FEAST YOUR EYES ON SOME REAL SAUCE!
?!?
1

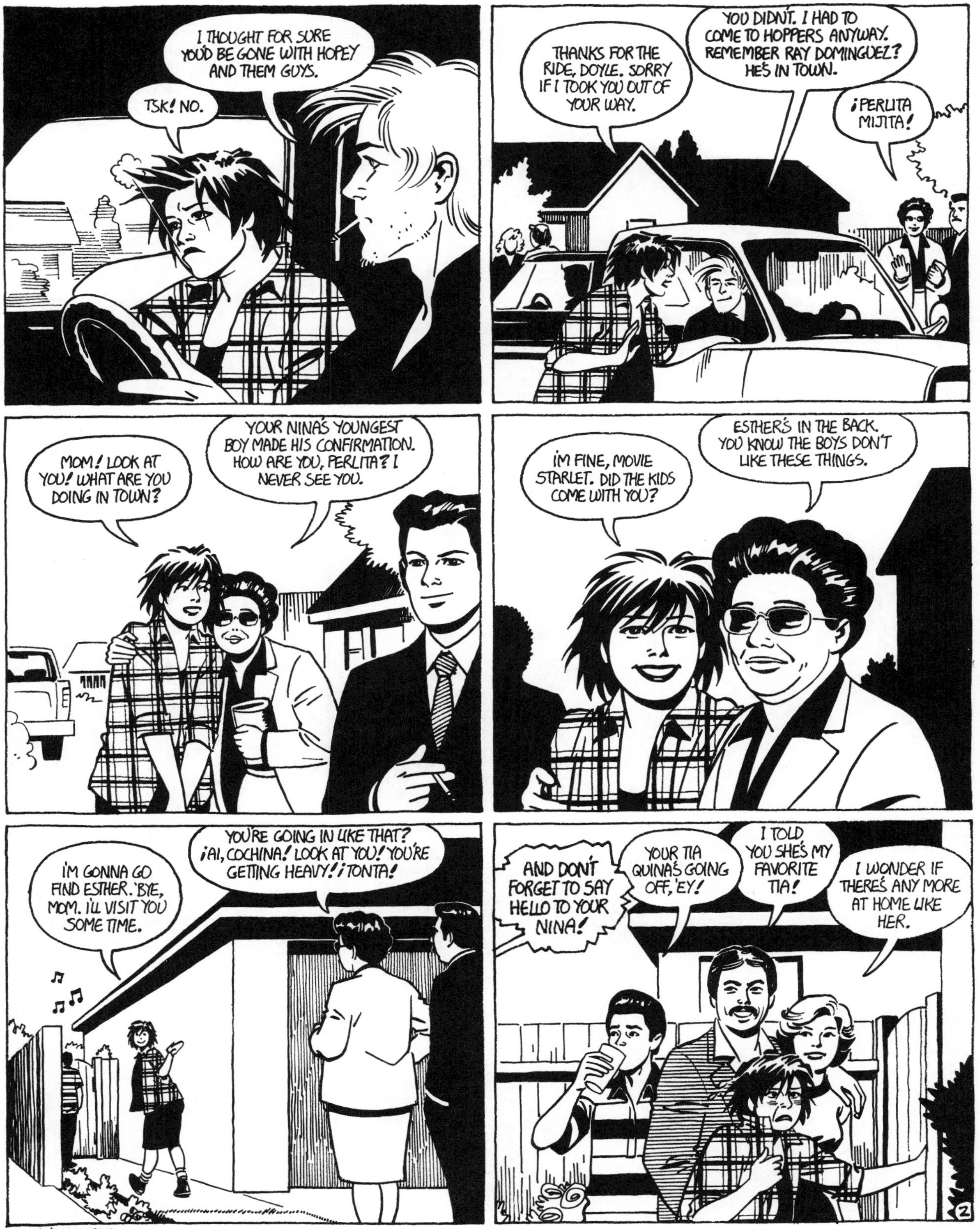
I THOUGHT FOR SURE YOU'D BE GONE WITH HOPEY AND THEM GUYS.
TSK! NO.
THANKS FOR THE RIDE, DOYLE. SORRY IF I TOOK YOU OUT OF YOUR WAY.
YOU DIDN'T. I HAD TO COME TO HOPPERS ANYWAY. REMEMBER RAY DOMINGUEZ? HE'S IN TOWN.
¡PERLITA MIJITA!
MOM! LOOK AT YOU! WHAT ARE YOU DOING IN TOWN?
YOUR NINA'S YOUNGEST BOY MADE HIS CONFIRMATION. HOW ARE YOU, PERLITA? I NEVER SEE YOU.
I'M FINE, MOVIE STARLET. DID THE KIDS COME WITH YOU?
ESTHER'S IN THE BACK. YOU KNOW THE BOYS DON'T LIKE THESE THINGS.
I'M GONNA GO FIND ESTHER. 'BYE, MOM. I'LL VISIT YOU SOME TIME.
YOU'RE GOING IN LIKE THAT? ¡AI, COCHINA! LOOK AT YOU! YOU'RE GETTING HEAVY! ¡TONTA!
AND DON'T FORGET TO SAY HELLO TO YOUR NINA!
YOUR TIA QUINA'S GOING OFF, 'EY!
I TOLD YOU SHE'S MY FAVORITE TIA!
I WONDER IF THERE'S ANY MORE AT HOME LIKE HER.
2

NINA/GODMOTHER

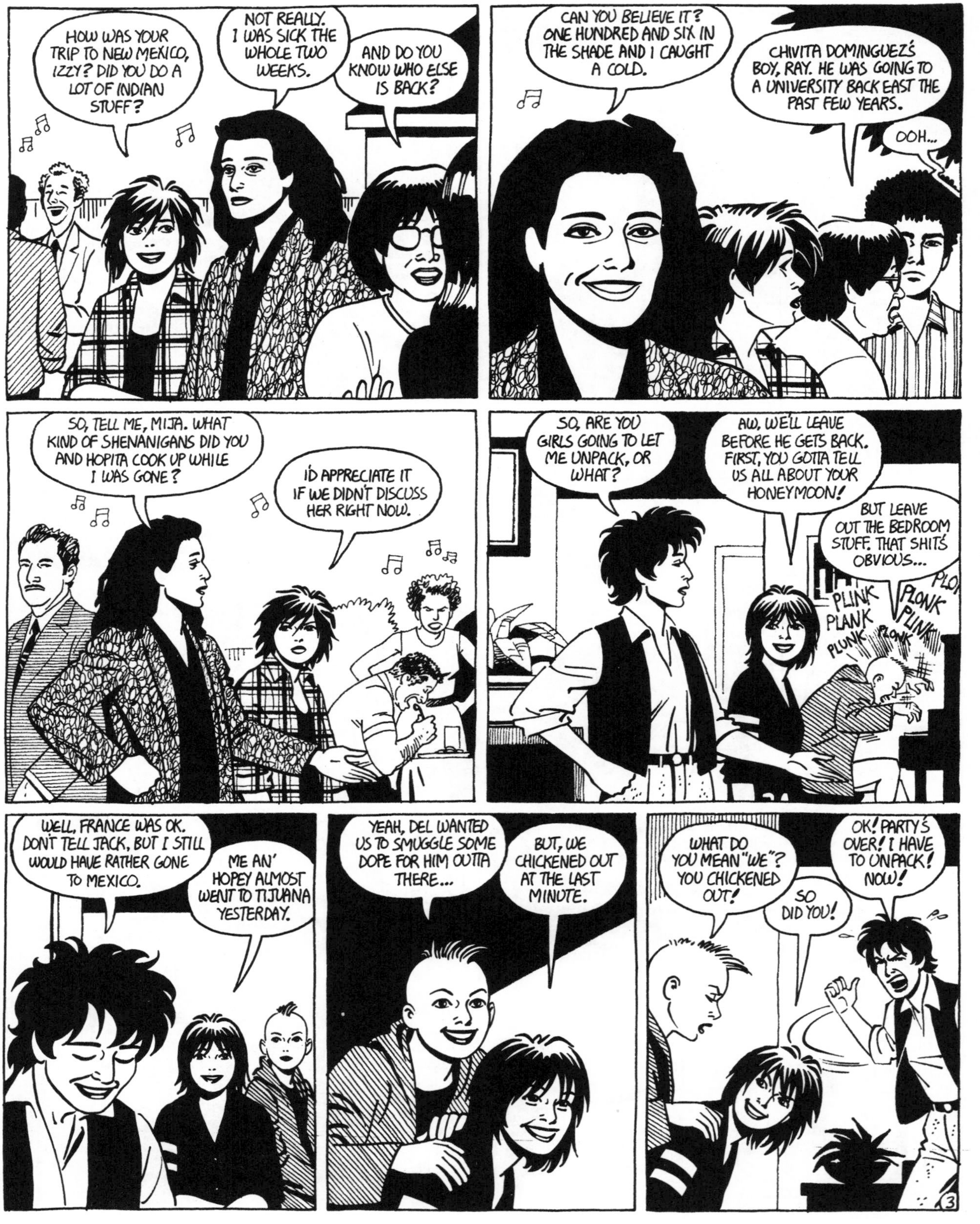
HOW WAS YOUR TRIP TO NEW MEXICO, IZZY? DID YOU DO A LOT OF INDIAN STUFF?
NOT REALLY. I WAS SICK THE WHOLE TWO WEEKS.
AND DO YOU KNOW WHO ELSE IS BACK?
CAN YOU BELIEVE IT? ONE HUNDRED AND SIX IN THE SHADE AND I CAUGHT A COLD.
CHIVITA DOMINGUEZ'S BOY, RAY. HE WAS GOING TO A UNIVERSITY BACK EAST THE PAST FEW YEARS.
OOH...
SO, TELL ME, MIJA. WHAT KIND OF SHENANIGANS DID YOU AND HOPITA COOK UP WHILE I WAS GONE?
I'D APPRECIATE IT IF WE DIDN'T DISCUSS HER RIGHT NOW.
SO, ARE YOU GIRLS GOING TO LET ME UNPACK, OR WHAT?
AW, WE'LL LEAVE BEFORE HE GETS BACK. FIRST, YOU GOTTA TELL US ALL ABOUT YOUR HONEYMOON!
BUT LEAVE OUT THE BEDROOM STUFF. THAT SHIT'S OBVIOUS...
PLINK PLANK PLUNK PLONK PLONK PLINK PLONK
WELL, FRANCE WAS OK. DON'T TELL JACK, BUT I STILL WOULD HAVE RATHER GONE TO MEXICO.
ME AN' HOPEY ALMOST WENT TO TIJUANA YESTERDAY.
YEAH, DEL WANTED US TO SMUGGLE SOME DOPE FOR HIM OUTTA THERE...
BUT, WE CHICKENED OUT AT THE LAST MINUTE.
WHAT DO YOU MEAN "WE"? YOU CHICKENED OUT!
SO DID YOU!
OK! PARTY'S OVER! I HAVE TO UNPACK! NOW!
3

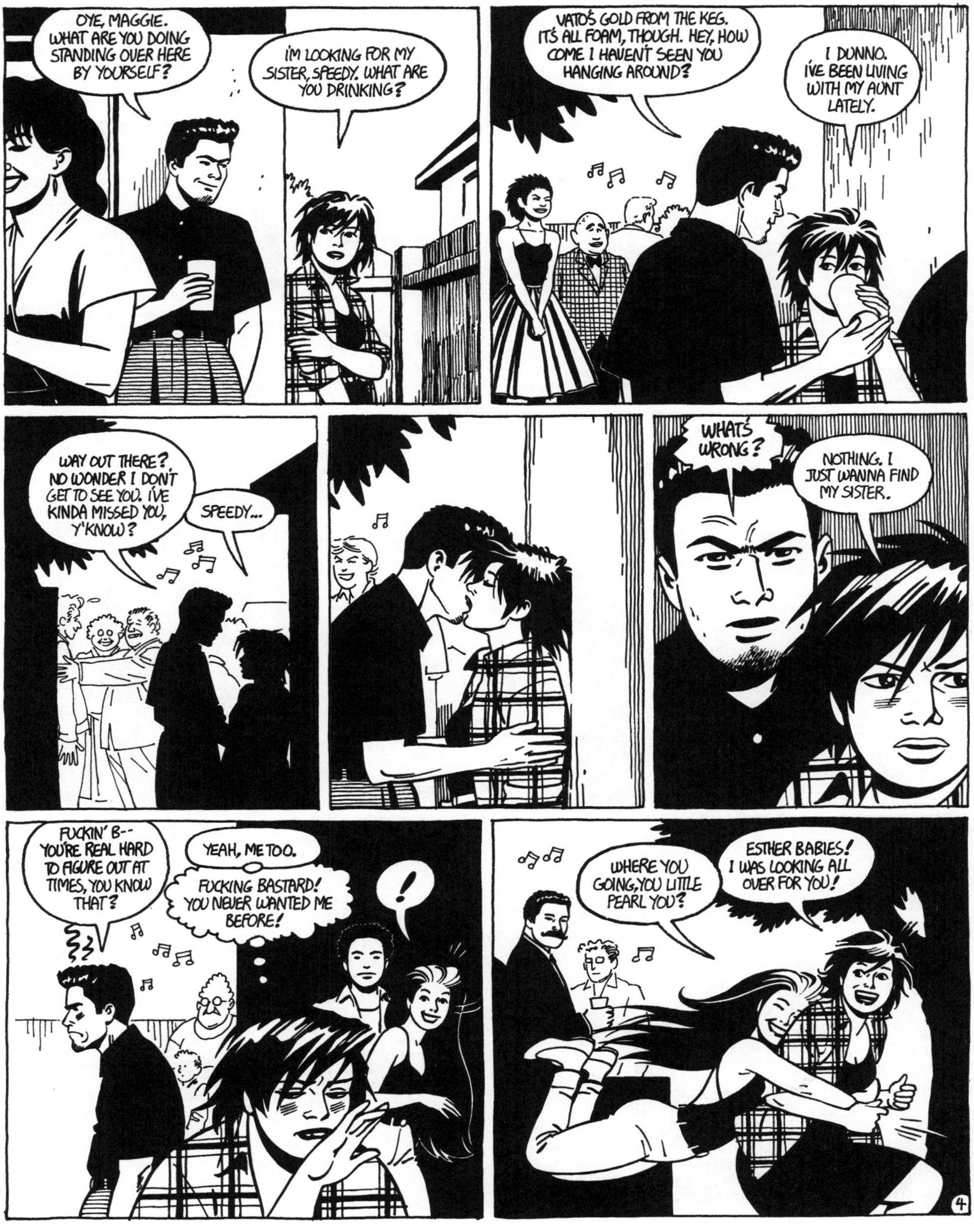
OYE, MAGGIE. WHAT ARE YOU DOING STANDING OVER HERE BY YOURSELF?
I'M LOOKING FOR MY SISTER, SPEEDY. WHAT ARE YOU DRINKING?
VATO'S GOLD FROM THE KEG. IT'S ALL FOAM, THOUGH. HEY, HOW COME I HAVEN'T SEEN YOU HANGING AROUND?
I DUNNO. I'VE BEEN LIVING WITH MY AUNT LATELY.
WAY OUT THERE? NO WONDER I DON'T GET TO SEE YOU. I'VE KINDA MISSED YOU, Y'KNOW?
SPEEDY...
WHAT'S WRONG?
NOTHING. I JUST WANNA FIND MY SISTER.
FUCKIN' B-- YOU'RE REAL HARD TO FIGURE OUT AT TIMES, YOU KNOW THAT?
YEAH, ME TOO.
FUCKING BASTARD! YOU NEVER WANTED ME BEFORE!
!
WHERE YOU GOING, YOU LITTLE PEARL YOU?
ESTHER BABIES! I WAS LOOKING ALL OVER FOR YOU!
4

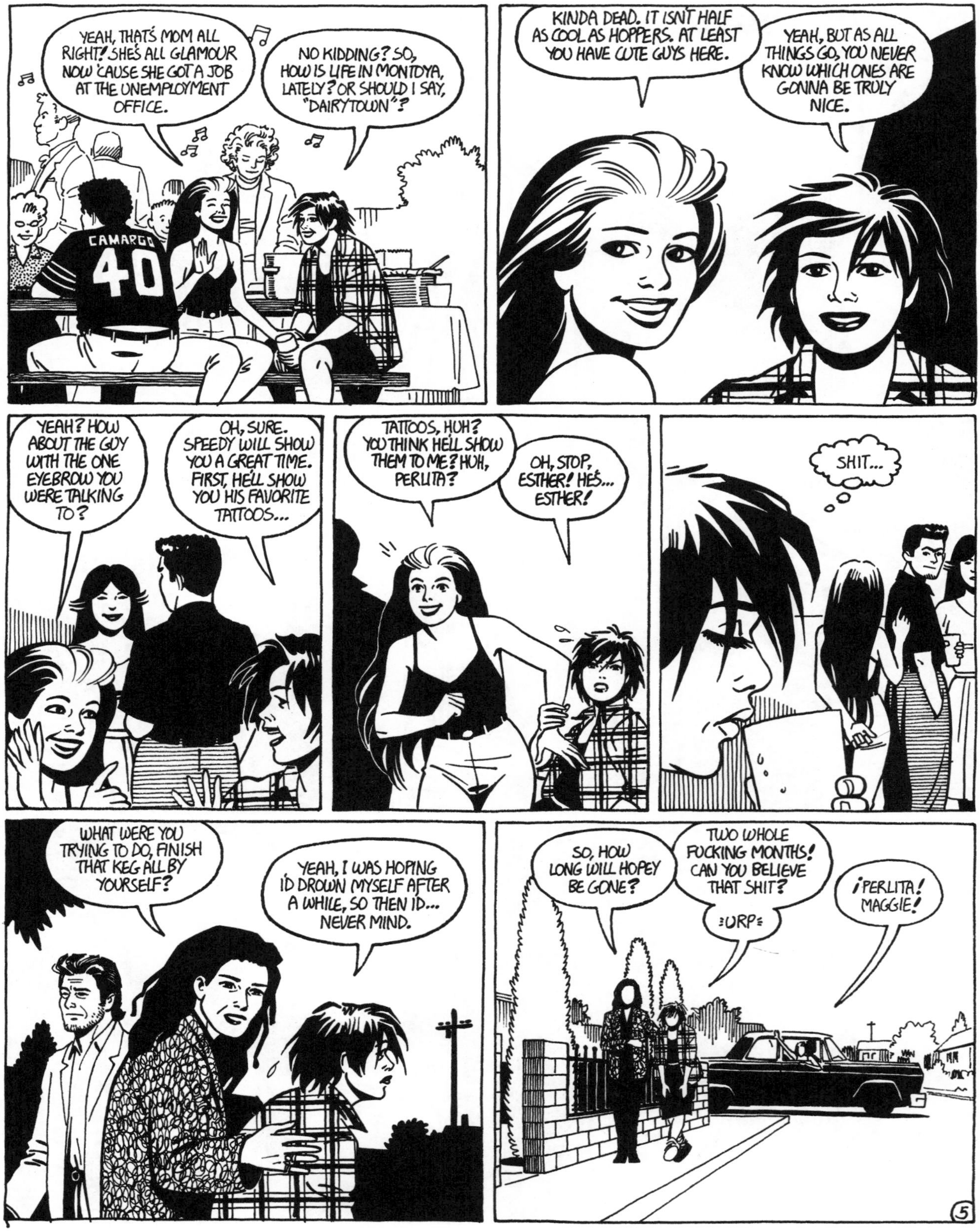
YEAH, THAT'S MOM ALL RIGHT! SHE'S ALL GLAMOUR NOW 'CAUSE SHE GOT A JOB AT THE UNEMPLOYMENT OFFICE.
NO KIDDING? SO, HOW IS LIFE IN MONTOYA, LATELY? OR SHOULD I SAY, "DAIRYTOWN"?
CAMARGO
40
KINDA DEAD. IT ISN'T HALF AS COOL AS HOPPERS. AT LEAST YOU HAVE CUTE GUYS HERE.
YEAH, BUT AS ALL THINGS GO, YOU NEVER KNOW WHICH ONES ARE GONNA BE TRULY NICE.
YEAH? HOW ABOUT THE GUY WITH THE ONE EYEBROW YOU WERE TALKING TO?
OH, SURE. SPEEDY WILL SHOW YOU A GREAT TIME. FIRST, HE'LL SHOW YOU HIS FAVORITE TATTOOS...
TATTOOS, HUH? YOU THINK HE'LL SHOW THEM TO ME? HUH, PERLITA?
OH, STOP, ESTHER! HE'S... ESTHER!
SHIT...
WHAT WERE YOU TRYING TO DO, FINISH THAT KEG ALL BY YOURSELF?
YEAH, I WAS HOPING I'D DROWN MYSELF AFTER A WHILE, SO THEN I'D... NEVER MIND.
SO, HOW LONG WILL HOPEY BE GONE?
TWO WHOLE FUCKING MONTHS! CAN YOU BELIEVE THAT SHIT?
URP
¡PERLITA! MAGGIE!
5

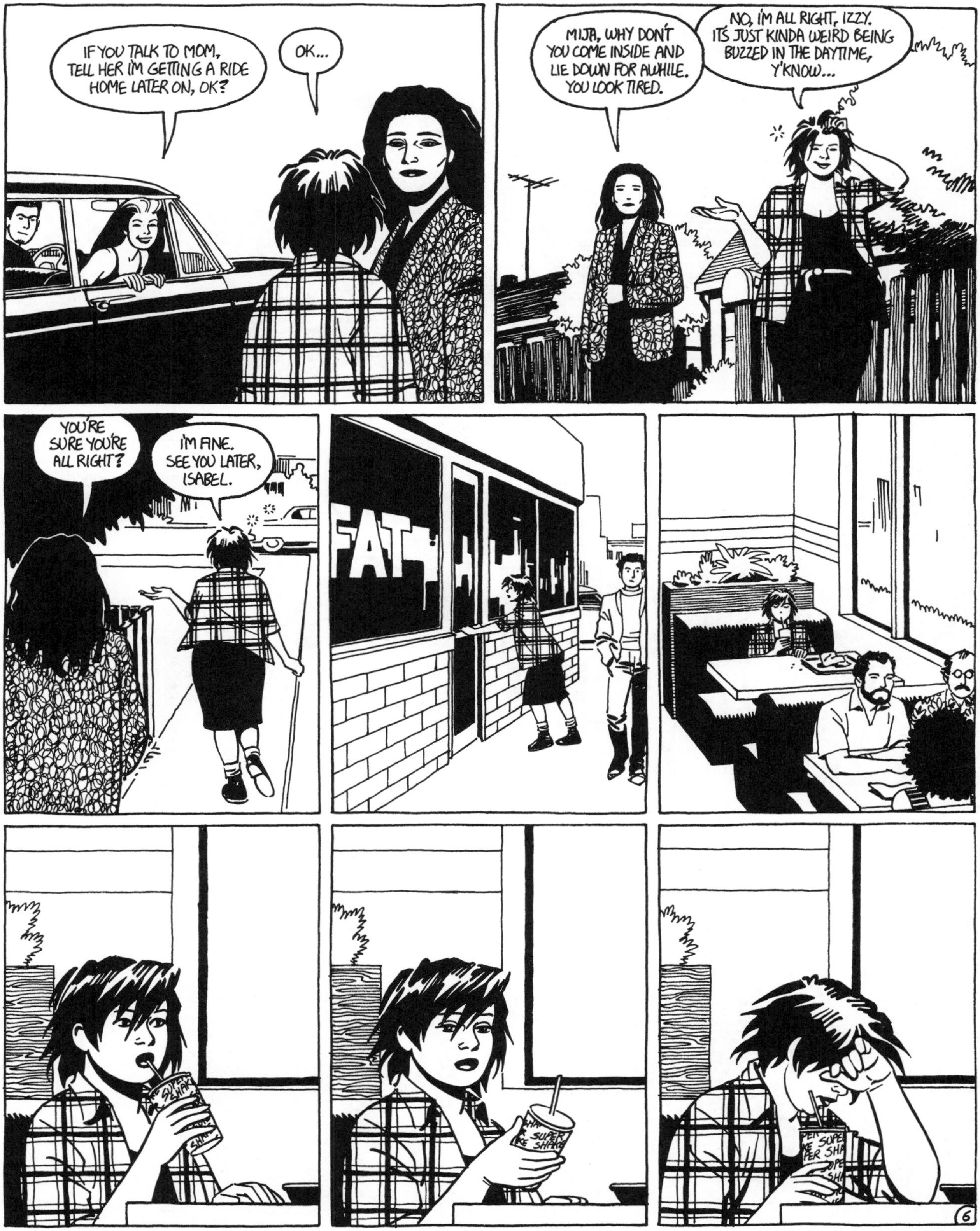

IF YOU TALK TO MOM, TELL HER I'M GETTING A RIDE HOME LATER ON, OK?
OK...
MIJA, WHY DON'T YOU COME INSIDE AND LIE DOWN FOR AWHILE. YOU LOOK TIRED.
NO, I'M ALL RIGHT, IZZY. IT'S JUST KINDA WEIRD BEING BUZZED IN THE DAYTIME, Y'KNOW...
YOU'RE SURE YOU'RE ALL RIGHT?
I'M FINE. SEE YOU LATER, ISABEL.
FAT
6

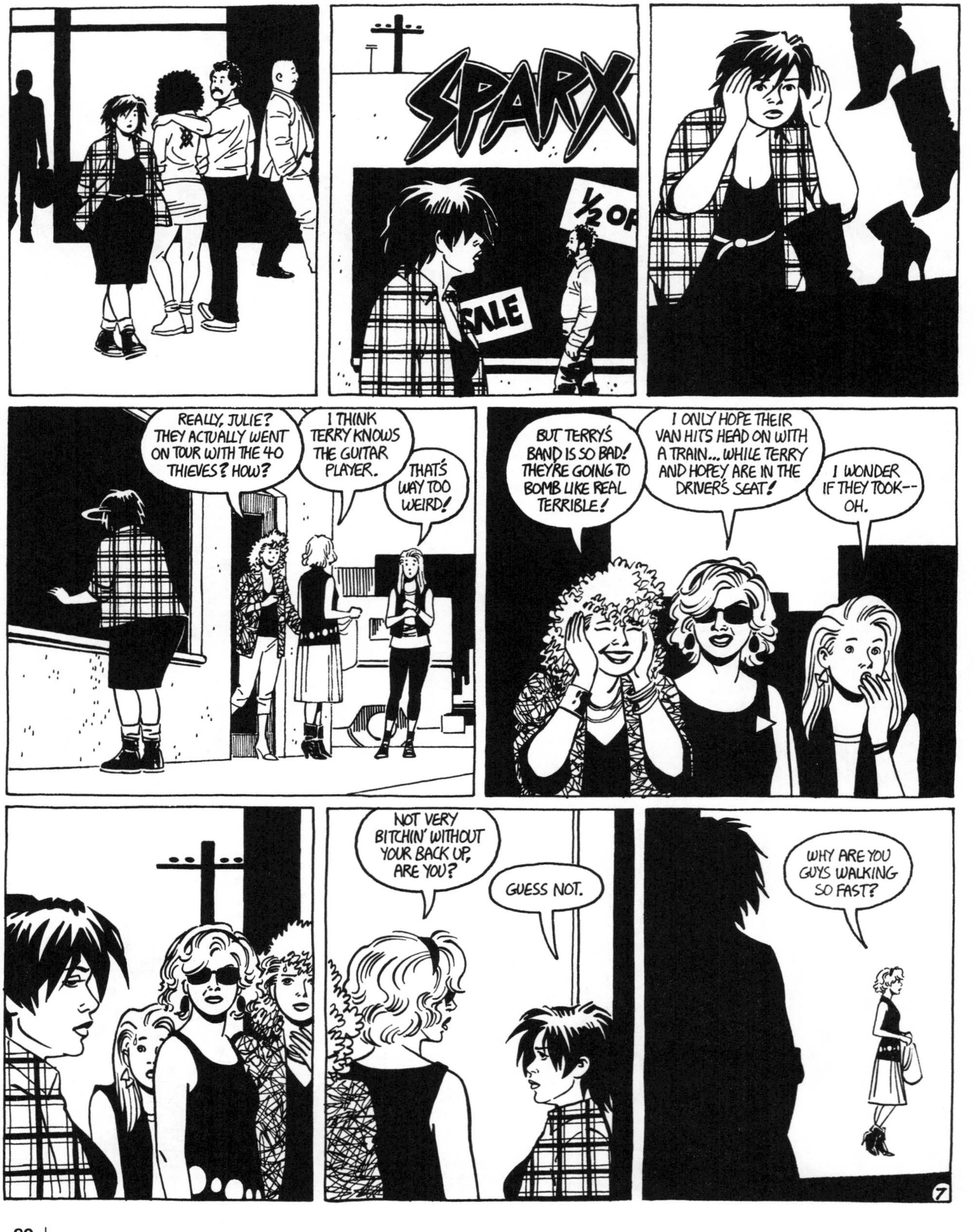
SPARX
1/2 OF
SALE
REALLY, JULIE? THEY ACTUALLY WENT ON TOUR WITH THE 40 THIEVES? HOW?
I THINK TERRY KNOWS THE GUITAR PLAYER.
THAT'S WAY TOO WEIRD!
BUT TERRY'S BAND IS SO BAD! THEY'RE GOING TO BOMB LIKE REAL TERRIBLE!
I ONLY HOPE THEIR VAN HITS HEAD ON WITH A TRAIN... WHILE TERRY AND HOPEY ARE IN THE DRIVER'S SEAT!
I WONDER IF THEY TOOK-- OH.
NOT VERY BITCHIN' WITHOUT YOUR BACK UP, ARE YOU?
GUESS NOT.
WHY ARE YOU GUYS WALKING SO FAST?
7

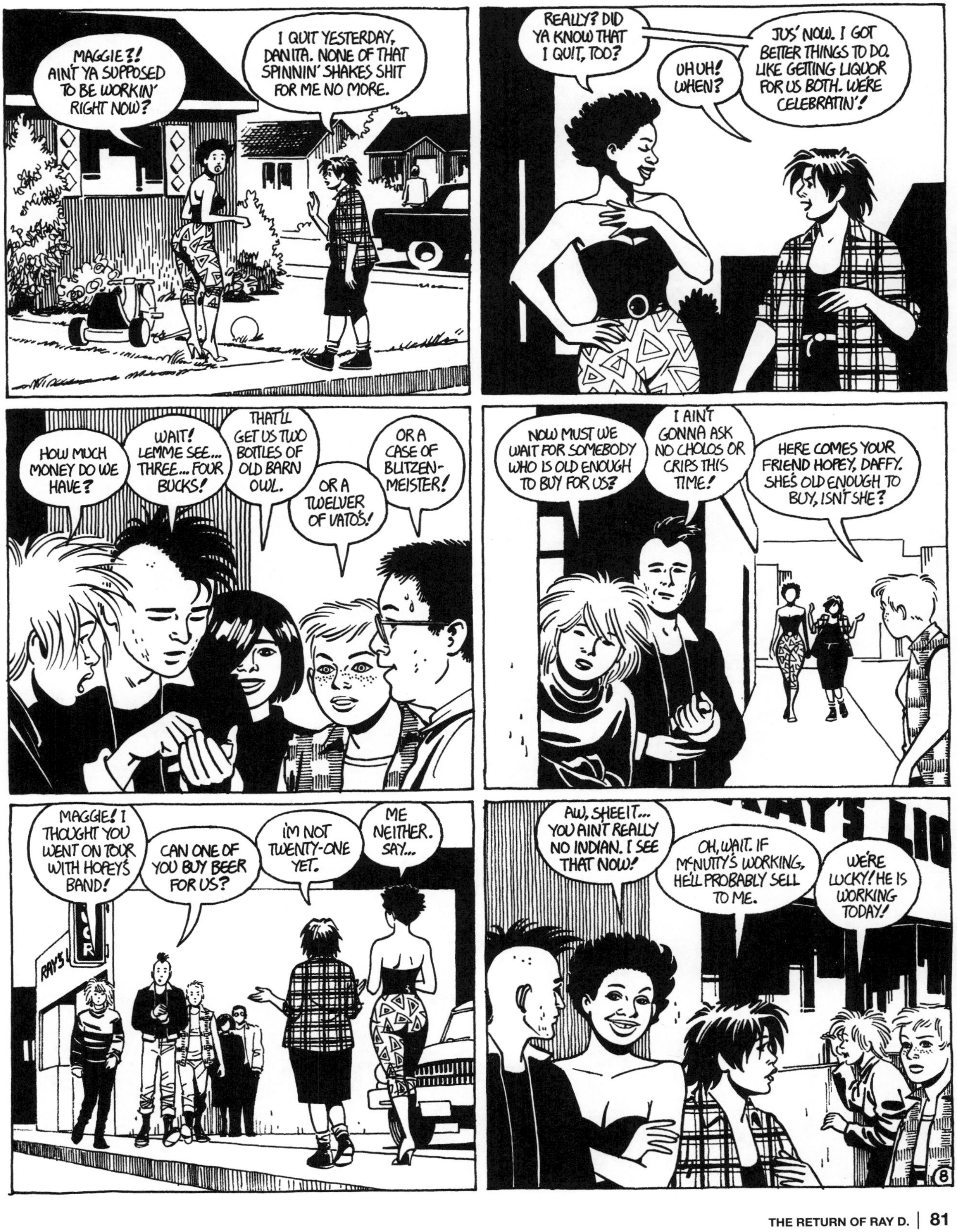
MAGGIE?! AIN'T YA SUPPOSED TO BE WORKIN' RIGHT NOW?
I QUIT YESTERDAY, DANITA. NONE OF THAT SPINNIN' SHAKES SHIT FOR ME NO MORE.
REALLY? DID YA KNOW THAT I QUIT, TOO?
UH UH! WHEN?
JUS' NOW. I GOT BETTER THINGS TO DO. LIKE GETTING LIQUOR FOR US BOTH. WE'RE CELEBRATIN'!
HOW MUCH MONEY DO WE HAVE?
WAIT! LEMME SEE... THREE... FOUR BUCKS!
THAT'LL GET US TWO BOTTLES OF OLD BARN OWL.
OR A TWELVER OF VATO'S!
OR A CASE OF BLITZEN-MEISTER!
NOW MUST WE WAIT FOR SOMEBODY WHO IS OLD ENOUGH TO BUY FOR US?
I AIN'T GONNA ASK NO CHOLOS OR CRIPS THIS TIME!
HERE COMES YOUR FRIEND HOPEY, DAFFY. SHE'S OLD ENOUGH TO BUY, ISN'T SHE?
MAGGIE! I THOUGHT YOU WENT ON TOUR WITH HOPEY'S BAND!
CAN ONE OF YOU BUY BEER FOR US?
I'M NOT TWENTY-ONE YET.
ME NEITHER. SAY...
RAY'S
AW, SHEEIT... YOU AIN'T REALLY NO INDIAN. I SEE THAT NOW!
OH, WAIT. IF McNUTTY'S WORKING, HE'LL PROBABLY SELL TO ME.
WE'RE LUCKY! HE IS WORKING TODAY!
8

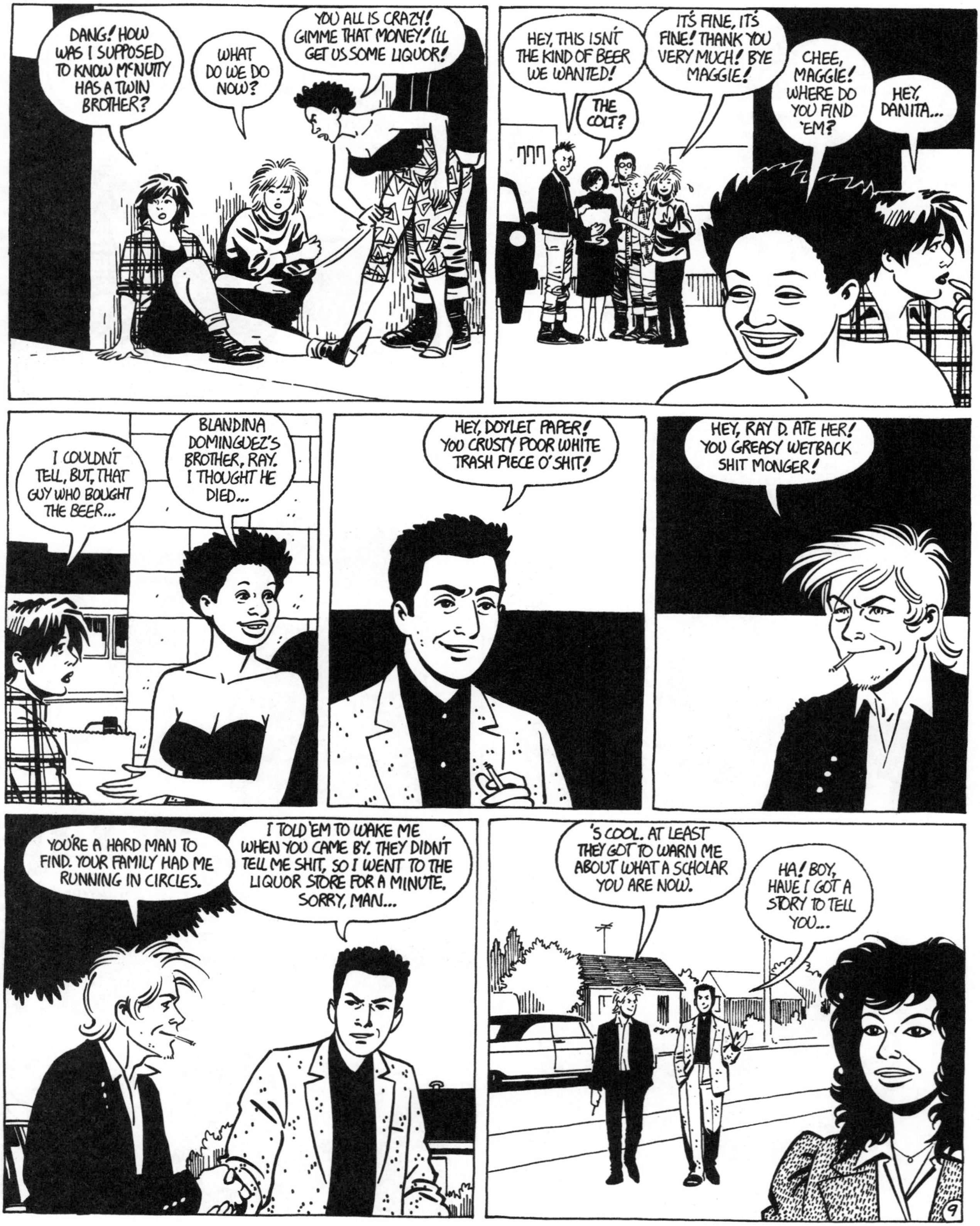
DANG! HOW WAS I SUPPOSED TO KNOW McNUTTY HAS A TWIN BROTHER?
WHAT DO WE DO NOW?
YOU ALL IS CRAZY! GIMME THAT MONEY! I'LL GET US SOME LIQUOR!
HEY, THIS ISN'T THE KIND OF BEER WE WANTED!
THE COLT?
IT'S FINE, IT'S FINE! THANK YOU VERY MUCH! BYE MAGGIE!
CHEE, MAGGIE! WHERE DO YOU FIND 'EM?
HEY, DANITA...
I COULDN'T TELL, BUT, THAT GUY WHO BOUGHT THE BEER...
BLANDINA DOMINGUEZ'S BROTHER, RAY. I THOUGHT HE DIED...
HEY, DOYLET PAPER! YOU CRUSTY POOR WHITE TRASH PIECE O' SHIT!
HEY, RAY D. ATE HER! YOU GREASY WETBACK SHIT MONGER!
YOU'RE A HARD MAN TO FIND. YOUR FAMILY HAD ME RUNNING IN CIRCLES.
I TOLD 'EM TO WAKE ME WHEN YOU CAME BY. THEY DIDN'T TELL ME SHIT, SO I WENT TO THE LIQUOR STORE FOR A MINUTE. SORRY, MAN...
'S COOL. AT LEAST THEY GOT TO WARN ME ABOUT WHAT A SCHOLAR YOU ARE NOW.
HA! BOY, HAVE I GOT A STORY TO TELL YOU...
9

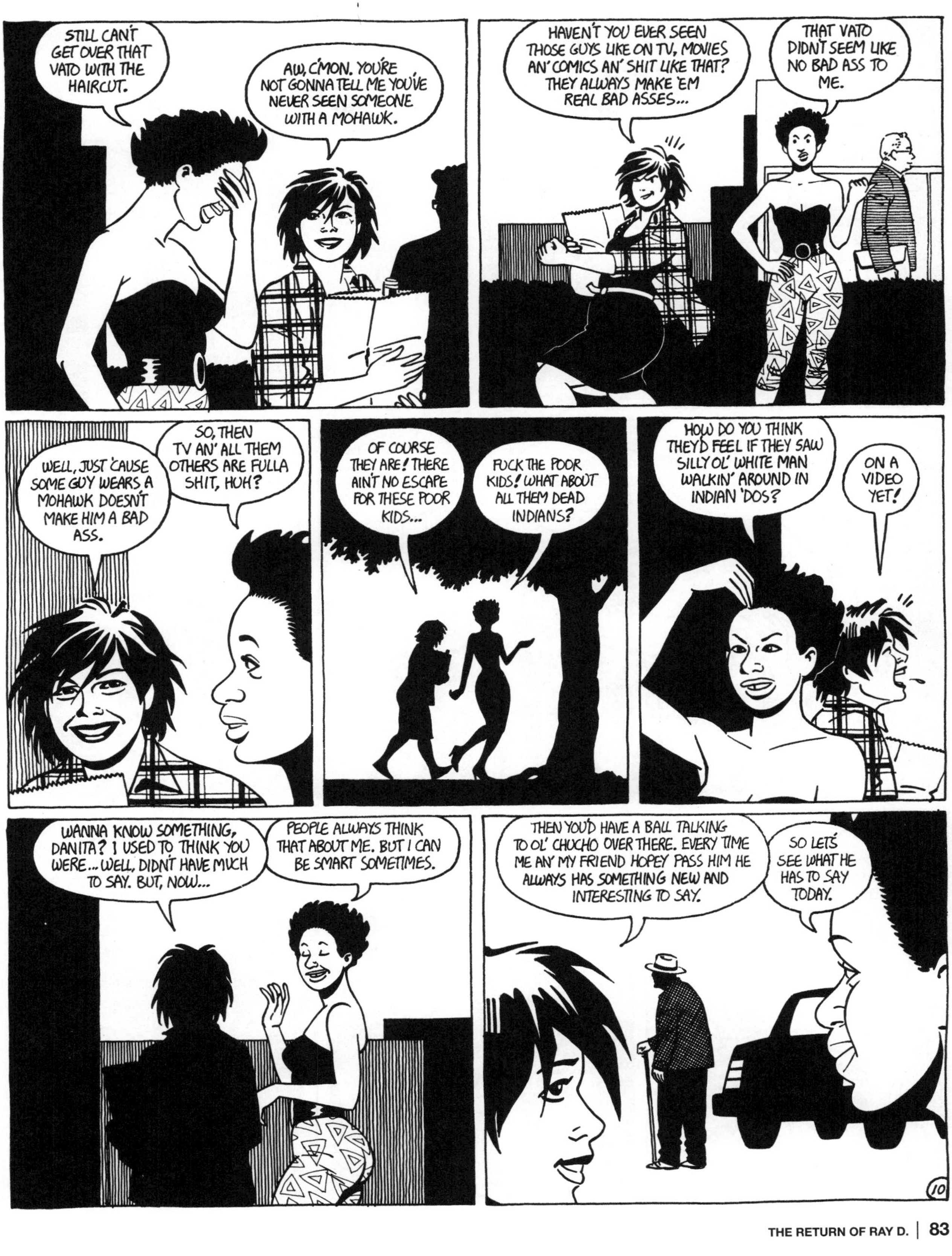
STILL CAN'T GET OVER THAT VATO WITH THE HAIRCUT.
AW, C'MON. YOU'RE NOT GONNA TELL ME YOU'VE NEVER SEEN SOMEONE WITH A MOHAWK.
HAVEN'T YOU EVER SEEN THOSE GUYS LIKE ON TV, MOVIES AN' COMICS AN' SHIT LIKE THAT? THEY ALWAYS MAKE 'EM REAL BAD ASSES...
THAT VATO DIDN'T SEEM LIKE NO BAD ASS TO ME.
WELL, JUST 'CAUSE SOME GUY WEARS A MOHAWK DOESN'T MAKE HIM A BAD ASS.
SO, THEN TV AN' ALL THEM OTHERS ARE FULLA SHIT, HUH?
OF COURSE THEY ARE! THERE AIN'T NO ESCAPE FOR THESE POOR KIDS...
FUCK THE POOR KIDS! WHAT ABOUT ALL THEM DEAD INDIANS?
HOW DO YOU THINK THEY'D FEEL IF THEY SAW SILLY OL' WHITE MAN WALKIN' AROUND IN INDIAN 'DOS?
ON A VIDEO YET!
WANNA KNOW SOMETHING, DANITA? I USED TO THINK YOU WERE... WELL, DIDN'T HAVE MUCH TO SAY. BUT, NOW...
PEOPLE ALWAYS THINK THAT ABOUT ME. BUT I CAN BE SMART SOMETIMES.
THEN YOU'D HAVE A BALL TALKING TO OL' CHUCHO OVER THERE. EVERY TIME ME AN' MY FRIEND HOPEY PASS HIM HE ALWAYS HAS SOMETHING NEW AND INTERESTING TO SAY.
SO LET'S SEE WHAT HE HAS TO SAY TODAY.
10

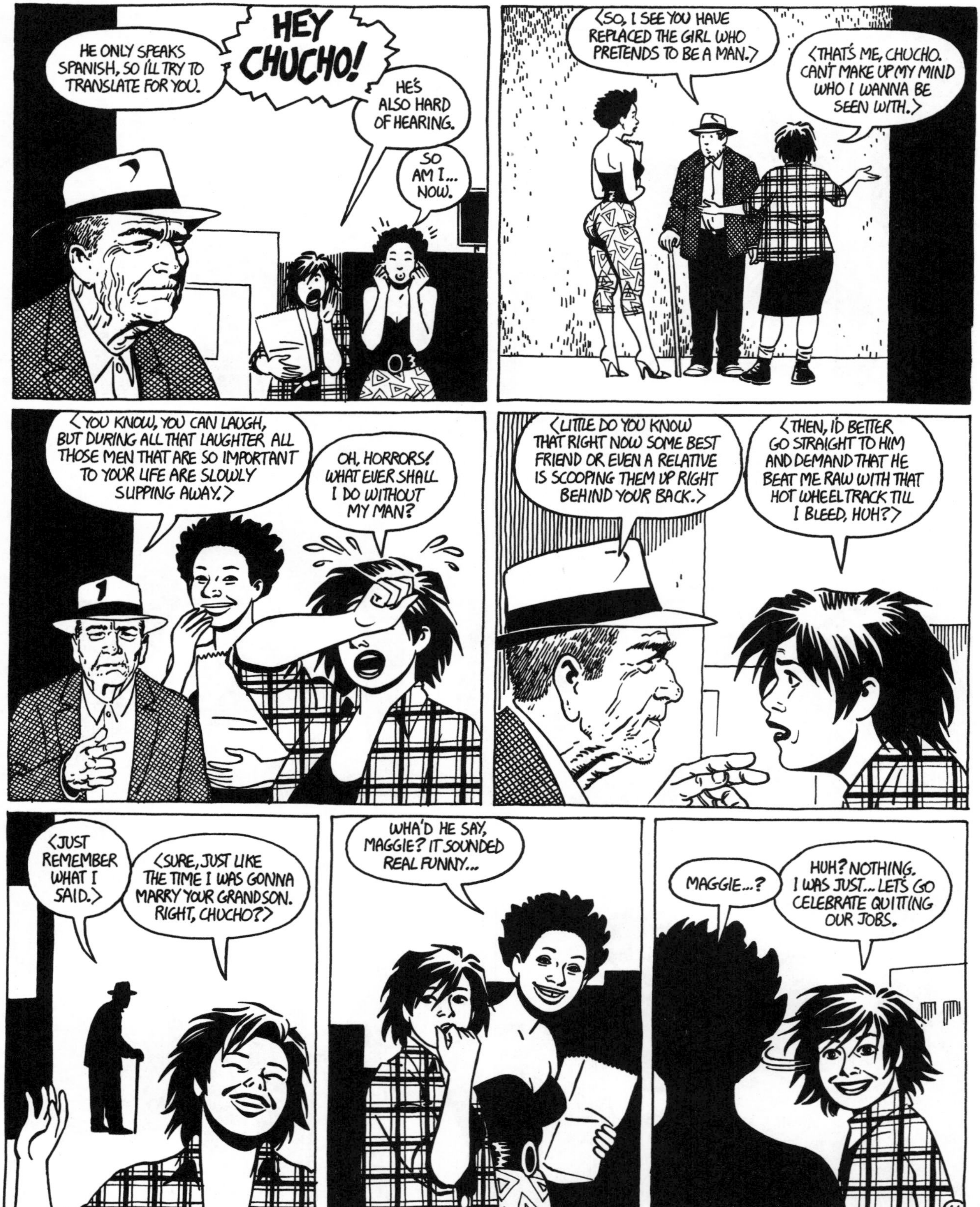
HE ONLY SPEAKS SPANISH, SO I'LL TRY TO TRANSLATE FOR YOU.
HEY CHUCHO!
HE'S ALSO HARD OF HEARING.
SO AM I... NOW.
<SO, I SEE YOU HAVE REPLACED THE GIRL WHO PRETENDS TO BE A MAN.>
<THAT'S ME, CHUCHO. CAN'T MAKE UP MY MIND WHO I WANNA BE SEEN WITH.>
<YOU KNOW, YOU CAN LAUGH, BUT DURING ALL THAT LAUGHTER ALL THOSE MEN THAT ARE SO IMPORTANT TO YOUR LIFE ARE SLOWLY SLIPPING AWAY.>
OH, HORRORS! WHAT EVER SHALL I DO WITHOUT MY MAN?
<LITTLE DO YOU KNOW THAT RIGHT NOW SOME BEST FRIEND OR EVEN A RELATIVE IS SCOOPING THEM UP RIGHT BEHIND YOUR BACK.>
<THEN, I'D BETTER GO STRAIGHT TO HIM AND DEMAND THAT HE BEAT ME RAW WITH THAT HOT WHEEL TRACK TILL I BLEED, HUH?>
<JUST REMEMBER WHAT I SAID.>
<SURE, JUST LIKE THE TIME I WAS GONNA MARRY YOUR GRANDSON. RIGHT, CHUCHO?>
WHA'D HE SAY, MAGGIE? IT SOUNDED REAL FUNNY...
MAGGIE...?
HUH? NOTHING. I WAS JUST... LET'S GO CELEBRATE QUITTING OUR JOBS.
11

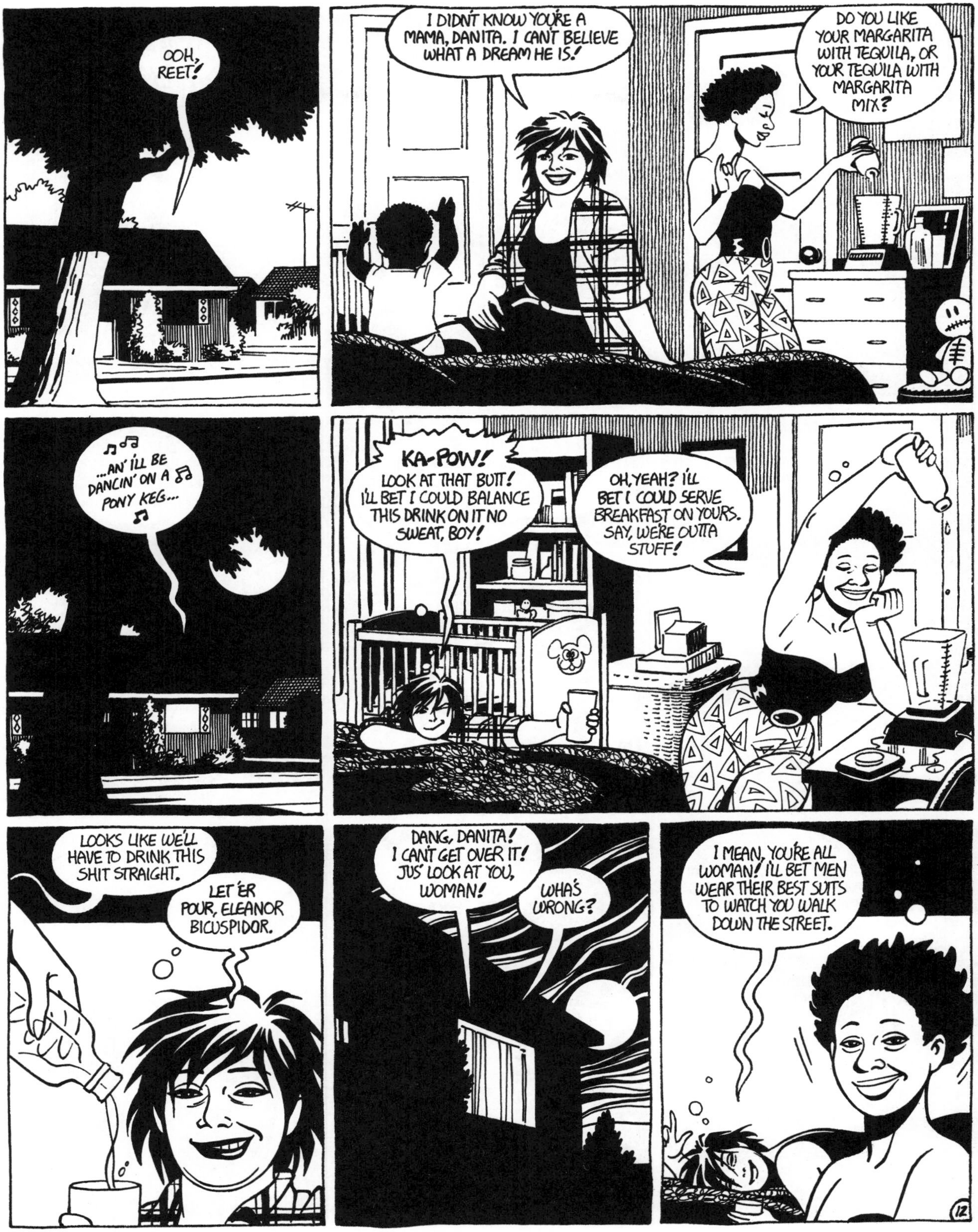
OOH, REET!
I DIDN'T KNOW YOU'RE A MAMA, DANITA. I CAN'T BELIEVE WHAT A DREAM HE IS!
DO YOU LIKE YOUR MARGARITA WITH TEQUILA, OR YOUR TEQUILA WITH MARGARITA MIX?
...AN' I'LL BE DANCIN' ON A PONY KEG...
KA-POW!
LOOK AT THAT BUTT! I'LL BET I COULD BALANCE THIS DRINK ON IT NO SWEAT, BOY!
OH, YEAH? I'LL BET I COULD SERVE BREAKFAST ON YOURS. SAY, WE'RE OUTTA STUFF!
LOOKS LIKE WE'LL HAVE TO DRINK THIS SHIT STRAIGHT.
LET 'ER POUR, ELEANOR BICUSPIDOR.
DANG, DANITA! I CAN'T GET OVER IT! JUS' LOOK AT YOU, WOMAN!
WHA'S WRONG?
I MEAN, YOU'RE ALL WOMAN! I'LL BET MEN WEAR THEIR BEST SUITS TO WATCH YOU WALK DOWN THE STREET.
12

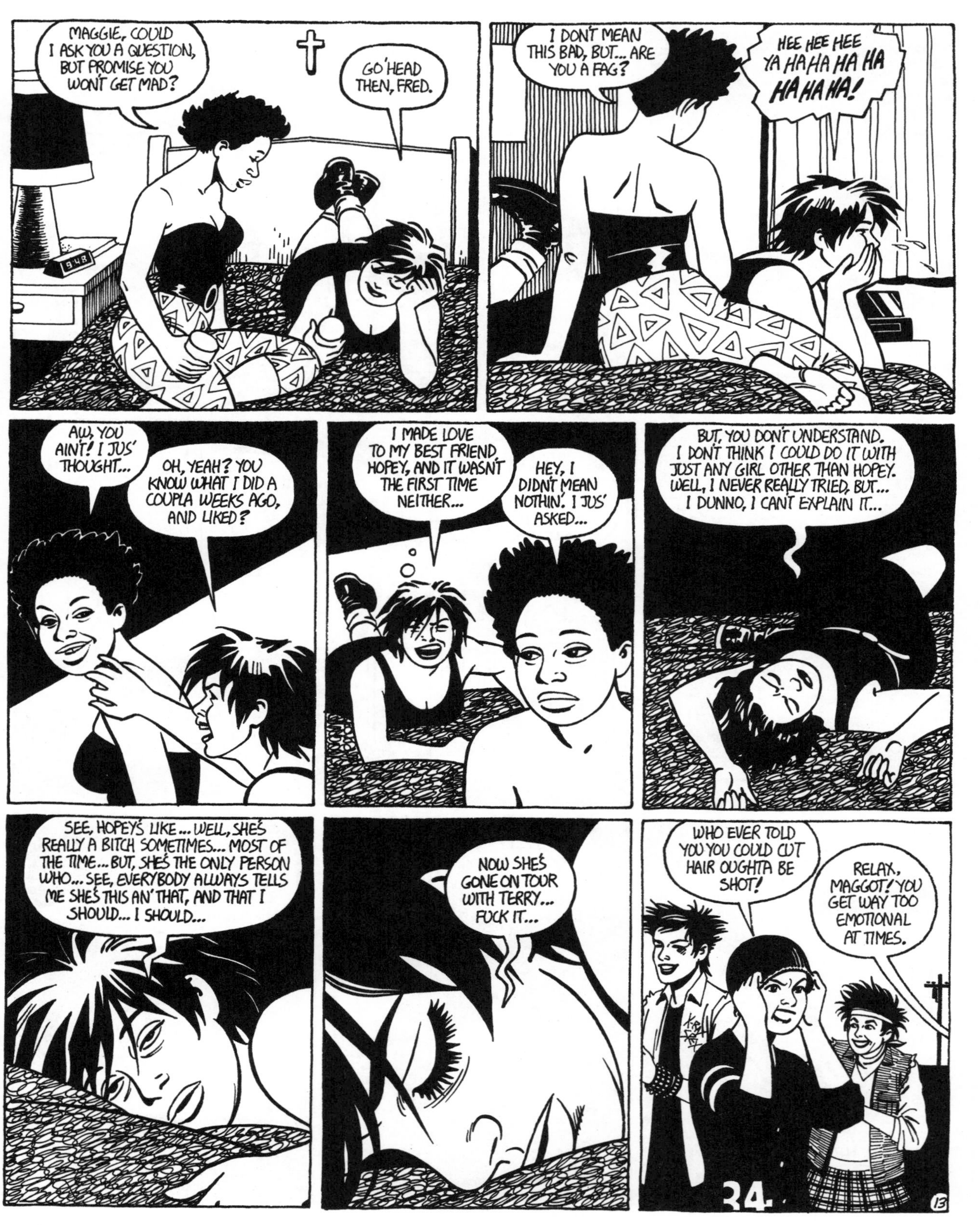
MAGGIE, COULD I ASK YOU A QUESTION, BUT PROMISE YOU WON'T GET MAD?
GO'HEAD THEN, FRED.
I DON'T MEAN THIS BAD, BUT... ARE YOU A FAG?
HEE HEE HEE YA HA HA HA HA HA HA HA!
AW, YOU AIN'T! I JUS' THOUGHT...
OH, YEAH? YOU KNOW WHAT I DID A COUPLA WEEKS AGO, AND LIKED?
I MADE LOVE TO MY BEST FRIEND HOPEY, AND IT WASN'T THE FIRST TIME NEITHER...
HEY, I DIDN'T MEAN NOTHIN'. I JUS' ASKED...
BUT, YOU DON'T UNDERSTAND. I DON'T THINK I COULD DO IT WITH JUST ANY GIRL OTHER THAN HOPEY. WELL, I NEVER REALLY TRIED, BUT... I DUNNO, I CAN'T EXPLAIN IT...
SEE, HOPEY'S LIKE... WELL, SHE'S REALLY A BITCH SOMETIMES... MOST OF THE TIME... BUT, SHE'S THE ONLY PERSON WHO... SEE, EVERYBODY ALWAYS TELLS ME SHE'S THIS AN' THAT, AND THAT I SHOULD... I SHOULD...
NOW SHE'S GONE ON TOUR WITH TERRY... FUCK IT...
WHO EVER TOLD YOU YOU COULD CUT HAIR OUGHTA BE SHOT!
RELAX, MAGGOT! YOU GET WAY TOO EMOTIONAL AT TIMES.
34
13

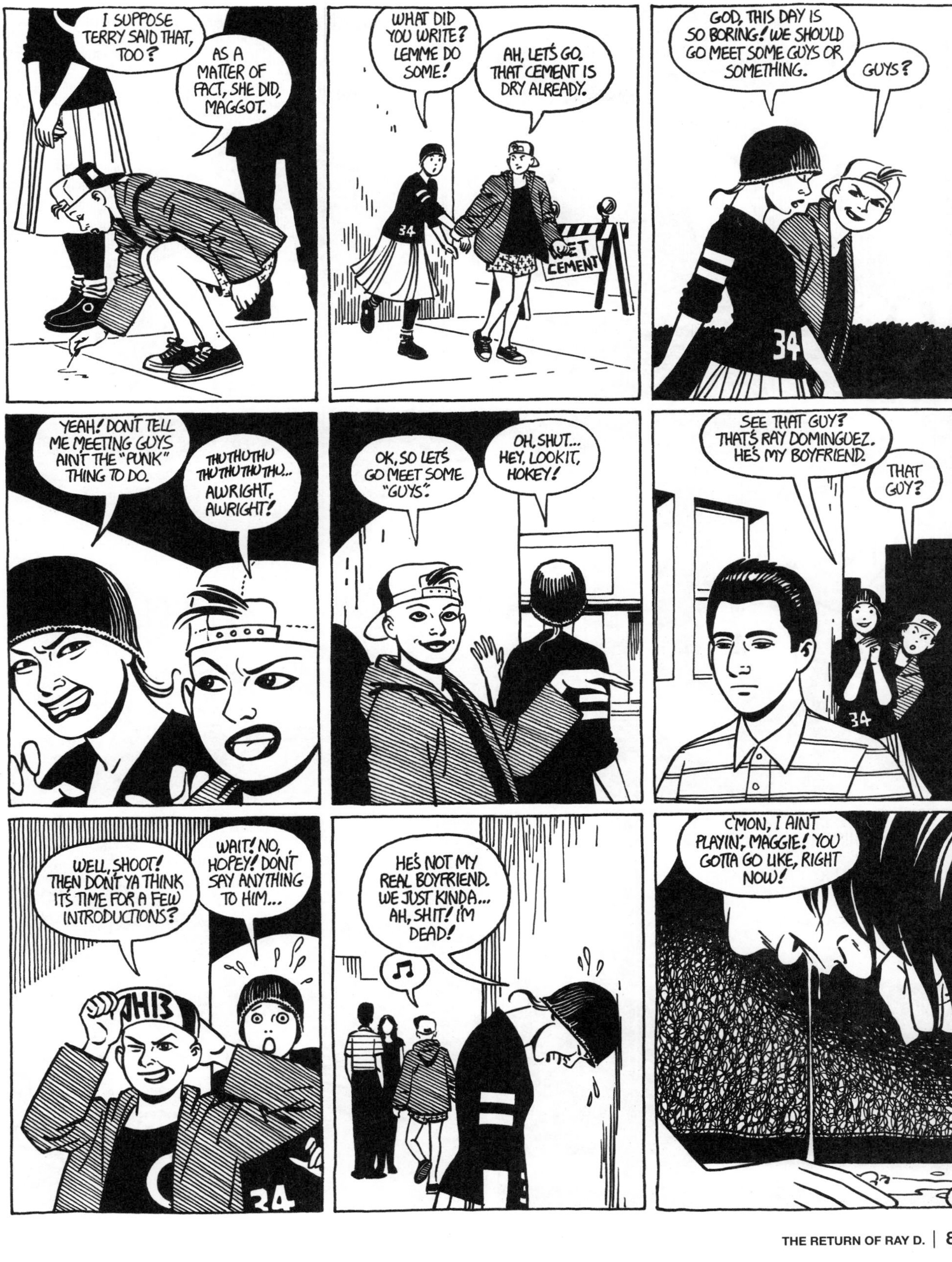
I SUPPOSE TERRY SAID THAT, TOO?
AS A MATTER OF FACT, SHE DID, MAGGOT.
WHAT DID YOU WRITE? LEMME DO SOME!
AH, LET'S GO. THAT CEMENT IS DRY ALREADY.
WET CEMENT
GOD, THIS DAY IS SO BORING! WE SHOULD GO MEET SOME GUYS OR SOMETHING.
GUYS?
YEAH! DON'T TELL ME MEETING GUYS AIN'T THE "PUNK" THING TO DO.
THUTHUTHU THUTHUTHUTHU... AWRIGHT, AWRIGHT!
OK, SO LET'S GO MEET SOME "GUYS".
OH, SHUT... HEY, LOOKIT, HOKEY!
SEE THAT GUY? THAT'S RAY DOMINGUEZ. HE'S MY BOYFRIEND.
THAT GUY?
WELL, SHOOT! THEN DON'T YA THINK IT'S TIME FOR A FEW INTRODUCTIONS?
WAIT! NO, HOPEY! DON'T SAY ANYTHING TO HIM...
HE'S NOT MY REAL BOYFRIEND. WE JUST KINDA... AH, SHIT! I'M DEAD!
C'MON, I AIN'T PLAYIN', MAGGIE! YOU GOTTA GO LIKE, RIGHT NOW!
14

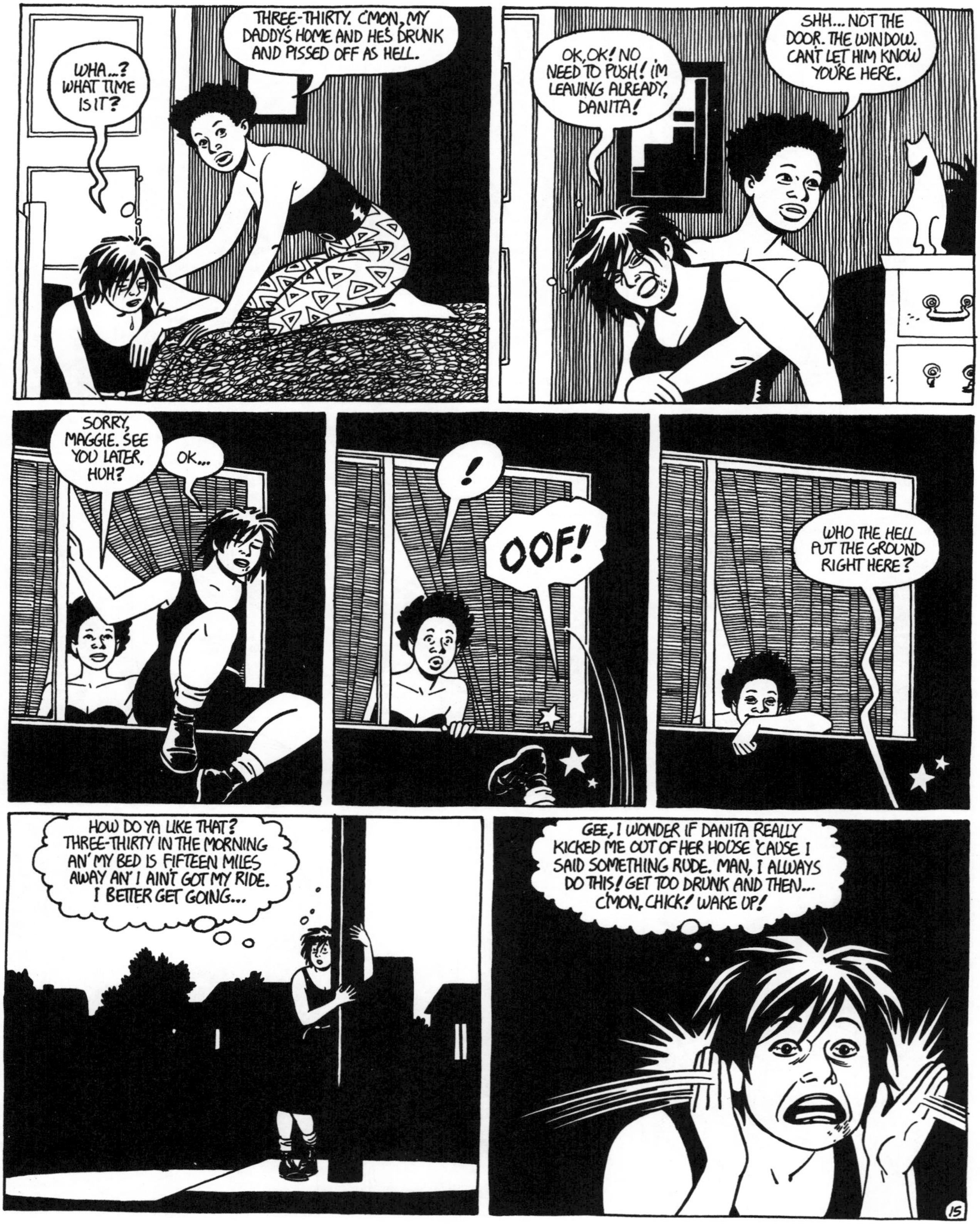
WHA...? WHAT TIME IS IT?
THREE-THIRTY. C'MON, MY DADDY'S HOME AND HE'S DRUNK AND PISSED OFF AS HELL.
OK, OK! NO NEED TO PUSH! I'M LEAVING ALREADY, DANITA!
SHH... NOT THE DOOR. THE WINDOW. CAN'T LET HIM KNOW YOU'RE HERE.
SORRY, MAGGIE. SEE YOU LATER, HUH?
OK...
!
OOF!
WHO THE HELL PUT THE GROUND RIGHT HERE?
HOW DO YA LIKE THAT? THREE-THIRTY IN THE MORNING AN' MY BED IS FIFTEEN MILES AWAY AN' I AIN'T GOT MY RIDE. I BETTER GET GOING...
GEE, I WONDER IF DANITA REALLY KICKED ME OUT OF HER HOUSE 'CAUSE I SAID SOMETHING RUDE. MAN, I ALWAYS DO THIS! GET TOO DRUNK AND THEN... C'MON, CHICK! WAKE UP!
15

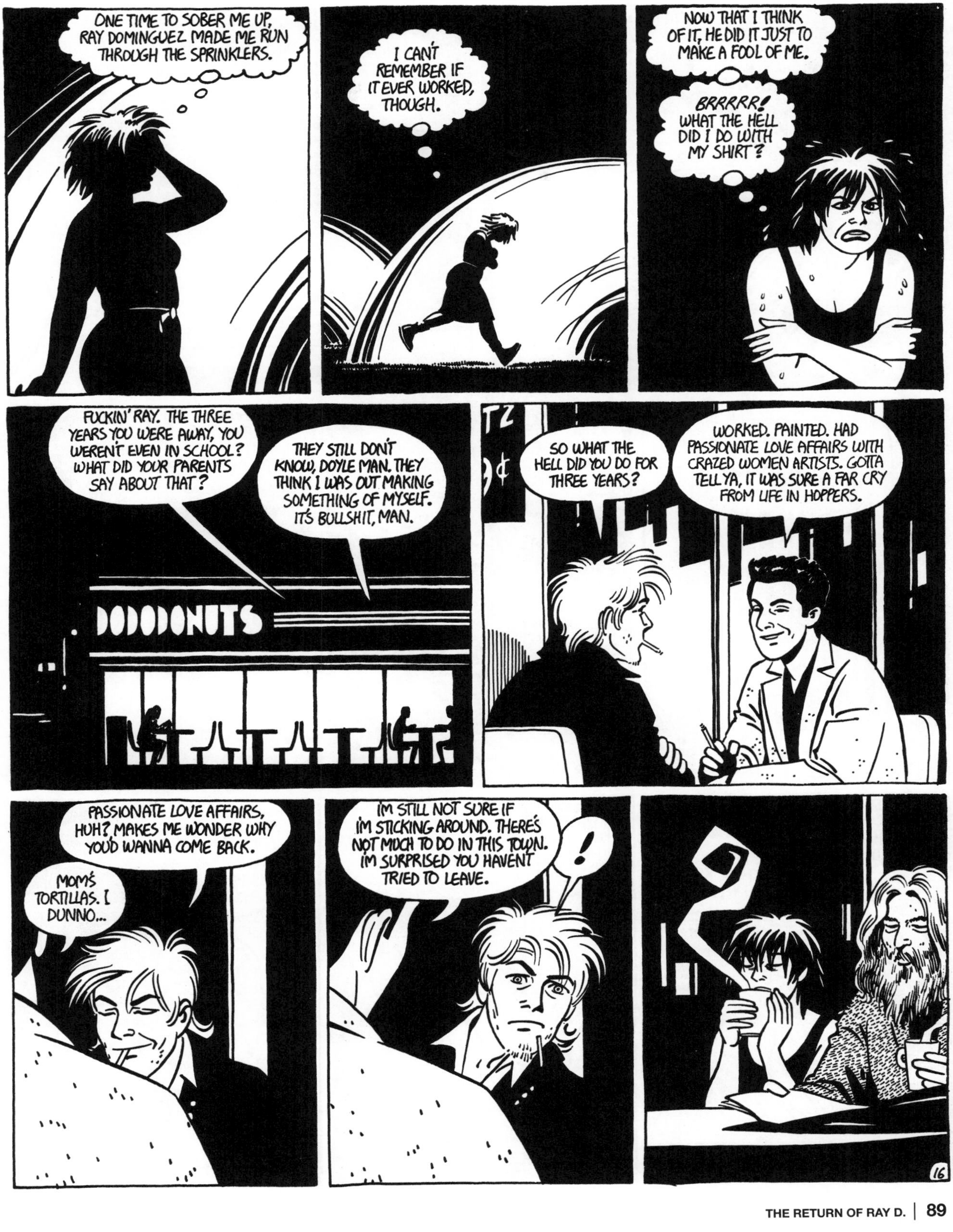
ONE TIME TO SOBER ME UP, RAY DOMINGUEZ MADE ME RUN THROUGH THE SPRINKLERS.
I CAN'T REMEMBER IF IT EVER WORKED, THOUGH.
NOW THAT I THINK OF IT, HE DID IT JUST TO MAKE A FOOL OF ME.
BRRRRR! WHAT THE HELL DID I DO WITH MY SHIRT?
FUCKIN' RAY. THE THREE YEARS YOU WERE AWAY, YOU WEREN'T EVEN IN SCHOOL? WHAT DID YOUR PARENTS SAY ABOUT THAT?
THEY STILL DON'T KNOW, DOYLE MAN. THEY THINK I WAS OUT MAKING SOMETHING OF MYSELF. IT'S BULLSHIT, MAN.
DODODONUTS
SO WHAT THE HELL DID YOU DO FOR THREE YEARS?
WORKED. PAINTED. HAD PASSIONATE LOVE AFFAIRS WITH CRAZED WOMEN ARTISTS. GOTTA TELL YA, IT WAS SURE A FAR CRY FROM LIFE IN HOPPERS.
PASSIONATE LOVE AFFAIRS, HUH? MAKES ME WONDER WHY YOU'D WANNA COME BACK.
MOM'S TORTILLAS. I DUNNO...
I'M STILL NOT SURE IF I'M STICKING AROUND. THERE'S NOT MUCH TO DO IN THIS TOWN. I'M SURPRISED YOU HAVEN'T TRIED TO LEAVE.
!
16

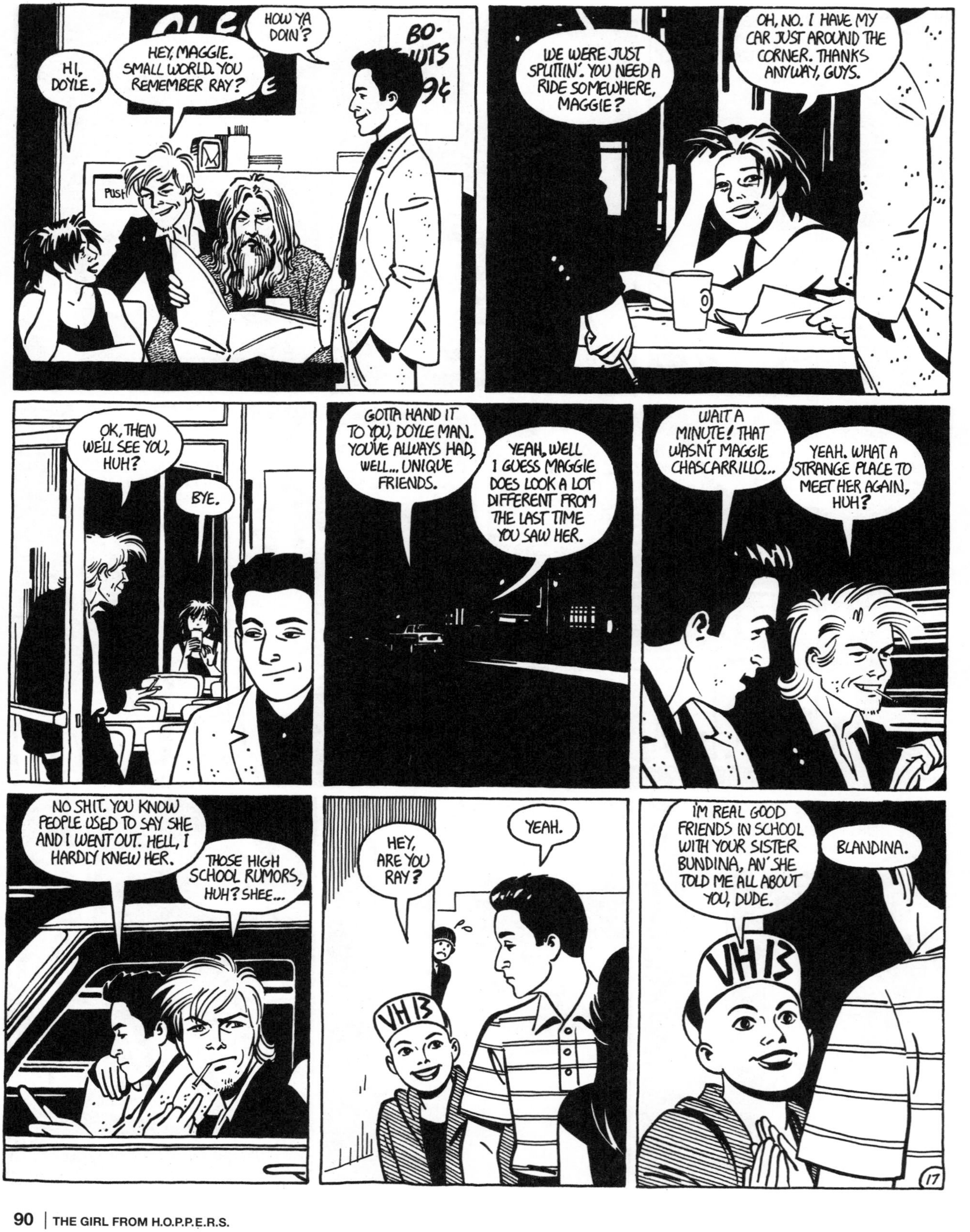

HI, DOYLE.
HEY, MAGGIE. SMALL WORLD. YOU REMEMBER RAY?
HOW YA DOIN'?
BO-NUTS 9¢
PUSH
WE WERE JUST SPLITTIN'. YOU NEED A RIDE SOMEWHERE, MAGGIE?
OH, NO. I HAVE MY CAR JUST AROUND THE CORNER. THANKS ANYWAY, GUYS.
OK, THEN WE'LL SEE YOU, HUH?
BYE.
GOTTA HAND IT TO YOU, DOYLE MAN. YOU'VE ALWAYS HAD, WELL... UNIQUE FRIENDS.
YEAH, WELL I GUESS MAGGIE DOES LOOK A LOT DIFFERENT FROM THE LAST TIME YOU SAW HER.
WAIT A MINUTE! THAT WASN'T MAGGIE CHASCARRILLO...
YEAH. WHAT A STRANGE PLACE TO MEET HER AGAIN, HUH?
NO SHIT. YOU KNOW PEOPLE USED TO SAY SHE AND I WENT OUT. HELL, I HARDLY KNEW HER.
THOSE HIGH SCHOOL RUMORS, HUH? SHEE...
HEY, ARE YOU RAY?
YEAH.
VH13
I'M REAL GOOD FRIENDS IN SCHOOL WITH YOUR SISTER BUNDINA, AN' SHE TOLD ME ALL ABOUT YOU, DUDE.
BLANDINA.
VH13
17

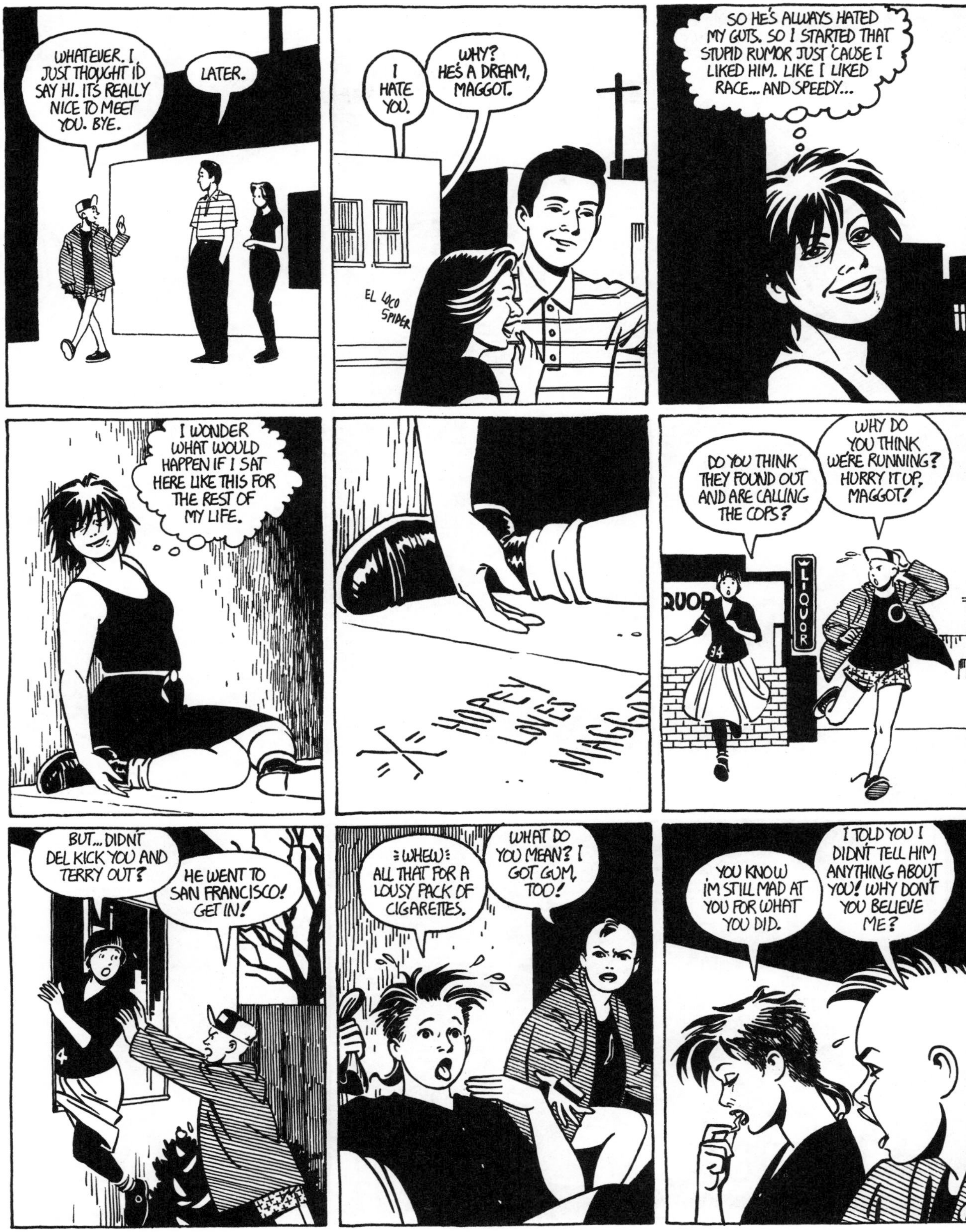
WHATEVER. I JUST THOUGHT I'D SAY HI. IT'S REALLY NICE TO MEET YOU. BYE.
LATER.
I HATE YOU.
WHY? HE'S A DREAM, MAGGOT.
EL LOCO SPIDER
SO HE'S ALWAYS HATED MY GUTS. SO I STARTED THAT STUPID RUMOR JUST 'CAUSE I LIKED HIM. LIKE I LIKED RACE... AND SPEEDY...
I WONDER WHAT WOULD HAPPEN IF I SAT HERE LIKE THIS FOR THE REST OF MY LIFE.
HOPEY LOVES MAGGO
DO YOU THINK THEY FOUND OUT AND ARE CALLING THE COPS?
WHY DO YOU THINK WE'RE RUNNING? HURRY IT UP, MAGGOT!
QUOR
LIQUOR
BUT... DIDN'T DEL KICK YOU AND TERRY OUT?
HE WENT TO SAN FRANCISCO! GET IN!
WHEW
ALL THAT FOR A LOUSY PACK OF CIGARETTES.
WHAT DO YOU MEAN? I GOT GUM, TOO!
YOU KNOW I'M STILL MAD AT YOU FOR WHAT YOU DID.
I TOLD YOU I DIDN'T TELL HIM ANYTHING ABOUT YOU! WHY DON'T YOU BELIEVE ME?
18

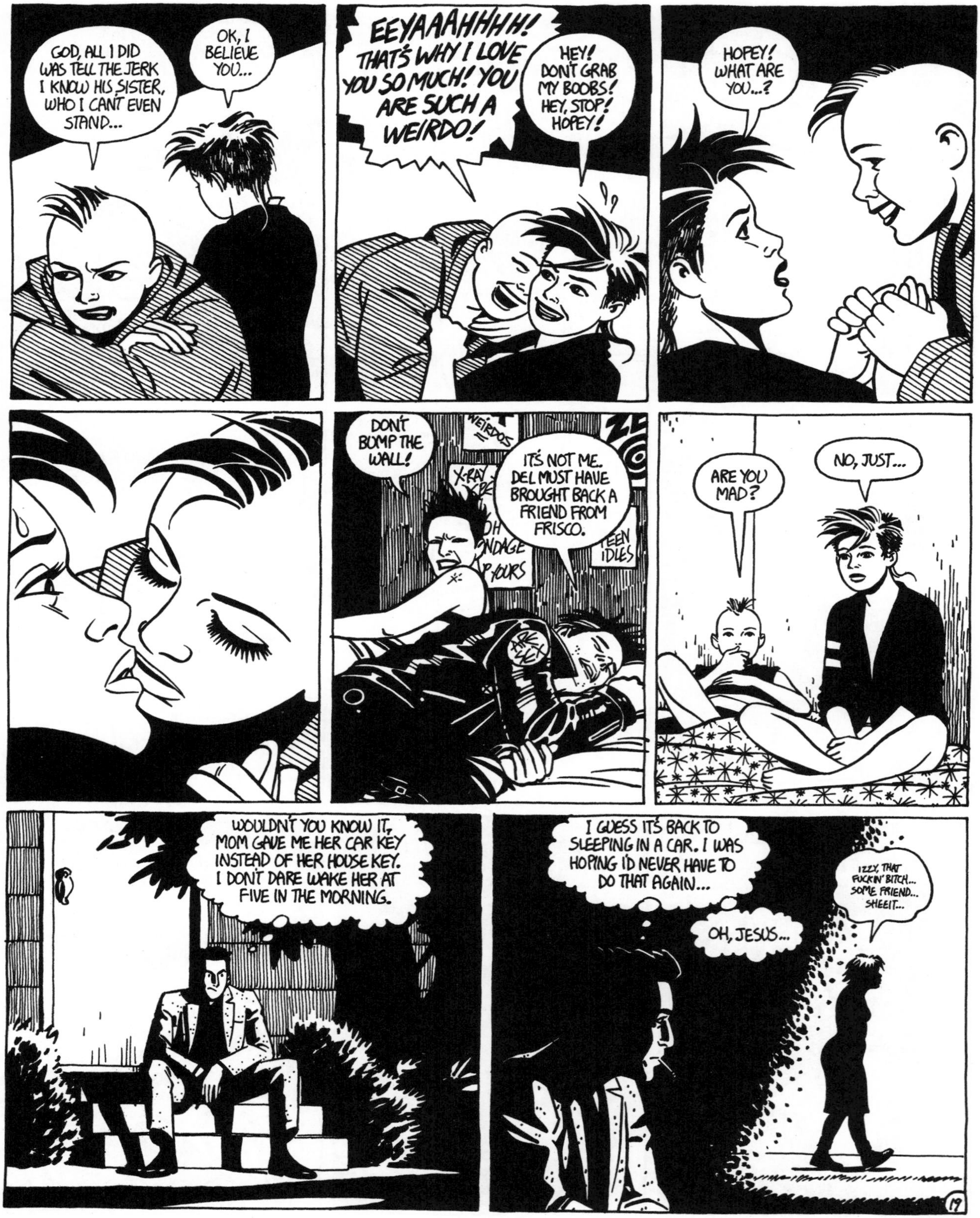
GOD, ALL I DID WAS TELL THE JERK I KNOW HIS SISTER, WHO I CAN'T EVEN STAND...
OK, I BELIEVE YOU...
EEYAAAHHHH! THAT'S WHY I LOVE YOU SO MUCH! YOU ARE SUCH A WEIRDO!
HEY! DON'T GRAB MY BOOBS! HEY, STOP! HOPEY!
HOPEY! WHAT ARE YOU...?
DON'T BUMP THE WALL!
WEIRDOS
IT'S NOT ME. DEL MUST HAVE BROUGHT BACK A FRIEND FROM FRISCO.
TEEN IDLES
ARE YOU MAD?
NO, JUST...
WOULDN'T YOU KNOW IT, MOM GAVE ME HER CAR KEY INSTEAD OF HER HOUSE KEY. I DON'T DARE WAKE HER AT FIVE IN THE MORNING.
I GUESS IT'S BACK TO SLEEPING IN A CAR. I WAS HOPING I'D NEVER HAVE TO DO THAT AGAIN...
OH, JESUS...
IZZY, THAT FUCKIN' BITCH... SOME FRIEND... SHEEIT...
19

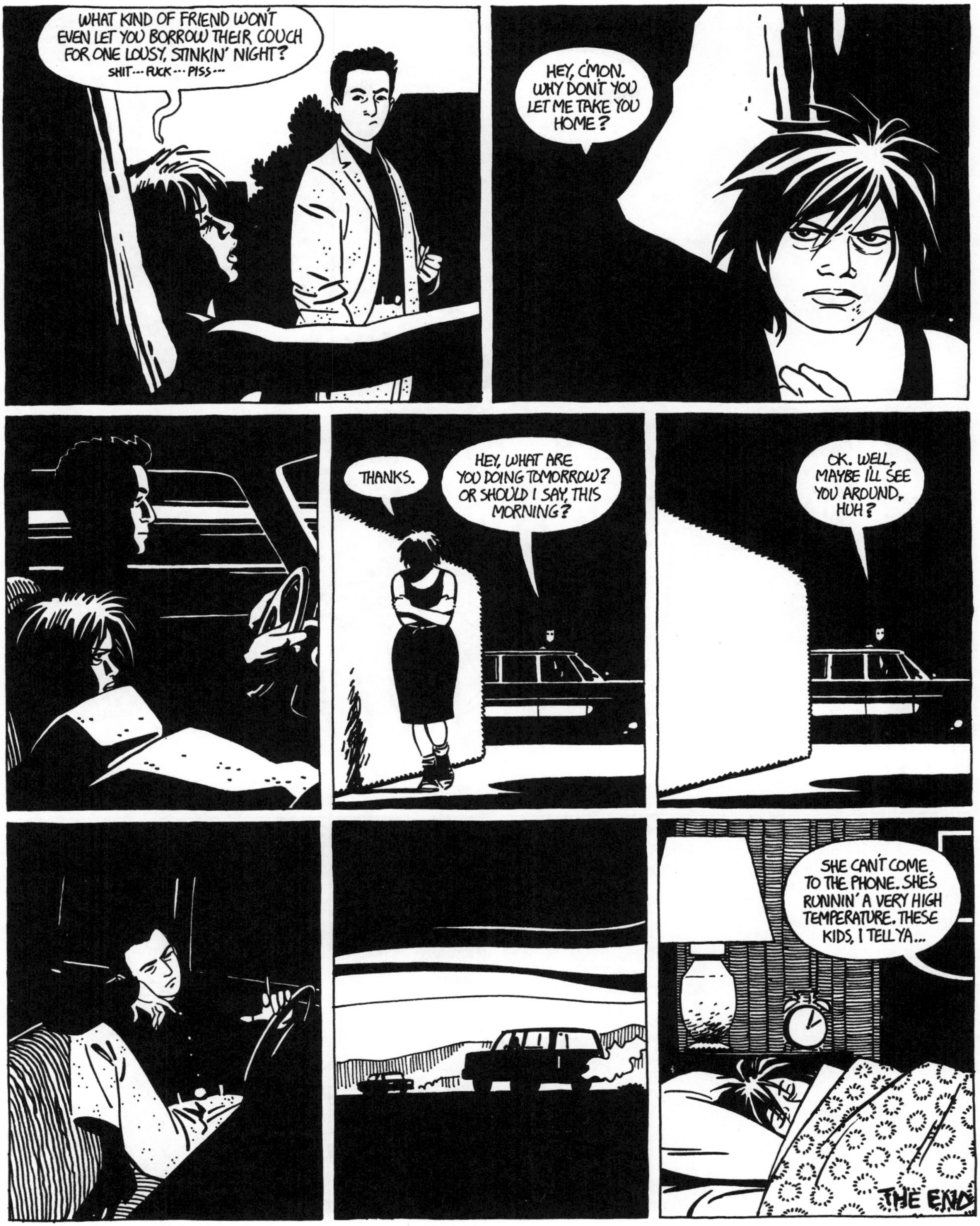
WHAT KIND OF FRIEND WON'T EVEN LET YOU BORROW THEIR COUCH FOR ONE LOUSY, STINKIN' NIGHT? SHIT--- FUCK --- PISS ---
HEY, C'MON. WHY DON'T YOU LET ME TAKE YOU HOME?
THANKS.
HEY, WHAT ARE YOU DOING TOMORROW? OR SHOULD I SAY, THIS MORNING?
OK. WELL, MAYBE I'LL SEE YOU AROUND, HUH?
SHE CAN'T COME TO THE PHONE. SHE'S RUNNIN' A VERY HIGH TEMPERATURE. THESE KIDS, I TELL YA...
THE END

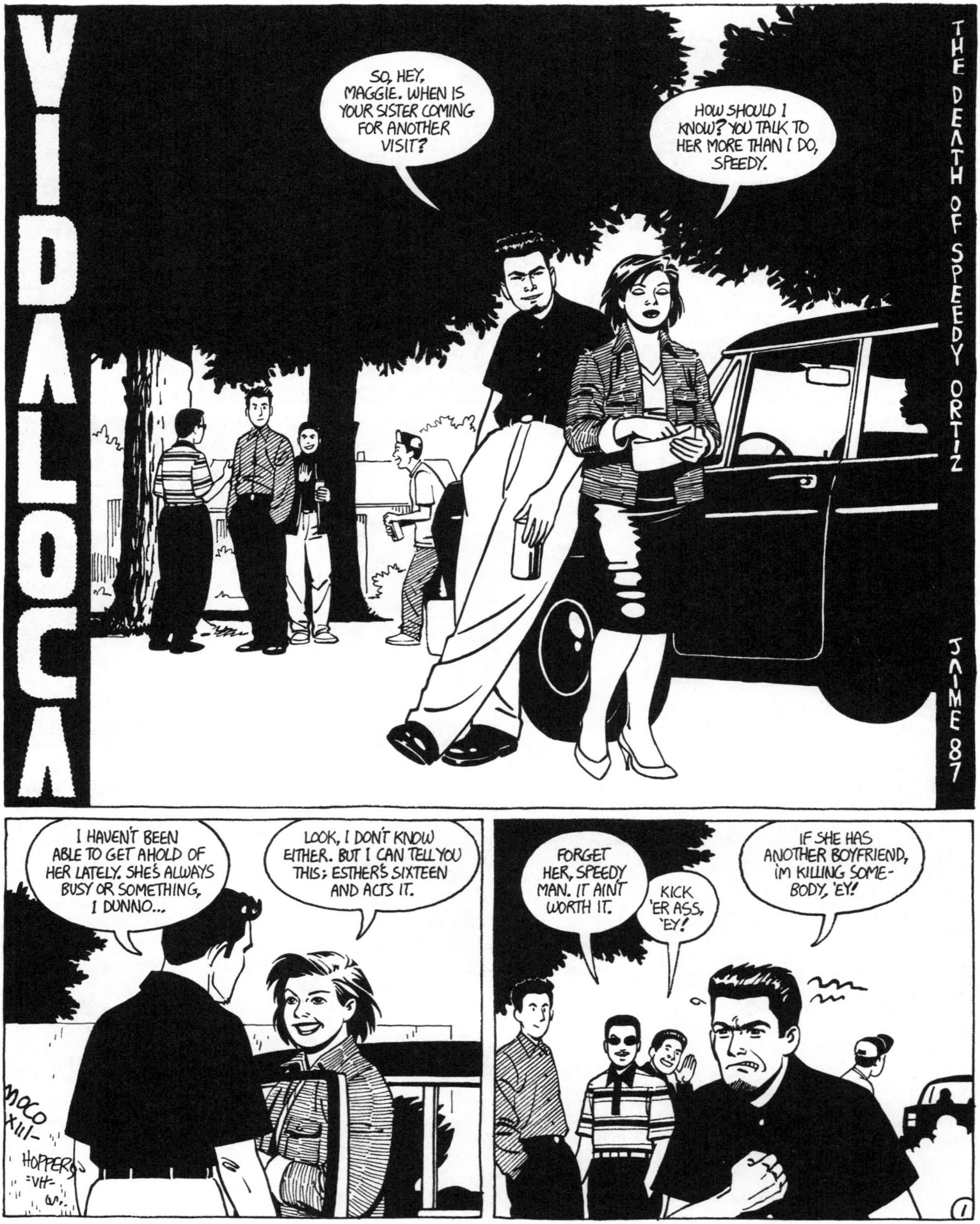
VIDALOCA
THE DEATH OF SPEEDY ORTIZ
SO, HEY, MAGGIE. WHEN IS YOUR SISTER COMING FOR ANOTHER VISIT?
HOW SHOULD I KNOW? YOU TALK TO HER MORE THAN I DO, SPEEDY.
JAIME 87
I HAVEN'T BEEN ABLE TO GET AHOLD OF HER LATELY. SHE'S ALWAYS BUSY OR SOMETHING, I DUNNO...
LOOK, I DON'T KNOW EITHER. BUT I CAN TELL YOU THIS; ESTHER'S SIXTEEN AND ACTS IT.
FORGET HER, SPEEDY MAN. IT AIN'T WORTH IT.
KICK 'ER ASS, 'EY!
IF SHE HAS ANOTHER BOYFRIEND, I'M KILLING SOME-BODY, 'EY!

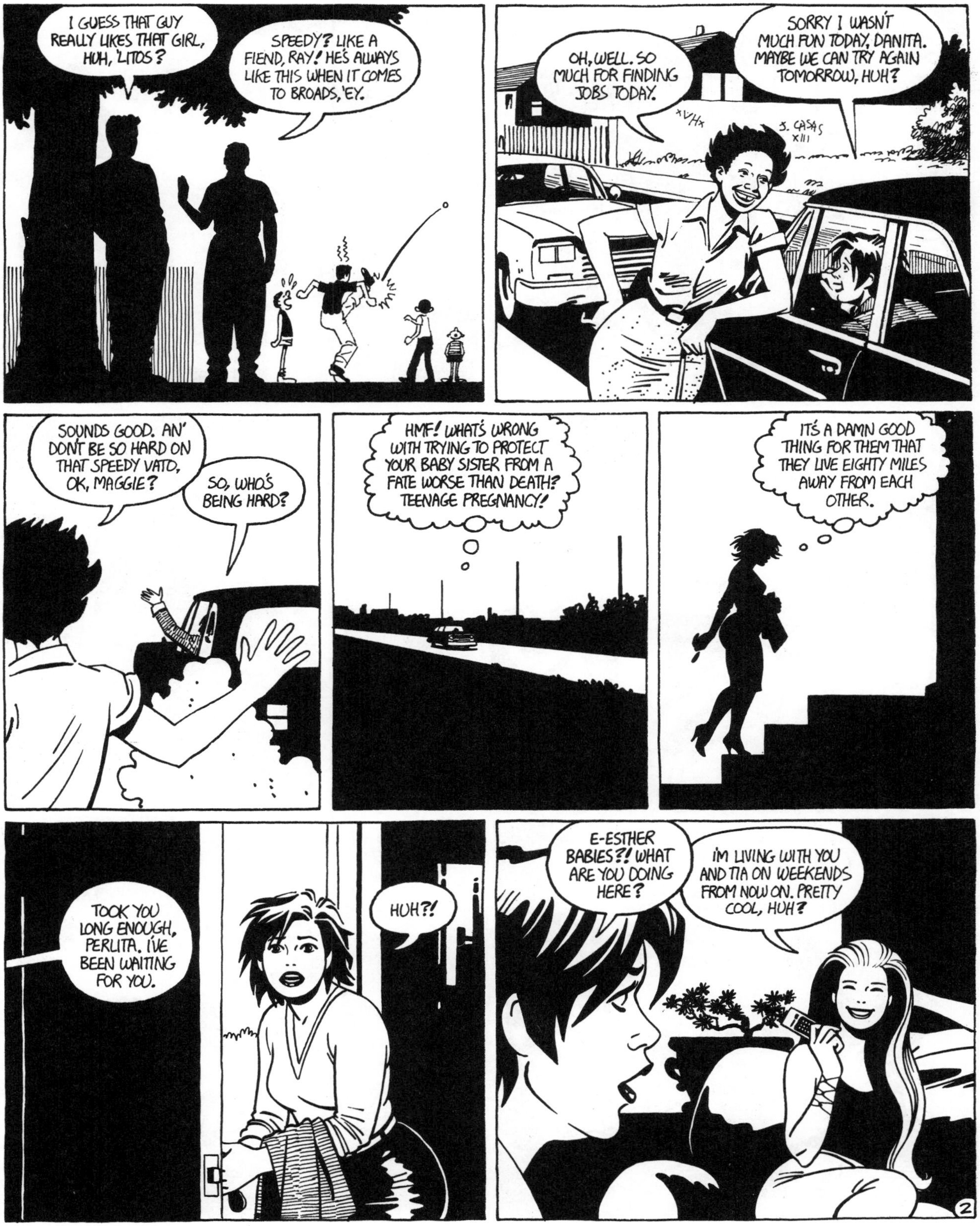
I GUESS THAT GUY REALLY LIKES THAT GIRL, HUH, 'LITOS?
SPEEDY? LIKE A FIEND, RAY! HE'S ALWAYS LIKE THIS WHEN IT COMES TO BROADS, 'EY.
OH, WELL. SO MUCH FOR FINDING JOBS TODAY.
SORRY I WASN'T MUCH FUN TODAY, DANITA. MAYBE WE CAN TRY AGAIN TOMORROW, HUH?
SOUNDS GOOD. AN' DON'T BE SO HARD ON THAT SPEEDY VATO, OK, MAGGIE?
SO, WHO'S BEING HARD?
HMF! WHAT'S WRONG WITH TRYING TO PROTECT YOUR BABY SISTER FROM A FATE WORSE THAN DEATH? TEENAGE PREGNANCY!
IT'S A DAMN GOOD THING FOR THEM THAT THEY LIVE EIGHTY MILES AWAY FROM EACH OTHER.
TOOK YOU LONG ENOUGH, PERLITA. I'VE BEEN WAITING FOR YOU.
HUH?!
E-ESTHER BABIES?! WHAT ARE YOU DOING HERE?
I'M LIVING WITH YOU AND TIA ON WEEKENDS FROM NOW ON. PRETTY COOL, HUH?
2

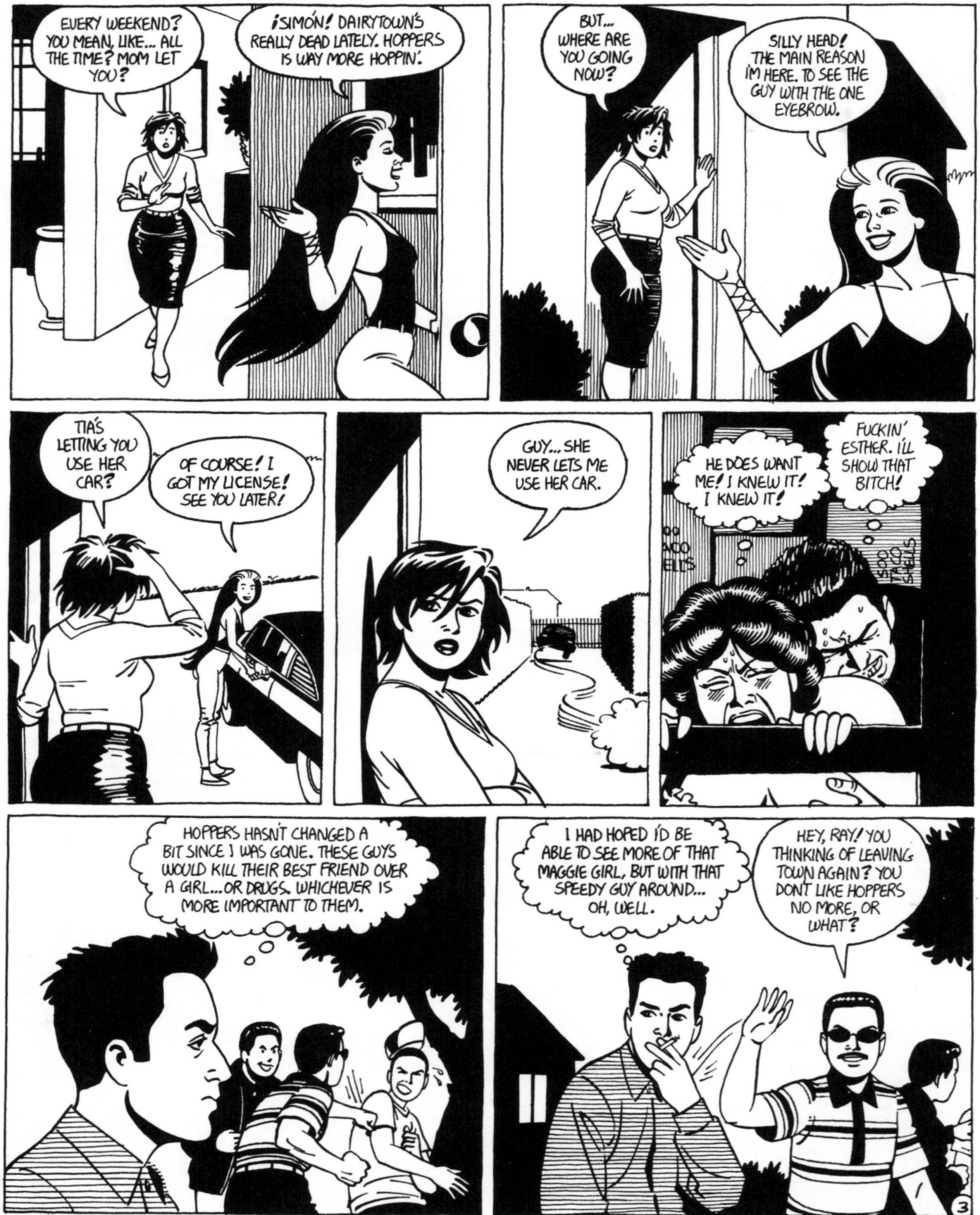
EVERY WEEKEND? YOU MEAN, LIKE... ALL THE TIME? MOM LET YOU?
¡SIMÓN! DAIRYTOWN'S REALLY DEAD LATELY. HOPPERS IS WAY MORE HOPPIN'.
BUT... WHERE ARE YOU GOING NOW?
SILLY HEAD! THE MAIN REASON I'M HERE. TO SEE THE GUY WITH THE ONE EYEBROW.
TIA'S LETTING YOU USE HER CAR?
OF COURSE! I GOT MY LICENSE! SEE YOU LATER!
GUY... SHE NEVER LETS ME USE HER CAR.
HE DOES WANT ME! I KNEW IT! I KNEW IT!
FUCKIN' ESTHER. I'LL SHOW THAT BITCH!
HOPPERS HASN'T CHANGED A BIT SINCE I WAS GONE. THESE GUYS WOULD KILL THEIR BEST FRIEND OVER A GIRL...OR DRUGS. WHICHEVER IS MORE IMPORTANT TO THEM.
I HAD HOPED I'D BE ABLE TO SEE MORE OF THAT MAGGIE GIRL, BUT WITH THAT SPEEDY GUY AROUND... OH, WELL.
HEY, RAY! YOU THINKING OF LEAVING TOWN AGAIN? YOU DON'T LIKE HOPPERS NO MORE, OR WHAT?
3

SIMÓN/OF COURSE!

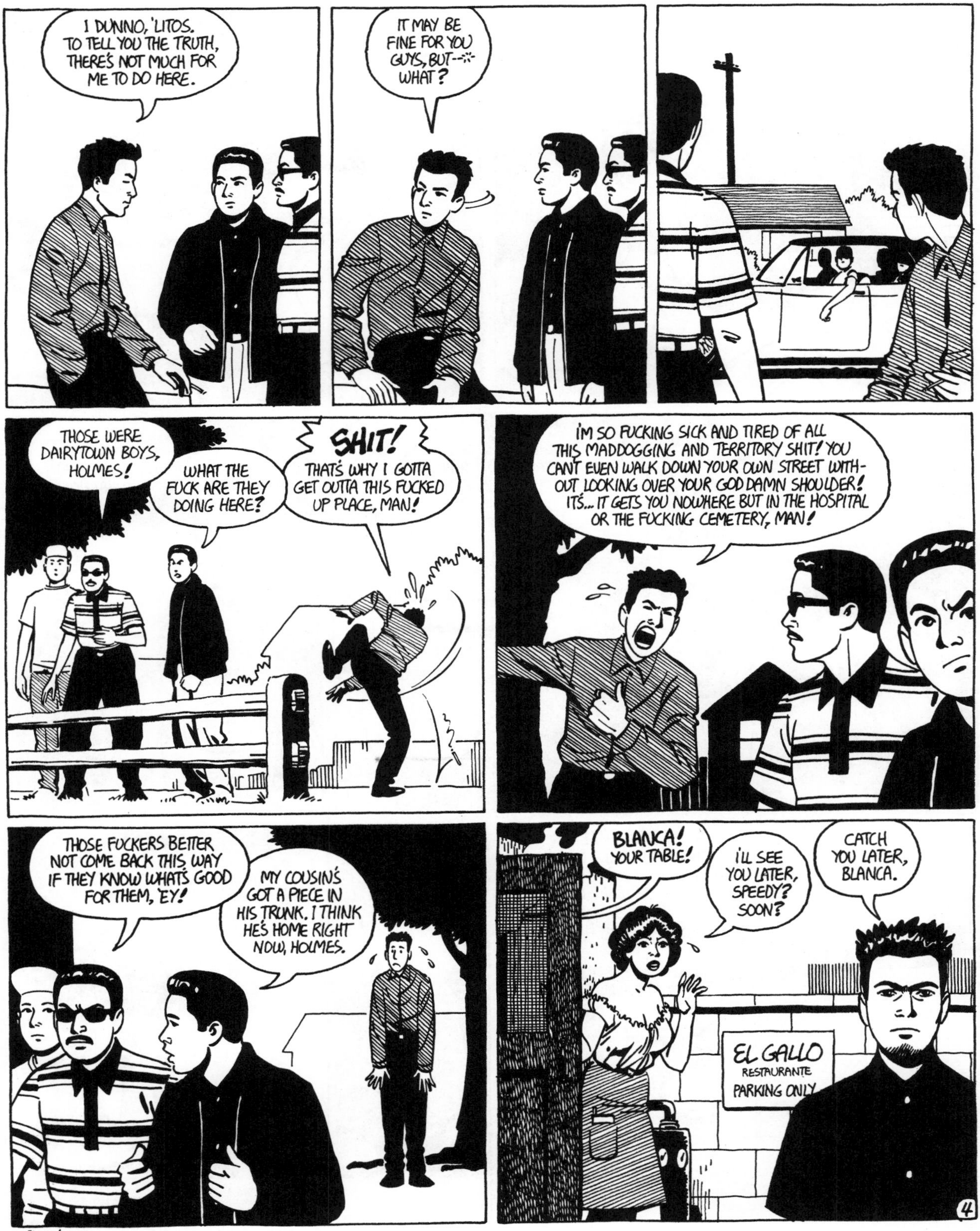
I DUNNO, 'LITOS. TO TELL YOU THE TRUTH, THERE'S NOT MUCH FOR ME TO DO HERE.
IT MAY BE FINE FOR YOU GUYS, BUT-- WHAT?
THOSE WERE DAIRYTOWN BOYS, HOLMES!
WHAT THE FUCK ARE THEY DOING HERE?
SHIT!
THAT'S WHY I GOTTA GET OUTTA THIS FUCKED UP PLACE, MAN!
I'M SO FUCKING SICK AND TIRED OF ALL THIS MADDOGGING AND TERRITORY SHIT! YOU CAN'T EVEN WALK DOWN YOUR OWN STREET WITH-OUT LOOKING OVER YOUR GOD DAMN SHOULDER! IT'S... IT GETS YOU NOWHERE BUT IN THE HOSPITAL OR THE FUCKING CEMETERY, MAN!
THOSE FUCKERS BETTER NOT COME BACK THIS WAY IF THEY KNOW WHAT'S GOOD FOR THEM, 'EY!
MY COUSIN'S GOT A PIECE IN HIS TRUNK. I THINK HE'S HOME RIGHT NOW, HOLMES.
BLANCA! YOUR TABLE!
I'LL SEE YOU LATER, SPEEDY? SOON?
CATCH YOU LATER, BLANCA.
EL GALLO
RESTAURANTE
PARKING ONLY
4

PIECE/GUN

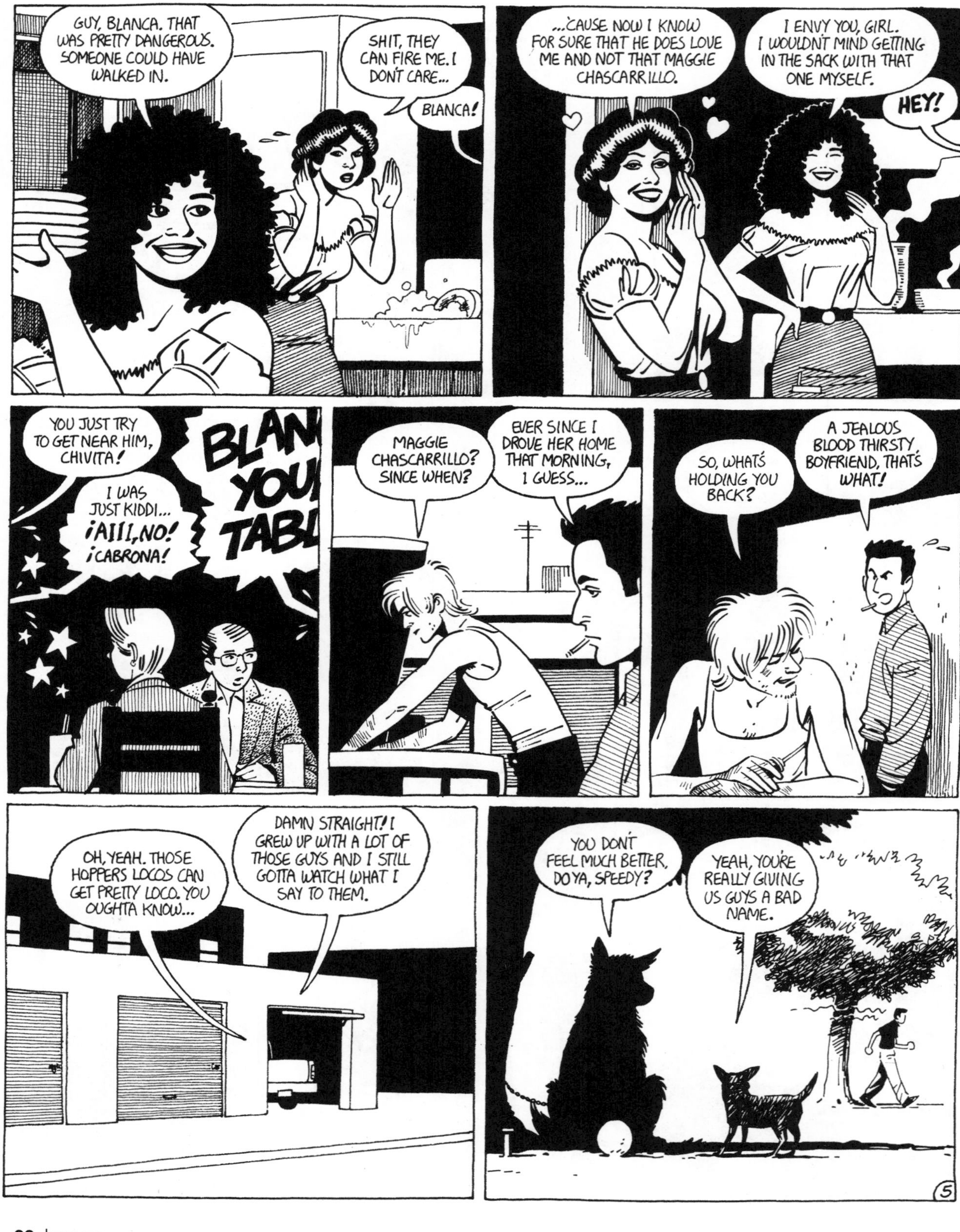

GUY, BLANCA. THAT WAS PRETTY DANGEROUS. SOMEONE COULD HAVE WALKED IN.
SHIT, THEY CAN FIRE ME. I DON'T CARE...
BLANCA!
...'CAUSE NOW I KNOW FOR SURE THAT HE DOES LOVE ME AND NOT THAT MAGGIE CHASCARRILLO.
I ENVY YOU, GIRL. I WOULDN'T MIND GETTING IN THE SACK WITH THAT ONE MYSELF.
HEY!
YOU JUST TRY TO GET NEAR HIM, CHIVITA!
I WAS JUST KIDDI... ¡AIII, NO! ¡CABRONA!
MAGGIE CHASCARRILLO? SINCE WHEN?
EVER SINCE I DROVE HER HOME THAT MORNING, I GUESS...
SO, WHAT'S HOLDING YOU BACK?
A JEALOUS BLOOD THIRSTY BOYFRIEND, THAT'S WHAT!
OH, YEAH. THOSE HOPPERS LOCOS CAN GET PRETTY LOCO. YOU OUGHTA KNOW...
DAMN STRAIGHT! I GREW UP WITH A LOT OF THOSE GUYS AND I STILL GOTTA WATCH WHAT I SAY TO THEM.
YOU DON'T FEEL MUCH BETTER, DO YA, SPEEDY?
YEAH, YOU'RE REALLY GIVING US GUYS A BAD NAME.
5

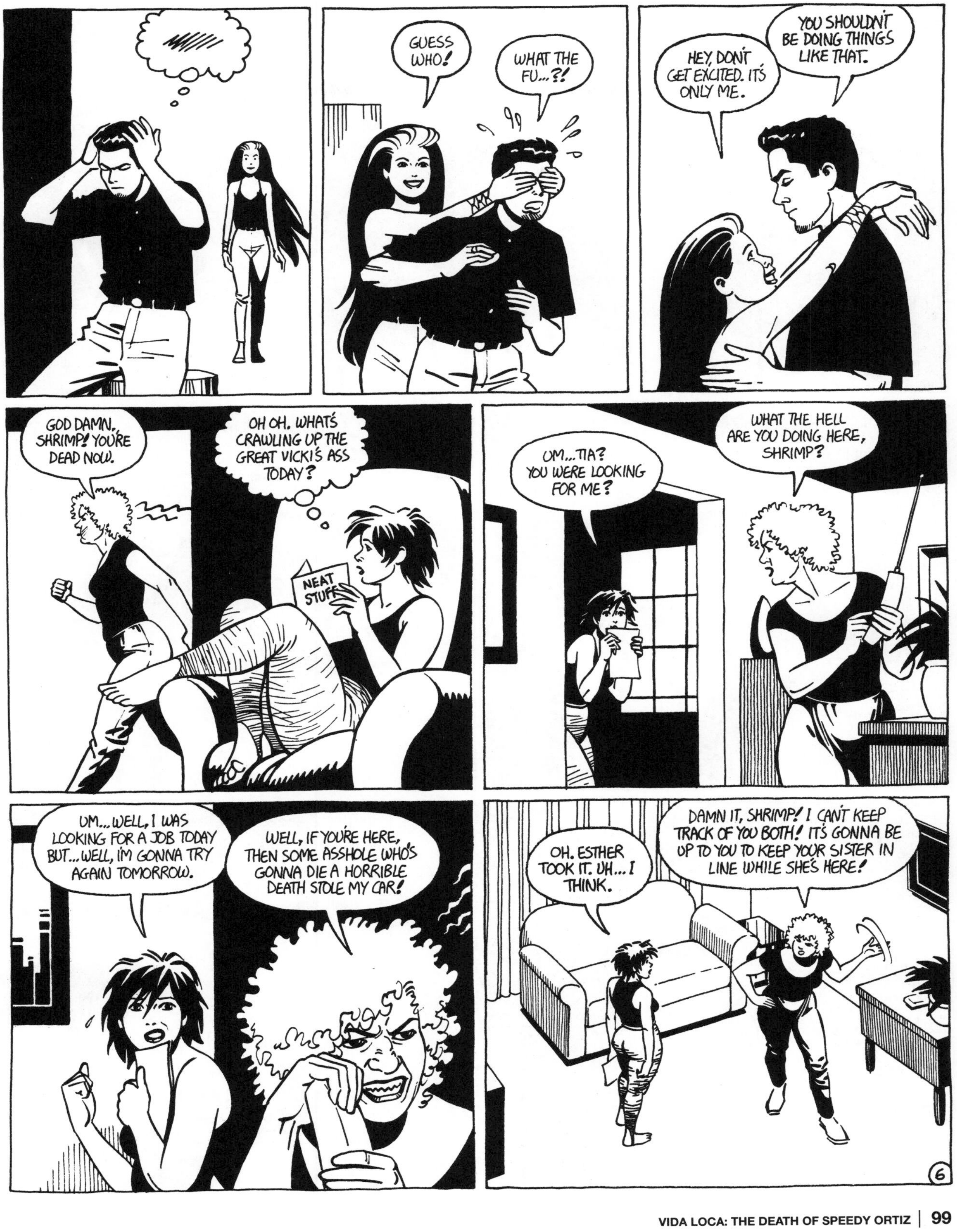
GUESS WHO!
WHAT THE FU...?!
HEY, DON'T GET EXCITED. IT'S ONLY ME.
YOU SHOULDN'T BE DOING THINGS LIKE THAT.
GOD DAMN, SHRIMP! YOU'RE DEAD NOW.
OH OH. WHAT'S CRAWLING UP THE GREAT VICKI'S ASS TODAY?
NEAT STUFF
UM...TIA? YOU WERE LOOKING FOR ME?
WHAT THE HELL ARE YOU DOING HERE, SHRIMP?
UM...WELL, I WAS LOOKING FOR A JOB TODAY BUT...WELL, I'M GONNA TRY AGAIN TOMORROW.
WELL, IF YOU'RE HERE, THEN SOME ASSHOLE WHO'S GONNA DIE A HORRIBLE DEATH STOLE MY CAR!
OH. ESTHER TOOK IT. UH...I THINK.
DAMN IT, SHRIMP! I CAN'T KEEP TRACK OF YOU BOTH! IT'S GONNA BE UP TO YOU TO KEEP YOUR SISTER IN LINE WHILE SHE'S HERE!
6

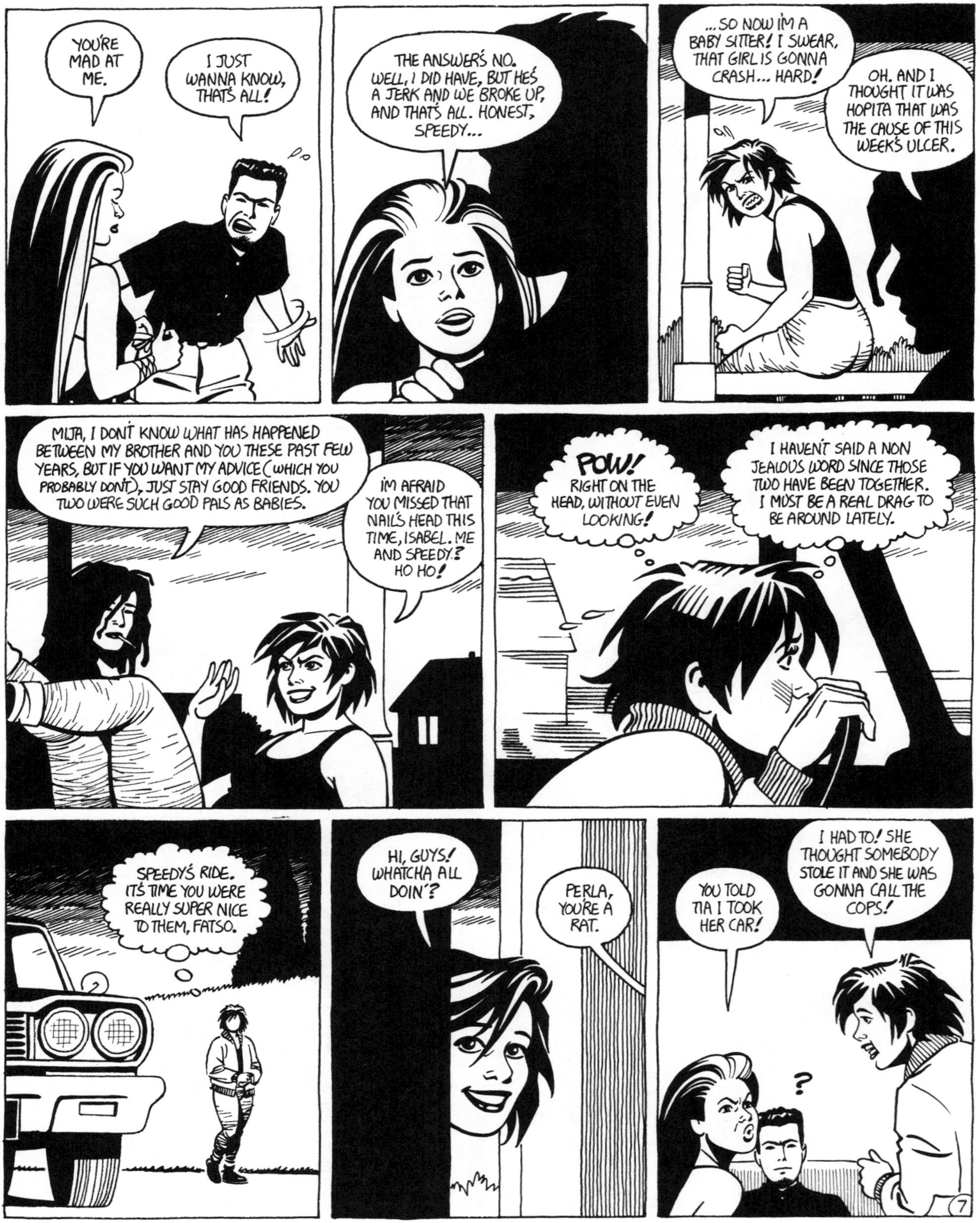
YOU'RE MAD AT ME.
I JUST WANNA KNOW, THAT'S ALL!
THE ANSWER'S NO. WELL, I DID HAVE, BUT HE'S A JERK AND WE BROKE UP, AND THAT'S ALL. HONEST, SPEEDY...
...SO NOW I'M A BABY SITTER! I SWEAR, THAT GIRL IS GONNA CRASH... HARD!
OH. AND I THOUGHT IT WAS HOPITA THAT WAS THE CAUSE OF THIS WEEK'S ULCER.
MIJA, I DON'T KNOW WHAT HAS HAPPENED BETWEEN MY BROTHER AND YOU THESE PAST FEW YEARS, BUT IF YOU WANT MY ADVICE (WHICH YOU PROBABLY DON'T), JUST STAY GOOD FRIENDS. YOU TWO WERE SUCH GOOD PALS AS BABIES.
I'M AFRAID YOU MISSED THAT NAIL'S HEAD THIS TIME, ISABEL. ME AND SPEEDY? HO HO!
POW! RIGHT ON THE HEAD, WITHOUT EVEN LOOKING!
I HAVEN'T SAID A NON JEALOUS WORD SINCE THOSE TWO HAVE BEEN TOGETHER. I MUST BE A REAL DRAG TO BE AROUND LATELY.
SPEEDY'S RIDE. IT'S TIME YOU WERE REALLY SUPER NICE TO THEM, FATSO.
HI, GUYS! WHATCHA ALL DOIN'?
PERLA, YOU'RE A RAT.
YOU TOLD TIA I TOOK HER CAR!
I HAD TO! SHE THOUGHT SOMEBODY STOLE IT AND SHE WAS GONNA CALL THE COPS!
?
7

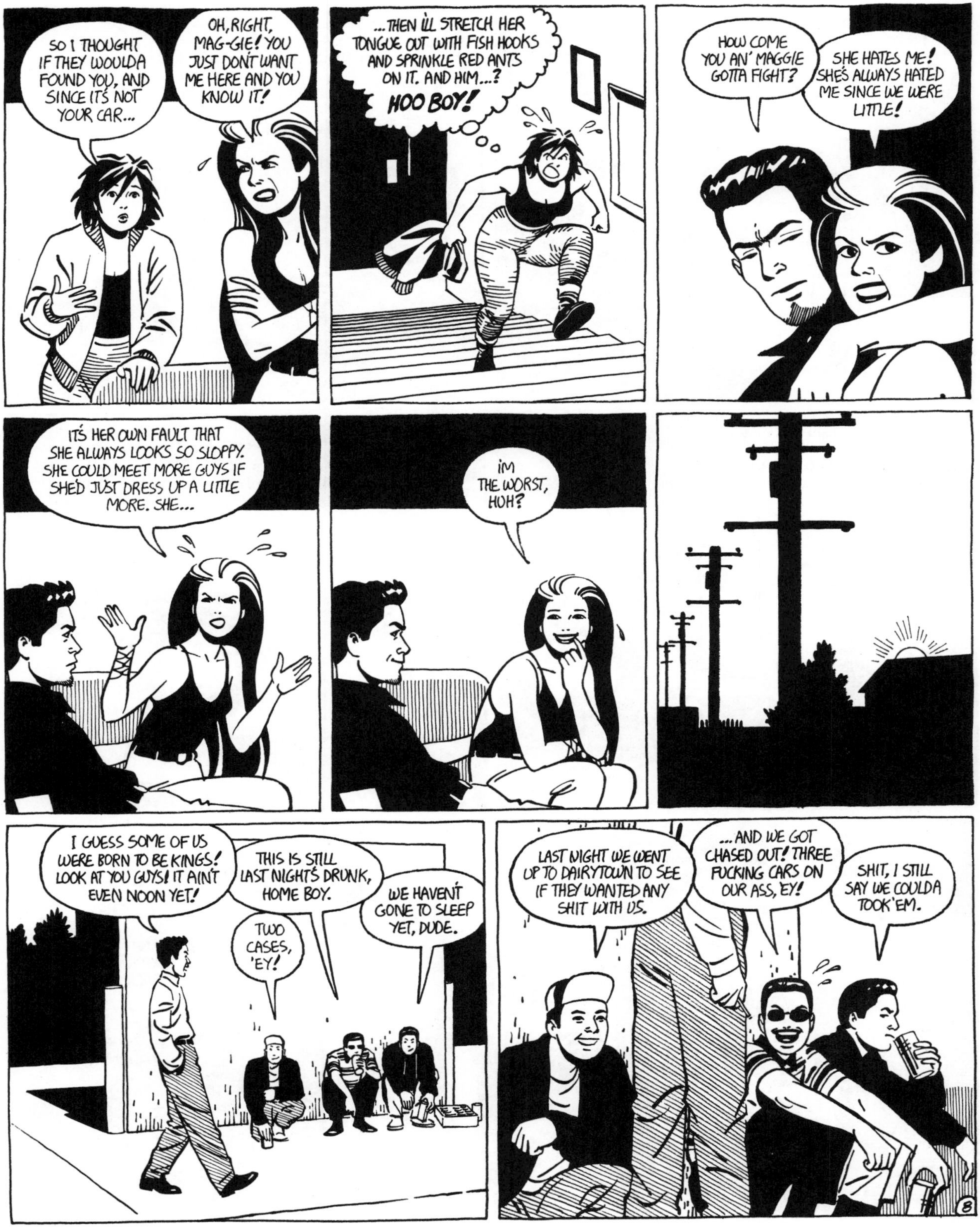
SO I THOUGHT IF THEY WOULDA FOUND YOU, AND SINCE IT'S NOT YOUR CAR...
OH, RIGHT, MAG-GIE! YOU JUST DON'T WANT ME HERE AND YOU KNOW IT!
...THEN I'LL STRETCH HER TONGUE OUT WITH FISH HOOKS AND SPRINKLE RED ANTS ON IT. AND HIM...? HOO BOY!
HOW COME YOU AN' MAGGIE GOTTA FIGHT?
SHE HATES ME! SHE'S ALWAYS HATED ME SINCE WE WERE LITTLE!
IT'S HER OWN FAULT THAT SHE ALWAYS LOOKS SO SLOPPY. SHE COULD MEET MORE GUYS IF SHE'D JUST DRESS UP A LITTLE MORE. SHE...
I'M THE WORST, HUH?
I GUESS SOME OF US WERE BORN TO BE KINGS! LOOK AT YOU GUYS! IT AIN'T EVEN NOON YET!
THIS IS STILL LAST NIGHT'S DRUNK, HOME BOY.
TWO CASES, 'EY!
WE HAVEN'T GONE TO SLEEP YET, DUDE.
LAST NIGHT WE WENT UP TO DAIRYTOWN TO SEE IF THEY WANTED ANY SHIT WITH US.
...AND WE GOT CHASED OUT! THREE FUCKING CARS ON OUR ASS, 'EY!
SHIT, I STILL SAY WE COULDA TOOK 'EM.
8

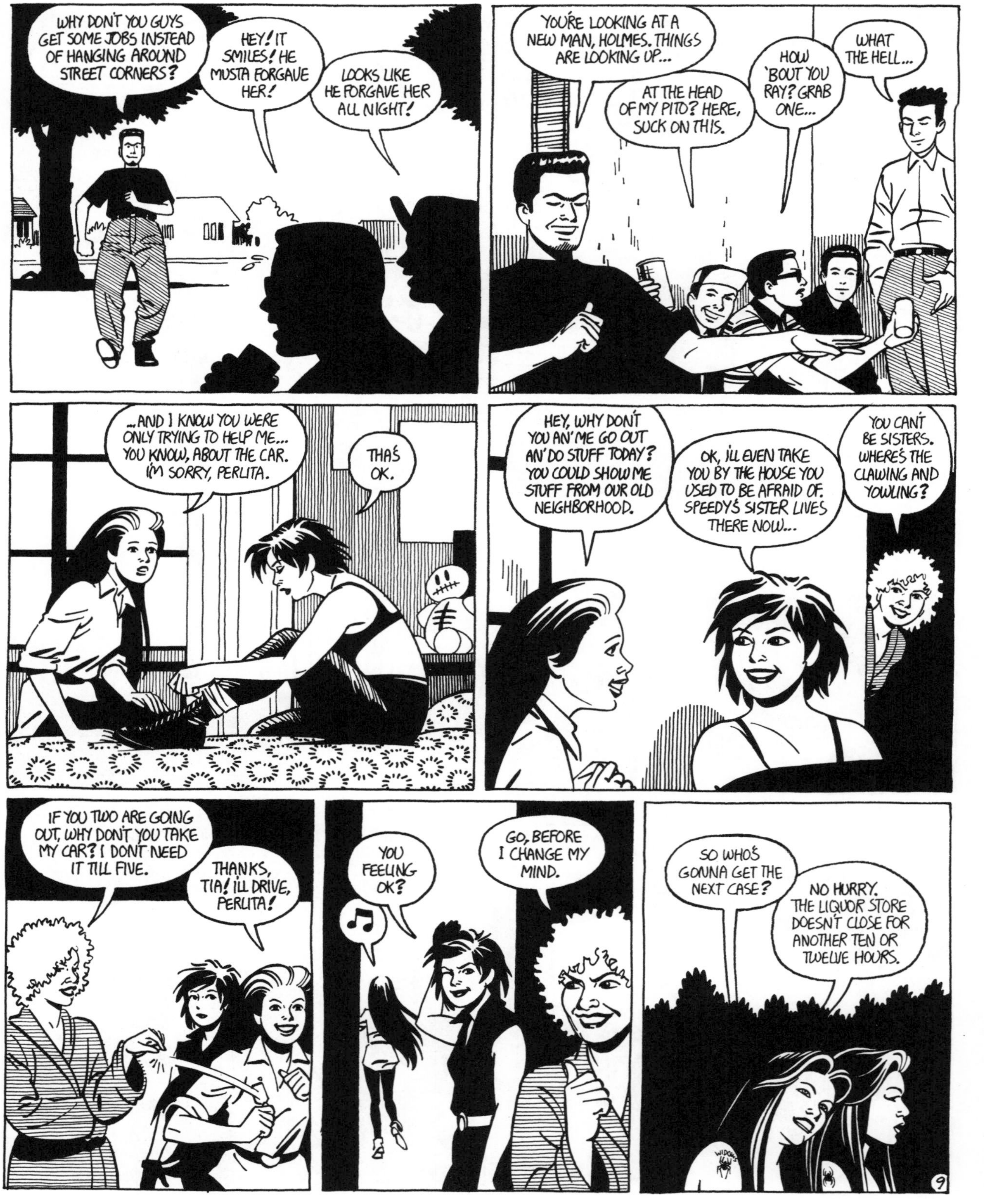
WHY DON'T YOU GUYS GET SOME JOBS INSTEAD OF HANGING AROUND STREET CORNERS?
HEY! IT SMILES! HE MUSTA FORGAVE HER!
LOOKS LIKE HE FORGAVE HER ALL NIGHT!
YOU'RE LOOKING AT A NEW MAN, HOLMES. THINGS ARE LOOKING UP...
AT THE HEAD OF MY PITO? HERE, SUCK ON THIS.
HOW 'BOUT YOU RAY? GRAB ONE...
WHAT THE HELL...
...AND I KNOW YOU WERE ONLY TRYING TO HELP ME... YOU KNOW, ABOUT THE CAR. I'M SORRY, PERLITA.
THAT'S OK.
HEY, WHY DON'T YOU AN' ME GO OUT AN' DO STUFF TODAY? YOU COULD SHOW ME STUFF FROM OUR OLD NEIGHBORHOOD.
OK, I'LL EVEN TAKE YOU BY THE HOUSE YOU USED TO BE AFRAID OF. SPEEDY'S SISTER LIVES THERE NOW...
YOU CAN'T BE SISTERS. WHERE'S THE CLAWING AND YOWLING?
IF YOU TWO ARE GOING OUT, WHY DON'T YOU TAKE MY CAR? I DON'T NEED IT TILL FIVE.
THANKS, TIA! I'LL DRIVE, PERLITA!
YOU FEELING OK?
GO, BEFORE I CHANGE MY MIND.
SO WHO'S GONNA GET THE NEXT CASE?
NO HURRY. THE LIQUOR STORE DOESN'T CLOSE FOR ANOTHER TEN OR TWELVE HOURS.
9

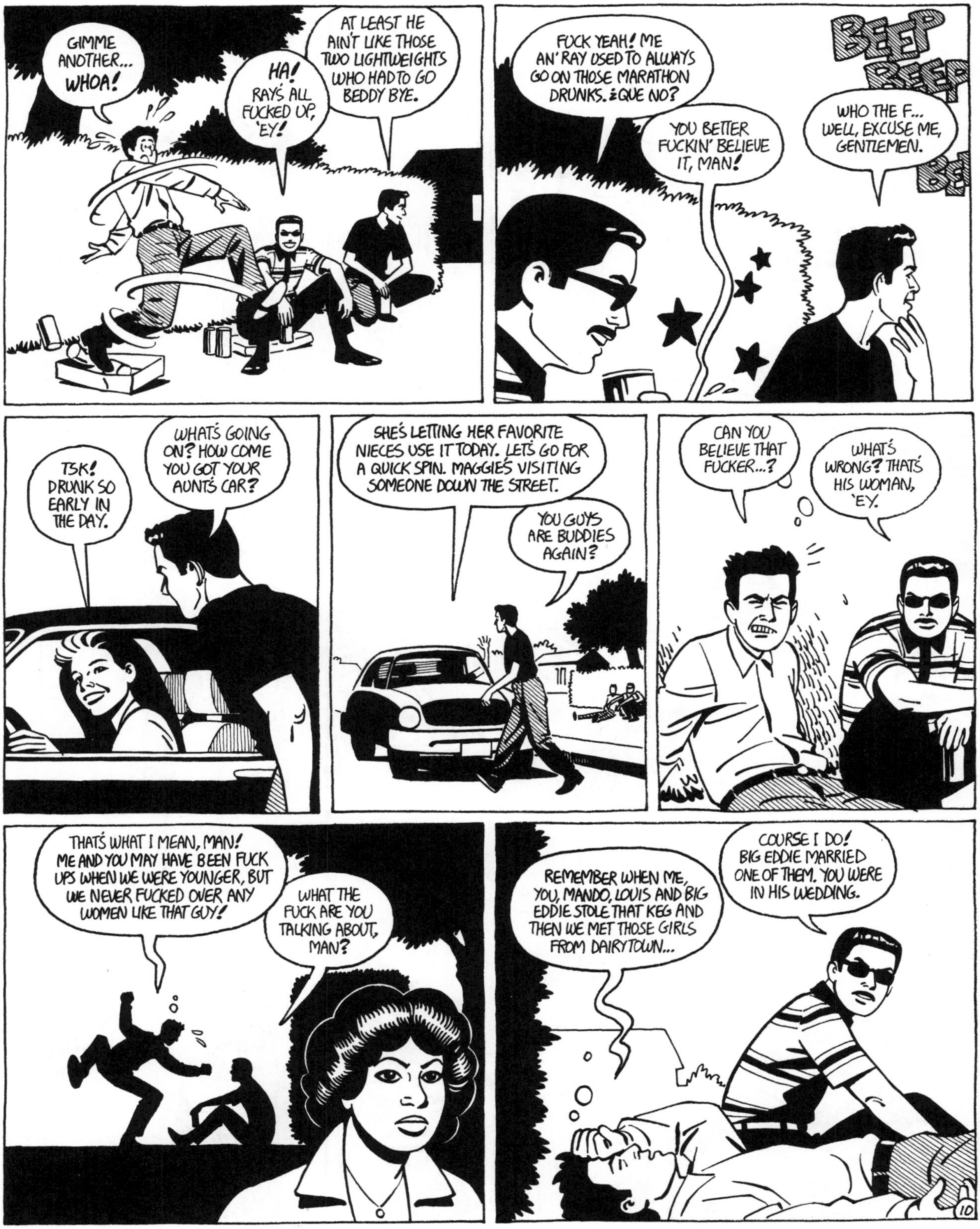
GIMME ANOTHER... WHOA!
HA! RAY'S ALL FUCKED UP, 'EY!
AT LEAST HE AIN'T LIKE THOSE TWO LIGHTWEIGHTS WHO HAD TO GO BEDDY BYE.
FUCK YEAH! ME AN' RAY USED TO ALWAYS GO ON THOSE MARATHON DRUNKS. ¿QUE NO?
YOU BETTER FUCKIN' BELIEVE IT, MAN!
BEEP BEEP
WHO THE F... WELL, EXCUSE ME, GENTLEMEN.
TSK! DRUNK SO EARLY IN THE DAY.
WHAT'S GOING ON? HOW COME YOU GOT YOUR AUNT'S CAR?
SHE'S LETTING HER FAVORITE NIECES USE IT TODAY. LET'S GO FOR A QUICK SPIN. MAGGIE'S VISITING SOMEONE DOWN THE STREET.
YOU GUYS ARE BUDDIES AGAIN?
CAN YOU BELIEVE THAT FUCKER...?
WHAT'S WRONG? THAT'S HIS WOMAN, 'EY.
THAT'S WHAT I MEAN, MAN! ME AND YOU MAY HAVE BEEN FUCK UPS WHEN WE WERE YOUNGER, BUT WE NEVER FUCKED OVER ANY WOMEN LIKE THAT GUY!
WHAT THE FUCK ARE YOU TALKING ABOUT, MAN?
REMEMBER WHEN ME, YOU, MANDO, LOUIS AND BIG EDDIE STOLE THAT KEG AND THEN WE MET THOSE GIRLS FROM DAIRYTOWN...
COURSE I DO! BIG EDDIE MARRIED ONE OF THEM. YOU WERE IN HIS WEDDING.
10

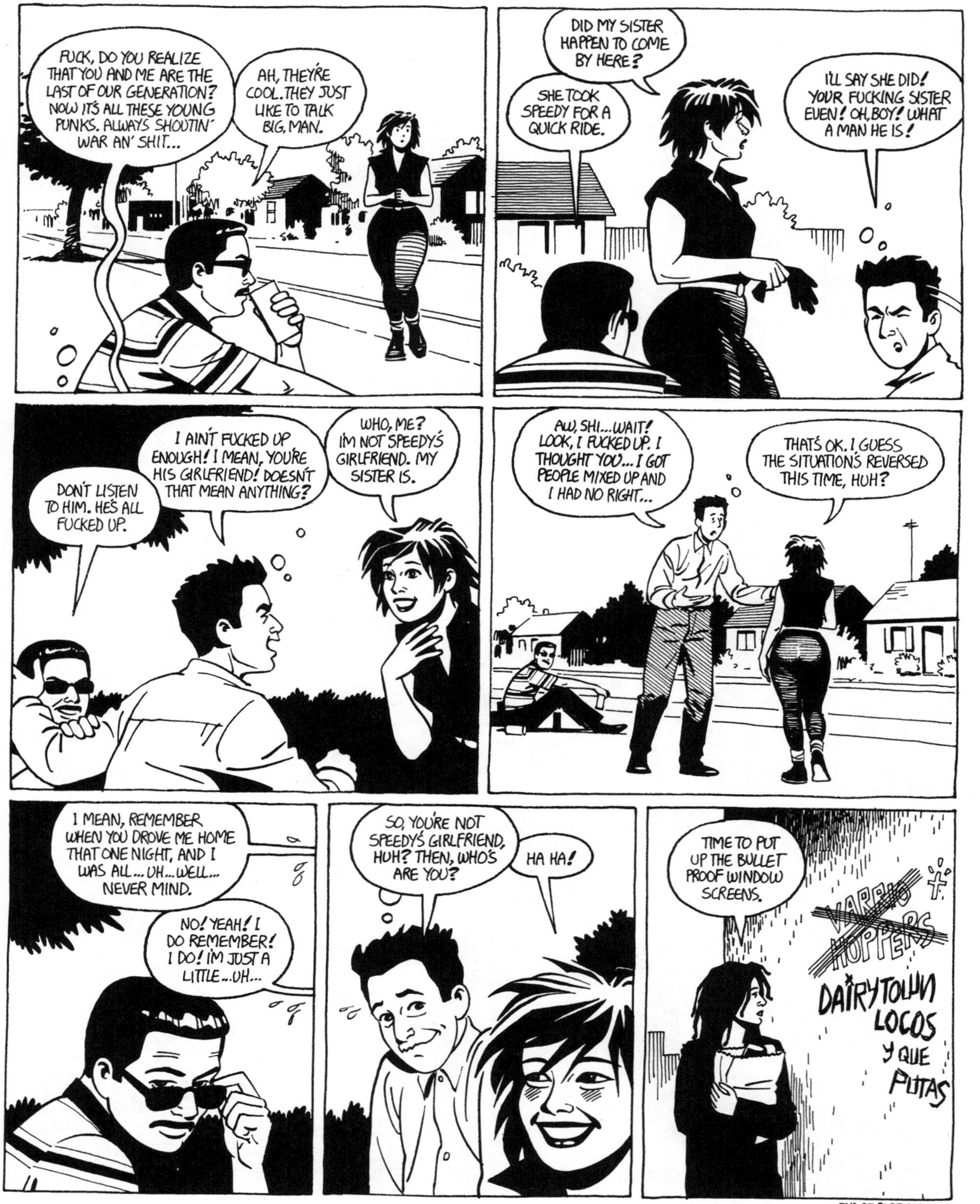
FUCK, DO YOU REALIZE THAT YOU AND ME ARE THE LAST OF OUR GENERATION? NOW IT'S ALL THESE YOUNG PUNKS. ALWAYS SHOUTIN' WAR AN' SHIT...
AH, THEY'RE COOL. THEY JUST LIKE TO TALK BIG, MAN.
DID MY SISTER HAPPEN TO COME BY HERE?
SHE TOOK SPEEDY FOR A QUICK RIDE.
I'LL SAY SHE DID! YOUR FUCKING SISTER EVEN! OH, BOY! WHAT A MAN HE IS!
DON'T LISTEN TO HIM. HE'S ALL FUCKED UP.
I AIN'T FUCKED UP ENOUGH! I MEAN, YOU'RE HIS GIRLFRIEND! DOESN'T THAT MEAN ANYTHING?
WHO, ME? I'M NOT SPEEDY'S GIRLFRIEND. MY SISTER IS.
AW, SHI... WAIT! LOOK, I FUCKED UP. I THOUGHT YOU... I GOT PEOPLE MIXED UP AND I HAD NO RIGHT...
THAT'S OK. I GUESS THE SITUATION'S REVERSED THIS TIME, HUH?
I MEAN, REMEMBER WHEN YOU DROVE ME HOME THAT ONE NIGHT, AND I WAS ALL... UH... WELL... NEVER MIND.
NO! YEAH! I DO REMEMBER! I DO! I'M JUST A LITTLE... UH...
SO, YOU'RE NOT SPEEDY'S GIRLFRIEND, HUH? THEN, WHO'S ARE YOU?
HA HA!
TIME TO PUT UP THE BULLET PROOF WINDOW SCREENS.
VARRIO HOPPERS
DAIRYTOWN LOCOS Y QUE PUTAS

END OF PART ONE

VIDA LOCA 2

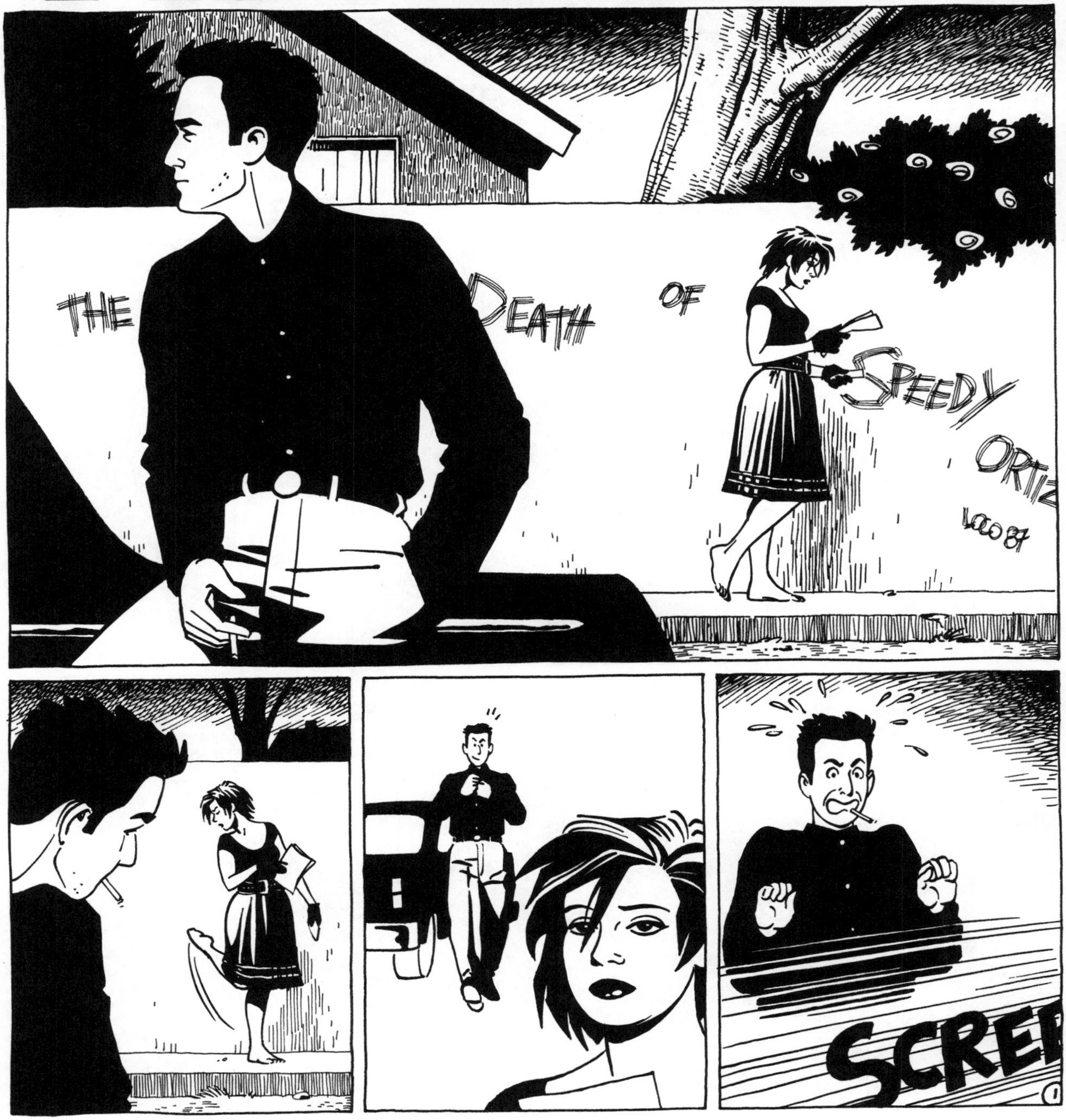
THE DEATH OF SPEEDY ORTIZ
SCRE

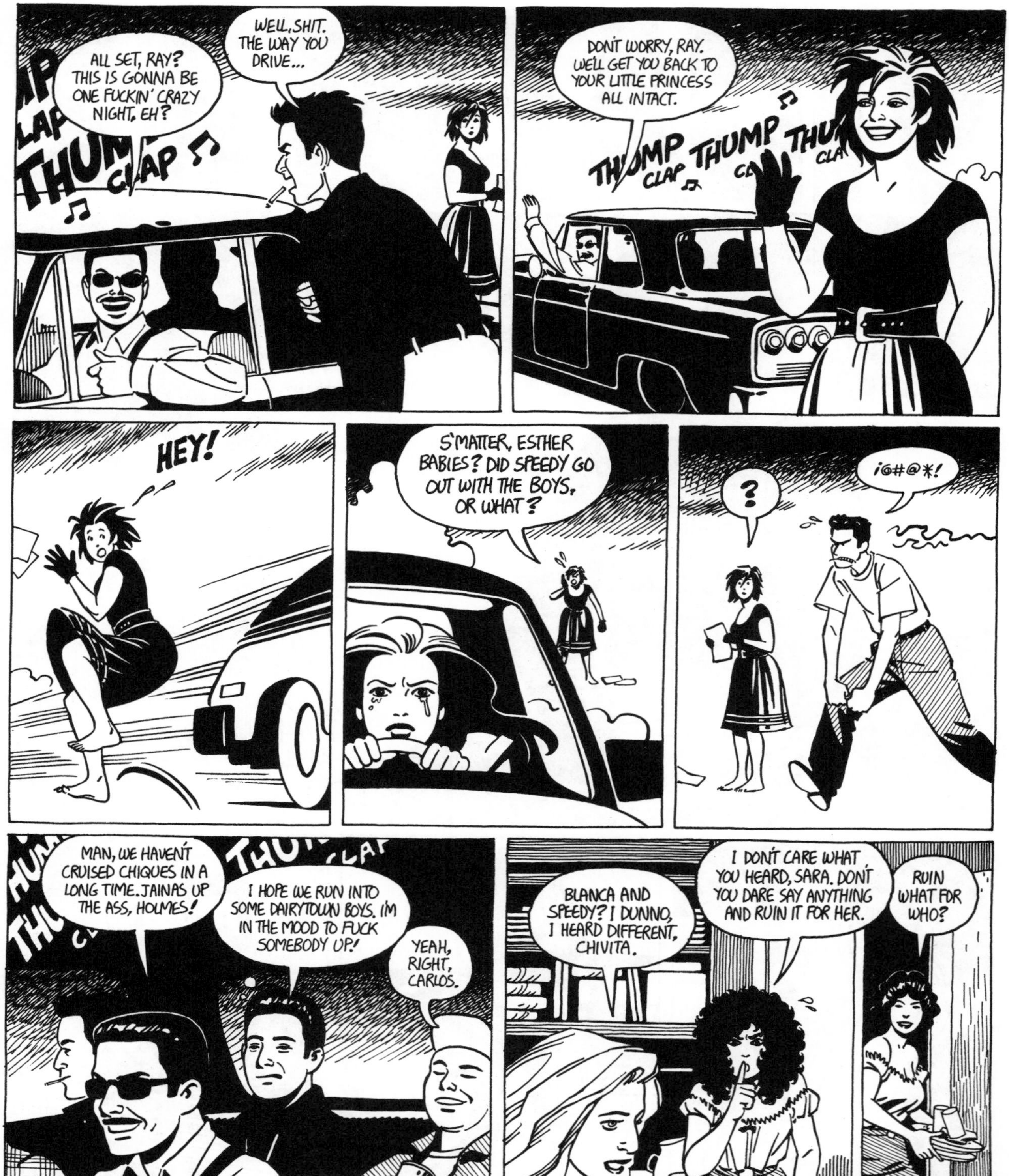
ALL SET, RAY? THIS IS GONNA BE ONE FUCKIN' CRAZY NIGHT, EH?
CLAP
WELL, SHIT. THE WAY YOU DRIVE...
DON'T WORRY, RAY. WE'LL GET YOU BACK TO YOUR LITTLE PRINCESS ALL INTACT.
THUMP CLAP THUMP
HEY!
S'MATTER, ESTHER BABIES? DID SPEEDY GO OUT WITH THE BOYS, OR WHAT?
?
¡@#@*!
MAN, WE HAVEN'T CRUISED CHIQUES IN A LONG TIME. JAINAS UP THE ASS, HOLMES!
I HOPE WE RUN INTO SOME DAIRYTOWN BOYS. I'M IN THE MOOD TO FUCK SOMEBODY UP!
YEAH, RIGHT, CARLOS.
BLANCA AND SPEEDY? I DUNNO, I HEARD DIFFERENT, CHIVITA.
I DON'T CARE WHAT YOU HEARD, SARA. DON'T YOU DARE SAY ANYTHING AND RUIN IT FOR HER.
RUIN WHAT FOR WHO?
2

JAINAS/GIRLS

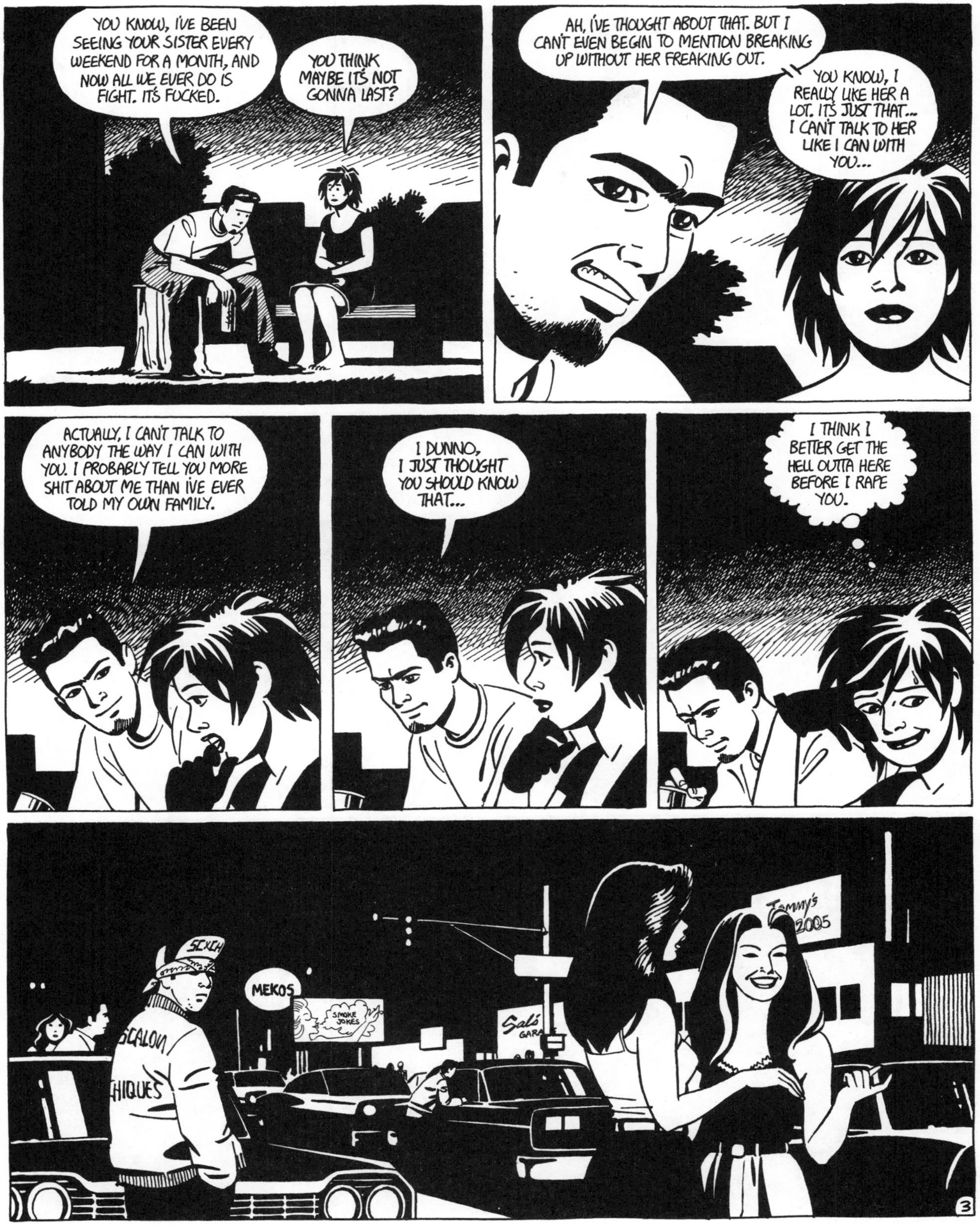
YOU KNOW, I'VE BEEN SEEING YOUR SISTER EVERY WEEKEND FOR A MONTH, AND NOW ALL WE EVER DO IS FIGHT. IT'S FUCKED.
YOU THINK MAYBE IT'S NOT GONNA LAST?
AH, I'VE THOUGHT ABOUT THAT. BUT I CAN'T EVEN BEGIN TO MENTION BREAKING UP WITHOUT HER FREAKING OUT.
YOU KNOW, I REALLY LIKE HER A LOT. IT'S JUST THAT... I CAN'T TALK TO HER LIKE I CAN WITH YOU...
ACTUALLY, I CAN'T TALK TO ANYBODY THE WAY I CAN WITH YOU. I PROBABLY TELL YOU MORE SHIT ABOUT ME THAN I'VE EVER TOLD MY OWN FAMILY.
I DUNNO, I JUST THOUGHT YOU SHOULD KNOW THAT...
I THINK I BETTER GET THE HELL OUTTA HERE BEFORE I RAPE YOU.
MEKOS
SMOKE JOKES
Tammy's
2005
3

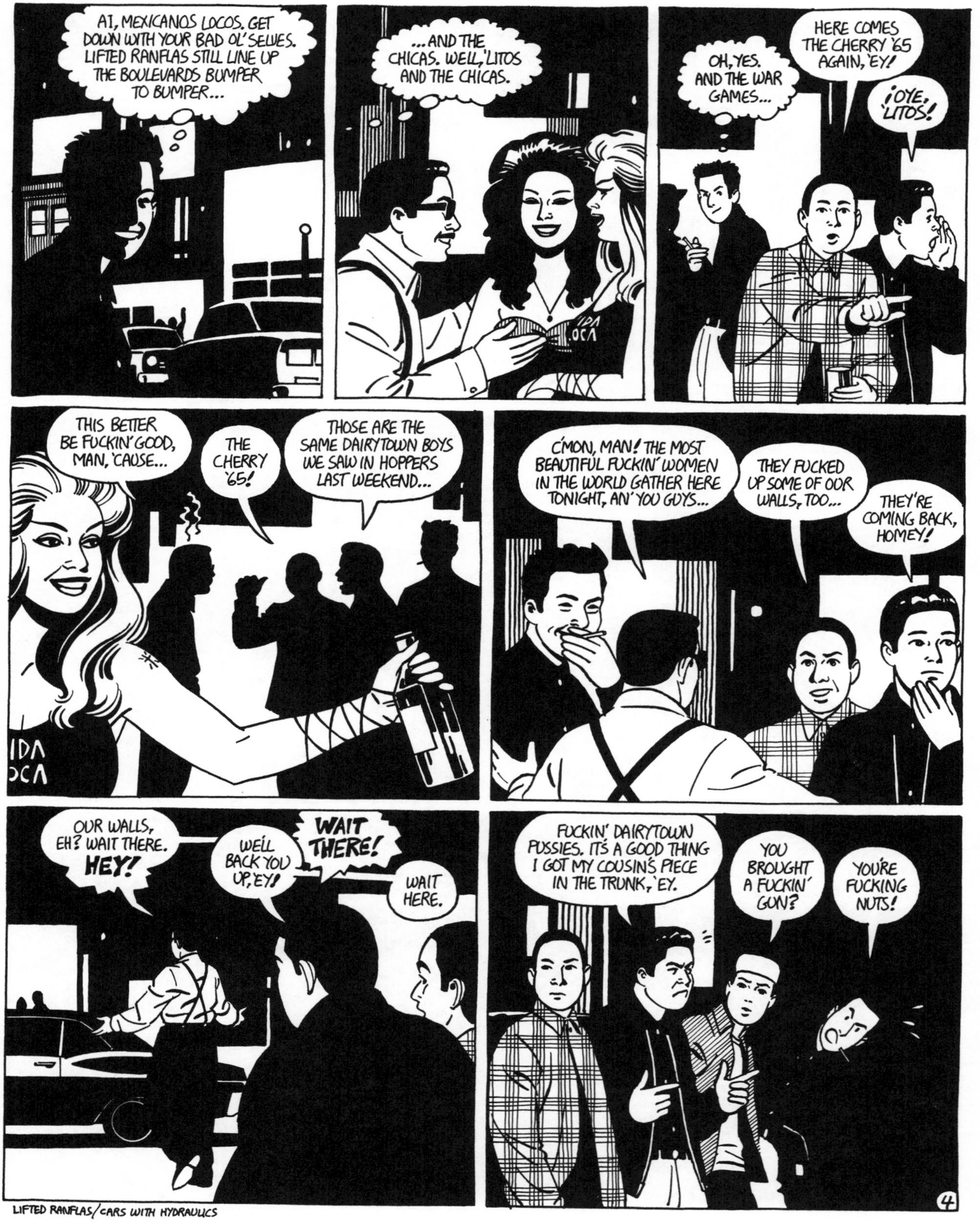
AI, MEXICANOS LOCOS. GET DOWN WITH YOUR BAD OL' SELVES. LIFTED RANFLAS STILL LINE UP THE BOULEVARDS BUMPER TO BUMPER...
...AND THE CHICAS. WELL, 'LITOS AND THE CHICAS.
OH, YES. AND THE WAR GAMES...
HERE COMES THE CHERRY '65 AGAIN, 'EY!
¡OYE, 'LITOS!
THIS BETTER BE FUCKIN' GOOD, MAN, 'CAUSE...
THE CHERRY '65!
THOSE ARE THE SAME DAIRYTOWN BOYS WE SAW IN HOPPERS LAST WEEKEND...
C'MON, MAN! THE MOST BEAUTIFUL FUCKIN' WOMEN IN THE WORLD GATHER HERE TONIGHT, AN' YOU GUYS...
THEY FUCKED UP SOME OF OUR WALLS, TOO...
THEY'RE COMING BACK, HOMEY!
OUR WALLS, EH? WAIT THERE. HEY!
WE'LL BACK YOU UP, 'EY!
WAIT THERE!
WAIT HERE.
FUCKIN' DAIRYTOWN PUSSIES. IT'S A GOOD THING I GOT MY COUSIN'S PIECE IN THE TRUNK, 'EY.
YOU BROUGHT A FUCKIN' GUN?
YOU'RE FUCKING NUTS!
4

LIFTED RANFLAS/CARS WITH HYDRAULICS

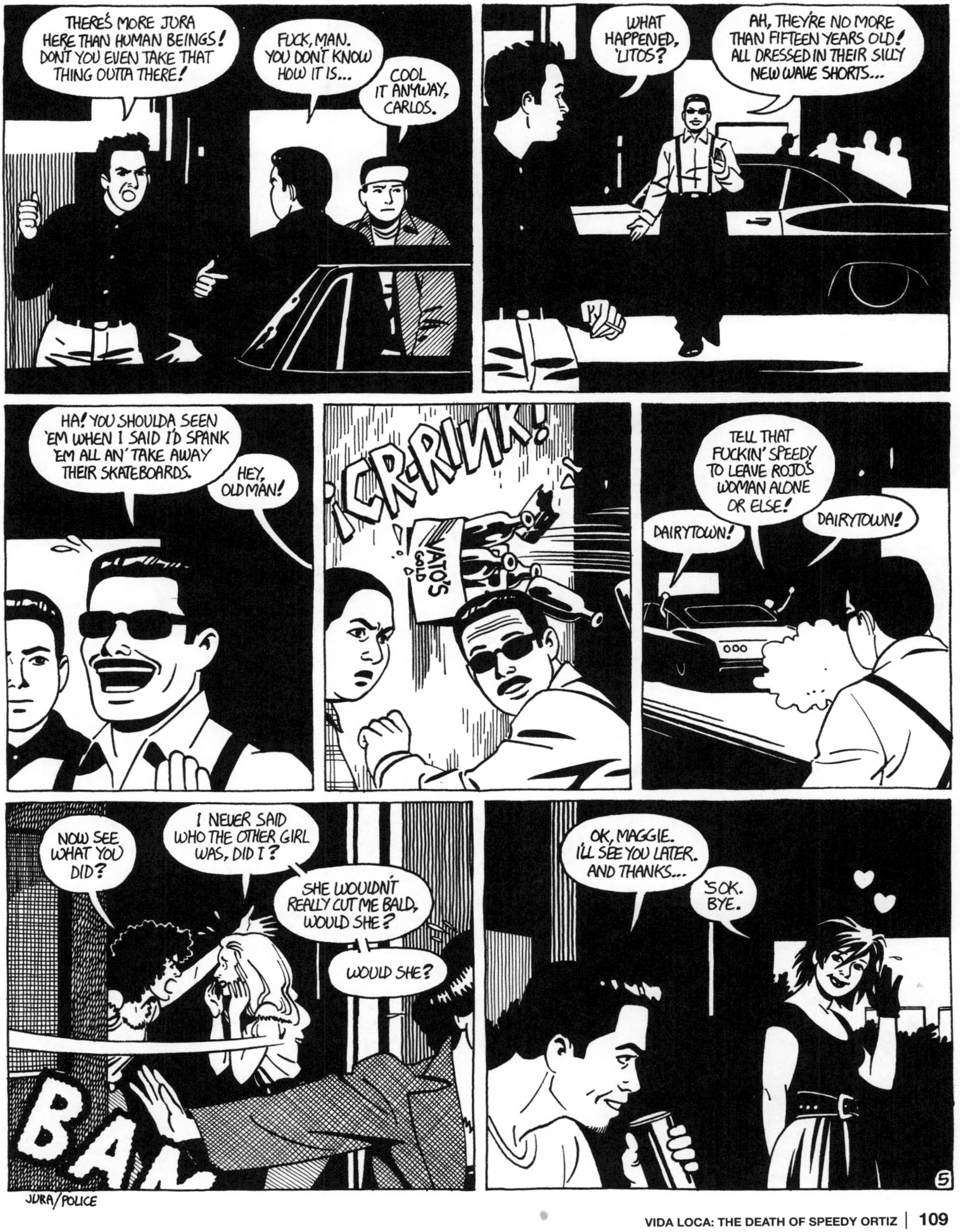
THERE'S MORE JURA HERE THAN HUMAN BEINGS! DON'T YOU EVEN TAKE THAT THING OUTTA THERE!
FUCK, MAN. YOU DON'T KNOW HOW IT IS...
COOL IT ANYWAY, CARLOS.
WHAT HAPPENED, 'LITOS?
AH, THEY'RE NO MORE THAN FIFTEEN YEARS OLD! ALL DRESSED IN THEIR SILLY NEW WAVE SHORTS...
HA! YOU SHOULDA SEEN 'EM WHEN I SAID I'D SPANK 'EM ALL AN' TAKE AWAY THEIR SKATEBOARDS.
HEY, OLD MAN!
¡CR-RINK!
VATO'S GOLD
TELL THAT FUCKIN' SPEEDY TO LEAVE ROJO'S WOMAN ALONE OR ELSE!
DAIRYTOWN!
DAIRYTOWN!
NOW SEE WHAT YOU DID?
I NEVER SAID WHO THE OTHER GIRL WAS, DID I?
SHE WOULDN'T REALLY CUT ME BALD, WOULD SHE?
WOULD SHE?
BAM
OK, MAGGIE. I'LL SEE YOU LATER. AND THANKS...
'S OK. BYE.
5
JURA/POLICE

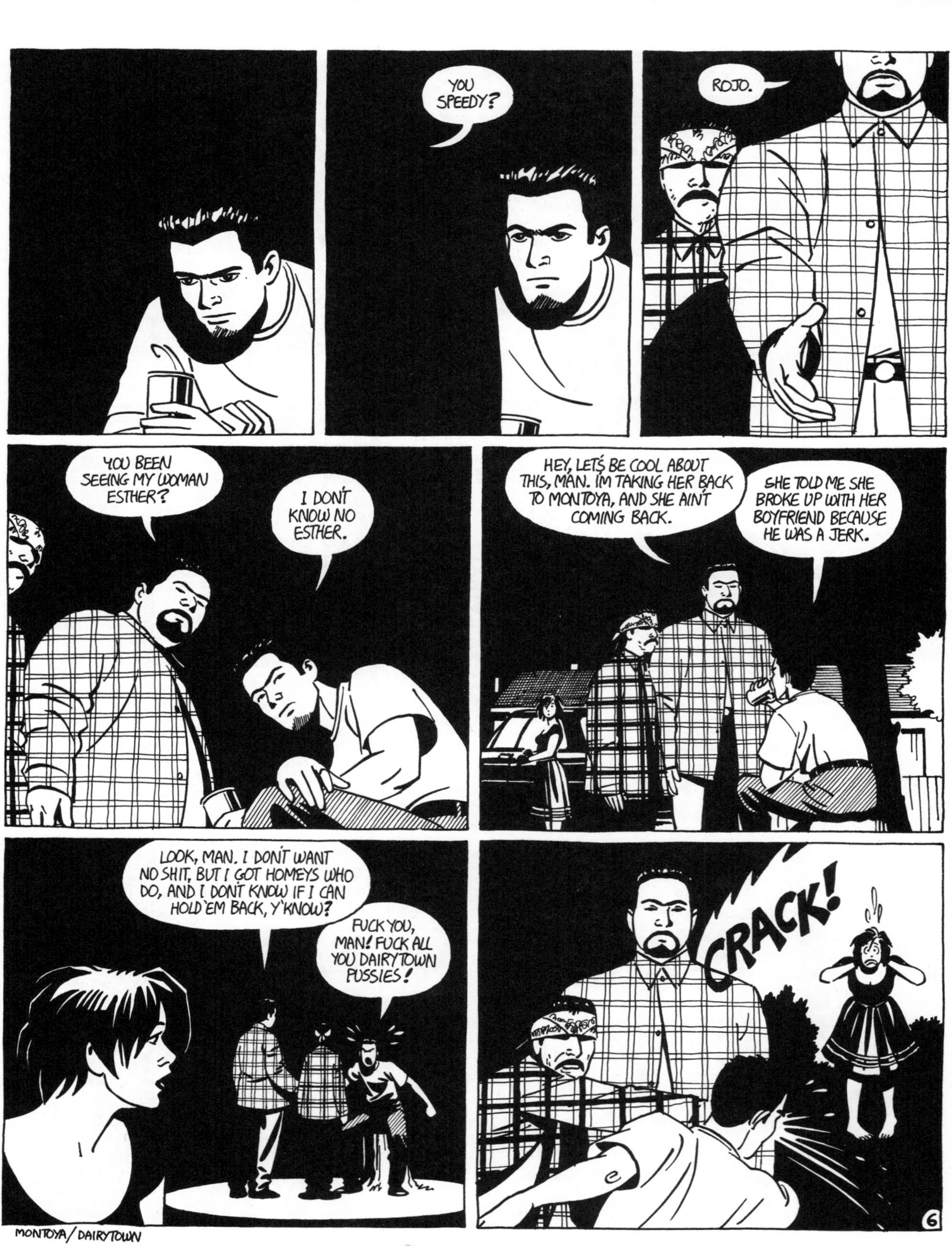
YOU SPEEDY?
ROJO.
YOU BEEN SEEING MY WOMAN ESTHER?
I DON'T KNOW NO ESTHER.
HEY, LET'S BE COOL ABOUT THIS, MAN. I'M TAKING HER BACK TO MONTOYA, AND SHE AIN'T COMING BACK.
SHE TOLD ME SHE BROKE UP WITH HER BOYFRIEND BECAUSE HE WAS A JERK.
LOOK, MAN. I DON'T WANT NO SHIT, BUT I GOT HOMEYS WHO DO, AND I DON'T KNOW IF I CAN HOLD 'EM BACK, Y'KNOW?
FUCK YOU, MAN! FUCK ALL YOU DAIRYTOWN PUSSIES!
CRACK!
6

MONTOYA/DAIRYTOWN

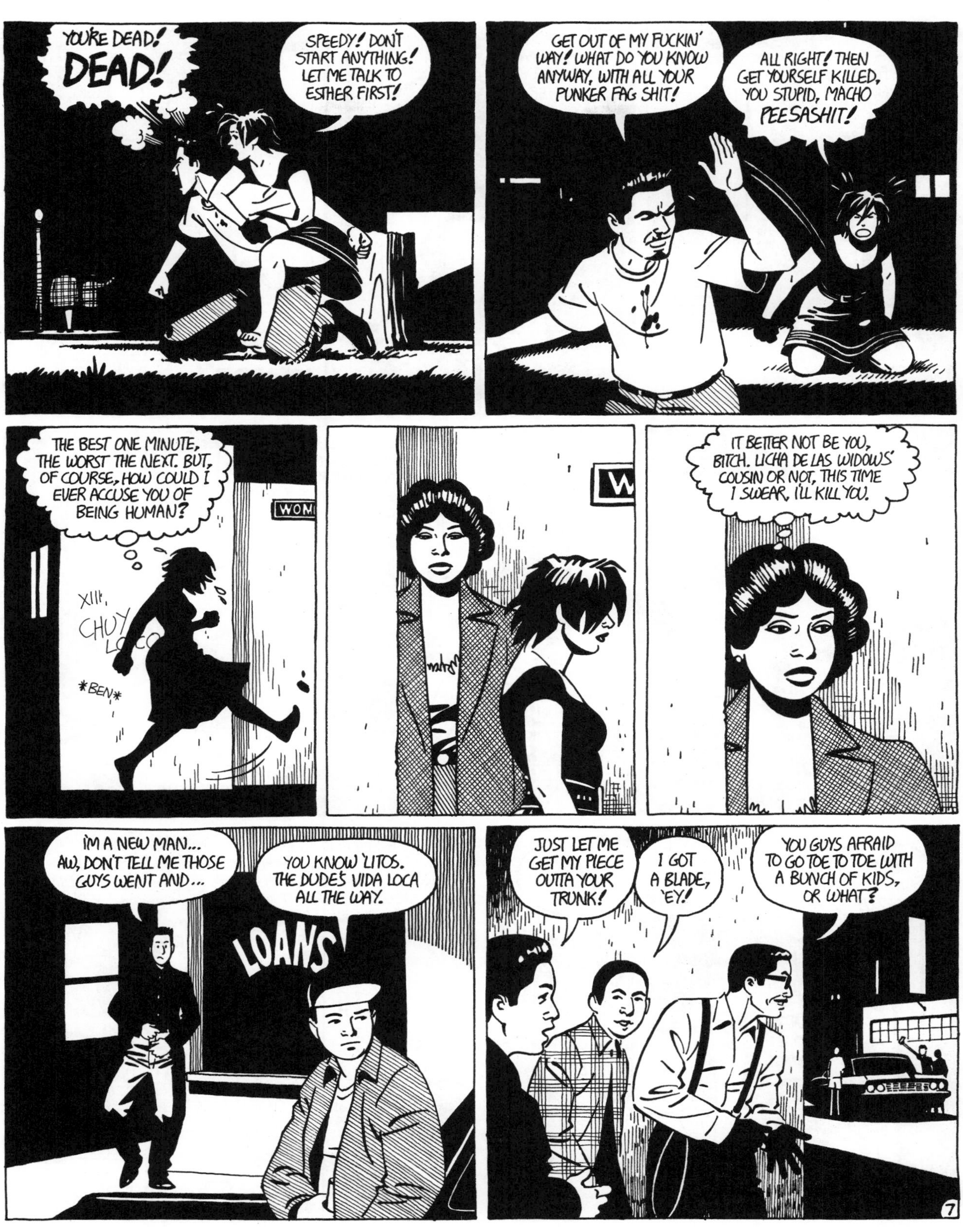
YOU'RE DEAD! DEAD!
SPEEDY! DON'T START ANYTHING! LET ME TALK TO ESTHER FIRST!
GET OUT OF MY FUCKIN' WAY! WHAT DO YOU KNOW ANYWAY, WITH ALL YOUR PUNKER FAG SHIT!
ALL RIGHT! THEN GET YOURSELF KILLED, YOU STUPID, MACHO PEESASHIT!
THE BEST ONE MINUTE, THE WORST THE NEXT. BUT, OF COURSE, HOW COULD I EVER ACCUSE YOU OF BEING HUMAN?
WOM
XIII
CHUY LOCO
BEN
W
IT BETTER NOT BE YOU, BITCH. LICHA DE LAS WIDOWS' COUSIN OR NOT, THIS TIME I SWEAR, I'LL KILL YOU.
I'M A NEW MAN... AW, DON'T TELL ME THOSE GUYS WENT AND...
YOU KNOW 'LITOS. THE DUDE'S VIDA LOCA ALL THE WAY.
LOANS
JUST LET ME GET MY PIECE OUTTA YOUR TRUNK!
I GOT A BLADE, 'EY!
YOU GUYS AFRAID TO GO TOE TO TOE WITH A BUNCH OF KIDS, OR WHAT?
7

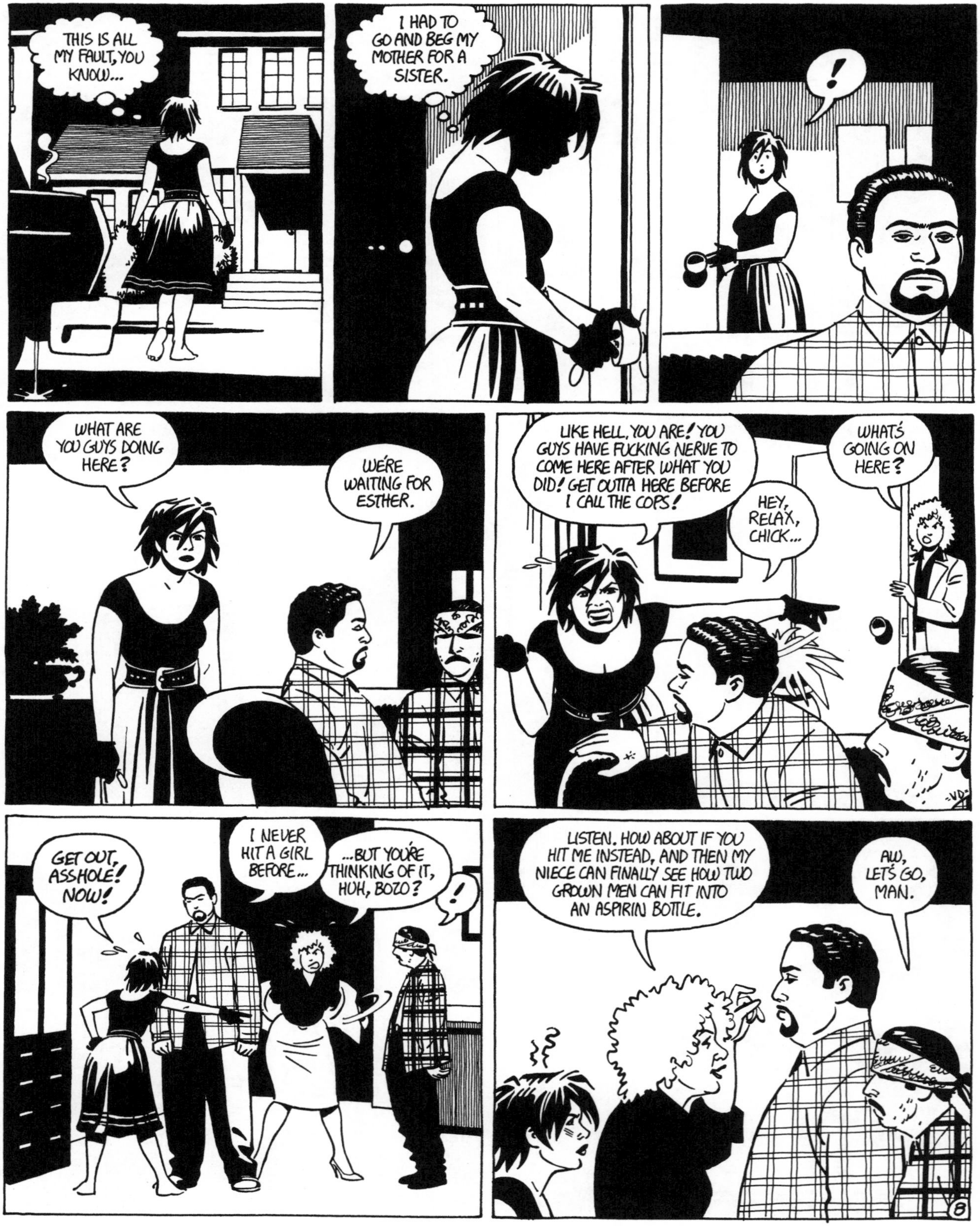
THIS IS ALL MY FAULT, YOU KNOW...
I HAD TO GO AND BEG MY MOTHER FOR A SISTER.
!
WHAT ARE YOU GUYS DOING HERE?
WE'RE WAITING FOR ESTHER.
LIKE HELL, YOU ARE! YOU GUYS HAVE FUCKING NERVE TO COME HERE AFTER WHAT YOU DID! GET OUTTA HERE BEFORE I CALL THE COPS!
HEY, RELAX, CHICK...
WHAT'S GOING ON HERE?
GET OUT, ASSHOLE! NOW!
I NEVER HIT A GIRL BEFORE...
...BUT YOU'RE THINKING OF IT, HUH, BOZO?
!
LISTEN. HOW ABOUT IF YOU HIT ME INSTEAD, AND THEN MY NIECE CAN FINALLY SEE HOW TWO GROWN MEN CAN FIT INTO AN ASPIRIN BOTTLE.
AW, LET'S GO, MAN.
8

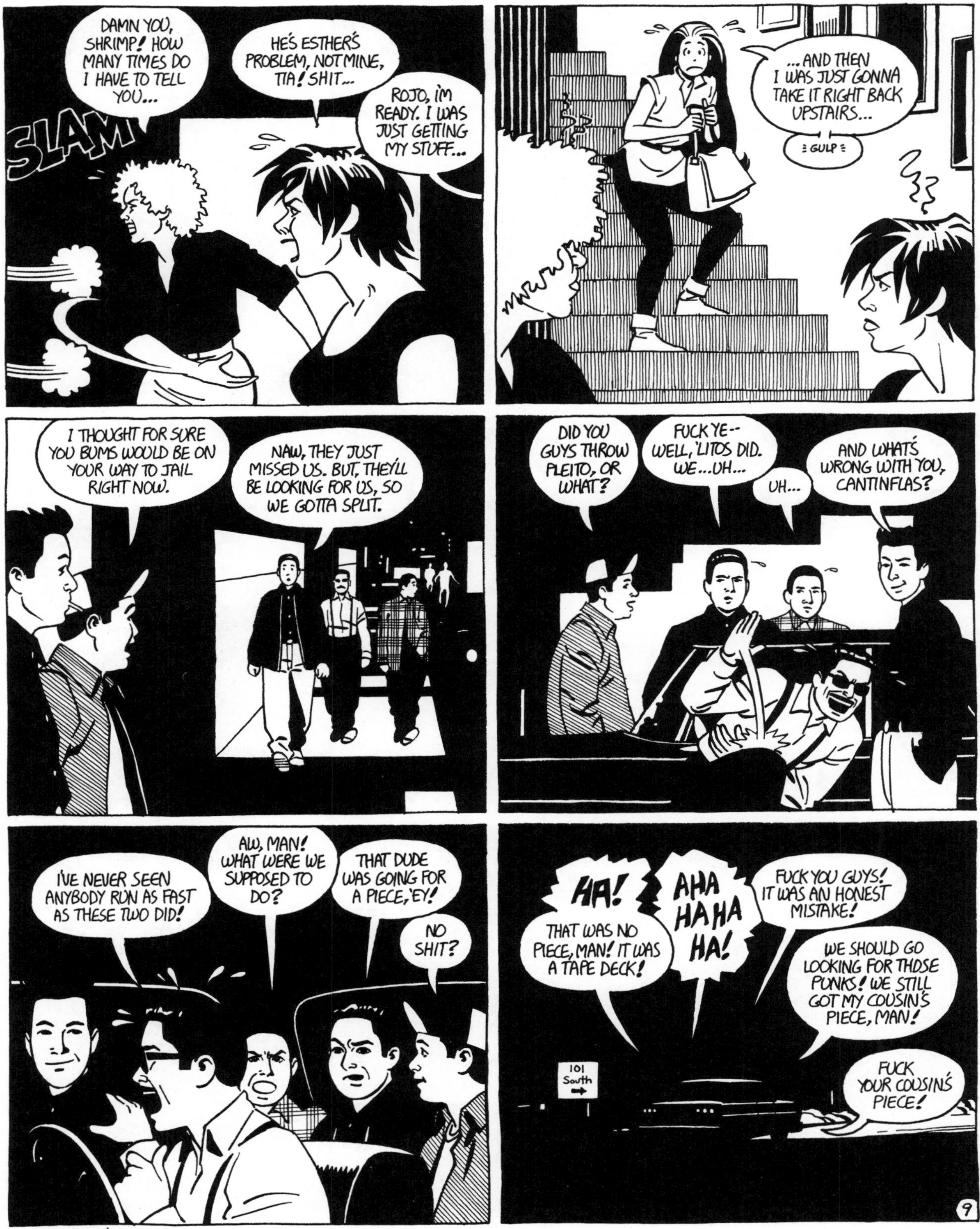

DAMN YOU, SHRIMP! HOW MANY TIMES DO I HAVE TO TELL YOU...
SLAM
HE'S ESTHER'S PROBLEM, NOT MINE, TIA! SHIT...
ROJO, I'M READY. I WAS JUST GETTING MY STUFF...
...AND THEN I WAS JUST GONNA TAKE IT RIGHT BACK UPSTAIRS...
GULP
I THOUGHT FOR SURE YOU BUMS WOULD BE ON YOUR WAY TO JAIL RIGHT NOW.
NAW, THEY JUST MISSED US. BUT, THEY'LL BE LOOKING FOR US, SO WE GOTTA SPLIT.
DID YOU GUYS THROW PLEITO, OR WHAT?
FUCK YE-- WELL, 'LITOS DID. WE...UH...
UH...
AND WHAT'S WRONG WITH YOU, CANTINFLAS?
I'VE NEVER SEEN ANYBODY RUN AS FAST AS THESE TWO DID!
AW, MAN! WHAT WERE WE SUPPOSED TO DO?
THAT DUDE WAS GOING FOR A PIECE, 'EY!
NO SHIT?
HA!
THAT WAS NO PIECE, MAN! IT WAS A TAPE DECK!
AHA HAHA HA!
FUCK YOU GUYS! IT WAS AN HONEST MISTAKE!
WE SHOULD GO LOOKING FOR THOSE PUNKS! WE STILL GOT MY COUSIN'S PIECE, MAN!
101 South
FUCK YOUR COUSIN'S PIECE!
9

THROW PLEITO/FIGHT

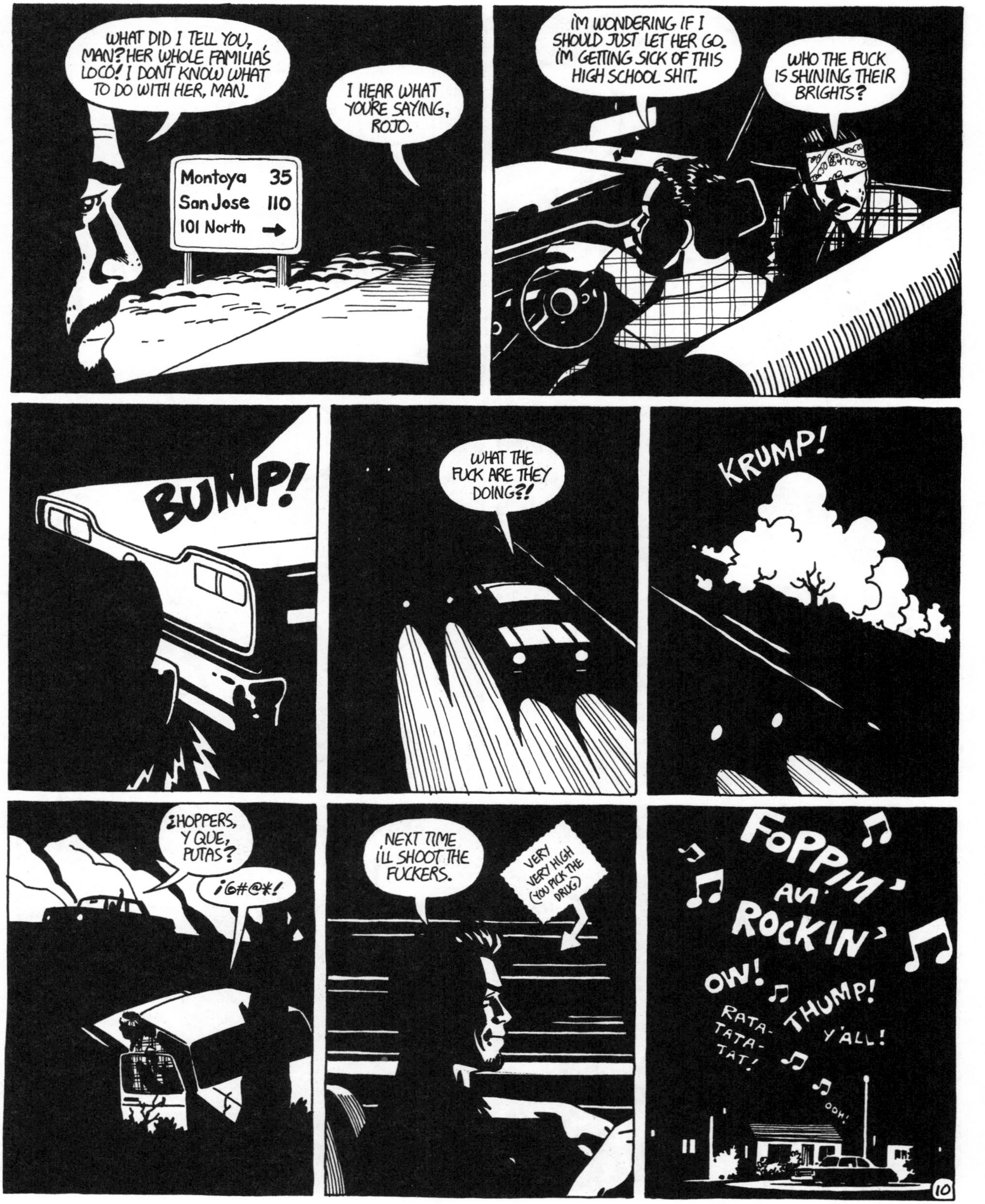

WHAT DID I TELL YOU, MAN? HER WHOLE FAMILIA'S LOCO! I DON'T KNOW WHAT TO DO WITH HER, MAN.
Montoya 35
San Jose 110
101 North
I HEAR WHAT YOU'RE SAYING, ROJO.
I'M WONDERING IF I SHOULD JUST LET HER GO. I'M GETTING SICK OF THIS HIGH SCHOOL SHIT.
WHO THE FUCK IS SHINING THEIR BRIGHTS?
BUMP!
WHAT THE FUCK ARE THEY DOING?!
KRUMP!
¿HOPPERS, Y QUE, PUTAS?
¡@#@*!
NEXT TIME I'LL SHOOT THE FUCKERS.
VERY VERY HIGH (YOU PICK THE DRUG)
FOPPIN' AN' ROCKIN'
OW!
THUMP!
RATA-TATA-TAT!
Y'ALL!
OOH!
10

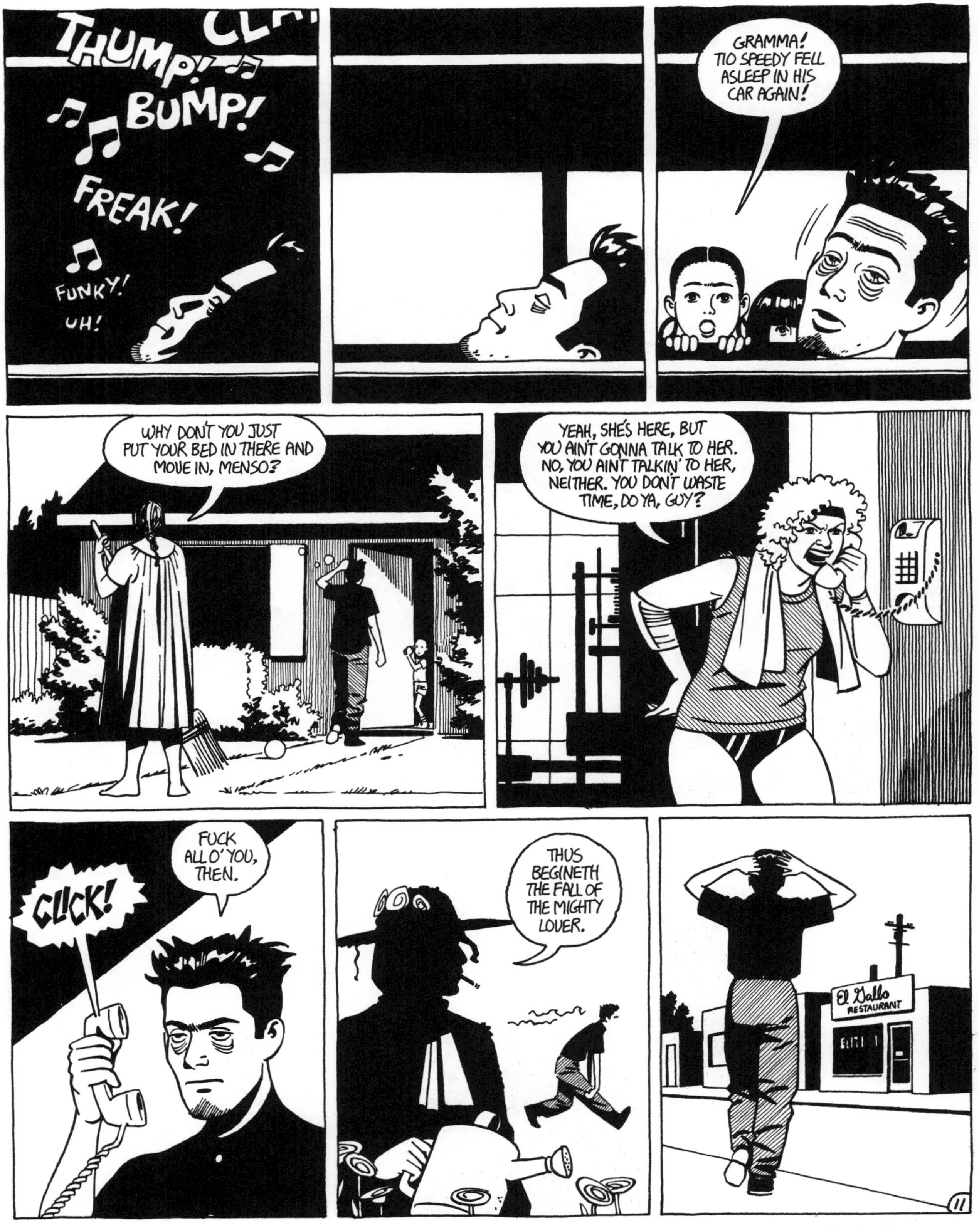
THUMP!
CLA
BUMP!
FREAK!
FUNKY!
UH!
GRAMMA! TIO SPEEDY FELL ASLEEP IN HIS CAR AGAIN!
WHY DON'T YOU JUST PUT YOUR BED IN THERE AND MOVE IN, MENSO?
YEAH, SHE'S HERE, BUT YOU AIN'T GONNA TALK TO HER. NO, YOU AINT TALKIN' TO HER, NEITHER. YOU DON'T WASTE TIME, DO YA, GUY?
CLICK!
FUCK ALL O' YOU, THEN.
THUS BEGINETH THE FALL OF THE MIGHTY LOVER.
El Gallo
RESTAURANT
11

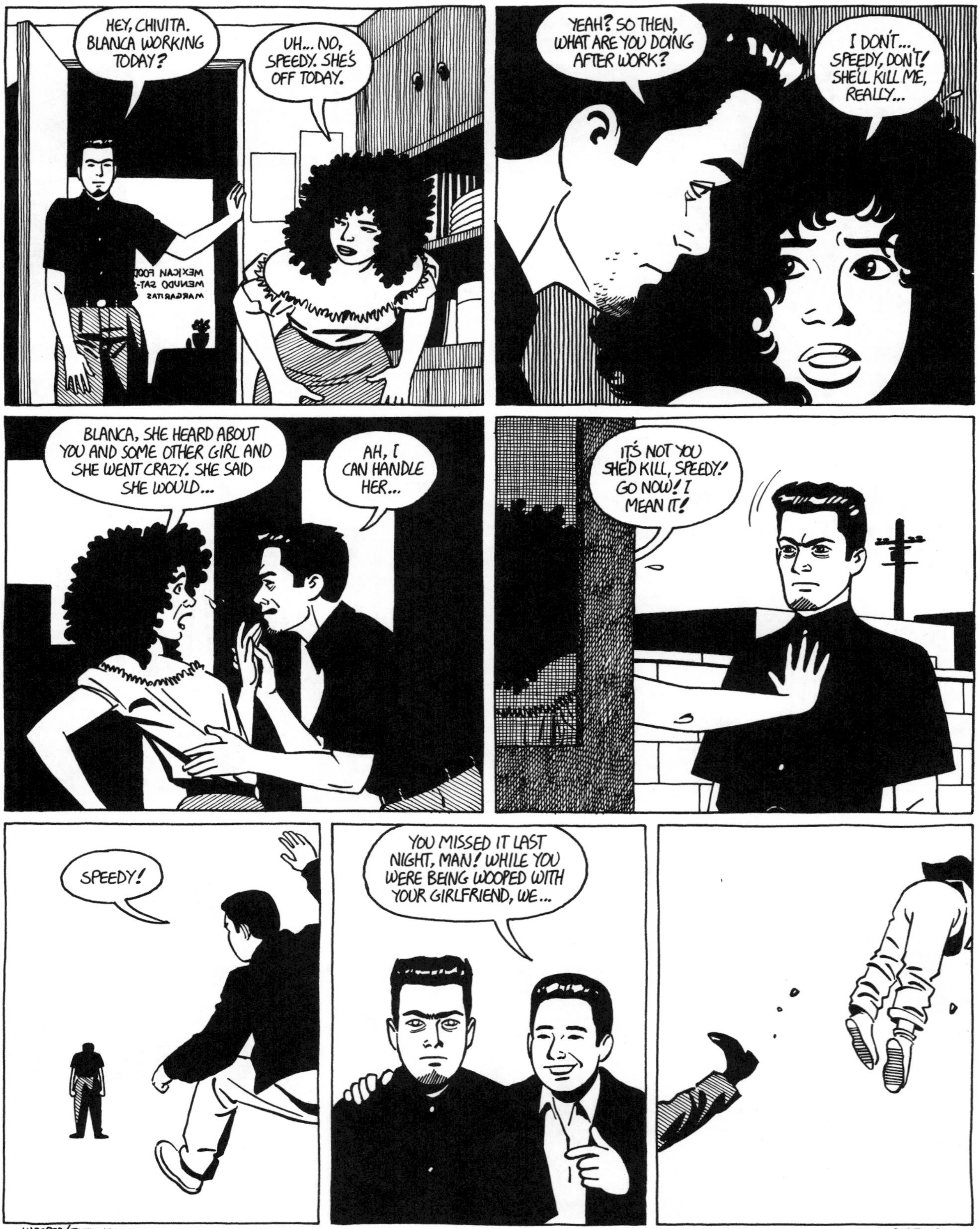
HEY, CHIVITA. BLANCA WORKING TODAY?
UH... NO, SPEEDY. SHE'S OFF TODAY.
YEAH? SO THEN, WHAT ARE YOU DOING AFTER WORK?
I DON'T... SPEEDY, DON'T! SHE'LL KILL ME, REALLY...
BLANCA, SHE HEARD ABOUT YOU AND SOME OTHER GIRL AND SHE WENT CRAZY. SHE SAID SHE WOULD...
AH, I CAN HANDLE HER...
IT'S NOT YOU SHE'D KILL, SPEEDY! GO NOW! I MEAN IT!
SPEEDY!
YOU MISSED IT LAST NIGHT, MAN! WHILE YOU WERE BEING WOOPED WITH YOUR GIRLFRIEND, WE...

WOOPED/ TOTALLY IN LOVE

END OF PART TWO

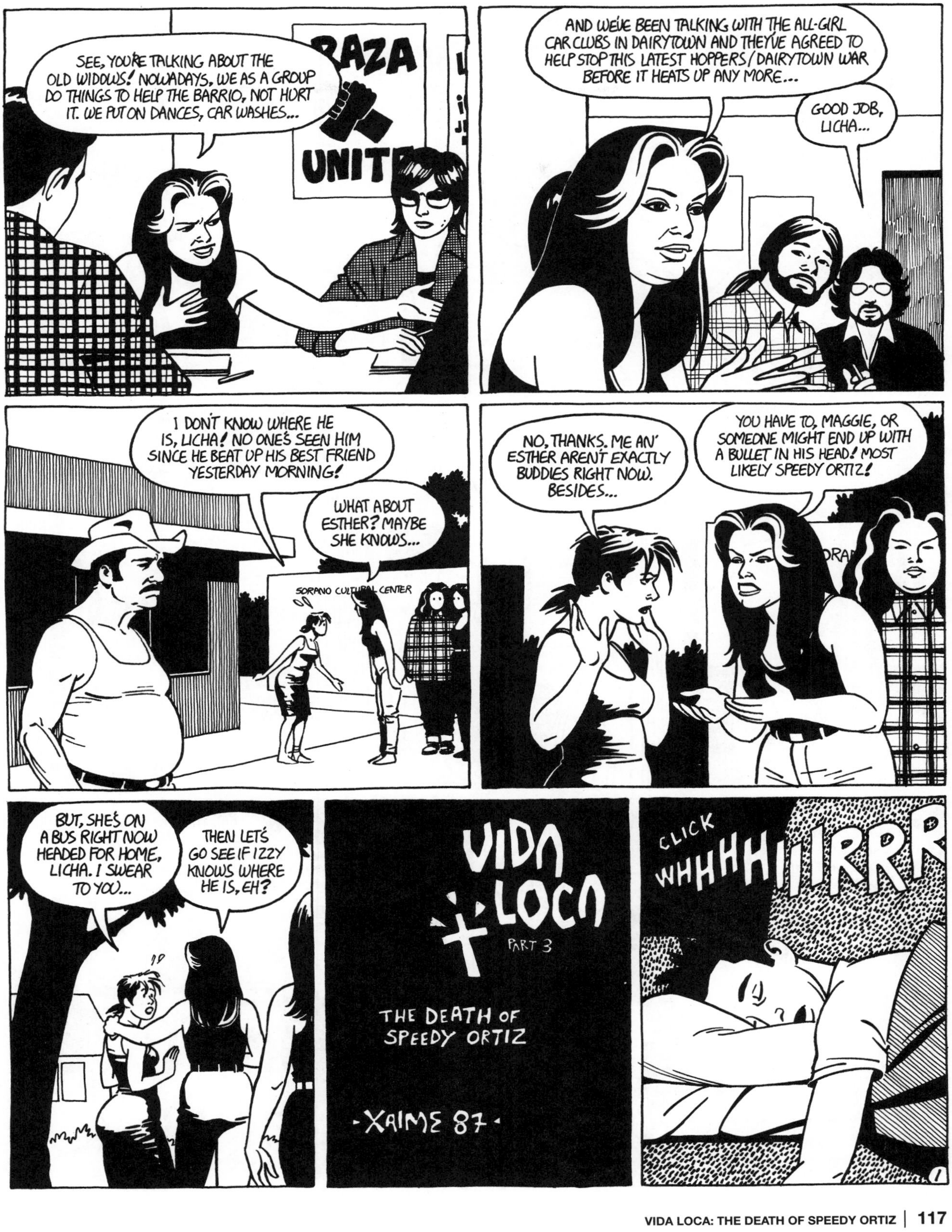
SEE, YOU'RE TALKING ABOUT THE OLD WIDOWS! NOWADAYS, WE AS A GROUP DO THINGS TO HELP THE BARRIO, NOT HURT IT. WE PUT ON DANCES, CAR WASHES...
RAZA
UNIT
AND WE'VE BEEN TALKING WITH THE ALL-GIRL CAR CLUBS IN DAIRYTOWN AND THEY'VE AGREED TO HELP STOP THIS LATEST HOPPERS/DAIRYTOWN WAR BEFORE IT HEATS UP ANY MORE...
GOOD JOB, LICHA...
I DON'T KNOW WHERE HE IS, LICHA! NO ONE'S SEEN HIM SINCE HE BEAT UP HIS BEST FRIEND YESTERDAY MORNING!
WHAT ABOUT ESTHER? MAYBE SHE KNOWS...
SORANO CULTURAL CENTER
NO, THANKS. ME AN' ESTHER AREN'T EXACTLY BUDDIES RIGHT NOW. BESIDES...
YOU HAVE TO, MAGGIE, OR SOMEONE MIGHT END UP WITH A BULLET IN HIS HEAD! MOST LIKELY SPEEDY ORTIZ!
BUT, SHE'S ON A BUS RIGHT NOW HEADED FOR HOME, LICHA. I SWEAR TO YOU...
THEN LET'S GO SEE IF IZZY KNOWS WHERE HE IS, EH?
VIDA LOCA
PART 3
THE DEATH OF SPEEDY ORTIZ
·XAIME 87·
CLICK
WHHHHIIIRRR
1

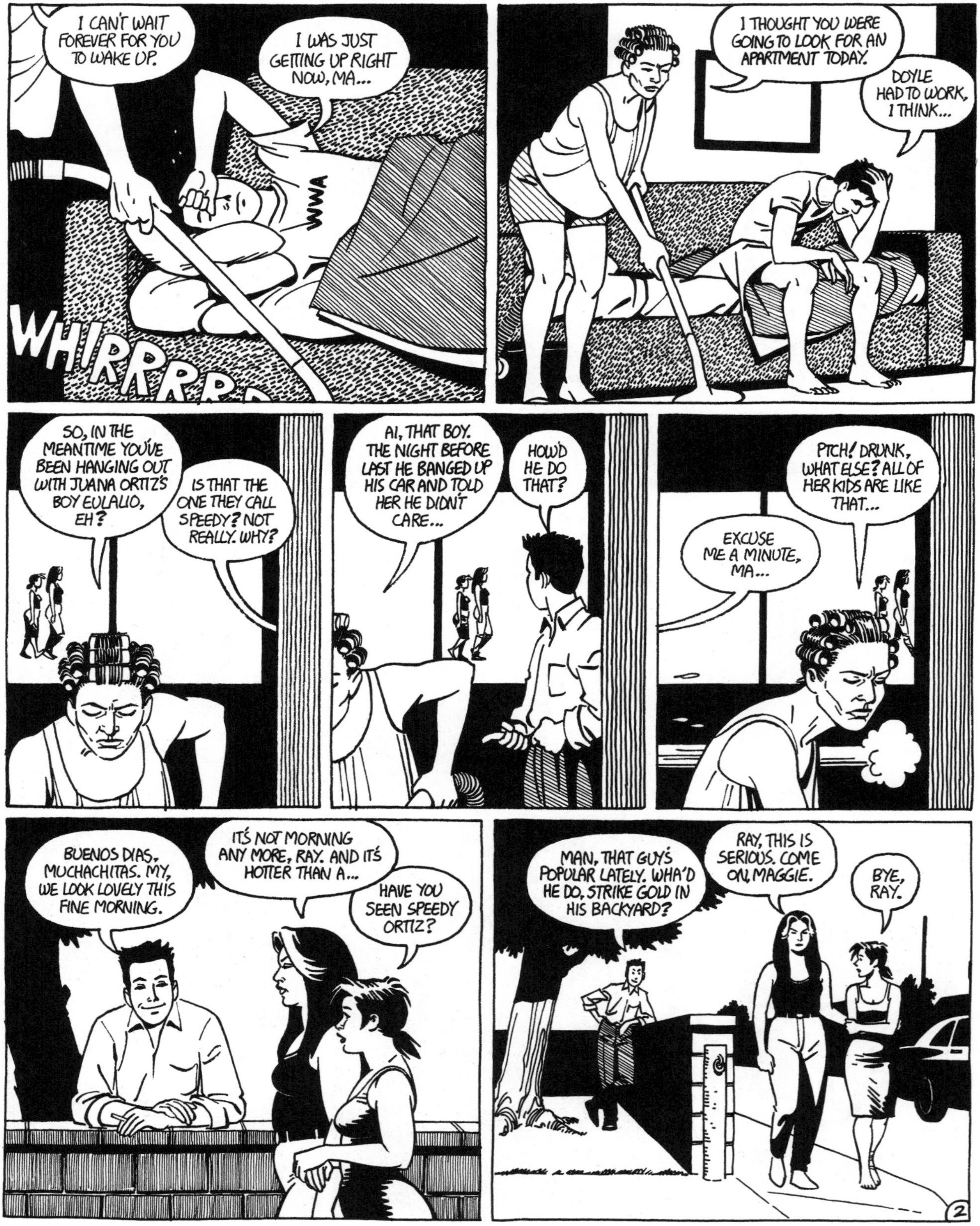
I CAN'T WAIT FOREVER FOR YOU TO WAKE UP.
I WAS JUST GETTING UP RIGHT NOW, MA...
WWA
WHIRRRRR
I THOUGHT YOU WERE GOING TO LOOK FOR AN APARTMENT TODAY.
DOYLE HAD TO WORK, I THINK...
SO, IN THE MEANTIME YOU'VE BEEN HANGING OUT WITH JUANA ORTIZ'S BOY EULALIO, EH?
IS THAT THE ONE THEY CALL SPEEDY? NOT REALLY. WHY?
AI, THAT BOY. THE NIGHT BEFORE LAST HE BANGED UP HIS CAR AND TOLD HER HE DIDN'T CARE...
HOW'D HE DO THAT?
PTCH! DRUNK, WHAT ELSE? ALL OF HER KIDS ARE LIKE THAT...
EXCUSE ME A MINUTE, MA...
BUENOS DIAS, MUCHACHITAS. MY, WE LOOK LOVELY THIS FINE MORNING.
IT'S NOT MORNING ANY MORE, RAY. AND IT'S HOTTER THAN A...
HAVE YOU SEEN SPEEDY ORTIZ?
MAN, THAT GUY'S POPULAR LATELY. WHA'D HE DO, STRIKE GOLD IN HIS BACKYARD?
RAY, THIS IS SERIOUS. COME ON, MAGGIE.
BYE, RAY.
2

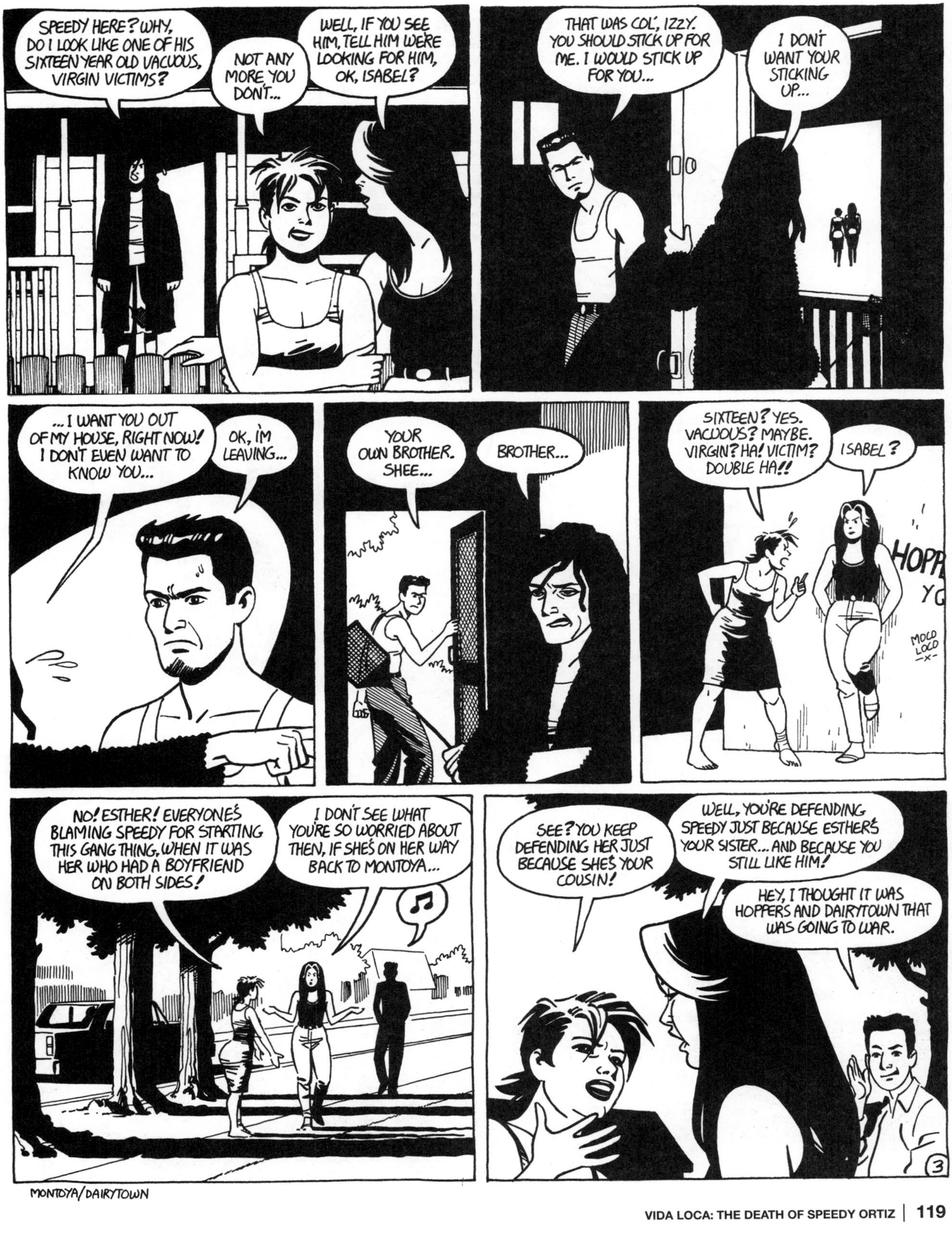
SPEEDY HERE? WHY, DO I LOOK LIKE ONE OF HIS SIXTEEN YEAR OLD VACUOUS, VIRGIN VICTIMS?
NOT ANY MORE YOU DON'T...
WELL, IF YOU SEE HIM, TELL HIM WE'RE LOOKING FOR HIM, OK, ISABEL?
THAT WAS COL', IZZY. YOU SHOULD STICK UP FOR ME. I WOULD STICK UP FOR YOU...
I DON'T WANT YOUR STICKING UP...
...I WANT YOU OUT OF MY HOUSE, RIGHT NOW! I DON'T EVEN WANT TO KNOW YOU...
OK, I'M LEAVING...
YOUR OWN BROTHER. SHEE...
BROTHER...
SIXTEEN? YES. VACUOUS? MAYBE. VIRGIN? HA! VICTIM? DOUBLE HA!!
ISABEL?
HOPP
YO
MOCO LOCO
NO! ESTHER! EVERYONE'S BLAMING SPEEDY FOR STARTING THIS GANG THING, WHEN IT WAS HER WHO HAD A BOYFRIEND ON BOTH SIDES!
I DON'T SEE WHAT YOU'RE SO WORRIED ABOUT THEN, IF SHE'S ON HER WAY BACK TO MONTOYA...
♪
SEE? YOU KEEP DEFENDING HER JUST BECAUSE SHE'S YOUR COUSIN!
WELL, YOU'RE DEFENDING SPEEDY JUST BECAUSE ESTHER'S YOUR SISTER... AND BECAUSE YOU STILL LIKE HIM!
HEY, I THOUGHT IT WAS HOPPERS AND DAIRYTOWN THAT WAS GOING TO WAR.
3
MONTOYA/DAIRYTOWN

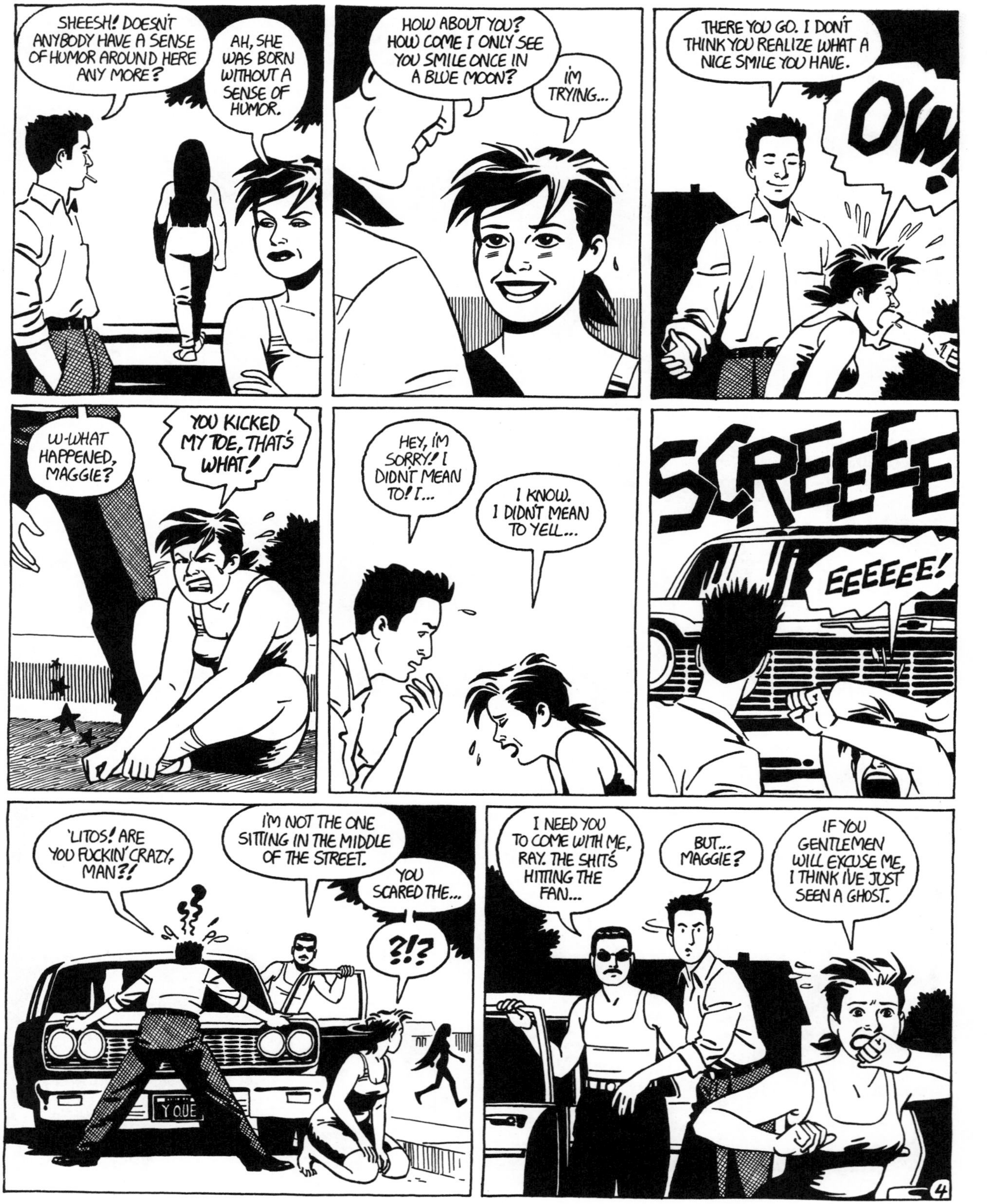
SHEESH! DOESN'T ANYBODY HAVE A SENSE OF HUMOR AROUND HERE ANY MORE?
AH, SHE WAS BORN WITHOUT A SENSE OF HUMOR.
HOW ABOUT YOU? HOW COME I ONLY SEE YOU SMILE ONCE IN A BLUE MOON?
I'M TRYING...
THERE YOU GO. I DON'T THINK YOU REALIZE WHAT A NICE SMILE YOU HAVE.
OW!
W-WHAT HAPPENED, MAGGIE?
YOU KICKED MY TOE, THAT'S WHAT!
HEY, I'M SORRY! I DIDN'T MEAN TO! I...
I KNOW. I DIDN'T MEAN TO YELL...
SCREEEE
EEEEEE!
'LITOS! ARE YOU FUCKIN' CRAZY, MAN?!
I'M NOT THE ONE SITTING IN THE MIDDLE OF THE STREET.
YOU SCARED THE...
?!?
I NEED YOU TO COME WITH ME, RAY. THE SHIT'S HITTING THE FAN...
BUT... MAGGIE?
IF YOU GENTLEMEN WILL EXCUSE ME, I THINK I'VE JUST SEEN A GHOST.
4

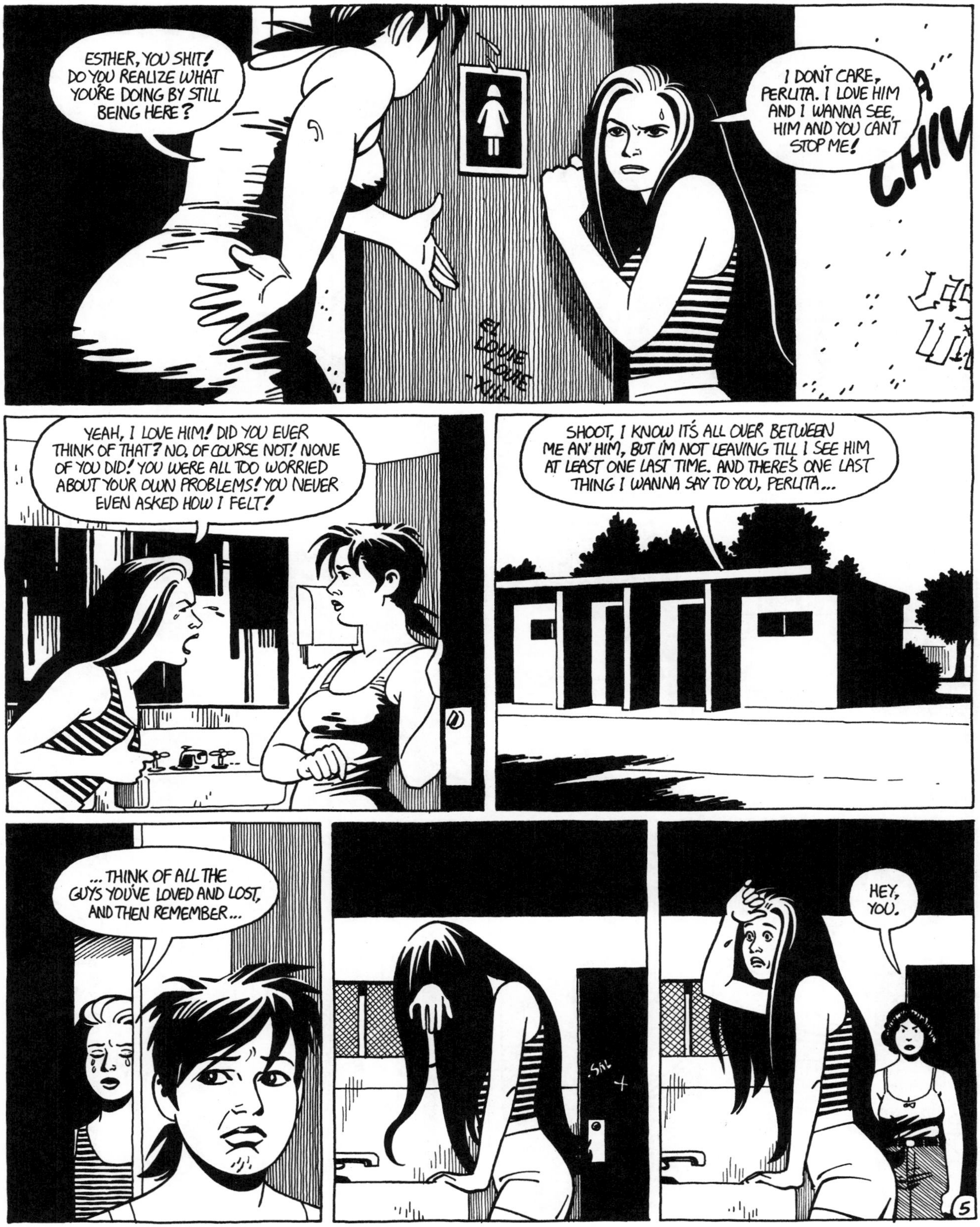
ESTHER, YOU SHIT! DO YOU REALIZE WHAT YOU'RE DOING BY STILL BEING HERE?
I DON'T CARE, PERLITA. I LOVE HIM AND I WANNA SEE, HIM AND YOU CAN'T STOP ME!
YEAH, I LOVE HIM! DID YOU EVER THINK OF THAT? NO, OF COURSE NOT! NONE OF YOU DID! YOU WERE ALL TOO WORRIED ABOUT YOUR OWN PROBLEMS! YOU NEVER EVEN ASKED HOW I FELT!
SHOOT, I KNOW IT'S ALL OVER BETWEEN ME AN' HIM, BUT I'M NOT LEAVING TILL I SEE HIM AT LEAST ONE LAST TIME. AND THERE'S ONE LAST THING I WANNA SAY TO YOU, PERLITA...
...THINK OF ALL THE GUYS YOU'VE LOVED AND LOST, AND THEN REMEMBER...
HEY, YOU.
5

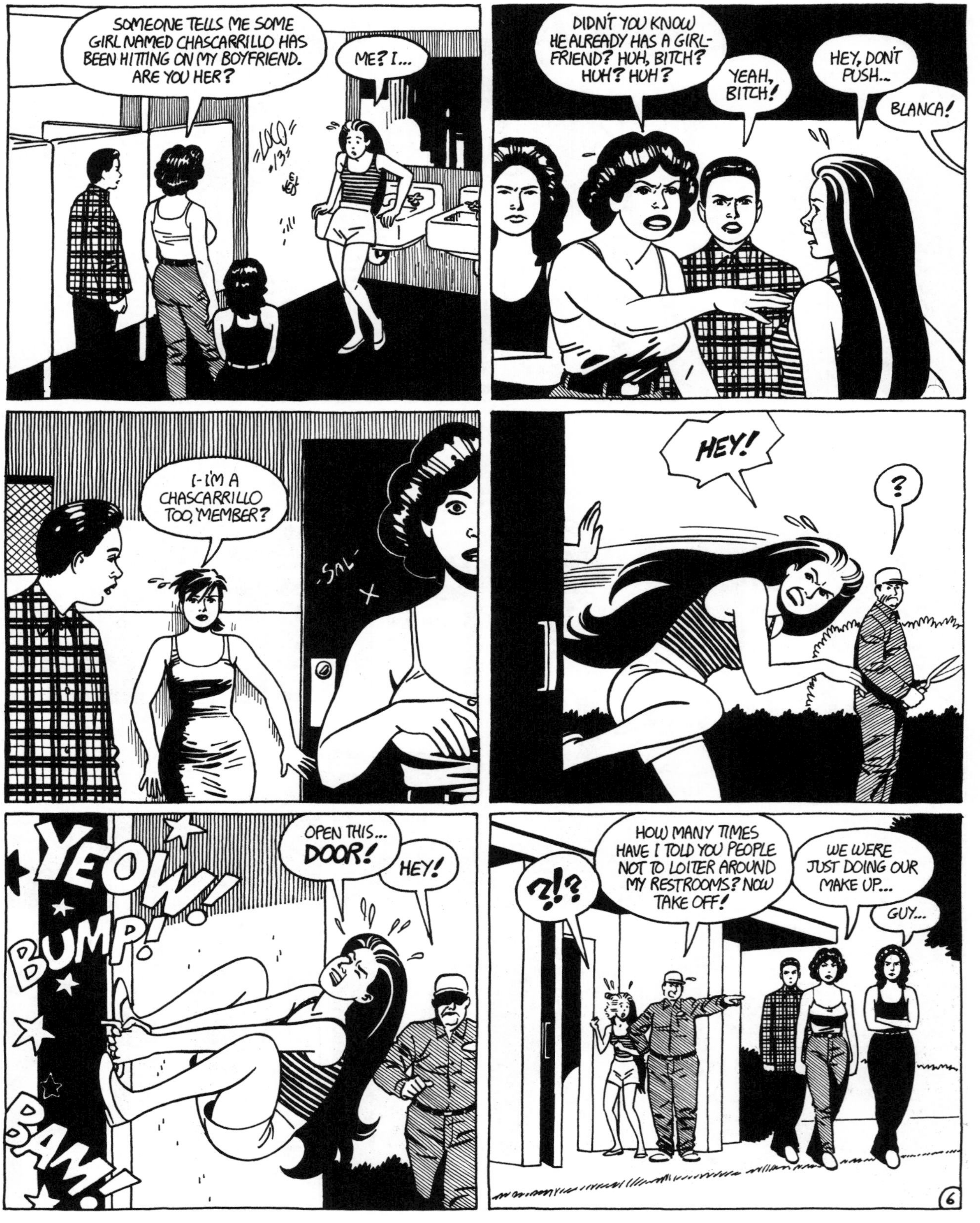
SOMEONE TELLS ME SOME GIRL NAMED CHASCARRILLO HAS BEEN HITTING ON MY BOYFRIEND. ARE YOU HER?
ME? I...
DIDN'T YOU KNOW HE ALREADY HAS A GIRL-FRIEND? HUH, BITCH? HUH? HUH?
YEAH, BITCH!
HEY, DON'T PUSH...
BLANCA!
I-I'M A CHASCARRILLO TOO, 'MEMBER?
HEY!
?
YEOW!
BUMP!
BAM!
OPEN THIS... DOOR!
HEY!
?!?
HOW MANY TIMES HAVE I TOLD YOU PEOPLE NOT TO LOITER AROUND MY RESTROOMS? NOW TAKE OFF!
WE WERE JUST DOING OUR MAKE UP...
GUY...
6

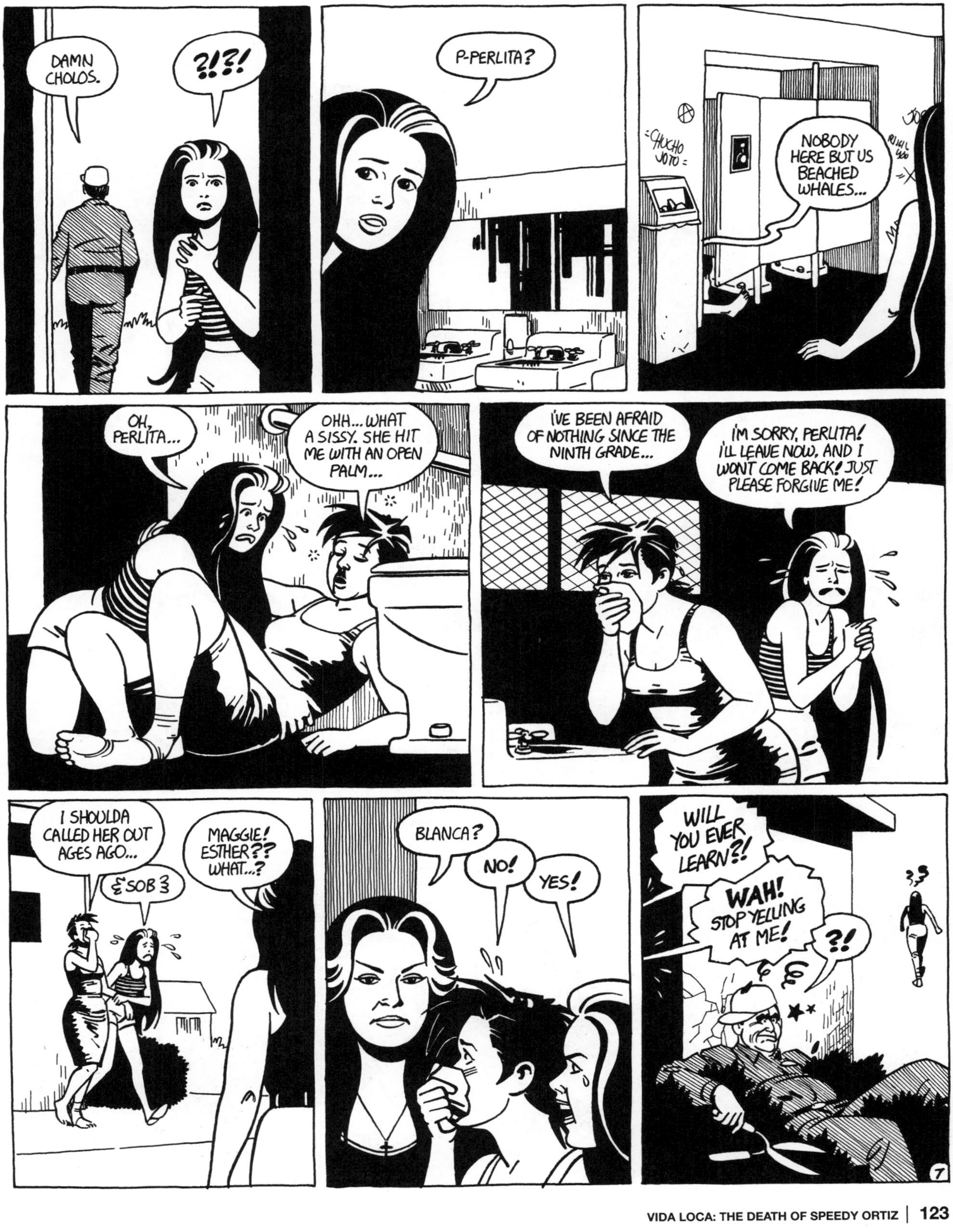
DAMN CHOLOS.
?!?!
P-PERLITA?
=CHUCHO JOTO=
NOBODY HERE BUT US BEACHED WHALES...
OH, PERLITA...
OHH... WHAT A SISSY. SHE HIT ME WITH AN OPEN PALM...
I'VE BEEN AFRAID OF NOTHING SINCE THE NINTH GRADE...
I'M SORRY, PERLITA! I'LL LEAVE NOW, AND I WON'T COME BACK! JUST PLEASE FORGIVE ME!
I SHOULDA CALLED HER OUT AGES AGO...
SOB
MAGGIE! ESTHER?? WHAT...?
BLANCA?
NO!
YES!
WILL YOU EVER LEARN?!
WAH! STOP YELLING AT ME!
?!
7

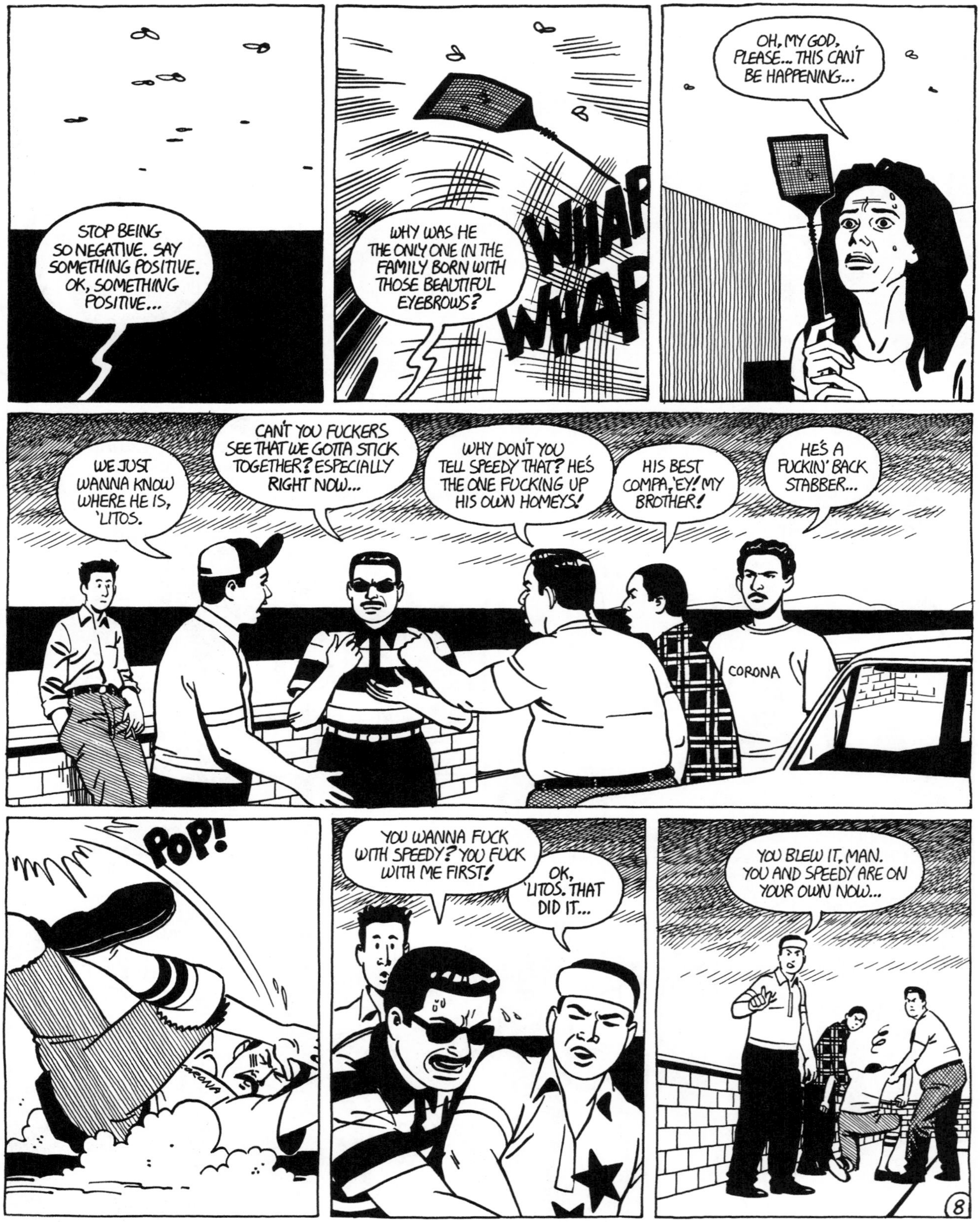
STOP BEING SO NEGATIVE. SAY SOMETHING POSITIVE. OK, SOMETHING POSITIVE...
WHY WAS HE THE ONLY ONE IN THE FAMILY BORN WITH THOSE BEAUTIFUL EYEBROWS?
WHAP
WHAP
OH, MY GOD, PLEASE... THIS CAN'T BE HAPPENING...
WE JUST WANNA KNOW WHERE HE IS, 'LITOS.
CAN'T YOU FUCKERS SEE THAT WE GOTTA STICK TOGETHER? ESPECIALLY RIGHT NOW...
WHY DON'T YOU TELL SPEEDY THAT? HE'S THE ONE FUCKING UP HIS OWN HOMEYS!
HIS BEST COMPA, 'EY! MY BROTHER!
HE'S A FUCKIN' BACK STABBER...
CORONA
POP!
CORONA
YOU WANNA FUCK WITH SPEEDY? YOU FUCK WITH ME FIRST!
OK, 'LITOS. THAT DID IT...
YOU BLEW IT, MAN. YOU AND SPEEDY ARE ON YOUR OWN NOW...
8

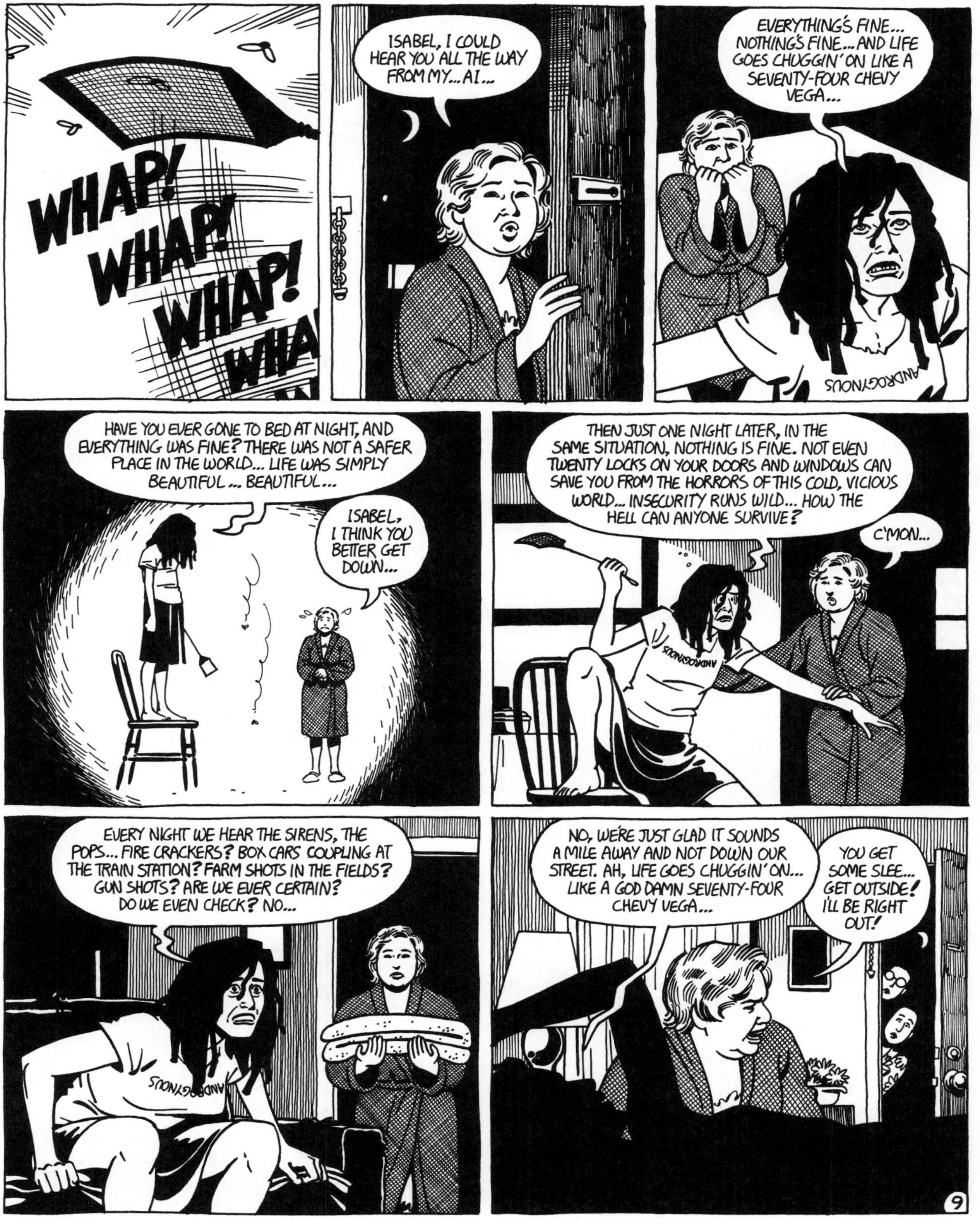
WHAP!
WHAP!
WHAP!
WHA
ISABEL, I COULD HEAR YOU ALL THE WAY FROM MY... AI...
EVERYTHING'S FINE... NOTHING'S FINE... AND LIFE GOES CHUGGIN' ON LIKE A SEVENTY-FOUR CHEVY VEGA...
HAVE YOU EVER GONE TO BED AT NIGHT, AND EVERYTHING WAS FINE? THERE WAS NOT A SAFER PLACE IN THE WORLD... LIFE WAS SIMPLY BEAUTIFUL ... BEAUTIFUL...
ISABEL, I THINK YOU BETTER GET DOWN...
THEN JUST ONE NIGHT LATER, IN THE SAME SITUATION, NOTHING IS FINE. NOT EVEN TWENTY LOCKS ON YOUR DOORS AND WINDOWS CAN SAVE YOU FROM THE HORRORS OF THIS COLD, VICIOUS WORLD... INSECURITY RUNS WILD... HOW THE HELL CAN ANYONE SURVIVE?
C'MON...
EVERY NIGHT WE HEAR THE SIRENS, THE POPS... FIRE CRACKERS? BOX CARS COUPLING AT THE TRAIN STATION? FARM SHOTS IN THE FIELDS? GUN SHOTS? ARE WE EVER CERTAIN? DO WE EVEN CHECK? NO...
NO, WE'RE JUST GLAD IT SOUNDS A MILE AWAY AND NOT DOWN OUR STREET. AH, LIFE GOES CHUGGIN' ON... LIKE A GOD DAMN SEVENTY-FOUR CHEVY VEGA...
YOU GET SOME SLEE... GET OUTSIDE! I'LL BE RIGHT OUT!
9

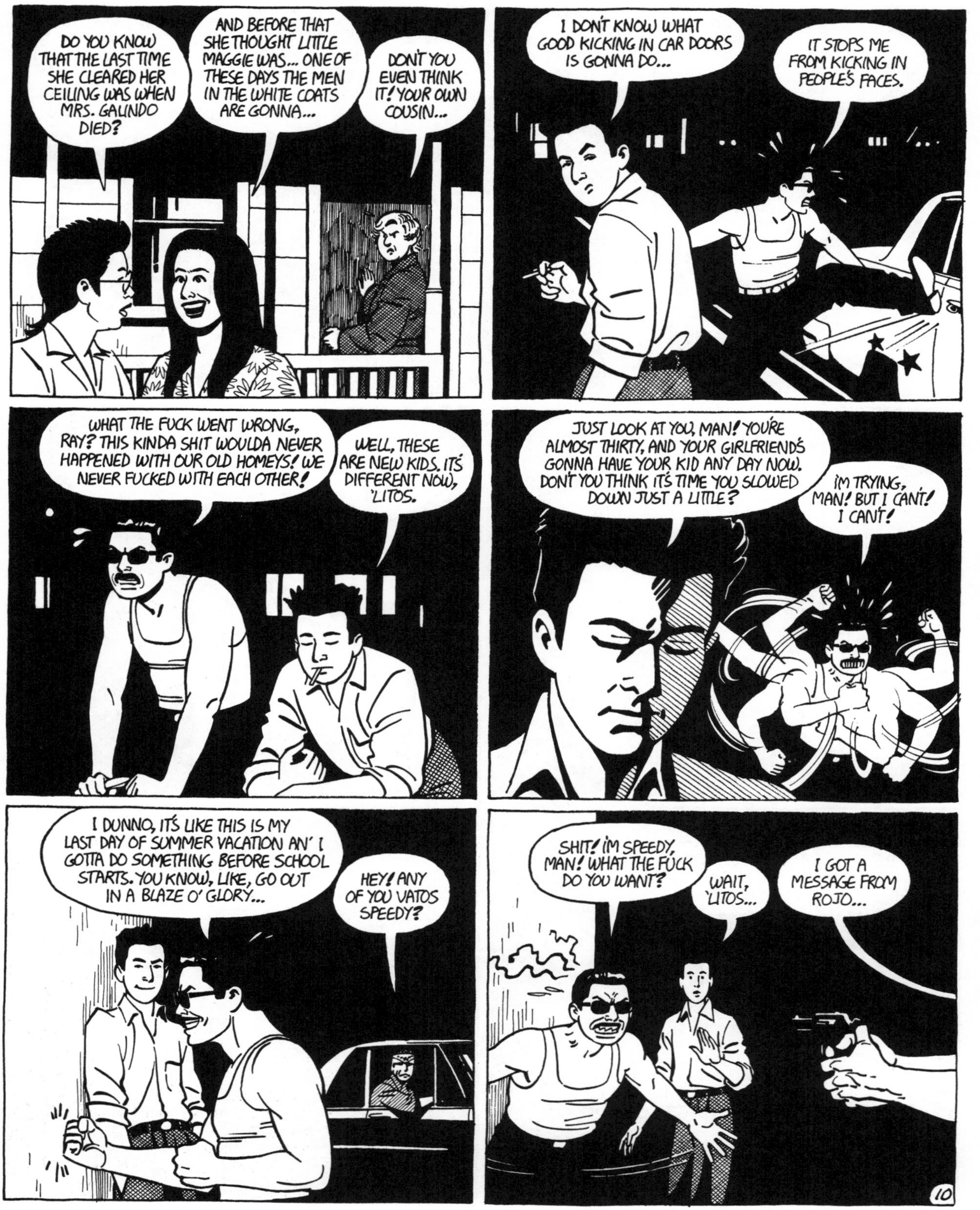

DO YOU KNOW THAT THE LAST TIME SHE CLEARED HER CEILING WAS WHEN MRS. GALINDO DIED?
AND BEFORE THAT SHE THOUGHT LITTLE MAGGIE WAS... ONE OF THESE DAYS THE MEN IN THE WHITE COATS ARE GONNA...
DON'T YOU EVEN THINK IT! YOUR OWN COUSIN...
I DON'T KNOW WHAT GOOD KICKING IN CAR DOORS IS GONNA DO...
IT STOPS ME FROM KICKING IN PEOPLE'S FACES.
WHAT THE FUCK WENT WRONG, RAY? THIS KINDA SHIT WOULDA NEVER HAPPENED WITH OUR OLD HOMEYS! WE NEVER FUCKED WITH EACH OTHER!
WELL, THESE ARE NEW KIDS. IT'S DIFFERENT NOW, 'LITOS.
JUST LOOK AT YOU, MAN! YOU'RE ALMOST THIRTY, AND YOUR GIRLFRIEND'S GONNA HAVE YOUR KID ANY DAY NOW. DON'T YOU THINK IT'S TIME YOU SLOWED DOWN JUST A LITTLE?
I'M TRYING, MAN! BUT I CAN'T! I CAN'T!
I DUNNO, IT'S LIKE THIS IS MY LAST DAY OF SUMMER VACATION AN' I GOTTA DO SOMETHING BEFORE SCHOOL STARTS. YOU KNOW, LIKE, GO OUT IN A BLAZE O' GLORY...
HEY! ANY OF YOU VATOS SPEEDY?
SHIT! I'M SPEEDY, MAN! WHAT THE FUCK DO YOU WANT?
WAIT, 'LITOS...
I GOT A MESSAGE FROM ROJO...
10

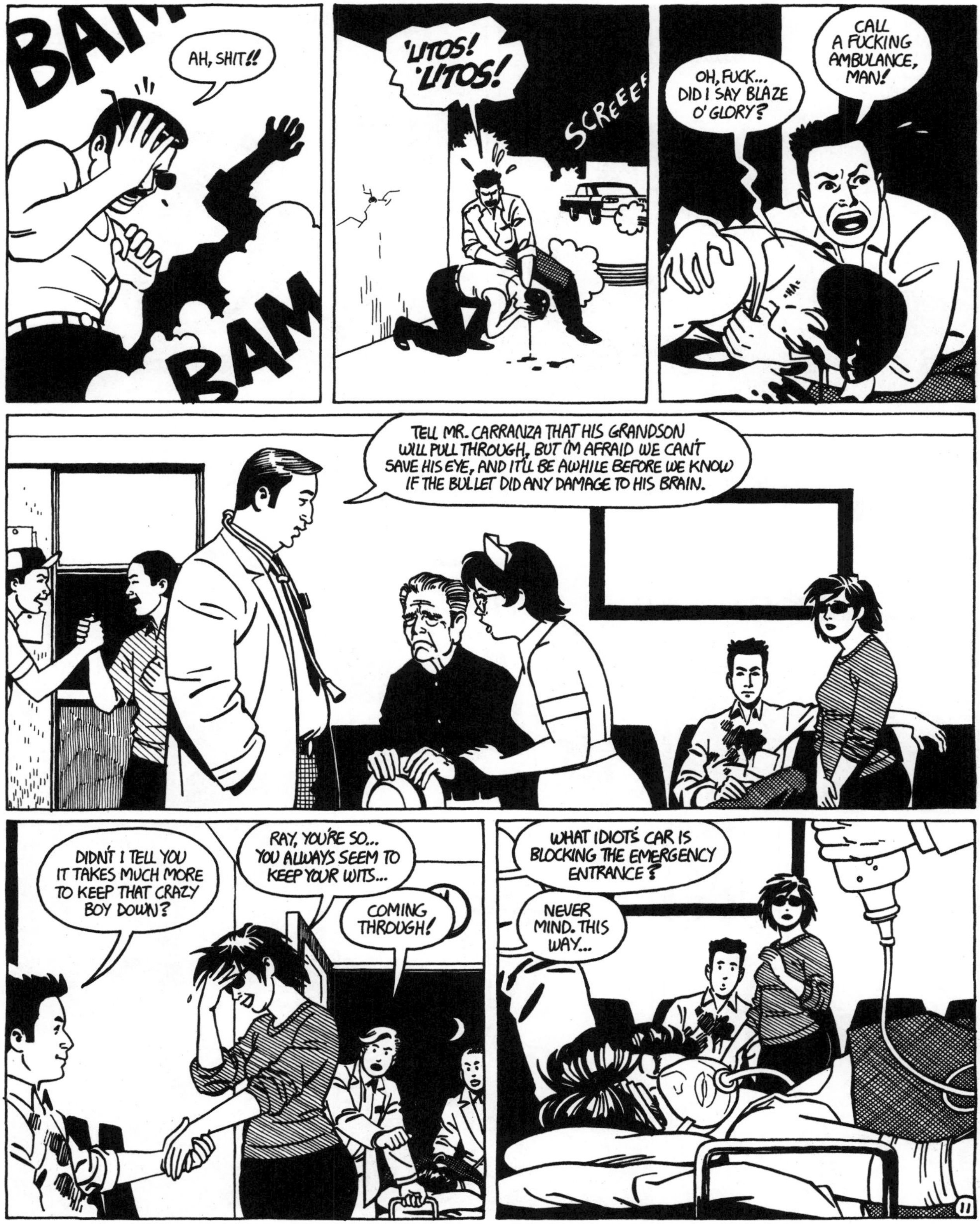
BAM
AH, SHIT!!
BAM
'LITOS! 'LITOS!
SCREEEE
OH, FUCK... DID I SAY BLAZE O' GLORY?
CALL A FUCKING AMBULANCE, MAN!
TELL MR. CARRANZA THAT HIS GRANDSON WILL PULL THROUGH, BUT I'M AFRAID WE CAN'T SAVE HIS EYE, AND IT'LL BE AWHILE BEFORE WE KNOW IF THE BULLET DID ANY DAMAGE TO HIS BRAIN.
DIDN'T I TELL YOU IT TAKES MUCH MORE TO KEEP THAT CRAZY BOY DOWN?
RAY, YOU'RE SO... YOU ALWAYS SEEM TO KEEP YOUR WITS...
COMING THROUGH!
WHAT IDIOT'S CAR IS BLOCKING THE EMERGENCY ENTRANCE?
NEVER MIND. THIS WAY...
11

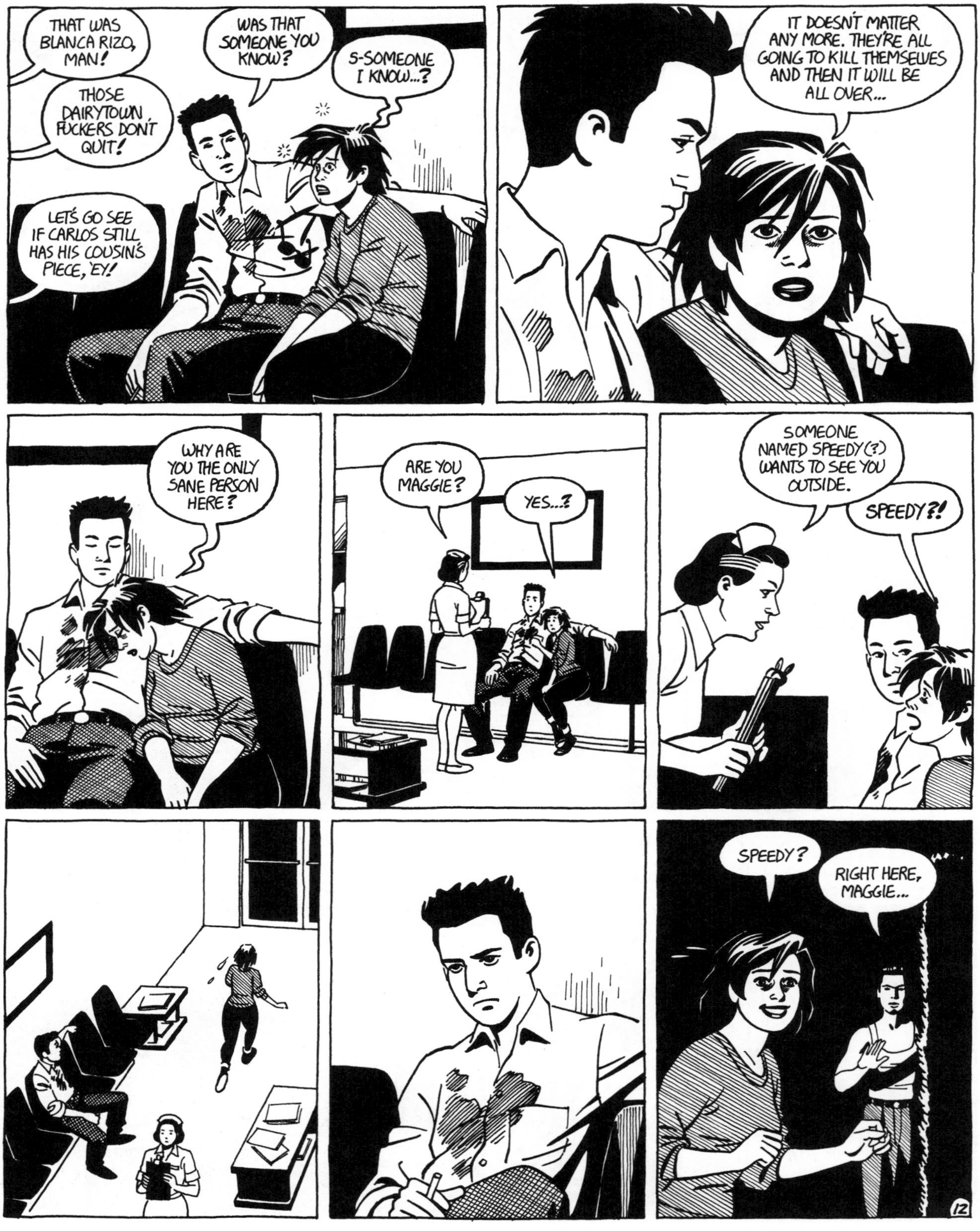
THAT WAS BLANCA RIZO, MAN!
THOSE DAIRYTOWN FUCKERS DON'T QUIT!
WAS THAT SOMEONE YOU KNOW?
S-SOMEONE I KNOW...?
LET'S GO SEE IF CARLOS STILL HAS HIS COUSIN'S PIECE, 'EY!
IT DOESN'T MATTER ANY MORE. THEY'RE ALL GOING TO KILL THEMSELVES AND THEN IT WILL BE ALL OVER...
WHY ARE YOU THE ONLY SANE PERSON HERE?
ARE YOU MAGGIE?
YES...?
SOMEONE NAMED SPEEDY (?) WANTS TO SEE YOU OUTSIDE.
SPEEDY?!
SPEEDY?
RIGHT HERE, MAGGIE...
12

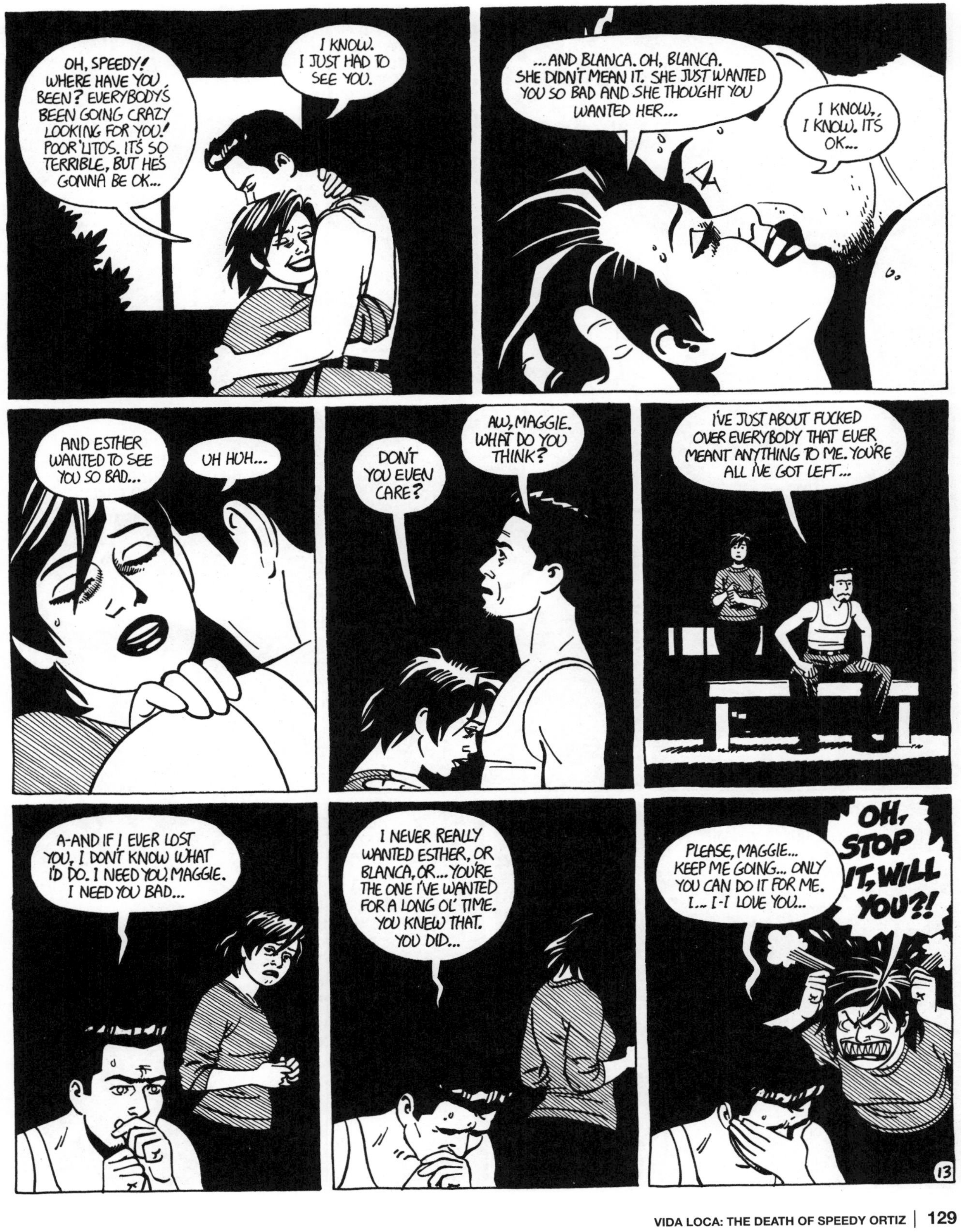
OH, SPEEDY! WHERE HAVE YOU BEEN? EVERYBODY'S BEEN GOING CRAZY LOOKING FOR YOU! POOR 'LITOS. IT'S SO TERRIBLE, BUT HE'S GONNA BE OK...
I KNOW. I JUST HAD TO SEE YOU.
...AND BLANCA. OH, BLANCA. SHE DIDN'T MEAN IT. SHE JUST WANTED YOU SO BAD AND SHE THOUGHT YOU WANTED HER...
I KNOW, I KNOW. IT'S OK...
AND ESTHER WANTED TO SEE YOU SO BAD...
UH HUH...
DON'T YOU EVEN CARE?
AW, MAGGIE. WHAT DO YOU THINK?
I'VE JUST ABOUT FUCKED OVER EVERYBODY THAT EVER MEANT ANYTHING TO ME. YOU'RE ALL I'VE GOT LEFT...
A-AND IF I EVER LOST YOU, I DON'T KNOW WHAT I'D DO. I NEED YOU, MAGGIE. I NEED YOU BAD...
I NEVER REALLY WANTED ESTHER, OR BLANCA, OR... YOU'RE THE ONE I'VE WANTED FOR A LONG OL' TIME. YOU KNEW THAT. YOU DID...
PLEASE, MAGGIE... KEEP ME GOING... ONLY YOU CAN DO IT FOR ME. I... I-I LOVE YOU...
OH, STOP IT, WILL YOU?!
13

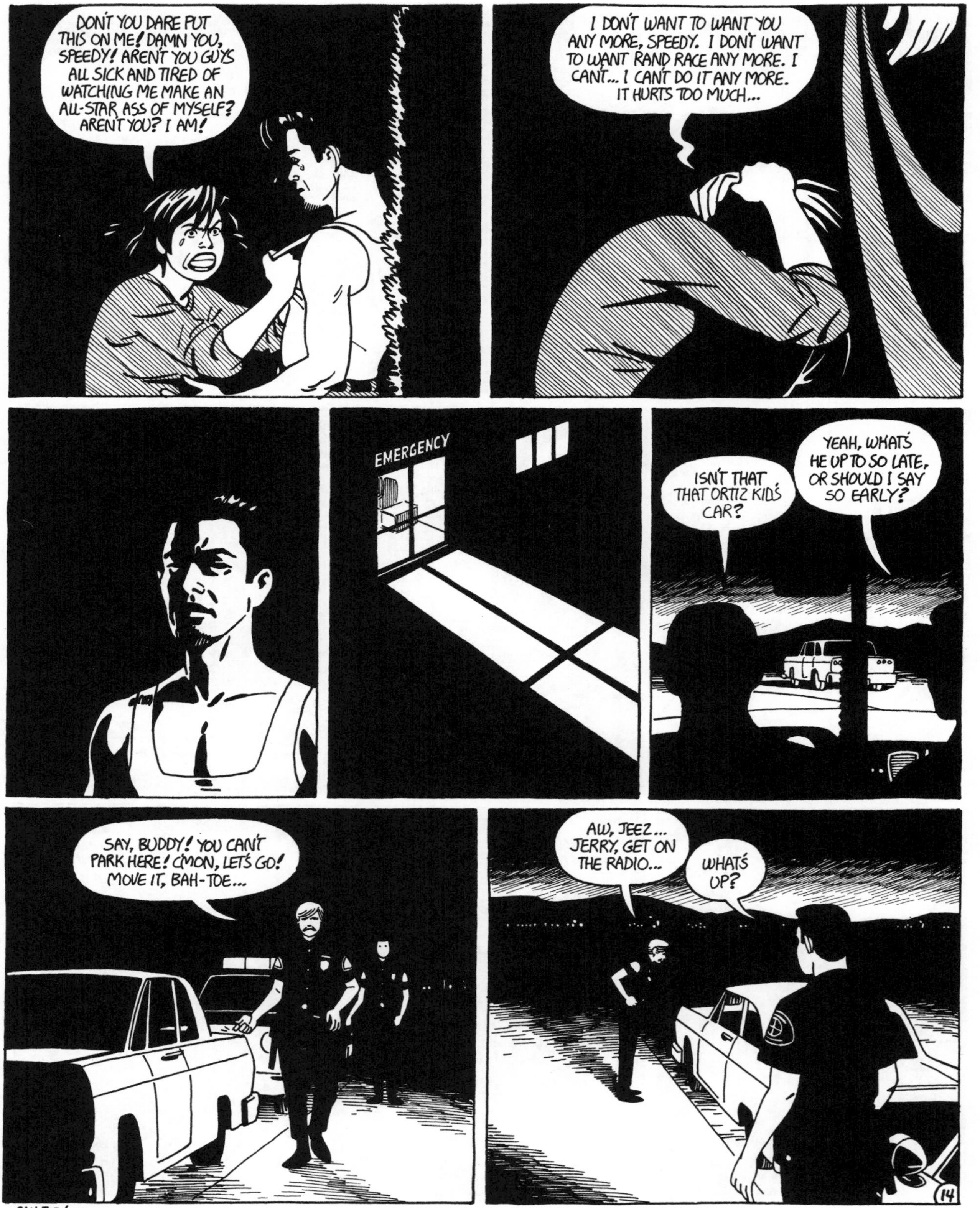
DON'T YOU DARE PUT THIS ON ME! DAMN YOU, SPEEDY! AREN'T YOU GUYS ALL SICK AND TIRED OF WATCHING ME MAKE AN ALL-STAR ASS OF MYSELF? AREN'T YOU? I AM!
I DON'T WANT TO WANT YOU ANY MORE, SPEEDY. I DON'T WANT TO WANT RAND RACE ANY MORE. I CAN'T... I CAN'T DO IT ANY MORE. IT HURTS TOO MUCH...
EMERGENCY
ISN'T THAT THAT ORTIZ KID'S CAR?
YEAH, WHAT'S HE UP TO SO LATE, OR SHOULD I SAY SO EARLY?
SAY, BUDDY! YOU CAN'T PARK HERE! C'MON, LET'S GO! MOVE IT, BAH-TOE...
AW, JEEZ... JERRY, GET ON THE RADIO...
WHAT'S UP?
14

BAH-TOE/VATO

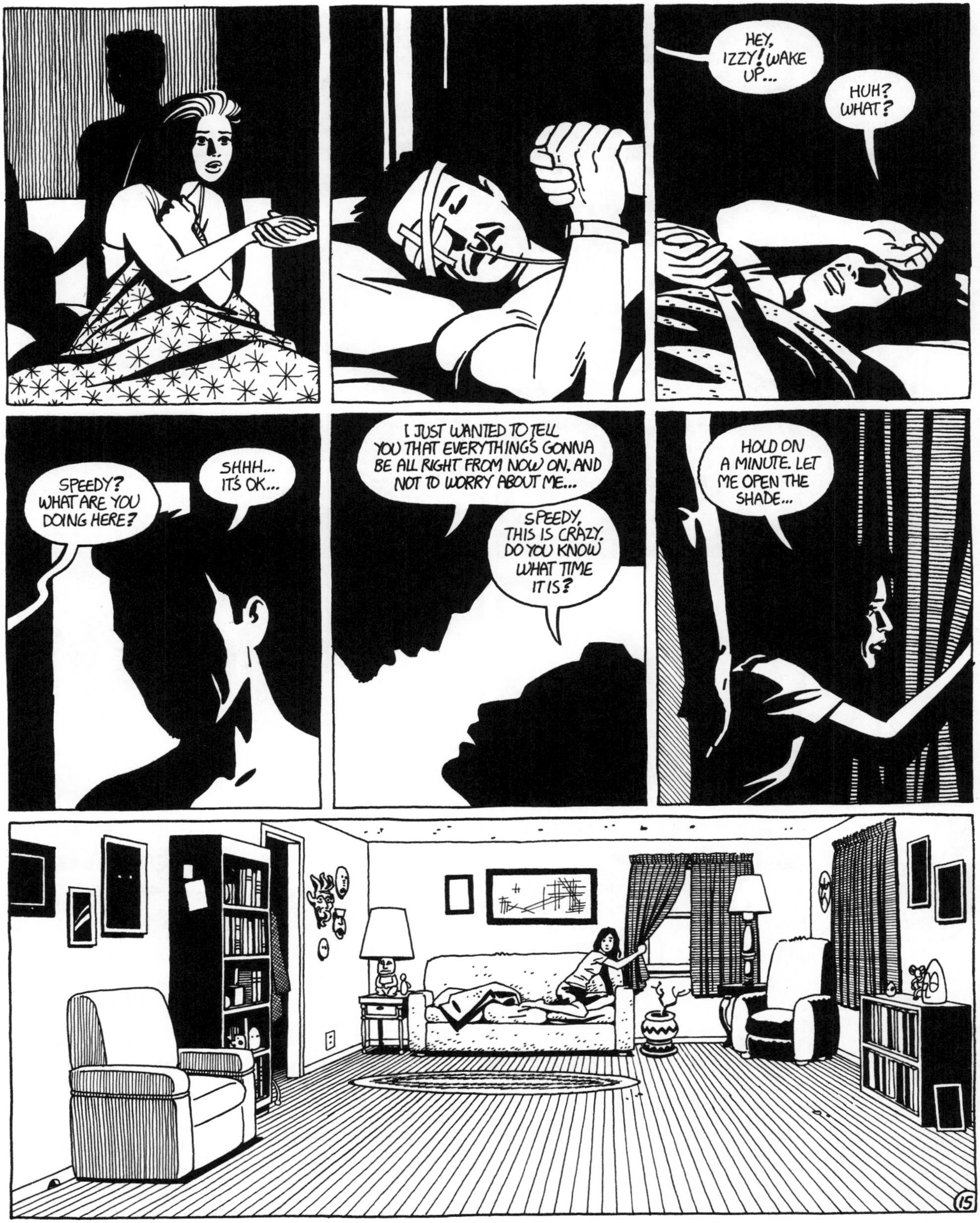
HEY, IZZY! WAKE UP...
HUH? WHAT?
SPEEDY? WHAT ARE YOU DOING HERE?
SHHH... IT'S OK...
I JUST WANTED TO TELL YOU THAT EVERYTHING'S GONNA BE ALL RIGHT FROM NOW ON, AND NOT TO WORRY ABOUT ME...
SPEEDY, THIS IS CRAZY. DO YOU KNOW WHAT TIME IT IS?
HOLD ON A MINUTE. LET ME OPEN THE SHADE...
15

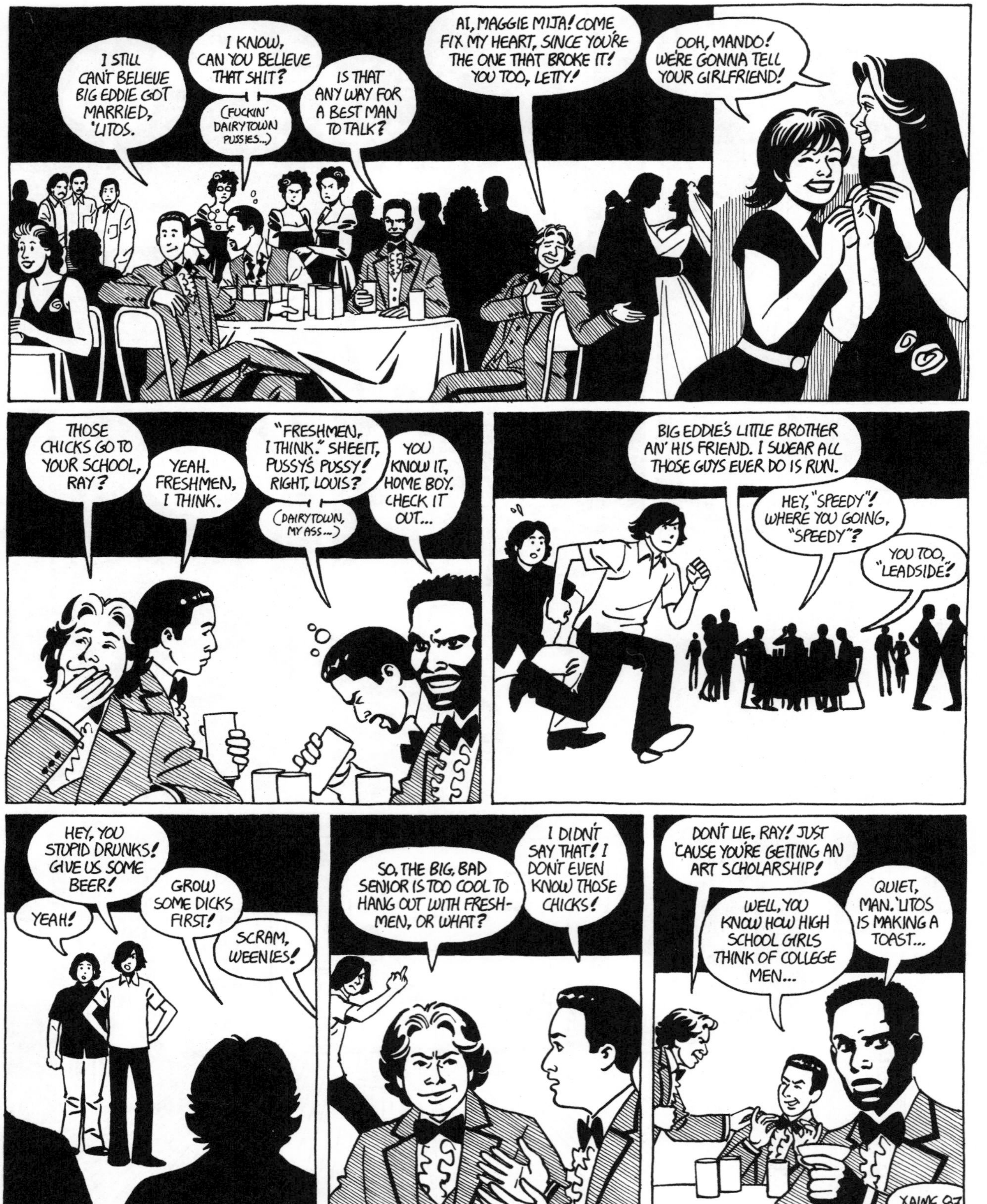
I STILL CAN'T BELIEVE BIG EDDIE GOT MARRIED, 'LITOS.
I KNOW, CAN YOU BELIEVE THAT SHIT?
(FUCKIN' DAIRYTOWN PUSSIES...)
IS THAT ANY WAY FOR A BEST MAN TO TALK?
AI, MAGGIE MIJA! COME FIX MY HEART, SINCE YOU'RE THE ONE THAT BROKE IT! YOU TOO, LETTY!
OOH, MANDO! WE'RE GONNA TELL YOUR GIRLFRIEND!
THOSE CHICKS GO TO YOUR SCHOOL, RAY?
YEAH. FRESHMEN, I THINK.
"FRESHMEN, I THINK." SHEEIT, PUSSY'S PUSSY! RIGHT, LOUIS?
(DAIRYTOWN, MY ASS...)
YOU KNOW IT, HOME BOY. CHECK IT OUT...
BIG EDDIE'S LITTLE BROTHER AN' HIS FRIEND. I SWEAR ALL THOSE GUYS EVER DO IS RUN.
HEY, "SPEEDY"! WHERE YOU GOING, "SPEEDY"?
YOU TOO, "LEADSIDE"!
HEY, YOU STUPID DRUNKS! GIVE US SOME BEER!
YEAH!
GROW SOME DICKS FIRST!
SCRAM, WEENIES!
SO, THE BIG, BAD SENIOR IS TOO COOL TO HANG OUT WITH FRESH-MEN, OR WHAT?
I DIDN'T SAY THAT! I DON'T EVEN KNOW THOSE CHICKS!
DON'T LIE, RAY! JUST 'CAUSE YOU'RE GETTING AN ART SCHOLARSHIP!
WELL, YOU KNOW HOW HIGH SCHOOL GIRLS THINK OF COLLEGE MEN...
QUIET, MAN. 'LITOS IS MAKING A TOAST...
XAIME 87

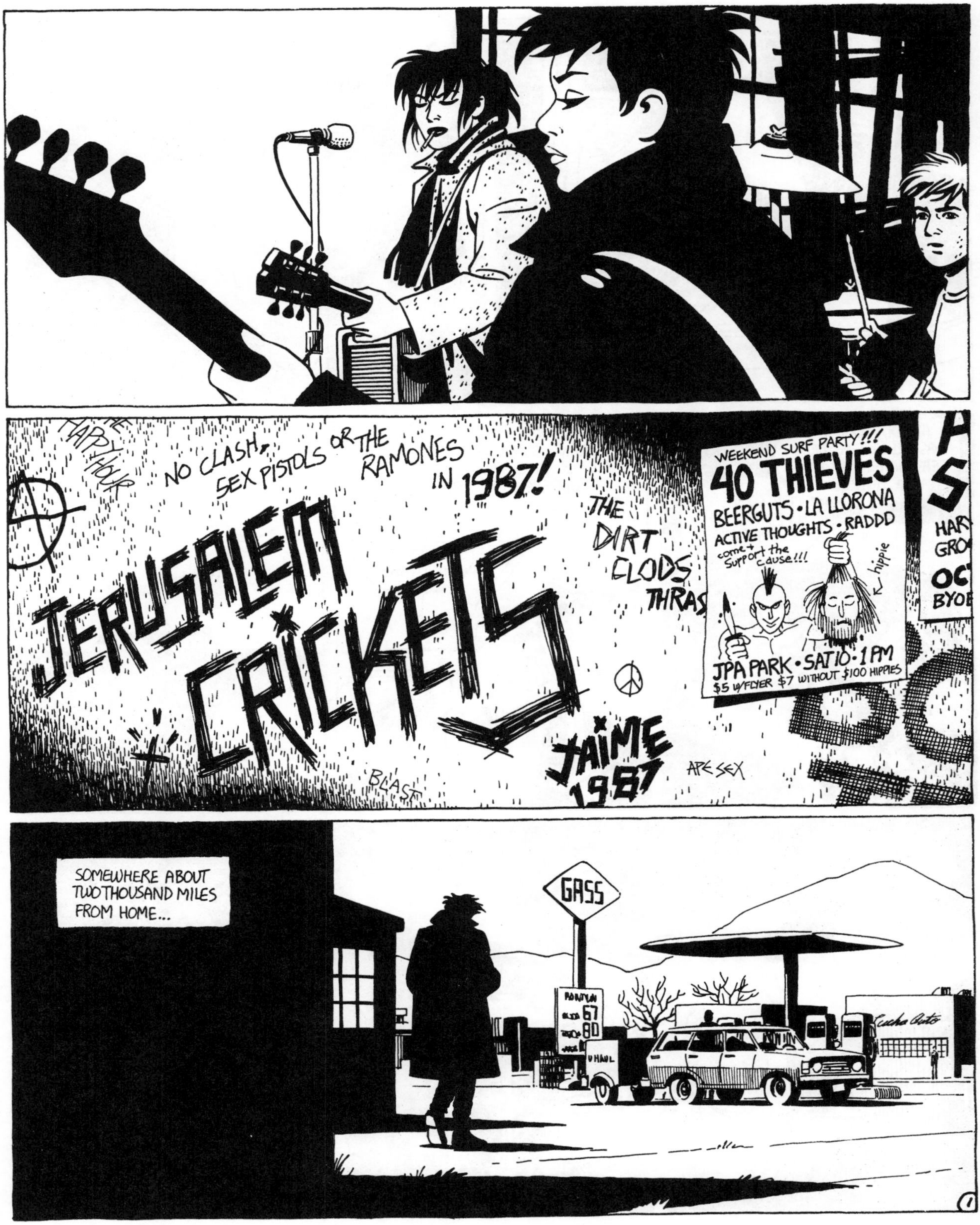
NO CLASH, SEX PISTOLS OR THE RAMONES IN 1987!
HAPPY HOUR
JERUSALEM CRICKETS
THE DIRT CLODS
WEEKEND SURF PARTY!!!
40 THIEVES
BEERGUTS • LA LLORONA
ACTIVE THOUGHTS • RADDD
come + support the cause!!!
hippie
JPA PARK • SAT 10 • 1 PM
$5 W/FLYER $7 WITHOUT $100 HIPPIES
BYOB
JAIME 1987
APE SEX
BLAST
SOMEWHERE ABOUT TWO THOUSAND MILES FROM HOME...
GASS
U HAUL

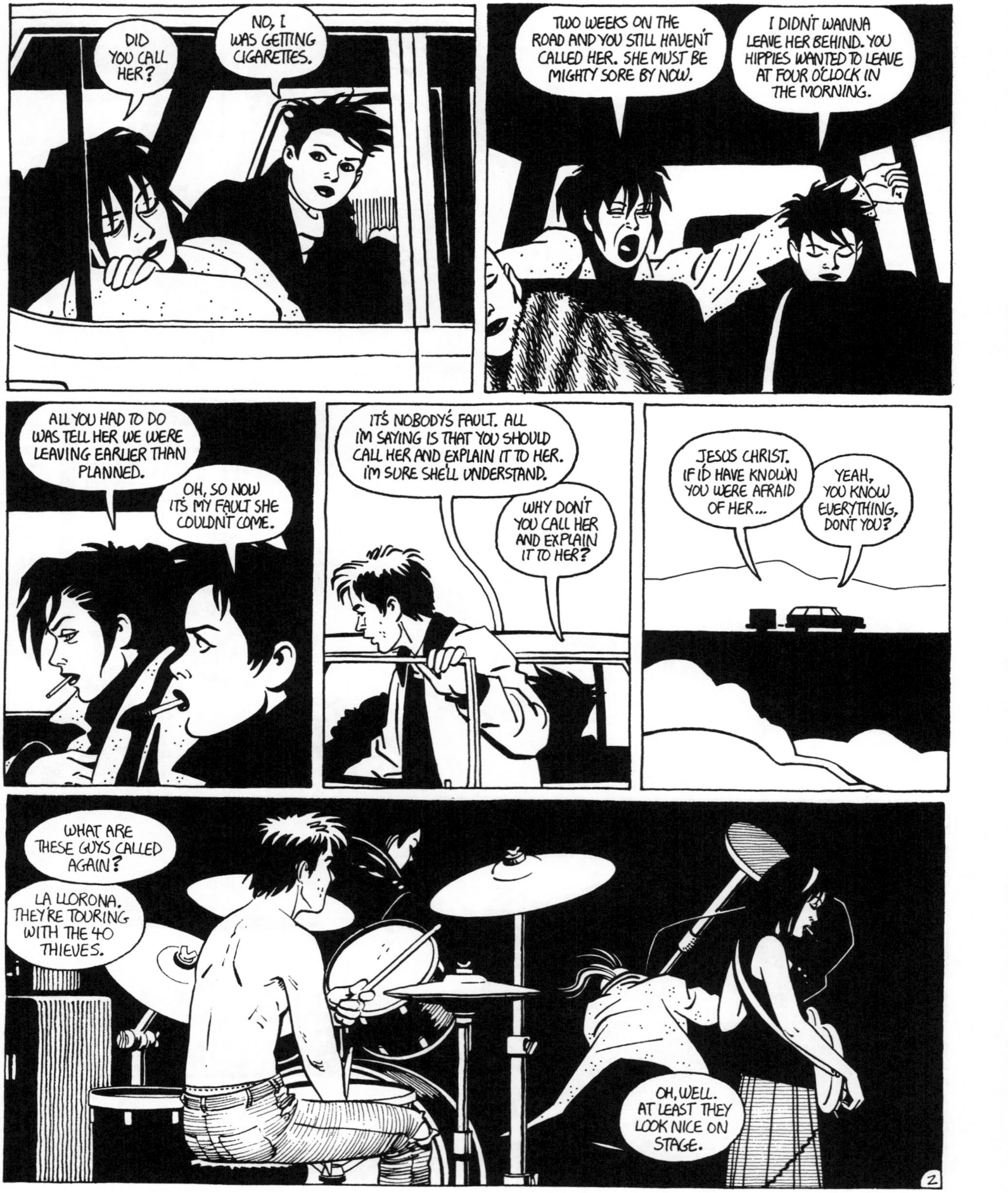
DID YOU CALL HER?
NO, I WAS GETTING CIGARETTES.
TWO WEEKS ON THE ROAD AND YOU STILL HAVEN'T CALLED HER. SHE MUST BE MIGHTY SORE BY NOW.
I DIDN'T WANNA LEAVE HER BEHIND. YOU HIPPIES WANTED TO LEAVE AT FOUR O'CLOCK IN THE MORNING.
ALL YOU HAD TO DO WAS TELL HER WE WERE LEAVING EARLIER THAN PLANNED.
OH, SO NOW IT'S MY FAULT SHE COULDN'T COME.
IT'S NOBODY'S FAULT. ALL I'M SAYING IS THAT YOU SHOULD CALL HER AND EXPLAIN IT TO HER. I'M SURE SHE'LL UNDERSTAND.
WHY DON'T YOU CALL HER AND EXPLAIN IT TO HER?
JESUS CHRIST. IF I'D HAVE KNOWN YOU WERE AFRAID OF HER...
YEAH, YOU KNOW EVERYTHING, DON'T YOU?
WHAT ARE THESE GUYS CALLED AGAIN?
LA LLORONA. THEY'RE TOURING WITH THE 40 THIEVES.
OH, WELL. AT LEAST THEY LOOK NICE ON STAGE.
2

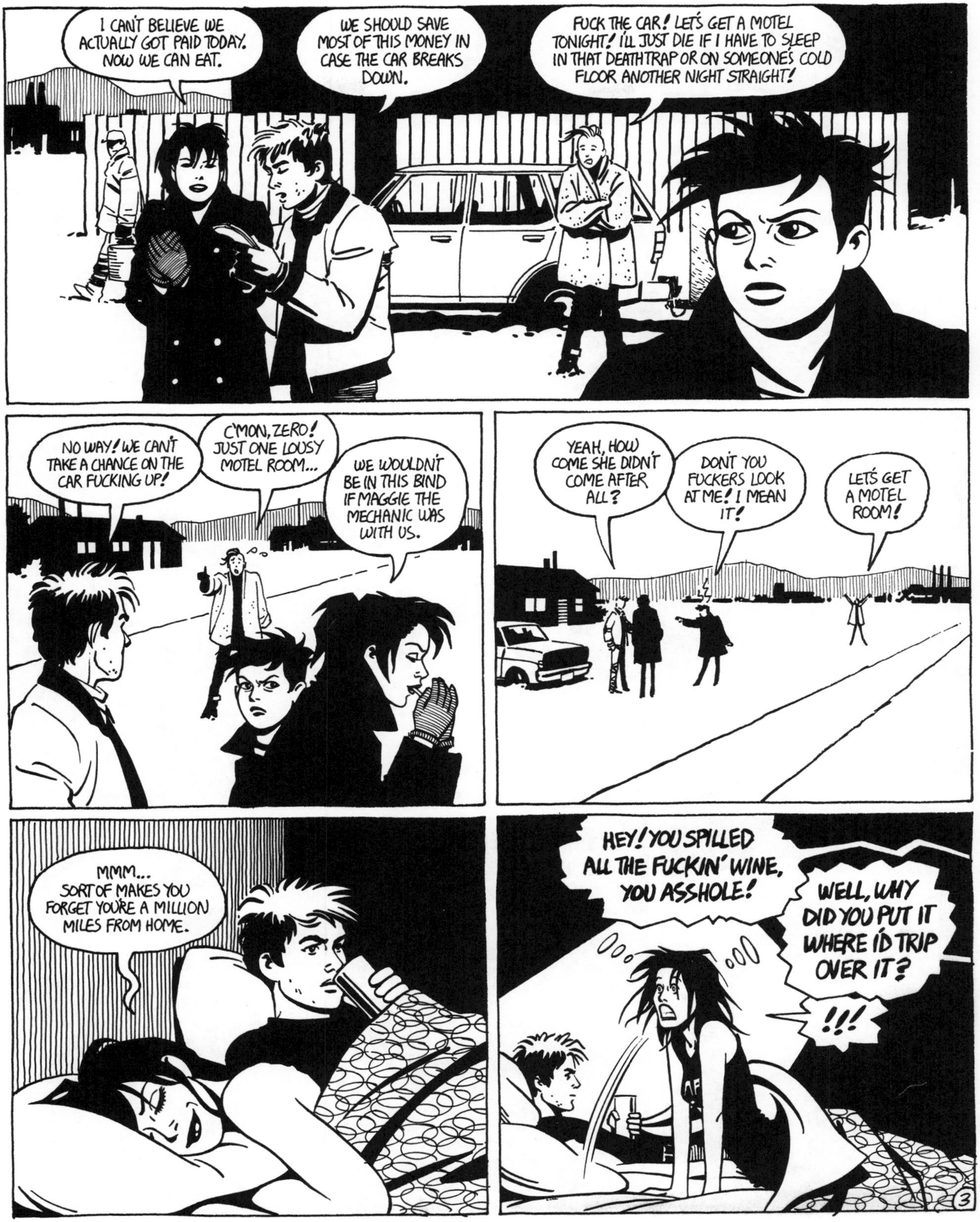
I CAN'T BELIEVE WE ACTUALLY GOT PAID TODAY. NOW WE CAN EAT.
WE SHOULD SAVE MOST OF THIS MONEY IN CASE THE CAR BREAKS DOWN.
FUCK THE CAR! LET'S GET A MOTEL TONIGHT! I'LL JUST DIE IF I HAVE TO SLEEP IN THAT DEATHTRAP OR ON SOMEONE'S COLD FLOOR ANOTHER NIGHT STRAIGHT!
NO WAY! WE CAN'T TAKE A CHANCE ON THE CAR FUCKING UP!
C'MON, ZERO! JUST ONE LOUSY MOTEL ROOM...
WE WOULDN'T BE IN THIS BIND IF MAGGIE THE MECHANIC WAS WITH US.
YEAH, HOW COME SHE DIDN'T COME AFTER ALL?
DON'T YOU FUCKERS LOOK AT ME! I MEAN IT!
LET'S GET A MOTEL ROOM!
MMM... SORT OF MAKES YOU FORGET YOU'RE A MILLION MILES FROM HOME.
HEY! YOU SPILLED ALL THE FUCKIN' WINE, YOU ASSHOLE!
WELL, WHY DID YOU PUT IT WHERE I'D TRIP OVER IT?
!!!
3

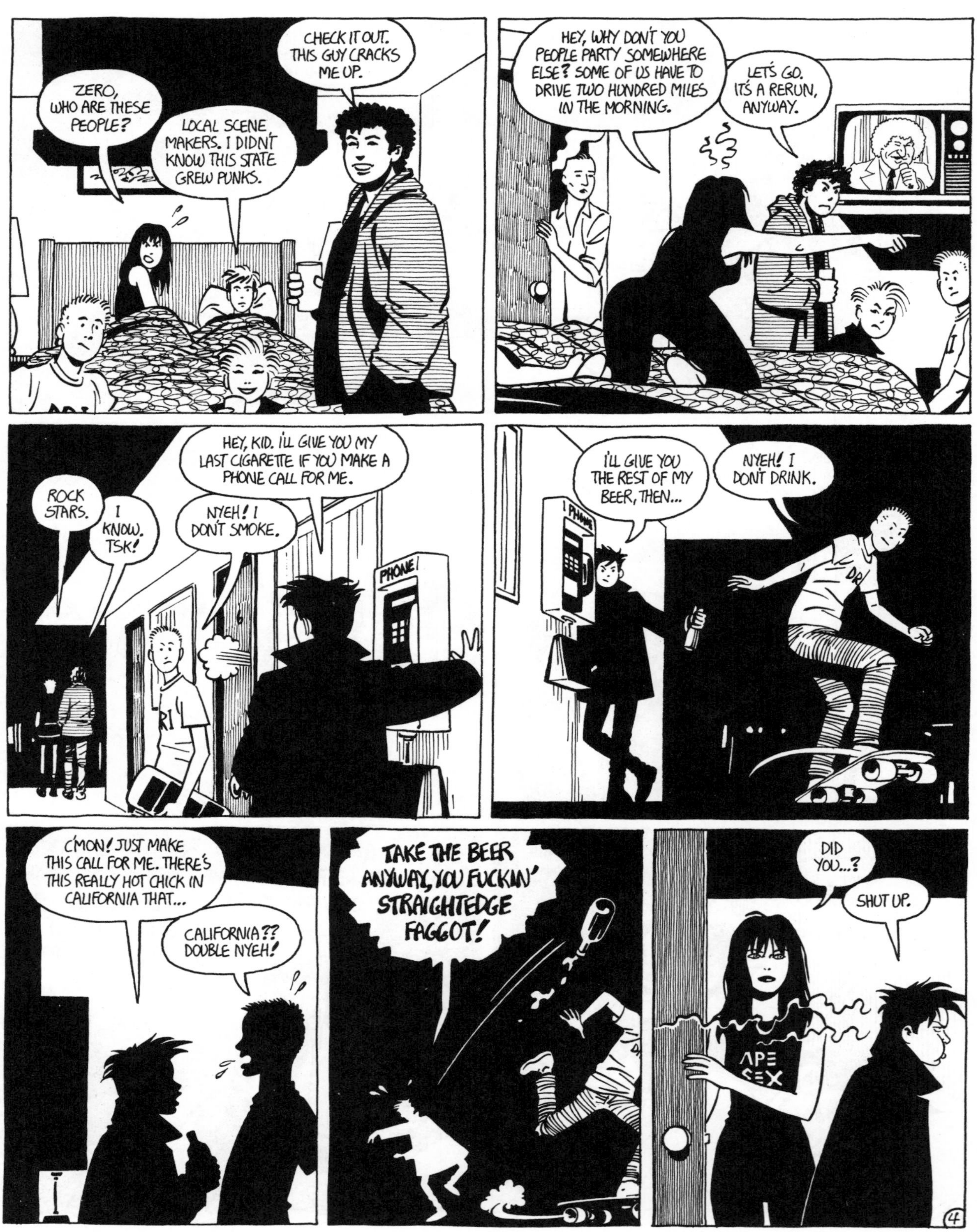
ZERO, WHO ARE THESE PEOPLE?
LOCAL SCENE MAKERS. I DIDN'T KNOW THIS STATE GREW PUNKS.
CHECK IT OUT. THIS GUY CRACKS ME UP.
HEY, WHY DON'T YOU PEOPLE PARTY SOMEWHERE ELSE? SOME OF US HAVE TO DRIVE TWO HUNDRED MILES IN THE MORNING.
LET'S GO. IT'S A RERUN, ANYWAY.
ROCK STARS.
I KNOW. TSK!
HEY, KID. I'LL GIVE YOU MY LAST CIGARETTE IF YOU MAKE A PHONE CALL FOR ME.
NYEH! I DON'T SMOKE.
PHONE
I'LL GIVE YOU THE REST OF MY BEER, THEN...
NYEH! I DON'T DRINK.
C'MON! JUST MAKE THIS CALL FOR ME. THERE'S THIS REALLY HOT CHICK IN CALIFORNIA THAT...
CALIFORNIA?? DOUBLE NYEH!
TAKE THE BEER ANYWAY, YOU FUCKIN' STRAIGHTEDGE FAGGOT!
DID YOU...?
SHUT UP.
APE SEX
4

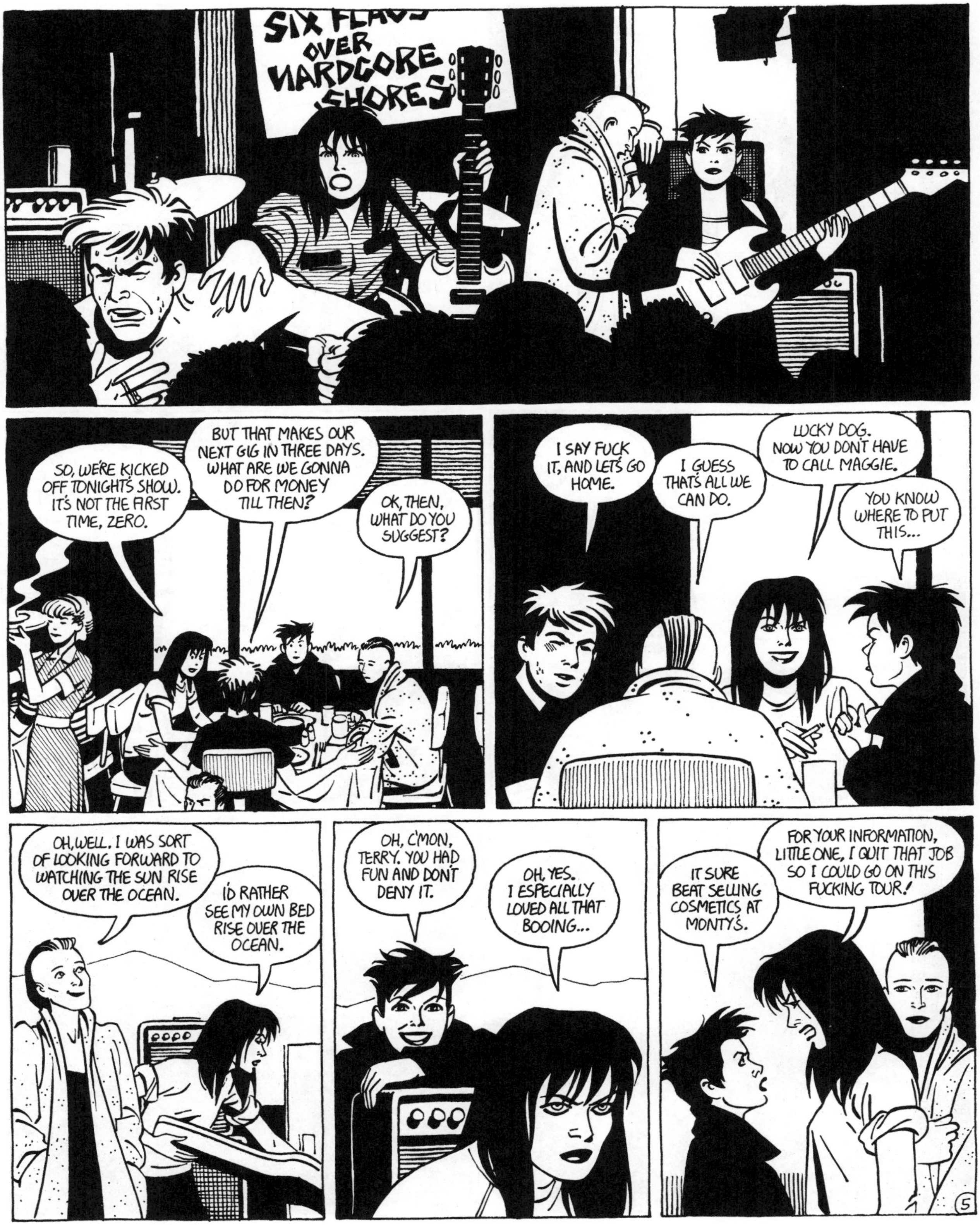
SIX FLAGS OVER HARDCORE SHORES
SO, WE'RE KICKED OFF TONIGHT'S SHOW. IT'S NOT THE FIRST TIME, ZERO.
BUT THAT MAKES OUR NEXT GIG IN THREE DAYS. WHAT ARE WE GONNA DO FOR MONEY TILL THEN?
OK, THEN, WHAT DO YOU SUGGEST?
I SAY FUCK IT, AND LET'S GO HOME.
I GUESS THAT'S ALL WE CAN DO.
LUCKY DOG. NOW YOU DON'T HAVE TO CALL MAGGIE.
YOU KNOW WHERE TO PUT THIS...
OH, WELL. I WAS SORT OF LOOKING FORWARD TO WATCHING THE SUN RISE OVER THE OCEAN.
I'D RATHER SEE MY OWN BED RISE OVER THE OCEAN.
OH, C'MON, TERRY. YOU HAD FUN AND DON'T DENY IT.
OH, YES. I ESPECIALLY LOVED ALL THAT BOOING...
IT SURE BEAT SELLING COSMETICS AT MONTY'S.
FOR YOUR INFORMATION, LITTLE ONE, I QUIT THAT JOB SO I COULD GO ON THIS FUCKING TOUR!
5

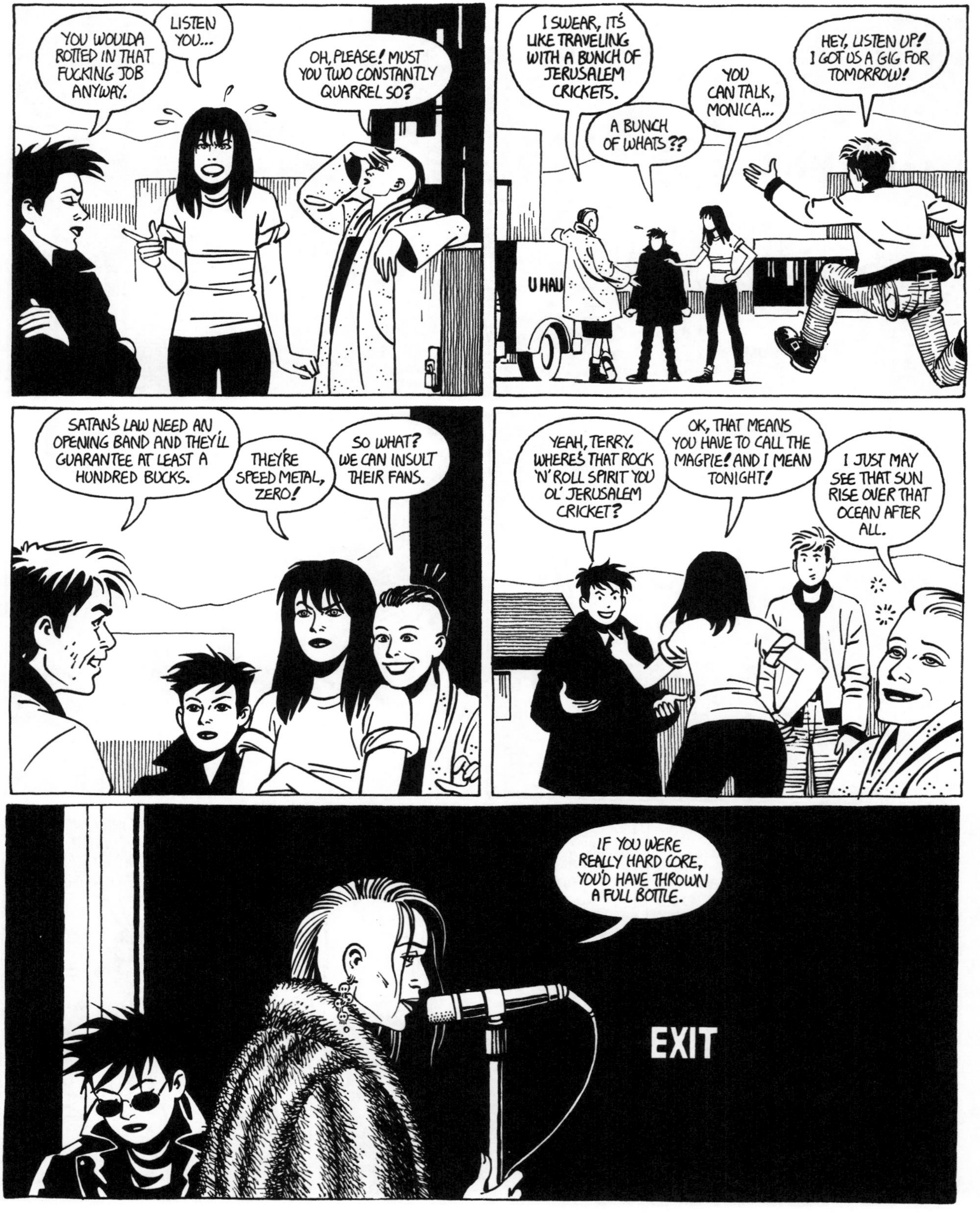
YOU WOULDA ROTTED IN THAT FUCKING JOB ANYWAY.
LISTEN YOU...
OH, PLEASE! MUST YOU TWO CONSTANTLY QUARREL SO?
I SWEAR, IT'S LIKE TRAVELING WITH A BUNCH OF JERUSALEM CRICKETS.
A BUNCH OF WHATS??
YOU CAN TALK, MONICA...
HEY, LISTEN UP! I GOT US A GIG FOR TOMORROW!
U HAU
SATAN'S LAW NEED AN OPENING BAND AND THEY'LL GUARANTEE AT LEAST A HUNDRED BUCKS.
THEY'RE SPEED METAL, ZERO!
SO WHAT? WE CAN INSULT THEIR FANS.
YEAH, TERRY. WHERE'S THAT ROCK 'N' ROLL SPIRIT YOU OL' JERUSALEM CRICKET?
OK, THAT MEANS YOU HAVE TO CALL THE MAGPIE! AND I MEAN TONIGHT!
I JUST MAY SEE THAT SUN RISE OVER THAT OCEAN AFTER ALL.
IF YOU WERE REALLY HARD CORE, YOU'D HAVE THROWN A FULL BOTTLE.
EXIT

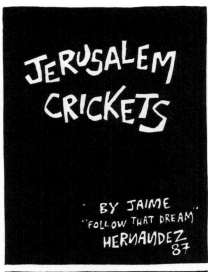

JERUSALEM CRICKETS

BY JAIME
"FOLLOW THAT DREAM"
HERNANDEZ
'87

TERRY, I GOTTA HELP LOAD UP OUR SHIT!

IT CAN WAIT. COME ON.

YOU HAVE A CHOICE. TELEPHONE OR LETTER.

LETTER.

WHY ARE YOU SO ANXIOUS FOR ME TO WRITE THE MAGPIE? YOU HATE HER!

YOU HAVE TO CLEAR MY GOOD NAME, LOVE...

YFM

I JUST KNOW SHE THINKS I'M THE ONE RESPONSIBLE FOR LEAVING HER BEHIND ON THIS TOUR.

I KNEW IT WAS MORE THAN JUST THINKING OF MAGGIE...

I AM THINKING OF MAGGIE. SHE STILL MUST BE HEARTBROKEN WITHOUT A WORD FROM YOU YET.

SURE, SURE, OK.

DAMN! HOW DOES ANYONE START ONE OF THESE THINGS?

"DEAREST MAGPIE..."

"SORRY I COULDN'T GET IN TOUCH WITH YOU EARLIER, BUT THIS PAST MONTH HAS BEEN VERY HECTIC FOR OUR BAND..."

HOW DO YOU SPELL "HECTIC"?

"BY THE WAY, WE'RE ALSO SORRY YOU COULDN'T COME WITH US, BUT WE HAD TO GET AN EARLY START, AND YOU..."

SHE'S NOT GONNA BUY THAT!

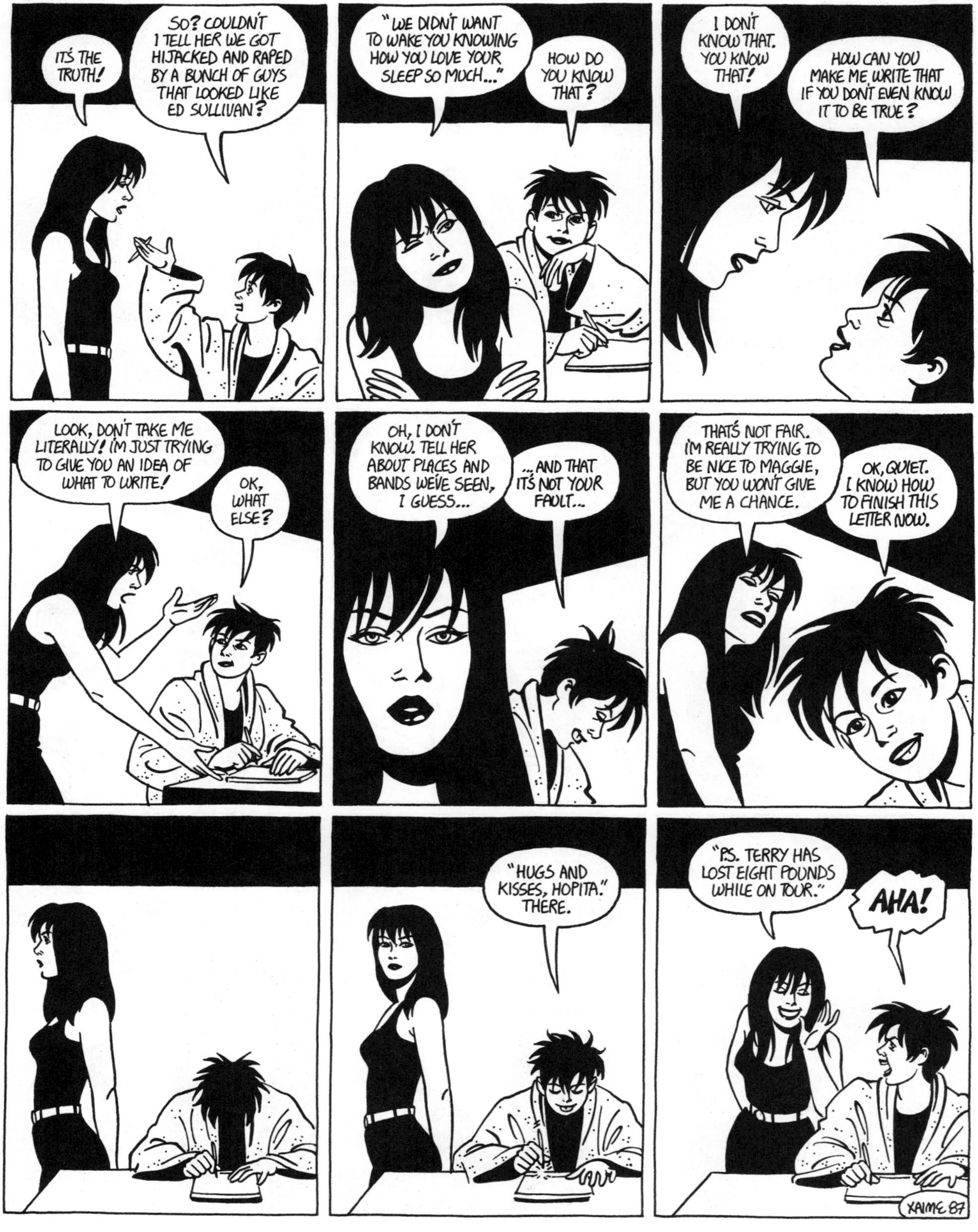
IT'S THE TRUTH!
SO? COULDN'T I TELL HER WE GOT HIJACKED AND RAPED BY A BUNCH OF GUYS THAT LOOKED LIKE ED SULLIVAN?
"WE DIDN'T WANT TO WAKE YOU KNOWING HOW YOU LOVE YOUR SLEEP SO MUCH..."
HOW DO YOU KNOW THAT?
I DON'T KNOW THAT. YOU KNOW THAT!
HOW CAN YOU MAKE ME WRITE THAT IF YOU DON'T EVEN KNOW IT TO BE TRUE?
LOOK, DON'T TAKE ME LITERALLY! I'M JUST TRYING TO GIVE YOU AN IDEA OF WHAT TO WRITE!
OK, WHAT ELSE?
OH, I DON'T KNOW. TELL HER ABOUT PLACES AND BANDS WE'VE SEEN, I GUESS...
...AND THAT IT'S NOT YOUR FAULT...
THAT'S NOT FAIR. I'M REALLY TRYING TO BE NICE TO MAGGIE, BUT YOU WON'T GIVE ME A CHANCE.
OK, QUIET. I KNOW HOW TO FINISH THIS LETTER NOW.
"HUGS AND KISSES, HOPITA." THERE.
"P.S. TERRY HAS LOST EIGHT POUNDS WHILE ON TOUR."
AHA!
XAIME 87

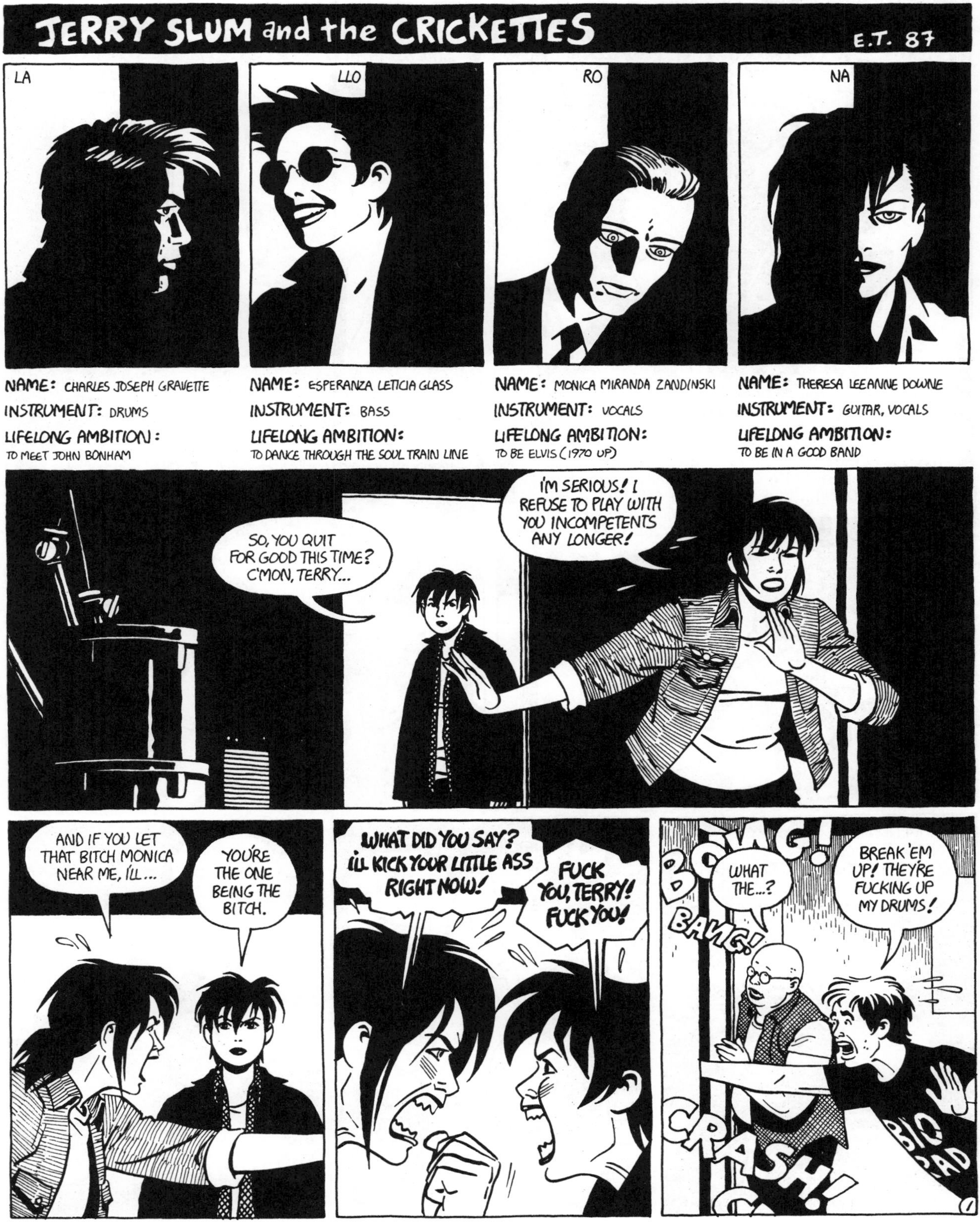
JERRY SLUM and the CRICKETTES
E.T. 87
LA
LLO
RO
NA
NAME: CHARLES JOSEPH GRAVETTE
INSTRUMENT: DRUMS
LIFELONG AMBITION: TO MEET JOHN BONHAM
NAME: ESPERANZA LETICIA GLASS
INSTRUMENT: BASS
LIFELONG AMBITION: TO DANCE THROUGH THE SOUL TRAIN LINE
NAME: MONICA MIRANDA ZANDINSKI
INSTRUMENT: VOCALS
LIFELONG AMBITION: TO BE ELVIS (1970 UP)
NAME: THERESA LEEANNE DOWNE
INSTRUMENT: GUITAR, VOCALS
LIFELONG AMBITION: TO BE IN A GOOD BAND
SO, YOU QUIT FOR GOOD THIS TIME? C'MON, TERRY...
I'M SERIOUS! I REFUSE TO PLAY WITH YOU INCOMPETENTS ANY LONGER!
AND IF YOU LET THAT BITCH MONICA NEAR ME, I'LL...
YOU'RE THE ONE BEING THE BITCH.
WHAT DID YOU SAY? I'LL KICK YOUR LITTLE ASS RIGHT NOW!
FUCK YOU, TERRY! FUCK YOU!
WHAT THE...?
BREAK 'EM UP! THEY'RE FUCKING UP MY DRUMS!
BANG!
CRASH!
1

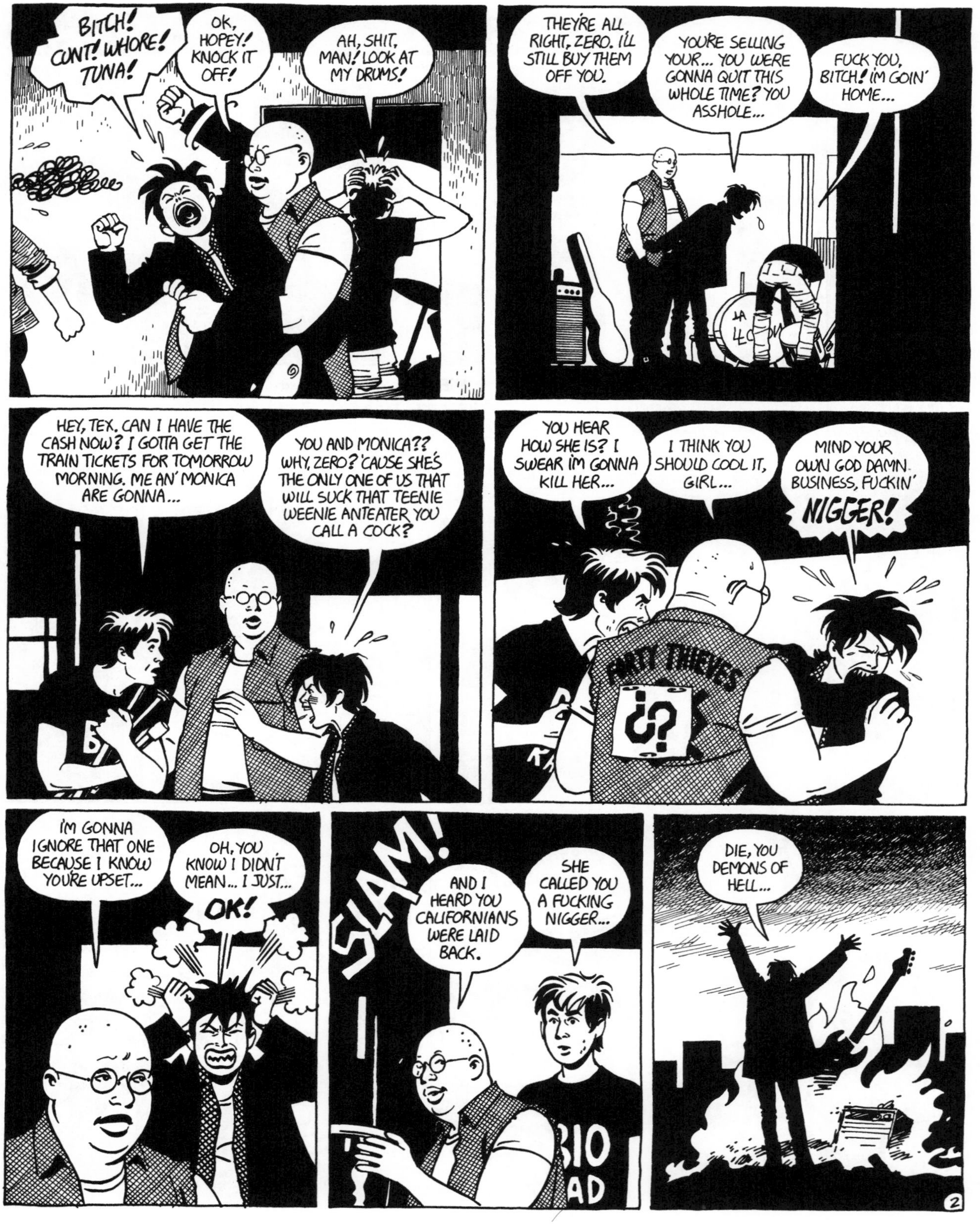
BITCH! CUNT! WHORE! TUNA!
OK, HOPEY! KNOCK IT OFF!
AH, SHIT, MAN! LOOK AT MY DRUMS!
THEY'RE ALL RIGHT, ZERO. I'LL STILL BUY THEM OFF YOU.
YOU'RE SELLING YOUR... YOU WERE GONNA QUIT THIS WHOLE TIME? YOU ASSHOLE...
FUCK YOU, BITCH! I'M GOIN' HOME...
HEY, TEX. CAN I HAVE THE CASH NOW? I GOTTA GET THE TRAIN TICKETS FOR TOMORROW MORNING. ME AN' MONICA ARE GONNA...
YOU AND MONICA?? WHY, ZERO? 'CAUSE SHE'S THE ONLY ONE OF US THAT WILL SUCK THAT TEENIE WEENIE ANTEATER YOU CALL A COCK?
YOU HEAR HOW SHE IS? I SWEAR I'M GONNA KILL HER...
I THINK YOU SHOULD COOL IT, GIRL...
MIND YOUR OWN GOD DAMN BUSINESS, FUCKIN' NIGGER!
I'M GONNA IGNORE THAT ONE BECAUSE I KNOW YOU'RE UPSET...
OH, YOU KNOW I DIDN'T MEAN... I JUST... OK!
SLAM!
AND I HEARD YOU CALIFORNIANS WERE LAID BACK.
SHE CALLED YOU A FUCKING NIGGER...
DIE, YOU DEMONS OF HELL...
2

YOU KNOW, YOU COULD HAVE SOLD THEM AND BOUGHT A TRAIN TICKET, TOO...
SHIT, I'D HAVE TO PAY SOMEONE TO TAKE 'EM.
I JUST CAME BY TO TELL YOU THAT TERRY JOINED THE FORTY THIEVES FOR THE REST OF THE TOUR, AND THEY'RE LEAVING THE CAR TO YOU...
OH, JOY. IT'S BEEN BROKEN DOWN FOR A WEEK. DAMN, WHERE'S A MECHANIC WHEN YOU NEED ONE?
COLE
KAFF
KAFF
KAFF
KAFF
KAFF
OOTAH! IF I SPEND ONE MORE NIGHT IN THIS THING, I'M SERIOUSLY GONNA TURN INTO HANK QUINLAN'S TWIN!
YOU GOT AN EXTRA BACK SEAT IN THERE?
KAFF KAFF
WHAT HAPPENED, TEXAS? YOU RUN AWAY FROM THE BATSHELDER HOTEL, OR WHAT?
PIGS RAIDED IT. I THINK I WAS THE ONLY ONE THAT GOT OUT... MINUS MY DRUMS!
3

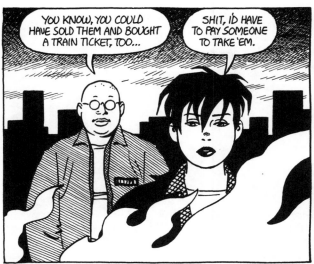

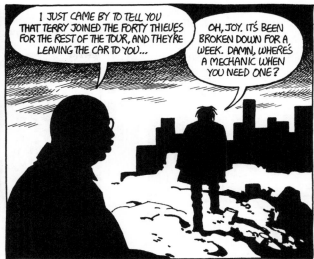

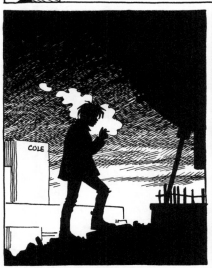

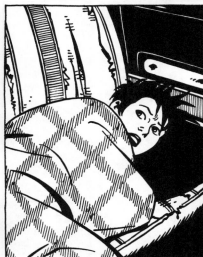

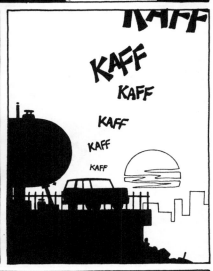

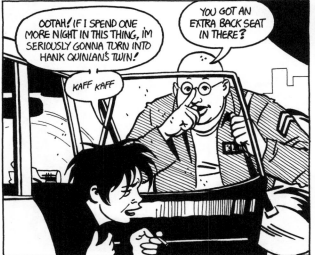

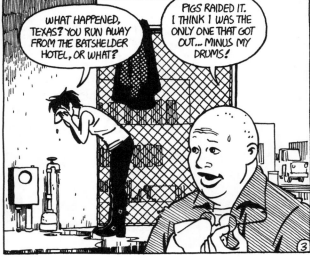

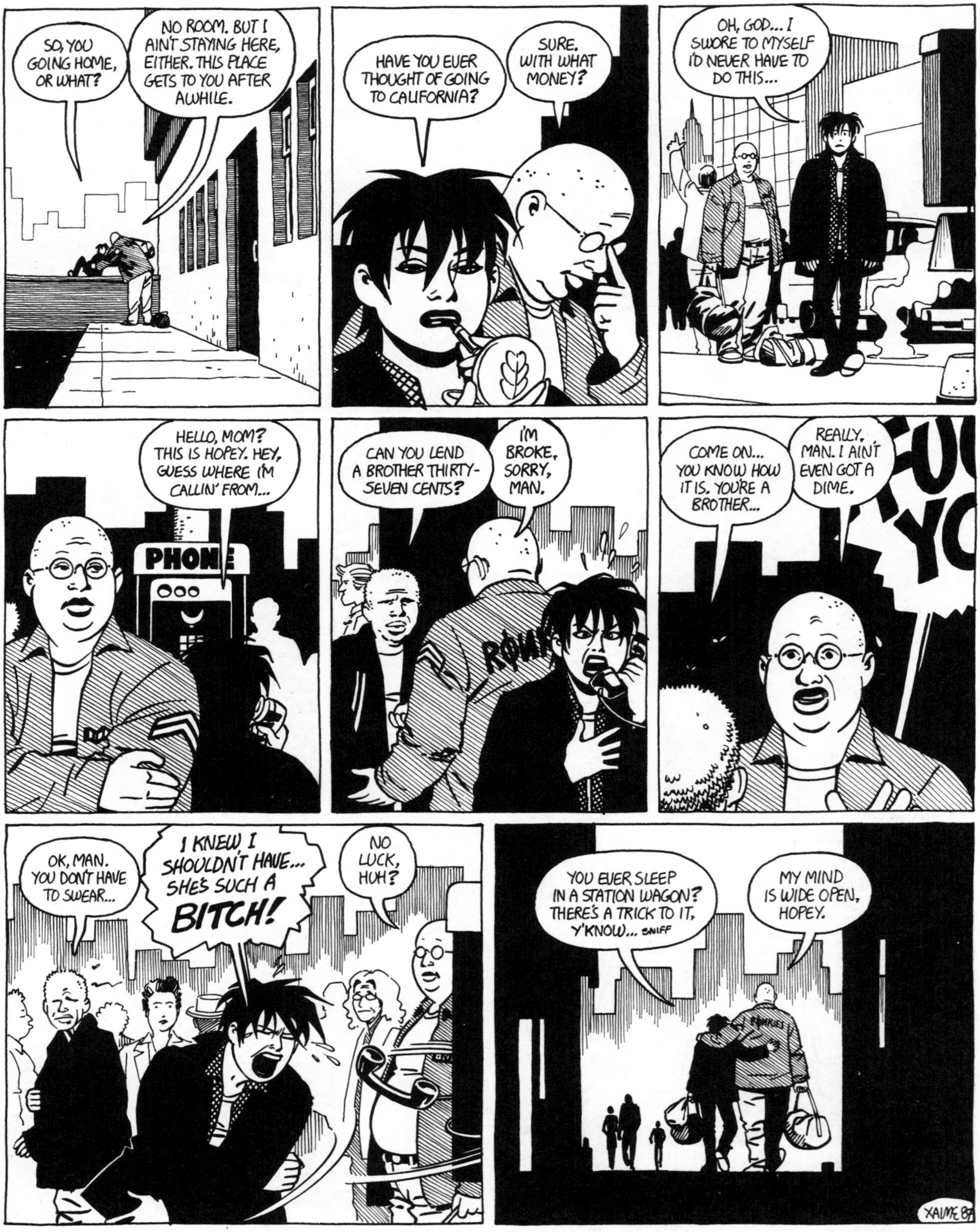
SO, YOU GOING HOME, OR WHAT?
NO ROOM. BUT I AIN'T STAYING HERE, EITHER. THIS PLACE GETS TO YOU AFTER AWHILE.
HAVE YOU EVER THOUGHT OF GOING TO CALIFORNIA?
SURE. WITH WHAT MONEY?
OH, GOD... I SWORE TO MYSELF I'D NEVER HAVE TO DO THIS...
HELLO, MOM? THIS IS HOPEY. HEY, GUESS WHERE I'M CALLIN' FROM...
PHONE
CAN YOU LEND A BROTHER THIRTY-SEVEN CENTS?
I'M BROKE, SORRY, MAN.
COME ON... YOU KNOW HOW IT IS. YOU'RE A BROTHER...
REALLY, MAN. I AIN'T EVEN GOT A DIME.
OK, MAN. YOU DON'T HAVE TO SWEAR...
I KNEW I SHOULDN'T HAVE... SHE'S SUCH A BITCH!
NO LUCK, HUH?
YOU EVER SLEEP IN A STATION WAGON? THERE'S A TRICK TO IT, Y'KNOW... SNIFF
MY MIND IS WIDE OPEN, HOPEY.
XAIME 87

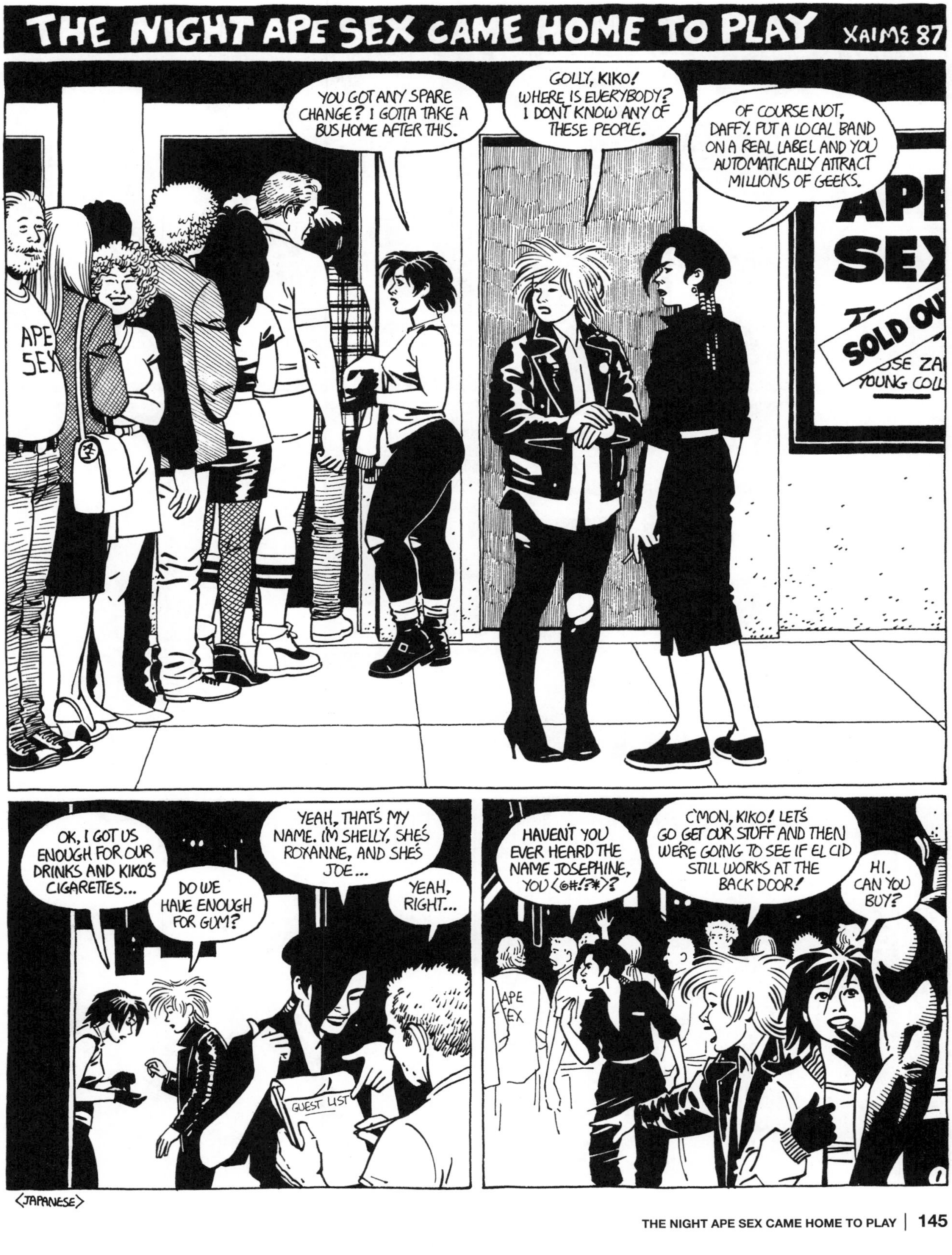
THE NIGHT APE SEX CAME HOME TO PLAY
XAIME 87
YOU GOT ANY SPARE CHANGE? I GOTTA TAKE A BUS HOME AFTER THIS.
GOLLY, KIKO! WHERE IS EVERYBODY? I DON'T KNOW ANY OF THESE PEOPLE.
OF COURSE NOT, DAFFY. PUT A LOCAL BAND ON A REAL LABEL AND YOU AUTOMATICALLY ATTRACT MILLIONS OF GEEKS.
APE SEX
SOLD OUT
APE SEX
OK, I GOT US ENOUGH FOR OUR DRINKS AND KIKO'S CIGARETTES...
DO WE HAVE ENOUGH FOR GUM?
YEAH, THAT'S MY NAME. I'M SHELLY, SHE'S ROXANNE, AND SHE'S JOE...
YEAH, RIGHT...
GUEST LIST
HAVEN'T YOU EVER HEARD THE NAME JOSEPHINE, YOU <@#!?*>?
C'MON, KIKO! LET'S GO GET OUR STUFF AND THEN WE'RE GOING TO SEE IF EL CID STILL WORKS AT THE BACK DOOR!
HI. CAN YOU BUY?
APE SEX
1
<JAPANESE>

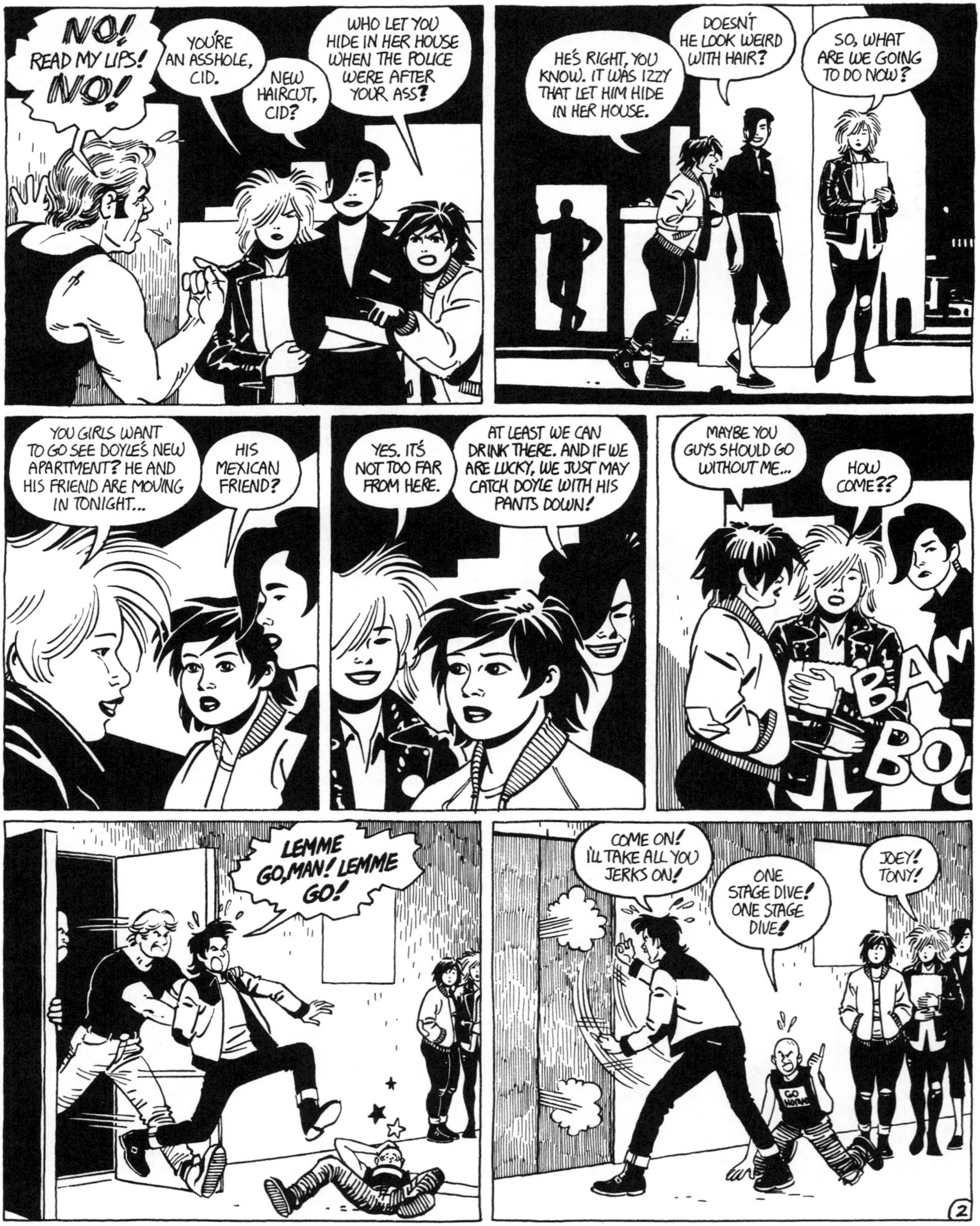
NO! READ MY LIPS! NO!
YOU'RE AN ASSHOLE, CID.
NEW HAIRCUT, CID?
WHO LET YOU HIDE IN HER HOUSE WHEN THE POLICE WERE AFTER YOUR ASS?
HE'S RIGHT, YOU KNOW. IT WAS IZZY THAT LET HIM HIDE IN HER HOUSE.
DOESN'T HE LOOK WEIRD WITH HAIR?
SO, WHAT ARE WE GOING TO DO NOW?
YOU GIRLS WANT TO GO SEE DOYLE'S NEW APARTMENT? HE AND HIS FRIEND ARE MOVING IN TONIGHT...
HIS MEXICAN FRIEND?
YES. IT'S NOT TOO FAR FROM HERE.
AT LEAST WE CAN DRINK THERE. AND IF WE ARE LUCKY, WE JUST MAY CATCH DOYLE WITH HIS PANTS DOWN!
MAYBE YOU GUYS SHOULD GO WITHOUT ME...
HOW COME??
BAM
BO
LEMME GO, MAN! LEMME GO!
COME ON! I'LL TAKE ALL YOU JERKS ON!
ONE STAGE DIVE! ONE STAGE DIVE!
JOEY! TONY!
2

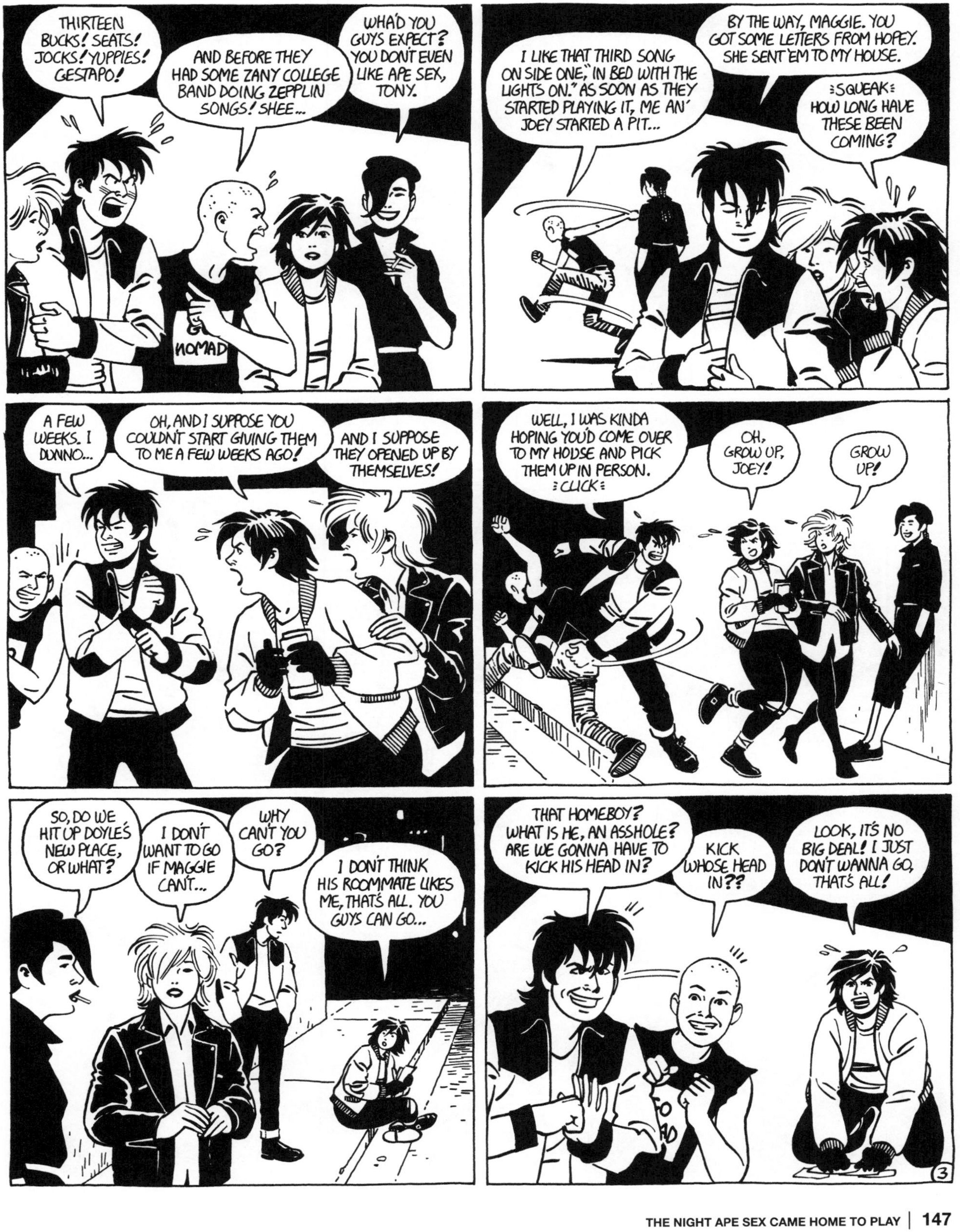
THIRTEEN BUCKS! SEATS! JOCKS! YUPPIES! GESTAPO!
AND BEFORE THEY HAD SOME ZANY COLLEGE BAND DOING ZEPPLIN SONGS! SHEE...
WHA'D YOU GUYS EXPECT? YOU DON'T EVEN LIKE APE SEX, TONY.
NOMAD
I LIKE THAT THIRD SONG ON SIDE ONE, "IN BED WITH THE LIGHTS ON." AS SOON AS THEY STARTED PLAYING IT, ME AN' JOEY STARTED A PIT...
BY THE WAY, MAGGIE. YOU GOT SOME LETTERS FROM HOPEY. SHE SENT 'EM TO MY HOUSE.
SQUEAK
HOW LONG HAVE THESE BEEN COMING?
A FEW WEEKS. I DUNNO...
OH, AND I SUPPOSE YOU COULDN'T START GIVING THEM TO ME A FEW WEEKS AGO!
AND I SUPPOSE THEY OPENED UP BY THEMSELVES!
WELL, I WAS KINDA HOPING YOU'D COME OVER TO MY HOUSE AND PICK THEM UP IN PERSON.
CLICK
OH, GROW UP, JOEY!
GROW UP!
SO, DO WE HIT UP DOYLE'S NEW PLACE, OR WHAT?
I DON'T WANT TO GO IF MAGGIE CAN'T...
WHY CAN'T YOU GO?
I DON'T THINK HIS ROOMMATE LIKES ME, THAT'S ALL. YOU GUYS CAN GO...
THAT HOMEBOY? WHAT IS HE, AN ASSHOLE? ARE WE GONNA HAVE TO KICK HIS HEAD IN?
KICK WHOSE HEAD IN??
LOOK, IT'S NO BIG DEAL! I JUST DON'T WANNA GO, THAT'S ALL!
3

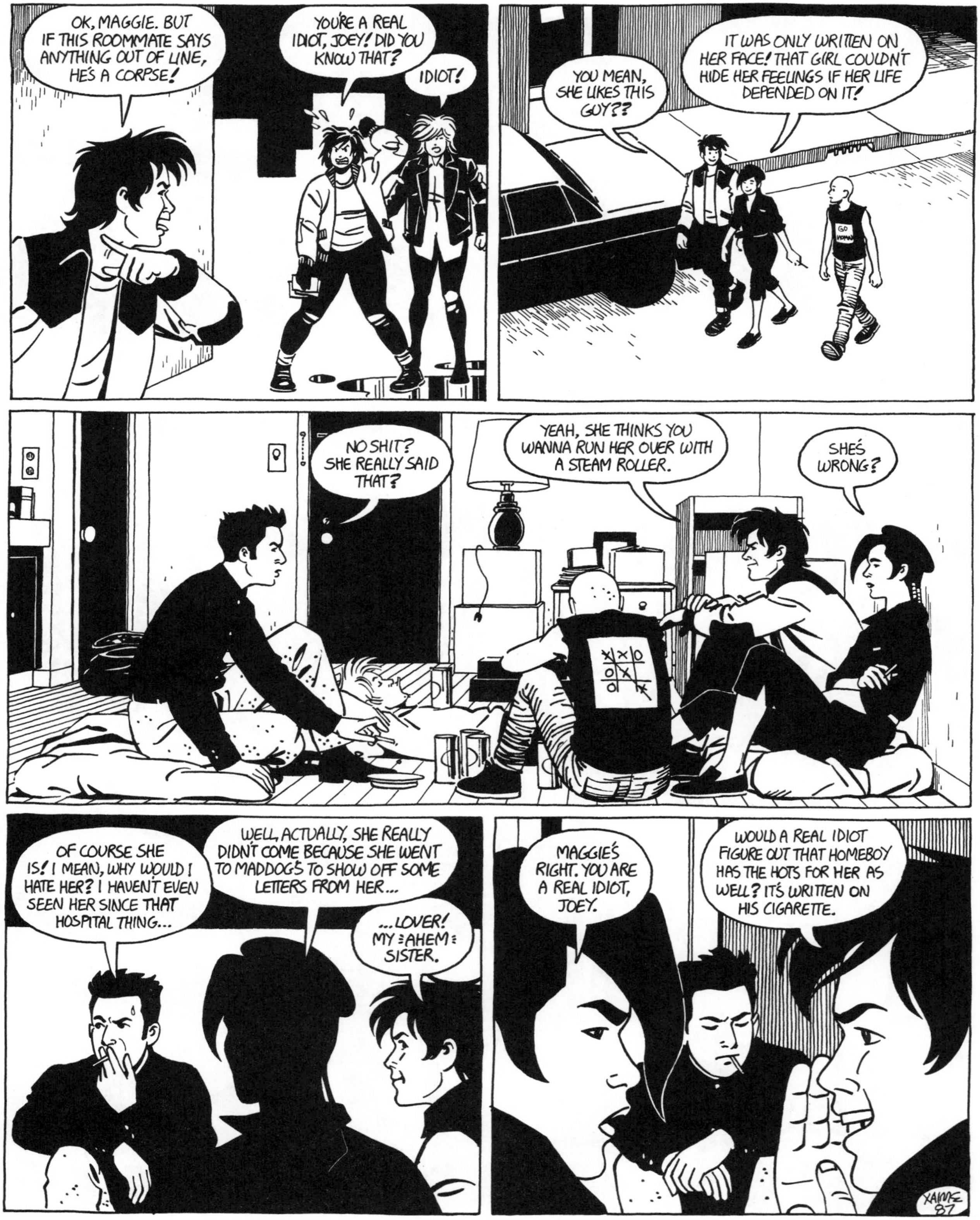
OK, MAGGIE. BUT IF THIS ROOMMATE SAYS ANYTHING OUT OF LINE, HE'S A CORPSE!
YOU'RE A REAL IDIOT, JOEY! DID YOU KNOW THAT?
IDIOT!
YOU MEAN, SHE LIKES THIS GUY??
IT WAS ONLY WRITTEN ON HER FACE! THAT GIRL COULDN'T HIDE HER FEELINGS IF HER LIFE DEPENDED ON IT!
GO WOMAN
NO SHIT? SHE REALLY SAID THAT?
YEAH, SHE THINKS YOU WANNA RUN HER OVER WITH A STEAM ROLLER.
SHE'S WRONG?
OF COURSE SHE IS! I MEAN, WHY WOULD I HATE HER? I HAVEN'T EVEN SEEN HER SINCE THAT HOSPITAL THING...
WELL, ACTUALLY, SHE REALLY DIDN'T COME BECAUSE SHE WENT TO MADDOG'S TO SHOW OFF SOME LETTERS FROM HER...
...LOVER! MY AHEM SISTER.
MAGGIE'S RIGHT. YOU ARE A REAL IDIOT, JOEY.
WOULD A REAL IDIOT FIGURE OUT THAT HOMEBOY HAS THE HOTS FOR HER AS WELL? IT'S WRITTEN ON HIS CIGARETTE.
XAIME 87

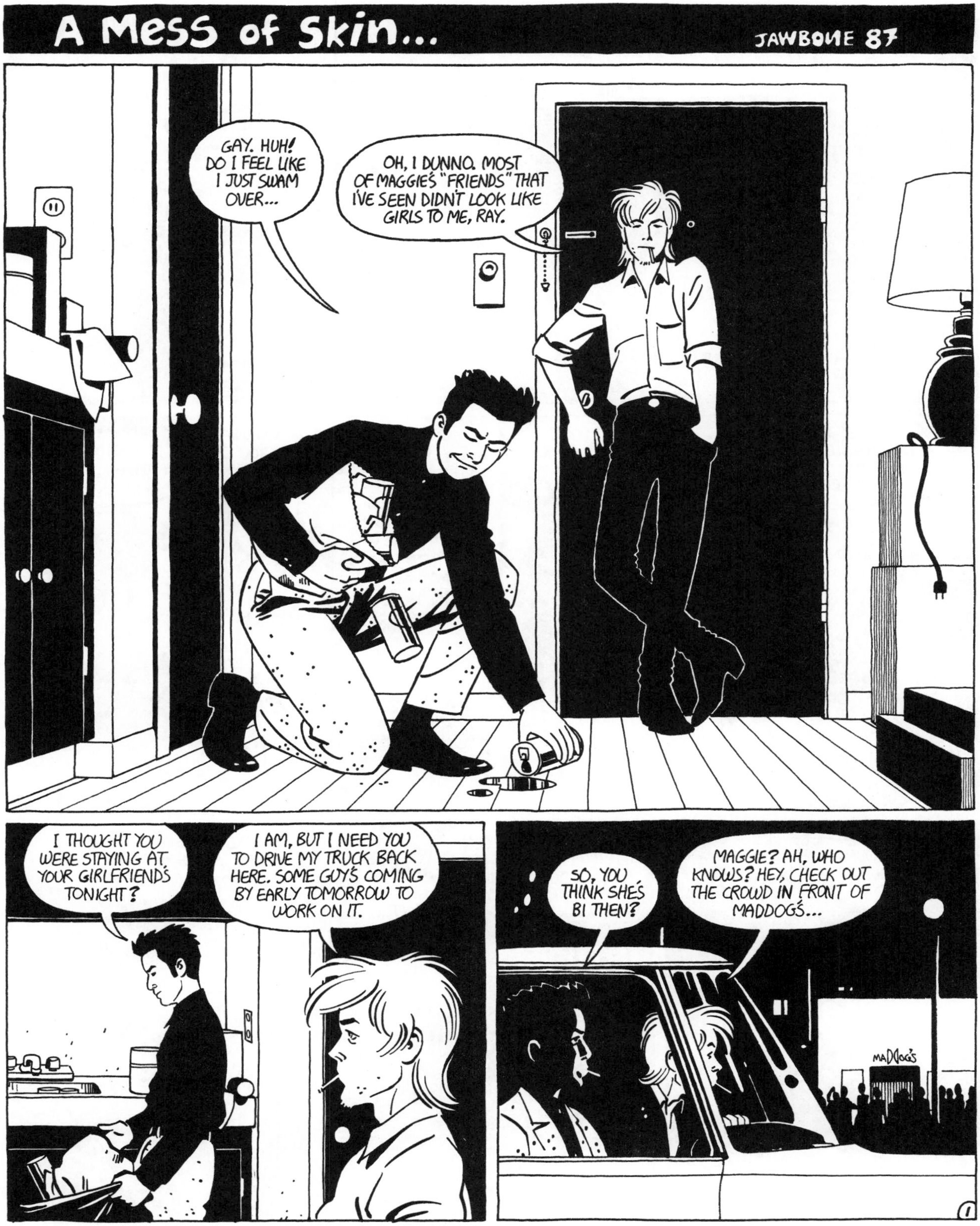
A Mess of Skin...
JAWBONE 87
GAY. HUH! DO I FEEL LIKE I JUST SWAM OVER...
OH, I DUNNO. MOST OF MAGGIE'S "FRIENDS" THAT I'VE SEEN DIDN'T LOOK LIKE GIRLS TO ME, RAY.
I THOUGHT YOU WERE STAYING AT YOUR GIRLFRIEND'S TONIGHT?
I AM, BUT I NEED YOU TO DRIVE MY TRUCK BACK HERE. SOME GUY'S COMING BY EARLY TOMORROW TO WORK ON IT.
SO, YOU THINK SHE'S BI THEN?
MAGGIE? AH, WHO KNOWS? HEY, CHECK OUT THE CROWD IN FRONT OF MADDOG'S...
MADDOG'S
1

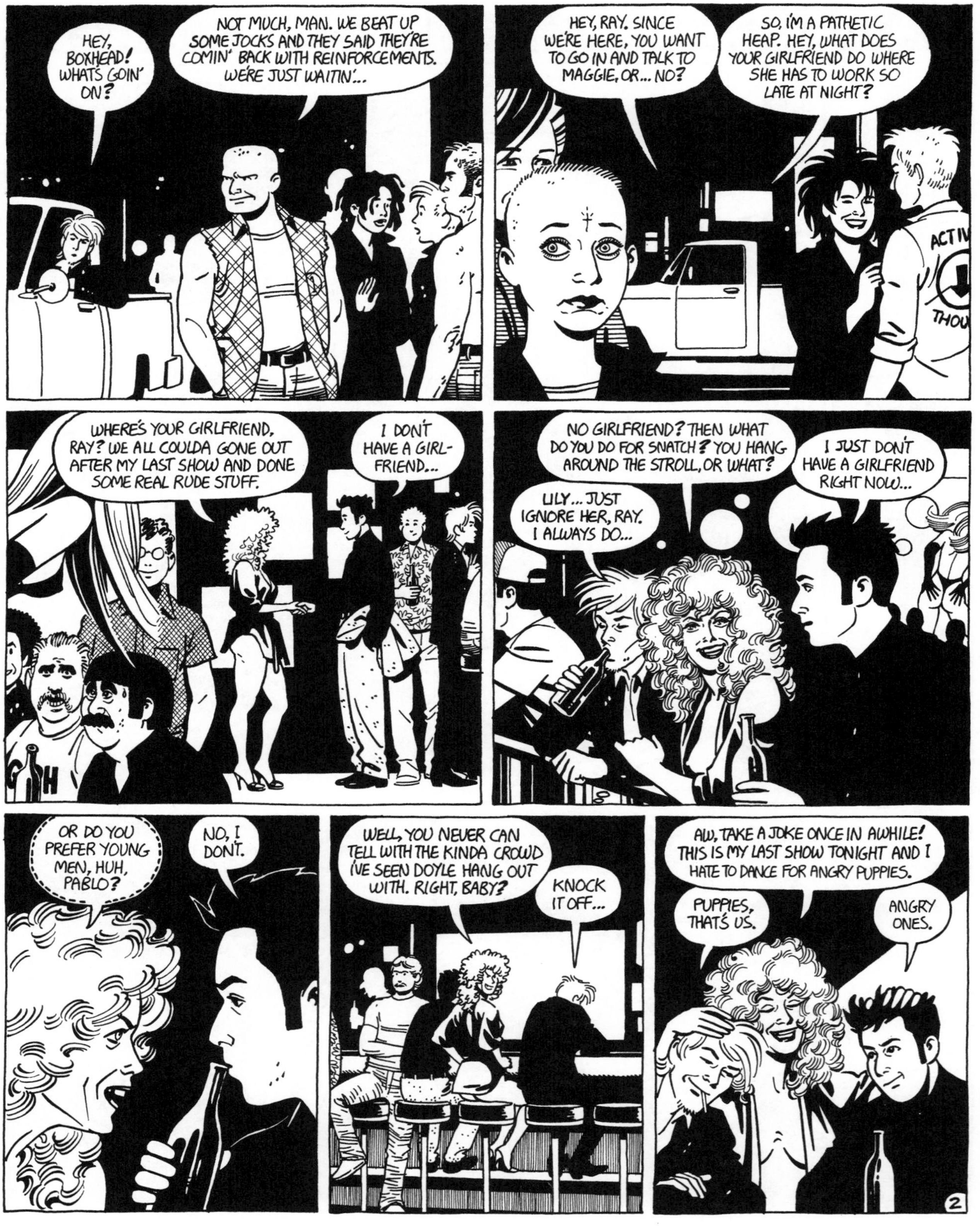
HEY, BOXHEAD! WHAT'S GOIN' ON?
NOT MUCH, MAN. WE BEAT UP SOME JOCKS AND THEY SAID THEY'RE COMIN' BACK WITH REINFORCEMENTS. WE'RE JUST WAITIN'...
HEY, RAY. SINCE WE'RE HERE, YOU WANT TO GO IN AND TALK TO MAGGIE, OR... NO?
SO, I'M A PATHETIC HEAP. HEY, WHAT DOES YOUR GIRLFRIEND DO WHERE SHE HAS TO WORK SO LATE AT NIGHT?
WHERE'S YOUR GIRLFRIEND, RAY? WE ALL COULDA GONE OUT AFTER MY LAST SHOW AND DONE SOME REAL RUDE STUFF.
I DON'T HAVE A GIRL-FRIEND...
NO GIRLFRIEND? THEN WHAT DO YOU DO FOR SNATCH? YOU HANG AROUND THE STROLL, OR WHAT?
LILY... JUST IGNORE HER, RAY. I ALWAYS DO...
I JUST DON'T HAVE A GIRLFRIEND RIGHT NOW...
OR DO YOU PREFER YOUNG MEN, HUH, PABLO?
NO, I DON'T.
WELL, YOU NEVER CAN TELL WITH THE KINDA CROWD I'VE SEEN DOYLE HANG OUT WITH. RIGHT, BABY?
KNOCK IT OFF...
AW, TAKE A JOKE ONCE IN AWHILE! THIS IS MY LAST SHOW TONIGHT AND I HATE TO DANCE FOR ANGRY PUPPIES.
PUPPIES, THAT'S US.
ANGRY ONES.
2

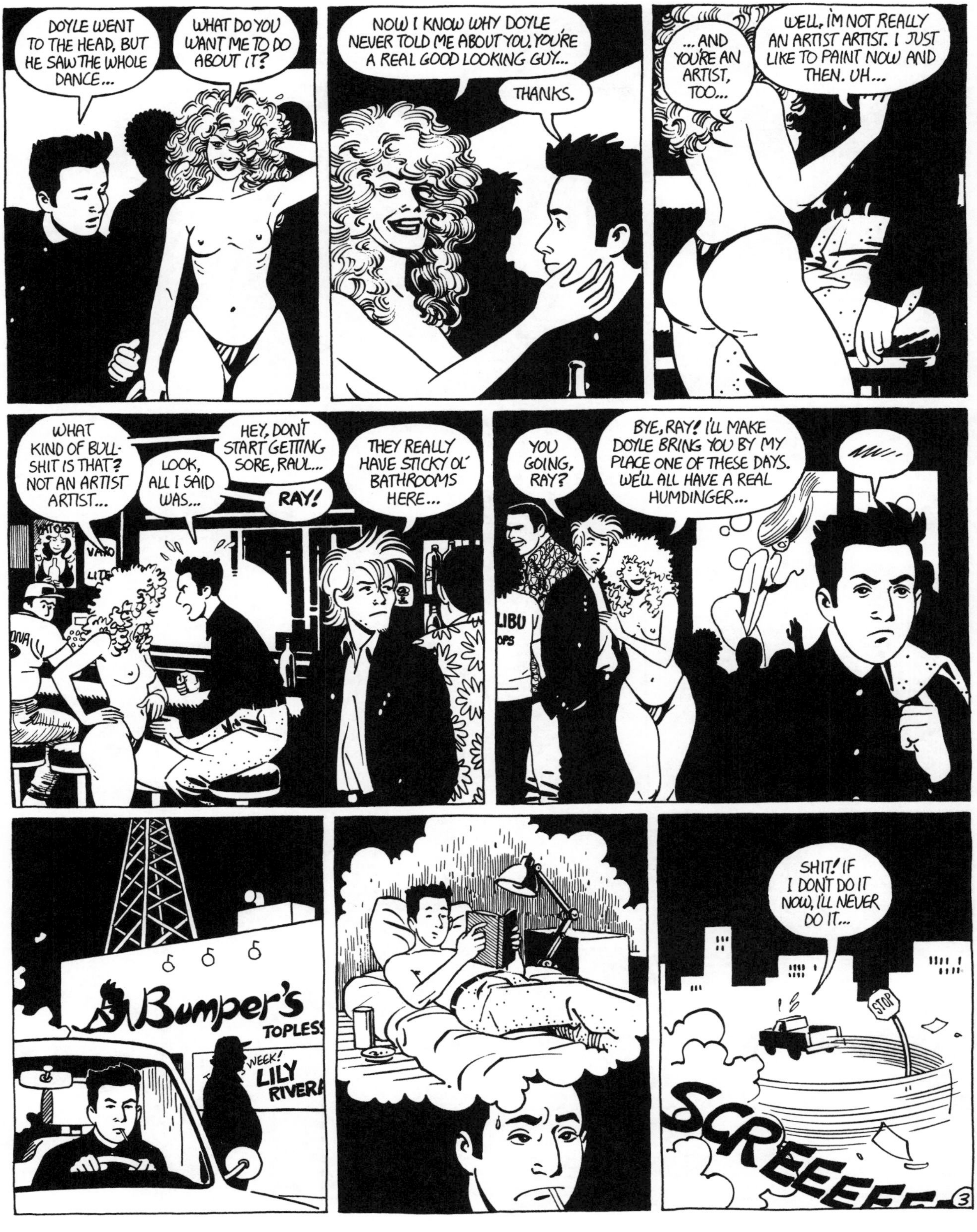
DOYLE WENT TO THE HEAD, BUT HE SAW THE WHOLE DANCE...
WHAT DO YOU WANT ME TO DO ABOUT IT?
NOW I KNOW WHY DOYLE NEVER TOLD ME ABOUT YOU. YOU'RE A REAL GOOD LOOKING GUY...
THANKS.
...AND YOU'RE AN ARTIST, TOO...
WELL, I'M NOT REALLY AN ARTIST ARTIST. I JUST LIKE TO PAINT NOW AND THEN. UH...
WHAT KIND OF BULL-SHIT IS THAT? NOT AN ARTIST ARTIST...
HEY, DON'T START GETTING SORE, RAUL...
LOOK, ALL I SAID WAS...
RAY!
THEY REALLY HAVE STICKY OL' BATHROOMS HERE...
YOU GOING, RAY?
BYE, RAY! I'LL MAKE DOYLE BRING YOU BY MY PLACE ONE OF THESE DAYS. WE'LL ALL HAVE A REAL HUMDINGER...
Bumper's
TOPLES
WEEK!
LILY
RIVERA
SHIT! IF I DON'T DO IT NOW, I'LL NEVER DO IT...
STOP
SCREEEEE
3

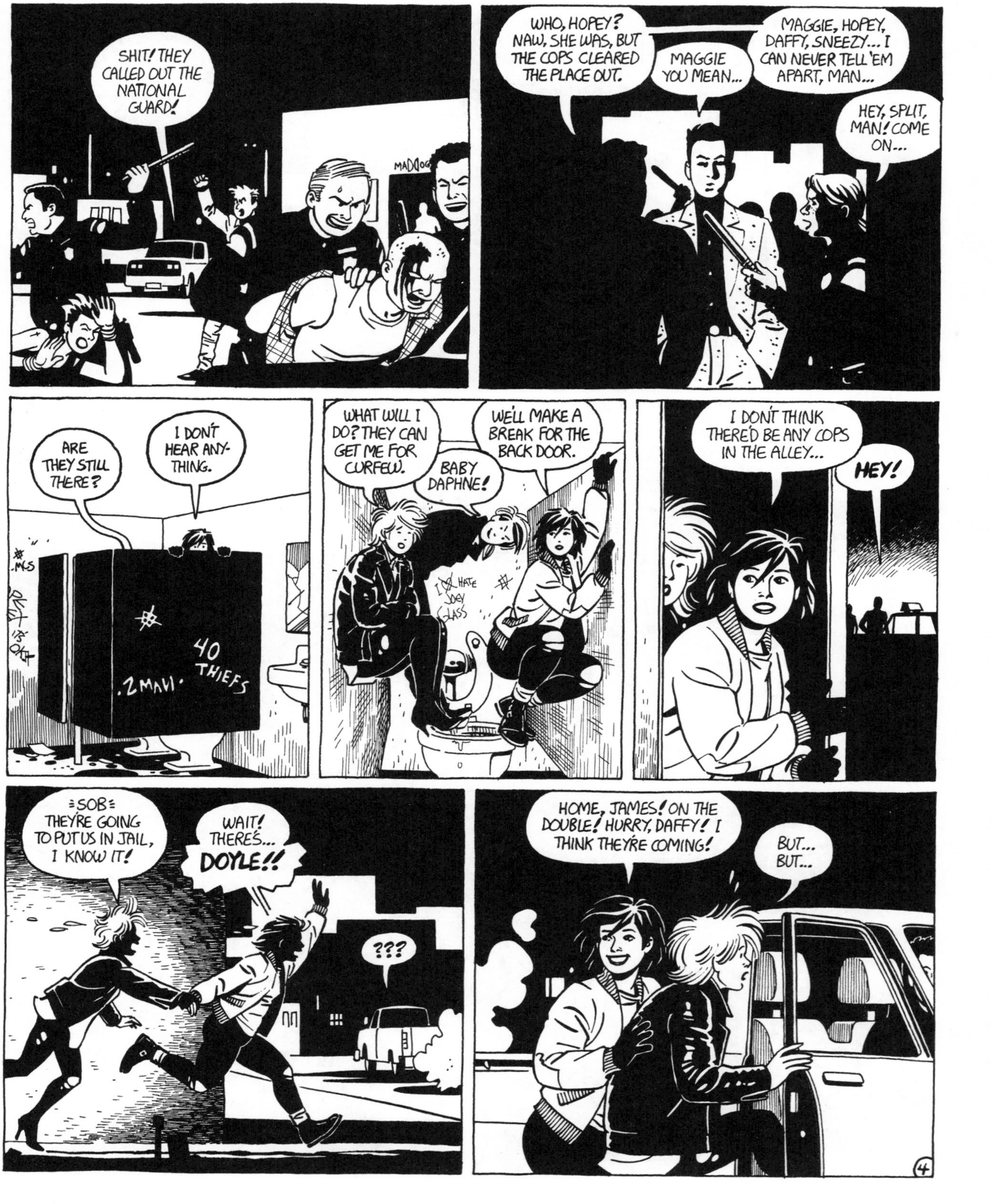
SHIT! THEY CALLED OUT THE NATIONAL GUARD!
WHO, HOPEY? NAW, SHE WAS, BUT THE COPS CLEARED THE PLACE OUT.
MAGGIE YOU MEAN...
MAGGIE, HOPEY, DAFFY, SNEEZY... I CAN NEVER TELL 'EM APART, MAN...
HEY, SPLIT, MAN! COME ON...
ARE THEY STILL THERE?
I DON'T HEAR ANY-THING.
40 THIEFS
WHAT WILL I DO? THEY CAN GET ME FOR CURFEW.
BABY DAPHNE!
WE'LL MAKE A BREAK FOR THE BACK DOOR.
I DON'T THINK THERE'D BE ANY COPS IN THE ALLEY...
HEY!
≈SOB≈ THEY'RE GOING TO PUT US IN JAIL, I KNOW IT!
WAIT! THERE'S... DOYLE!!
???
HOME, JAMES! ON THE DOUBLE! HURRY, DAFFY! I THINK THEY'RE COMING!
BUT... BUT...
4

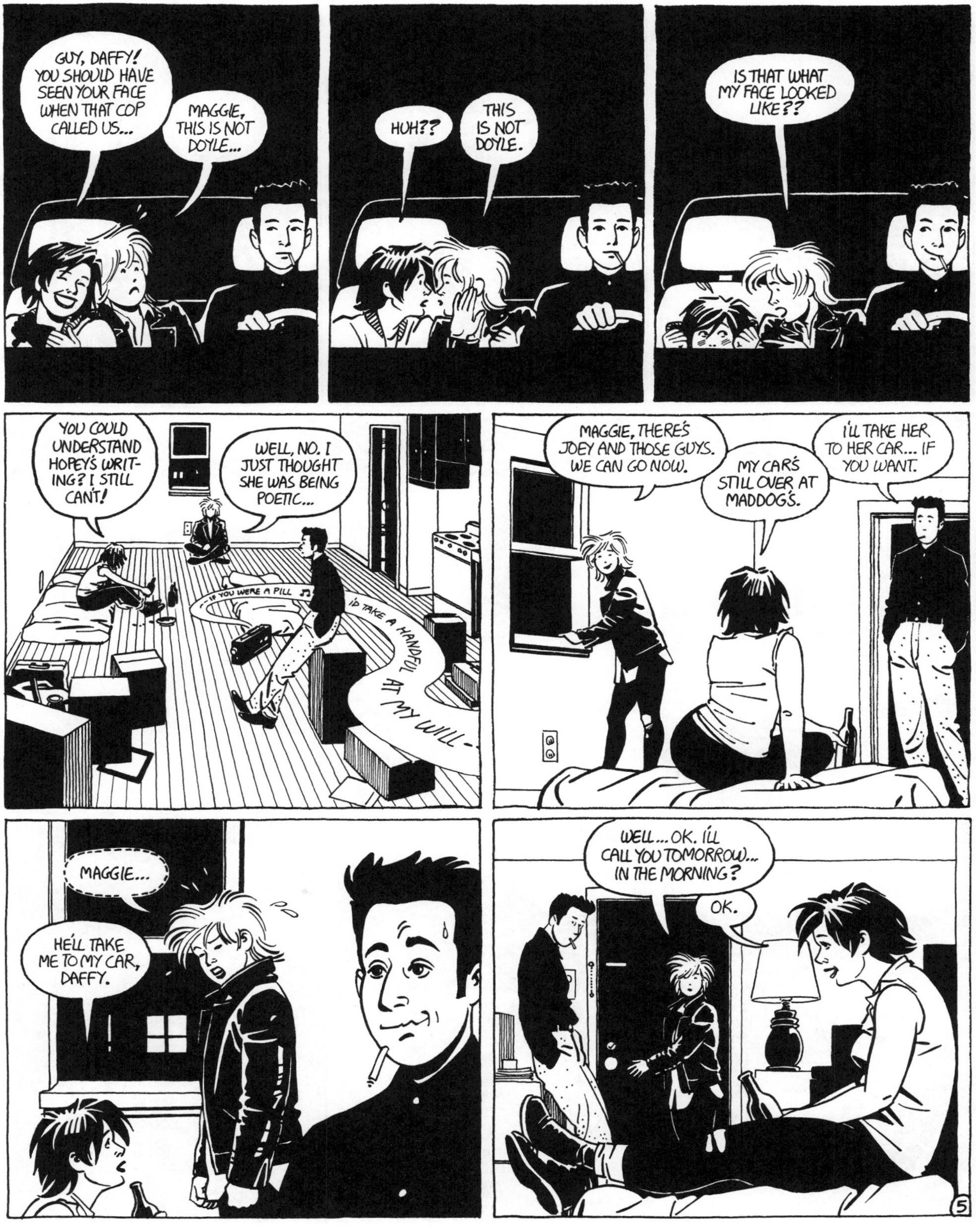
GUY, DAFFY! YOU SHOULD HAVE SEEN YOUR FACE WHEN THAT COP CALLED US...
MAGGIE, THIS IS NOT DOYLE...
HUH??
THIS IS NOT DOYLE.
IS THAT WHAT MY FACE LOOKED LIKE??
YOU COULD UNDERSTAND HOPEY'S WRITING? I STILL CAN'T!
WELL, NO. I JUST THOUGHT SHE WAS BEING POETIC...
--IF YOU WERE A PILL ♫ I'D TAKE A HANDFUL AT MY WILL--
MAGGIE, THERE'S JOEY AND THOSE GUYS. WE CAN GO NOW.
MY CAR'S STILL OVER AT MADDOG'S.
I'LL TAKE HER TO HER CAR... IF YOU WANT.
MAGGIE...
HE'LL TAKE ME TO MY CAR, DAFFY.
WELL... OK. I'LL CALL YOU TOMORROW... IN THE MORNING?
OK.
5

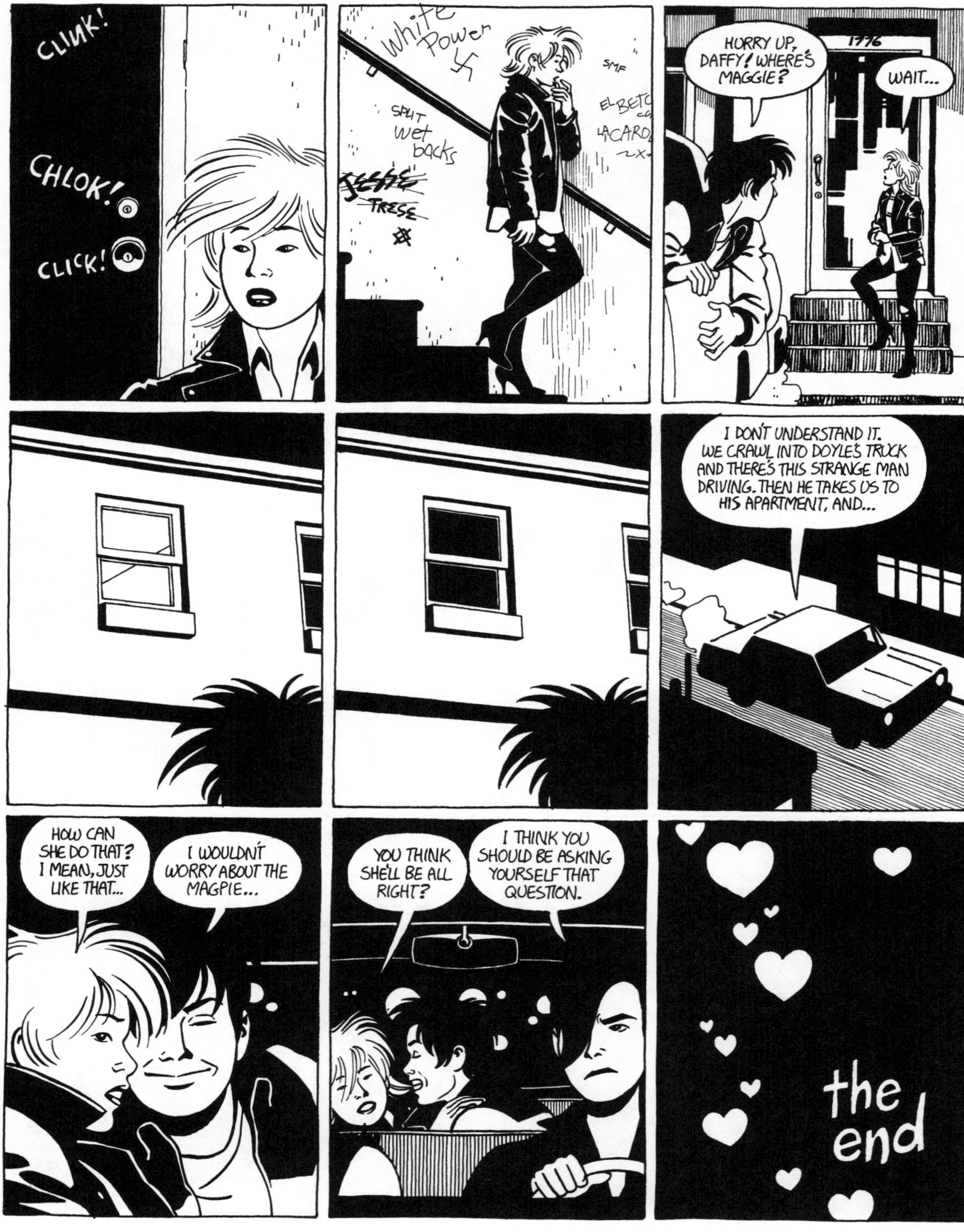
CLINK!
CHLOK!
CLICK!
white Power
SMF
SPLIT wet backs
TRESE
HURRY UP, DAFFY! WHERE'S MAGGIE?
WAIT...
I DON'T UNDERSTAND IT. WE CRAWL INTO DOYLE'S TRUCK AND THERE'S THIS STRANGE MAN DRIVING. THEN HE TAKES US TO HIS APARTMENT, AND...
HOW CAN SHE DO THAT? I MEAN, JUST LIKE THAT...
I WOULDN'T WORRY ABOUT THE MAGPIE...
YOU THINK SHE'LL BE ALL RIGHT?
I THINK YOU SHOULD BE ASKING YOURSELF THAT QUESTION.
the end

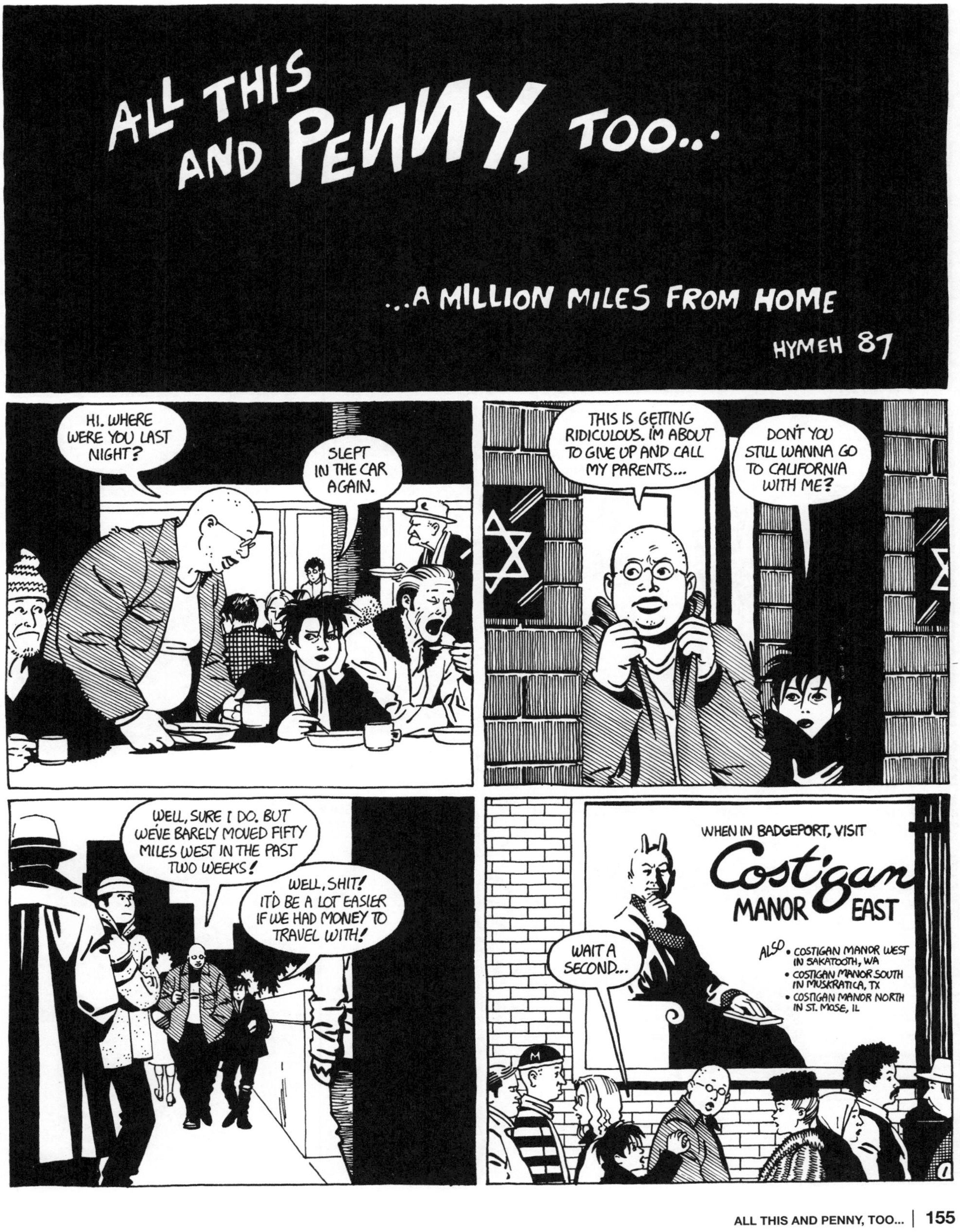
ALL THIS AND PENNY, TOO...
...A MILLION MILES FROM HOME
HYMEH 87
HI. WHERE WERE YOU LAST NIGHT?
SLEPT IN THE CAR AGAIN.
THIS IS GETTING RIDICULOUS. I'M ABOUT TO GIVE UP AND CALL MY PARENTS...
DON'T YOU STILL WANNA GO TO CALIFORNIA WITH ME?
WELL, SURE I DO. BUT WE'VE BARELY MOVED FIFTY MILES WEST IN THE PAST TWO WEEKS!
WELL, SHIT! IT'D BE A LOT EASIER IF WE HAD MONEY TO TRAVEL WITH!
WHEN IN BADGEPORT, VISIT
Costigan MANOR EAST
ALSO • COSTIGAN MANOR WEST IN SAKATOOTH, WA
• COSTIGAN MANOR SOUTH IN MUSKRATICA, TX
• COSTIGAN MANOR NORTH IN ST. MOSE, IL
WAIT A SECOND...
1

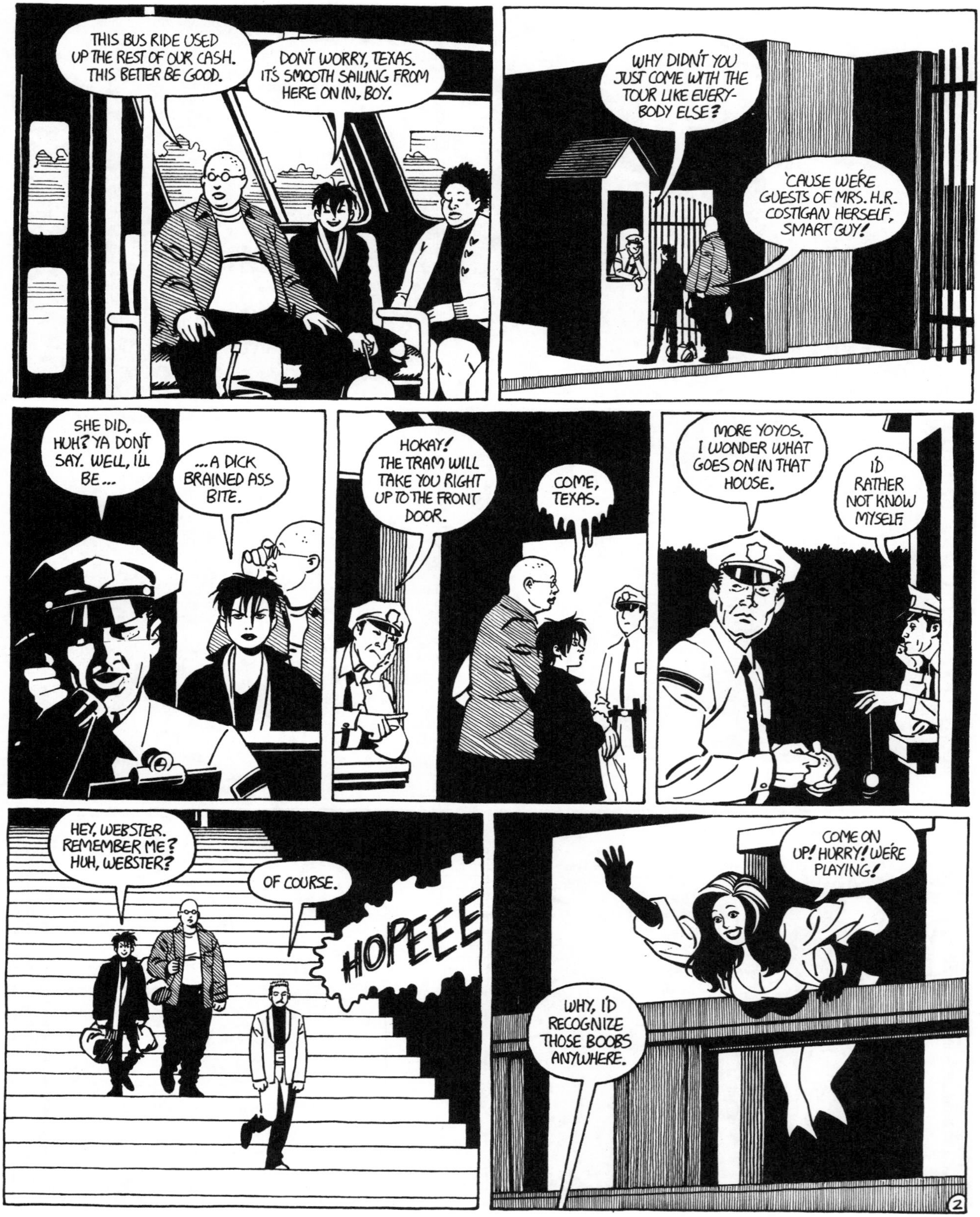
THIS BUS RIDE USED UP THE REST OF OUR CASH. THIS BETTER BE GOOD.
DON'T WORRY, TEXAS. IT'S SMOOTH SAILING FROM HERE ON IN, BOY.
WHY DIDN'T YOU JUST COME WITH THE TOUR LIKE EVERY-BODY ELSE?
'CAUSE WE'RE GUESTS OF MRS. H.R. COSTIGAN HERSELF, SMART GUY!
SHE DID, HUH? YA DON'T SAY. WELL, I'LL BE...
...A DICK BRAINED ASS BITE.
HOKAY! THE TRAM WILL TAKE YOU RIGHT UP TO THE FRONT DOOR.
COME, TEXAS.
MORE YOYOS. I WONDER WHAT GOES ON IN THAT HOUSE.
I'D RATHER NOT KNOW MYSELF.
HEY, WEBSTER. REMEMBER ME? HUH, WEBSTER?
OF COURSE.
HOPEEE
COME ON UP! HURRY! WE'RE PLAYING!
WHY, I'D RECOGNIZE THOSE BOOBS ANYWHERE.
2

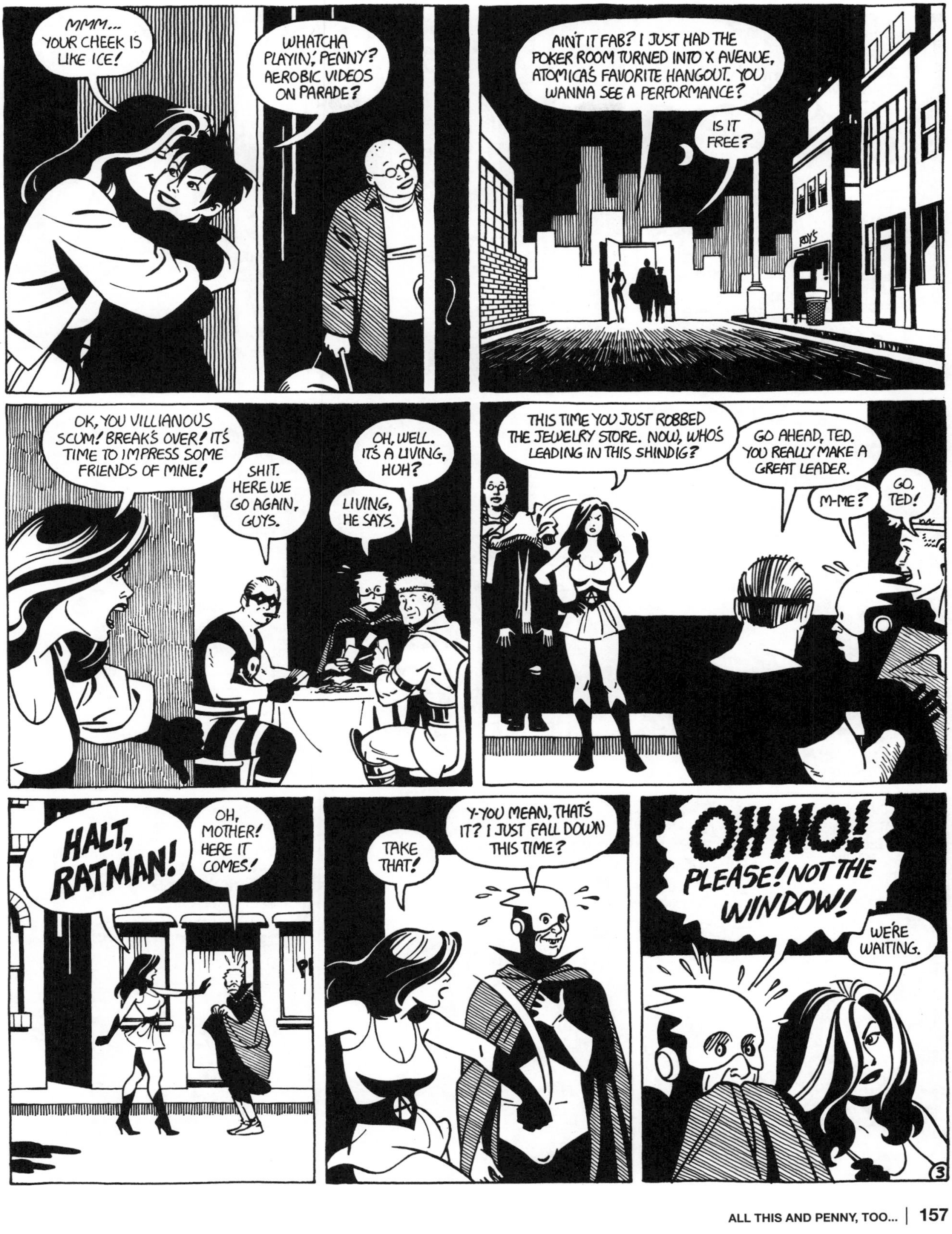
MMM... YOUR CHEEK IS LIKE ICE!
WHATCHA PLAYIN,' PENNY? AEROBIC VIDEOS ON PARADE?
AIN'T IT FAB? I JUST HAD THE POKER ROOM TURNED INTO X AVENUE, ATOMICA'S FAVORITE HANGOUT. YOU WANNA SEE A PERFORMANCE?
IS IT FREE?
ROY'S
OK, YOU VILLIANOUS SCUM! BREAK'S OVER! IT'S TIME TO IMPRESS SOME FRIENDS OF MINE!
SHIT. HERE WE GO AGAIN, GUYS.
OH, WELL. IT'S A LIVING, HUH?
LIVING, HE SAYS.
THIS TIME YOU JUST ROBBED THE JEWELRY STORE. NOW, WHO'S LEADING IN THIS SHINDIG?
GO AHEAD, TED. YOU REALLY MAKE A GREAT LEADER.
M-ME?
GO, TED!
HALT, RATMAN!
OH, MOTHER! HERE IT COMES!
TAKE THAT!
Y-YOU MEAN, THAT'S IT? I JUST FALL DOWN THIS TIME?
OH NO! PLEASE! NOT THE WINDOW!
WE'RE WAITING.
3

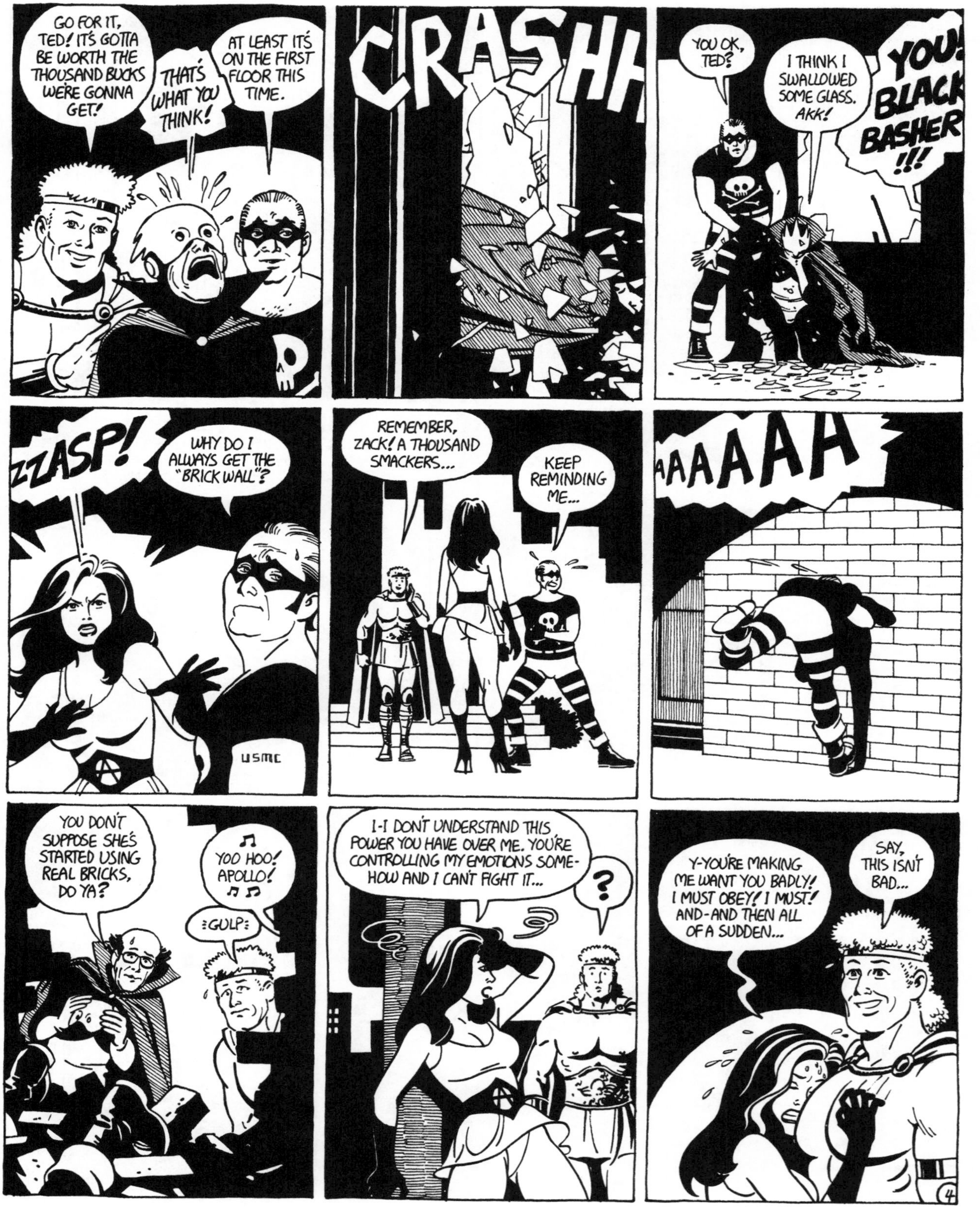

GO FOR IT, TED! IT'S GOTTA BE WORTH THE THOUSAND BUCKS WE'RE GONNA GET!
THAT'S WHAT YOU THINK!
AT LEAST IT'S ON THE FIRST FLOOR THIS TIME.
CRASHH
YOU OK, TED?
I THINK I SWALLOWED SOME GLASS. AKK!
YOU! BLACK BASHER!!!
ZZASP!
WHY DO I ALWAYS GET THE "BRICK WALL"?
USMC
REMEMBER, ZACK! A THOUSAND SMACKERS...
KEEP REMINDING ME...
AAAAAAA
YOU DON'T SUPPOSE SHE'S STARTED USING REAL BRICKS, DO YA?
YOO HOO! APOLLO!
GULP
I-I DON'T UNDERSTAND THIS POWER YOU HAVE OVER ME. YOU'RE CONTROLLING MY EMOTIONS SOMEHOW AND I CAN'T FIGHT IT...
?
Y-YOU'RE MAKING ME WANT YOU BADLY! I MUST OBEY! I MUST! AND-AND THEN ALL OF A SUDDEN...
SAY, THIS ISN'T BAD...
4

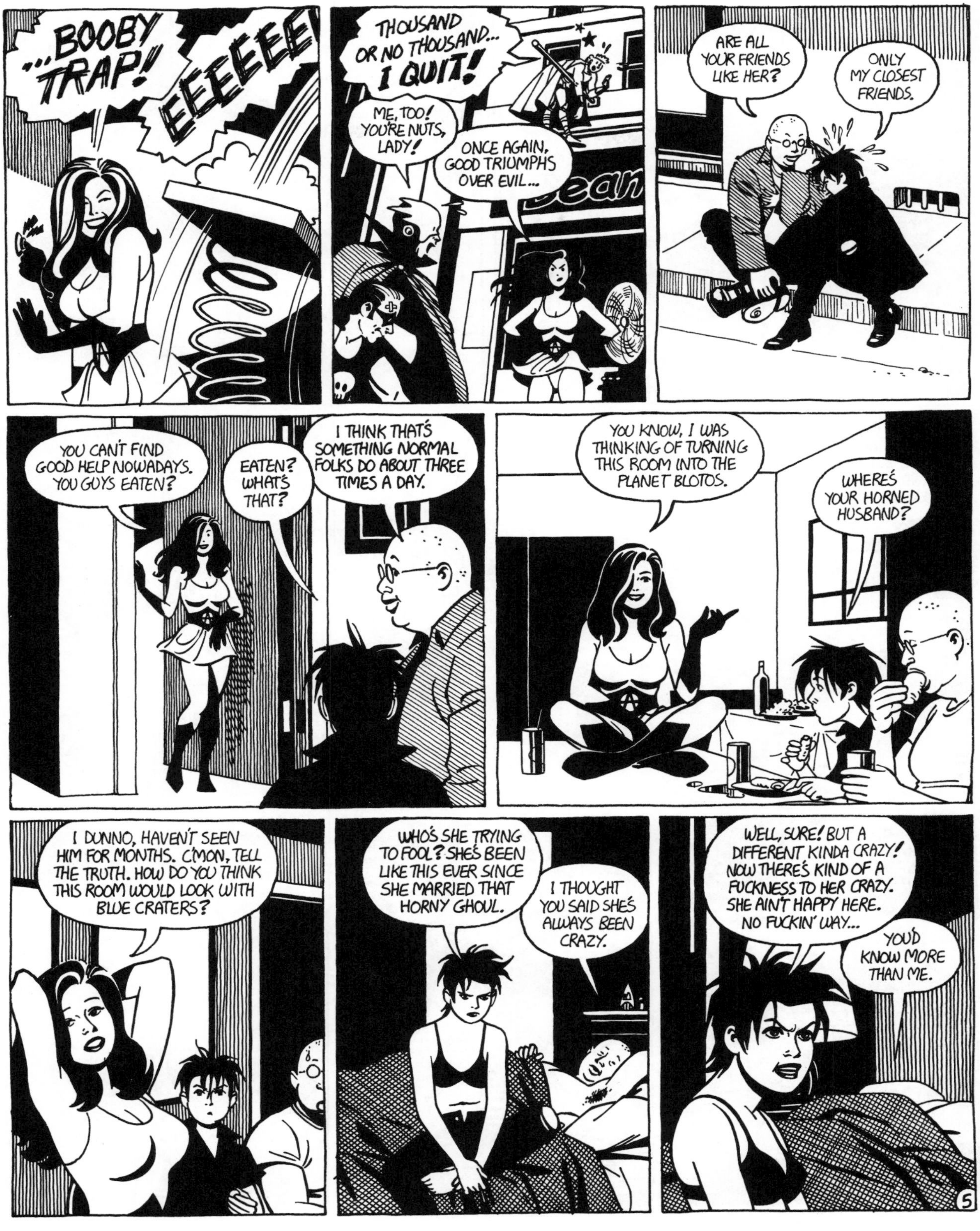
...BOOBY TRAP!
EEEEEEE
THOUSAND OR NO THOUSAND... I QUIT!
ME, TOO! YOU'RE NUTS, LADY!
ONCE AGAIN, GOOD TRIUMPHS OVER EVIL...
ARE ALL YOUR FRIENDS LIKE HER?
ONLY MY CLOSEST FRIENDS.
YOU CAN'T FIND GOOD HELP NOWADAYS. YOU GUYS EATEN?
EATEN? WHAT'S THAT?
I THINK THAT'S SOMETHING NORMAL FOLKS DO ABOUT THREE TIMES A DAY.
YOU KNOW, I WAS THINKING OF TURNING THIS ROOM INTO THE PLANET BLOTOS.
WHERE'S YOUR HORNED HUSBAND?
I DUNNO, HAVEN'T SEEN HIM FOR MONTHS. C'MON, TELL THE TRUTH. HOW DO YOU THINK THIS ROOM WOULD LOOK WITH BLUE CRATERS?
WHO'S SHE TRYING TO FOOL? SHE'S BEEN LIKE THIS EVER SINCE SHE MARRIED THAT HORNY GHOUL.
I THOUGHT YOU SAID SHE'S ALWAYS BEEN CRAZY.
WELL, SURE! BUT A DIFFERENT KINDA CRAZY! NOW THERE'S KIND OF A FUCKNESS TO HER CRAZY. SHE AIN'T HAPPY HERE. NO FUCKIN' WAY...
YOU'D KNOW MORE THAN ME.
5

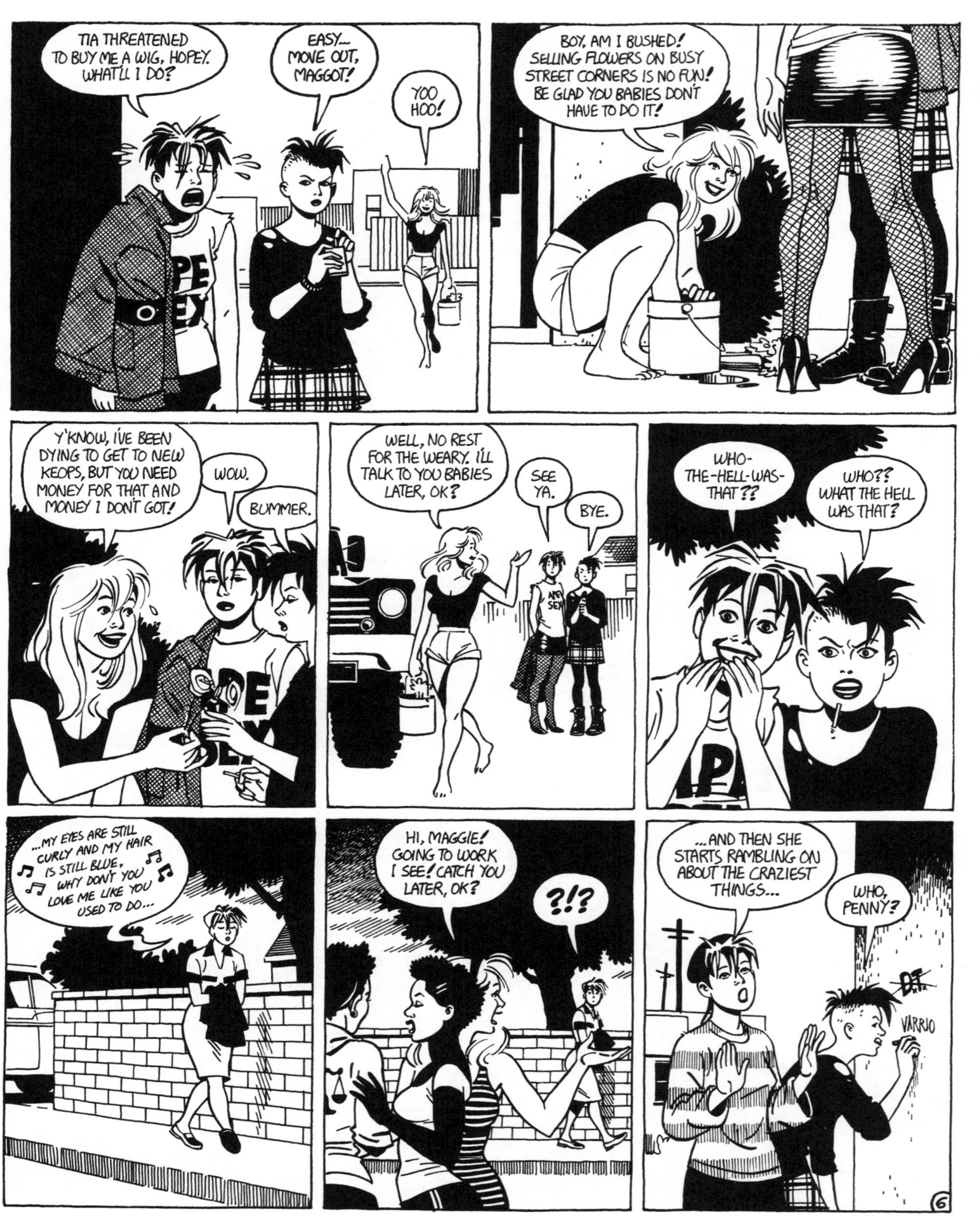
TIA THREATENED TO BUY ME A WIG, HOPEY. WHAT'LL I DO?
EASY... MOVE OUT, MAGGOT!
YOO HOO!
BOY, AM I BUSHED! SELLING FLOWERS ON BUSY STREET CORNERS IS NO FUN! BE GLAD YOU BABIES DON'T HAVE TO DO IT!
Y'KNOW, I'VE BEEN DYING TO GET TO NEW KEOPS, BUT YOU NEED MONEY FOR THAT AND MONEY I DON'T GOT!
WOW.
BUMMER.
WELL, NO REST FOR THE WEARY. I'LL TALK TO YOU BABIES LATER, OK?
SEE YA.
BYE.
WHO-THE-HELL-WAS-THAT??
WHO?? WHAT THE HELL WAS THAT?
...MY EYES ARE STILL CURLY AND MY HAIR IS STILL BLUE, WHY DON'T YOU LOVE ME LIKE YOU USED TO DO...
HI, MAGGIE! GOING TO WORK I SEE! CATCH YOU LATER, OK?
?!?
...AND THEN SHE STARTS RAMBLING ON ABOUT THE CRAZIEST THINGS...
WHO, PENNY?
D.T.
VARRIO
6

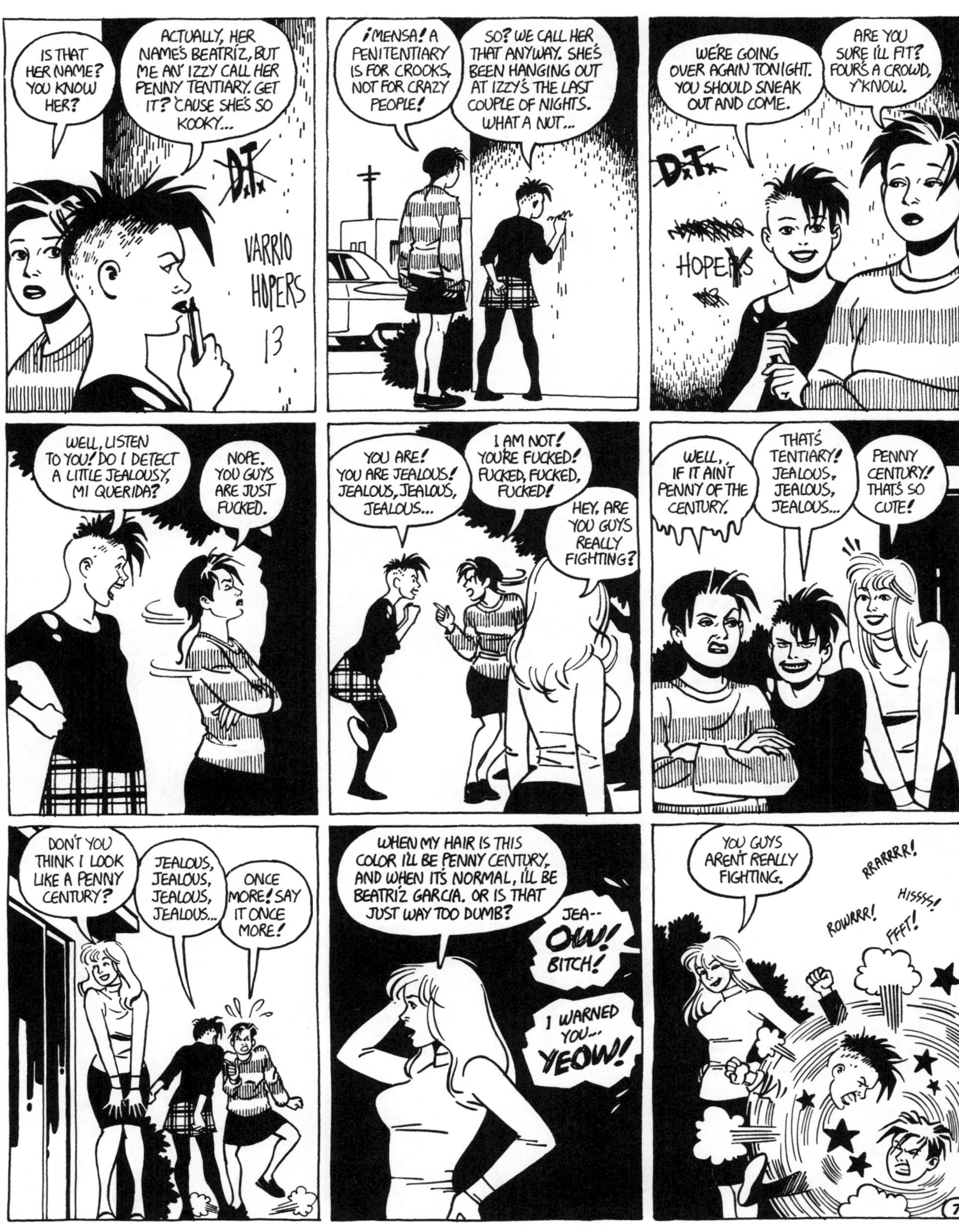
IS THAT HER NAME? YOU KNOW HER?
ACTUALLY, HER NAME'S BEATRÍZ, BUT ME AN' IZZY CALL HER PENNY TENTIARY. GET IT? 'CAUSE SHE'S SO KOOKY...
D.T.
VARRIO HOPERS 13
¡MENSA! A PENITENTIARY IS FOR CROOKS, NOT FOR CRAZY PEOPLE!
SO? WE CALL HER THAT ANYWAY. SHE'S BEEN HANGING OUT AT IZZY'S THE LAST COUPLE OF NIGHTS. WHAT A NUT...
WE'RE GOING OVER AGAIN TONIGHT. YOU SHOULD SNEAK OUT AND COME.
ARE YOU SURE I'LL FIT? FOUR'S A CROWD, Y'KNOW.
WELL, LISTEN TO YOU! DO I DETECT A LITTLE JEALOUSY, MI QUERIDA?
NOPE. YOU GUYS ARE JUST FUCKED.
YOU ARE! YOU ARE JEALOUS! JEALOUS, JEALOUS, JEALOUS...
I AM NOT! YOU'RE FUCKED! FUCKED, FUCKED, FUCKED!
HEY, ARE YOU GUYS REALLY FIGHTING?
WELL, IF IT AIN'T PENNY OF THE CENTURY.
THAT'S TENTIARY! JEALOUS, JEALOUS, JEALOUS...
PENNY CENTURY! THAT'S SO CUTE!
DON'T YOU THINK I LOOK LIKE A PENNY CENTURY?
JEALOUS, JEALOUS, JEALOUS, JEALOUS...
ONCE MORE! SAY IT ONCE MORE!
WHEN MY HAIR IS THIS COLOR I'LL BE PENNY CENTURY, AND WHEN IT'S NORMAL, I'LL BE BEATRÍZ GARCIA. OR IS THAT JUST WAY TOO DUMB?
JEA-- OW! BITCH!
I WARNED YOU... YEOW!
YOU GUYS AREN'T REALLY FIGHTING.
RRARRRR!
HISSSS!
ROWRRR!
FFFT!
7

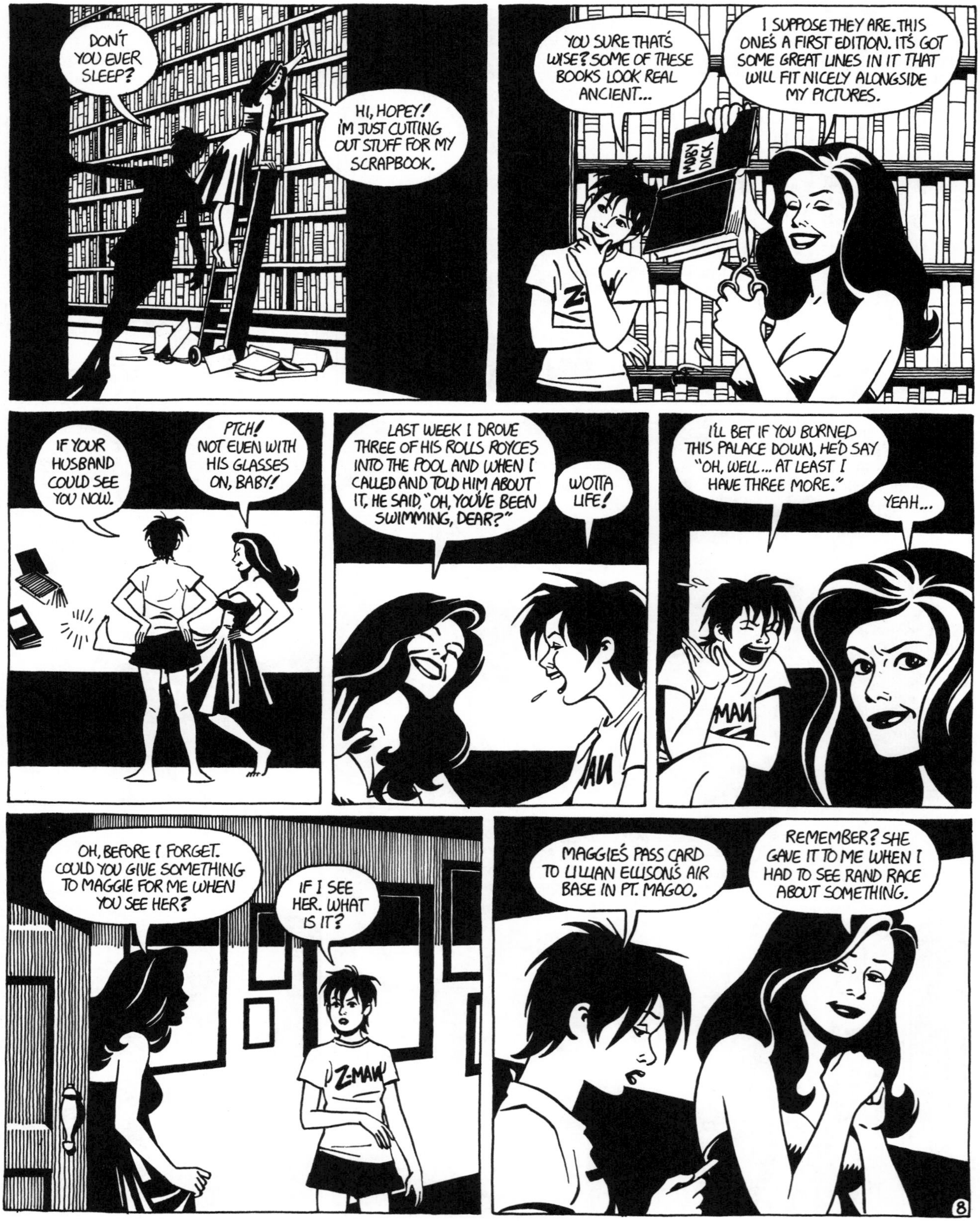
DON'T YOU EVER SLEEP?
HI, HOPEY! I'M JUST CUTTING OUT STUFF FOR MY SCRAPBOOK.
YOU SURE THAT'S WISE? SOME OF THESE BOOKS LOOK REAL ANCIENT...
I SUPPOSE THEY ARE. THIS ONE'S A FIRST EDITION. IT'S GOT SOME GREAT LINES IN IT THAT WILL FIT NICELY ALONGSIDE MY PICTURES.
MOBY DICK
Z-MAN
IF YOUR HUSBAND COULD SEE YOU NOW.
PTCH! NOT EVEN WITH HIS GLASSES ON, BABY!
LAST WEEK I DROVE THREE OF HIS ROLLS ROYCES INTO THE POOL AND WHEN I CALLED AND TOLD HIM ABOUT IT, HE SAID, "OH, YOU'VE BEEN SWIMMING, DEAR?"
WOTTA LIFE!
I'LL BET IF YOU BURNED THIS PALACE DOWN, HE'D SAY "OH, WELL... AT LEAST I HAVE THREE MORE."
YEAH...
OH, BEFORE I FORGET. COULD YOU GIVE SOMETHING TO MAGGIE FOR ME WHEN YOU SEE HER?
IF I SEE HER. WHAT IS IT?
Z-MAN
MAGGIE'S PASS CARD TO LILLIAN ELLISON'S AIR BASE IN PT. MAGOO.
REMEMBER? SHE GAVE IT TO ME WHEN I HAD TO SEE RAND RACE ABOUT SOMETHING.
8

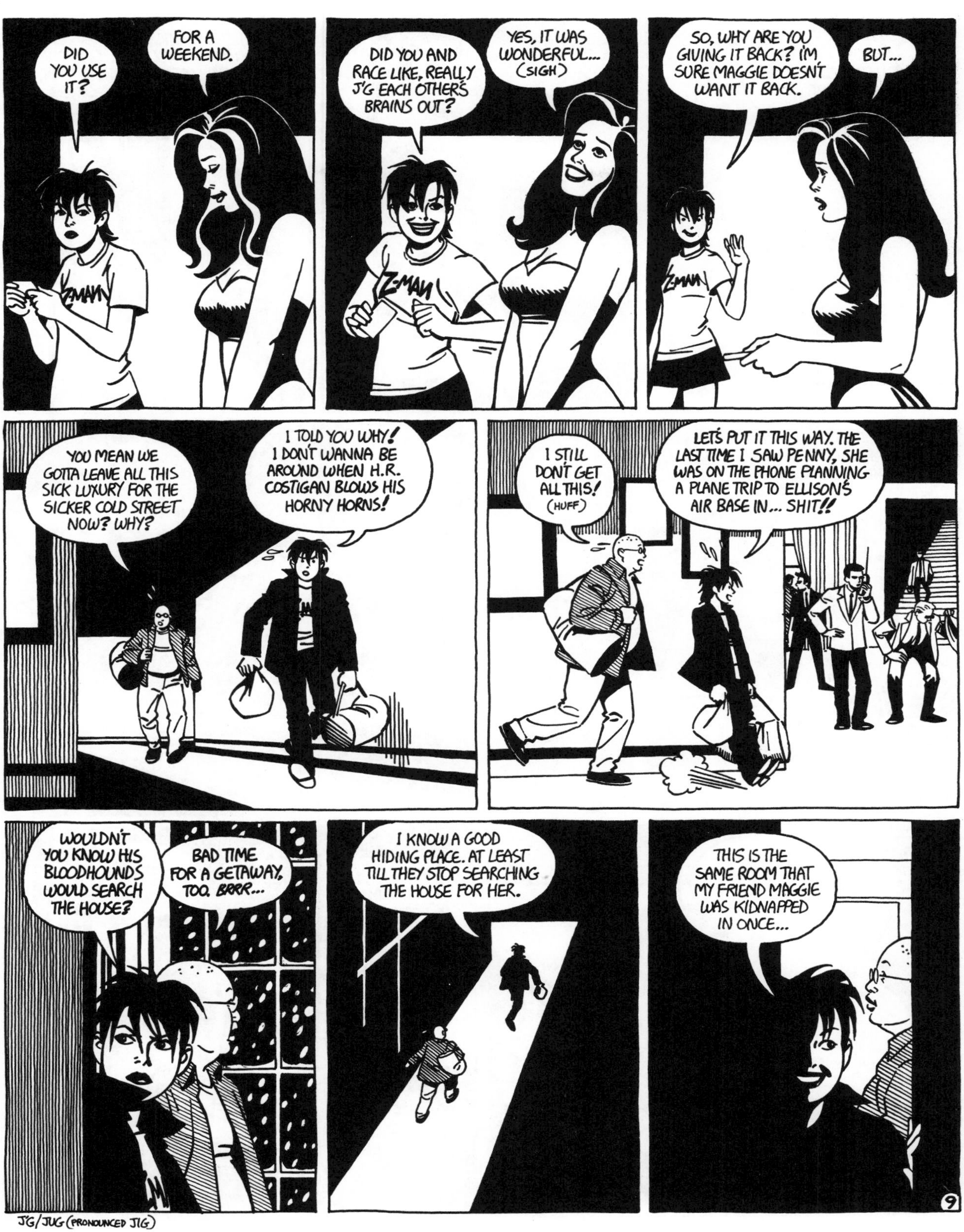
DID YOU USE IT?
FOR A WEEKEND.
DID YOU AND RACE LIKE, REALLY J'G EACH OTHER'S BRAINS OUT?
YES, IT WAS WONDERFUL... (SIGH)
SO, WHY ARE YOU GIVING IT BACK? I'M SURE MAGGIE DOESN'T WANT IT BACK.
BUT...
YOU MEAN WE GOTTA LEAVE ALL THIS SICK LUXURY FOR THE SICKER COLD STREET NOW? WHY?
I TOLD YOU WHY! I DON'T WANNA BE AROUND WHEN H.R. COSTIGAN BLOWS HIS HORNY HORNS!
I STILL DON'T GET ALL THIS! (HUFF)
LET'S PUT IT THIS WAY. THE LAST TIME I SAW PENNY, SHE WAS ON THE PHONE PLANNING A PLANE TRIP TO ELLISON'S AIR BASE IN... SHIT!!
WOULDN'T YOU KNOW HIS BLOODHOUNDS WOULD SEARCH THE HOUSE?
BAD TIME FOR A GETAWAY, TOO. BRRR...
I KNOW A GOOD HIDING PLACE. AT LEAST TILL THEY STOP SEARCHING THE HOUSE FOR HER.
THIS IS THE SAME ROOM THAT MY FRIEND MAGGIE WAS KIDNAPPED IN ONCE...
9

J'G/JUG (PRONOUNCED J'G)

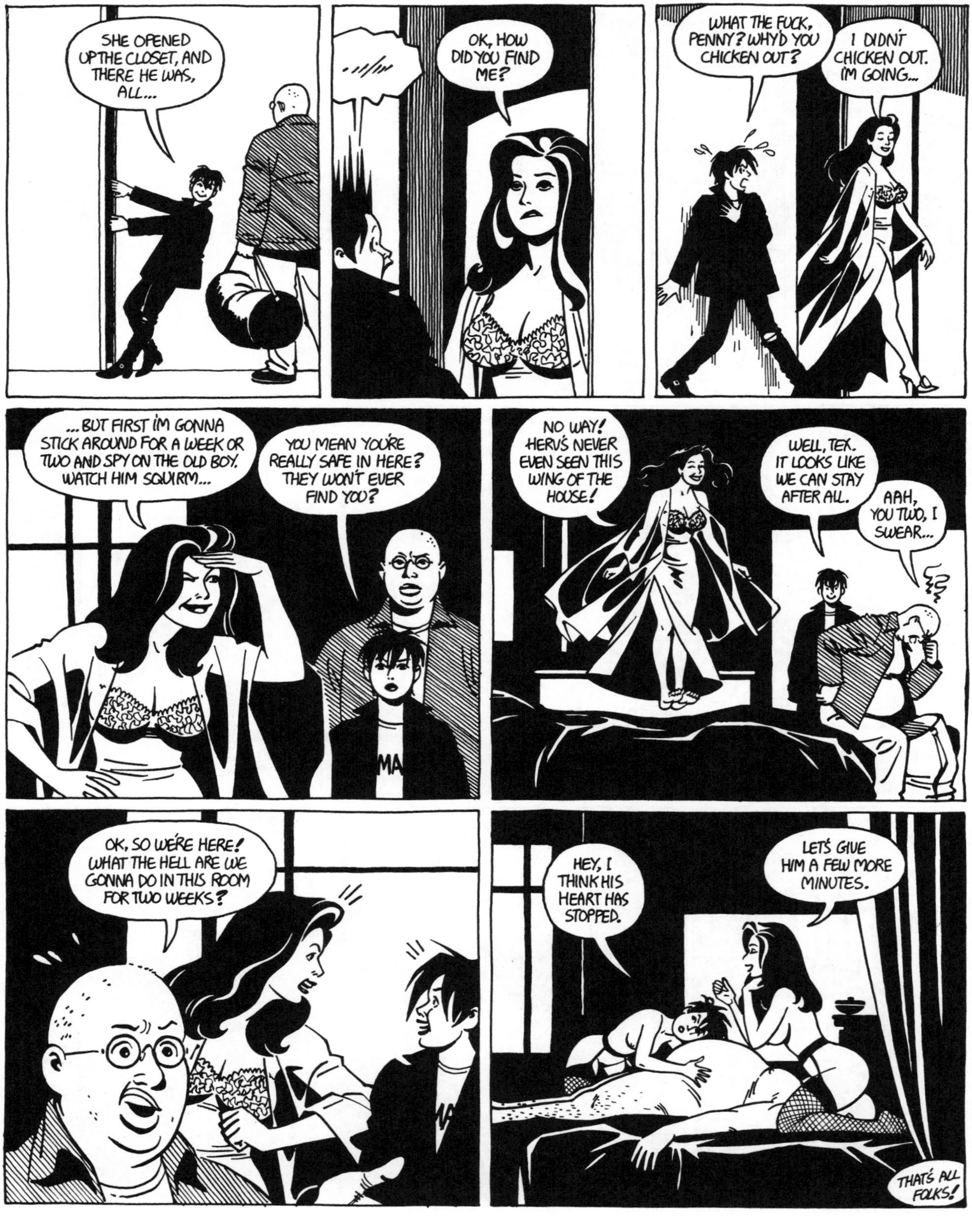
SHE OPENED UP THE CLOSET, AND THERE HE WAS, ALL...
OK, HOW DID YOU FIND ME?
WHAT THE FUCK, PENNY? WHY'D YOU CHICKEN OUT?
I DIDN'T CHICKEN OUT. I'M GOING...
...BUT FIRST I'M GONNA STICK AROUND FOR A WEEK OR TWO AND SPY ON THE OLD BOY. WATCH HIM SQUIRM...
YOU MEAN YOU'RE REALLY SAFE IN HERE? THEY WON'T EVER FIND YOU?
NO WAY! HERV'S NEVER EVEN SEEN THIS WING OF THE HOUSE!
WELL, TEX. IT LOOKS LIKE WE CAN STAY AFTER ALL.
AAH, YOU TWO, I SWEAR...
OK, SO WE'RE HERE! WHAT THE HELL ARE WE GONNA DO IN THIS ROOM FOR TWO WEEKS?
HEY, I THINK HIS HEART HAS STOPPED.
LET'S GIVE HIM A FEW MORE MINUTES.
THAT'S ALL FOLKS!

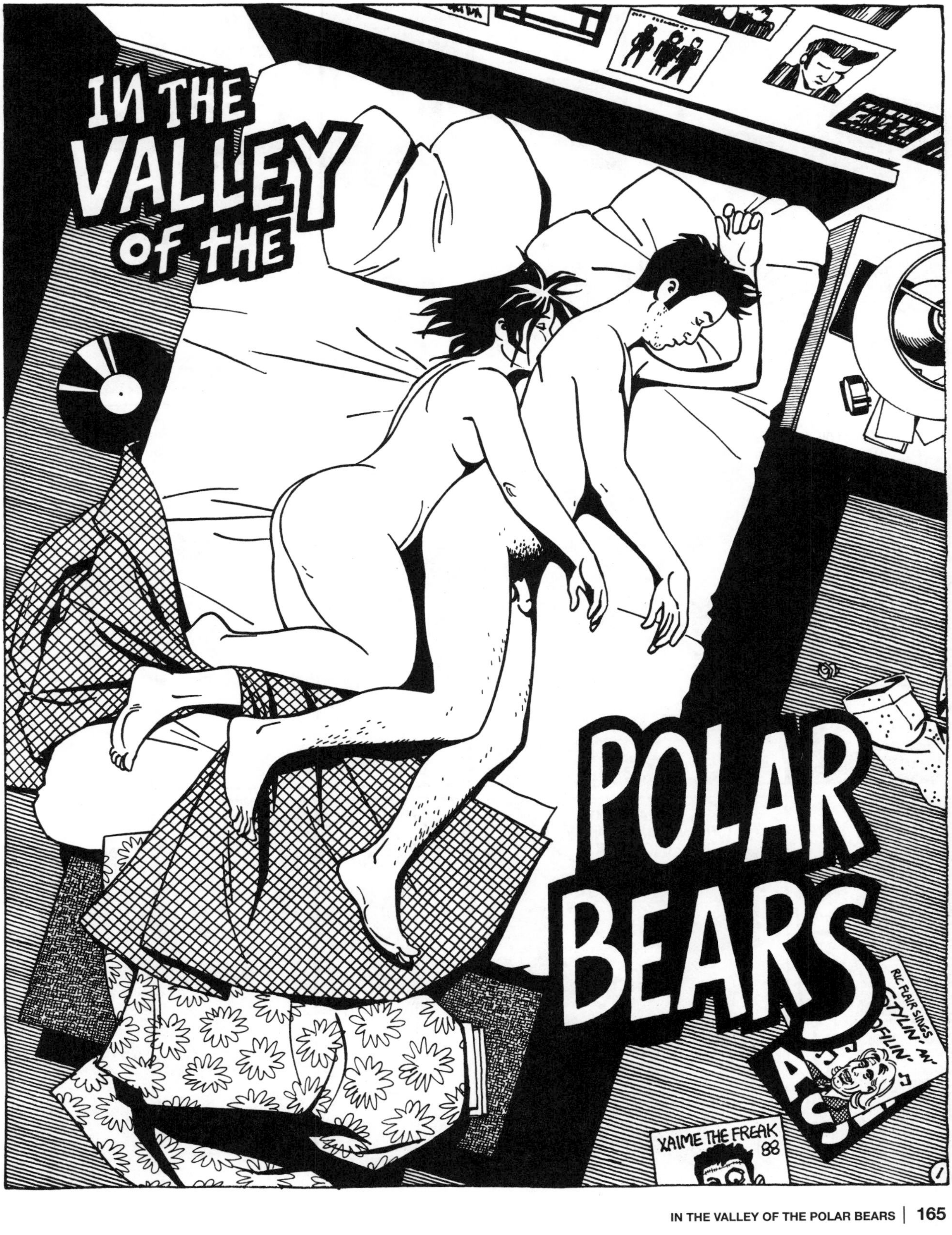
IN THE VALLEY of the
POLAR BEARS
RIC FLAIR SINGS
XAIME THE FREAK
88
1

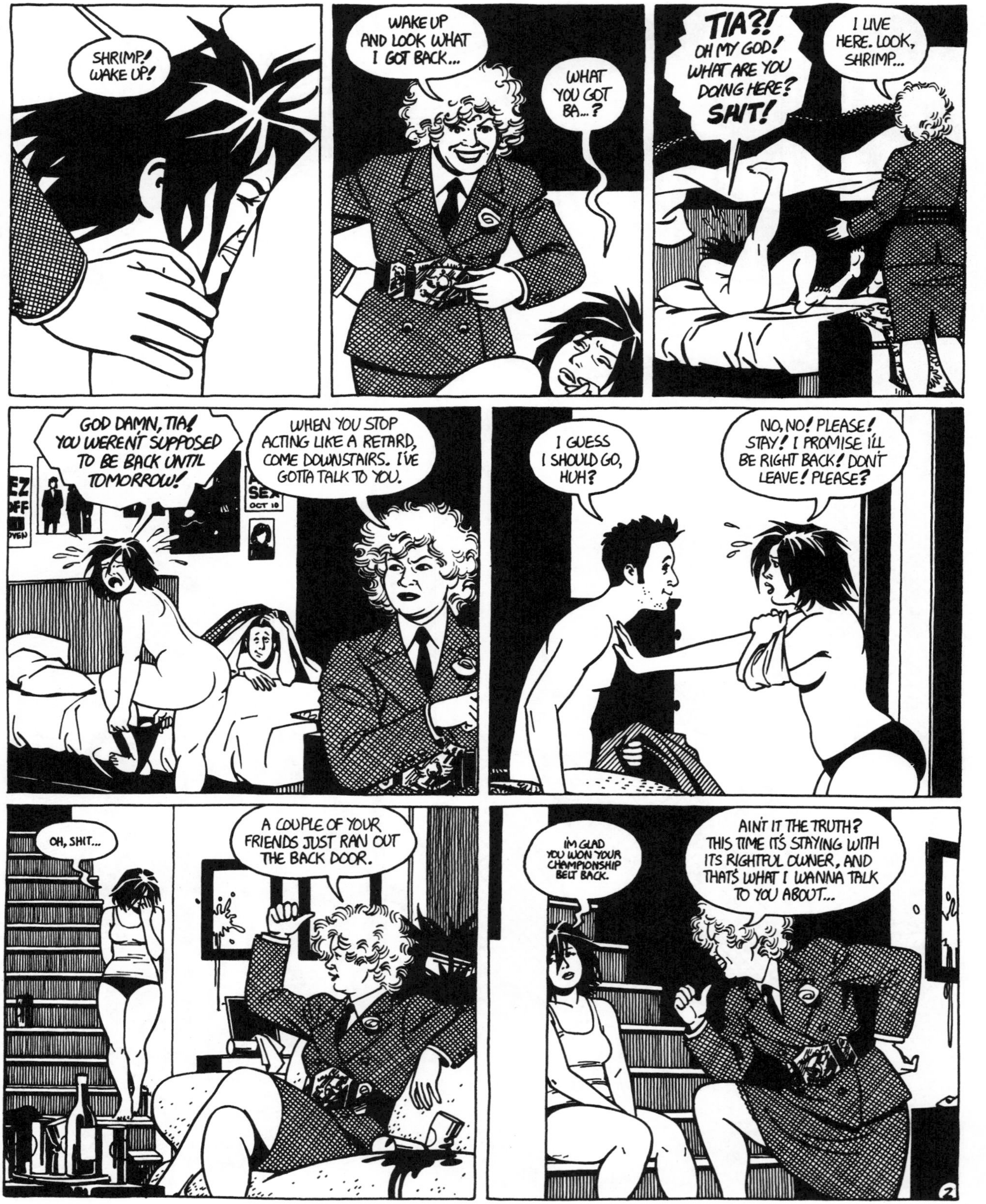
SHRIMP! WAKE UP!
WAKE UP AND LOOK WHAT I GOT BACK...
WHAT YOU GOT BA...?
TIA?! OH MY GOD! WHAT ARE YOU DOING HERE? SHIT!
I LIVE HERE. LOOK, SHRIMP...
GOD DAMN, TIA! YOU WEREN'T SUPPOSED TO BE BACK UNTIL TOMORROW!
WHEN YOU STOP ACTING LIKE A RETARD, COME DOWNSTAIRS. I'VE GOTTA TALK TO YOU.
I GUESS I SHOULD GO, HUH?
NO, NO! PLEASE! STAY! I PROMISE I'LL BE RIGHT BACK! DON'T LEAVE! PLEASE?
OH, SHIT...
A COUPLE OF YOUR FRIENDS JUST RAN OUT THE BACK DOOR.
I'M GLAD YOU WON YOUR CHAMPIONSHIP BELT BACK.
AIN'T IT THE TRUTH? THIS TIME IT'S STAYING WITH ITS RIGHTFUL OWNER, AND THAT'S WHAT I WANNA TALK TO YOU ABOUT...
2

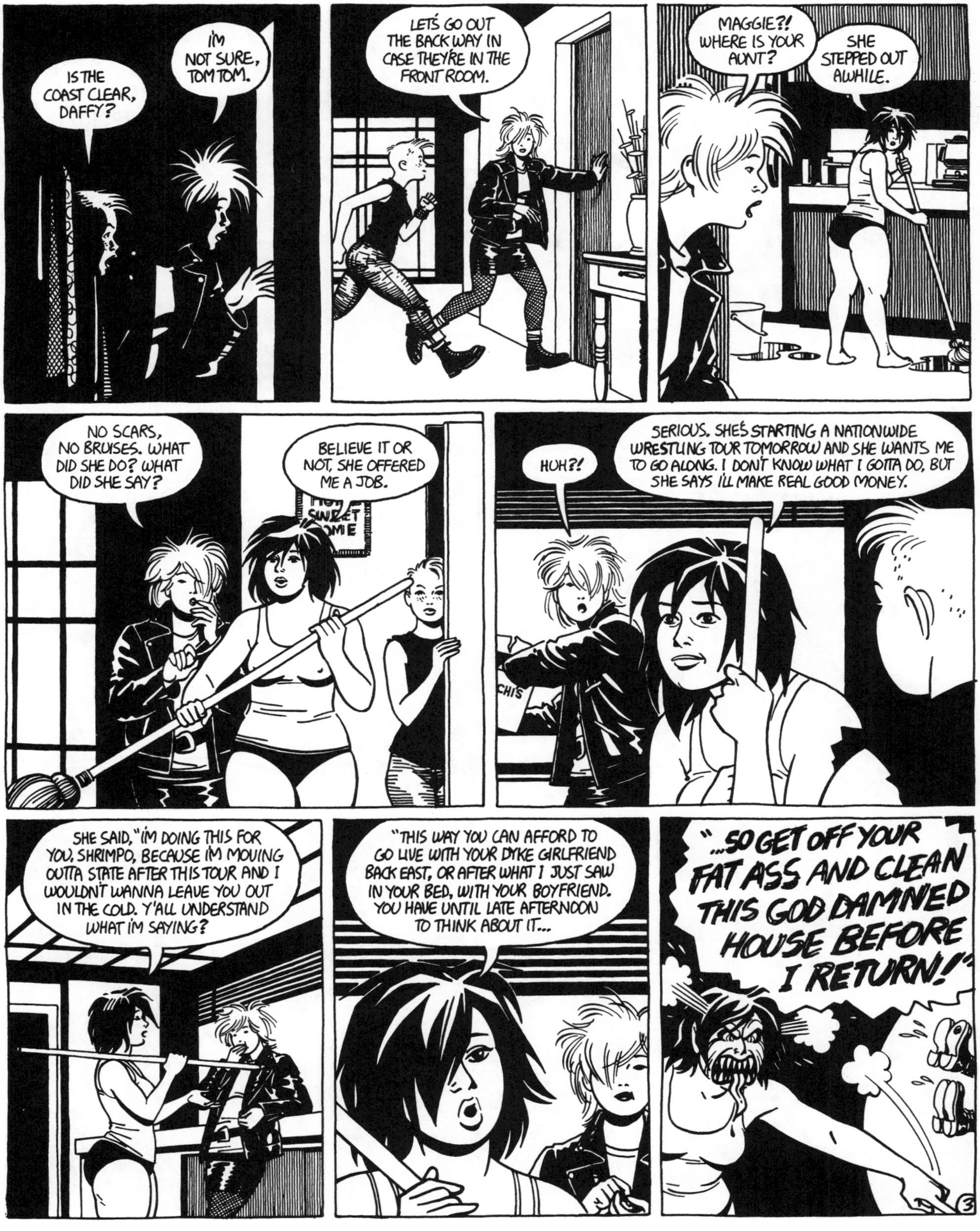
IS THE COAST CLEAR, DAFFY?
I'M NOT SURE, TOM TOM.
LET'S GO OUT THE BACK WAY IN CASE THEY'RE IN THE FRONT ROOM.
MAGGIE?! WHERE IS YOUR AUNT?
SHE STEPPED OUT AWHILE.
NO SCARS, NO BRUISES. WHAT DID SHE DO? WHAT DID SHE SAY?
BELIEVE IT OR NOT, SHE OFFERED ME A JOB.
HUH?!
SERIOUS. SHE'S STARTING A NATIONWIDE WRESTLING TOUR TOMORROW AND SHE WANTS ME TO GO ALONG. I DON'T KNOW WHAT I GOTTA DO, BUT SHE SAYS I'LL MAKE REAL GOOD MONEY.
SHE SAID, "I'M DOING THIS FOR YOU, SHRIMPO, BECAUSE I'M MOVING OUTTA STATE AFTER THIS TOUR AND I WOULDN'T WANNA LEAVE YOU OUT IN THE COLD. Y'ALL UNDERSTAND WHAT I'M SAYING?
"THIS WAY YOU CAN AFFORD TO GO LIVE WITH YOUR DYKE GIRLFRIEND BACK EAST, OR AFTER WHAT I JUST SAW IN YOUR BED, WITH YOUR BOYFRIEND. YOU HAVE UNTIL LATE AFTERNOON TO THINK ABOUT IT...
"...SO GET OFF YOUR FAT ASS AND CLEAN THIS GOD DAMNED HOUSE BEFORE I RETURN!"
3

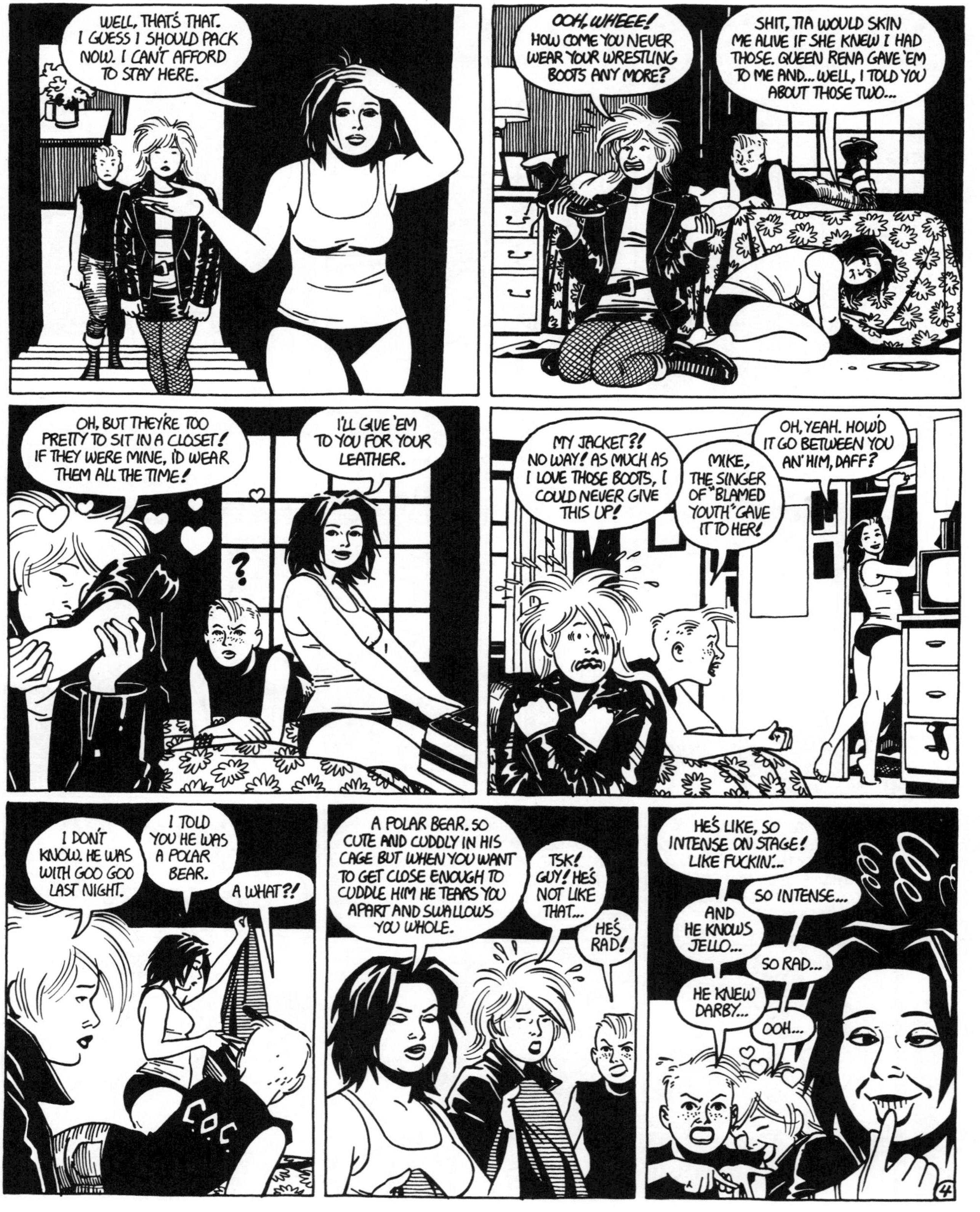
WELL, THAT'S THAT. I GUESS I SHOULD PACK NOW. I CAN'T AFFORD TO STAY HERE.
OOH, WHEEE! HOW COME YOU NEVER WEAR YOUR WRESTLING BOOTS ANY MORE?
SHIT, TIA WOULD SKIN ME ALIVE IF SHE KNEW I HAD THOSE. QUEEN RENA GAVE 'EM TO ME AND... WELL, I TOLD YOU ABOUT THOSE TWO...
OH, BUT THEY'RE TOO PRETTY TO SIT IN A CLOSET! IF THEY WERE MINE, I'D WEAR THEM ALL THE TIME!
I'LL GIVE 'EM TO YOU FOR YOUR LEATHER.
?
MY JACKET?! NO WAY! AS MUCH AS I LOVE THOSE BOOTS, I COULD NEVER GIVE THIS UP!
MIKE, THE SINGER OF "BLAMED YOUTH" GAVE IT TO HER!
OH, YEAH. HOW'D IT GO BETWEEN YOU AN' HIM, DAFF?
I DON'T KNOW. HE WAS WITH GOO GOO LAST NIGHT.
I TOLD YOU HE WAS A POLAR BEAR.
A WHAT?!
C.O.C.
A POLAR BEAR. SO CUTE AND CUDDLY IN HIS CAGE BUT WHEN YOU WANT TO GET CLOSE ENOUGH TO CUDDLE HIM HE TEARS YOU APART AND SWALLOWS YOU WHOLE.
TSK! GUY! HE'S NOT LIKE THAT...
HE'S RAD!
HE'S LIKE, SO INTENSE ON STAGE! LIKE FUCKIN'...
SO INTENSE...
AND HE KNOWS JELLO...
SO RAD...
HE KNEW DARBY...
OOH...
4

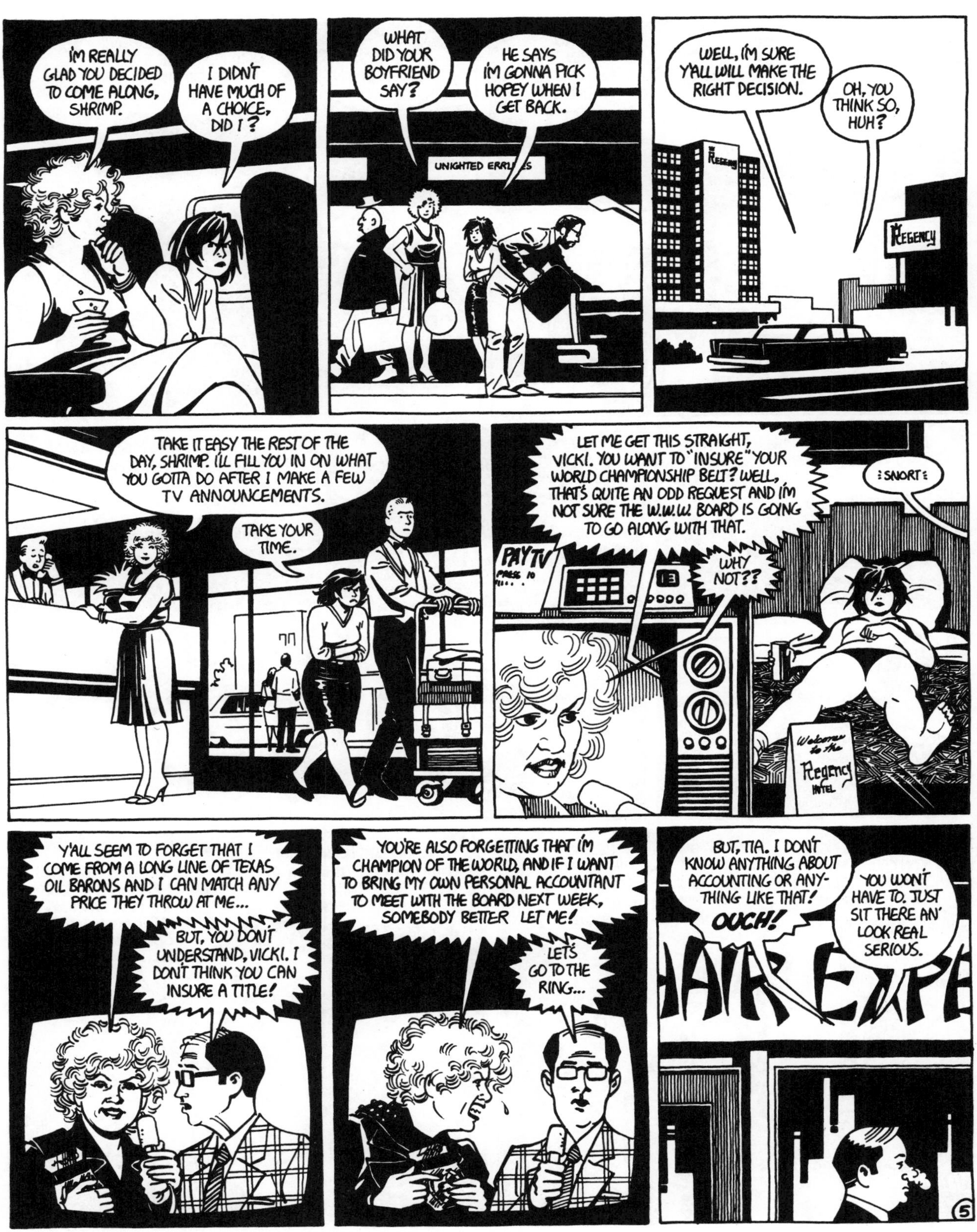

I'M REALLY GLAD YOU DECIDED TO COME ALONG, SHRIMP.
I DIDN'T HAVE MUCH OF A CHOICE, DID I?
WHAT DID YOUR BOYFRIEND SAY?
HE SAYS I'M GONNA PICK HOPEY WHEN I GET BACK.
UNIGHTED ERRL
WELL, I'M SURE Y'ALL WILL MAKE THE RIGHT DECISION.
OH, YOU THINK SO, HUH?
REGENCY
TAKE IT EASY THE REST OF THE DAY, SHRIMP. I'LL FILL YOU IN ON WHAT YOU GOTTA DO AFTER I MAKE A FEW TV ANNOUNCEMENTS.
TAKE YOUR TIME.
LET ME GET THIS STRAIGHT, VICKI. YOU WANT TO "INSURE" YOUR WORLD CHAMPIONSHIP BELT? WELL, THAT'S QUITE AN ODD REQUEST AND I'M NOT SURE THE W.W.W. BOARD IS GOING TO GO ALONG WITH THAT.
WHY NOT??
PAY TV
SNORT
Welcome to the Regency Hotel
Y'ALL SEEM TO FORGET THAT I COME FROM A LONG LINE OF TEXAS OIL BARONS AND I CAN MATCH ANY PRICE THEY THROW AT ME...
BUT, YOU DON'T UNDERSTAND, VICKI. I DON'T THINK YOU CAN INSURE A TITLE!
YOU'RE ALSO FORGETTING THAT I'M CHAMPION OF THE WORLD, AND IF I WANT TO BRING MY OWN PERSONAL ACCOUNTANT TO MEET WITH THE BOARD NEXT WEEK, SOMEBODY BETTER LET ME!
LET'S GO TO THE RING...
BUT, TIA. I DON'T KNOW ANYTHING ABOUT ACCOUNTING OR ANYTHING LIKE THAT! OUCH!
YOU WON'T HAVE TO. JUST SIT THERE AN' LOOK REAL SERIOUS.
HAIR EXPE
5

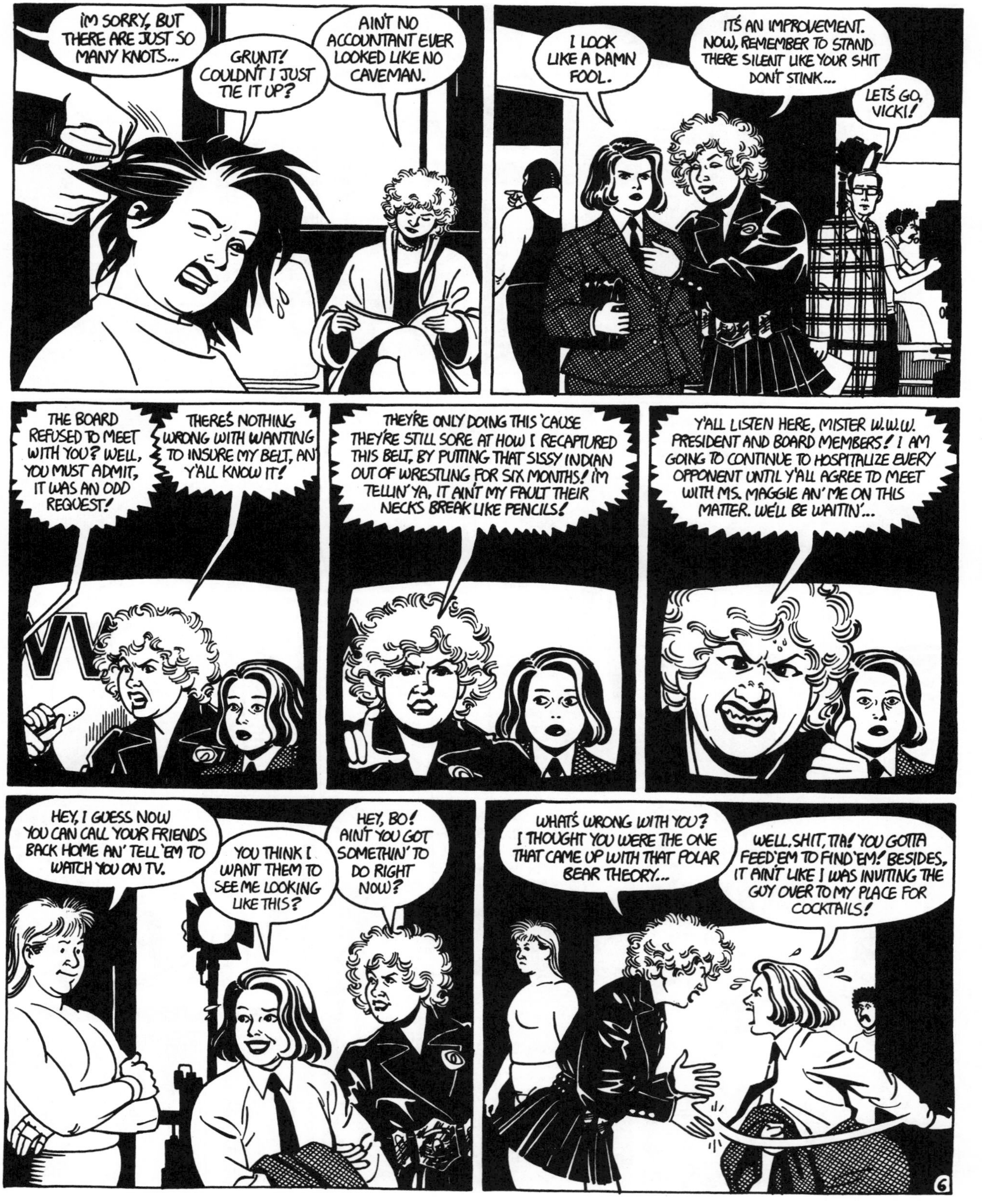
I'M SORRY, BUT THERE ARE JUST SO MANY KNOTS...
GRUNT! COULDN'T I JUST TIE IT UP?
AIN'T NO ACCOUNTANT EVER LOOKED LIKE NO CAVEMAN.
I LOOK LIKE A DAMN FOOL.
IT'S AN IMPROVEMENT. NOW, REMEMBER TO STAND THERE SILENT LIKE YOUR SHIT DON'T STINK...
LET'S GO, VICKI!
THE BOARD REFUSED TO MEET WITH YOU? WELL, YOU MUST ADMIT, IT WAS AN ODD REQUEST!
THERE'S NOTHING WRONG WITH WANTING TO INSURE MY BELT, AN' Y'ALL KNOW IT!
THEY'RE ONLY DOING THIS 'CAUSE THEY'RE STILL SORE AT HOW I RECAPTURED THIS BELT, BY PUTTING THAT SISSY INDIAN OUT OF WRESTLING FOR SIX MONTHS! I'M TELLIN' YA, IT AIN'T MY FAULT THEIR NECKS BREAK LIKE PENCILS!
Y'ALL LISTEN HERE, MISTER W.W.W. PRESIDENT AND BOARD MEMBERS! I AM GOING TO CONTINUE TO HOSPITALIZE EVERY OPPONENT UNTIL Y'ALL AGREE TO MEET WITH MS. MAGGIE AN' ME ON THIS MATTER. WE'LL BE WAITIN'...
HEY, I GUESS NOW YOU CAN CALL YOUR FRIENDS BACK HOME AN' TELL 'EM TO WATCH YOU ON TV.
YOU THINK I WANT THEM TO SEE ME LOOKING LIKE THIS?
HEY, BO! AIN'T YOU GOT SOMETHIN' TO DO RIGHT NOW?
WHAT'S WRONG WITH YOU? I THOUGHT YOU WERE THE ONE THAT CAME UP WITH THAT POLAR BEAR THEORY...
WELL, SHIT, TIA! YOU GOTTA FEED 'EM TO FIND 'EM! BESIDES, IT AIN'T LIKE I WAS INVITING THE GUY OVER TO MY PLACE FOR COCKTAILS!
6

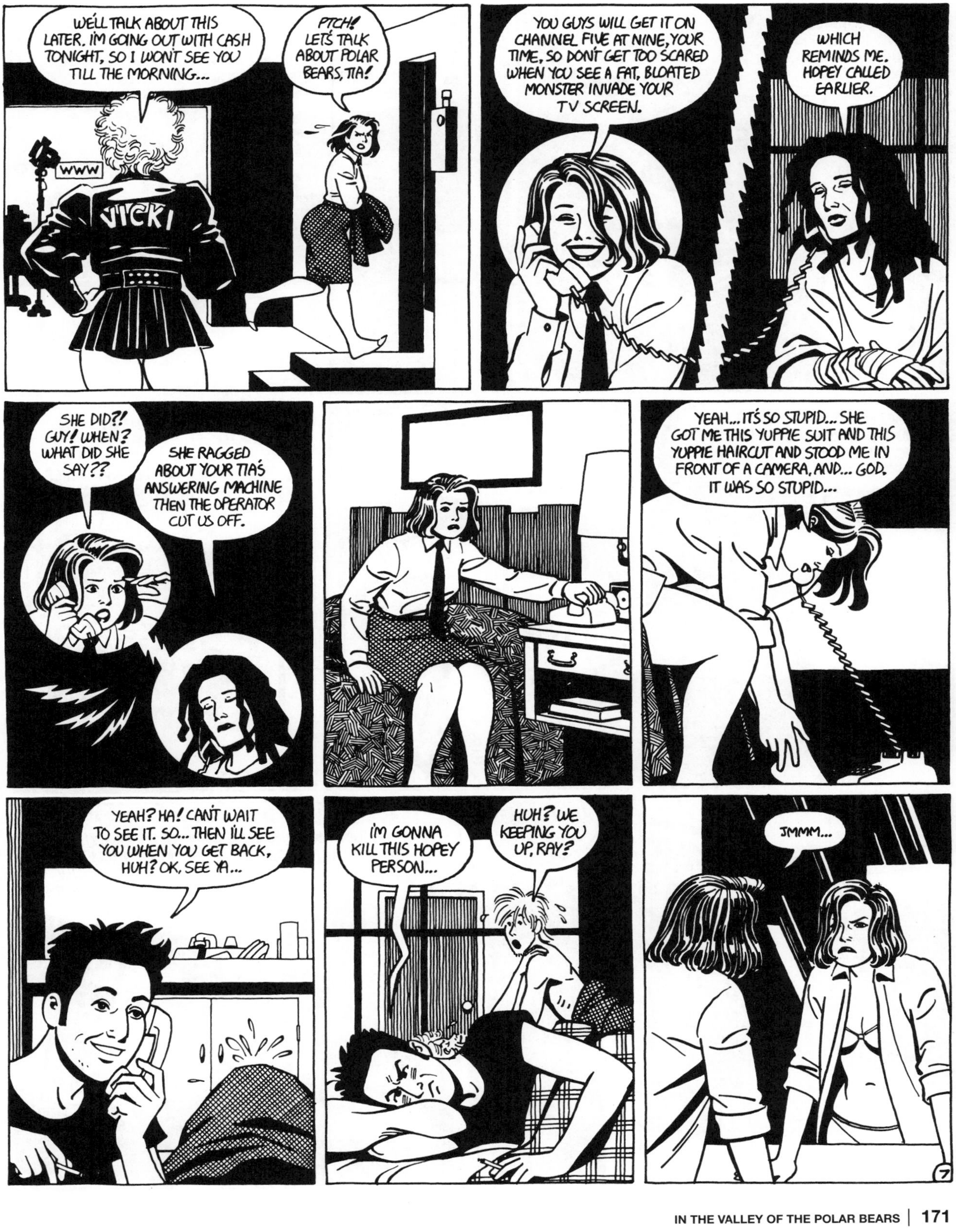
WE'LL TALK ABOUT THIS LATER. I'M GOING OUT WITH CASH TONIGHT, SO I WON'T SEE YOU TILL THE MORNING...
WWW
VICKI
PTCH! LET'S TALK ABOUT POLAR BEARS, TIA!
YOU GUYS WILL GET IT ON CHANNEL FIVE AT NINE, YOUR TIME, SO DON'T GET TOO SCARED WHEN YOU SEE A FAT, BLOATED MONSTER INVADE YOUR TV SCREEN.
WHICH REMINDS ME. HOPEY CALLED EARLIER.
SHE DID?! GUY! WHEN? WHAT DID SHE SAY??
SHE RAGGED ABOUT YOUR TIA'S ANSWERING MACHINE THEN THE OPERATOR CUT US OFF.
YEAH... IT'S SO STUPID... SHE GOT ME THIS YUPPIE SUIT AND THIS YUPPIE HAIRCUT AND STOOD ME IN FRONT OF A CAMERA, AND... GOD. IT WAS SO STUPID...
YEAH? HA! CAN'T WAIT TO SEE IT. SO... THEN I'LL SEE YOU WHEN YOU GET BACK, HUH? OK, SEE YA...
I'M GONNA KILL THIS HOPEY PERSON...
HUH? WE KEEPING YOU UP, RAY?
JMMM...
7

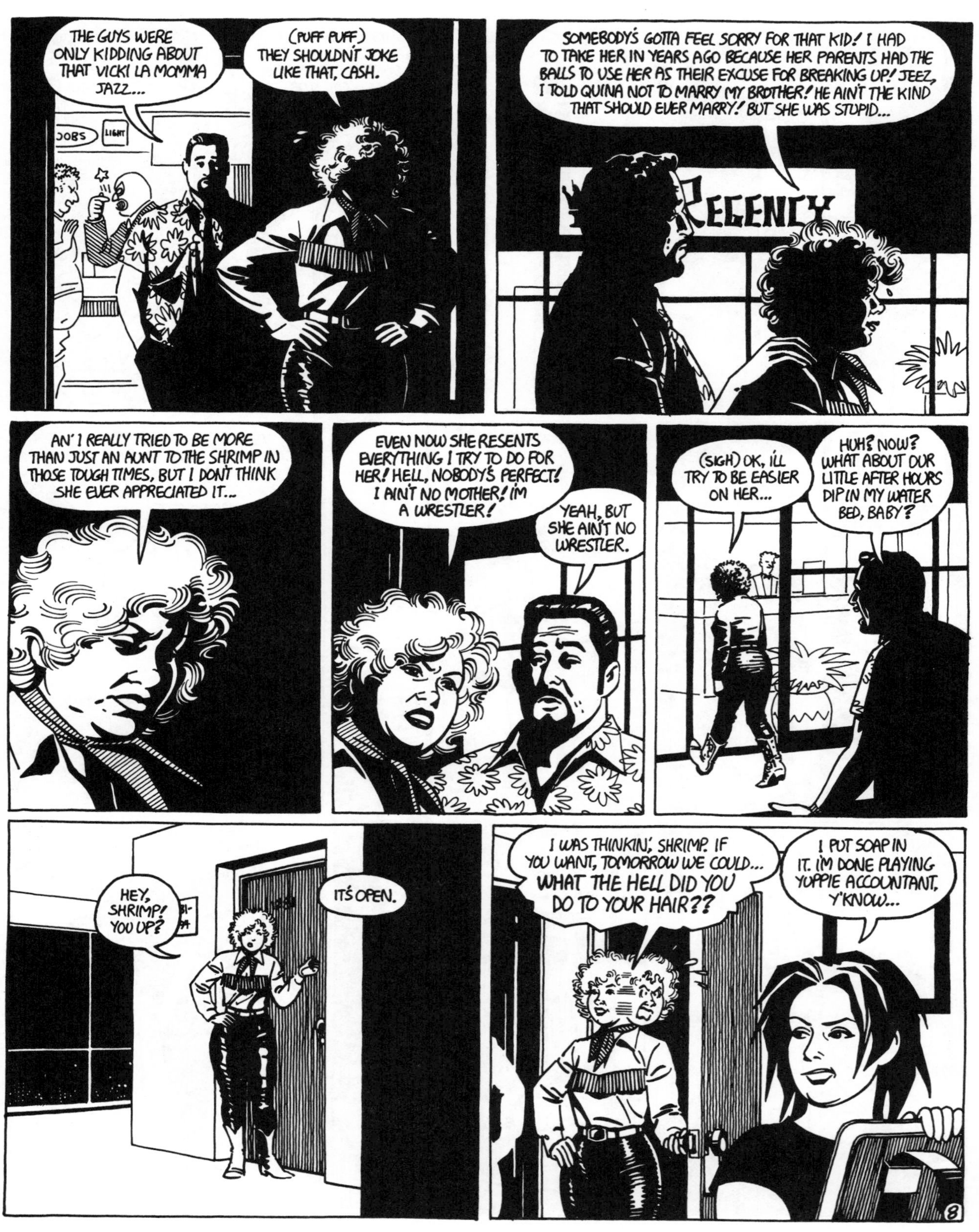
THE GUYS WERE ONLY KIDDING ABOUT THAT VICKI LA MOMMA JAZZ...
(PUFF PUFF) THEY SHOULDN'T JOKE LIKE THAT, CASH.
JOBS
LIGHT
SOMEBODY'S GOTTA FEEL SORRY FOR THAT KID! I HAD TO TAKE HER IN YEARS AGO BECAUSE HER PARENTS HAD THE BALLS TO USE HER AS THEIR EXCUSE FOR BREAKING UP! JEEZ, I TOLD QUINA NOT TO MARRY MY BROTHER! HE AIN'T THE KIND THAT SHOULD EVER MARRY! BUT SHE WAS STUPID...
REGENCY
AN' I REALLY TRIED TO BE MORE THAN JUST AN AUNT TO THE SHRIMP IN THOSE TOUGH TIMES, BUT I DON'T THINK SHE EVER APPRECIATED IT...
EVEN NOW SHE RESENTS EVERYTHING I TRY TO DO FOR HER! HELL, NOBODY'S PERFECT! I AIN'T NO MOTHER! I'M A WRESTLER!
YEAH, BUT SHE AIN'T NO WRESTLER.
(SIGH) OK, I'LL TRY TO BE EASIER ON HER...
HUH? NOW? WHAT ABOUT OUR LITTLE AFTER HOURS DIP IN MY WATER BED, BABY?
HEY, SHRIMP! YOU UP?
IT'S OPEN.
I WAS THINKIN', SHRIMP. IF YOU WANT, TOMORROW WE COULD... WHAT THE HELL DID YOU DO TO YOUR HAIR??
I PUT SOAP IN IT. I'M DONE PLAYING YUPPIE ACCOUNTANT, Y'KNOW...
8

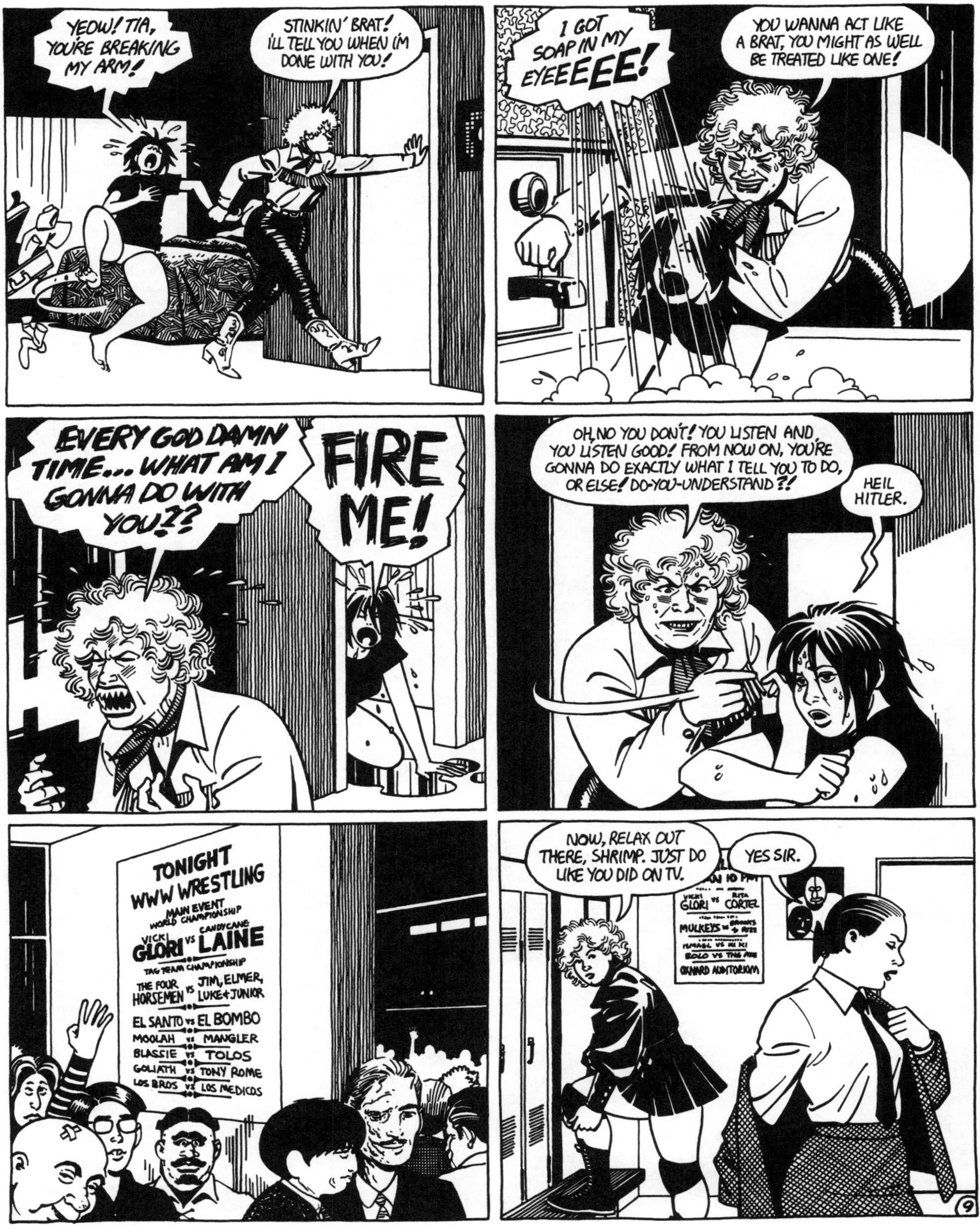
YEOW! TIA, YOU'RE BREAKING MY ARM!
STINKIN' BRAT! I'LL TELL YOU WHEN I'M DONE WITH YOU!
I GOT SOAP IN MY EYEEEEEE!
YOU WANNA ACT LIKE A BRAT, YOU MIGHT AS WELL BE TREATED LIKE ONE!
EVERY GOD DAMN TIME... WHAT AM I GONNA DO WITH YOU??
FIRE ME!
OH, NO YOU DON'T! YOU LISTEN AND YOU LISTEN GOOD! FROM NOW ON, YOU'RE GONNA DO EXACTLY WHAT I TELL YOU TO DO, OR ELSE! DO-YOU-UNDERSTAND?!
HEIL HITLER.
TONIGHT
WWW WRESTLING
MAIN EVENT
WORLD CHAMPIONSHIP
VICKI GLORI vs CANDYCANE LAINE
TAG TEAM CHAMPIONSHIP
THE FOUR HORSEMEN vs JIM, ELMER, LUKE & JUNIOR
EL SANTO vs EL BOMBO
MOOLAH vs MANGLER
BLASSIE vs TOLOS
GOLIATH vs TONY ROME
LOS BROS vs LOS MEDICOS
NOW, RELAX OUT THERE, SHRIMP. JUST DO LIKE YOU DID ON TV.
YES SIR.
9

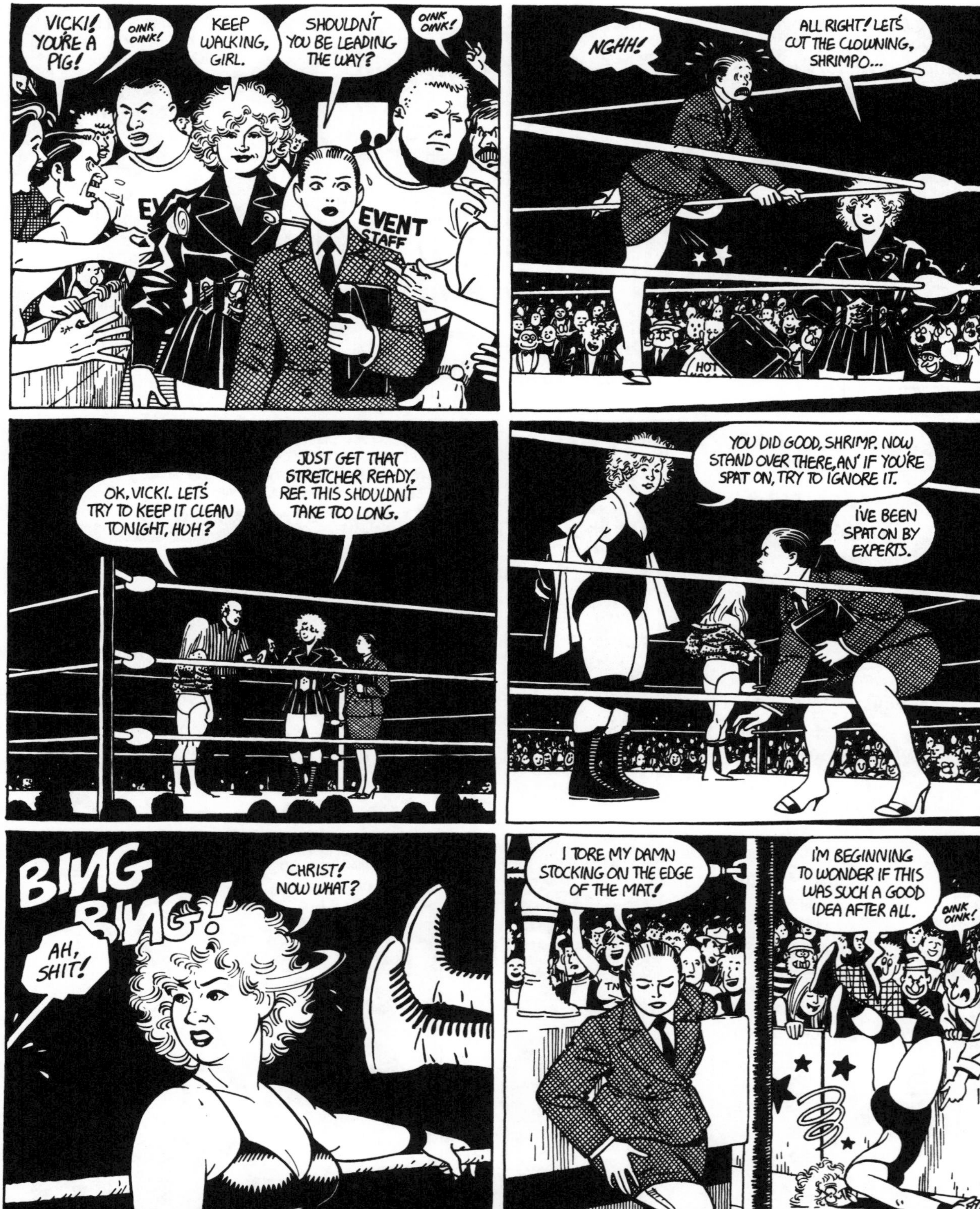
VICKI! YOU'RE A PIG!
OINK OINK!
KEEP WALKING, GIRL.
SHOULDN'T YOU BE LEADING THE WAY?
OINK OINK!
EVENT STAFF
NGHH!
ALL RIGHT! LET'S CUT THE CLOWNING, SHRIMPO...
OK, VICKI. LET'S TRY TO KEEP IT CLEAN TONIGHT, HUH?
JUST GET THAT STRETCHER READY, REF. THIS SHOULDN'T TAKE TOO LONG.
YOU DID GOOD, SHRIMP. NOW STAND OVER THERE, AN' IF YOU'RE SPAT ON, TRY TO IGNORE IT.
I'VE BEEN SPAT ON BY EXPERTS.
BING BING!
AH, SHIT!
CHRIST! NOW WHAT?
I TORE MY DAMN STOCKING ON THE EDGE OF THE MAT!
I'M BEGINNING TO WONDER IF THIS WAS SUCH A GOOD IDEA AFTER ALL.
OINK OINK!
END OF PART I

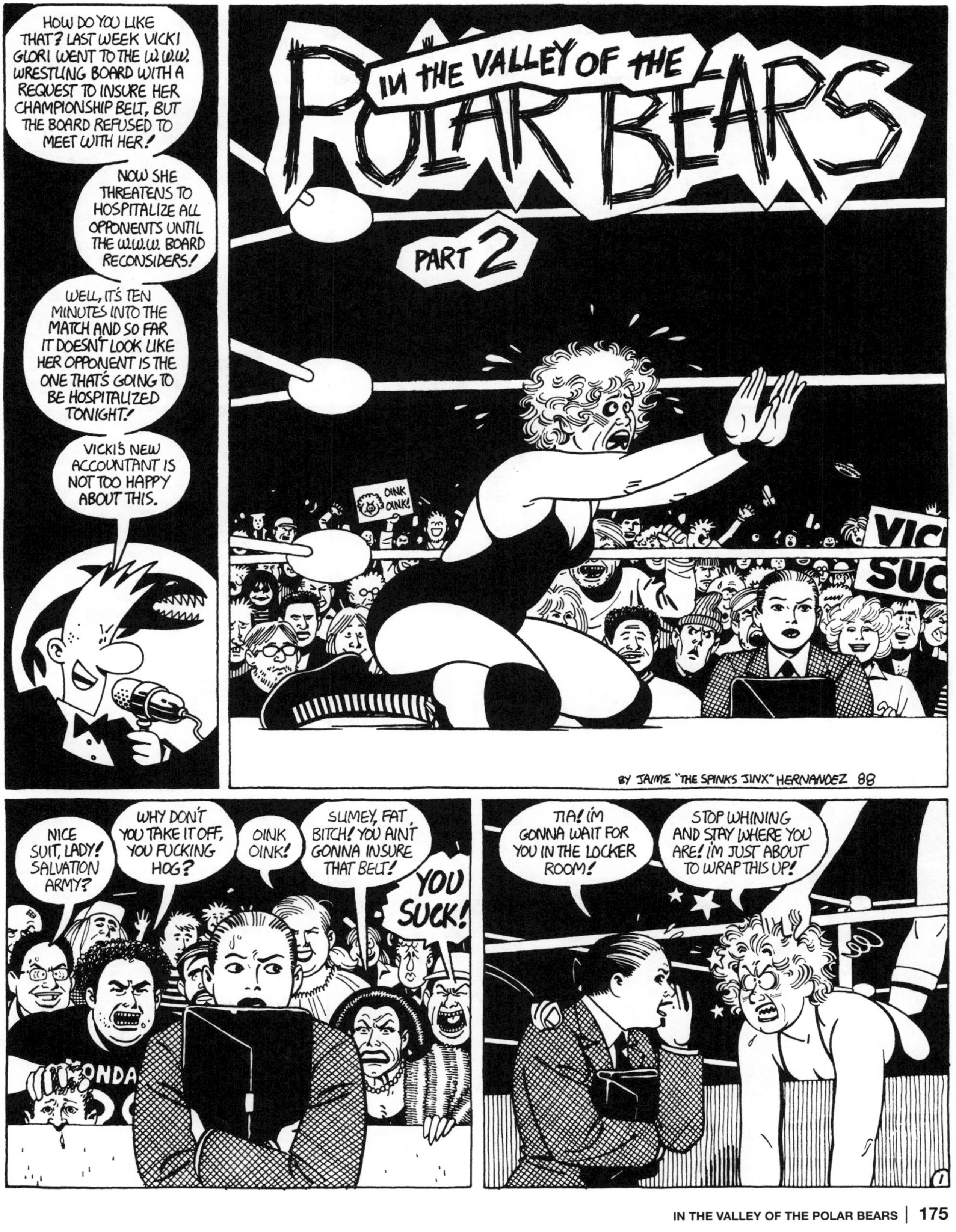
IN THE VALLEY OF THE
POLAR BEARS
PART 2
HOW DO YOU LIKE THAT? LAST WEEK VICKI GLORI WENT TO THE W.W.W. WRESTLING BOARD WITH A REQUEST TO INSURE HER CHAMPIONSHIP BELT, BUT THE BOARD REFUSED TO MEET WITH HER!
NOW SHE THREATENS TO HOSPITALIZE ALL OPPONENTS UNTIL THE W.W.W. BOARD RECONSIDERS!
WELL, IT'S TEN MINUTES INTO THE MATCH AND SO FAR IT DOESN'T LOOK LIKE HER OPPONENT IS THE ONE THAT'S GOING TO BE HOSPITALIZED TONIGHT!
VICKI'S NEW ACCOUNTANT IS NOT TOO HAPPY ABOUT THIS.
OINK OINK!
VIC
SUC
BY JAIME "THE SPINKS JINX" HERNANDEZ 88
NICE SUIT, LADY! SALVATION ARMY?
WHY DON'T YOU TAKE IT OFF, YOU FUCKING HOG?
OINK OINK!
SLIMEY, FAT BITCH! YOU AIN'T GONNA INSURE THAT BELT!
YOU SUCK!
TIA! I'M GONNA WAIT FOR YOU IN THE LOCKER ROOM!
STOP WHINING AND STAY WHERE YOU ARE! I'M JUST ABOUT TO WRAP THIS UP!
1

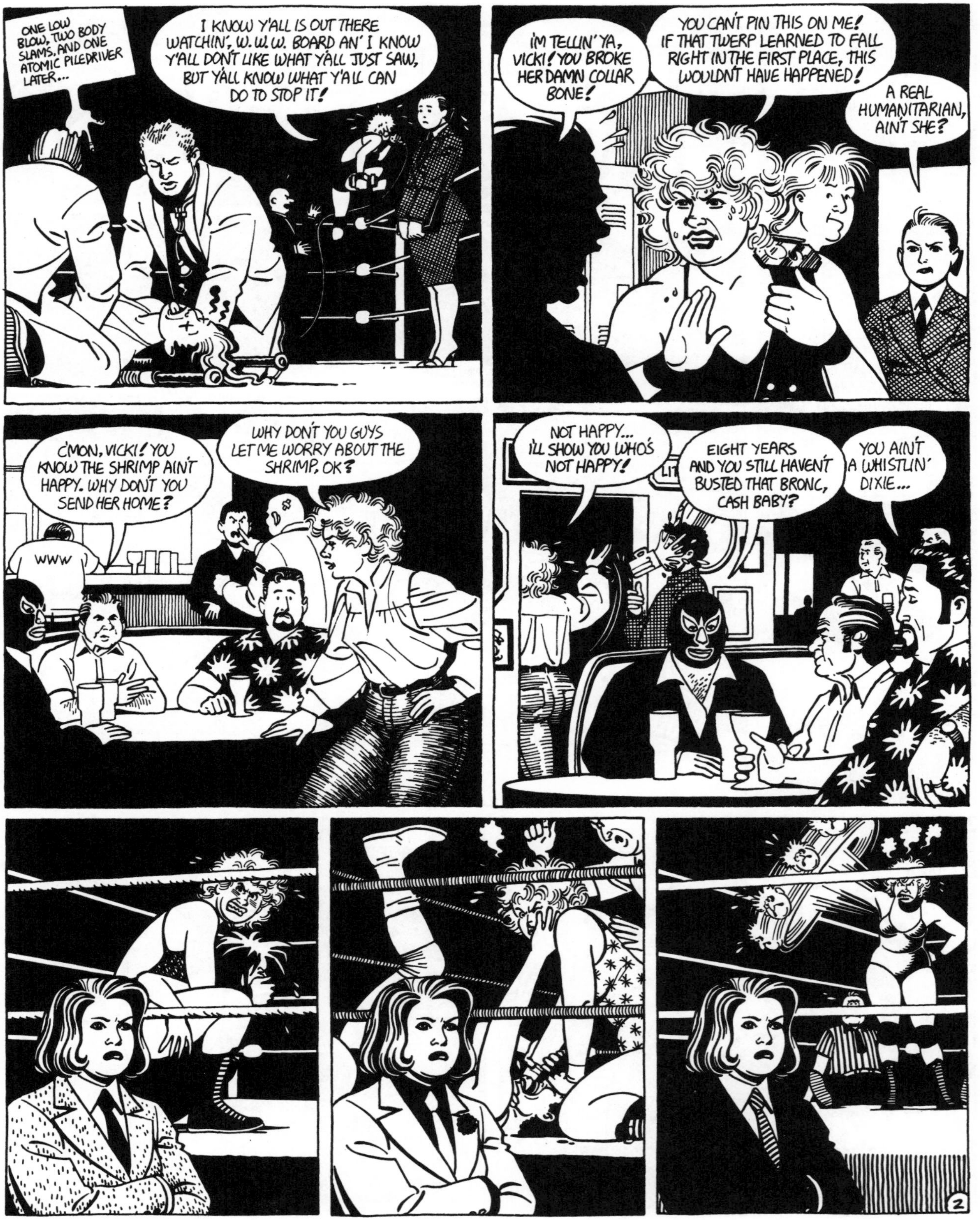

ONE LOW BLOW, TWO BODY SLAMS, AND ONE ATOMIC PILEDRIVER LATER...
I KNOW Y'ALL IS OUT THERE WATCHIN', W.W.W. BOARD AN' I KNOW Y'ALL DON'T LIKE WHAT Y'ALL JUST SAW, BUT Y'ALL KNOW WHAT Y'ALL CAN DO TO STOP IT!
I'M TELLIN' YA, VICKI! YOU BROKE HER DAMN COLLAR BONE!
YOU CAN'T PIN THIS ON ME! IF THAT TWERP LEARNED TO FALL RIGHT IN THE FIRST PLACE, THIS WOULDN'T HAVE HAPPENED!
A REAL HUMANITARIAN, AIN'T SHE?
C'MON, VICKI! YOU KNOW THE SHRIMP AIN'T HAPPY. WHY DON'T YOU SEND HER HOME?
WHY DON'T YOU GUYS LET ME WORRY ABOUT THE SHRIMP, OK?
WWW
NOT HAPPY... I'LL SHOW YOU WHO'S NOT HAPPY!
EIGHT YEARS AND YOU STILL HAVEN'T BUSTED THAT BRONC, CASH BABY?
YOU AIN'T A WHISTLIN' DIXIE...
2

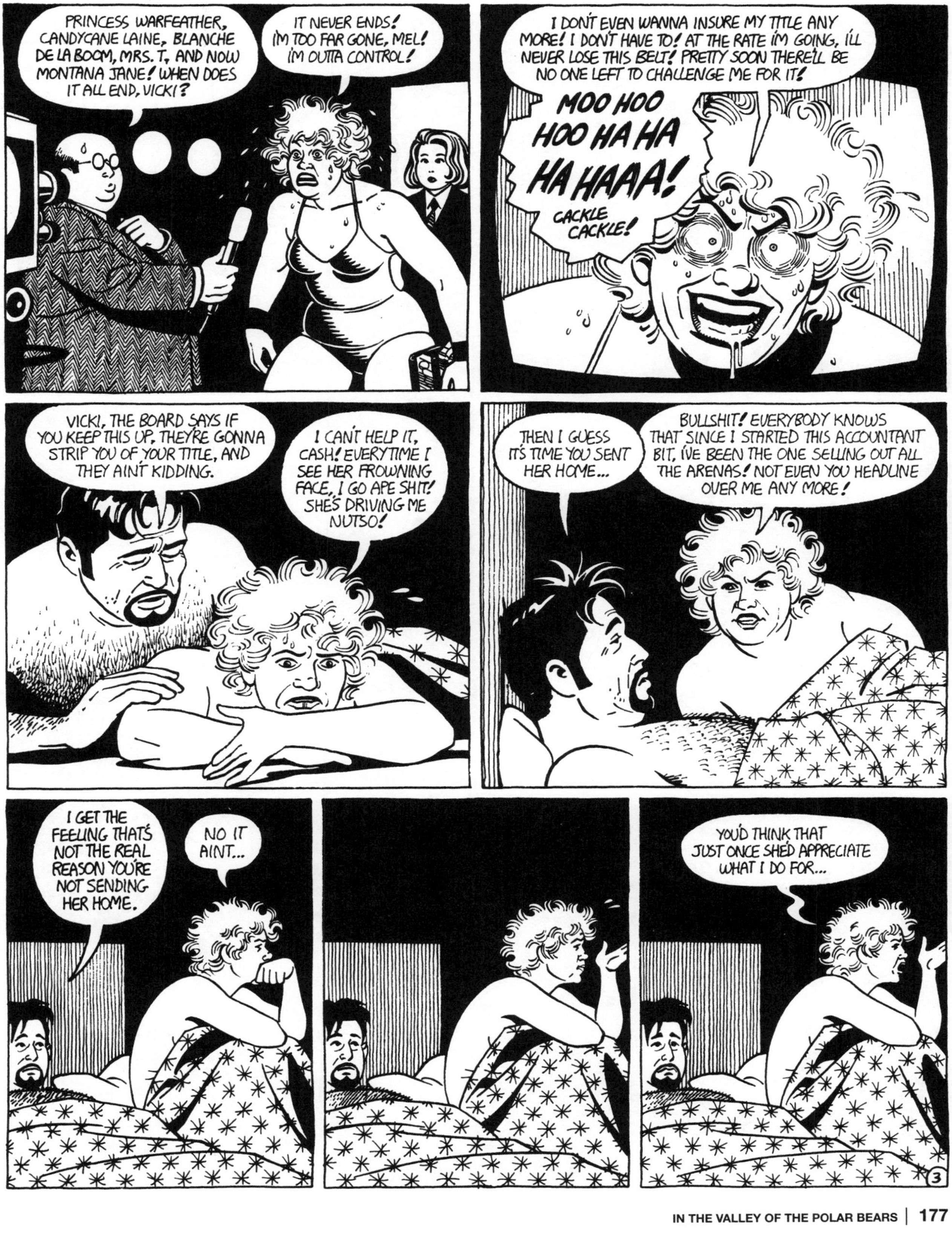
PRINCESS WARFEATHER, CANDYCANE LAINE, BLANCHE DE LA BOOM, MRS. T, AND NOW MONTANA JANE! WHEN DOES IT ALL END, VICKI?
IT NEVER ENDS! I'M TOO FAR GONE, MEL! I'M OUTTA CONTROL!
I DON'T EVEN WANNA INSURE MY TITLE ANY MORE! I DON'T HAVE TO! AT THE RATE I'M GOING, I'LL NEVER LOSE THIS BELT! PRETTY SOON THERE'LL BE NO ONE LEFT TO CHALLENGE ME FOR IT!
MOO HOO HOO HA HA HA HAAA!
CACKLE CACKLE!
VICKI, THE BOARD SAYS IF YOU KEEP THIS UP, THEY'RE GONNA STRIP YOU OF YOUR TITLE, AND THEY AIN'T KIDDING.
I CAN'T HELP IT, CASH! EVERYTIME I SEE HER FROWNING FACE, I GO APE SHIT! SHE'S DRIVING ME NUTSO!
THEN I GUESS IT'S TIME YOU SENT HER HOME...
BULLSHIT! EVERYBODY KNOWS THAT SINCE I STARTED THIS ACCOUNTANT BIT, I'VE BEEN THE ONE SELLING OUT ALL THE ARENAS! NOT EVEN YOU HEADLINE OVER ME ANY MORE!
I GET THE FEELING THAT'S NOT THE REAL REASON YOU'RE NOT SENDING HER HOME.
NO IT AINT...
YOU'D THINK THAT JUST ONCE SHE'D APPRECIATE WHAT I DO FOR...
3

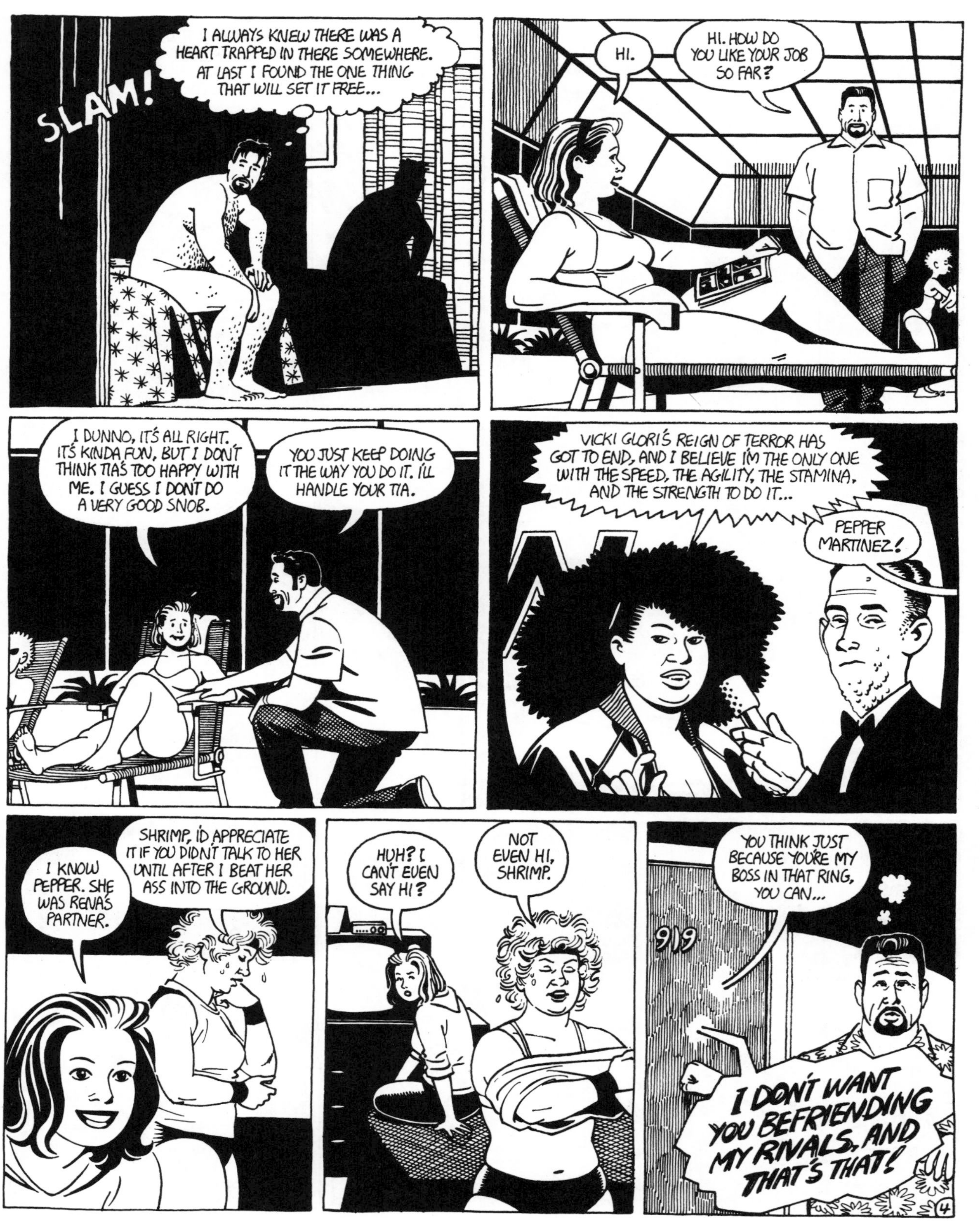
SLAM!
I ALWAYS KNEW THERE WAS A HEART TRAPPED IN THERE SOMEWHERE. AT LAST I FOUND THE ONE THING THAT WILL SET IT FREE...
HI.
HI. HOW DO YOU LIKE YOUR JOB SO FAR?
I DUNNO, IT'S ALL RIGHT. IT'S KINDA FUN, BUT I DON'T THINK TIA'S TOO HAPPY WITH ME. I GUESS I DON'T DO A VERY GOOD SNOB.
YOU JUST KEEP DOING IT THE WAY YOU DO IT. I'LL HANDLE YOUR TIA.
VICKI GLORI'S REIGN OF TERROR HAS GOT TO END, AND I BELIEVE I'M THE ONLY ONE WITH THE SPEED, THE AGILITY, THE STAMINA, AND THE STRENGTH TO DO IT...
PEPPER MARTINEZ!
I KNOW PEPPER. SHE WAS RENA'S PARTNER.
SHRIMP, I'D APPRECIATE IT IF YOU DIDN'T TALK TO HER UNTIL AFTER I BEAT HER ASS INTO THE GROUND.
HUH? I CAN'T EVEN SAY HI?
NOT EVEN HI, SHRIMP.
YOU THINK JUST BECAUSE YOU'RE MY BOSS IN THAT RING, YOU CAN...
919
I DON'T WANT YOU BEFRIENDING MY RIVALS, AND THAT'S THAT!
4

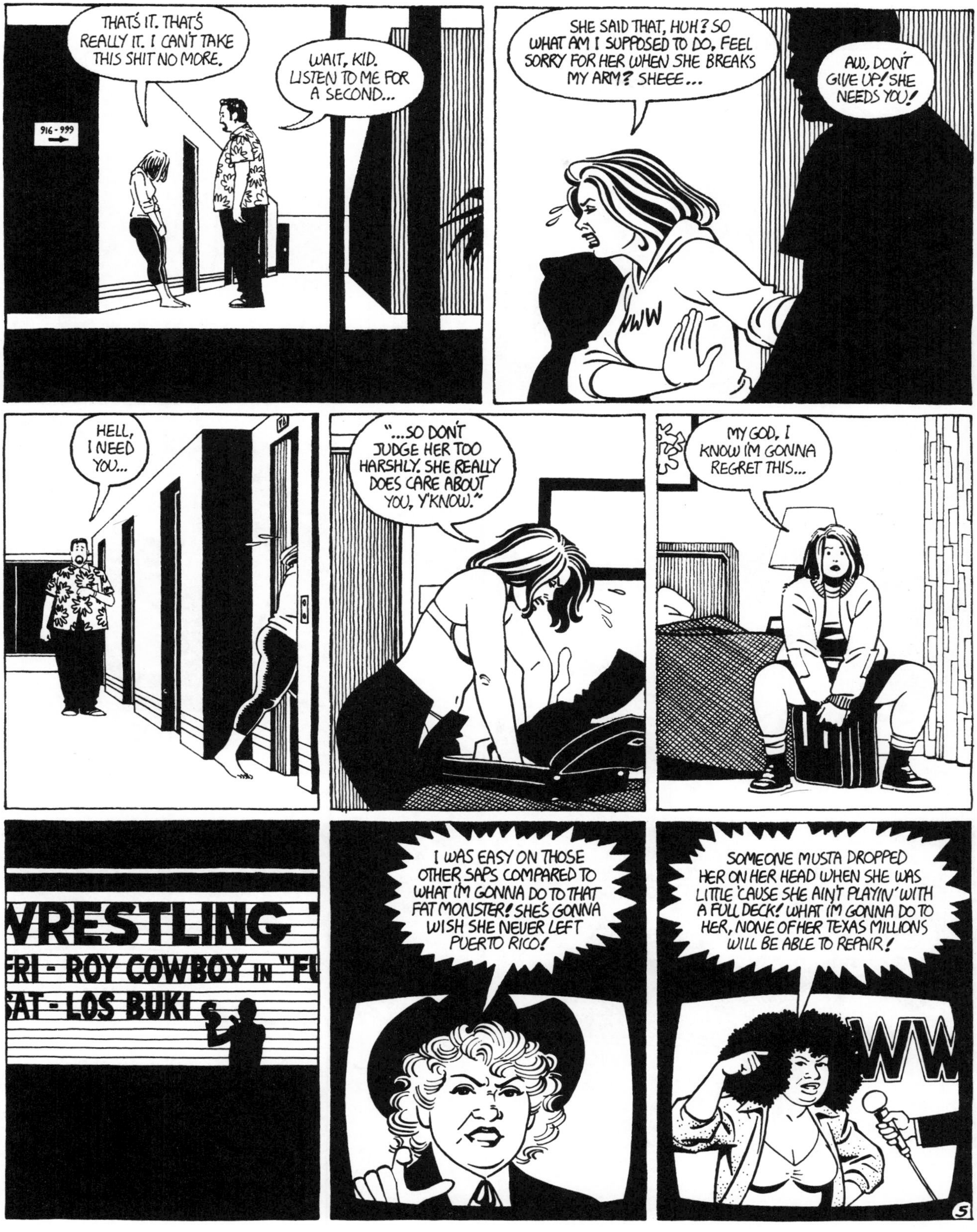

THAT'S IT. THAT'S REALLY IT. I CAN'T TAKE THIS SHIT NO MORE.
916-999
WAIT, KID. LISTEN TO ME FOR A SECOND...
SHE SAID THAT, HUH? SO WHAT AM I SUPPOSED TO DO, FEEL SORRY FOR HER WHEN SHE BREAKS MY ARM? SHEEE...
AW, DON'T GIVE UP! SHE NEEDS YOU!
HELL, I NEED YOU...
"...SO DON'T JUDGE HER TOO HARSHLY. SHE REALLY DOES CARE ABOUT YOU, Y'KNOW."
MY GOD, I KNOW I'M GONNA REGRET THIS...
WRESTLING
FRI - ROY COWBOY IN "FU
SAT - LOS BUKI
I WAS EASY ON THOSE OTHER SAPS COMPARED TO WHAT I'M GONNA DO TO THAT FAT MONSTER! SHE'S GONNA WISH SHE NEVER LEFT PUERTO RICO!
SOMEONE MUSTA DROPPED HER ON HER HEAD WHEN SHE WAS LITTLE 'CAUSE SHE AIN'T PLAYIN' WITH A FULL DECK! WHAT I'M GONNA DO TO HER, NONE OF HER TEXAS MILLIONS WILL BE ABLE TO REPAIR!
5

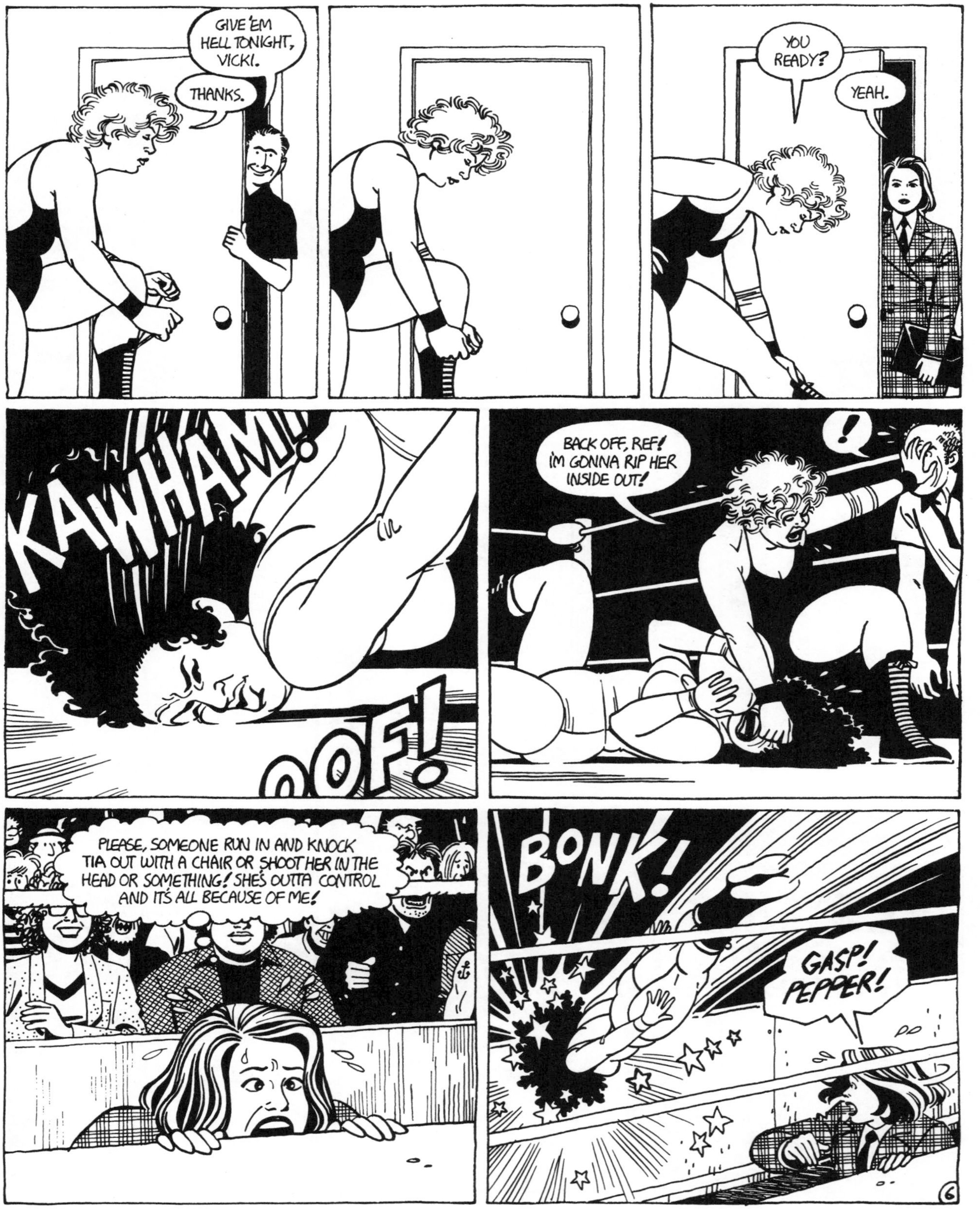

GIVE 'EM HELL TONIGHT, VICKI.
THANKS.
YOU READY?
YEAH.
KAWHAM!!
OOF!
BACK OFF, REF! I'M GONNA RIP HER INSIDE OUT!
!
PLEASE, SOMEONE RUN IN AND KNOCK TIA OUT WITH A CHAIR OR SHOOT HER IN THE HEAD OR SOMETHING! SHE'S OUTTA CONTROL AND IT'S ALL BECAUSE OF ME!
BONK!
GASP! PEPPER!
6

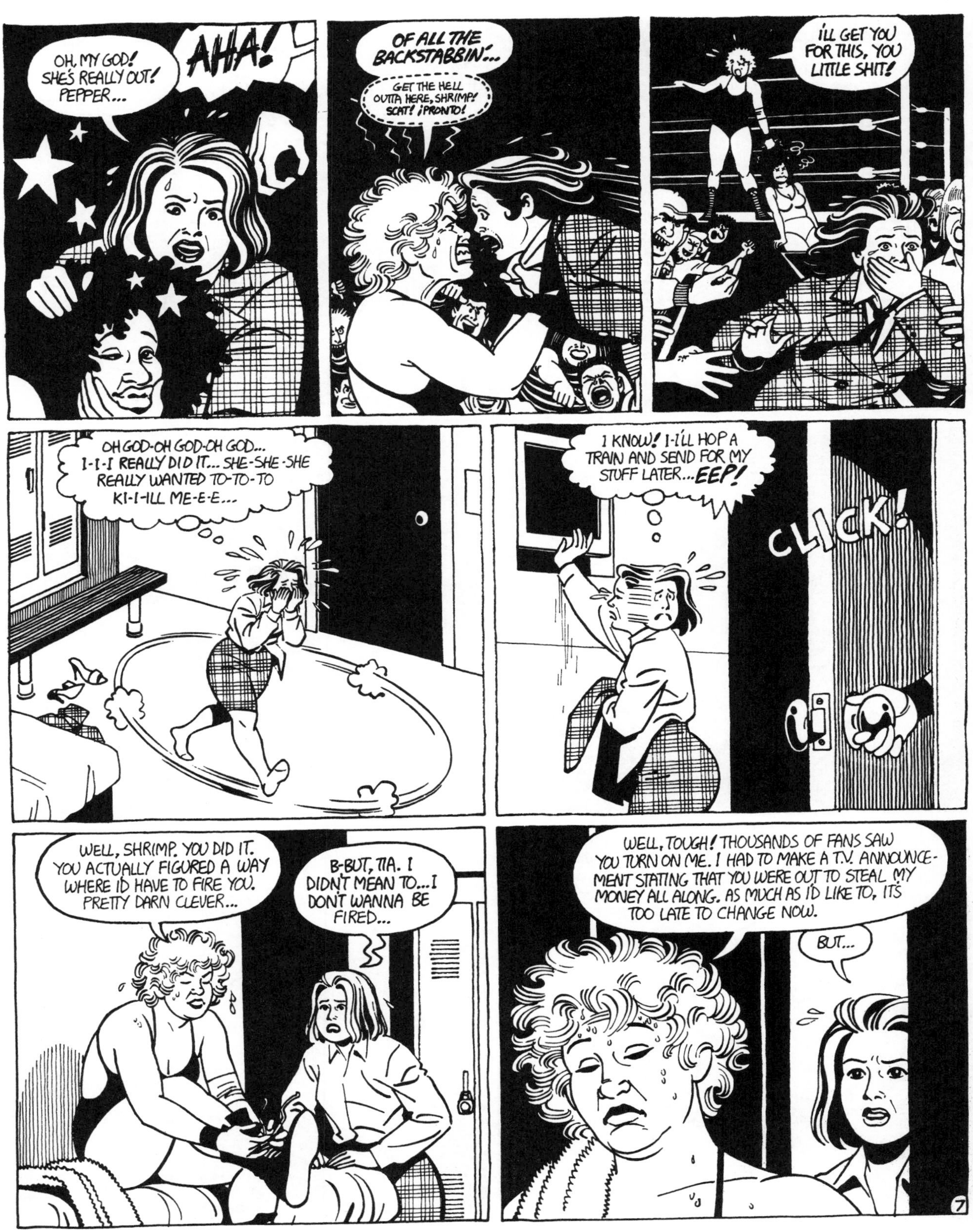
OH, MY GOD! SHE'S REALLY OUT! PEPPER...
AHA!
OF ALL THE BACKSTABBIN'...
GET THE HELL OUTTA HERE, SHRIMP! SCAT! ¡PRONTO!
I'LL GET YOU FOR THIS, YOU LITTLE SHIT!
OH GOD-OH GOD-OH GOD... I-I-I REALLY DID IT... SHE-SHE-SHE REALLY WANTED TO-TO-TO KI-I-ILL ME-E-E...
I KNOW! I-I'LL HOP A TRAIN AND SEND FOR MY STUFF LATER... EEP!
CLICK!
WELL, SHRIMP. YOU DID IT. YOU ACTUALLY FIGURED A WAY WHERE I'D HAVE TO FIRE YOU. PRETTY DARN CLEVER...
B-BUT, TIA. I DIDN'T MEAN TO... I DON'T WANNA BE FIRED...
WELL, TOUGH! THOUSANDS OF FANS SAW YOU TURN ON ME. I HAD TO MAKE A T.V. ANNOUNCE-MENT STATING THAT YOU WERE OUT TO STEAL MY MONEY ALL ALONG. AS MUCH AS I'D LIKE TO, IT'S TOO LATE TO CHANGE NOW.
BUT...
7

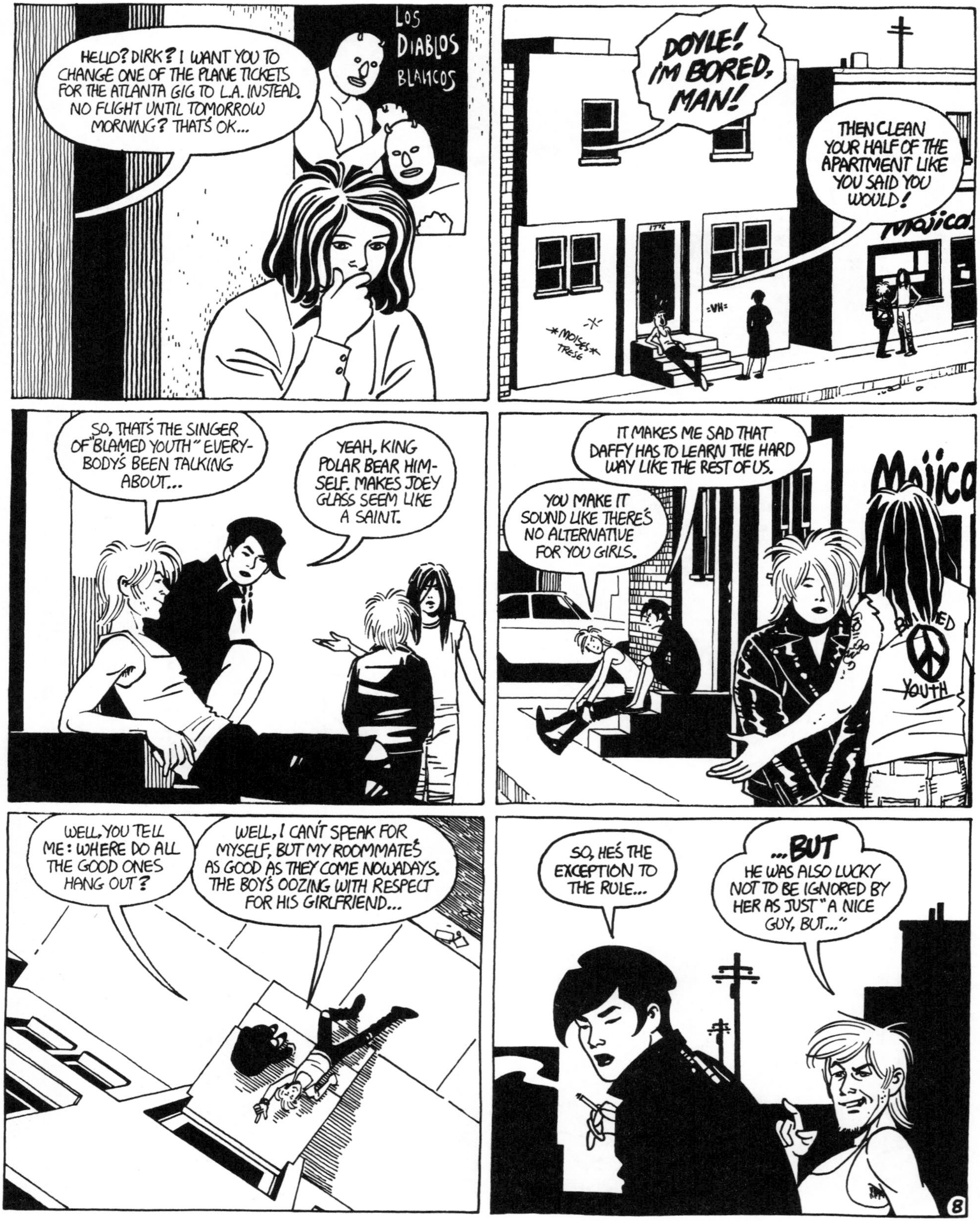

LOS DIABLOS BLANCOS
HELLO? DIRK? I WANT YOU TO CHANGE ONE OF THE PLANE TICKETS FOR THE ATLANTA GIG TO L.A. INSTEAD. NO FLIGHT UNTIL TOMORROW MORNING? THAT'S OK...
DOYLE! I'M BORED, MAN!
THEN CLEAN YOUR HALF OF THE APARTMENT LIKE YOU SAID YOU WOULD!
SO, THAT'S THE SINGER OF "BLAMED YOUTH" EVERYBODY'S BEEN TALKING ABOUT...
YEAH, KING POLAR BEAR HIMSELF. MAKES JOEY GLASS SEEM LIKE A SAINT.
IT MAKES ME SAD THAT DAFFY HAS TO LEARN THE HARD WAY LIKE THE REST OF US.
YOU MAKE IT SOUND LIKE THERE'S NO ALTERNATIVE FOR YOU GIRLS.
WELL, YOU TELL ME: WHERE DO ALL THE GOOD ONES HANG OUT?
WELL, I CAN'T SPEAK FOR MYSELF, BUT MY ROOMMATE'S AS GOOD AS THEY COME NOWADAYS. THE BOY'S OOZING WITH RESPECT FOR HIS GIRLFRIEND...
SO, HE'S THE EXCEPTION TO THE RULE...
...BUT HE WAS ALSO LUCKY NOT TO BE IGNORED BY HER AS JUST "A NICE GUY, BUT..."
8

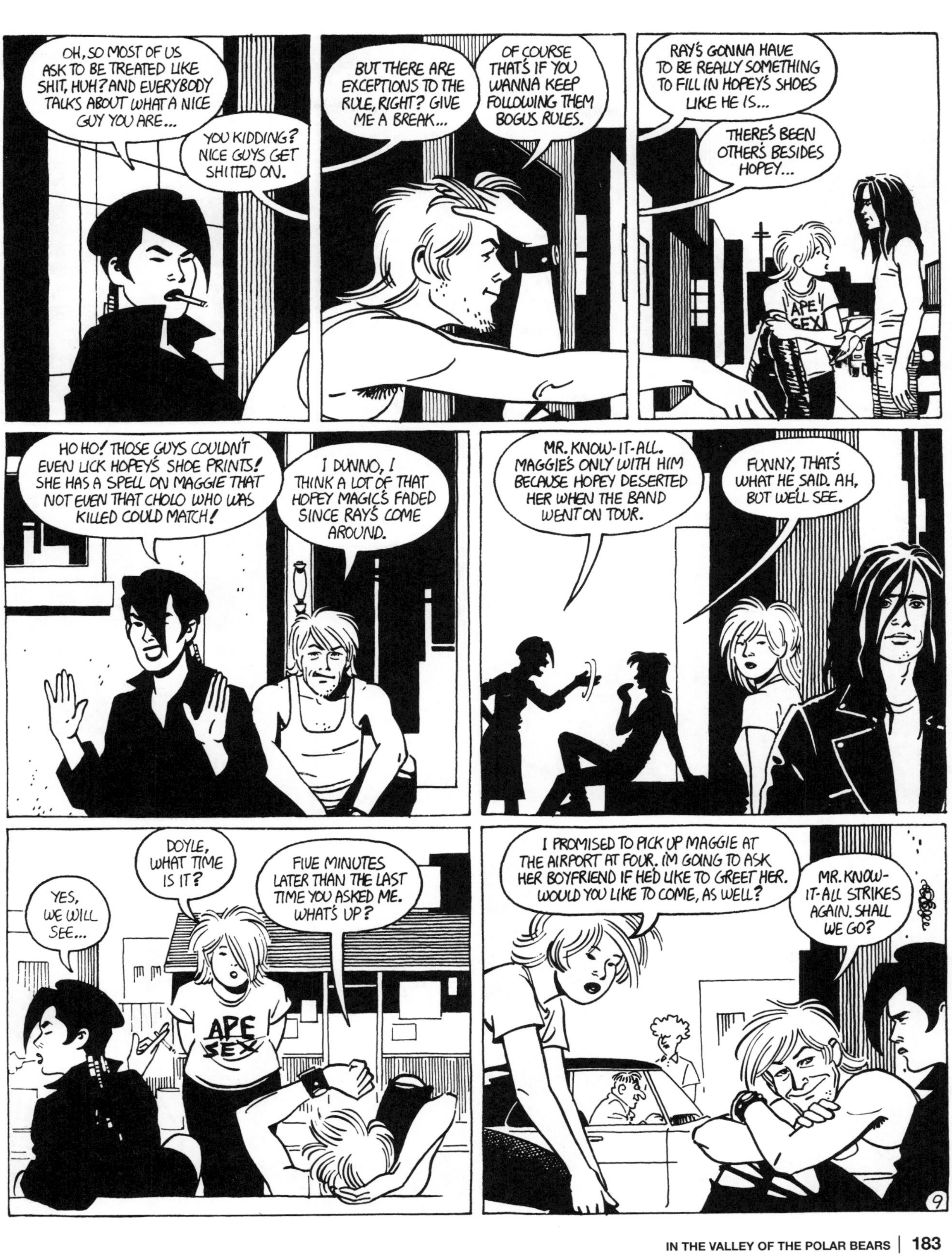
OH, SO MOST OF US ASK TO BE TREATED LIKE SHIT, HUH? AND EVERYBODY TALKS ABOUT WHAT A NICE GUY YOU ARE...
YOU KIDDING? NICE GUYS GET SHITTED ON.
BUT THERE ARE EXCEPTIONS TO THE RULE, RIGHT? GIVE ME A BREAK...
OF COURSE THAT'S IF YOU WANNA KEEP FOLLOWING THEM BOGUS RULES.
RAY'S GONNA HAVE TO BE REALLY SOMETHING TO FILL IN HOPEY'S SHOES LIKE HE IS...
THERE'S BEEN OTHER'S BESIDES HOPEY...
APE SEX
HO HO! THOSE GUYS COULDN'T EVEN LICK HOPEY'S SHOE PRINTS! SHE HAS A SPELL ON MAGGIE THAT NOT EVEN THAT CHOLO WHO WAS KILLED COULD MATCH!
I DUNNO, I THINK A LOT OF THAT HOPEY MAGIC'S FADED SINCE RAY'S COME AROUND.
MR. KNOW-IT-ALL. MAGGIE'S ONLY WITH HIM BECAUSE HOPEY DESERTED HER WHEN THE BAND WENT ON TOUR.
FUNNY, THAT'S WHAT HE SAID. AH, BUT WE'LL SEE.
YES, WE WILL SEE...
DOYLE, WHAT TIME IS IT?
FIVE MINUTES LATER THAN THE LAST TIME YOU ASKED ME. WHAT'S UP?
APE SEX
I PROMISED TO PICK UP MAGGIE AT THE AIRPORT AT FOUR. I'M GOING TO ASK HER BOYFRIEND IF HE'D LIKE TO GREET HER. WOULD YOU LIKE TO COME, AS WELL?
MR. KNOW-IT-ALL STRIKES AGAIN. SHALL WE GO?
9

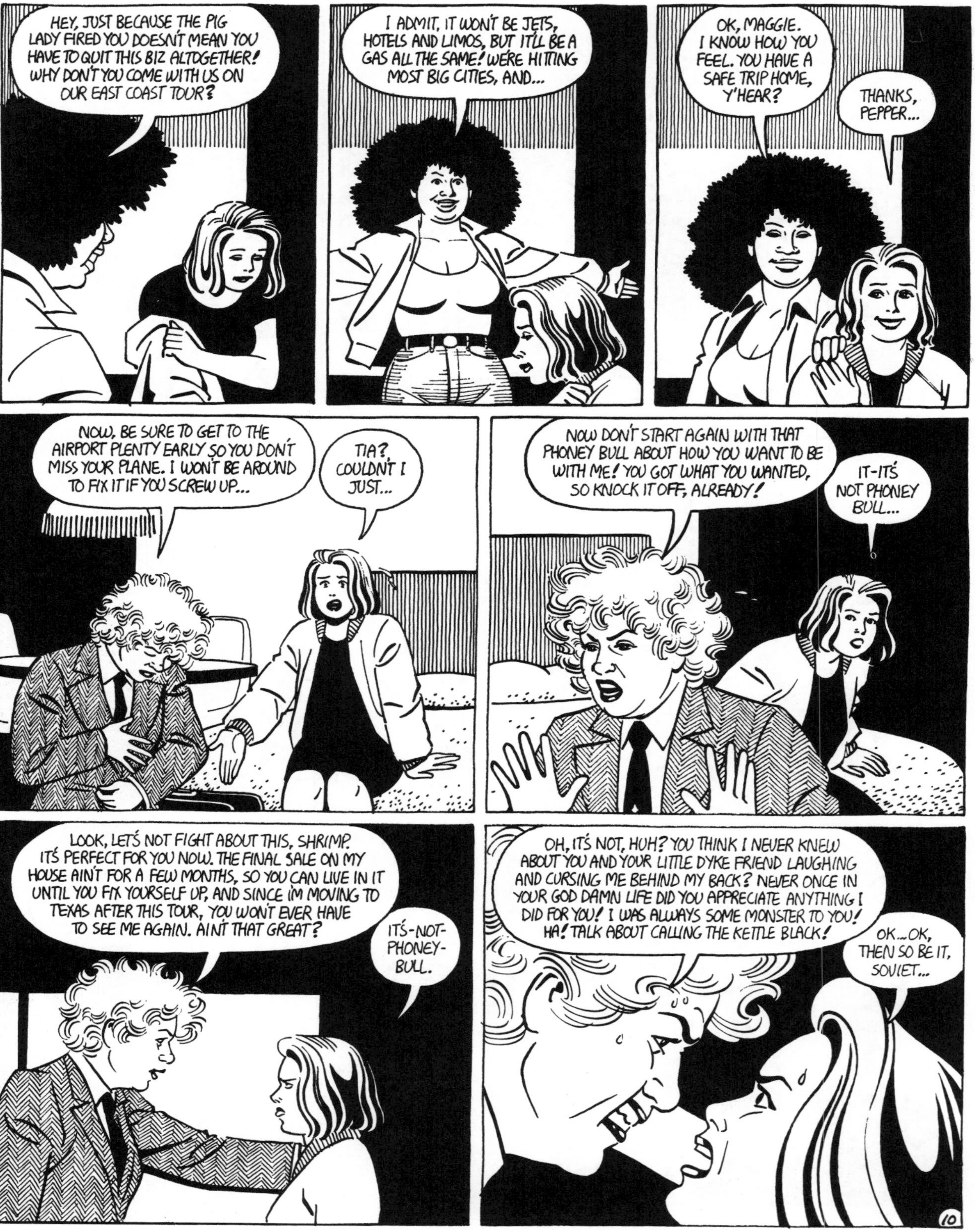
HEY, JUST BECAUSE THE PIG LADY FIRED YOU DOESN'T MEAN YOU HAVE TO QUIT THIS BIZ ALTOGETHER! WHY DON'T YOU COME WITH US ON OUR EAST COAST TOUR?
I ADMIT, IT WON'T BE JETS, HOTELS AND LIMOS, BUT IT'LL BE A GAS ALL THE SAME! WE'RE HITTING MOST BIG CITIES, AND...
OK, MAGGIE. I KNOW HOW YOU FEEL. YOU HAVE A SAFE TRIP HOME, Y'HEAR?
THANKS, PEPPER...
NOW, BE SURE TO GET TO THE AIRPORT PLENTY EARLY SO YOU DON'T MISS YOUR PLANE. I WON'T BE AROUND TO FIX IT IF YOU SCREW UP...
TIA? COULDN'T I JUST...
NOW DON'T START AGAIN WITH THAT PHONEY BULL ABOUT HOW YOU WANT TO BE WITH ME! YOU GOT WHAT YOU WANTED, SO KNOCK IT OFF, ALREADY!
IT-IT'S NOT PHONEY BULL...
LOOK, LET'S NOT FIGHT ABOUT THIS, SHRIMP. IT'S PERFECT FOR YOU NOW. THE FINAL SALE ON MY HOUSE AIN'T FOR A FEW MONTHS, SO YOU CAN LIVE IN IT UNTIL YOU FIX YOURSELF UP, AND SINCE I'M MOVING TO TEXAS AFTER THIS TOUR, YOU WON'T EVER HAVE TO SEE ME AGAIN. AIN'T THAT GREAT?
IT'S-NOT-PHONEY-BULL.
OH, IT'S NOT, HUH? YOU THINK I NEVER KNEW ABOUT YOU AND YOUR LITTLE DYKE FRIEND LAUGHING AND CURSING ME BEHIND MY BACK? NEVER ONCE IN YOUR GOD DAMN LIFE DID YOU APPRECIATE ANYTHING I DID FOR YOU! I WAS ALWAYS SOME MONSTER TO YOU! HA! TALK ABOUT CALLING THE KETTLE BLACK!
OK...OK, THEN SO BE IT, SOVIET...
10

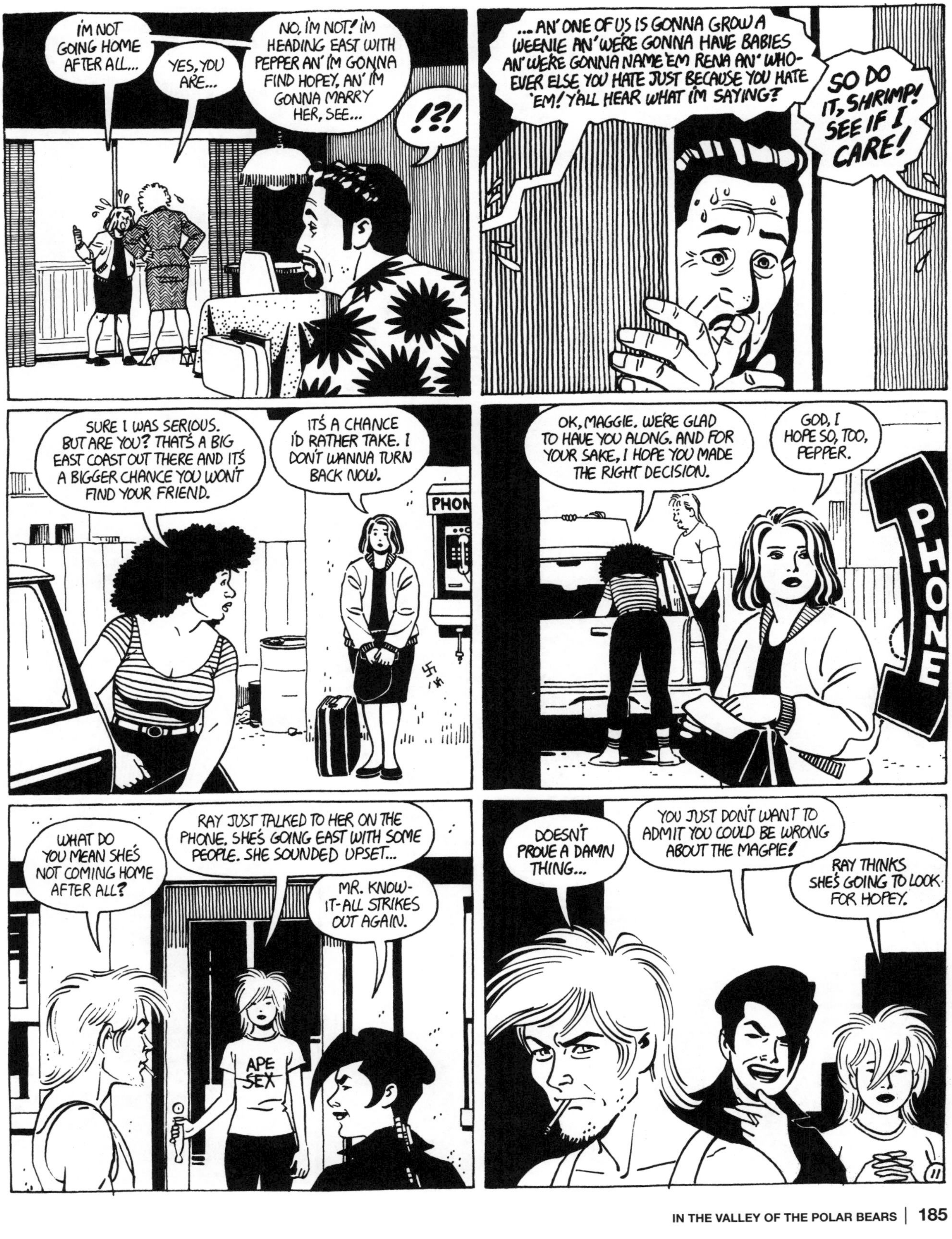
I'M NOT GOING HOME AFTER ALL...
YES, YOU ARE...
NO, I'M NOT! I'M HEADING EAST WITH PEPPER AN' I'M GONNA FIND HOPEY, AN' I'M GONNA MARRY HER, SEE...
!?!
...AN' ONE OF US IS GONNA GROW A WEENIE AN' WE'RE GONNA HAVE BABIES AN' WE'RE GONNA NAME 'EM RENA AN' WHO-EVER ELSE YOU HATE JUST BECAUSE YOU HATE 'EM! Y'ALL HEAR WHAT I'M SAYING?
SO DO IT, SHRIMP! SEE IF I CARE!
SURE I WAS SERIOUS. BUT ARE YOU? THAT'S A BIG EAST COAST OUT THERE AND IT'S A BIGGER CHANCE YOU WON'T FIND YOUR FRIEND.
IT'S A CHANCE I'D RATHER TAKE. I DON'T WANNA TURN BACK NOW.
PHON
OK, MAGGIE. WE'RE GLAD TO HAVE YOU ALONG. AND FOR YOUR SAKE, I HOPE YOU MADE THE RIGHT DECISION.
GOD, I HOPE SO, TOO, PEPPER.
PHONE
WHAT DO YOU MEAN SHE'S NOT COMING HOME AFTER ALL?
RAY JUST TALKED TO HER ON THE PHONE. SHE'S GOING EAST WITH SOME PEOPLE. SHE SOUNDED UPSET...
MR. KNOW-IT-ALL STRIKES OUT AGAIN.
APE SEX
DOESN'T PROVE A DAMN THING...
YOU JUST DON'T WANT TO ADMIT YOU COULD BE WRONG ABOUT THE MAGPIE!
RAY THINKS SHE'S GOING TO LOOK FOR HOPEY.
11

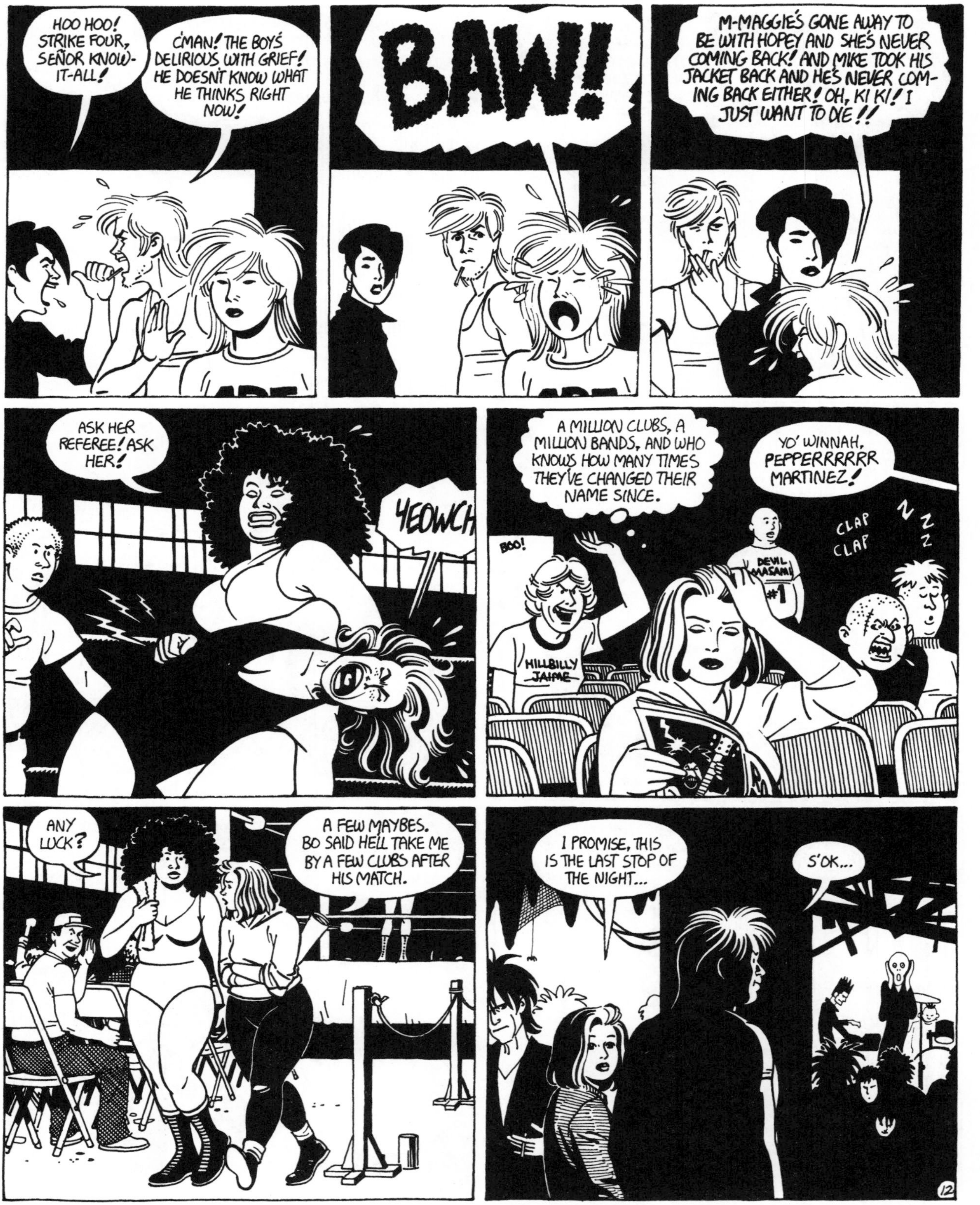
HOO HOO! STRIKE FOUR, SEÑOR KNOW-IT-ALL!
C'MAN! THE BOY'S DELIRIOUS WITH GRIEF! HE DOESN'T KNOW WHAT HE THINKS RIGHT NOW!
BAW!
M-MAGGIE'S GONE AWAY TO BE WITH HOPEY AND SHE'S NEVER COMING BACK! AND MIKE TOOK HIS JACKET BACK AND HE'S NEVER COMING BACK EITHER! OH, KI KI! I JUST WANT TO DIE!!
ASK HER REFEREE! ASK HER!
YEOWCH
A MILLION CLUBS, A MILLION BANDS, AND WHO KNOWS HOW MANY TIMES THEY'VE CHANGED THEIR NAME SINCE.
YO' WINNAH, PEPPERRRRRR MARTINEZ!
BOO!
CLAP CLAP
Z Z Z
DEVIL MASAMI #1
HILLBILLY JAIME
ANY LUCK?
A FEW MAYBES. BO SAID HE'LL TAKE ME BY A FEW CLUBS AFTER HIS MATCH.
I PROMISE, THIS IS THE LAST STOP OF THE NIGHT...
S'OK...
12

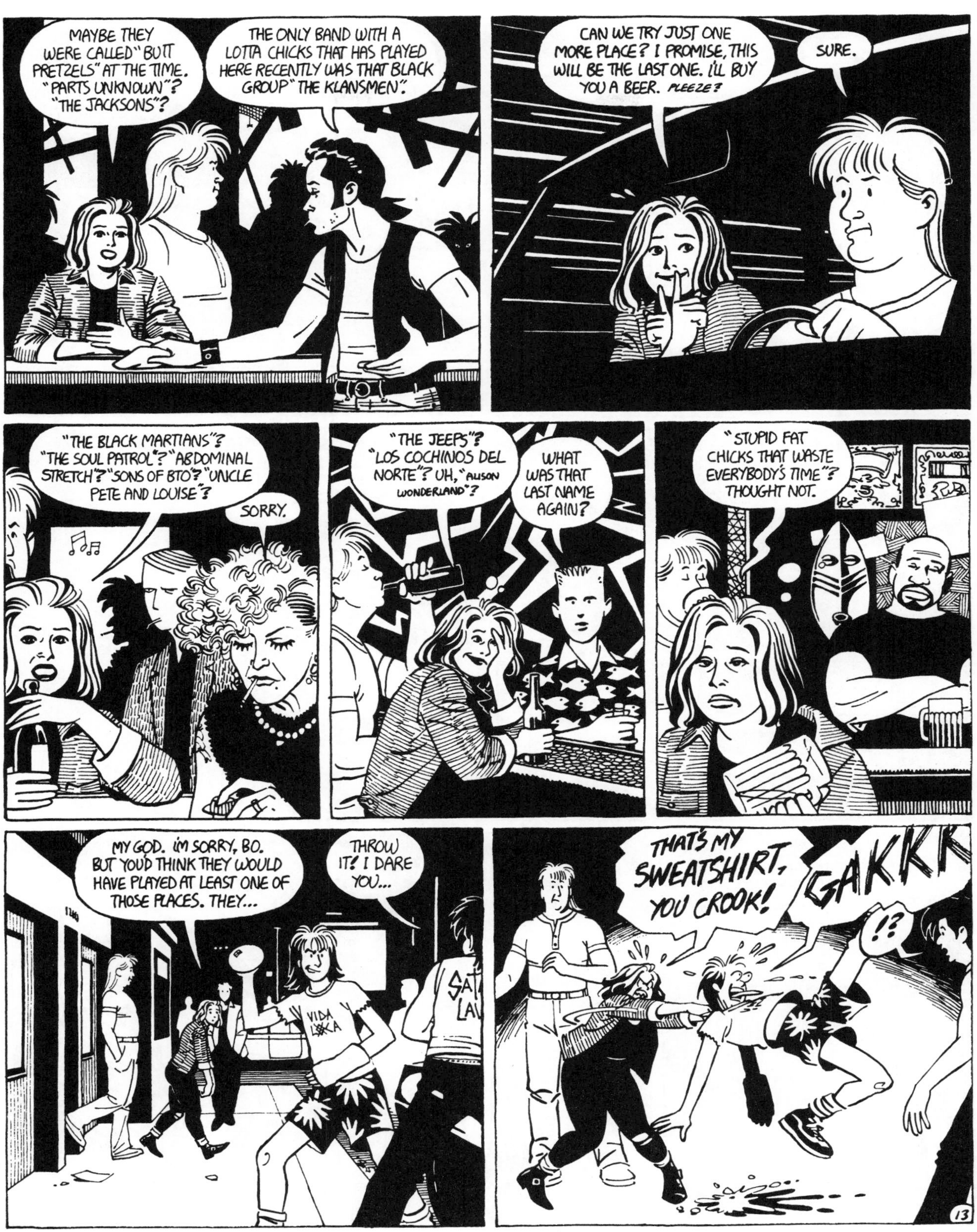
MAYBE THEY WERE CALLED "BUTT PRETZELS" AT THE TIME. "PARTS UNKNOWN"? "THE JACKSONS"?
THE ONLY BAND WITH A LOTTA CHICKS THAT HAS PLAYED HERE RECENTLY WAS THAT BLACK GROUP "THE KLANSMEN".
CAN WE TRY JUST ONE MORE PLACE? I PROMISE, THIS WILL BE THE LAST ONE. I'LL BUY YOU A BEER. PLEEZE?
SURE.
"THE BLACK MARTIANS"? "THE SOUL PATROL"? "ABDOMINAL STRETCH"? "SONS OF BTO"? "UNCLE PETE AND LOUISE"?
SORRY.
"THE JEEPS"? "LOS COCHINOS DEL NORTE"? UH, "ALISON WONDERLAND"?
WHAT WAS THAT LAST NAME AGAIN?
"STUPID FAT CHICKS THAT WASTE EVERYBODY'S TIME"? THOUGHT NOT.
MY GOD. I'M SORRY, BO. BUT YOU'D THINK THEY WOULD HAVE PLAYED AT LEAST ONE OF THOSE PLACES. THEY...
THROW IT! I DARE YOU...
VIDA LOCA
THAT'S MY SWEATSHIRT, YOU CROOK!
GAKKK
!?
13

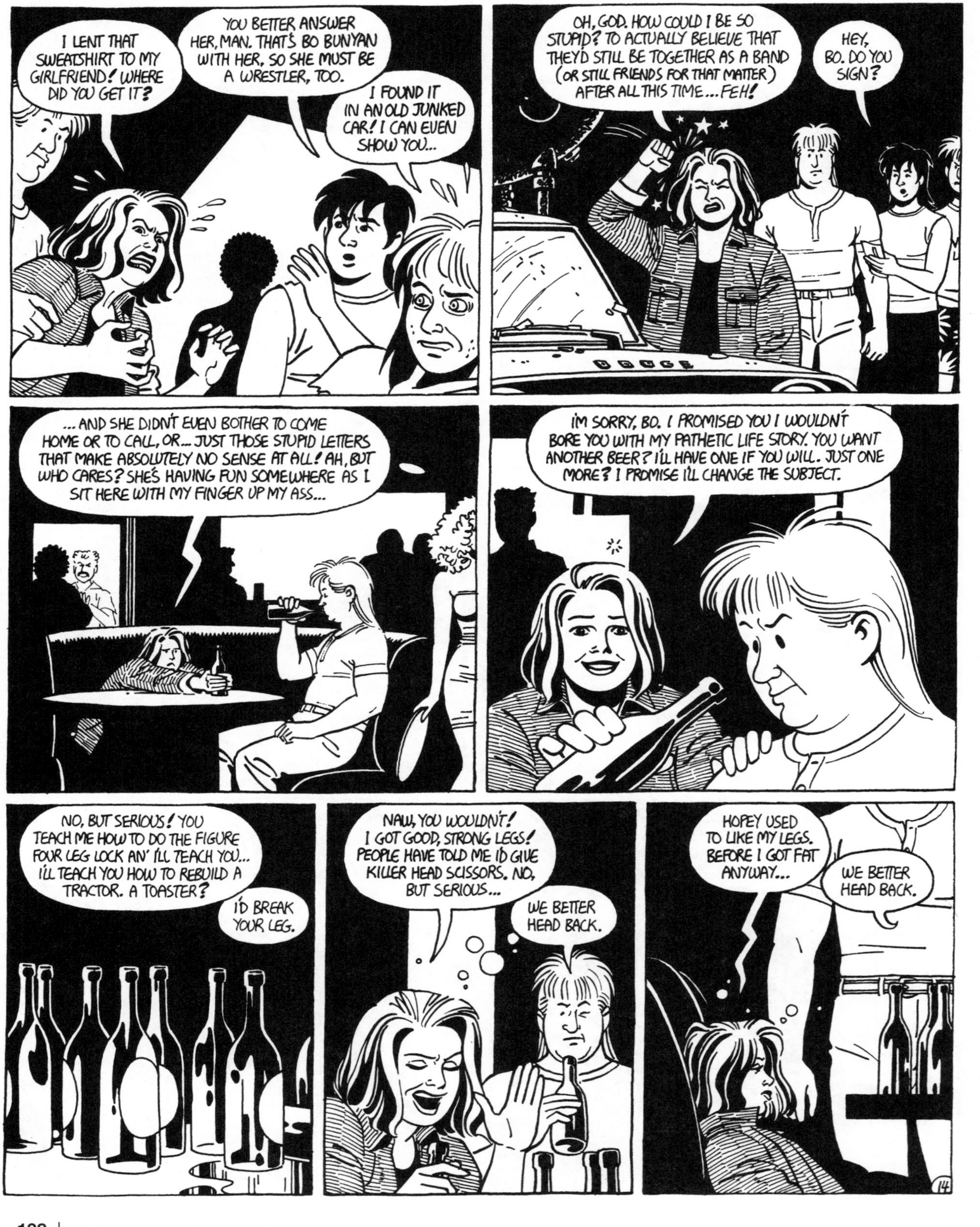
I LENT THAT SWEATSHIRT TO MY GIRLFRIEND! WHERE DID YOU GET IT?
YOU BETTER ANSWER HER, MAN. THAT'S BO BUNYAN WITH HER, SO SHE MUST BE A WRESTLER, TOO.
I FOUND IT IN AN OLD JUNKED CAR! I CAN EVEN SHOW YOU...
OH, GOD. HOW COULD I BE SO STUPID? TO ACTUALLY BELIEVE THAT THEY'D STILL BE TOGETHER AS A BAND (OR STILL FRIENDS FOR THAT MATTER) AFTER ALL THIS TIME... FEH!
HEY, BO. DO YOU SIGN?
DODGE
... AND SHE DIDN'T EVEN BOTHER TO COME HOME OR TO CALL, OR... JUST THOSE STUPID LETTERS THAT MAKE ABSOLUTELY NO SENSE AT ALL! AH, BUT WHO CARES? SHE'S HAVING FUN SOMEWHERE AS I SIT HERE WITH MY FINGER UP MY ASS...
I'M SORRY, BO. I PROMISED YOU I WOULDN'T BORE YOU WITH MY PATHETIC LIFE STORY. YOU WANT ANOTHER BEER? I'LL HAVE ONE IF YOU WILL. JUST ONE MORE? I PROMISE I'LL CHANGE THE SUBJECT.
NO, BUT SERIOUS! YOU TEACH ME HOW TO DO THE FIGURE FOUR LEG LOCK AN' I'LL TEACH YOU... I'LL TEACH YOU HOW TO REBUILD A TRACTOR. A TOASTER?
I'D BREAK YOUR LEG.
NAW, YOU WOULDN'T! I GOT GOOD, STRONG LEGS! PEOPLE HAVE TOLD ME I'D GIVE KILLER HEAD SCISSORS. NO, BUT SERIOUS...
WE BETTER HEAD BACK.
HOPEY USED TO LIKE MY LEGS. BEFORE I GOT FAT ANYWAY...
WE BETTER HEAD BACK.
14

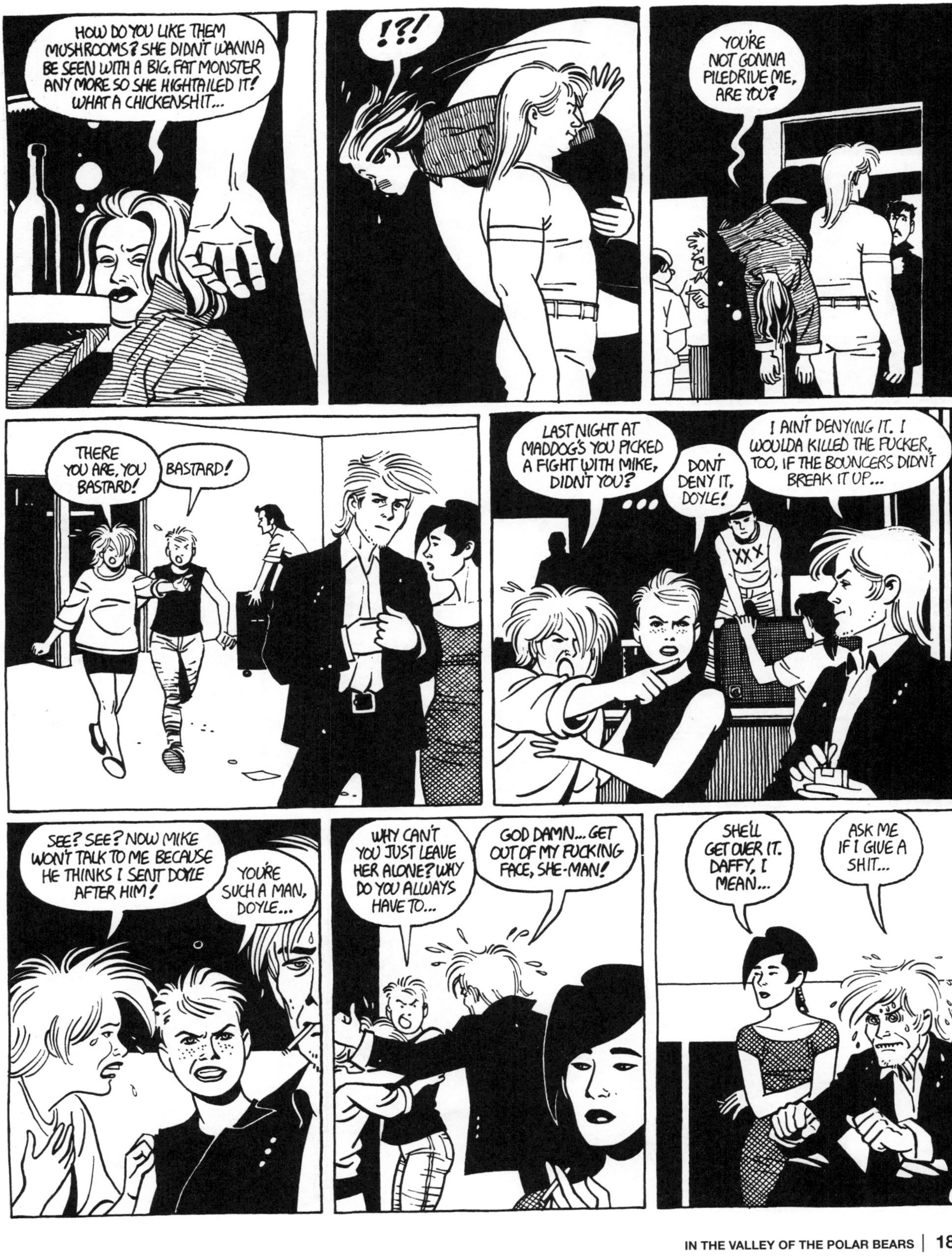
HOW DO YOU LIKE THEM MUSHROOMS? SHE DIDN'T WANNA BE SEEN WITH A BIG, FAT MONSTER ANY MORE SO SHE HIGHTAILED IT! WHAT A CHICKENSHIT...
!?!
YOU'RE NOT GONNA PILEDRIVE ME, ARE YOU?
THERE YOU ARE, YOU BASTARD!
BASTARD!
LAST NIGHT AT MADDOG'S YOU PICKED A FIGHT WITH MIKE, DIDN'T YOU?
...
DON'T DENY IT, DOYLE!
I AIN'T DENYING IT. I WOULDA KILLED THE FUCKER, TOO, IF THE BOUNCERS DIDN'T BREAK IT UP...
XXX
SEE? SEE? NOW MIKE WON'T TALK TO ME BECAUSE HE THINKS I SENT DOYLE AFTER HIM!
YOU'RE SUCH A MAN, DOYLE...
WHY CAN'T YOU JUST LEAVE HER ALONE? WHY DO YOU ALWAYS HAVE TO...
GOD DAMN... GET OUT OF MY FUCKING FACE, SHE-MAN!
SHE'LL GET OVER IT. DAFFY, I MEAN...
ASK ME IF I GIVE A SHIT...
15

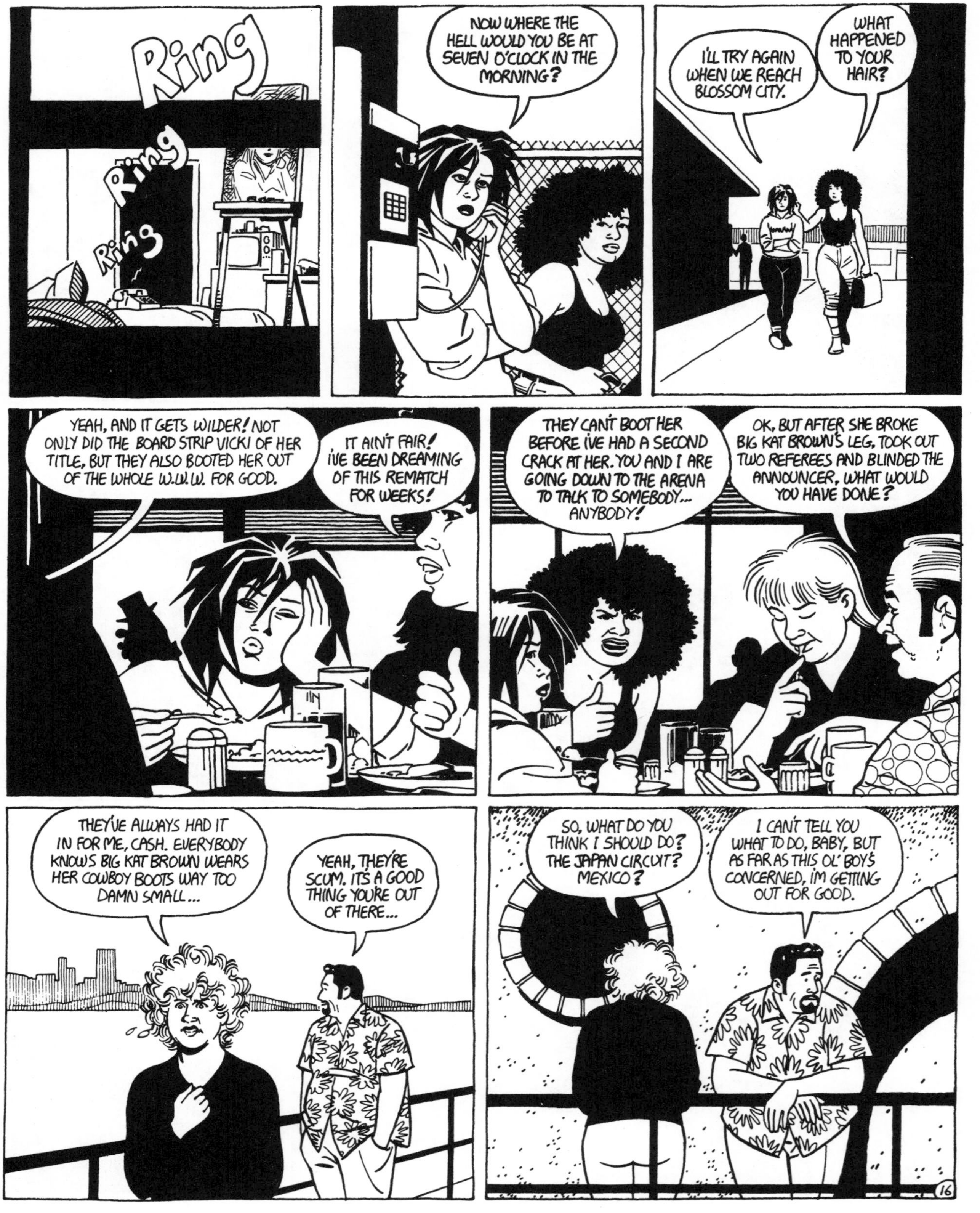
Ring
Ring
Ring
NOW WHERE THE HELL WOULD YOU BE AT SEVEN O'CLOCK IN THE MORNING?
I'LL TRY AGAIN WHEN WE REACH BLOSSOM CITY.
WHAT HAPPENED TO YOUR HAIR?
YEAH, AND IT GETS WILDER! NOT ONLY DID THE BOARD STRIP VICKI OF HER TITLE, BUT THEY ALSO BOOTED HER OUT OF THE WHOLE W.W.W. FOR GOOD.
IT AIN'T FAIR! I'VE BEEN DREAMING OF THIS REMATCH FOR WEEKS!
THEY CAN'T BOOT HER BEFORE I'VE HAD A SECOND CRACK AT HER. YOU AND I ARE GOING DOWN TO THE ARENA TO TALK TO SOMEBODY... ANYBODY!
OK, BUT AFTER SHE BROKE BIG KAT BROWN'S LEG, TOOK OUT TWO REFEREES AND BLINDED THE ANNOUNCER, WHAT WOULD YOU HAVE DONE?
THEY'VE ALWAYS HAD IT IN FOR ME, CASH. EVERYBODY KNOWS BIG KAT BROWN WEARS HER COWBOY BOOTS WAY TOO DAMN SMALL...
YEAH, THEY'RE SCUM. IT'S A GOOD THING YOU'RE OUT OF THERE...
SO, WHAT DO YOU THINK I SHOULD DO? THE JAPAN CIRCUIT? MEXICO?
I CAN'T TELL YOU WHAT TO DO, BABY, BUT AS FAR AS THIS OL' BOY'S CONCERNED, I'M GETTING OUT FOR GOOD.
16

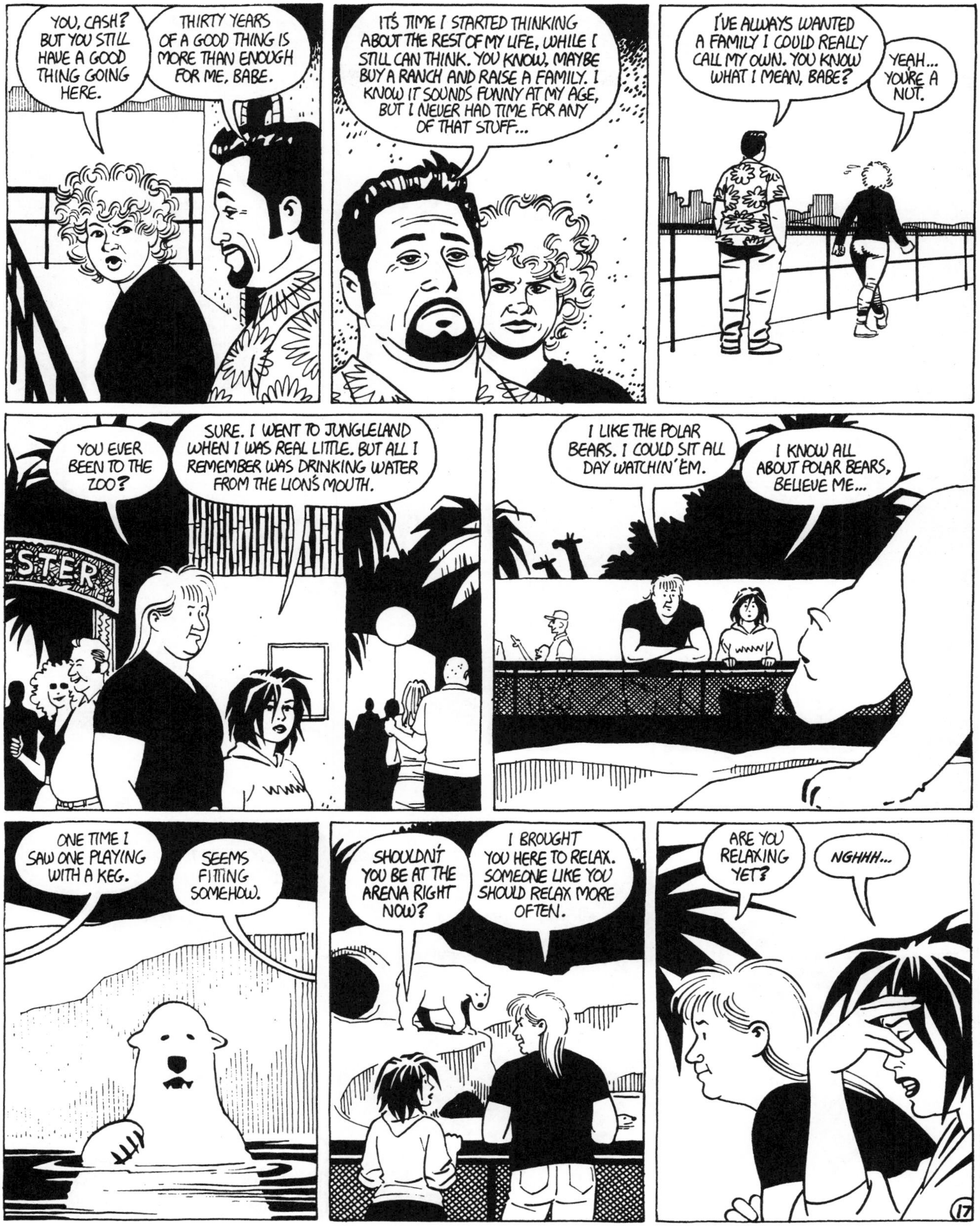
YOU, CASH? BUT YOU STILL HAVE A GOOD THING GOING HERE.
THIRTY YEARS OF A GOOD THING IS MORE THAN ENOUGH FOR ME, BABE.
IT'S TIME I STARTED THINKING ABOUT THE REST OF MY LIFE, WHILE I STILL CAN THINK. YOU KNOW, MAYBE BUY A RANCH AND RAISE A FAMILY. I KNOW IT SOUNDS FUNNY AT MY AGE, BUT I NEVER HAD TIME FOR ANY OF THAT STUFF...
I'VE ALWAYS WANTED A FAMILY I COULD REALLY CALL MY OWN. YOU KNOW WHAT I MEAN, BABE?
YEAH... YOU'RE A NUT.
YOU EVER BEEN TO THE ZOO?
SURE. I WENT TO JUNGLELAND WHEN I WAS REAL LITTLE. BUT ALL I REMEMBER WAS DRINKING WATER FROM THE LION'S MOUTH.
STER
I LIKE THE POLAR BEARS. I COULD SIT ALL DAY WATCHIN' 'EM.
I KNOW ALL ABOUT POLAR BEARS, BELIEVE ME...
ONE TIME I SAW ONE PLAYING WITH A KEG.
SEEMS FITTING SOMEHOW.
SHOULDN'T YOU BE AT THE ARENA RIGHT NOW?
I BROUGHT YOU HERE TO RELAX. SOMEONE LIKE YOU SHOULD RELAX MORE OFTEN.
ARE YOU RELAXING YET?
NGHHH...
17

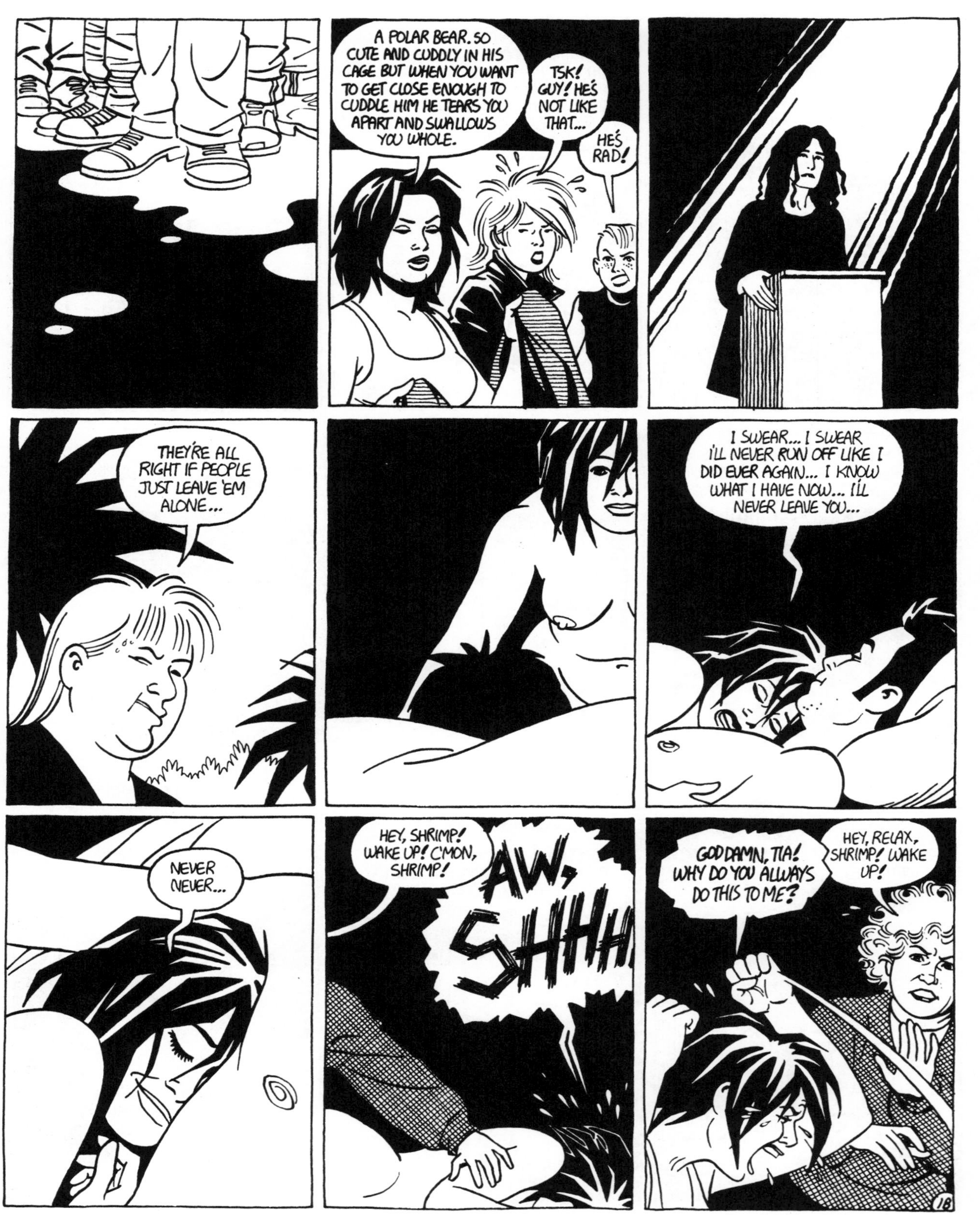
A POLAR BEAR. SO CUTE AND CUDDLY IN HIS CAGE BUT WHEN YOU WANT TO GET CLOSE ENOUGH TO CUDDLE HIM HE TEARS YOU APART AND SWALLOWS YOU WHOLE.
TSK! GUY! HE'S NOT LIKE THAT...
HE'S RAD!
THEY'RE ALL RIGHT IF PEOPLE JUST LEAVE 'EM ALONE...
I SWEAR... I SWEAR I'LL NEVER RUN OFF LIKE I DID EVER AGAIN... I KNOW WHAT I HAVE NOW... I'LL NEVER LEAVE YOU...
NEVER NEVER...
HEY, SHRIMP! WAKE UP! C'MON, SHRIMP!
AW, SHHH
GOD DAMN, TIA! WHY DO YOU ALWAYS DO THIS TO ME?
HEY, RELAX, SHRIMP! WAKE UP!
18

T-T-TIA...? WHAT...?
WHAT ARE YOU CRYING ABOUT, SHRIMP? LOOK AT YOU, YOU'RE SWEATING LIKE A DAMN PIG...
OH, YEAH... THAT'S RIGHT. I WASN'T FEELING WELL, SO I MADE BO BRING ME BACK TO THE HOTEL AND... WHOA...
SHRIMP, I GOTTA BE IN VEGAS IN ONE HOUR, SO... UM, AREN'T YOU GONNA ASK ME WHAT I'M DOING HERE?
WELL, THE THOUGHT HAD CROSSED MY MIND. LOSING YOUR BELT AND ALL THAT... I FIGURED YOU'D BE UP FOR MURDER ONE BY NOW...
I'M... MARRYING CASH.
HO! WAIT! HOLD ON A SECOND! I MUST BE STILL SLEEPING...
LOOK, SHRIMP! I WAS HOPING TO COME HERE AND... BUT IF YOU WANNA BE NASTY, LET'S JUST FORGET IT, OK?
GUY, I WAS JUST KIDDING. WHAT DO YOU WANT ME TO SAY?
THAT YOU'RE HAPPY FOR ME! I DON'T DO SOMETHING LIKE THIS EVERY-DAY, Y'KNOW!
WELL, OF COURSE I'M HAPPY FOR YOU, TIA.
OH, THANKS, SHRIMP! THAT'S JUST WHAT I HAD TO HEAR! UM...
I'M PRETTY DARN NERVOUS ABOUT THE WHOLE THING, AND I DON'T THINK I COULD GO THROUGH WITH IT IF I DIDN'T HAVE YOUR BLESSING, Y'KNOW?
UH HUH.
UM...
19

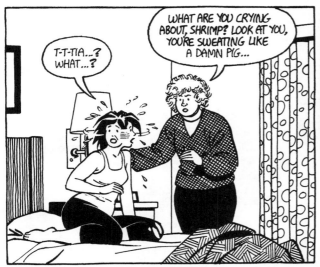

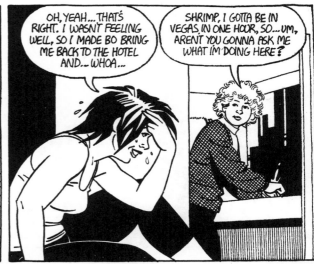

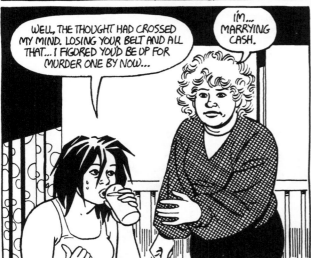

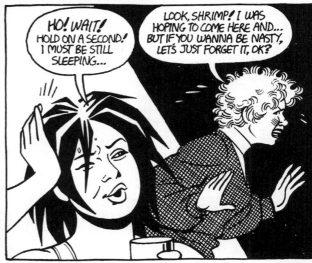

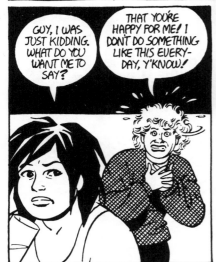

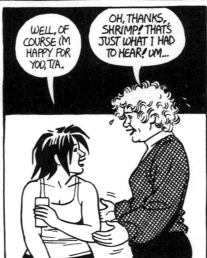

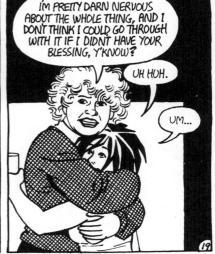

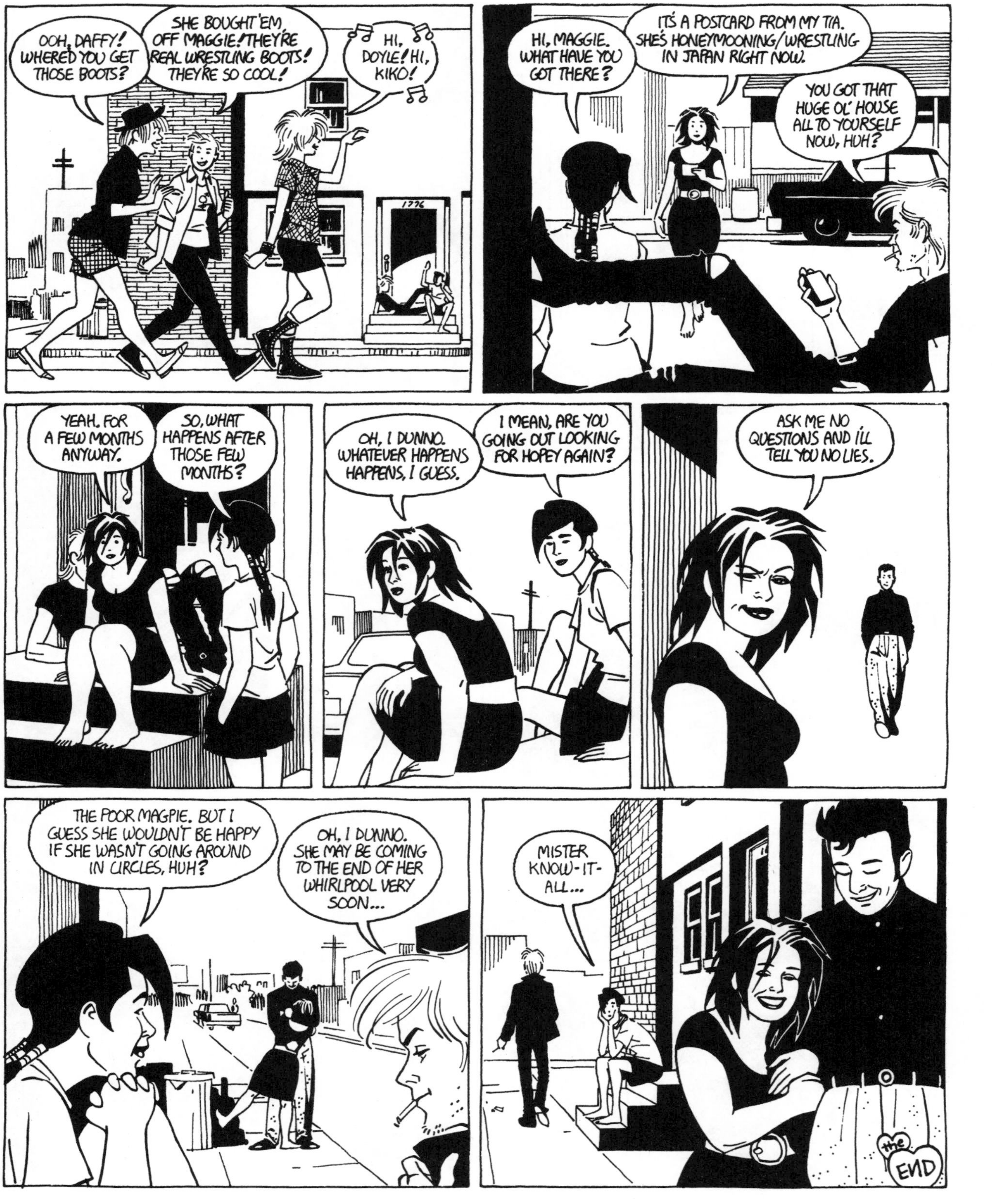
OOH, DAFFY! WHERE'D YOU GET THOSE BOOTS?
SHE BOUGHT 'EM OFF MAGGIE! THEY'RE REAL WRESTLING BOOTS! THEY'RE SO COOL!
HI, DOYLE! HI, KIKO!
1776
HI, MAGGIE. WHAT HAVE YOU GOT THERE?
IT'S A POSTCARD FROM MY TIA. SHE'S HONEYMOONING/WRESTLING IN JAPAN RIGHT NOW.
YOU GOT THAT HUGE OL' HOUSE ALL TO YOURSELF NOW, HUH?
YEAH. FOR A FEW MONTHS ANYWAY.
SO, WHAT HAPPENS AFTER THOSE FEW MONTHS?
OH, I DUNNO. WHATEVER HAPPENS HAPPENS, I GUESS.
I MEAN, ARE YOU GOING OUT LOOKING FOR HOPEY AGAIN?
ASK ME NO QUESTIONS AND I'LL TELL YOU NO LIES.
THE POOR MAGPIE. BUT I GUESS SHE WOULDN'T BE HAPPY IF SHE WASN'T GOING AROUND IN CIRCLES, HUH?
OH, I DUNNO. SHE MAY BE COMING TO THE END OF HER WHIRLPOOL VERY SOON...
MISTER KNOW-IT-ALL...
the END

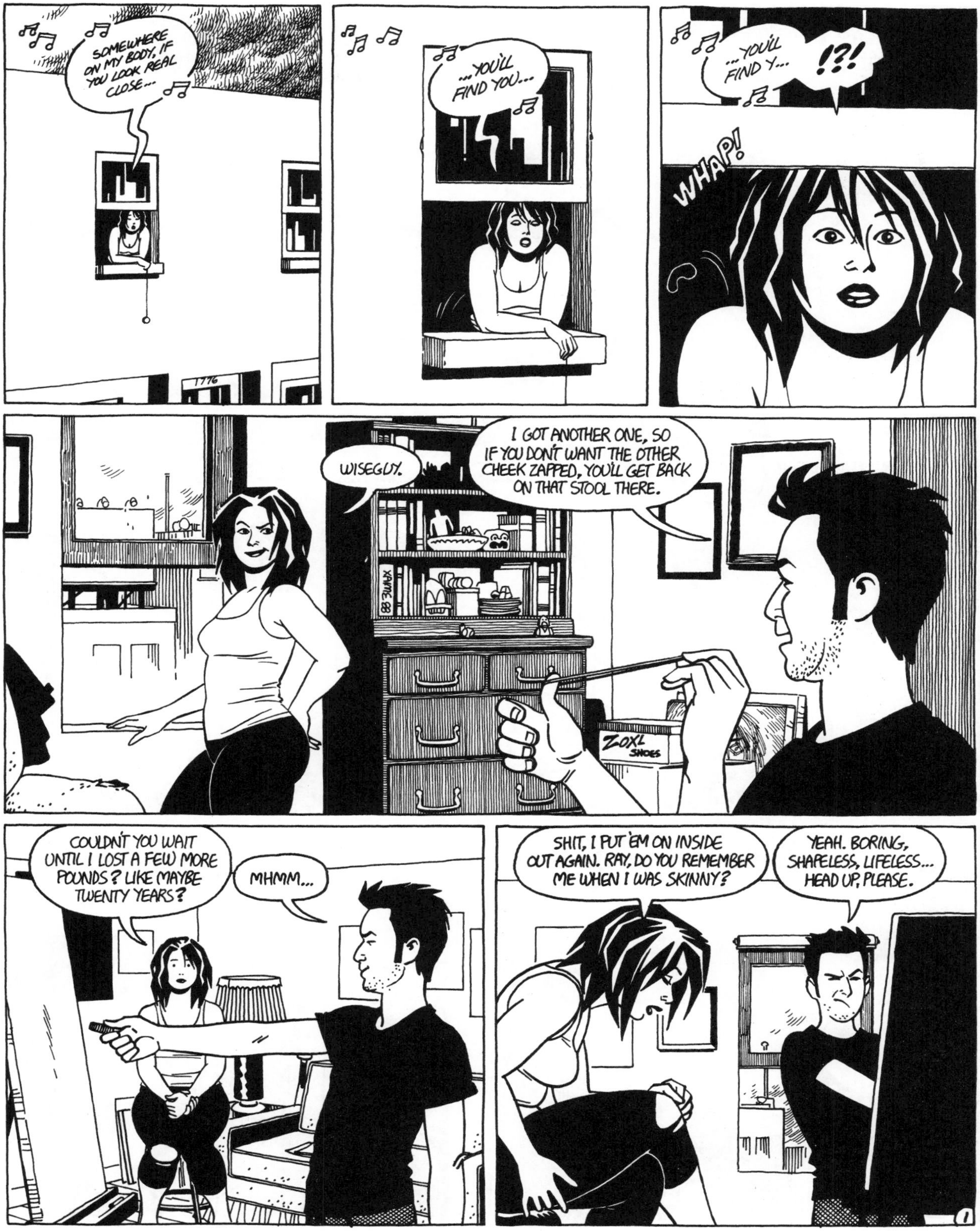
SOMEWHERE ON MY BODY, IF YOU LOOK REAL CLOSE...
...YOU'LL FIND YOU...
...YOU'LL FIND Y...
!?!
WHAP!
WISEGUY.
I GOT ANOTHER ONE, SO IF YOU DON'T WANT THE OTHER CHEEK ZAPPED, YOU'LL GET BACK ON THAT STOOL THERE.
ZOXL SHOES
COULDN'T YOU WAIT UNTIL I LOST A FEW MORE POUNDS? LIKE MAYBE TWENTY YEARS?
MHMM...
SHIT, I PUT 'EM ON INSIDE OUT AGAIN. RAY, DO YOU REMEMBER ME WHEN I WAS SKINNY?
YEAH. BORING, SHAPELESS, LIFELESS... HEAD UP, PLEASE.

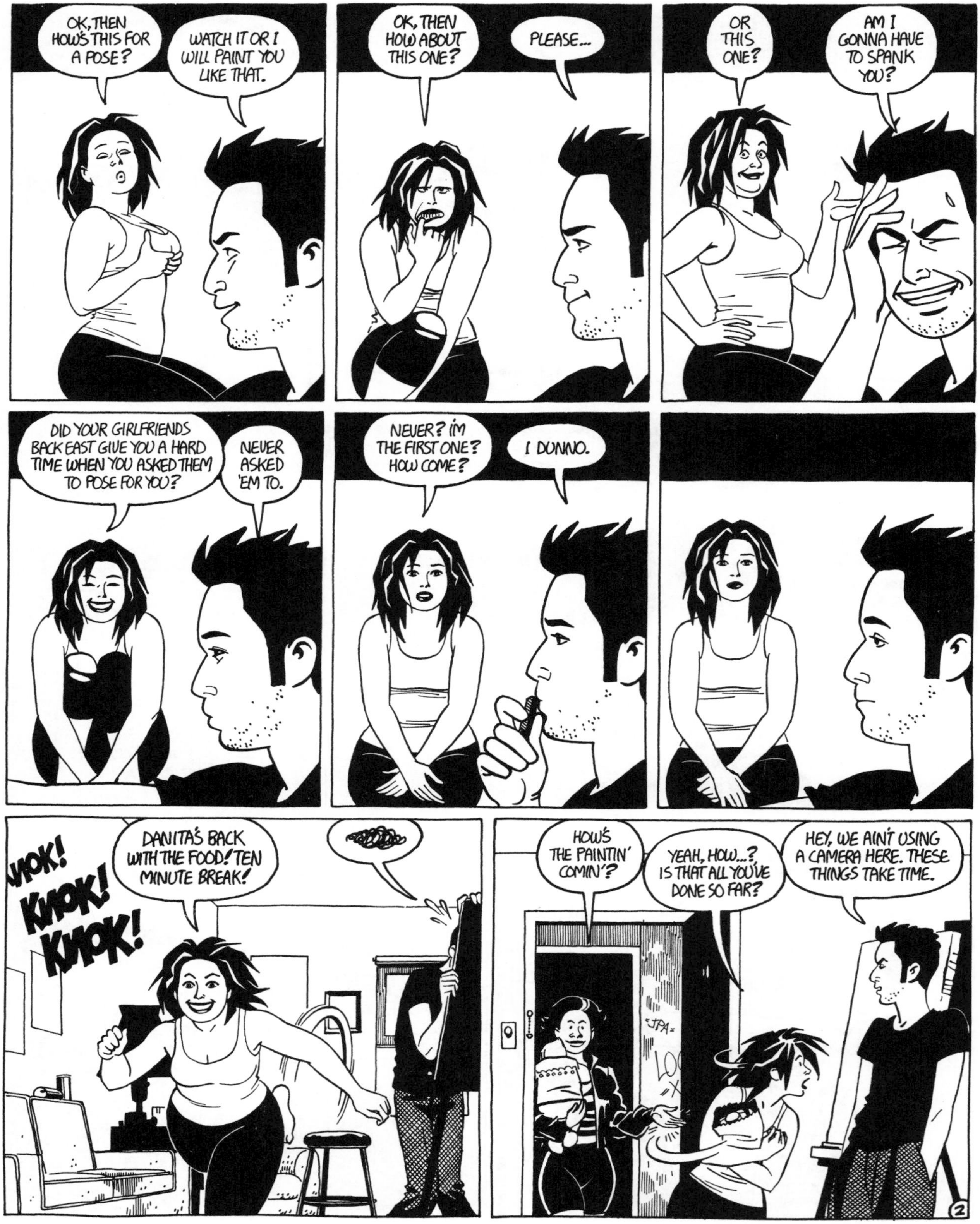

OK, THEN HOW'S THIS FOR A POSE?
WATCH IT OR I WILL PAINT YOU LIKE THAT.
OK, THEN HOW ABOUT THIS ONE?
PLEASE...
OR THIS ONE?
AM I GONNA HAVE TO SPANK YOU?
DID YOUR GIRLFRIENDS BACK EAST GIVE YOU A HARD TIME WHEN YOU ASKED THEM TO POSE FOR YOU?
NEVER ASKED 'EM TO.
NEVER? I'M THE FIRST ONE? HOW COME?
I DUNNO.
KNOK! KNOK! KNOK!
DANITA'S BACK WITH THE FOOD! TEN MINUTE BREAK!
HOW'S THE PAINTIN' COMIN'?
YEAH, HOW...? IS THAT ALL YOU'VE DONE SO FAR?
HEY, WE AIN'T USING A CAMERA HERE. THESE THINGS TAKE TIME.
2

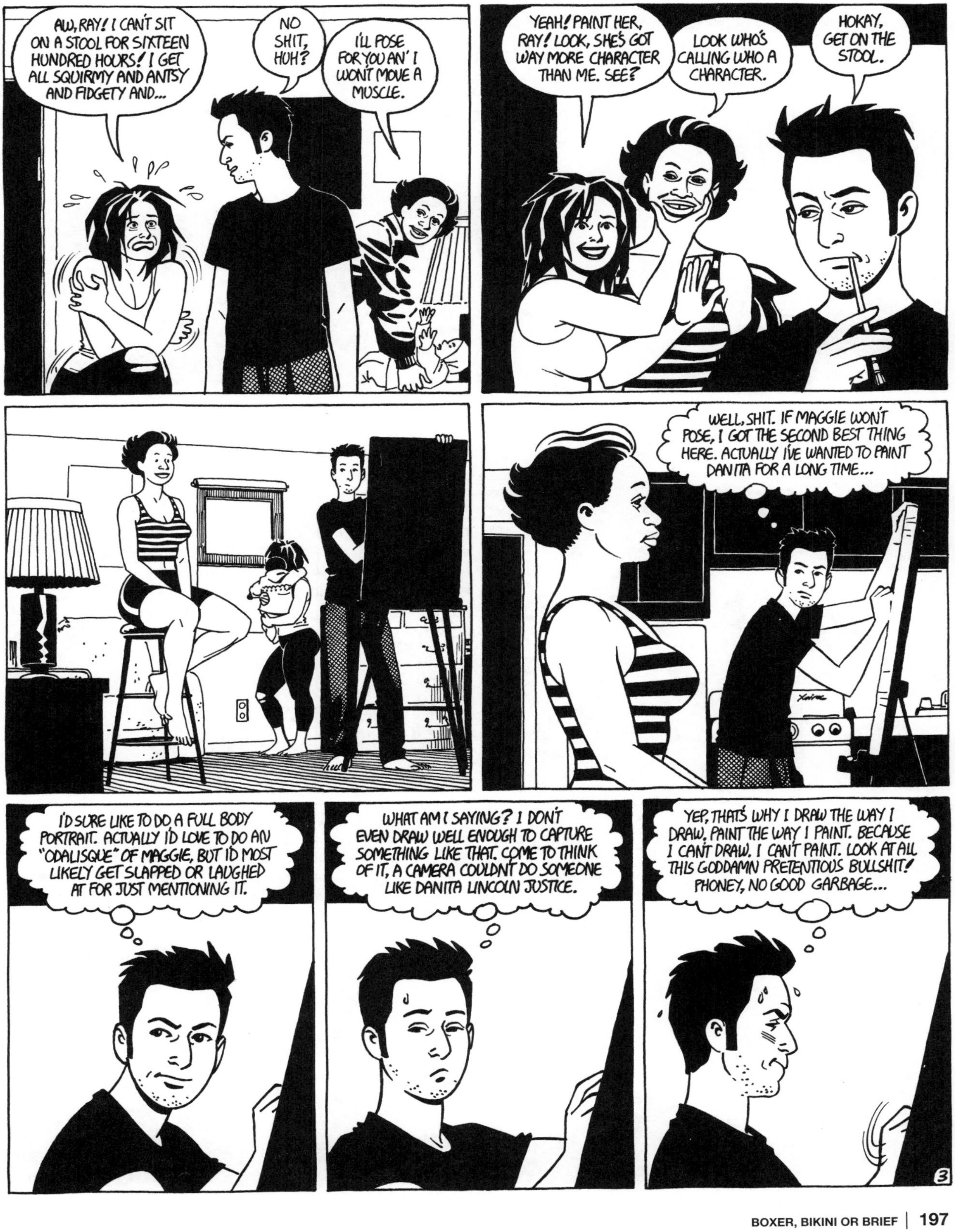
AW, RAY! I CAN'T SIT ON A STOOL FOR SIXTEEN HUNDRED HOURS! I GET ALL SQUIRMY AND ANTSY AND FIDGETY AND...
NO SHIT, HUH?
I'LL POSE FOR YOU AN' I WON'T MOVE A MUSCLE.
YEAH! PAINT HER, RAY! LOOK, SHE'S GOT WAY MORE CHARACTER THAN ME. SEE?
LOOK WHO'S CALLING WHO A CHARACTER.
HOKAY, GET ON THE STOOL.
WELL, SHIT. IF MAGGIE WON'T POSE, I GOT THE SECOND BEST THING HERE. ACTUALLY I'VE WANTED TO PAINT DANITA FOR A LONG TIME...
I'D SURE LIKE TO DO A FULL BODY PORTRAIT. ACTUALLY I'D LOVE TO DO AN "ODALISQUE" OF MAGGIE, BUT I'D MOST LIKELY GET SLAPPED OR LAUGHED AT FOR JUST MENTIONING IT.
WHAT AM I SAYING? I DON'T EVEN DRAW WELL ENOUGH TO CAPTURE SOMETHING LIKE THAT. COME TO THINK OF IT, A CAMERA COULDN'T DO SOMEONE LIKE DANITA LINCOLN JUSTICE.
YEP, THAT'S WHY I DRAW THE WAY I DRAW, PAINT THE WAY I PAINT. BECAUSE I CAN'T DRAW. I CAN'T PAINT. LOOK AT ALL THIS GODDAMN PRETENTIOUS BULLSHIT! PHONEY, NO GOOD GARBAGE...
3

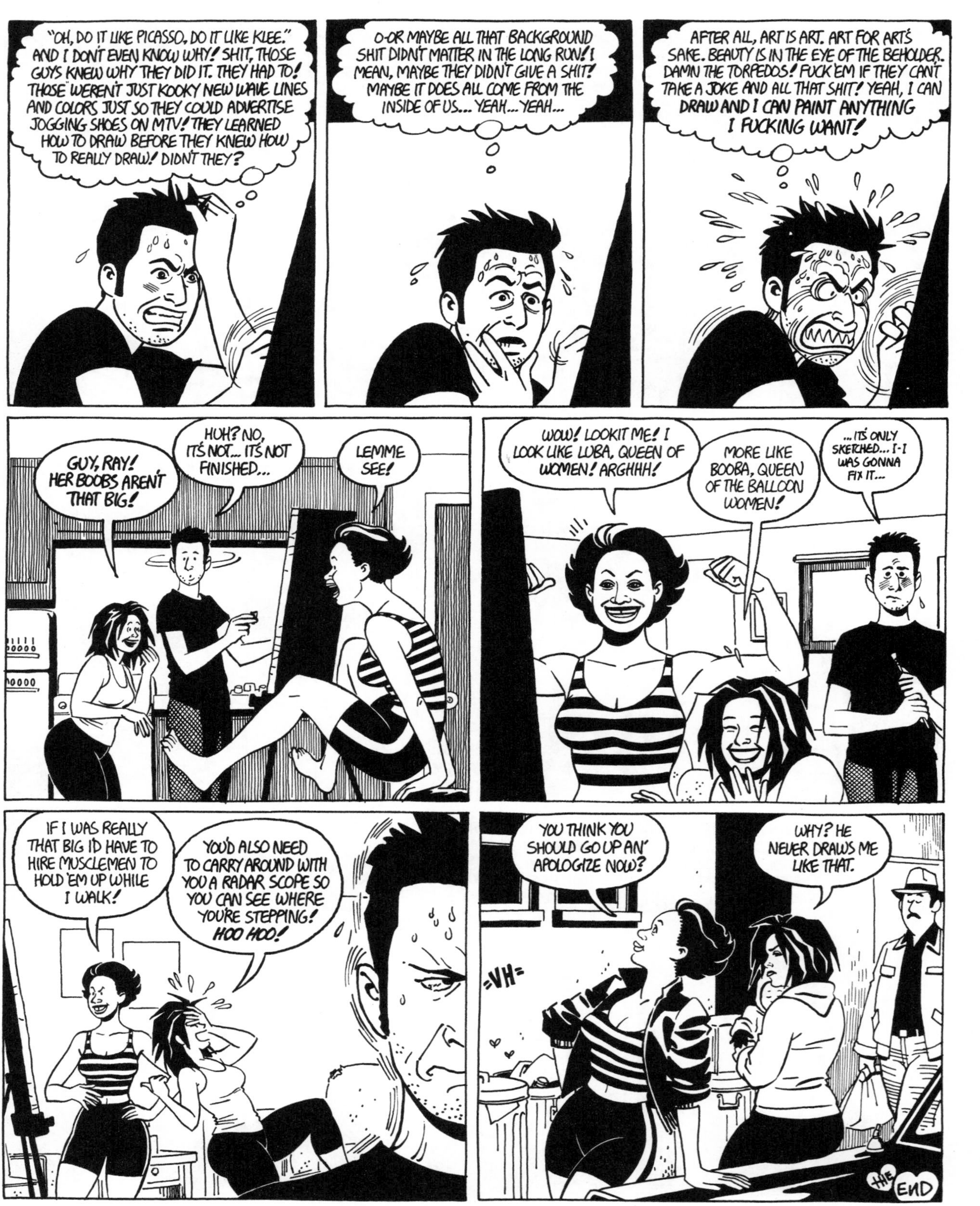
"OH, DO IT LIKE PICASSO, DO IT LIKE KLEE." AND I DON'T EVEN KNOW WHY! SHIT, THOSE GUYS KNEW WHY THEY DID IT. THEY HAD TO! THOSE WEREN'T JUST KOOKY NEW WAVE LINES AND COLORS JUST SO THEY COULD ADVERTISE JOGGING SHOES ON MTV! THEY LEARNED HOW TO DRAW BEFORE THEY KNEW HOW TO REALLY DRAW! DIDN'T THEY?
O-OR MAYBE ALL THAT BACKGROUND SHIT DIDN'T MATTER IN THE LONG RUN! I MEAN, MAYBE THEY DIDN'T GIVE A SHIT! MAYBE IT DOES ALL COME FROM THE INSIDE OF US... YEAH... YEAH...
AFTER ALL, ART IS ART. ART FOR ART'S SAKE. BEAUTY IS IN THE EYE OF THE BEHOLDER. DAMN THE TORPEDOS! FUCK 'EM IF THEY CAN'T TAKE A JOKE AND ALL THAT SHIT! YEAH, I CAN DRAW AND I CAN PAINT ANYTHING I FUCKING WANT!
GUY, RAY! HER BOOBS AREN'T THAT BIG!
HUH? NO, IT'S NOT... IT'S NOT FINISHED...
LEMME SEE!
WOW! LOOKIT ME! I LOOK LIKE LUBA, QUEEN OF WOMEN! ARGHHH!
MORE LIKE BOOBA, QUEEN OF THE BALLOON WOMEN!
...IT'S ONLY SKETCHED... I-I WAS GONNA FIX IT...
IF I WAS REALLY THAT BIG I'D HAVE TO HIRE MUSCLEMEN TO HOLD 'EM UP WHILE I WALK!
YOU'D ALSO NEED TO CARRY AROUND WITH YOU A RADAR SCOPE SO YOU CAN SEE WHERE YOU'RE STEPPING! HOO HOO!
YOU THINK YOU SHOULD GO UP AN' APOLOGIZE NOW?
=VH=
WHY? HE NEVER DRAWS ME LIKE THAT.
THE END

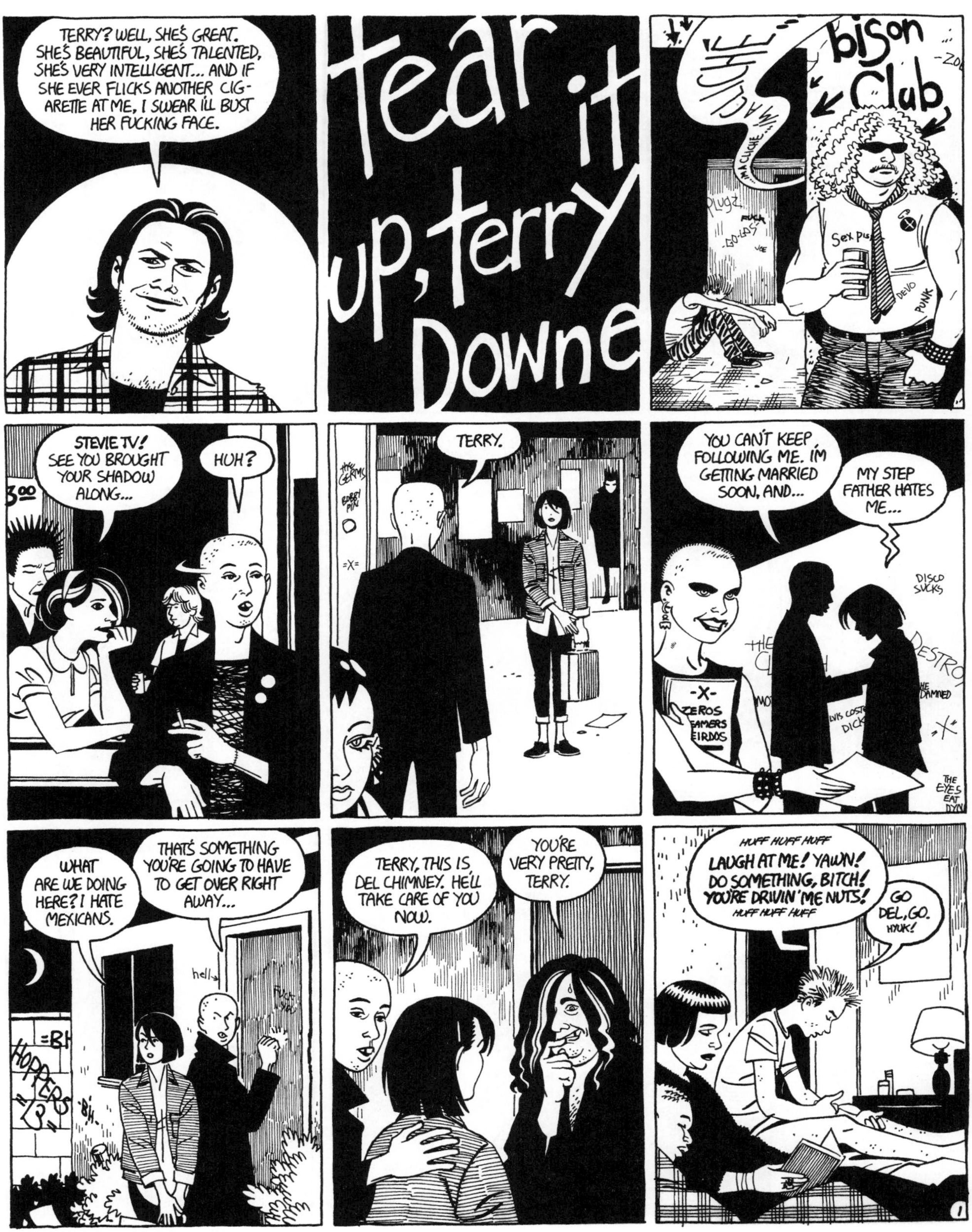
TERRY? WELL, SHE'S GREAT. SHE'S BEAUTIFUL, SHE'S TALENTED, SHE'S VERY INTELLIGENT... AND IF SHE EVER FLICKS ANOTHER CIG-ARETTE AT ME, I SWEAR I'LL BUST HER FUCKING FACE.
tear it up, terry Downe
bison Club
STEVIE TV! SEE YOU BROUGHT YOUR SHADOW ALONG...
HUH?
TERRY.
YOU CAN'T KEEP FOLLOWING ME. I'M GETTING MARRIED SOON, AND...
MY STEP FATHER HATES ME...
DISCO SUCKS
WHAT ARE WE DOING HERE? I HATE MEXICANS.
THAT'S SOMETHING YOU'RE GOING TO HAVE TO GET OVER RIGHT AWAY...
TERRY, THIS IS DEL CHIMNEY. HE'LL TAKE CARE OF YOU NOW.
YOU'RE VERY PRETTY, TERRY.
HUFF HUFF HUFF
LAUGH AT ME! YAWN! DO SOMETHING, BITCH! YOU'RE DRIVIN' ME NUTS!
HUFF HUFF HUFF
GO DEL, GO. HYUK!
1

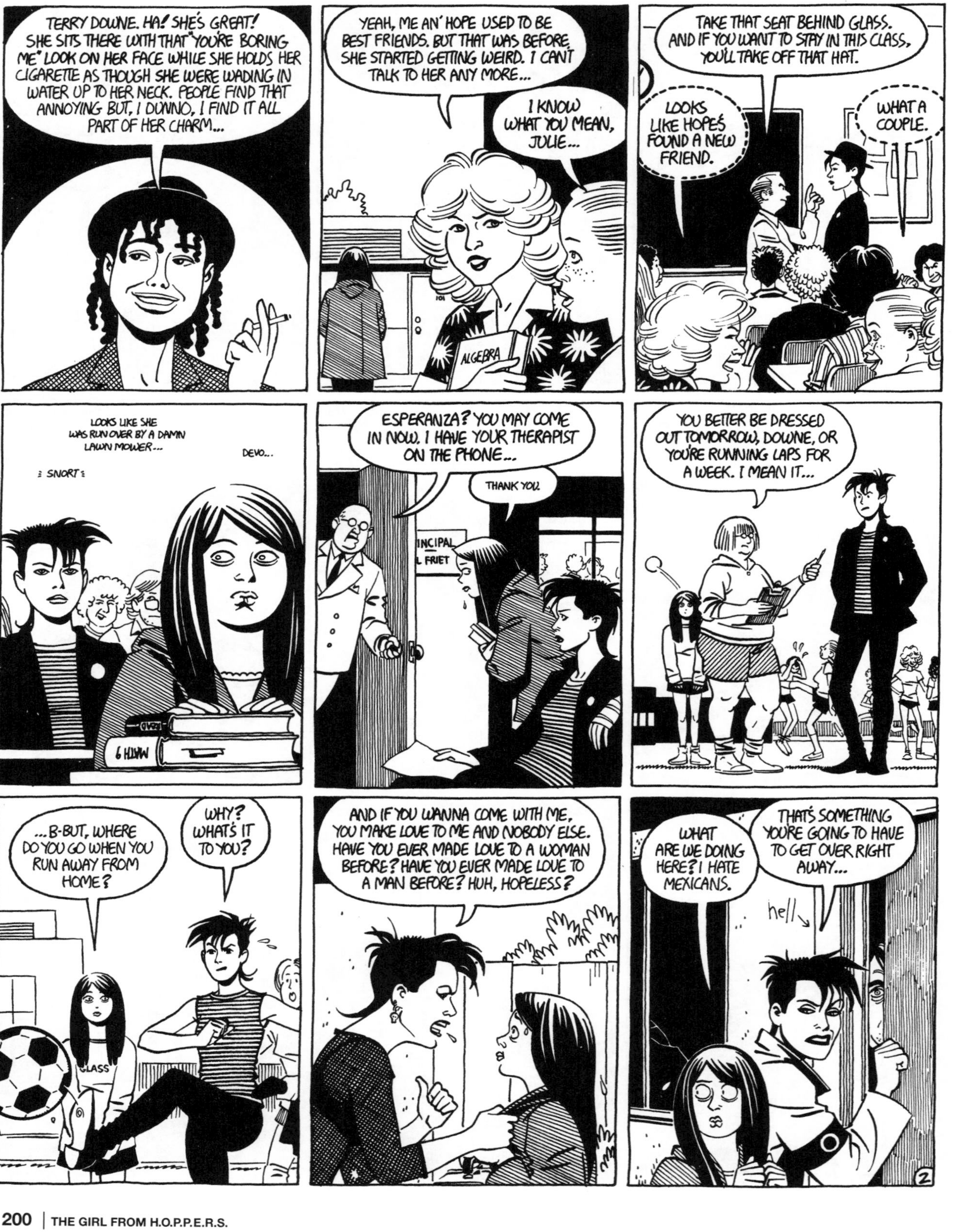
TERRY DOWNE. HA! SHE'S GREAT! SHE SITS THERE WITH THAT "YOU'RE BORING ME" LOOK ON HER FACE WHILE SHE HOLDS HER CIGARETTE AS THOUGH SHE WERE WADING IN WATER UP TO HER NECK. PEOPLE FIND THAT ANNOYING BUT, I DUNNO, I FIND IT ALL PART OF HER CHARM...
YEAH, ME AN' HOPE USED TO BE BEST FRIENDS. BUT THAT WAS BEFORE SHE STARTED GETTING WEIRD. I CAN'T TALK TO HER ANY MORE...
I KNOW WHAT YOU MEAN, JULIE...
ALGEBRA
TAKE THAT SEAT BEHIND GLASS. AND IF YOU WANT TO STAY IN THIS CLASS, YOU'LL TAKE OFF THAT HAT.
LOOKS LIKE HOPE'S FOUND A NEW FRIEND.
WHAT A COUPLE.
LOOKS LIKE SHE WAS RUN OVER BY A DAMN LAWN MOWER...
DEVO...
SNORT
MATH 9
ESPERANZA? YOU MAY COME IN NOW. I HAVE YOUR THERAPIST ON THE PHONE...
THANK YOU.
YOU BETTER BE DRESSED OUT TOMORROW, DOWNE, OR YOU'RE RUNNING LAPS FOR A WEEK. I MEAN IT...
...B-BUT, WHERE DO YOU GO WHEN YOU RUN AWAY FROM HOME?
WHY? WHAT'S IT TO YOU?
GLASS
AND IF YOU WANNA COME WITH ME, YOU MAKE LOVE TO ME AND NOBODY ELSE. HAVE YOU EVER MADE LOVE TO A WOMAN BEFORE? HAVE YOU EVER MADE LOVE TO A MAN BEFORE? HUH, HOPELESS?
WHAT ARE WE DOING HERE? I HATE MEXICANS.
THAT'S SOMETHING YOU'RE GOING TO HAVE TO GET OVER RIGHT AWAY...
hell
2

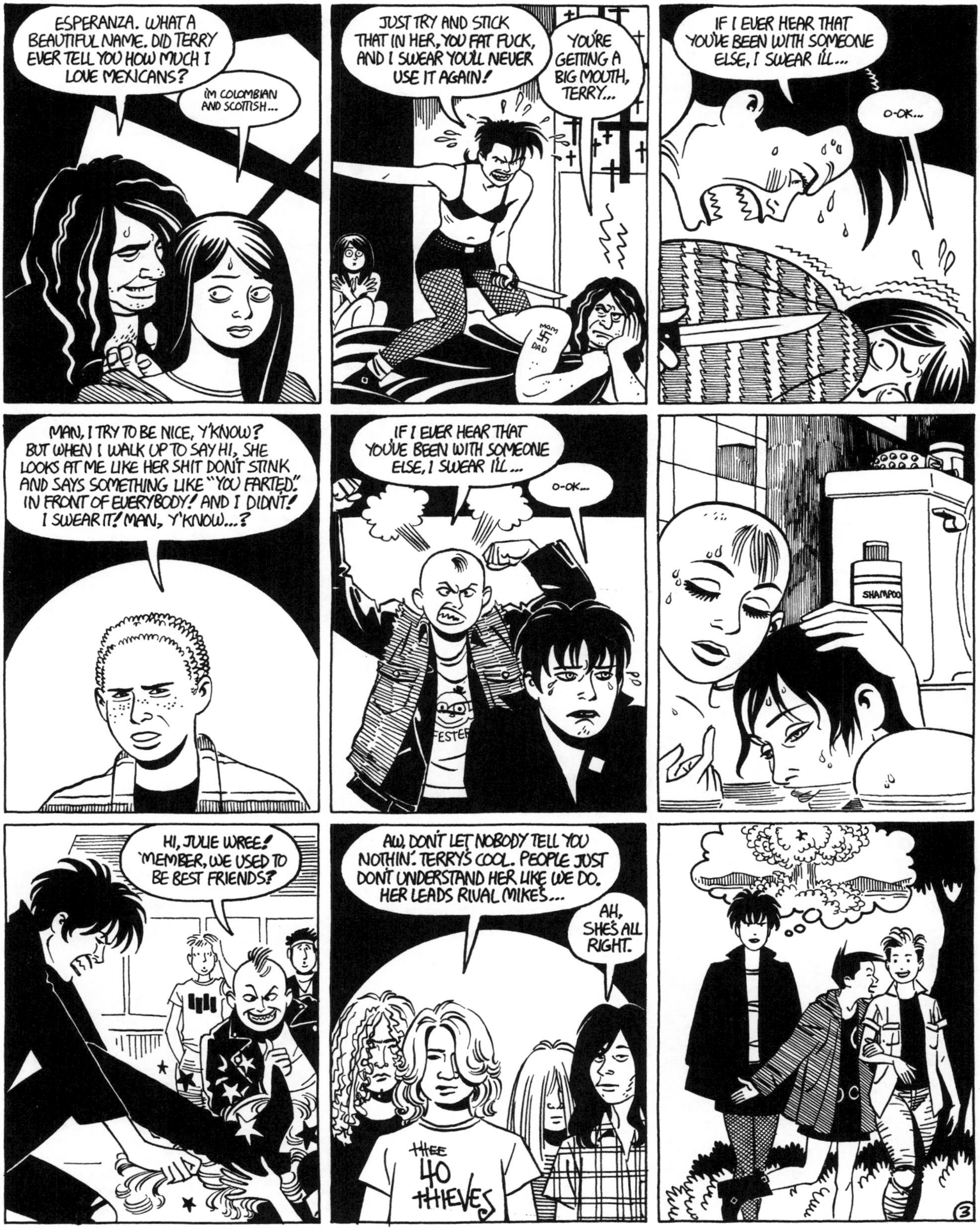
ESPERANZA. WHAT A BEAUTIFUL NAME. DID TERRY EVER TELL YOU HOW MUCH I LOVE MEXICANS?
I'M COLOMBIAN AND SCOTTISH...
JUST TRY AND STICK THAT IN HER, YOU FAT FUCK, AND I SWEAR YOU'LL NEVER USE IT AGAIN!
YOU'RE GETTING A BIG MOUTH, TERRY...
MOM
DAD
IF I EVER HEAR THAT YOU'VE BEEN WITH SOMEONE ELSE, I SWEAR I'LL...
O-OK...
MAN, I TRY TO BE NICE, Y'KNOW? BUT WHEN I WALK UP TO SAY HI, SHE LOOKS AT ME LIKE HER SHIT DON'T STINK AND SAYS SOMETHING LIKE "YOU FARTED." IN FRONT OF EVERYBODY! AND I DIDN'T! I SWEAR IT! MAN, Y'KNOW...?
IF I EVER HEAR THAT YOU'VE BEEN WITH SOMEONE ELSE, I SWEAR I'LL...
O-OK...
FESTER
SHAMPOO
HI, JULIE WREE! 'MEMBER, WE USED TO BE BEST FRIENDS?
AW, DON'T LET NOBODY TELL YOU NOTHIN'. TERRY'S COOL. PEOPLE JUST DON'T UNDERSTAND HER LIKE WE DO. HER LEADS RIVAL MIKE'S...
AH, SHE'S ALL RIGHT.
THEE 40 THIEVES
3

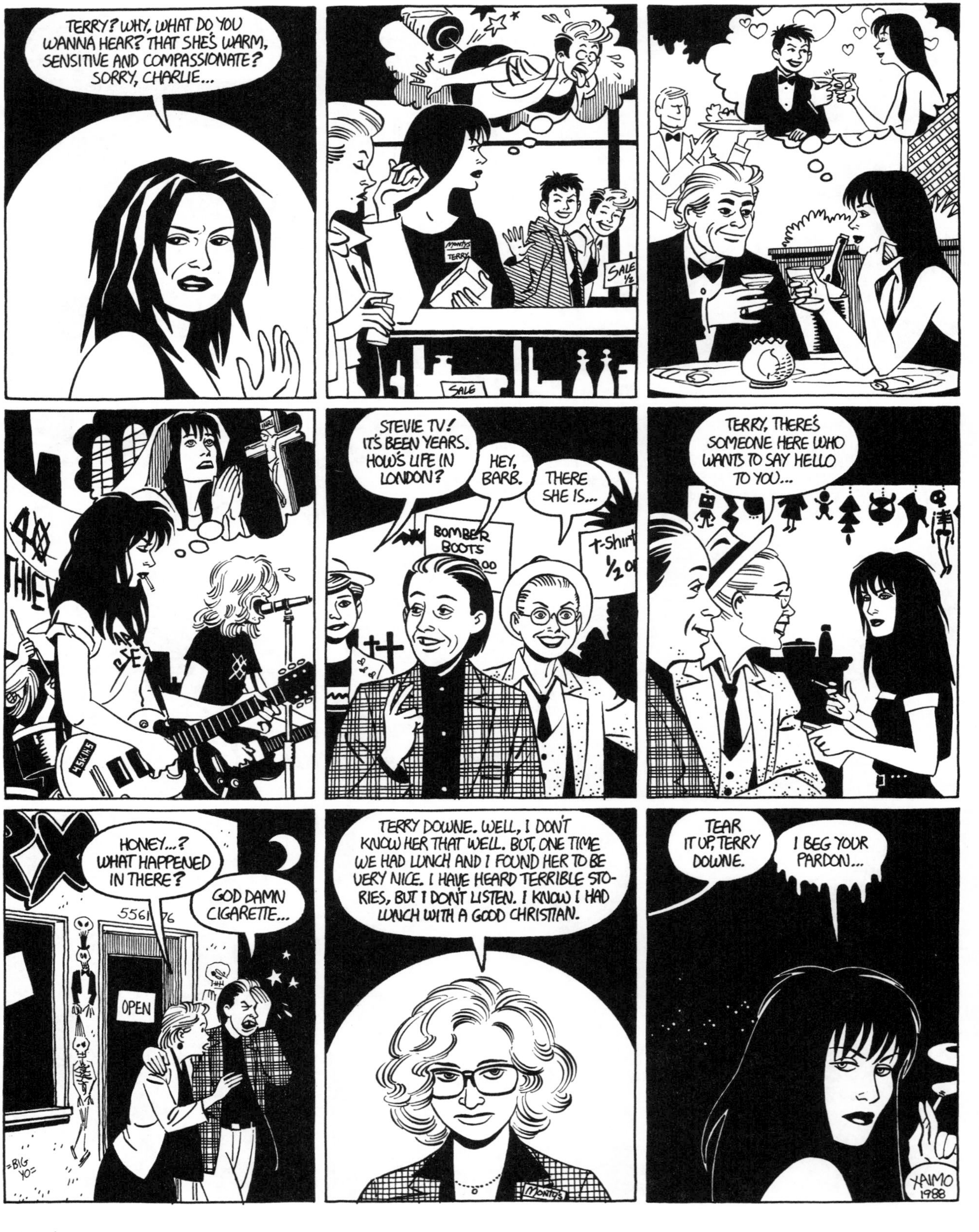
TERRY? WHY, WHAT DO YOU WANNA HEAR? THAT SHE'S WARM, SENSITIVE AND COMPASSIONATE? SORRY, CHARLIE...
MONTY'S
TERRY
SALE 1/2
SALE
STEVIE TV! IT'S BEEN YEARS. HOW'S LIFE IN LONDON?
HEY, BARB.
THERE SHE IS...
BOMBER BOOTS
TERRY, THERE'S SOMEONE HERE WHO WANTS TO SAY HELLO TO YOU...
HONEY...? WHAT HAPPENED IN THERE?
GOD DAMN CIGARETTE...
5561 76
OPEN
=BIG YO=
TERRY DOWNE. WELL, I DON'T KNOW HER THAT WELL. BUT, ONE TIME WE HAD LUNCH AND I FOUND HER TO BE VERY NICE. I HAVE HEARD TERRIBLE STORIES, BUT I DON'T LISTEN. I KNOW I HAD LUNCH WITH A GOOD CHRISTIAN.
MONTY'S
TEAR IT UP, TERRY DOWNE.
I BEG YOUR PARDON...
XAIMO 1988

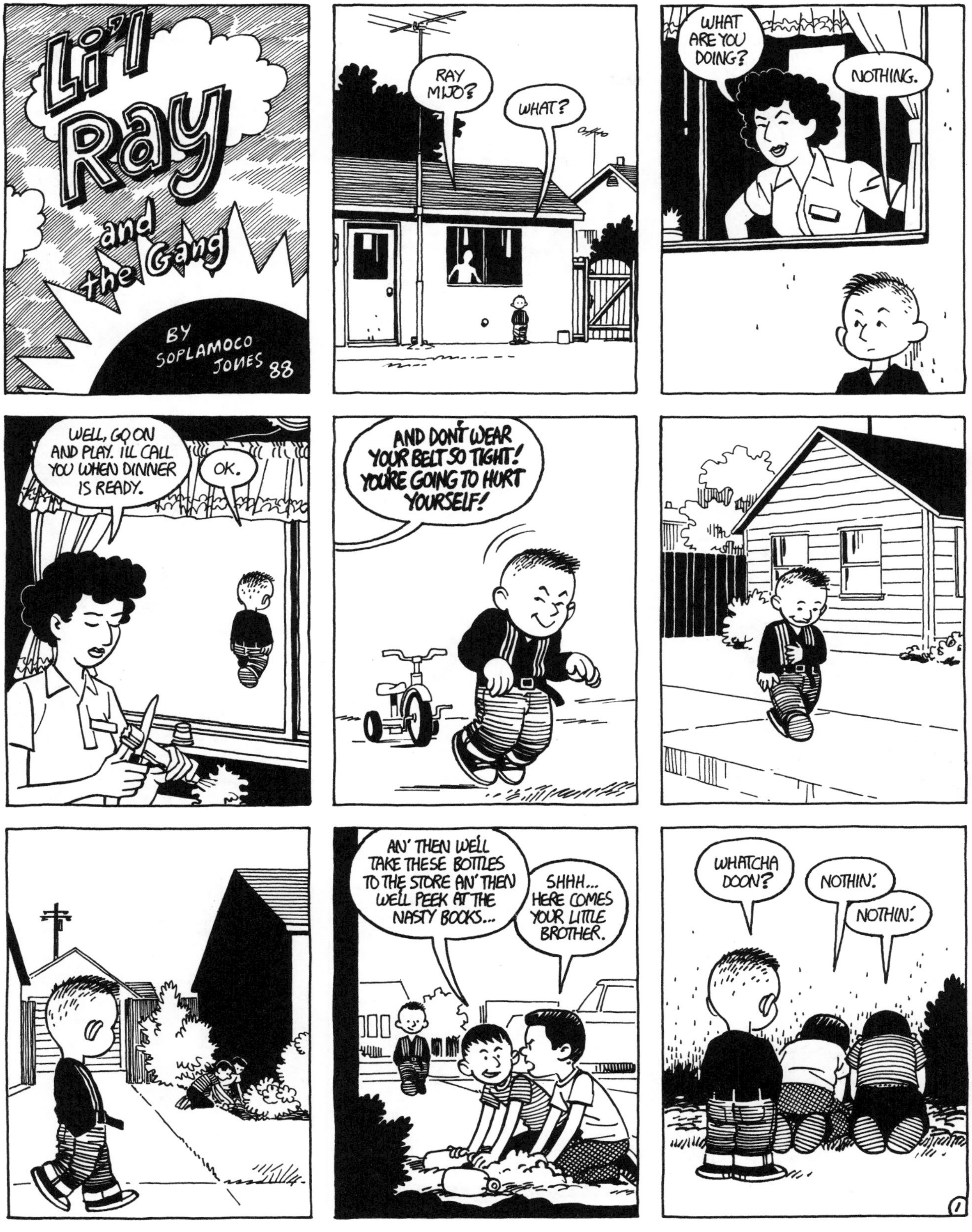
Li'l Ray
and the Gang
BY SOPLAMOCO JONES 88
RAY MIJO?
WHAT?
WHAT ARE YOU DOING?
NOTHING.
WELL, GO ON AND PLAY. I'LL CALL YOU WHEN DINNER IS READY.
OK.
AND DON'T WEAR YOUR BELT SO TIGHT! YOU'RE GOING TO HURT YOURSELF!
AN' THEN WE'LL TAKE THESE BOTTLES TO THE STORE AN' THEN WE'LL PEEK AT THE NASTY BOOKS...
SHHH... HERE COMES YOUR LITTLE BROTHER.
WHATCHA DOON?
NOTHIN'.
NOTHIN'.
1

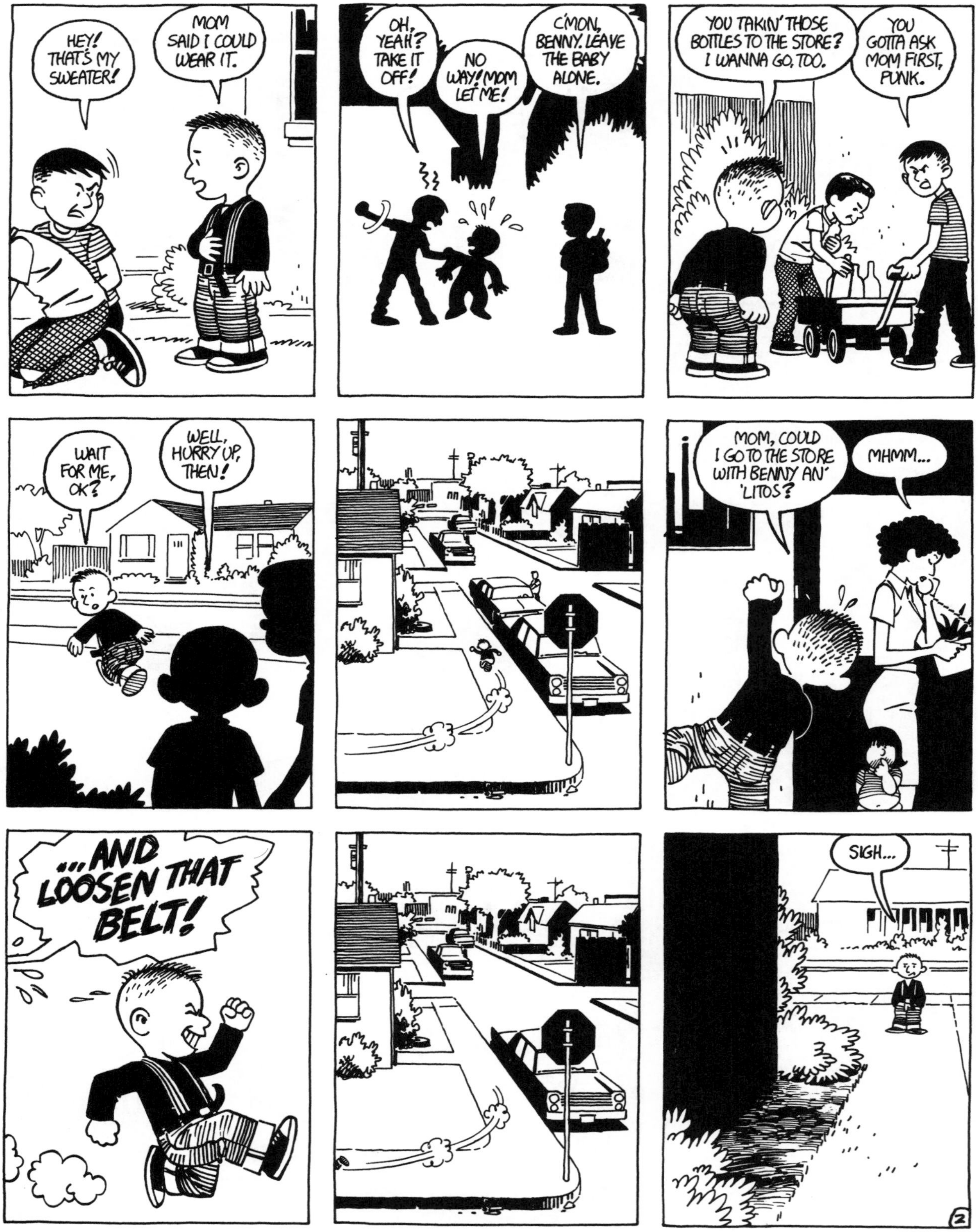
HEY! THAT'S MY SWEATER!
MOM SAID I COULD WEAR IT.
OH, YEAH? TAKE IT OFF!
NO WAY! MOM LET ME!
C'MON, BENNY. LEAVE THE BABY ALONE.
YOU TAKIN' THOSE BOTTLES TO THE STORE? I WANNA GO, TOO.
YOU GOTTA ASK MOM FIRST, PUNK.
WAIT FOR ME, OK?
WELL, HURRY UP, THEN!
MOM, COULD I GO TO THE STORE WITH BENNY AN' 'LITOS?
MHMM...
...AND LOOSEN THAT BELT!
SIGH...
2

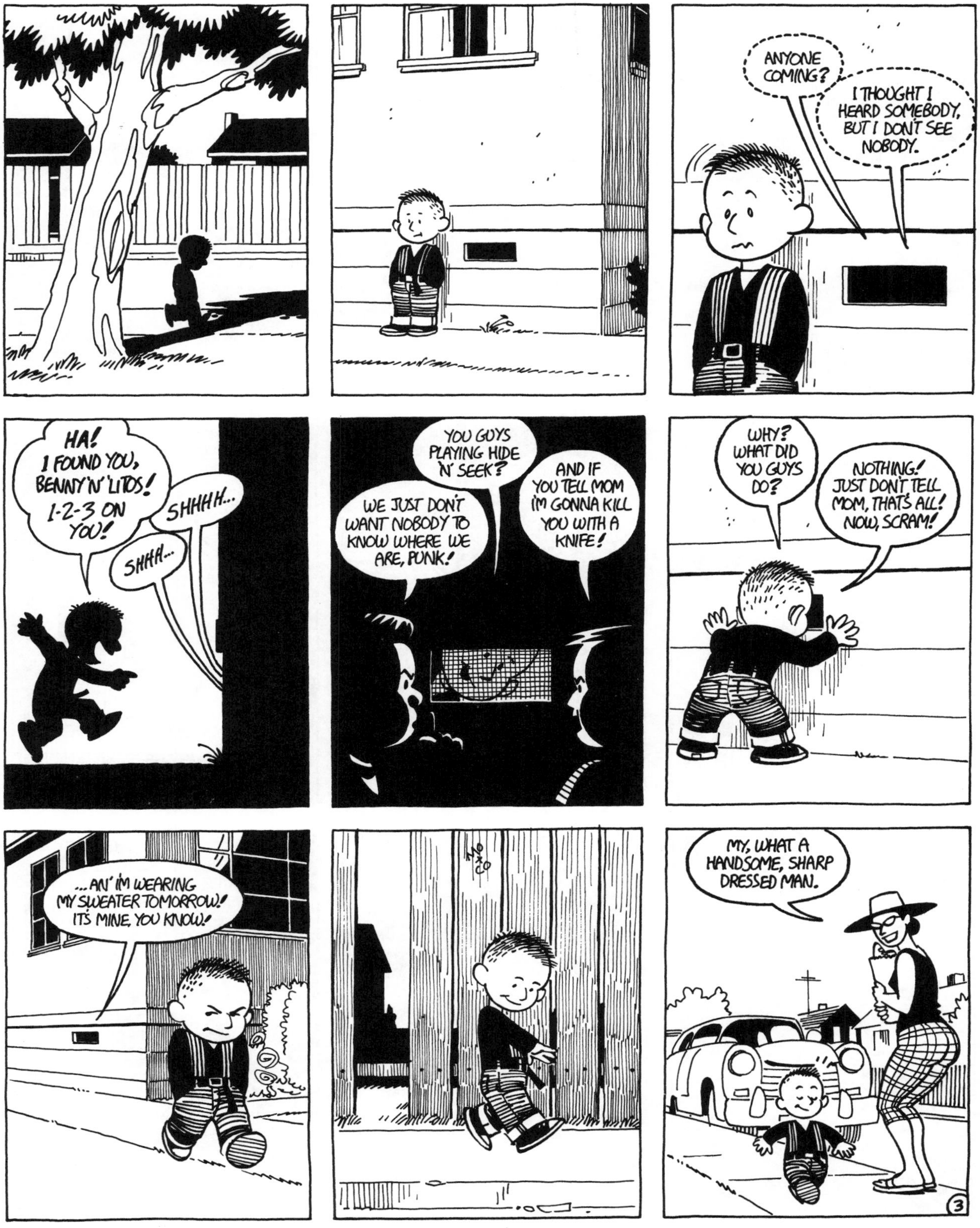
ANYONE COMING?
I THOUGHT I HEARD SOMEBODY, BUT I DON'T SEE NOBODY.
HA! I FOUND YOU, BENNY 'N' LITOS! 1-2-3 ON YOU!
SHHHH...
SHHH...
YOU GUYS PLAYING HIDE 'N' SEEK?
WE JUST DON'T WANT NOBODY TO KNOW WHERE WE ARE, PUNK!
AND IF YOU TELL MOM I'M GONNA KILL YOU WITH A KNIFE!
WHY? WHAT DID YOU GUYS DO?
NOTHING! JUST DON'T TELL MOM, THAT'S ALL! NOW, SCRAM!
...AN' I'M WEARING MY SWEATER TOMORROW! IT'S MINE, YOU KNOW!
MY, WHAT A HANDSOME, SHARP DRESSED MAN.
3

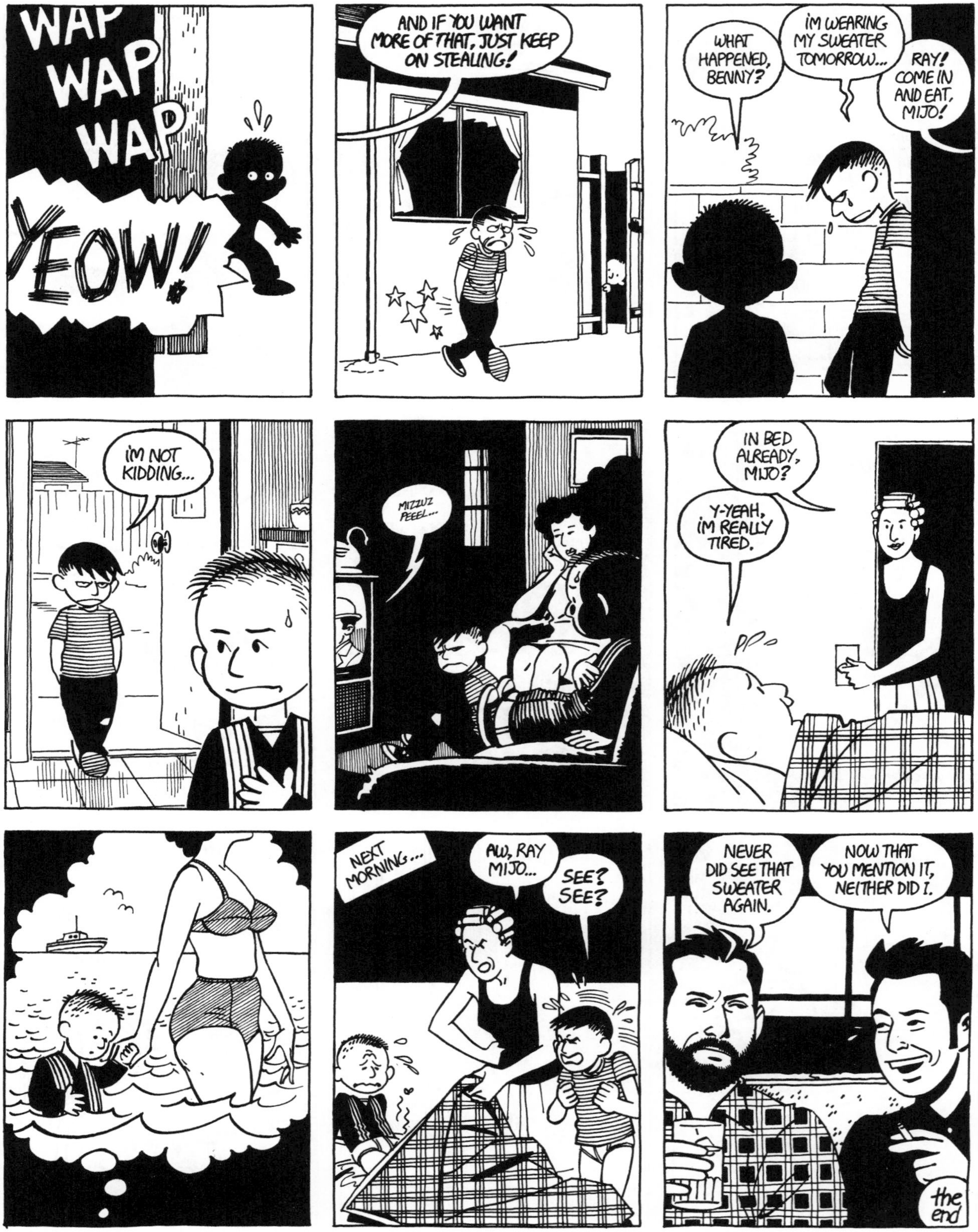
WAP
WAP
WAP
YEOW!
AND IF YOU WANT MORE OF THAT, JUST KEEP ON STEALING!
WHAT HAPPENED, BENNY?
I'M WEARING MY SWEATER TOMORROW...
RAY! COME IN AND EAT, MIJO!
I'M NOT KIDDING...
MIZZUZ PEEEL...
IN BED ALREADY, MIJO?
Y-YEAH, I'M REALLY TIRED.
NEXT MORNING...
AW, RAY MIJO...
SEE? SEE?
NEVER DID SEE THAT SWEATER AGAIN.
NOW THAT YOU MENTION IT, NEITHER DID I.
the end

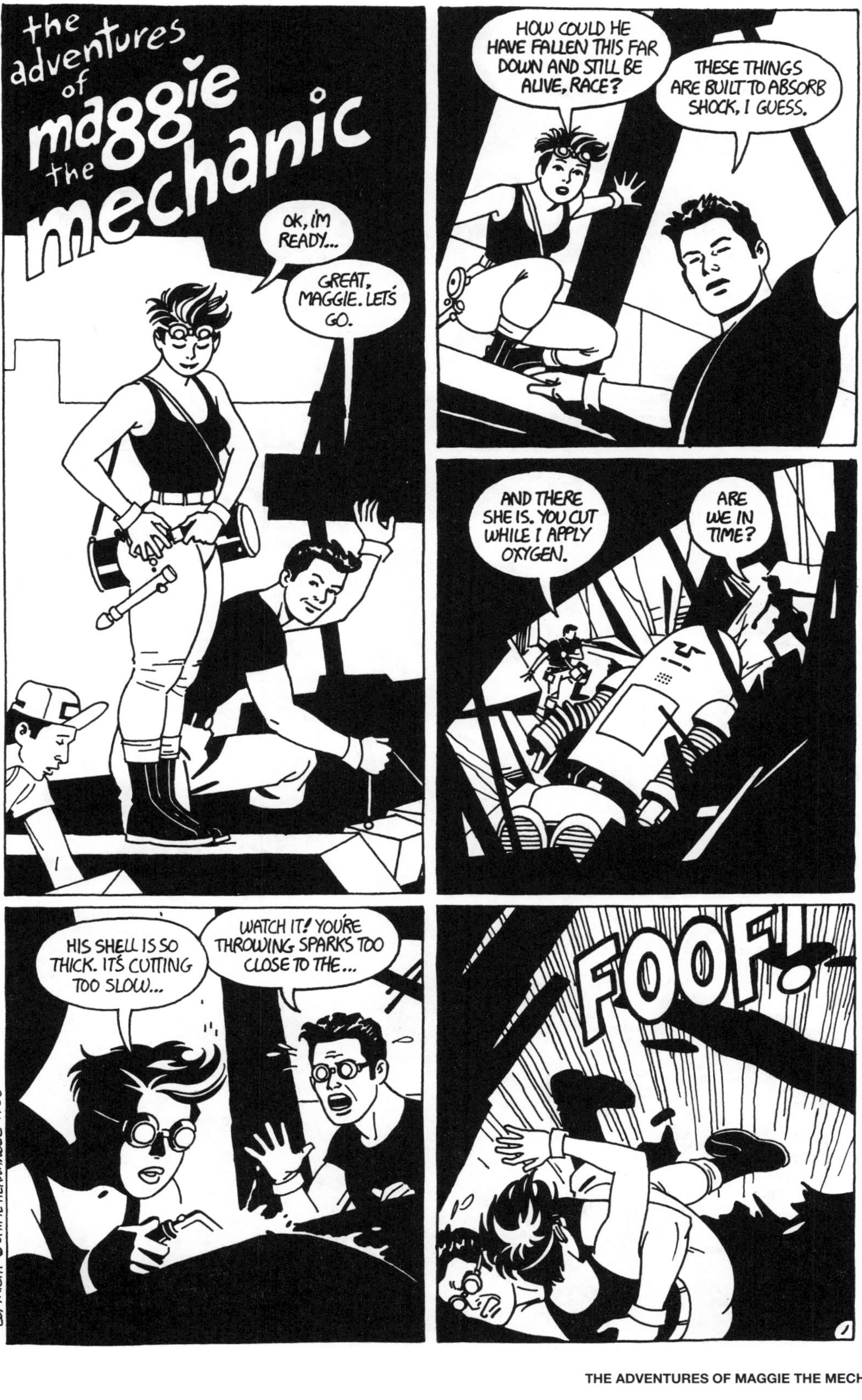
the adventures of maggie the mechanic
OK, I'M READY...
GREAT, MAGGIE. LET'S GO.
HOW COULD HE HAVE FALLEN THIS FAR DOWN AND STILL BE ALIVE, RACE?
THESE THINGS ARE BUILT TO ABSORB SHOCK, I GUESS.
AND THERE SHE IS. YOU CUT WHILE I APPLY OXYGEN.
ARE WE IN TIME?
HIS SHELL IS SO THICK. IT'S CUTTING TOO SLOW...
WATCH IT! YOU'RE THROWING SPARKS TOO CLOSE TO THE...
FOOF!
COPYRIGHT © JAIME HERNANDEZ 1988
1

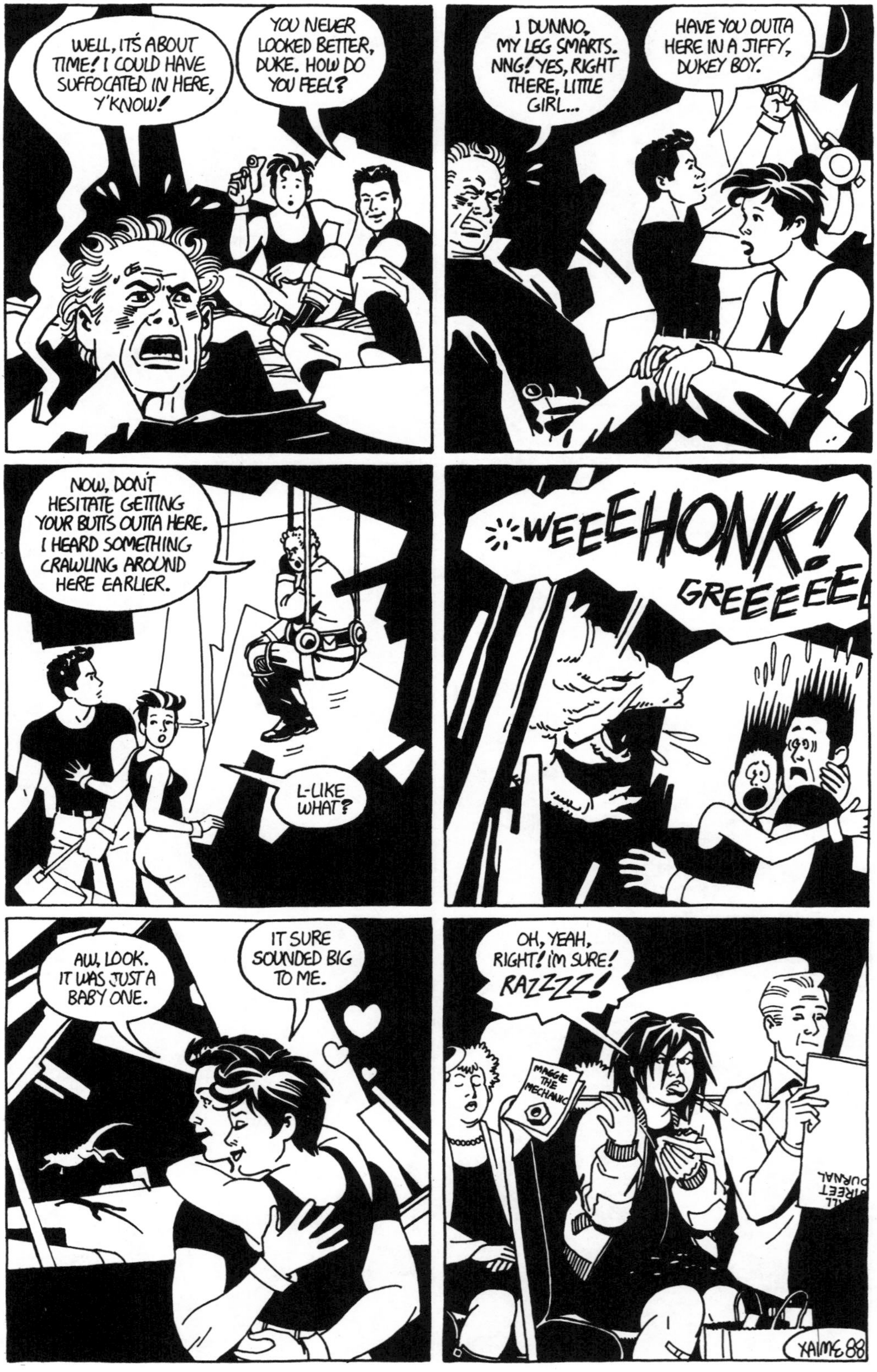
WELL, IT'S ABOUT TIME! I COULD HAVE SUFFOCATED IN HERE, Y'KNOW!
YOU NEVER LOOKED BETTER, DUKE. HOW DO YOU FEEL?
I DUNNO, MY LEG SMARTS. NNG! YES, RIGHT THERE, LITTLE GIRL...
HAVE YOU OUTTA HERE IN A JIFFY, DUKEY BOY.
NOW, DON'T HESITATE GETTING YOUR BUTTS OUTTA HERE. I HEARD SOMETHING CRAWLING AROUND HERE EARLIER.
L-LIKE WHAT?
WEEEHONK!
GREEEEEE
AW, LOOK. IT WAS JUST A BABY ONE.
IT SURE SOUNDED BIG TO ME.
OH, YEAH, RIGHT! I'M SURE! RAZZZZ!
MAGGIE THE MECHANIC
XAIME '88

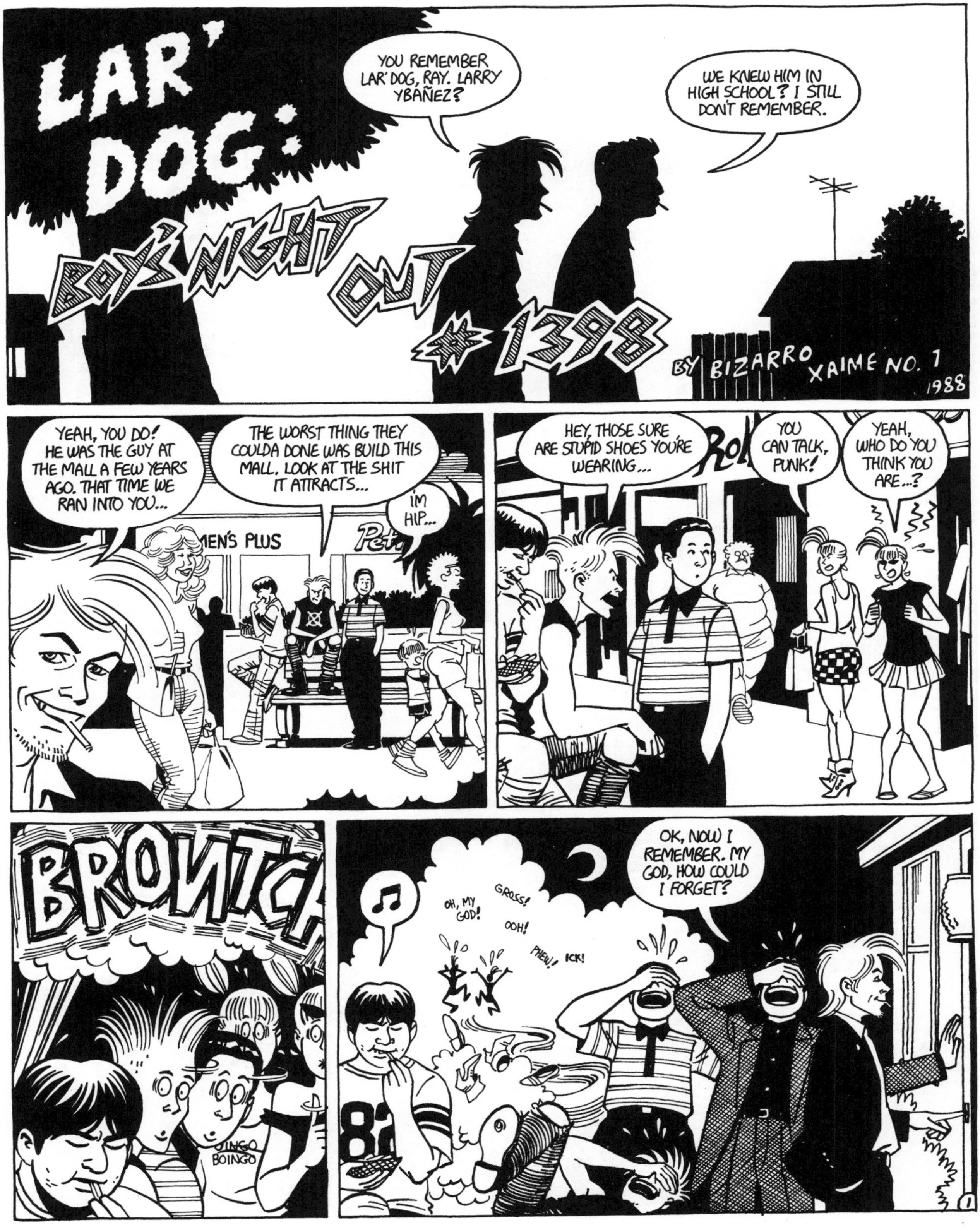
LAR' DOG:
BOY'S NIGHT OUT #1398
YOU REMEMBER LAR' DOG, RAY. LARRY YBAÑEZ?
WE KNEW HIM IN HIGH SCHOOL? I STILL DON'T REMEMBER.
BY BIZARRO XAIME NO. 1
1988
YEAH, YOU DO! HE WAS THE GUY AT THE MALL A FEW YEARS AGO. THAT TIME WE RAN INTO YOU...
THE WORST THING THEY COULDA DONE WAS BUILD THIS MALL. LOOK AT THE SHIT IT ATTRACTS...
I'M HIP...
MEN'S PLUS
HEY, THOSE SURE ARE STUPID SHOES YOU'RE WEARING...
YOU CAN TALK, PUNK!
YEAH, WHO DO YOU THINK YOU ARE...?
BRONTCH
OINGO BOINGO
OK, NOW I REMEMBER. MY GOD, HOW COULD I FORGET?
OH, MY GOD!
GROSS!
OOH!
PHEW!
ICK!
82

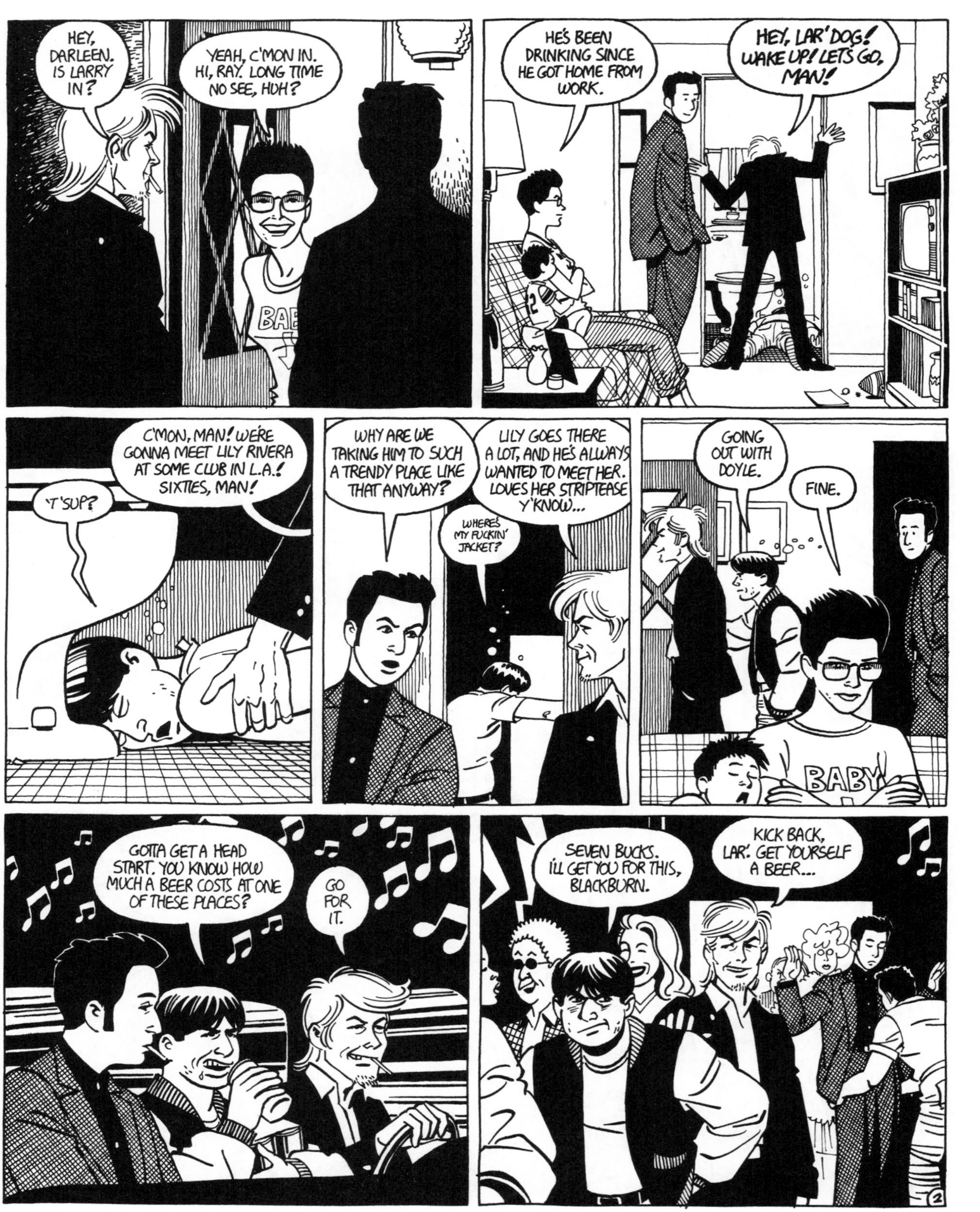
HEY, DARLEEN. IS LARRY IN?
YEAH, C'MON IN. HI, RAY. LONG TIME NO SEE, HUH?
HE'S BEEN DRINKING SINCE HE GOT HOME FROM WORK.
HEY, LAR'DOG! WAKE UP! LET'S GO, MAN!
'T'SUP?
C'MON, MAN! WE'RE GONNA MEET LILY RIVERA AT SOME CLUB IN L.A.! SIXTIES, MAN!
WHY ARE WE TAKING HIM TO SUCH A TRENDY PLACE LIKE THAT ANYWAY?
LILY GOES THERE A LOT, AND HE'S ALWAYS WANTED TO MEET HER. LOVES HER STRIPTEASE Y'KNOW...
WHERE'S MY FUCKIN' JACKET?
GOING OUT WITH DOYLE.
FINE.
GOTTA GET A HEAD START. YOU KNOW HOW MUCH A BEER COSTS AT ONE OF THESE PLACES?
GO FOR IT.
SEVEN BUCKS. I'LL GET YOU FOR THIS, BLACKBURN.
KICK BACK, LAR'. GET YOURSELF A BEER...
2

SO, THIS IS WHERE ALL THE HIP MOVIE AND MUSIC PEOPLE HANG OUT, HUH?

YEAH, I ALREADY SPOTTED THAT ENGLISH ASSHOLE THAT BUTCHERS MOTOWN SONGS.

OH, YEAH. THAT GUY'S EVERYWHERE. I'LL BET MAGGIE LIKES HIM BUT WON'T ADMIT IT. TO ME, ANYWAY. YEESH...

AND I'LL BET SHE'S SUPPOSED TO BE SOMEONE...

DON'T TELL ME, SHE'S IN THE LATEST "MICHAEL GEORGE" VIDEO...

AND CHECK OUT HER DATE...

FUCK, ALL THIS HOLLYWOOD SHIT! NOT EVEN THE BABES ARE TURNING ME ON.

I GOTTA GET THE FUCK OUTTA HERE...

HEY, WHAT TIME IS IT?

HEY, I KNOW YOU HAVE A WATCH. COULD YOU TELL ME THE TIME, SWEETY?

AW, JEEZ...

HEY, I PROMISE I AIN'T TRYING TO COME BETWEEN YOU AND THAT FAGGOT OVER THERE. I REALLY WANNA KNOW THE TIME...

OH GOD, WHAT DID I DO TO DESERVE THIS?

③

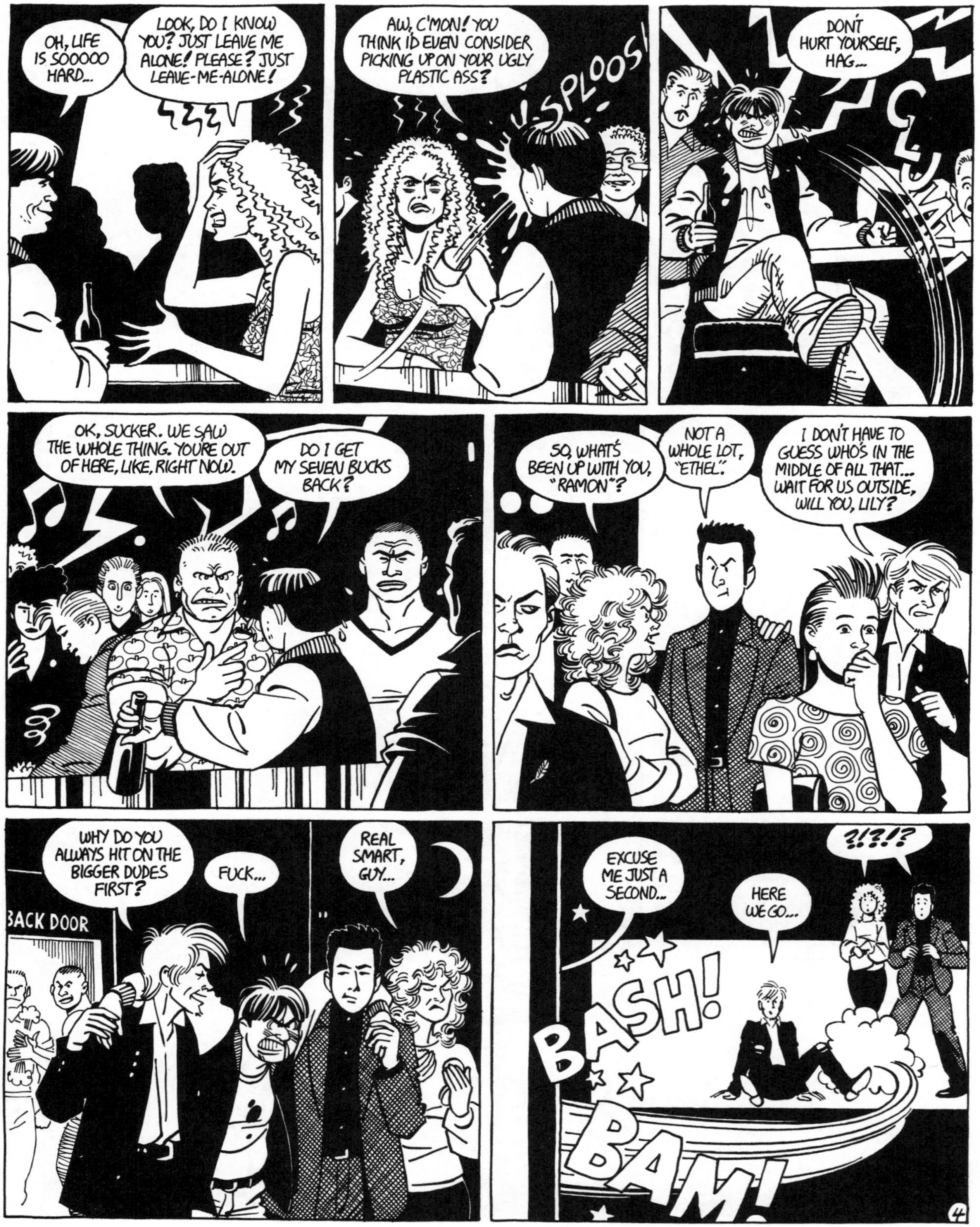
OH, LIFE IS SOOOOO HARD...
LOOK, DO I KNOW YOU? JUST LEAVE ME ALONE! PLEASE? JUST LEAVE-ME-ALONE!
AW, C'MON! YOU THINK I'D EVEN CONSIDER PICKING UP ON YOUR UGLY PLASTIC ASS?
SPLOOSH!
DON'T HURT YOURSELF, HAG...
CLUNK!
OK, SUCKER. WE SAW THE WHOLE THING. YOU'RE OUT OF HERE, LIKE, RIGHT NOW.
DO I GET MY SEVEN BUCKS BACK?
SO, WHAT'S BEEN UP WITH YOU, "RAMON"?
NOT A WHOLE LOT, "ETHEL."
I DON'T HAVE TO GUESS WHO'S IN THE MIDDLE OF ALL THAT... WAIT FOR US OUTSIDE, WILL YOU, LILY?
WHY DO YOU ALWAYS HIT ON THE BIGGER DUDES FIRST?
FUCK...
REAL SMART, GUY...
BACK DOOR
EXCUSE ME JUST A SECOND...
HERE WE GO...
?!?!?
BASH!
BAM!
4

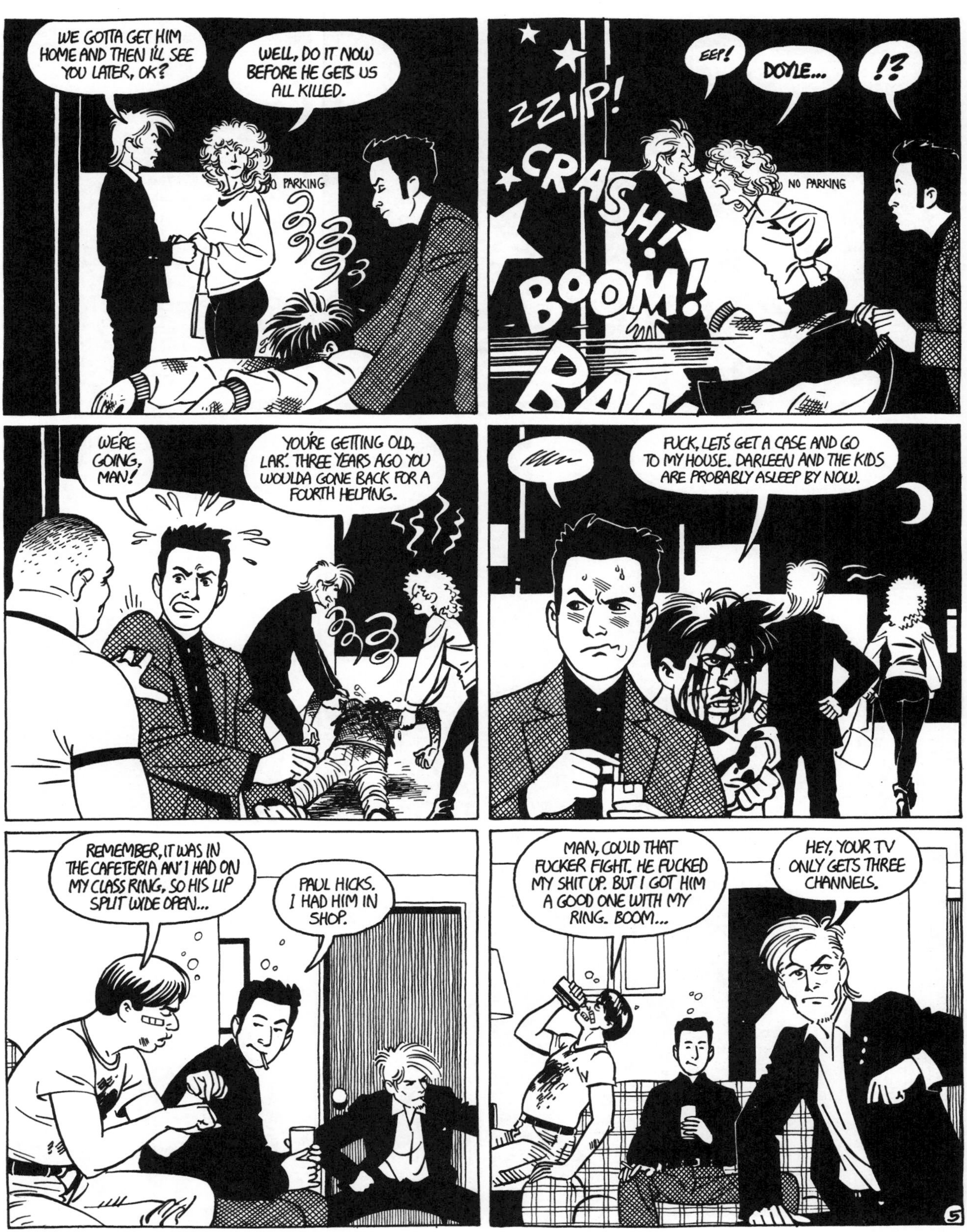
WE GOTTA GET HIM HOME AND THEN I'LL SEE YOU LATER, OK?
WELL, DO IT NOW BEFORE HE GETS US ALL KILLED.
NO PARKING
EEP!
DOYLE...
!?
ZZIP!
CRASH!
BOOM!
NO PARKING
WE'RE GOING, MAN!
YOU'RE GETTING OLD, LAR'. THREE YEARS AGO YOU WOULDA GONE BACK FOR A FOURTH HELPING.
FUCK, LET'S GET A CASE AND GO TO MY HOUSE. DARLEEN AND THE KIDS ARE PROBABLY ASLEEP BY NOW.
REMEMBER, IT WAS IN THE CAFETERIA AN' I HAD ON MY CLASS RING, SO HIS LIP SPLIT WIDE OPEN...
PAUL HICKS. I HAD HIM IN SHOP.
MAN, COULD THAT FUCKER FIGHT. HE FUCKED MY SHIT UP. BUT I GOT HIM A GOOD ONE WITH MY RING. BOOM...
HEY, YOUR TV ONLY GETS THREE CHANNELS.
5

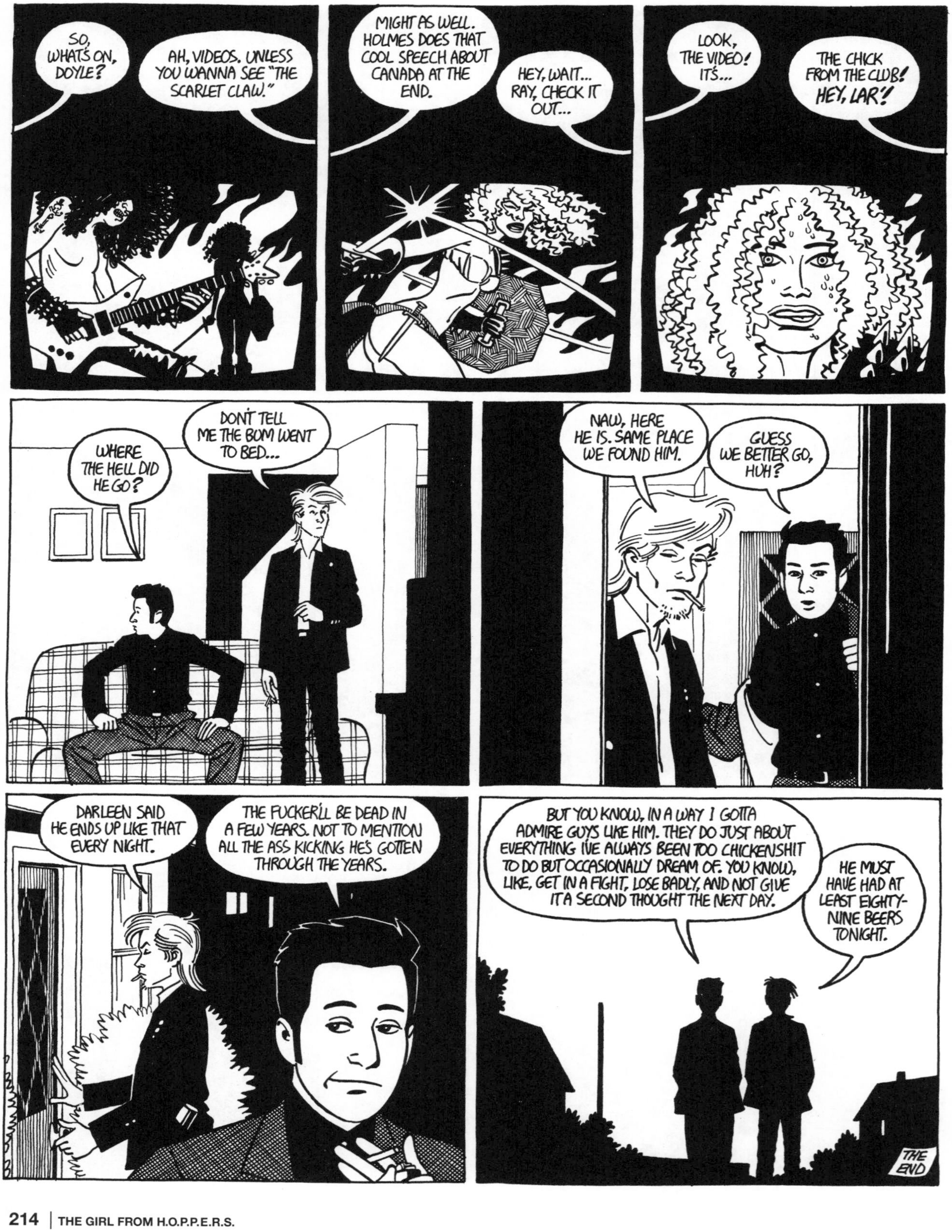
SO, WHAT'S ON, DOYLE?
AH, VIDEOS. UNLESS YOU WANNA SEE "THE SCARLET CLAW."
MIGHT AS WELL. HOLMES DOES THAT COOL SPEECH ABOUT CANADA AT THE END.
HEY, WAIT... RAY, CHECK IT OUT...
LOOK, THE VIDEO! IT'S...
THE CHICK FROM THE CLUB! HEY, LAR'!
WHERE THE HELL DID HE GO?
DON'T TELL ME THE BUM WENT TO BED...
NAW, HERE HE IS. SAME PLACE WE FOUND HIM.
GUESS WE BETTER GO, HUH?
DARLEEN SAID HE ENDS UP LIKE THAT EVERY NIGHT.
THE FUCKER'LL BE DEAD IN A FEW YEARS. NOT TO MENTION ALL THE ASS KICKING HE'S GOTTEN THROUGH THE YEARS.
BUT YOU KNOW, IN A WAY I GOTTA ADMIRE GUYS LIKE HIM. THEY DO JUST ABOUT EVERYTHING I'VE ALWAYS BEEN TOO CHICKENSHIT TO DO BUT OCCASIONALLY DREAM OF. YOU KNOW, LIKE, GET IN A FIGHT, LOSE BADLY, AND NOT GIVE IT A SECOND THOUGHT THE NEXT DAY.
HE MUST HAVE HAD AT LEAST EIGHTY-NINE BEERS TONIGHT.
THE END

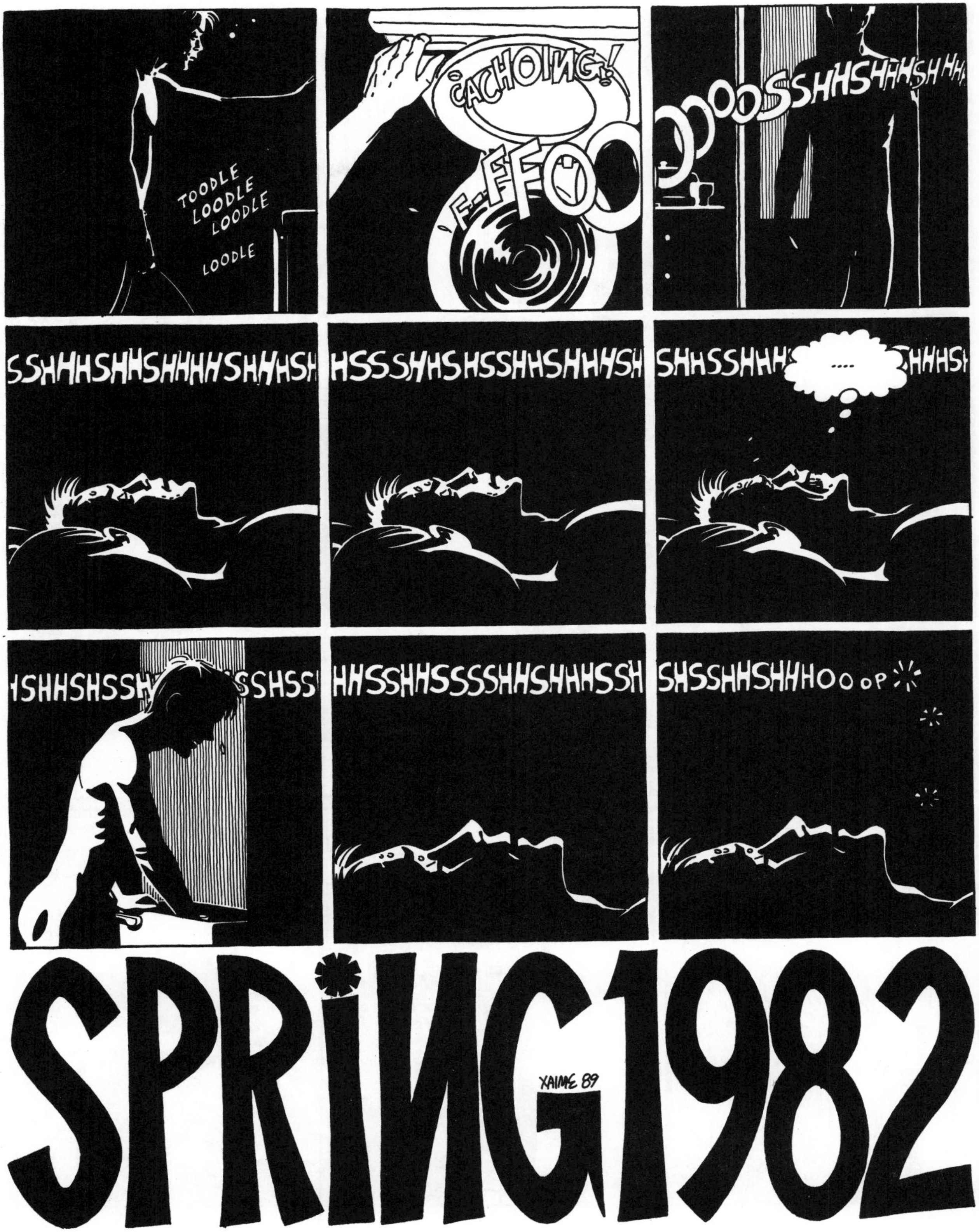
TOODLE
LOODLE
LOODLE
LOODLE
CACHOING!
F-FFOO
OOOOSSHHSHHHSHHH
SSHHHSHHSHHHHSHHHSH
HSSSHHSHSSHHSHHHSH
SHHSSHHH
HHHSH
HSHHSHSSH
SSHSS
HHSSHHSSSSHHSHHHSSH
SHSSHHSHHHOO OP
SPRING 1982
XAIME 89

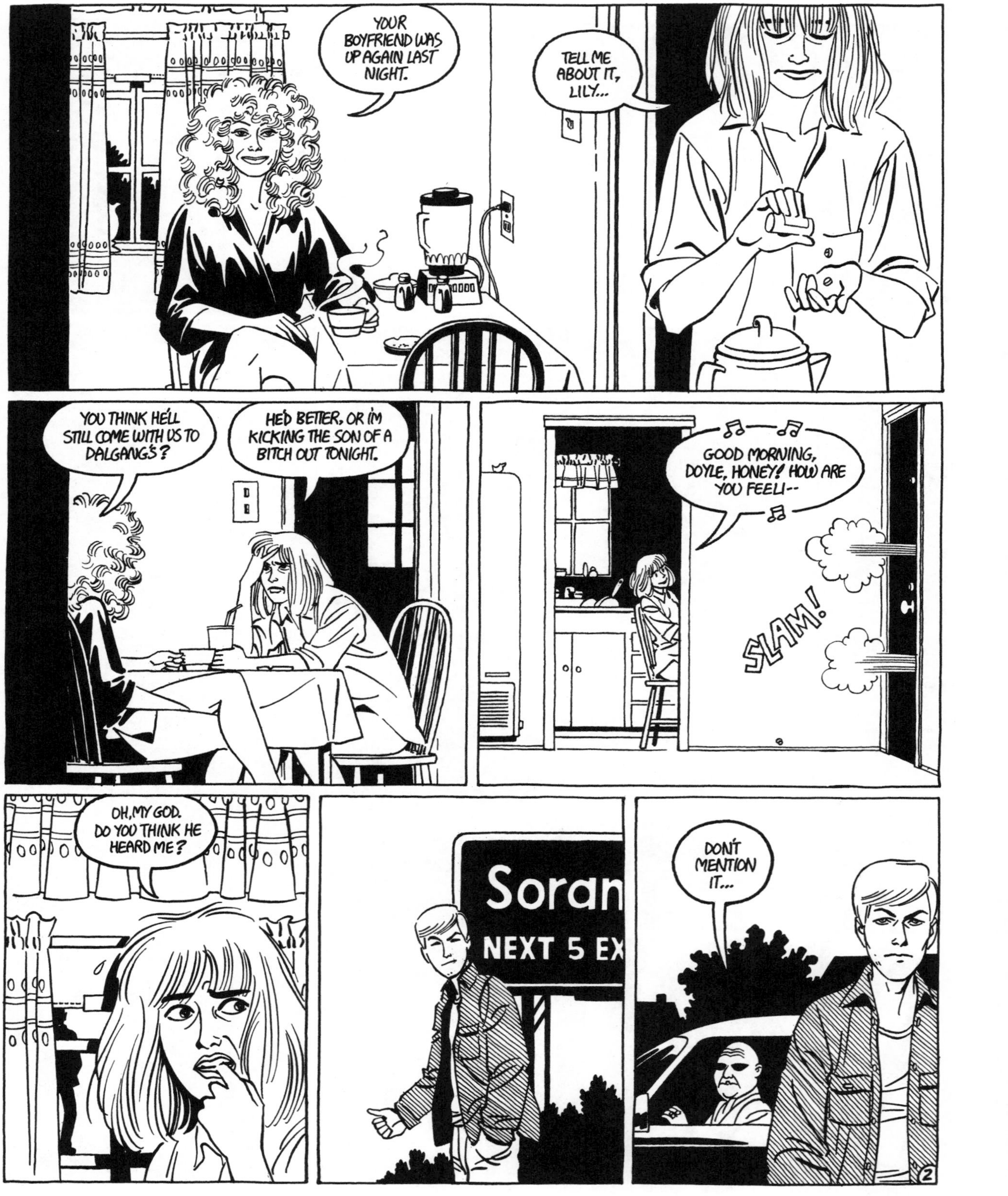
YOUR BOYFRIEND WAS UP AGAIN LAST NIGHT.
TELL ME ABOUT IT, LILY...
YOU THINK HE'LL STILL COME WITH US TO DALGANG'S?
HE'D BETTER, OR I'M KICKING THE SON OF A BITCH OUT TONIGHT.
GOOD MORNING, DOYLE, HONEY! HOW ARE YOU FEELI--
SLAM!
OH, MY GOD. DO YOU THINK HE HEARD ME?
Soran
NEXT 5 EX
DON'T MENTION IT...
2

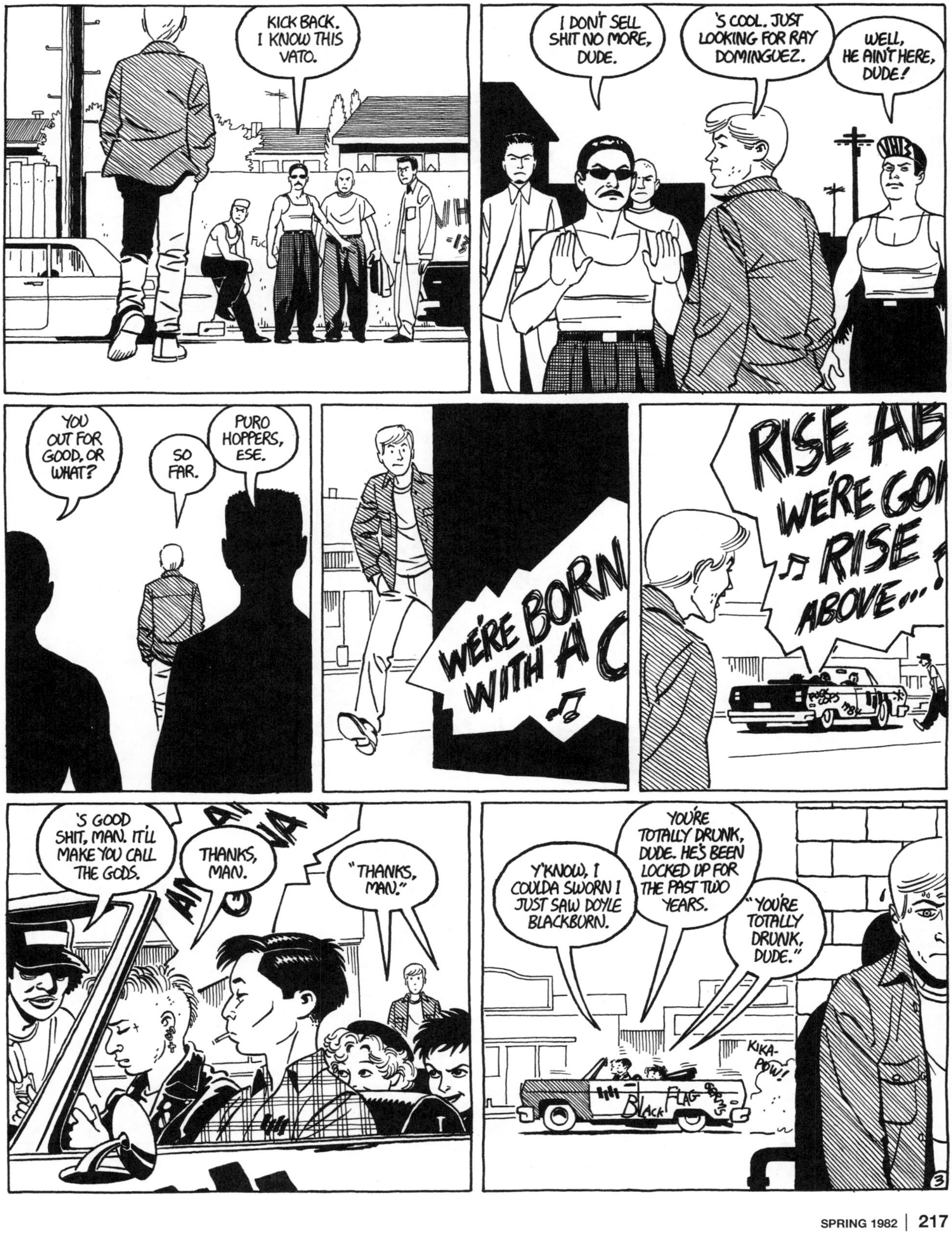

KICK BACK. I KNOW THIS VATO.
I DON'T SELL SHIT NO MORE, DUDE.
'S COOL. JUST LOOKING FOR RAY DOMINGUEZ.
WELL, HE AIN'T HERE, DUDE!
YOU OUT FOR GOOD, OR WHAT?
SO FAR.
PURO HOPPERS, ESE.
WE'RE BORN WITH A C
RISE AB
WE'RE GO
RISE
ABOVE...
'S GOOD SHIT, MAN. IT'LL MAKE YOU CALL THE GODS.
THANKS, MAN.
"THANKS, MAN."
Y'KNOW, I COULDA SWORN I JUST SAW DOYLE BLACKBURN.
YOU'RE TOTALLY DRUNK, DUDE. HE'S BEEN LOCKED UP FOR THE PAST TWO YEARS.
"YOU'RE TOTALLY DRUNK, DUDE."
KIKA-POW!
BLACK FLAG
3

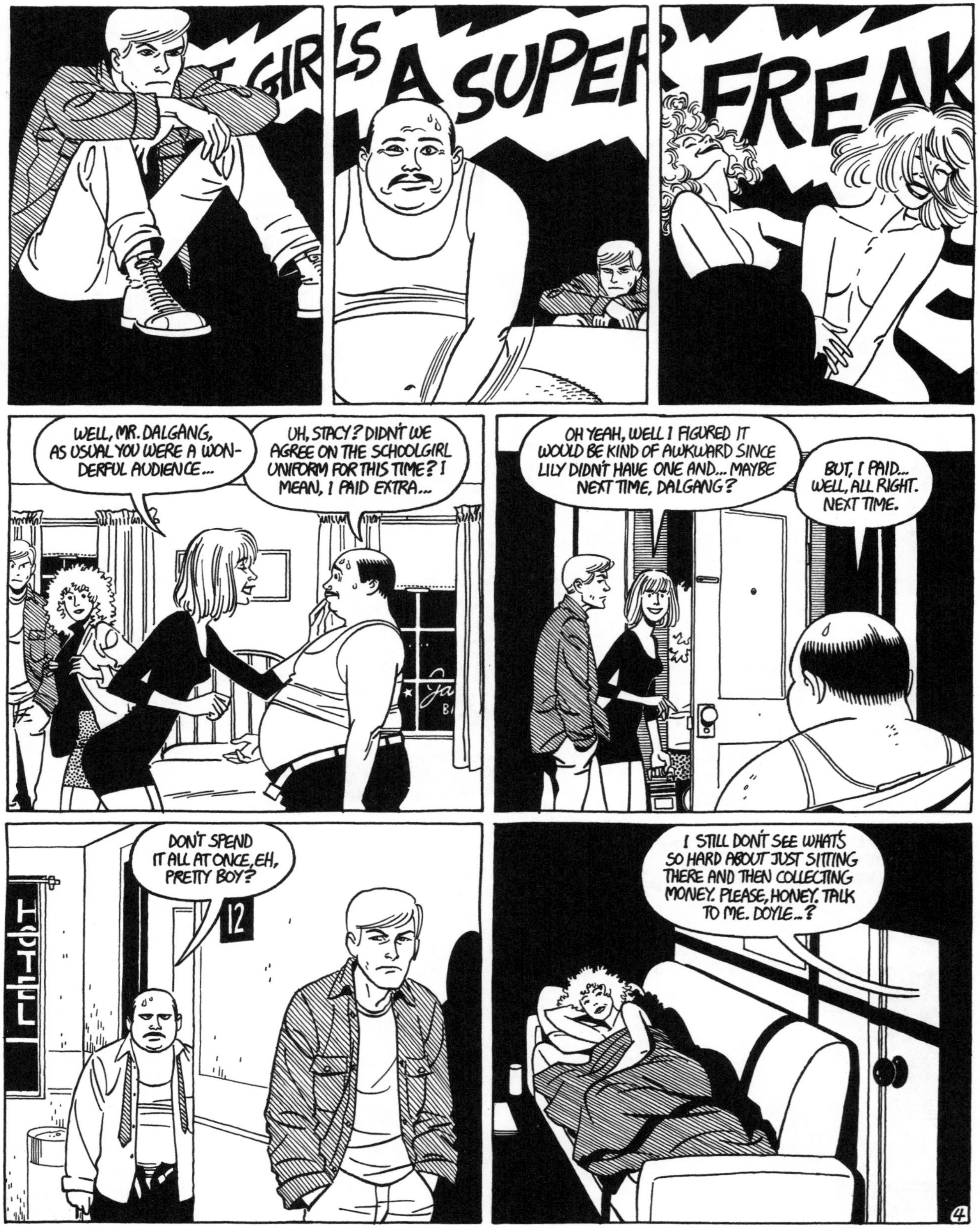
GIRLS A SUPER FREAK
WELL, MR. DALGANG, AS USUAL YOU WERE A WONDERFUL AUDIENCE...
UH, STACY? DIDN'T WE AGREE ON THE SCHOOLGIRL UNIFORM FOR THIS TIME? I MEAN, I PAID EXTRA...
OH YEAH, WELL I FIGURED IT WOULD BE KIND OF AWKWARD SINCE LILY DIDN'T HAVE ONE AND... MAYBE NEXT TIME, DALGANG?
BUT, I PAID... WELL, ALL RIGHT. NEXT TIME.
HOTEL
12
DON'T SPEND IT ALL AT ONCE, EH, PRETTY BOY?
I STILL DON'T SEE WHAT'S SO HARD ABOUT JUST SITTING THERE AND THEN COLLECTING MONEY. PLEASE, HONEY. TALK TO ME. DOYLE...?
4

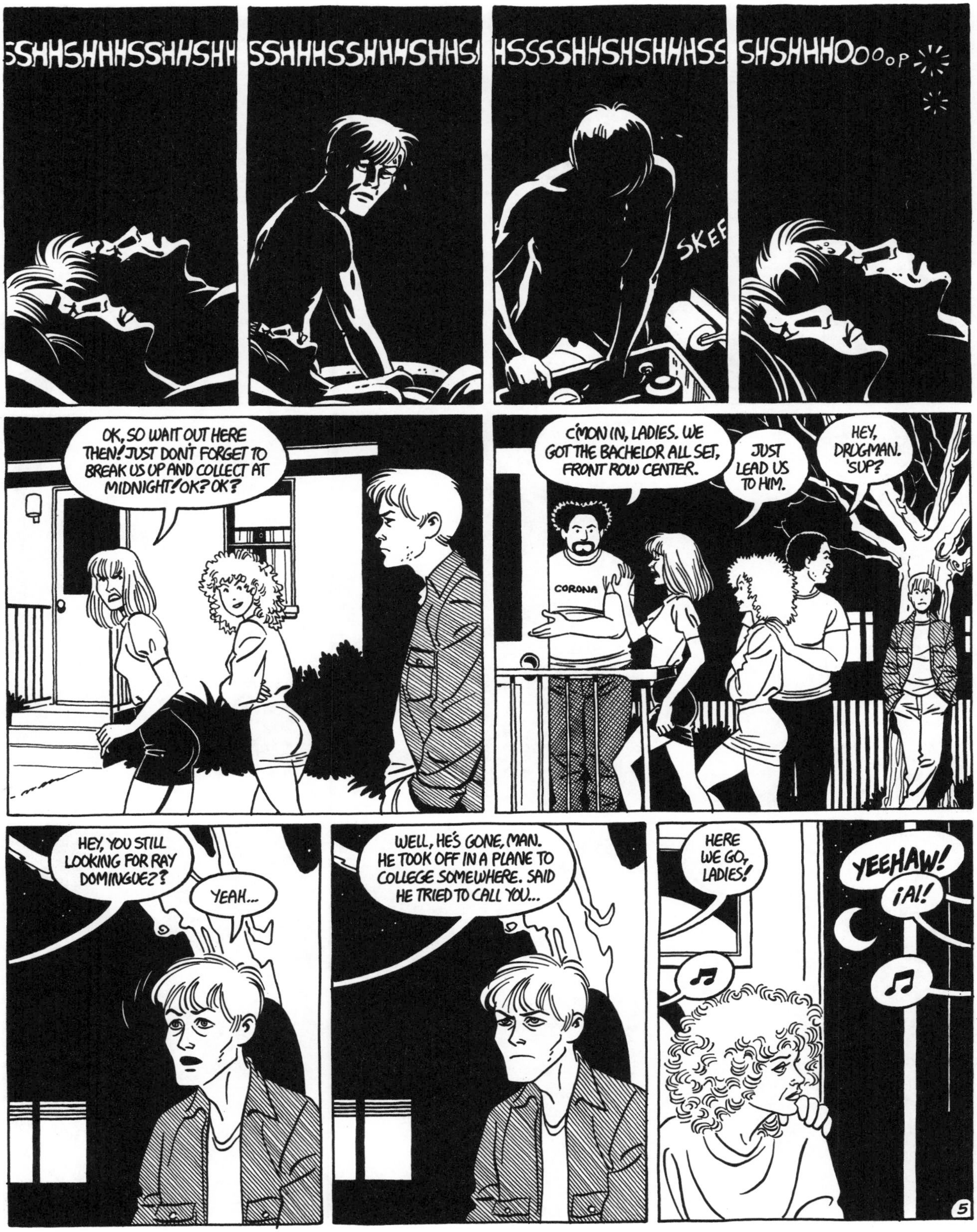
SSHHSHHHSSHHSHH
SSHHHSSHHHSHHS
HSSSSHHSHSHHHSS
SHSHHHOooop
SKEE
OK, SO WAIT OUT HERE THEN! JUST DON'T FORGET TO BREAK US UP AND COLLECT AT MIDNIGHT! OK? OK?
C'MON IN, LADIES. WE GOT THE BACHELOR ALL SET, FRONT ROW CENTER.
JUST LEAD US TO HIM.
HEY, DRUGMAN. 'SUP?
CORONA
HEY, YOU STILL LOOKING FOR RAY DOMINGUEZ?
YEAH...
WELL, HE'S GONE, MAN. HE TOOK OFF IN A PLANE TO COLLEGE SOMEWHERE. SAID HE TRIED TO CALL YOU...
HERE WE GO, LADIES!
YEEHAW!
¡AI!
5

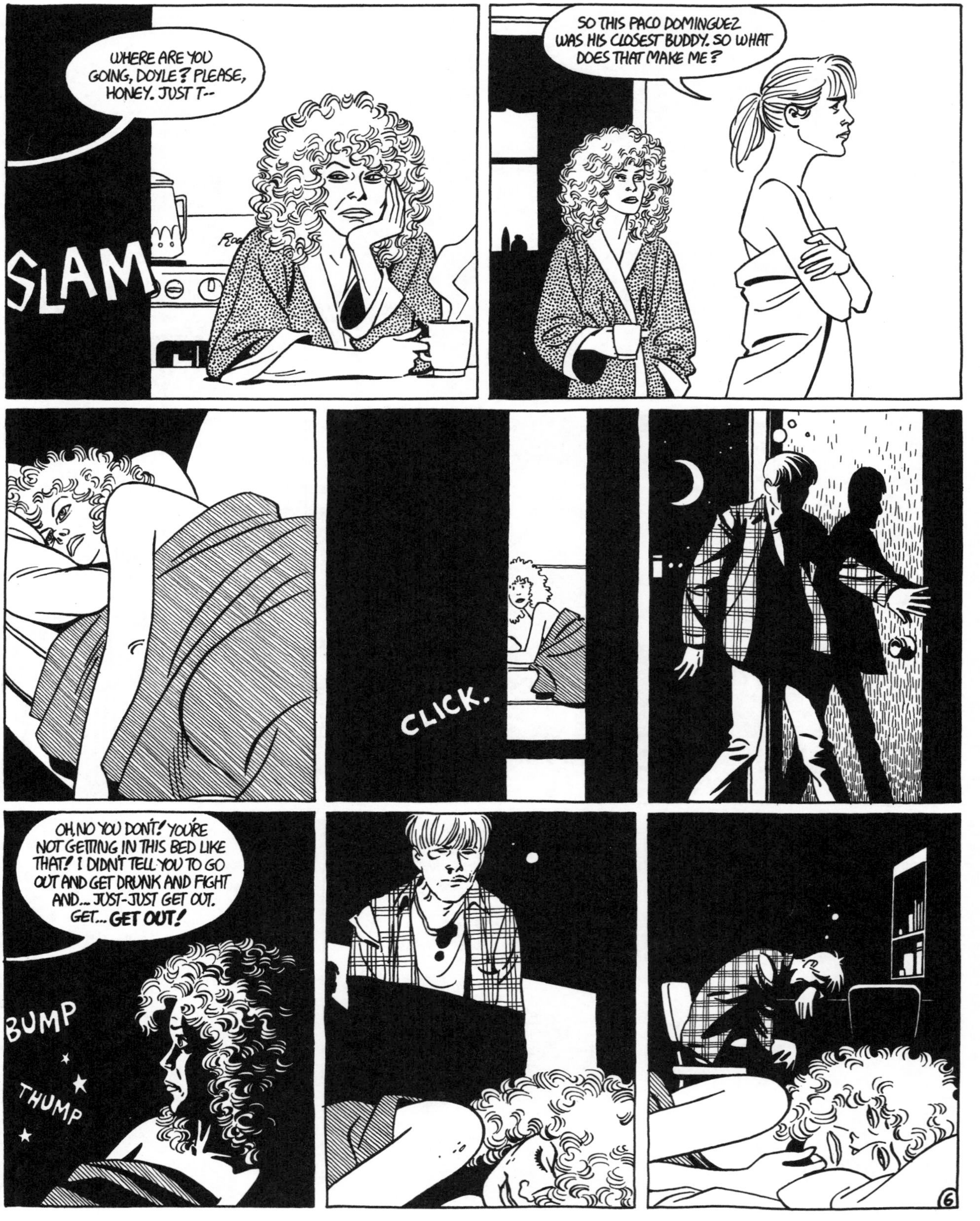
WHERE ARE YOU GOING, DOYLE? PLEASE, HONEY. JUST T--
SLAM
SO THIS PACO DOMINGUEZ WAS HIS CLOSEST BUDDY. SO WHAT DOES THAT MAKE ME?
CLICK.
OH, NO YOU DON'T! YOU'RE NOT GETTING IN THIS BED LIKE THAT! I DIDN'T TELL YOU TO GO OUT AND GET DRUNK AND FIGHT AND... JUST-JUST GET OUT. GET... GET OUT!
BUMP
THUMP
6

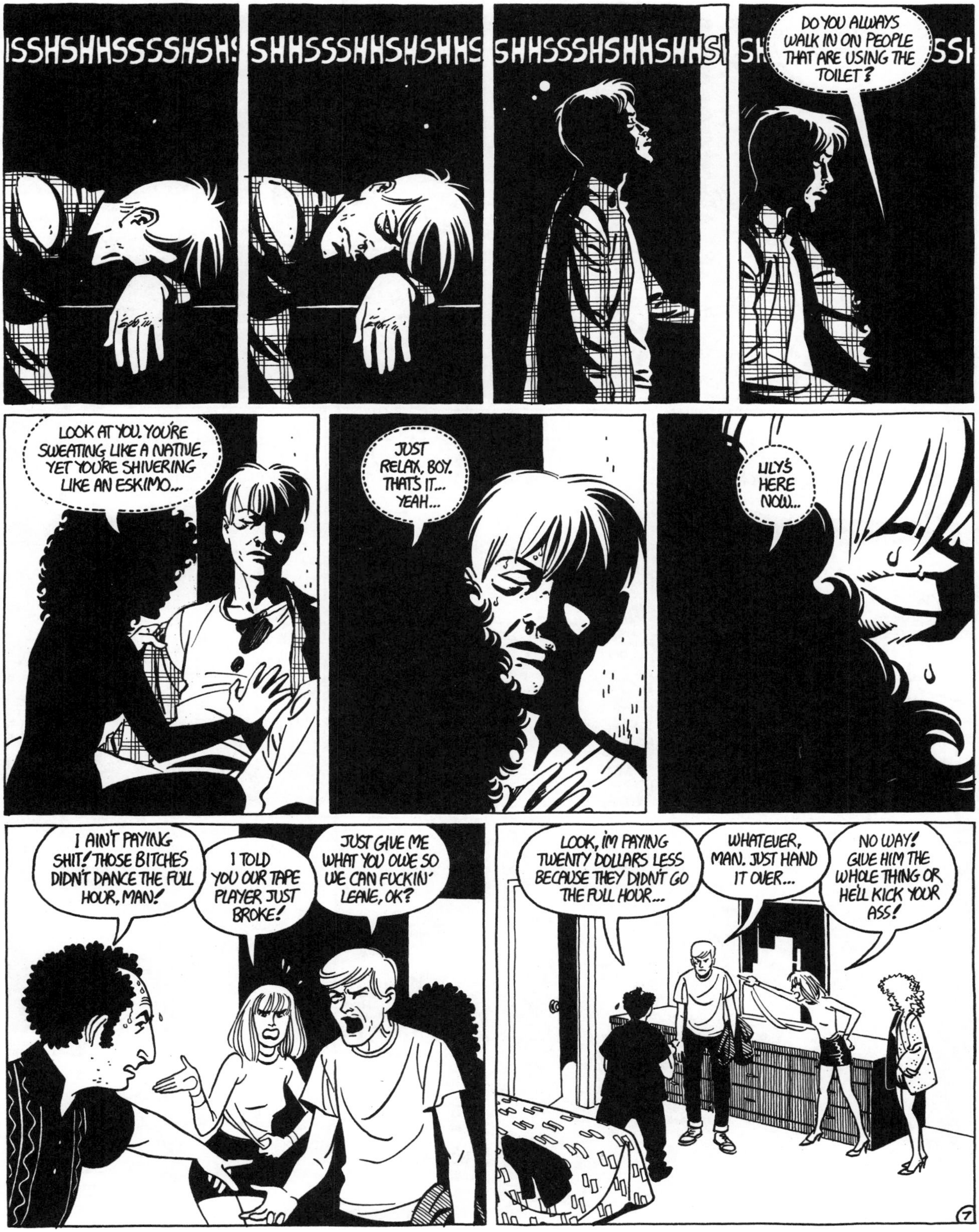
ISSHSHHSSSSHSHS
SHHSSSHHSHSHHS
SHHSSSHSHHSHHS
SH
SSH
DO YOU ALWAYS WALK IN ON PEOPLE THAT ARE USING THE TOILET?
LOOK AT YOU. YOU'RE SWEATING LIKE A NATIVE, YET YOU'RE SHIVERING LIKE AN ESKIMO...
JUST RELAX, BOY. THAT'S IT... YEAH...
LILY'S HERE NOW...
I AIN'T PAYING SHIT! THOSE BITCHES DIDN'T DANCE THE FULL HOUR, MAN!
I TOLD YOU OUR TAPE PLAYER JUST BROKE!
JUST GIVE ME WHAT YOU OWE SO WE CAN FUCKIN' LEAVE, OK?
LOOK, I'M PAYING TWENTY DOLLARS LESS BECAUSE THEY DIDN'T GO THE FULL HOUR...
WHATEVER, MAN. JUST HAND IT OVER...
NO WAY! GIVE HIM THE WHOLE THING OR HE'LL KICK YOUR ASS!
7

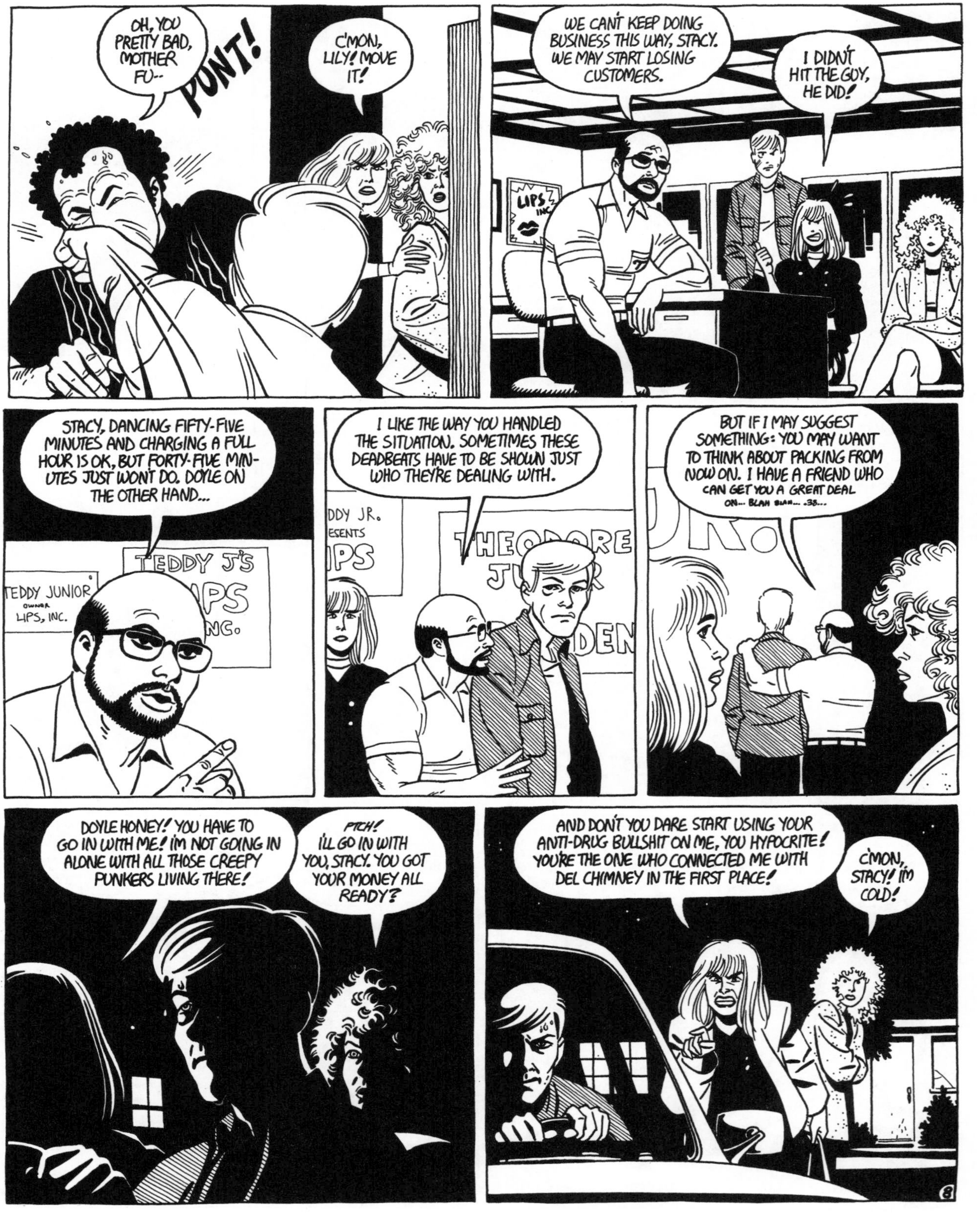
OH, YOU PRETTY BAD, MOTHER FU--
PONT!
C'MON, LILY! MOVE IT!
WE CAN'T KEEP DOING BUSINESS THIS WAY, STACY. WE MAY START LOSING CUSTOMERS.
I DIDN'T HIT THE GUY, HE DID!
LIPS INC
STACY, DANCING FIFTY-FIVE MINUTES AND CHARGING A FULL HOUR IS OK, BUT FORTY-FIVE MINUTES JUST WON'T DO. DOYLE ON THE OTHER HAND...
TEDDY J'S
TEDDY JUNIOR OWNER LIPS, INC.
I LIKE THE WAY YOU HANDLED THE SITUATION. SOMETIMES THESE DEADBEATS HAVE TO BE SHOWN JUST WHO THEY'RE DEALING WITH.
BUT IF I MAY SUGGEST SOMETHING: YOU MAY WANT TO THINK ABOUT PACKING FROM NOW ON. I HAVE A FRIEND WHO CAN GET YOU A GREAT DEAL ON... BLAH BLAH... .38...
DOYLE HONEY! YOU HAVE TO GO IN WITH ME! I'M NOT GOING IN ALONE WITH ALL THOSE CREEPY PUNKERS LIVING THERE!
PTCH! I'LL GO IN WITH YOU, STACY. YOU GOT YOUR MONEY ALL READY?
AND DON'T YOU DARE START USING YOUR ANTI-DRUG BULLSHIT ON ME, YOU HYPOCRITE! YOU'RE THE ONE WHO CONNECTED ME WITH DEL CHIMNEY IN THE FIRST PLACE!
C'MON, STACY! I'M COLD!
8

I CAN'T DO IT. I CAN'T KEEP ON TRYING TO STAY STRAIGHT WHILE I'M SURROUNDED BY ALL THIS... SHIT.
SO WHY DON'T YOU LEAVE ALL THIS SHIT?
I DUNNO... WOULD YOU COME WITH ME?
NO. I COULDN'T LEAVE STACY EVEN IF YOU COULD.
YOU FUCK HER BOYFRIEND IN THE BATH-ROOM.
BOYFRIEND? BOYFRIEND??
YOU TWO HAVEN'T BEEN BOYFRIEND AND GIRLFRIEND SINCE YOU GOT OUT AND YOU BOTH KNOW IT...
THEN YOU FEEL SORRY FOR STACY, TOO?
SORRY, MAN. PRIVATE PARTY.
UH, CAME TO PICK UP THE CHICKS, MAN. YOUR TIME'S UP.
WHAT? NO WAY!
GET LOST FOR ANOTHER TWO HOURS OR SO, GUY!
C'MON, MAN! IT'S MIDNIGHT! I GOTTA COLLECT NOW! HEY, DON'T FUCK...
GET LOST, MAN! WE AIN'T FUCKING DONE HERE YET!
SPLIT!
!?!
GET OUT!
AIN'T NOBODY COLLECTING DIDDLEY, MOTHER FUCKER.
TELL 'IM ABOUT IT, ACE!
DOYLE! WHAT ARE YOU DOING?
STACY, SHUT UP!
DOYLE, DON'T...
LOOK, GUYS. WE'RE JUST GONNA LEAVE, ALL RIGHT? WE'RE JUST GONNA WALK OUT...
SO LEAVE. YOU TOO, SHIT LICKER.
HAW!
9

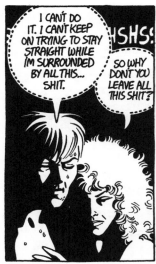

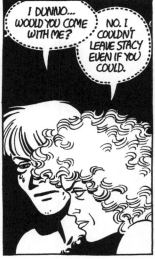

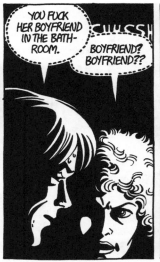

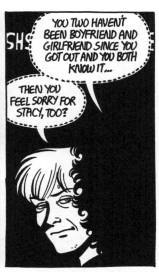

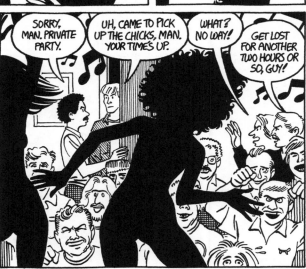

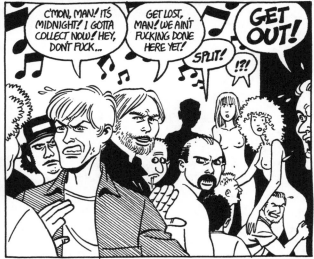

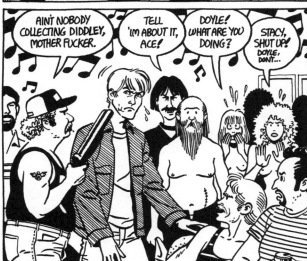

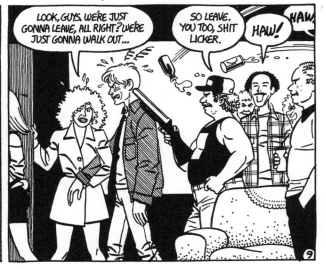

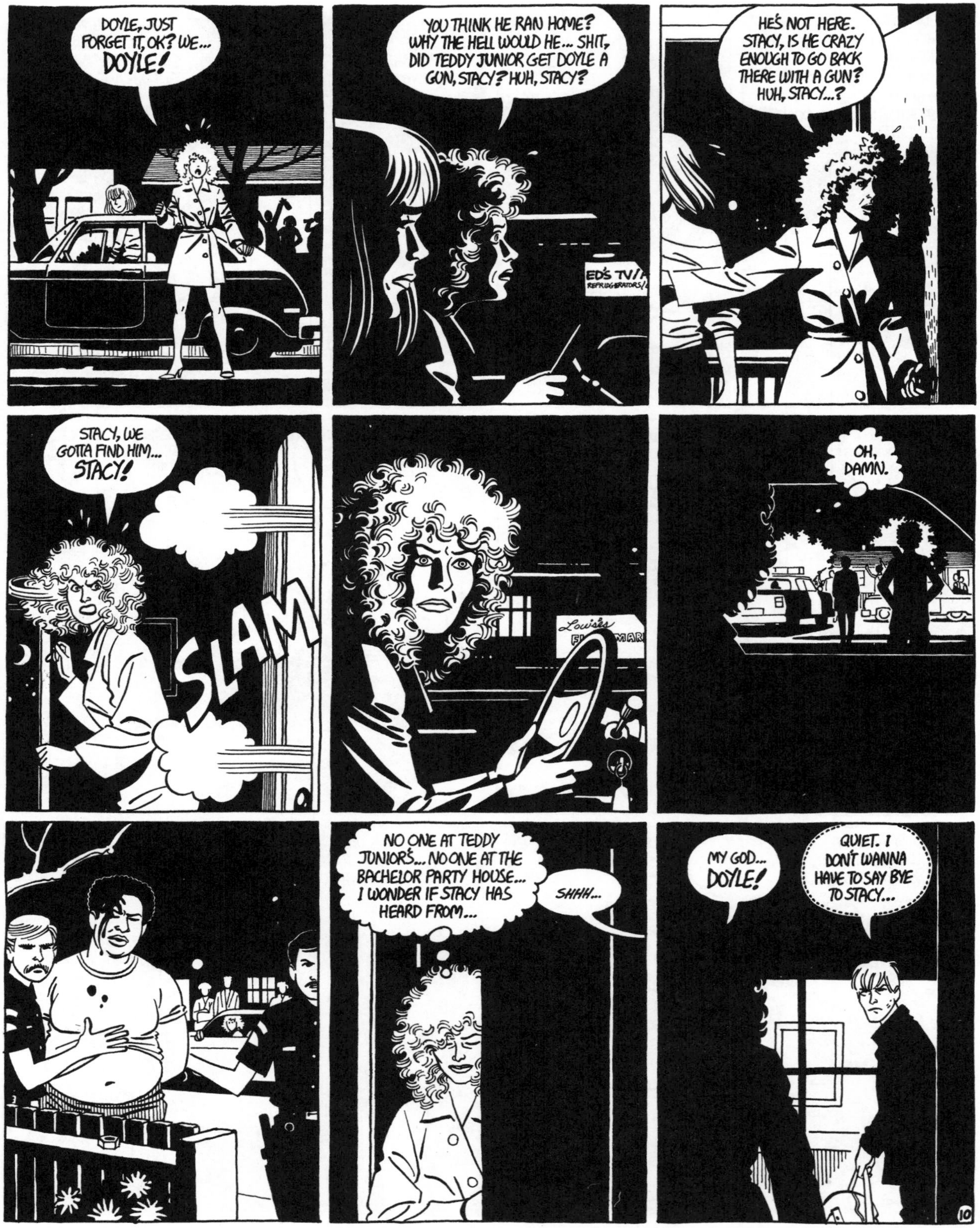
DOYLE, JUST FORGET IT, OK? WE... DOYLE!
YOU THINK HE RAN HOME? WHY THE HELL WOULD HE... SHIT, DID TEDDY JUNIOR GET DOYLE A GUN, STACY? HUH, STACY?
ED'S TV/
REFRIGERATORS/
HE'S NOT HERE. STACY, IS HE CRAZY ENOUGH TO GO BACK THERE WITH A GUN? HUH, STACY...?
STACY, WE GOTTA FIND HIM... STACY!
SLAM
Louise's
OH, DAMN.
NO ONE AT TEDDY JUNIOR'S... NO ONE AT THE BACHELOR PARTY HOUSE... I WONDER IF STACY HAS HEARD FROM...
SHHH...
MY GOD... DOYLE!
QUIET. I DON'T WANNA HAVE TO SAY BYE TO STACY...
10

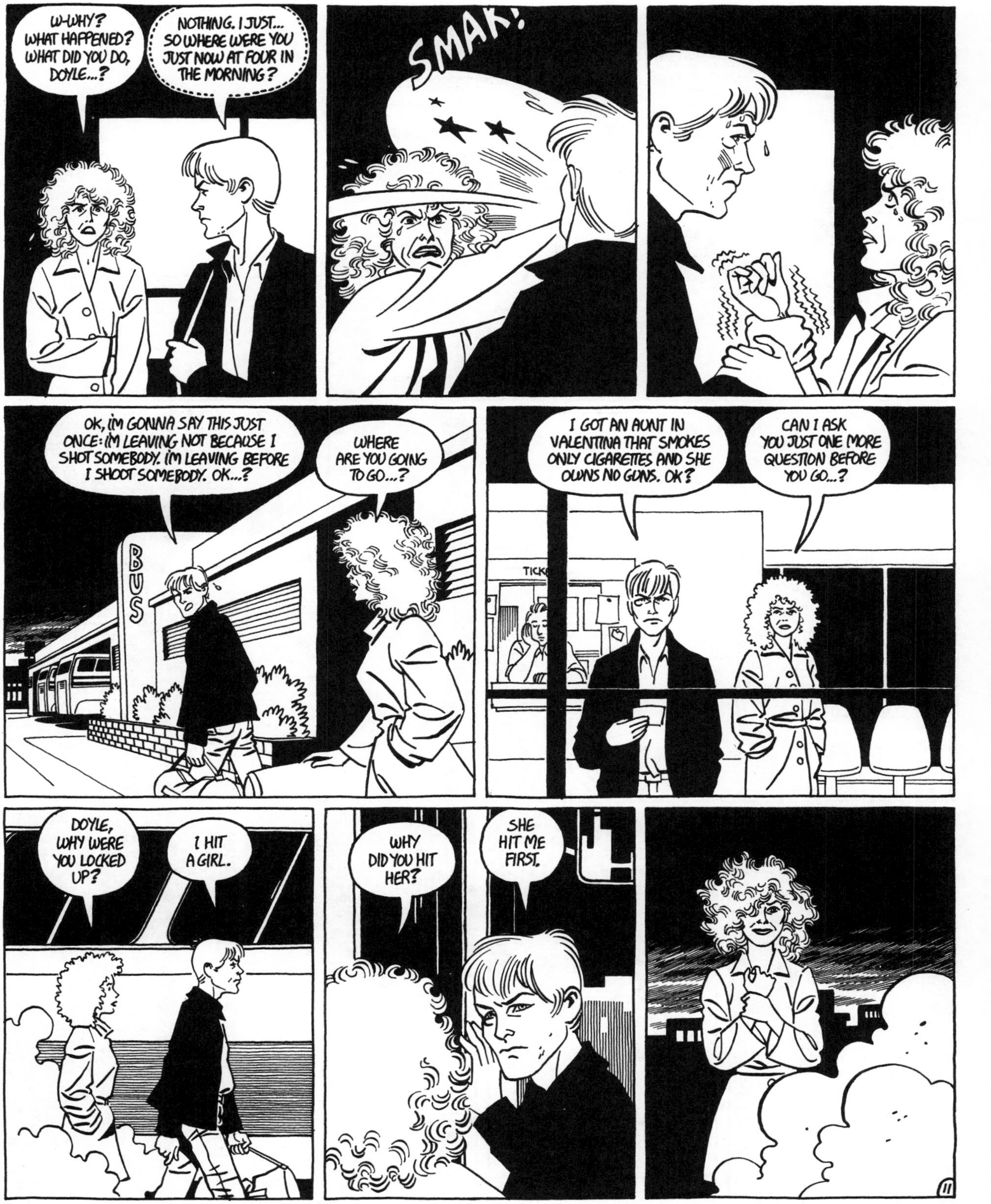
W-WHY? WHAT HAPPENED? WHAT DID YOU DO, DOYLE...?
NOTHING. I JUST... SO WHERE WERE YOU JUST NOW AT FOUR IN THE MORNING?
SMAK!
OK, I'M GONNA SAY THIS JUST ONCE: I'M LEAVING NOT BECAUSE I SHOT SOMEBODY. I'M LEAVING BEFORE I SHOOT SOMEBODY. OK...?
WHERE ARE YOU GOING TO GO...?
BUS
I GOT AN AUNT IN VALENTINA THAT SMOKES ONLY CIGARETTES AND SHE OWNS NO GUNS. OK?
CAN I ASK YOU JUST ONE MORE QUESTION BEFORE YOU GO...?
DOYLE, WHY WERE YOU LOCKED UP?
I HIT A GIRL.
WHY DID YOU HIT HER?
SHE HIT ME FIRST.
11

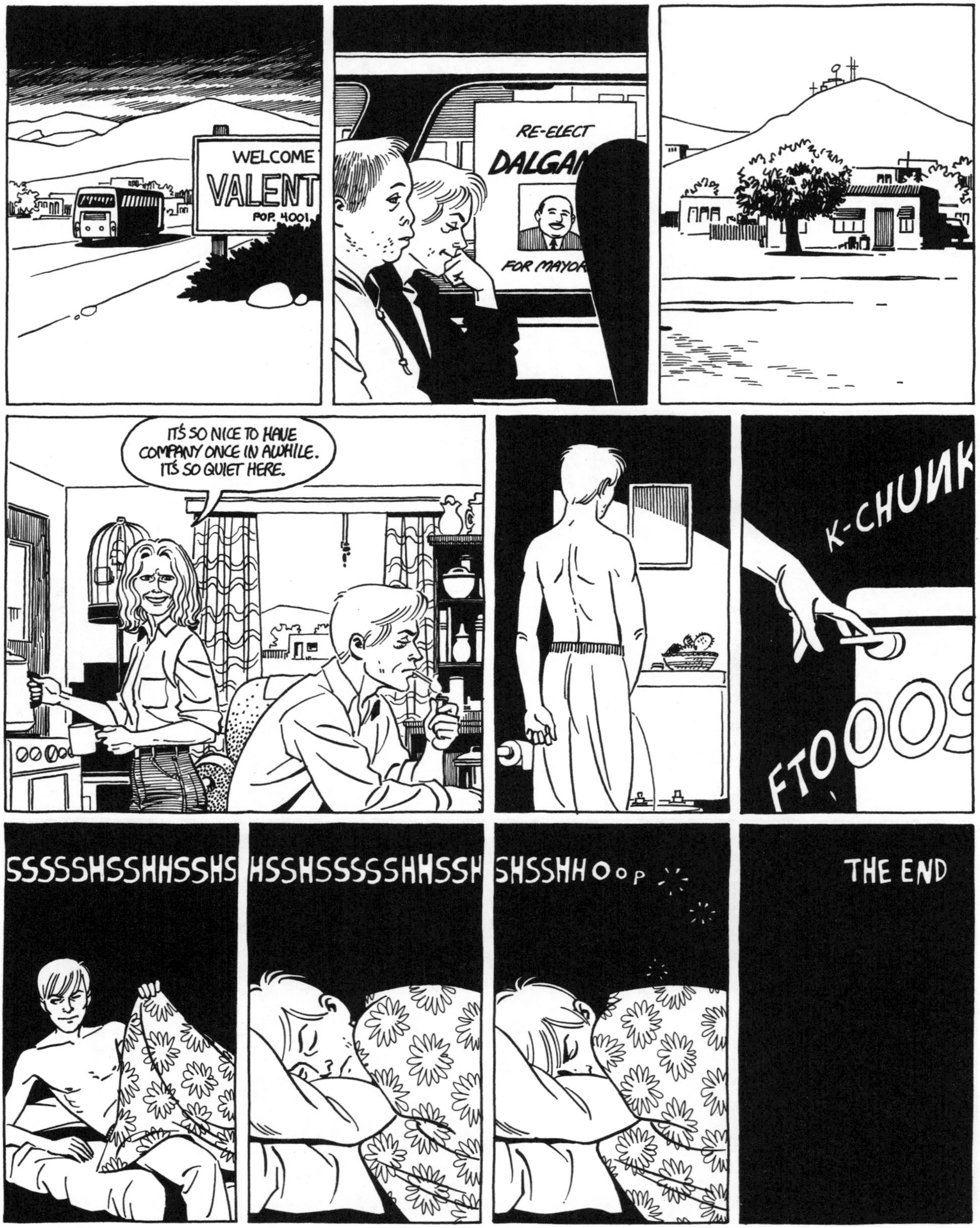
WELCOME
VALENT
POP. 4001
RE-ELECT
DALGA
FOR MAYOR
IT'S SO NICE TO HAVE COMPANY ONCE IN AWHILE. IT'S SO QUIET HERE.
K-CHUNK
FTOOOS
SSSSSHSSHHSSHS
HSSHSSSSSHHSSH
SHSSHHOOP
THE END

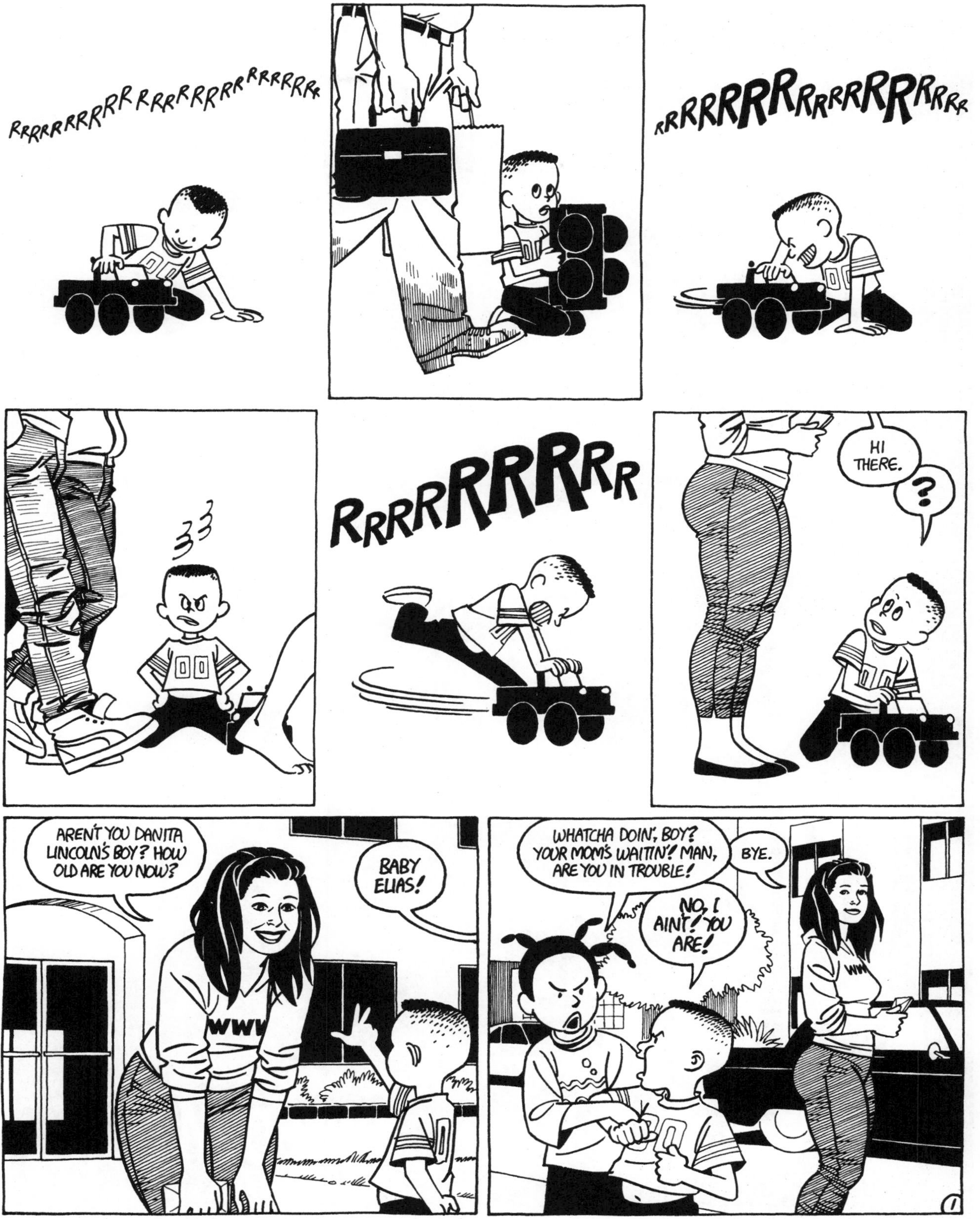
HI THERE.
?
AREN'T YOU DANITA LINCOLN'S BOY? HOW OLD ARE YOU NOW?
BABY ELIAS!
WHATCHA DOIN', BOY? YOUR MOM'S WAITIN'! MAN, ARE YOU IN TROUBLE!
BYE.
NO, I AIN'T! YOU ARE!
1

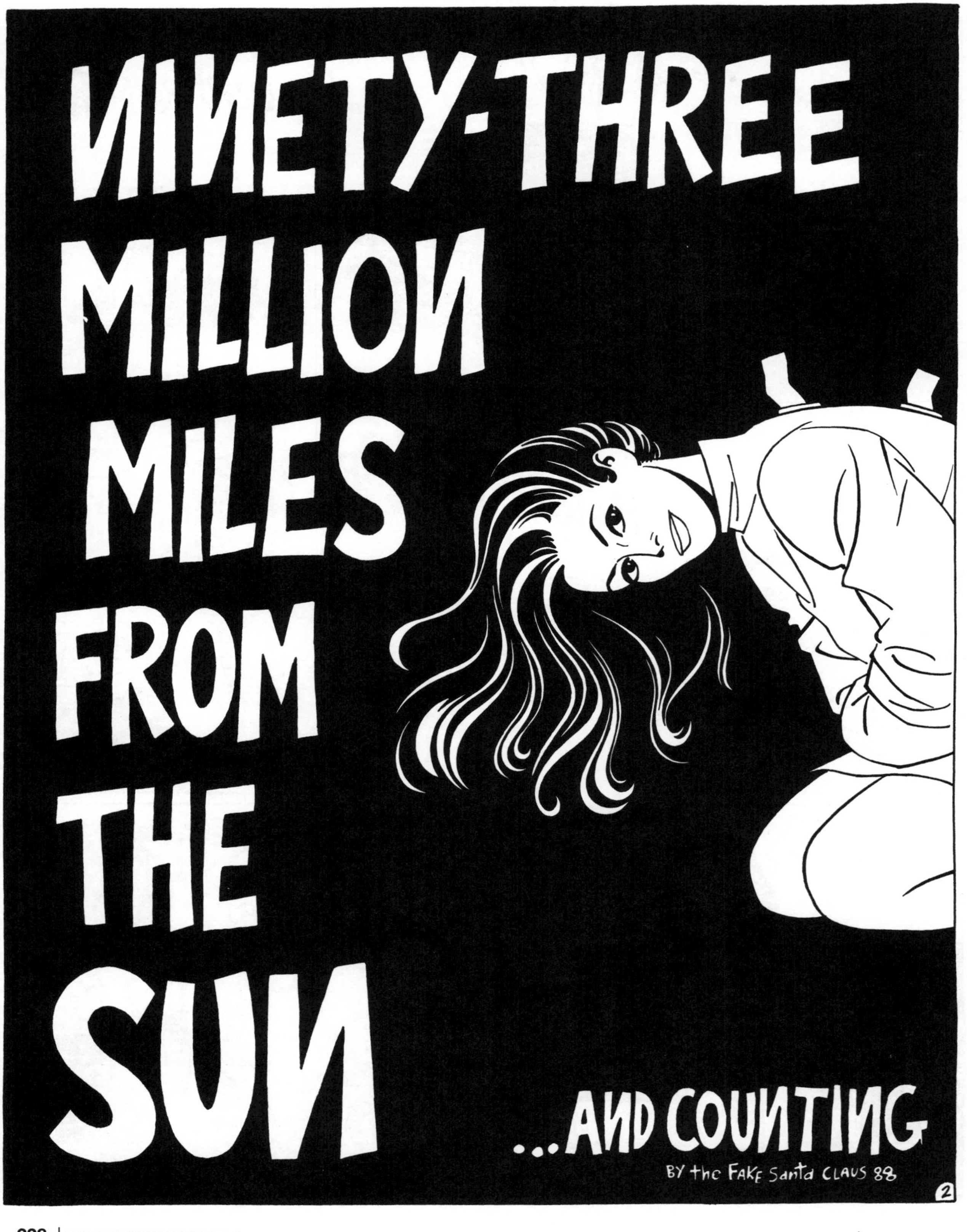
NINETY-THREE MILLION MILES FROM THE SUN
...AND COUNTING
BY the FAKE Santa CLAUS 88
2

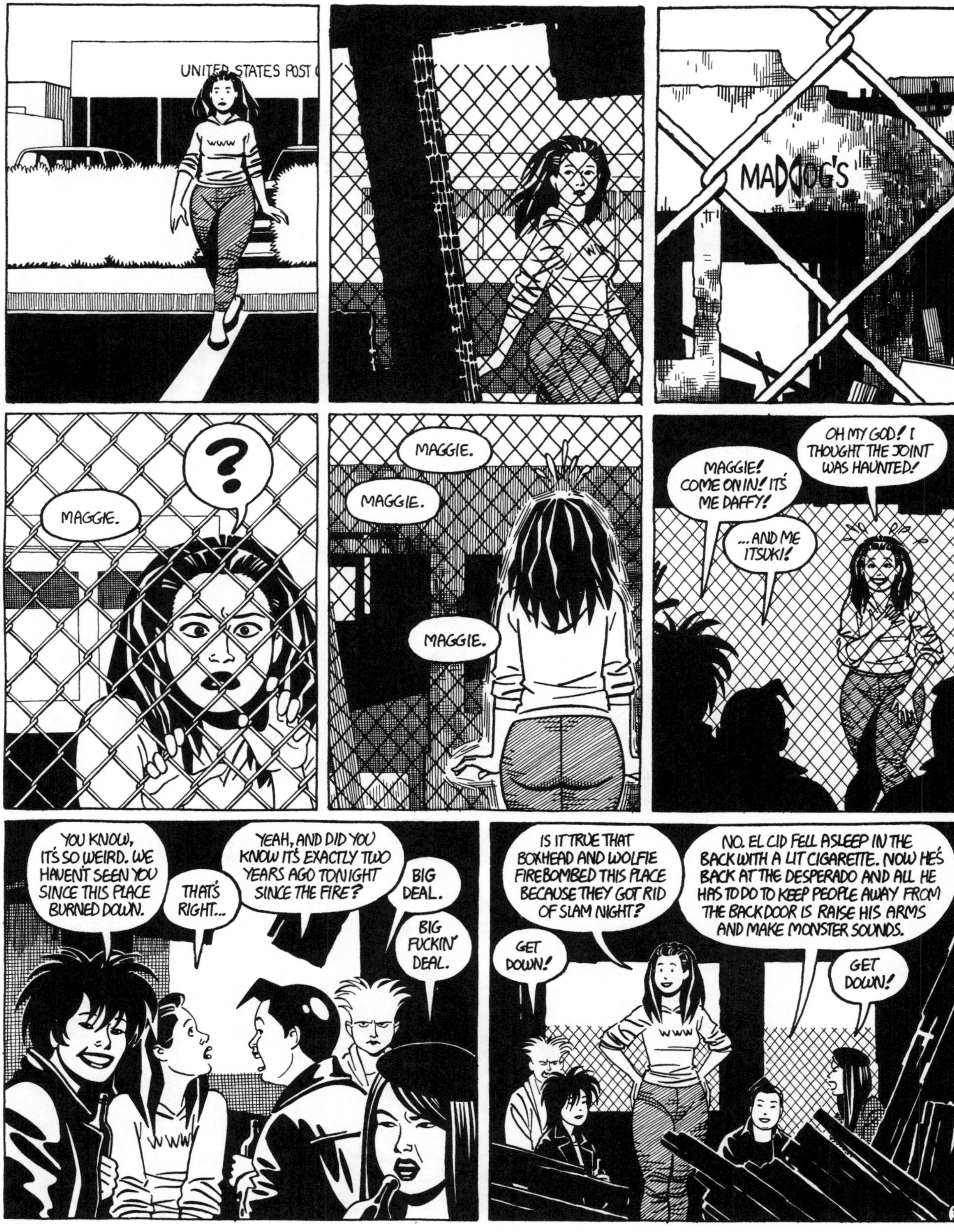
UNITED STATES POST
MADDOG'S
MAGGIE.
?
MAGGIE.
MAGGIE.
MAGGIE.
MAGGIE! COME ON IN! IT'S ME DAFFY!
OH MY GOD! I THOUGHT THE JOINT WAS HAUNTED!
...AND ME ITSUKI!
YOU KNOW, IT'S SO WEIRD. WE HAVEN'T SEEN YOU SINCE THIS PLACE BURNED DOWN.
THAT'S RIGHT...
YEAH, AND DID YOU KNOW IT'S EXACTLY TWO YEARS AGO TONIGHT SINCE THE FIRE?
BIG DEAL.
BIG FUCKIN' DEAL.
IS IT TRUE THAT BOXHEAD AND WOLFIE FIREBOMBED THIS PLACE BECAUSE THEY GOT RID OF SLAM NIGHT?
NO. EL CID FELL ASLEEP IN THE BACK WITH A LIT CIGARETTE. NOW HE'S BACK AT THE DESPERADO AND ALL HE HAS TO DO TO KEEP PEOPLE AWAY FROM THE BACK DOOR IS RAISE HIS ARMS AND MAKE MONSTER SOUNDS.
GET DOWN!
GET DOWN!

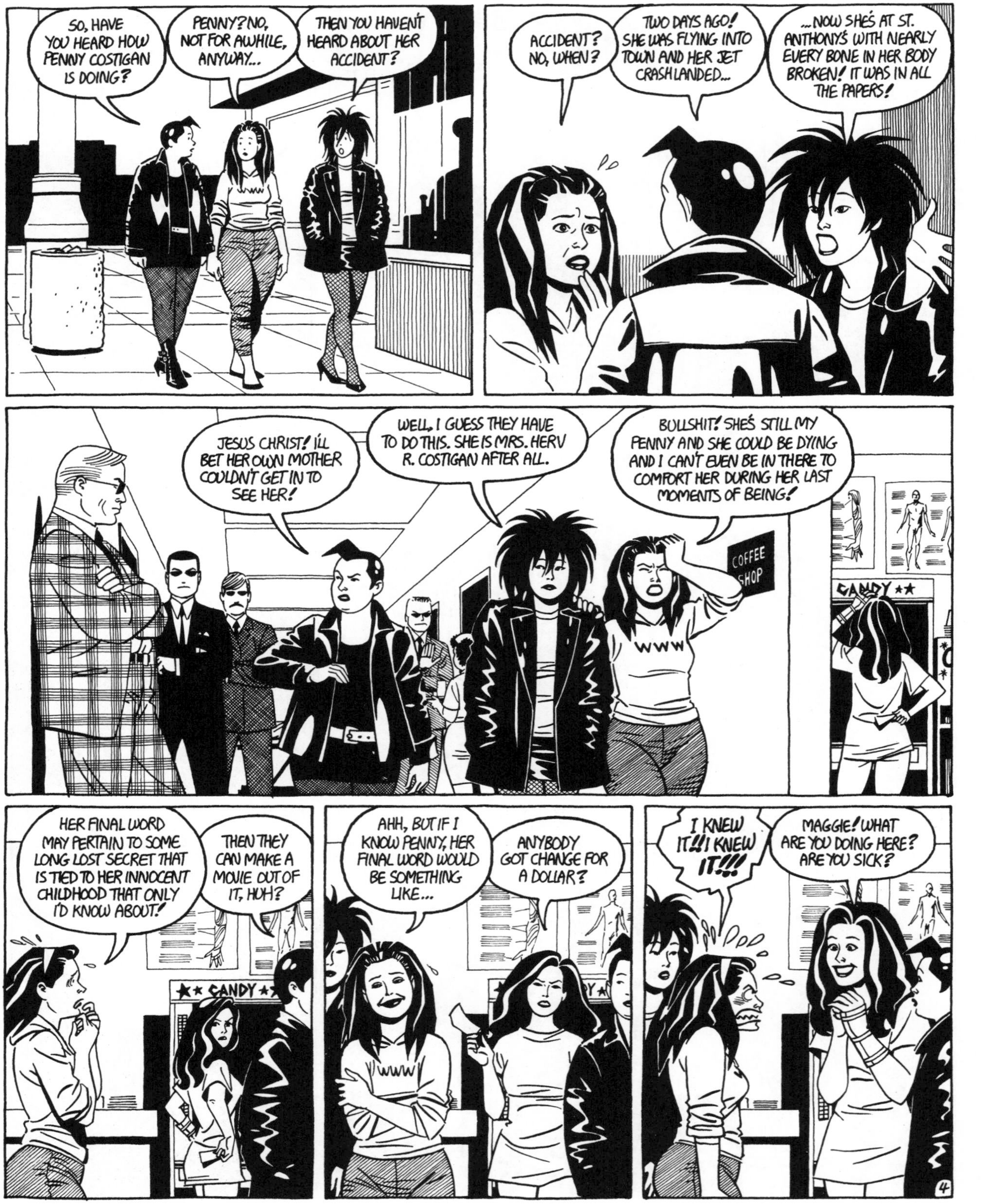
SO, HAVE YOU HEARD HOW PENNY COSTIGAN IS DOING?
PENNY? NO, NOT FOR AWHILE, ANYWAY...
THEN YOU HAVEN'T HEARD ABOUT HER ACCIDENT?
ACCIDENT? NO, WHEN?
TWO DAYS AGO! SHE WAS FLYING INTO TOWN AND HER JET CRASHLANDED...
...NOW SHE'S AT ST. ANTHONY'S WITH NEARLY EVERY BONE IN HER BODY BROKEN! IT WAS IN ALL THE PAPERS!
JESUS CHRIST! I'LL BET HER OWN MOTHER COULDN'T GET IN TO SEE HER!
WELL, I GUESS THEY HAVE TO DO THIS. SHE IS MRS. HERV R. COSTIGAN AFTER ALL.
BULLSHIT! SHE'S STILL MY PENNY AND SHE COULD BE DYING AND I CAN'T EVEN BE IN THERE TO COMFORT HER DURING HER LAST MOMENTS OF BEING!
COFFEE SHOP
CANDY
WWW
HER FINAL WORD MAY PERTAIN TO SOME LONG LOST SECRET THAT IS TIED TO HER INNOCENT CHILDHOOD THAT ONLY I'D KNOW ABOUT!
THEN THEY CAN MAKE A MOVIE OUT OF IT, HUH?
CANDY
AHH, BUT IF I KNOW PENNY, HER FINAL WORD WOULD BE SOMETHING LIKE...
ANYBODY GOT CHANGE FOR A DOLLAR?
WWW
I KNEW IT!!! I KNEW IT!!!
MAGGIE! WHAT ARE YOU DOING HERE? ARE YOU SICK?
4

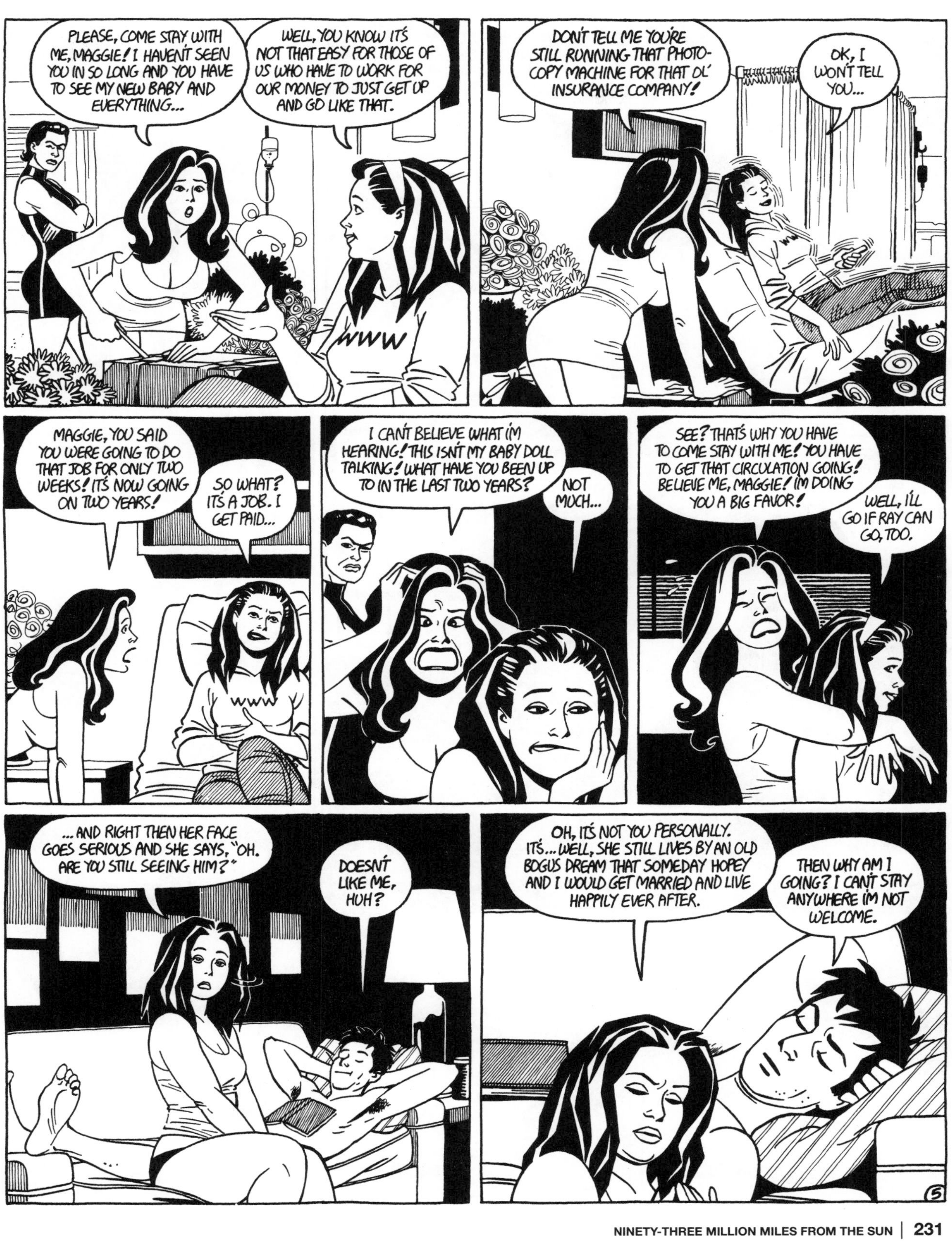
PLEASE, COME STAY WITH ME, MAGGIE! I HAVEN'T SEEN YOU IN SO LONG AND YOU HAVE TO SEE MY NEW BABY AND EVERYTHING...
WELL, YOU KNOW IT'S NOT THAT EASY FOR THOSE OF US WHO HAVE TO WORK FOR OUR MONEY TO JUST GET UP AND GO LIKE THAT.
DON'T TELL ME YOU'RE STILL RUNNING THAT PHOTO-COPY MACHINE FOR THAT OL' INSURANCE COMPANY!
OK, I WON'T TELL YOU...
MAGGIE, YOU SAID YOU WERE GOING TO DO THAT JOB FOR ONLY TWO WEEKS! IT'S NOW GOING ON TWO YEARS!
SO WHAT? IT'S A JOB. I GET PAID...
I CAN'T BELIEVE WHAT I'M HEARING! THIS ISN'T MY BABY DOLL TALKING! WHAT HAVE YOU BEEN UP TO IN THE LAST TWO YEARS?
NOT MUCH...
SEE? THAT'S WHY YOU HAVE TO COME STAY WITH ME! YOU HAVE TO GET THAT CIRCULATION GOING! BELIEVE ME, MAGGIE! I'M DOING YOU A BIG FAVOR!
WELL, I'LL GO IF RAY CAN GO, TOO.
...AND RIGHT THEN HER FACE GOES SERIOUS AND SHE SAYS, "OH. ARE YOU STILL SEEING HIM?"
DOESN'T LIKE ME, HUH?
OH, IT'S NOT YOU PERSONALLY. IT'S... WELL, SHE STILL LIVES BY AN OLD BOGUS DREAM THAT SOMEDAY HOPEY AND I WOULD GET MARRIED AND LIVE HAPPILY EVER AFTER.
THEN WHY AM I GOING? I CAN'T STAY ANYWHERE I'M NOT WELCOME.
5

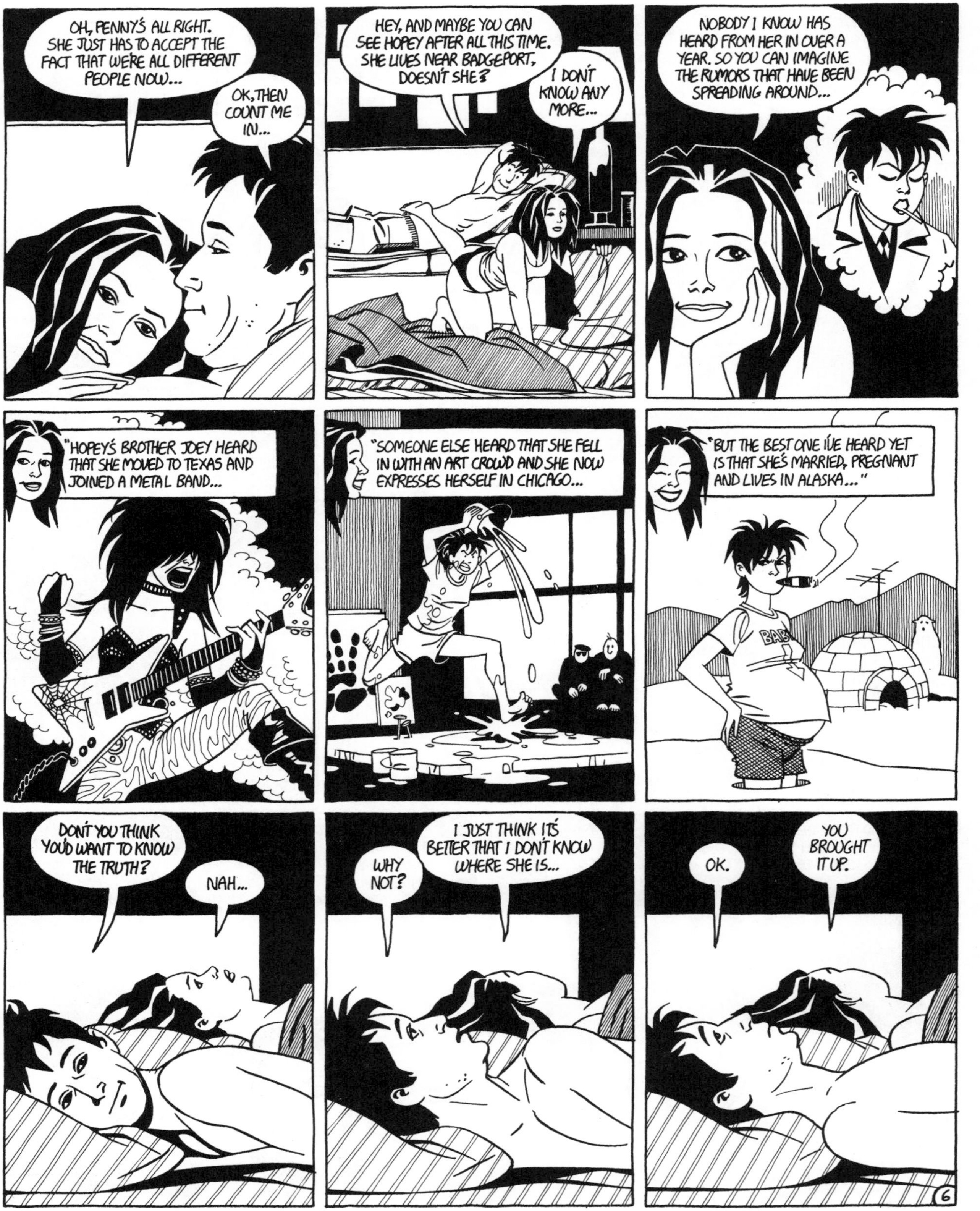

OH, PENNY'S ALL RIGHT. SHE JUST HAS TO ACCEPT THE FACT THAT WE'RE ALL DIFFERENT PEOPLE NOW...
OK, THEN COUNT ME IN...
HEY, AND MAYBE YOU CAN SEE HOPEY AFTER ALL THIS TIME. SHE LIVES NEAR BADGEPORT, DOESN'T SHE?
I DON'T KNOW ANY MORE...
NOBODY I KNOW HAS HEARD FROM HER IN OVER A YEAR. SO YOU CAN IMAGINE THE RUMORS THAT HAVE BEEN SPREADING AROUND...
"HOPEY'S BROTHER JOEY HEARD THAT SHE MOVED TO TEXAS AND JOINED A METAL BAND...
"SOMEONE ELSE HEARD THAT SHE FELL IN WITH AN ART CROWD AND SHE NOW EXPRESSES HERSELF IN CHICAGO...
"BUT THE BEST ONE I'VE HEARD YET IS THAT SHE'S MARRIED, PREGNANT AND LIVES IN ALASKA..."
DON'T YOU THINK YOU'D WANT TO KNOW THE TRUTH?
NAH...
WHY NOT?
I JUST THINK IT'S BETTER THAT I DON'T KNOW WHERE SHE IS...
OK.
YOU BROUGHT IT UP.
6

HI, WEBSTER. DO YOU HAVE MY FRIEND'S ROOM ALL READY?

YES, MRS. COSTIGAN. BUT, WHERE...?

THEY WENT LOOKING FOR THE HEAD. TEN TO ONE THE FOOLS ARE LOST.

NOW, LET'S SEE IF I REMEMBER... WHILE LOOKING FOR A BATHROOM, ALWAYS FOLLOW ONE OR TWO SIMPLE BUT IMPORTANT RULES. ONE: GO WITH SOMEONE WHO KNOWS THEIR WAY AROUND. JMMM...

MAGGIE, PLEASE! I'M ABOUT TO PASS OUT...

... BUT IF YOU CAN'T DO THAT, FOLLOW RULE NUMBER TWO...

I'M AFRAID I CAN'T WAIT FOR RULE NUMBER TWO. THE FIRST ROOM I COME ACROSS WILL HAVE TO BE THE UNFORTUNATE FLOOD VICTIM.

OOSH...

DID YOU KNOW THERE ARE PEOPLE INHABITING THESE ROOMS?

RAY, YOU DIDN'T...

NOT YET I DIDN'T. SO, I'M AFRAID A DARK CORNER WILL HAVE TO DO...

BOMBS AWAY...

7

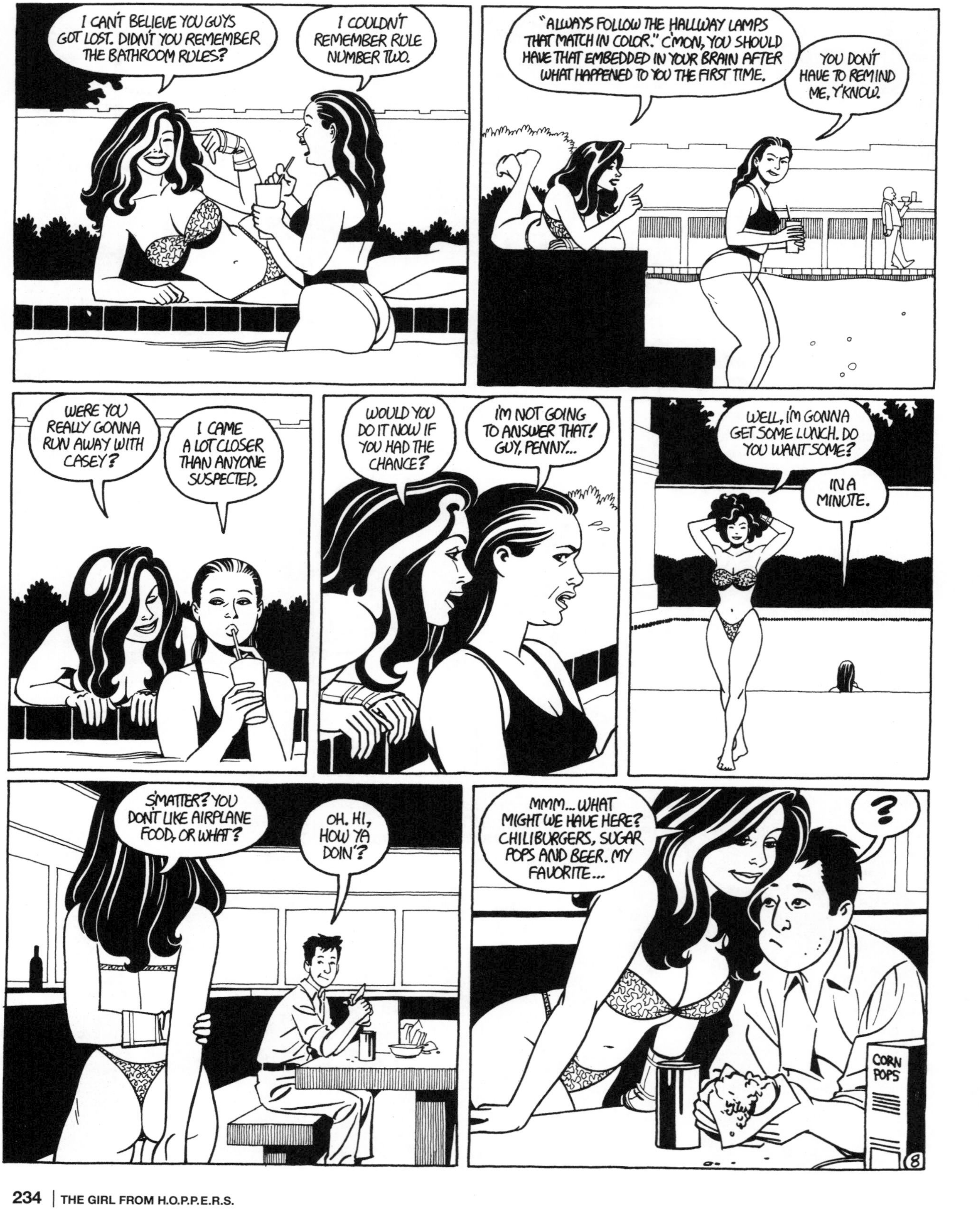
I CAN'T BELIEVE YOU GUYS GOT LOST. DIDN'T YOU REMEMBER THE BATHROOM RULES?
I COULDN'T REMEMBER RULE NUMBER TWO.
"ALWAYS FOLLOW THE HALLWAY LAMPS THAT MATCH IN COLOR." C'MON, YOU SHOULD HAVE THAT EMBEDDED IN YOUR BRAIN AFTER WHAT HAPPENED TO YOU THE FIRST TIME.
YOU DON'T HAVE TO REMIND ME, Y'KNOW.
WERE YOU REALLY GONNA RUN AWAY WITH CASEY?
I CAME A LOT CLOSER THAN ANYONE SUSPECTED.
WOULD YOU DO IT NOW IF YOU HAD THE CHANCE?
I'M NOT GOING TO ANSWER THAT! GUY, PENNY...
WELL, I'M GONNA GET SOME LUNCH. DO YOU WANT SOME?
IN A MINUTE.
S'MATTER? YOU DON'T LIKE AIRPLANE FOOD, OR WHAT?
OH. HI, HOW YA DOIN'?
MMM... WHAT MIGHT WE HAVE HERE? CHILIBURGERS, SUGAR POPS AND BEER. MY FAVORITE...
?
CORN POPS
8

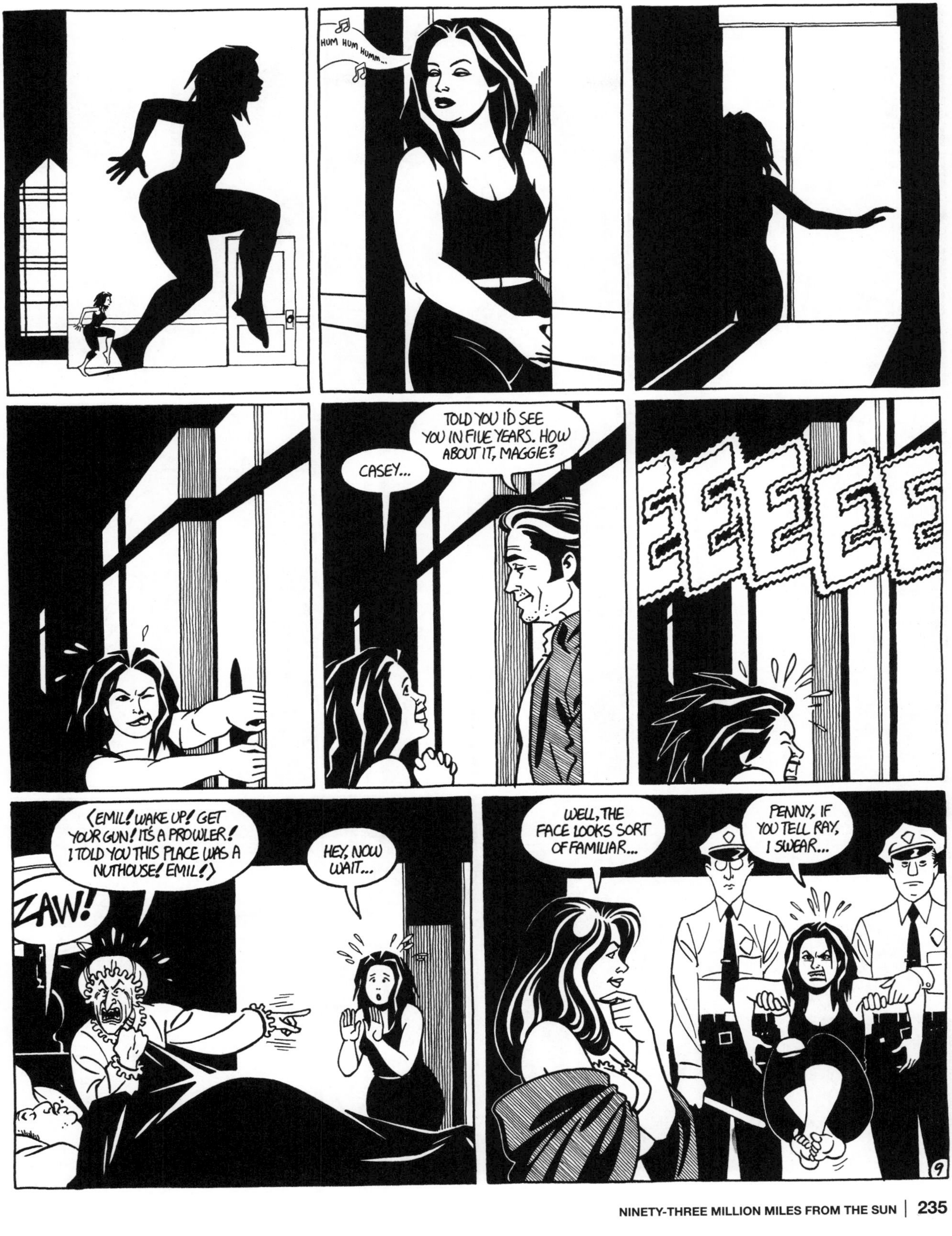
HUM HUM HUMM...
CASEY...
TOLD YOU I'D SEE YOU IN FIVE YEARS. HOW ABOUT IT, MAGGIE?
EEEEE
<EMIL! WAKE UP! GET YOUR GUN! IT'S A PROWLER! I TOLD YOU THIS PLACE WAS A NUTHOUSE! EMIL!>
ZAW!
HEY, NOW WAIT...
WELL, THE FACE LOOKS SORT OF FAMILIAR...
PENNY, IF YOU TELL RAY, I SWEAR...
9

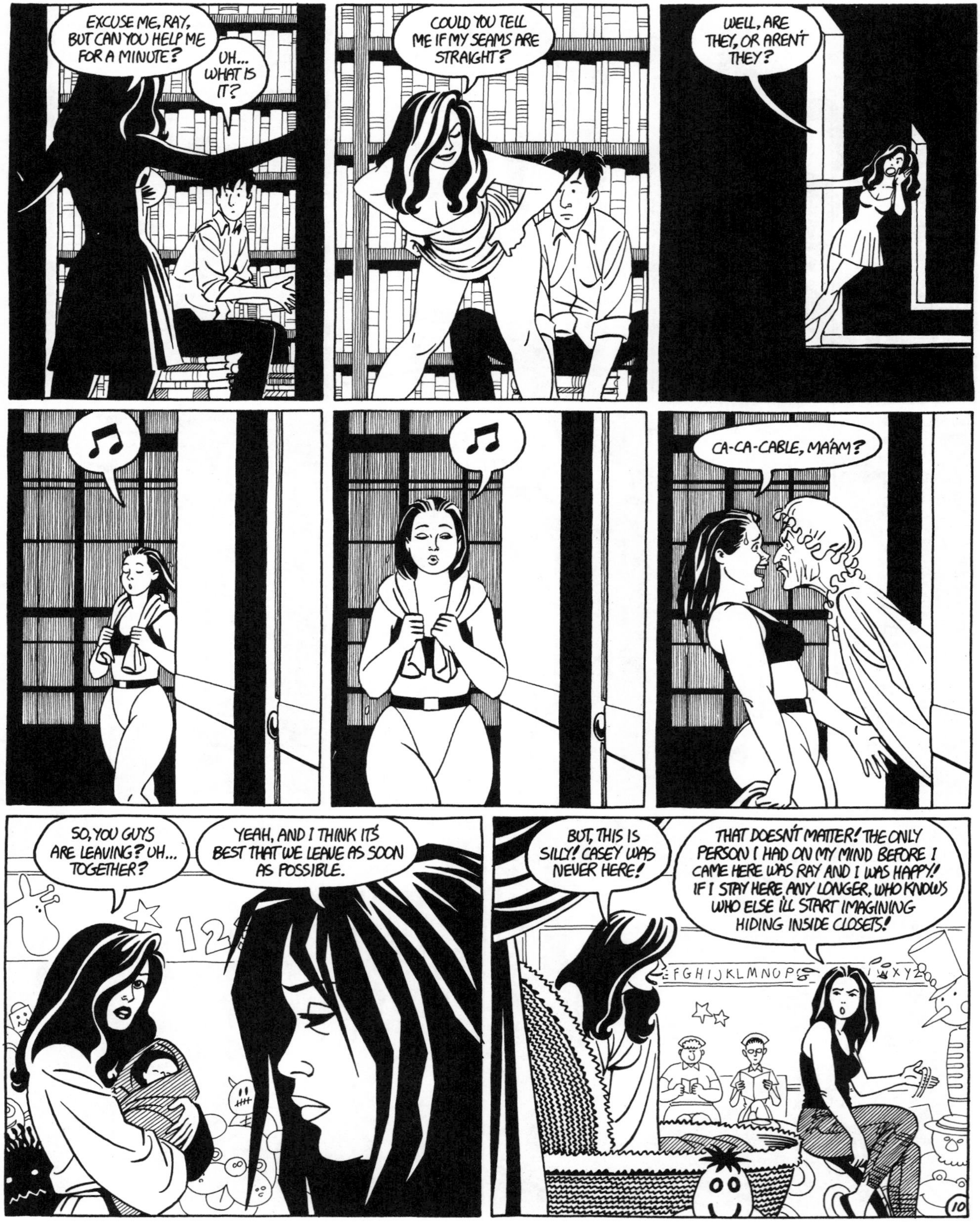
EXCUSE ME, RAY, BUT CAN YOU HELP ME FOR A MINUTE?
UH... WHAT IS IT?
COULD YOU TELL ME IF MY SEAMS ARE STRAIGHT?
WELL, ARE THEY, OR AREN'T THEY?
CA-CA-CABLE, MA'AM?
SO, YOU GUYS ARE LEAVING? UH... TOGETHER?
YEAH, AND I THINK IT'S BEST THAT WE LEAVE AS SOON AS POSSIBLE.
BUT, THIS IS SILLY! CASEY WAS NEVER HERE!
THAT DOESN'T MATTER! THE ONLY PERSON I HAD ON MY MIND BEFORE I CAME HERE WAS RAY AND I WAS HAPPY! IF I STAY HERE ANY LONGER, WHO KNOWS WHO ELSE I'LL START IMAGINING HIDING INSIDE CLOSETS!
10

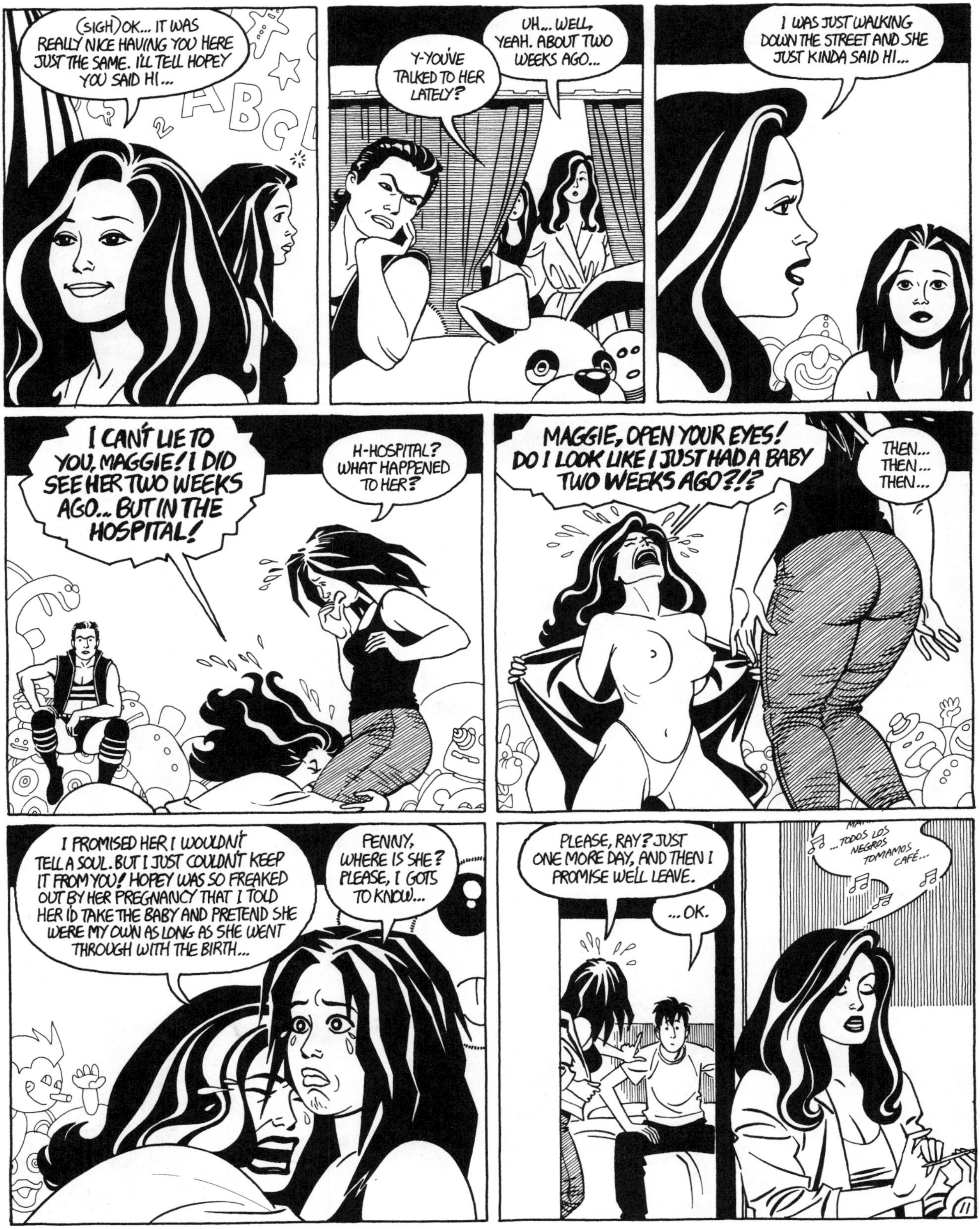
(SIGH) OK... IT WAS REALLY NICE HAVING YOU HERE JUST THE SAME. I'LL TELL HOPEY YOU SAID HI...
Y-YOU'VE TALKED TO HER LATELY?
UH... WELL, YEAH. ABOUT TWO WEEKS AGO...
I WAS JUST WALKING DOWN THE STREET AND SHE JUST KINDA SAID HI...
I CAN'T LIE TO YOU, MAGGIE! I DID SEE HER TWO WEEKS AGO... BUT IN THE HOSPITAL!
H-HOSPITAL? WHAT HAPPENED TO HER?
MAGGIE, OPEN YOUR EYES! DO I LOOK LIKE I JUST HAD A BABY TWO WEEKS AGO?!?
THEN... THEN... THEN...
I PROMISED HER I WOULDN'T TELL A SOUL. BUT I JUST COULDN'T KEEP IT FROM YOU! HOPEY WAS SO FREAKED OUT BY HER PREGNANCY THAT I TOLD HER I'D TAKE THE BABY AND PRETEND SHE WERE MY OWN AS LONG AS SHE WENT THROUGH WITH THE BIRTH...
PENNY, WHERE IS SHE? PLEASE, I GOTS TO KNOW...
PLEASE, RAY? JUST ONE MORE DAY, AND THEN I PROMISE WE'LL LEAVE.
...OK.
...TODOS LOS NEGROS TOMAMOS CAFÉ...

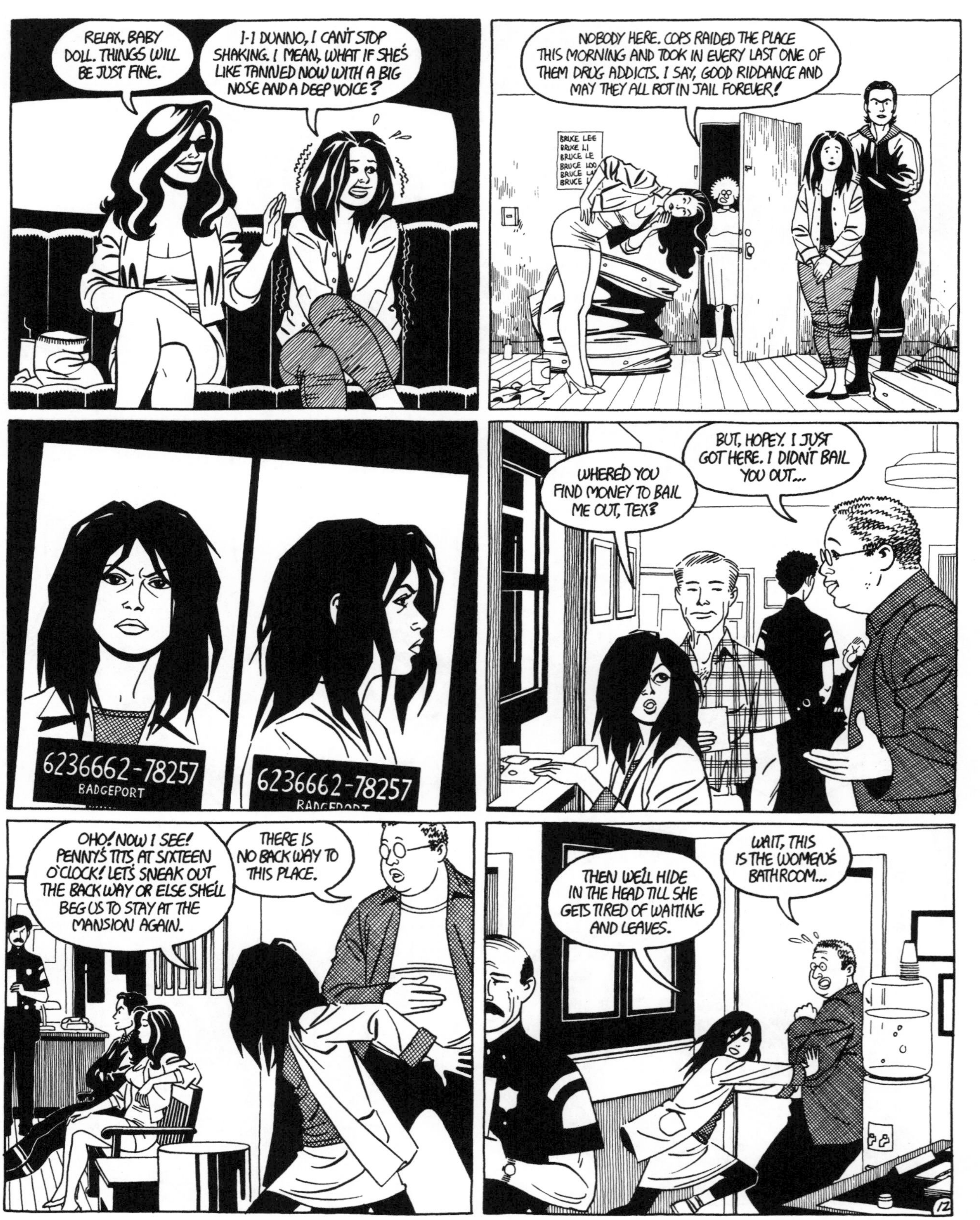
RELAX, BABY DOLL. THINGS WILL BE JUST FINE.
I-I DUNNO, I CAN'T STOP SHAKING. I MEAN, WHAT IF SHE'S LIKE TANNED NOW WITH A BIG NOSE AND A DEEP VOICE?
NOBODY HERE. COPS RAIDED THE PLACE THIS MORNING AND TOOK IN EVERY LAST ONE OF THEM DRUG ADDICTS. I SAY, GOOD RIDDANCE AND MAY THEY ALL ROT IN JAIL FOREVER!
BRUCE LEE
BRUCE LI
BRUCE LE
6236662-78257
BADGEPORT
6236662-78257
WHERE'D YOU FIND MONEY TO BAIL ME OUT, TEX?
BUT, HOPEY. I JUST GOT HERE. I DIDN'T BAIL YOU OUT...
OHO! NOW I SEE! PENNY'S TITS AT SIXTEEN O'CLOCK! LET'S SNEAK OUT THE BACK WAY OR ELSE SHE'LL BEG US TO STAY AT THE MANSION AGAIN.
THERE IS NO BACK WAY TO THIS PLACE.
THEN WE'LL HIDE IN THE HEAD TILL SHE GETS TIRED OF WAITING AND LEAVES.
WAIT, THIS IS THE WOMEN'S BATHROOM...
12

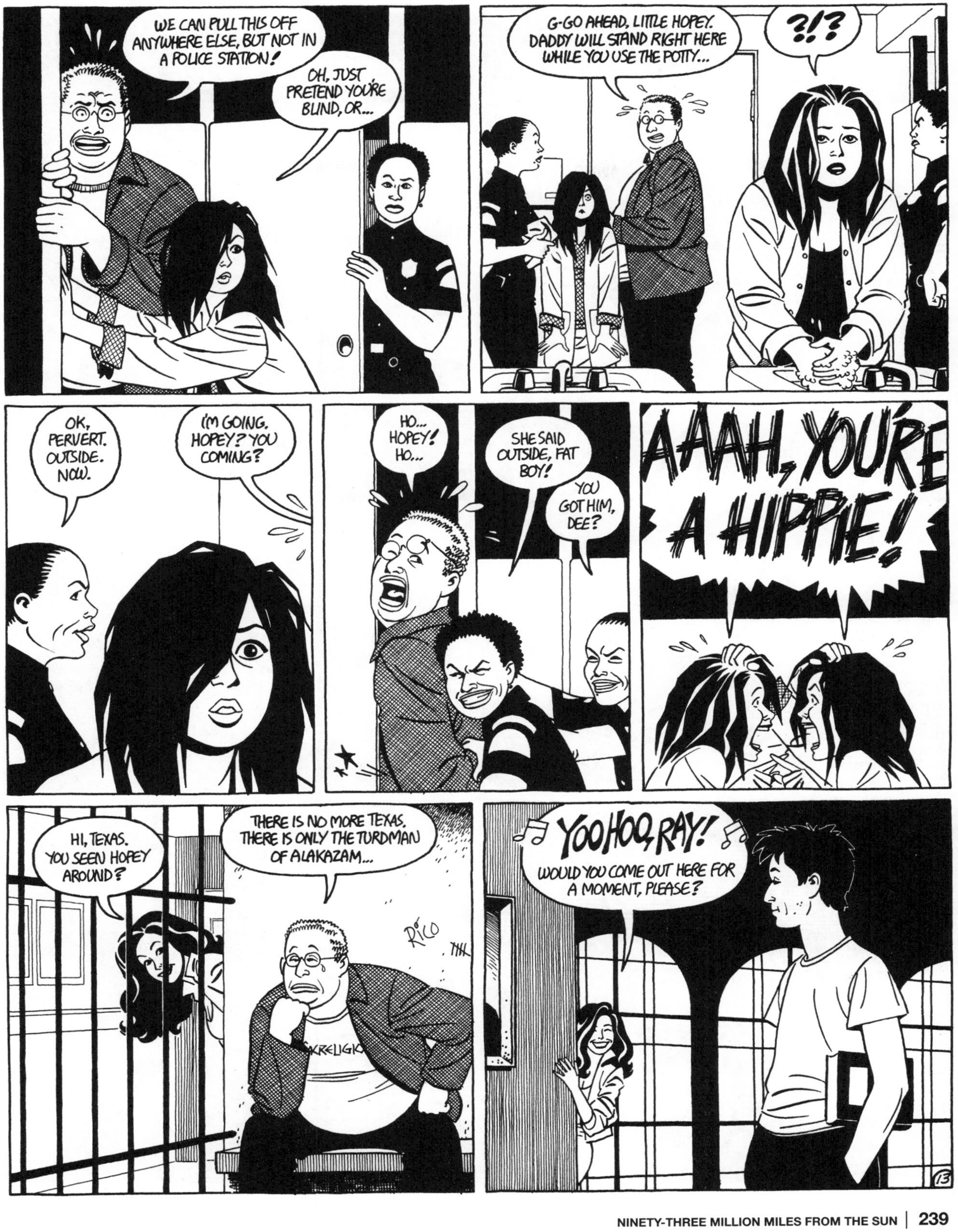
WE CAN PULL THIS OFF ANYWHERE ELSE, BUT NOT IN A POLICE STATION!
OH, JUST PRETEND YOU'RE BLIND, OR...
G-GO AHEAD, LITTLE HOPEY. DADDY WILL STAND RIGHT HERE WHILE YOU USE THE POTTY...
?!?
OK, PERVERT. OUTSIDE. NOW.
I'M GOING. HOPEY? YOU COMING?
HO... HOPEY! HO...
SHE SAID OUTSIDE, FAT BOY!
YOU GOT HIM, DEE?
AAAH, YOU'RE A HIPPIE!
HI, TEXAS. YOU SEEN HOPEY AROUND?
THERE IS NO MORE TEXAS. THERE IS ONLY THE TURDMAN OF ALAKAZAM...
YOOHOO, RAY!
WOULD YOU COME OUT HERE FOR A MOMENT, PLEASE?

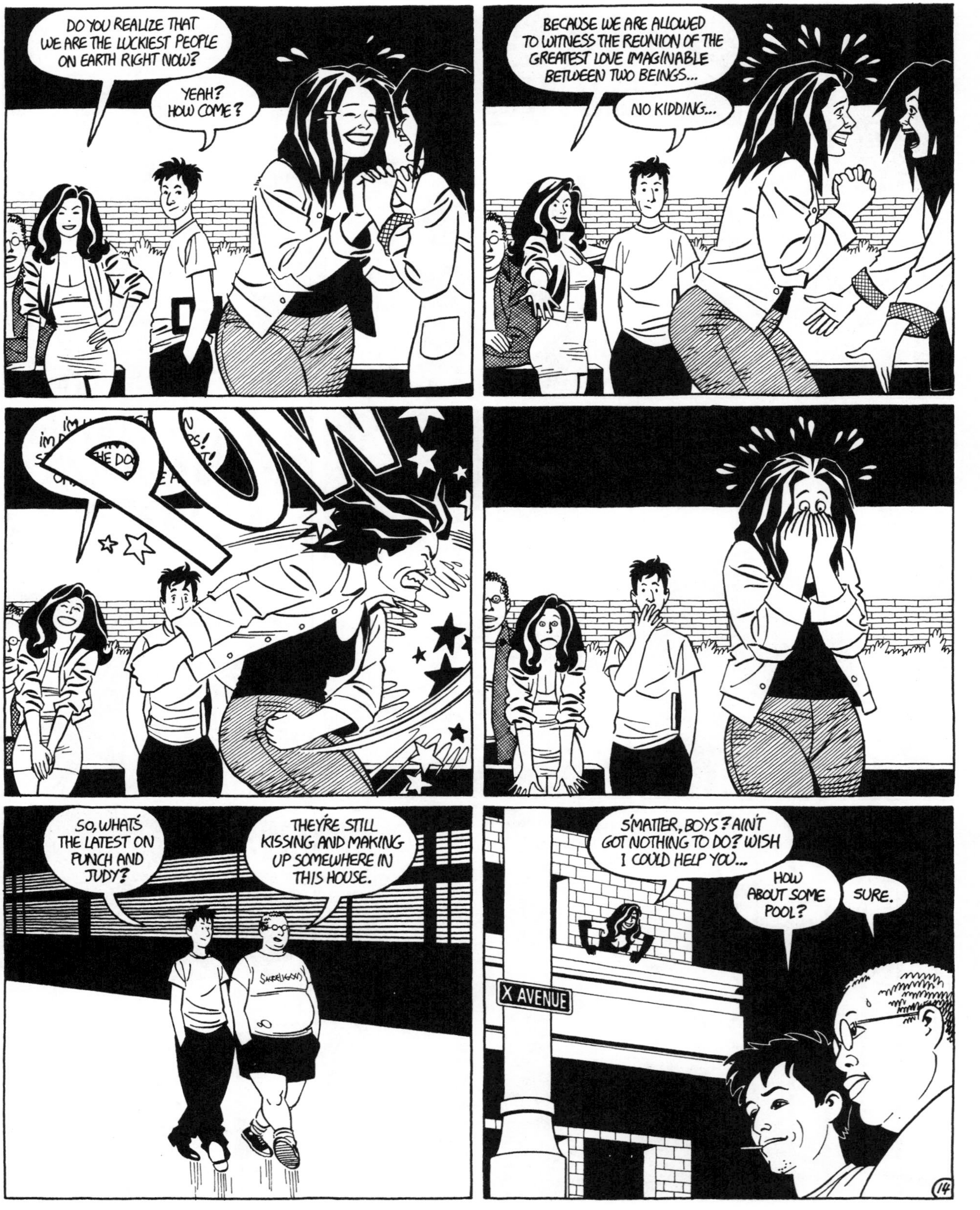
DO YOU REALIZE THAT WE ARE THE LUCKIEST PEOPLE ON EARTH RIGHT NOW?
YEAH? HOW COME?
BECAUSE WE ARE ALLOWED TO WITNESS THE REUNION OF THE GREATEST LOVE IMAGINABLE BETWEEN TWO BEINGS...
NO KIDDING...
POW
SO, WHAT'S THE LATEST ON PUNCH AND JUDY?
THEY'RE STILL KISSING AND MAKING UP SOMEWHERE IN THIS HOUSE.
X AVENUE
S'MATTER, BOYS? AIN'T GOT NOTHING TO DO? WISH I COULD HELP YOU...
HOW ABOUT SOME POOL?
SURE.
14

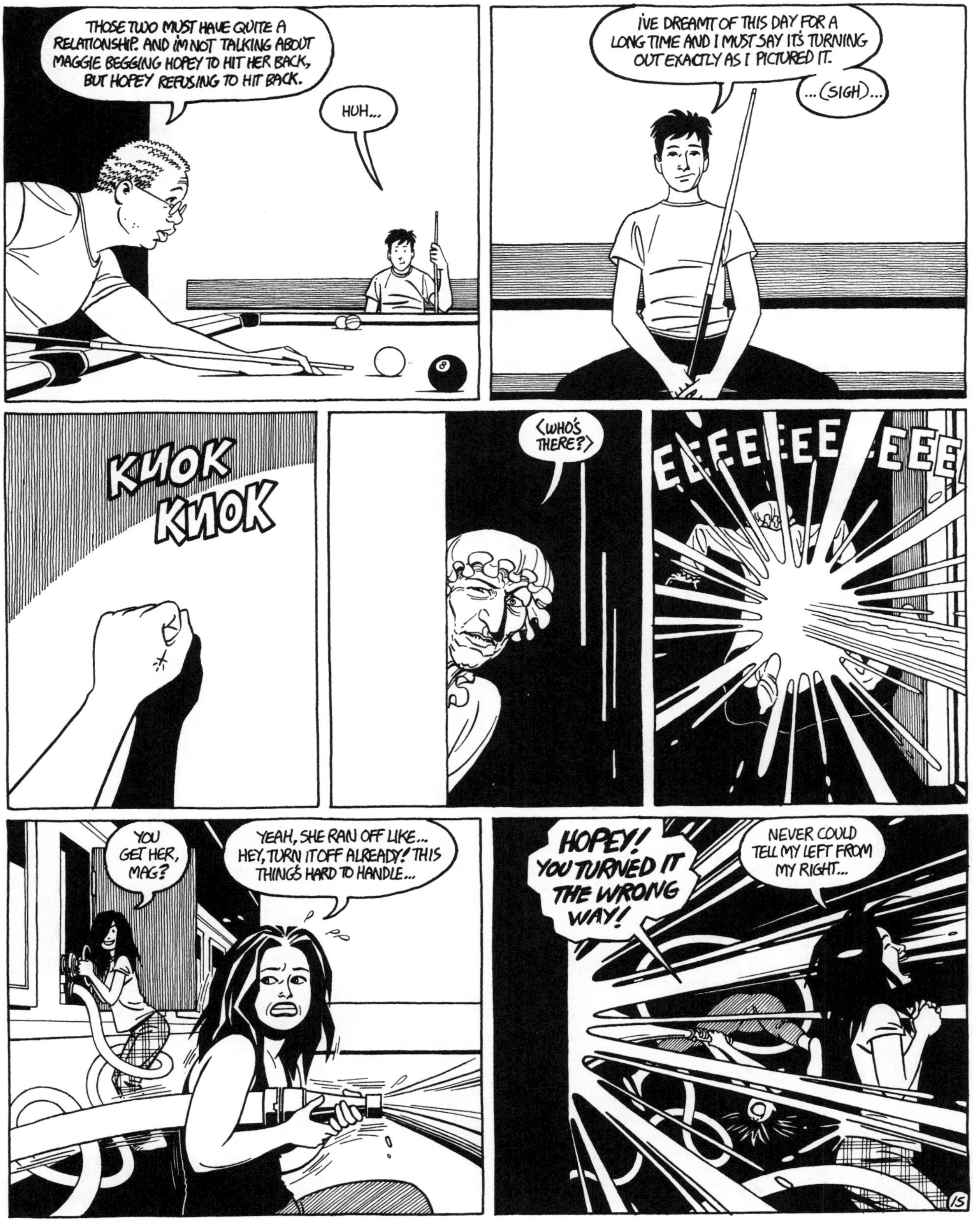
THOSE TWO MUST HAVE QUITE A RELATIONSHIP. AND I'M NOT TALKING ABOUT MAGGIE BEGGING HOPEY TO HIT HER BACK, BUT HOPEY REFUSING TO HIT BACK.
HUH...
I'VE DREAMT OF THIS DAY FOR A LONG TIME AND I MUST SAY IT'S TURNING OUT EXACTLY AS I PICTURED IT.
...(SIGH)...
KNOK KNOK
<WHO'S THERE?>
EEEEEEE EEE
YOU GET HER, MAG?
YEAH, SHE RAN OFF LIKE... HEY, TURN IT OFF ALREADY! THIS THING'S HARD TO HANDLE...
HOPEY! YOU TURNED IT THE WRONG WAY!
NEVER COULD TELL MY LEFT FROM MY RIGHT...
15

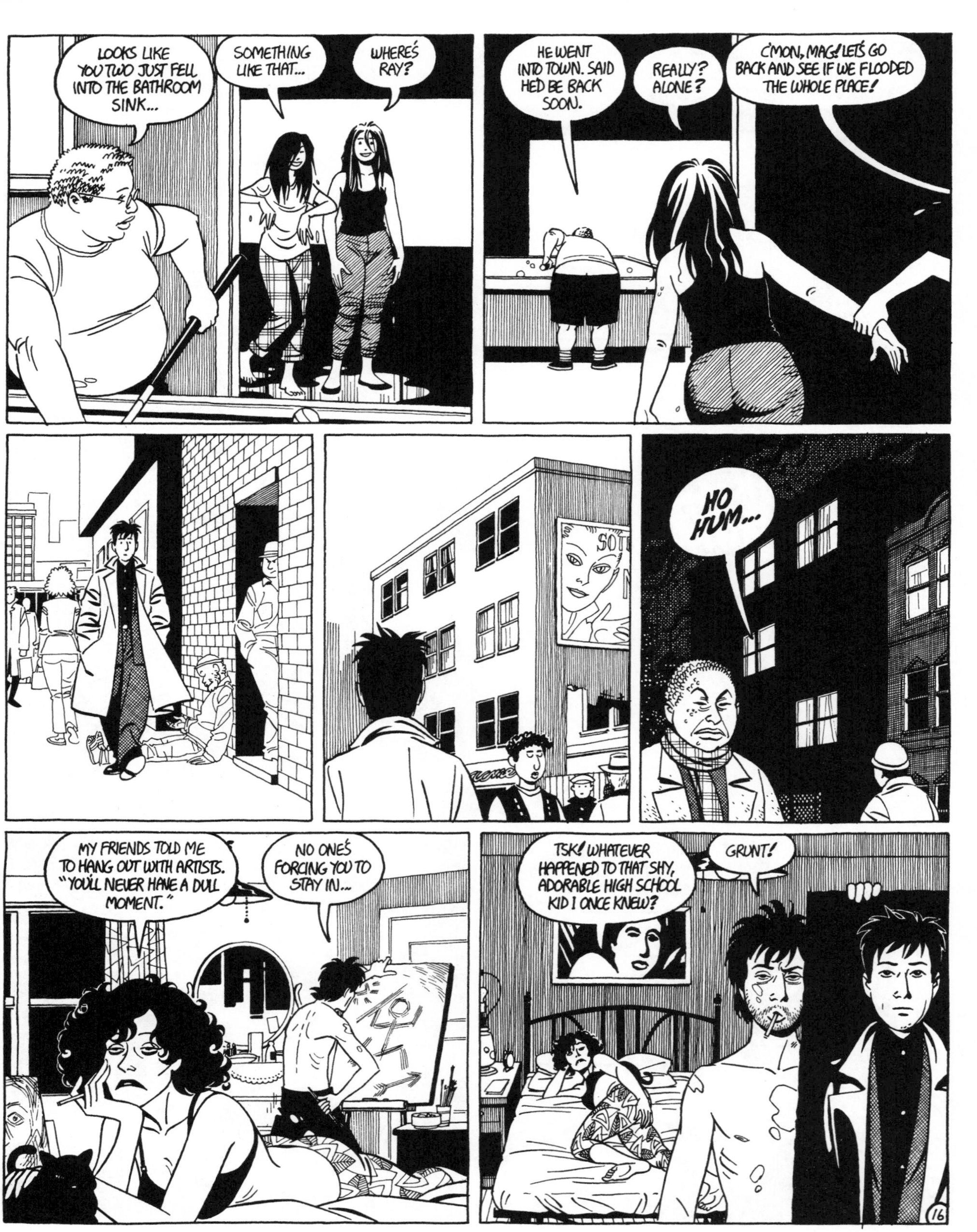
LOOKS LIKE YOU TWO JUST FELL INTO THE BATHROOM SINK...
SOMETHING LIKE THAT...
WHERE'S RAY?
HE WENT INTO TOWN. SAID HE'D BE BACK SOON.
REALLY? ALONE?
C'MON, MAG! LET'S GO BACK AND SEE IF WE FLOODED THE WHOLE PLACE!
HO HUM...
MY FRIENDS TOLD ME TO HANG OUT WITH ARTISTS. "YOU'LL NEVER HAVE A DULL MOMENT."
NO ONE'S FORCING YOU TO STAY IN...
TSK! WHATEVER HAPPENED TO THAT SHY, ADORABLE HIGH SCHOOL KID I ONCE KNEW?
GRUNT!
16

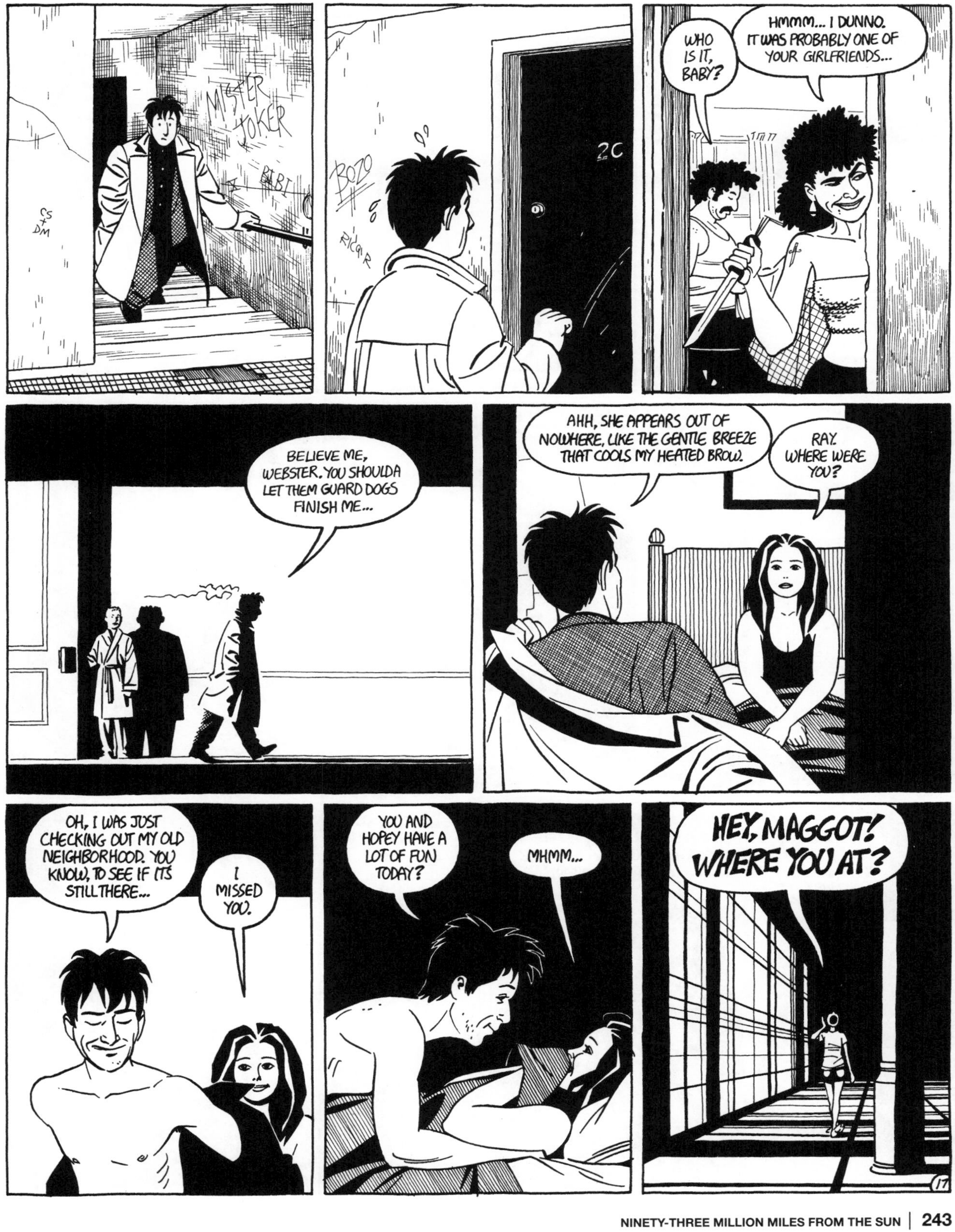
MISTER JOKER
BOZO
2C
WHO IS IT, BABY?
HMMM... I DUNNO. IT WAS PROBABLY ONE OF YOUR GIRLFRIENDS...
BELIEVE ME, WEBSTER. YOU SHOULDA LET THEM GUARD DOGS FINISH ME...
AHH, SHE APPEARS OUT OF NOWHERE, LIKE THE GENTLE BREEZE THAT COOLS MY HEATED BROW.
RAY. WHERE WERE YOU?
OH, I WAS JUST CHECKING OUT MY OLD NEIGHBORHOOD. YOU KNOW, TO SEE IF ITS STILL THERE...
I MISSED YOU.
YOU AND HOPEY HAVE A LOT OF FUN TODAY?
MHMM...
HEY, MAGGOT! WHERE YOU AT?
17

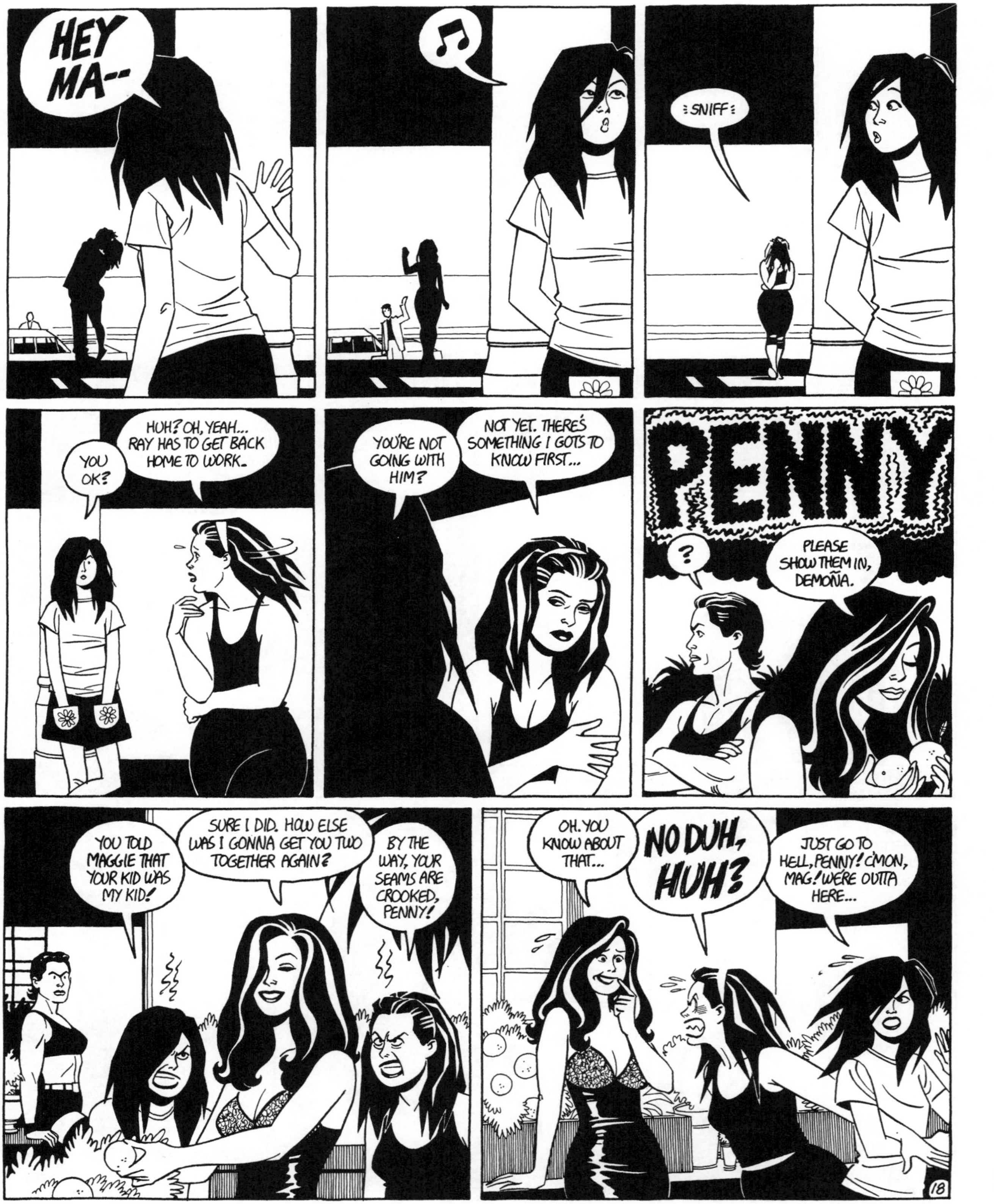
HEY MA--
♫
SNIFF
YOU OK?
HUH? OH, YEAH... RAY HAS TO GET BACK HOME TO WORK.
YOU'RE NOT GOING WITH HIM?
NOT YET. THERE'S SOMETHING I GOTS TO KNOW FIRST...
PENNY
?
PLEASE SHOW THEM IN, DEMOÑA.
YOU TOLD MAGGIE THAT YOUR KID WAS MY KID!
SURE I DID. HOW ELSE WAS I GONNA GET YOU TWO TOGETHER AGAIN?
BY THE WAY, YOUR SEAMS ARE CROOKED, PENNY!
OH. YOU KNOW ABOUT THAT...
NO DUH, HUH?
JUST GO TO HELL, PENNY! C'MON, MAG! WE'RE OUTTA HERE...
18

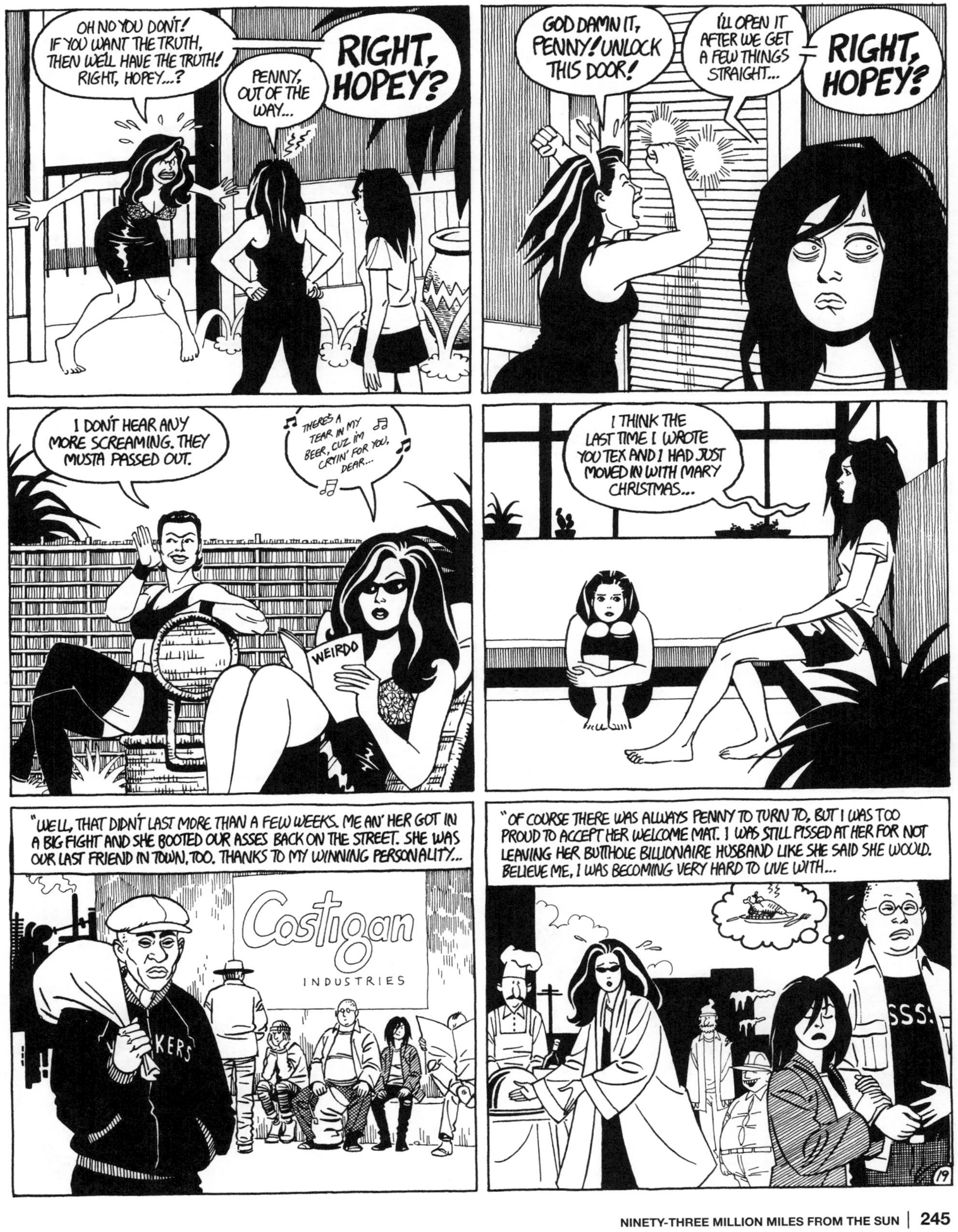
OH NO YOU DON'T! IF YOU WANT THE TRUTH, THEN WE'LL HAVE THE TRUTH! RIGHT, HOPEY...?
PENNY, OUT OF THE WAY...
RIGHT, HOPEY?
GOD DAMN IT, PENNY! UNLOCK THIS DOOR!
I'LL OPEN IT AFTER WE GET A FEW THINGS STRAIGHT...
RIGHT, HOPEY?
I DON'T HEAR ANY MORE SCREAMING. THEY MUSTA PASSED OUT.
THERE'S A TEAR IN MY BEER, CUZ I'M CRYIN' FOR YOU, DEAR...
WEIRDO
I THINK THE LAST TIME I WROTE YOU TEX AND I HAD JUST MOVED IN WITH MARY CHRISTMAS...
"WELL, THAT DIDN'T LAST MORE THAN A FEW WEEKS. ME AN' HER GOT IN A BIG FIGHT AND SHE BOOTED OUR ASSES BACK ON THE STREET. SHE WAS OUR LAST FRIEND IN TOWN, TOO. THANKS TO MY WINNING PERSONALITY...
Costigan INDUSTRIES
"OF COURSE THERE WAS ALWAYS PENNY TO TURN TO, BUT I WAS TOO PROUD TO ACCEPT HER WELCOME MAT. I WAS STILL PISSED AT HER FOR NOT LEAVING HER BUTTHOLE BILLIONAIRE HUSBAND LIKE SHE SAID SHE WOULD. BELIEVE ME, I WAS BECOMING VERY HARD TO LIVE WITH...
19

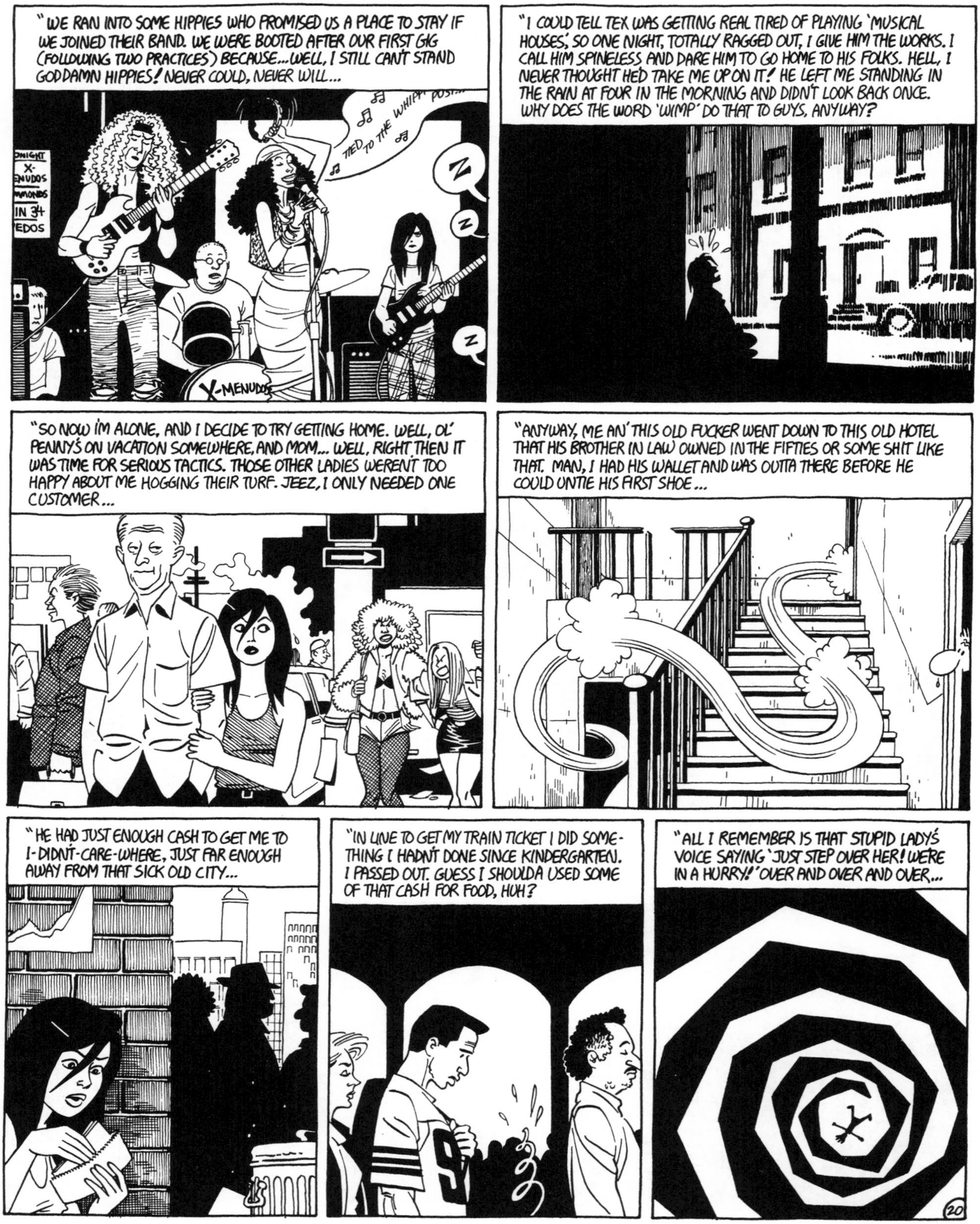
"WE RAN INTO SOME HIPPIES WHO PROMISED US A PLACE TO STAY IF WE JOINED THEIR BAND. WE WERE BOOTED AFTER OUR FIRST GIG (FOLLOWING TWO PRACTICES) BECAUSE... WELL, I STILL CAN'T STAND GODDAMN HIPPIES! NEVER COULD, NEVER WILL...
X-MENUDOS
Z
Z
Z
"I COULD TELL TEX WAS GETTING REAL TIRED OF PLAYING 'MUSICAL HOUSES,' SO ONE NIGHT, TOTALLY RAGGED OUT, I GIVE HIM THE WORKS. I CALL HIM SPINELESS AND DARE HIM TO GO HOME TO HIS FOLKS. HELL, I NEVER THOUGHT HE'D TAKE ME UP ON IT! HE LEFT ME STANDING IN THE RAIN AT FOUR IN THE MORNING AND DIDN'T LOOK BACK ONCE. WHY DOES THE WORD 'WIMP' DO THAT TO GUYS, ANYWAY?
"SO NOW I'M ALONE, AND I DECIDE TO TRY GETTING HOME. WELL, OL' PENNY'S ON VACATION SOMEWHERE, AND MOM... WELL, RIGHT THEN IT WAS TIME FOR SERIOUS TACTICS. THOSE OTHER LADIES WEREN'T TOO HAPPY ABOUT ME HOGGING THEIR TURF. JEEZ, I ONLY NEEDED ONE CUSTOMER...
"ANYWAY, ME AN' THIS OLD FUCKER WENT DOWN TO THIS OLD HOTEL THAT HIS BROTHER IN LAW OWNED IN THE FIFTIES OR SOME SHIT LIKE THAT. MAN, I HAD HIS WALLET AND WAS OUTTA THERE BEFORE HE COULD UNTIE HIS FIRST SHOE...
"HE HAD JUST ENOUGH CASH TO GET ME TO I-DIDN'T-CARE-WHERE, JUST FAR ENOUGH AWAY FROM THAT SICK OLD CITY...
"IN LINE TO GET MY TRAIN TICKET I DID SOMETHING I HADN'T DONE SINCE KINDERGARTEN. I PASSED OUT. GUESS I SHOULDA USED SOME OF THAT CASH FOR FOOD, HUH?
"ALL I REMEMBER IS THAT STUPID LADY'S VOICE SAYING 'JUST STEP OVER HER! WE'RE IN A HURRY!' OVER AND OVER AND OVER...
20

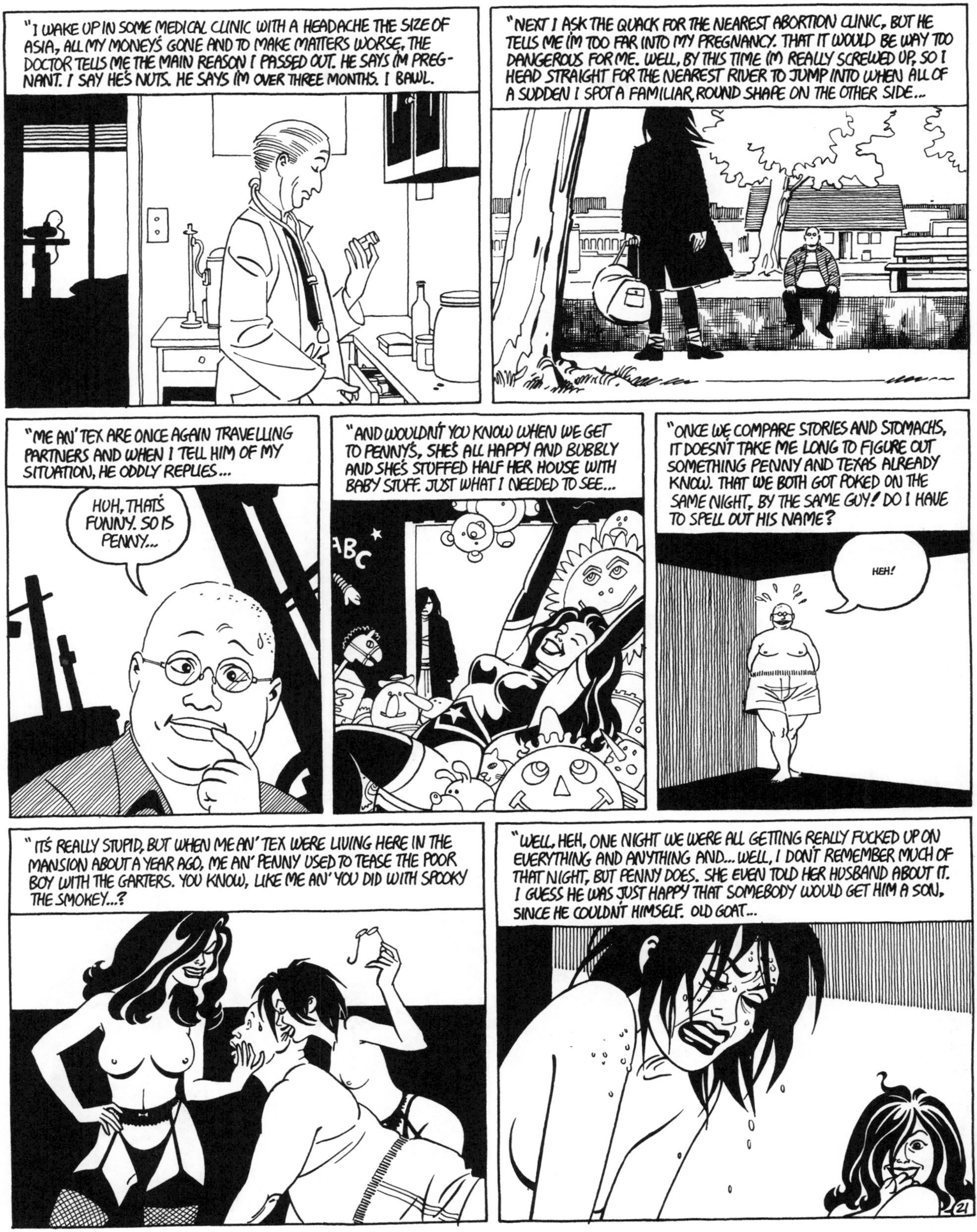
"I WAKE UP IN SOME MEDICAL CLINIC WITH A HEADACHE THE SIZE OF ASIA, ALL MY MONEY'S GONE AND TO MAKE MATTERS WORSE, THE DOCTOR TELLS ME THE MAIN REASON I PASSED OUT. HE SAYS I'M PREGNANT. I SAY HE'S NUTS. HE SAYS I'M OVER THREE MONTHS. I BAWL.
"NEXT I ASK THE QUACK FOR THE NEAREST ABORTION CLINIC, BUT HE TELLS ME I'M TOO FAR INTO MY PREGNANCY. THAT IT WOULD BE WAY TOO DANGEROUS FOR ME. WELL, BY THIS TIME I'M REALLY SCREWED UP, SO I HEAD STRAIGHT FOR THE NEAREST RIVER TO JUMP INTO WHEN ALL OF A SUDDEN I SPOT A FAMILIAR, ROUND SHAPE ON THE OTHER SIDE...
"ME AN' TEX ARE ONCE AGAIN TRAVELLING PARTNERS AND WHEN I TELL HIM OF MY SITUATION, HE ODDLY REPLIES...
HUH, THAT'S FUNNY. SO IS PENNY...
"AND WOULDN'T YOU KNOW WHEN WE GET TO PENNY'S, SHE'S ALL HAPPY AND BUBBLY AND SHE'S STUFFED HALF HER HOUSE WITH BABY STUFF. JUST WHAT I NEEDED TO SEE...
ABC
"ONCE WE COMPARE STORIES AND STOMACHS, IT DOESN'T TAKE ME LONG TO FIGURE OUT SOMETHING PENNY AND TEXAS ALREADY KNOW. THAT WE BOTH GOT POKED ON THE SAME NIGHT, BY THE SAME GUY! DO I HAVE TO SPELL OUT HIS NAME?
HEH!
"IT'S REALLY STUPID, BUT WHEN ME AN' TEX WERE LIVING HERE IN THE MANSION ABOUT A YEAR AGO, ME AN' PENNY USED TO TEASE THE POOR BOY WITH THE GARTERS. YOU KNOW, LIKE ME AN' YOU DID WITH SPOOKY THE SMOKEY...?
"WELL, HEH, ONE NIGHT WE WERE ALL GETTING REALLY FUCKED UP ON EVERYTHING AND ANYTHING AND... WELL, I DON'T REMEMBER MUCH OF THAT NIGHT, BUT PENNY DOES. SHE EVEN TOLD HER HUSBAND ABOUT IT. I GUESS HE WAS JUST HAPPY THAT SOMEBODY WOULD GET HIM A SON, SINCE HE COULDN'T HIMSELF. OLD GOAT...
21

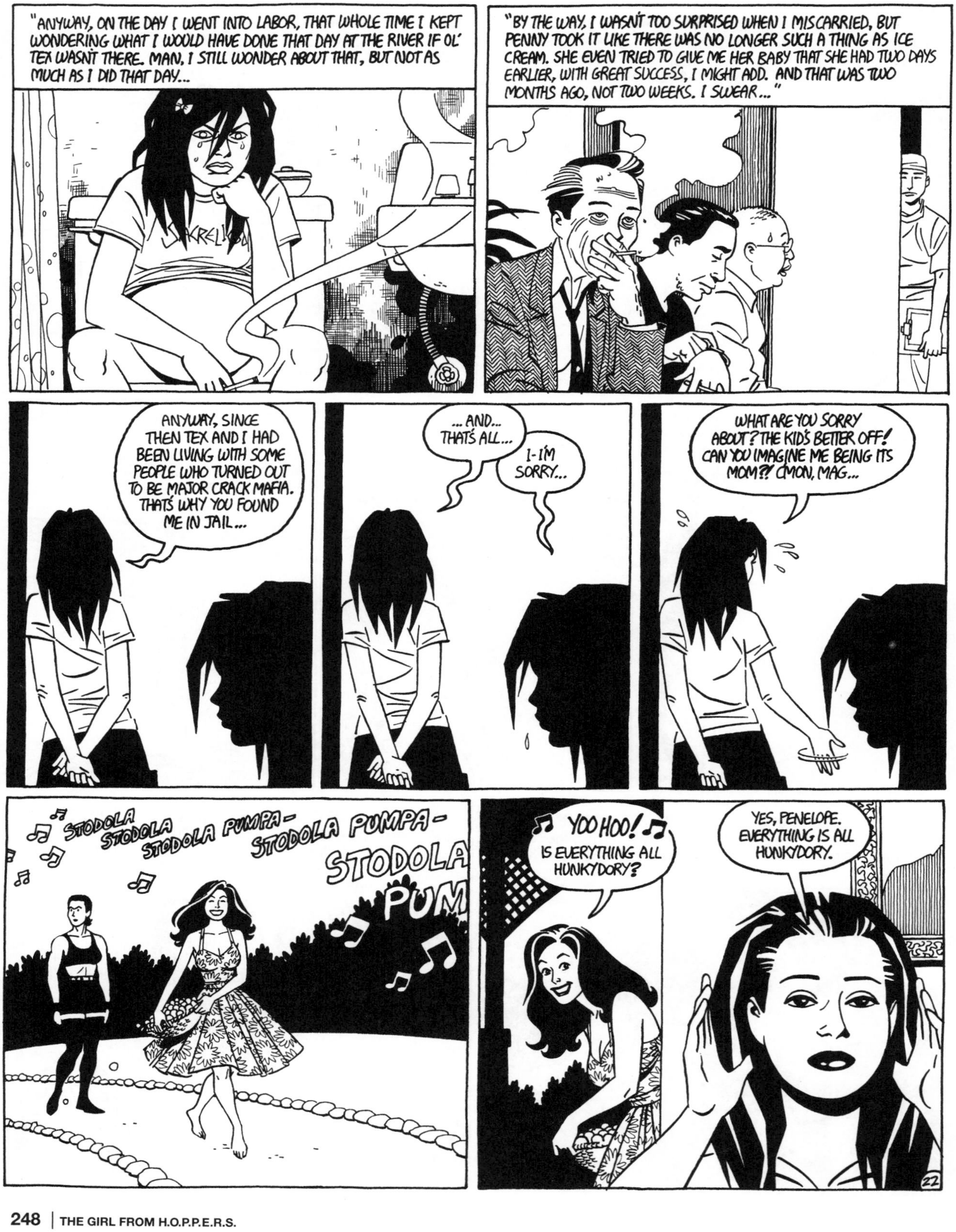
"ANYWAY, ON THE DAY I WENT INTO LABOR, THAT WHOLE TIME I KEPT WONDERING WHAT I WOULD HAVE DONE THAT DAY AT THE RIVER IF OL' TEX WASN'T THERE. MAN, I STILL WONDER ABOUT THAT, BUT NOT AS MUCH AS I DID THAT DAY...
"BY THE WAY, I WASN'T TOO SURPRISED WHEN I MISCARRIED, BUT PENNY TOOK IT LIKE THERE WAS NO LONGER SUCH A THING AS ICE CREAM. SHE EVEN TRIED TO GIVE ME HER BABY THAT SHE HAD TWO DAYS EARLIER, WITH GREAT SUCCESS, I MIGHT ADD. AND THAT WAS TWO MONTHS AGO, NOT TWO WEEKS. I SWEAR..."
ANYWAY, SINCE THEN TEX AND I HAD BEEN LIVING WITH SOME PEOPLE WHO TURNED OUT TO BE MAJOR CRACK MAFIA. THAT'S WHY YOU FOUND ME IN JAIL...
...AND... THAT'S ALL...
I-I'M SORRY...
WHAT ARE YOU SORRY ABOUT? THE KID'S BETTER OFF! CAN YOU IMAGINE ME BEING ITS MOM?! C'MON, MAG...
STODOLA STODOLA STODOLA PUMPA- STODOLA PUMPA- STODOLA PUM
YOO HOO!
IS EVERYTHING ALL HUNKYDORY?
YES, PENELOPE. EVERYTHING IS ALL HUNKYDORY.
22

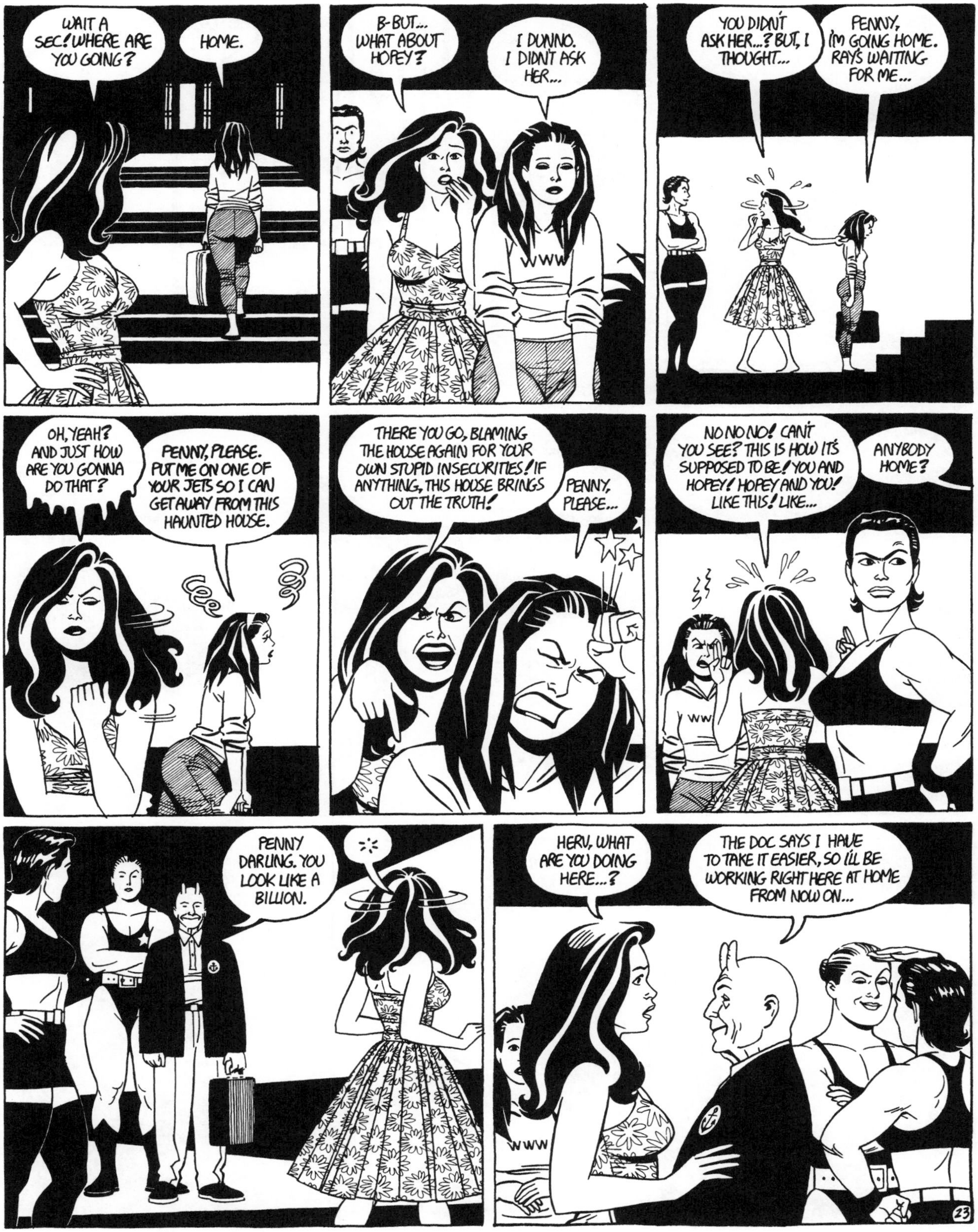
WAIT A SEC! WHERE ARE YOU GOING?
HOME.
B-BUT... WHAT ABOUT HOPEY?
I DUNNO. I DIDN'T ASK HER...
YOU DIDN'T ASK HER...? BUT, I THOUGHT...
PENNY, I'M GOING HOME. RAY'S WAITING FOR ME...
OH, YEAH? AND JUST HOW ARE YOU GONNA DO THAT?
PENNY, PLEASE. PUT ME ON ONE OF YOUR JETS SO I CAN GET AWAY FROM THIS HAUNTED HOUSE.
THERE YOU GO, BLAMING THE HOUSE AGAIN FOR YOUR OWN STUPID INSECURITIES! IF ANYTHING, THIS HOUSE BRINGS OUT THE TRUTH!
PENNY, PLEASE...
NO NO NO! CAN'T YOU SEE? THIS IS HOW IT'S SUPPOSED TO BE! YOU AND HOPEY! HOPEY AND YOU! LIKE THIS! LIKE...
ANYBODY HOME?
PENNY DARLING. YOU LOOK LIKE A BILLION.
HERV, WHAT ARE YOU DOING HERE...?
THE DOC SAYS I HAVE TO TAKE IT EASIER, SO I'LL BE WORKING RIGHT HERE AT HOME FROM NOW ON...
23

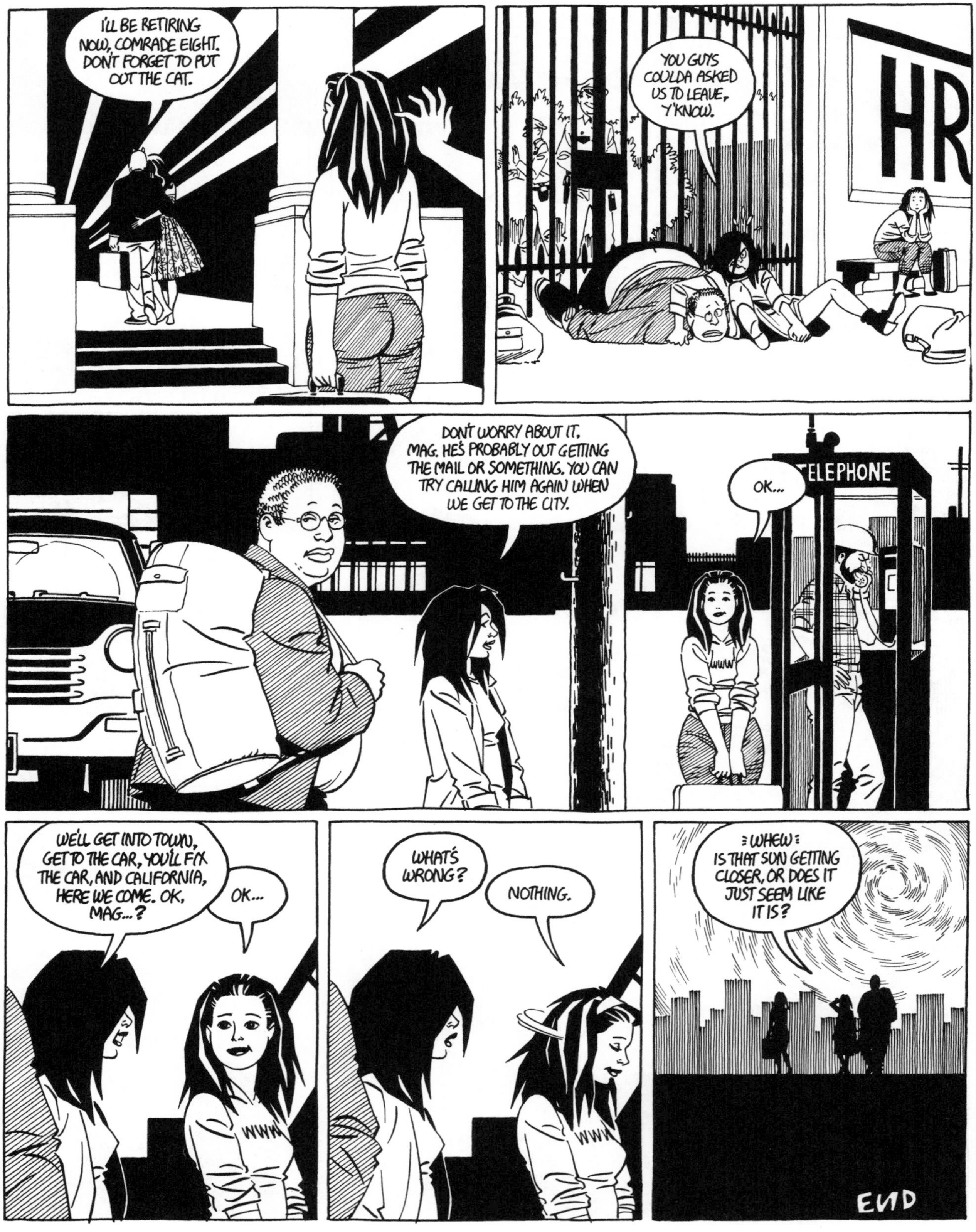
I'LL BE RETIRING NOW, COMRADE EIGHT. DON'T FORGET TO PUT OUT THE CAT.
YOU GUYS COULDA ASKED US TO LEAVE, Y'KNOW.
HR
DON'T WORRY ABOUT IT, MAG. HE'S PROBABLY OUT GETTING THE MAIL OR SOMETHING. YOU CAN TRY CALLING HIM AGAIN WHEN WE GET TO THE CITY.
OK...
TELEPHONE
WE'LL GET INTO TOWN, GET TO THE CAR, YOU'LL FIX THE CAR, AND CALIFORNIA, HERE WE COME. OK, MAG...?
OK...
WHAT'S WRONG?
NOTHING.
WHEW
IS THAT SUN GETTING CLOSER, OR DOES IT JUST SEEM LIKE IT IS?
END

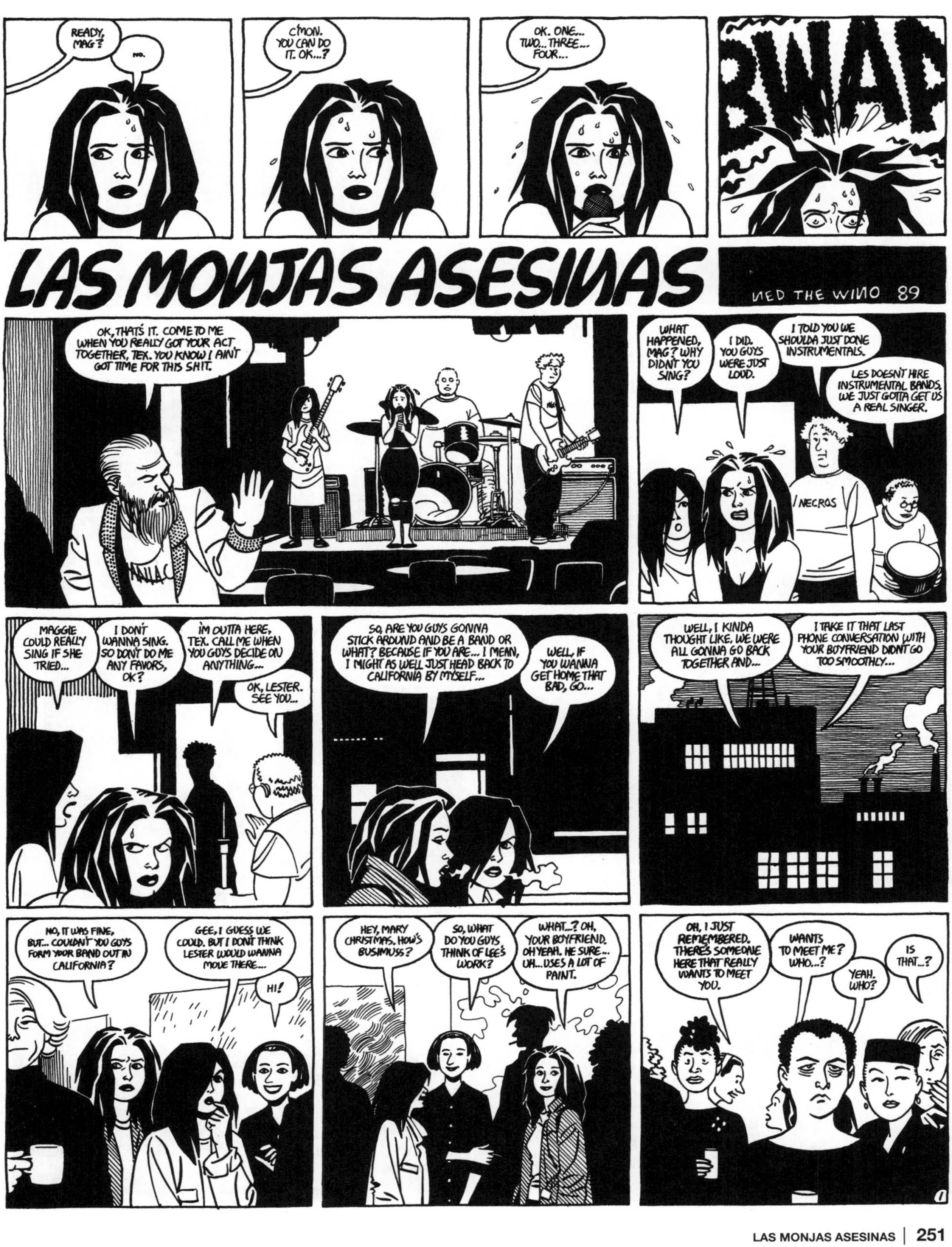
READY, MAG?
NO.
C'MON. YOU CAN DO IT. OK...?
OK. ONE... TWO... THREE... FOUR...
BWAP
LAS MONJAS ASESINAS
NED THE WINO 89
OK, THAT'S IT. COME TO ME WHEN YOU REALLY GOT YOUR ACT TOGETHER, TEX. YOU KNOW I AIN'T GOT TIME FOR THIS SHIT.
WHAT HAPPENED, MAG? WHY DIDN'T YOU SING?
I DID. YOU GUYS WERE JUST LOUD.
I TOLD YOU WE SHOULDA JUST DONE INSTRUMENTALS.
LES DOESN'T HIRE INSTRUMENTAL BANDS. WE JUST GOTTA GET US A REAL SINGER.
NECROS
MAGGIE COULD REALLY SING IF SHE TRIED...
I DON'T WANNA SING. SO DON'T DO ME ANY FAVORS, OK?
I'M OUTTA HERE, TEX. CALL ME WHEN YOU GUYS DECIDE ON ANYTHING...
OK, LESTER. SEE YOU...
SO, ARE YOU GUYS GONNA STICK AROUND AND BE A BAND OR WHAT? BECAUSE IF YOU ARE... I MEAN, I MIGHT AS WELL JUST HEAD BACK TO CALIFORNIA BY MYSELF...
WELL, IF YOU WANNA GET HOME THAT BAD, GO...
WELL, I KINDA THOUGHT LIKE, WE WERE ALL GONNA GO BACK TOGETHER AND...
I TAKE IT THAT LAST PHONE CONVERSATION WITH YOUR BOYFRIEND DIDN'T GO TOO SMOOTHLY...
NO, IT WAS FINE, BUT... COULDN'T YOU GUYS FORM YOUR BAND OUT IN CALIFORNIA?
GEE, I GUESS WE COULD. BUT I DON'T THINK LESTER WOULD WANNA MOVE THERE...
HI!
HEY, MARY CHRISTMAS. HOW'S BUSINUSS?
SO, WHAT DO YOU GUYS THINK OF LEE'S WORK?
WHAT...? OH, YOUR BOYFRIEND. OH YEAH. HE SURE... UH... USES A LOT OF PAINT.
OH, I JUST REMEMBERED. THERE'S SOMEONE HERE THAT REALLY WANTS TO MEET YOU.
WANTS TO MEET ME? WHO...?
YEAH. WHO?
IS THAT...?
1

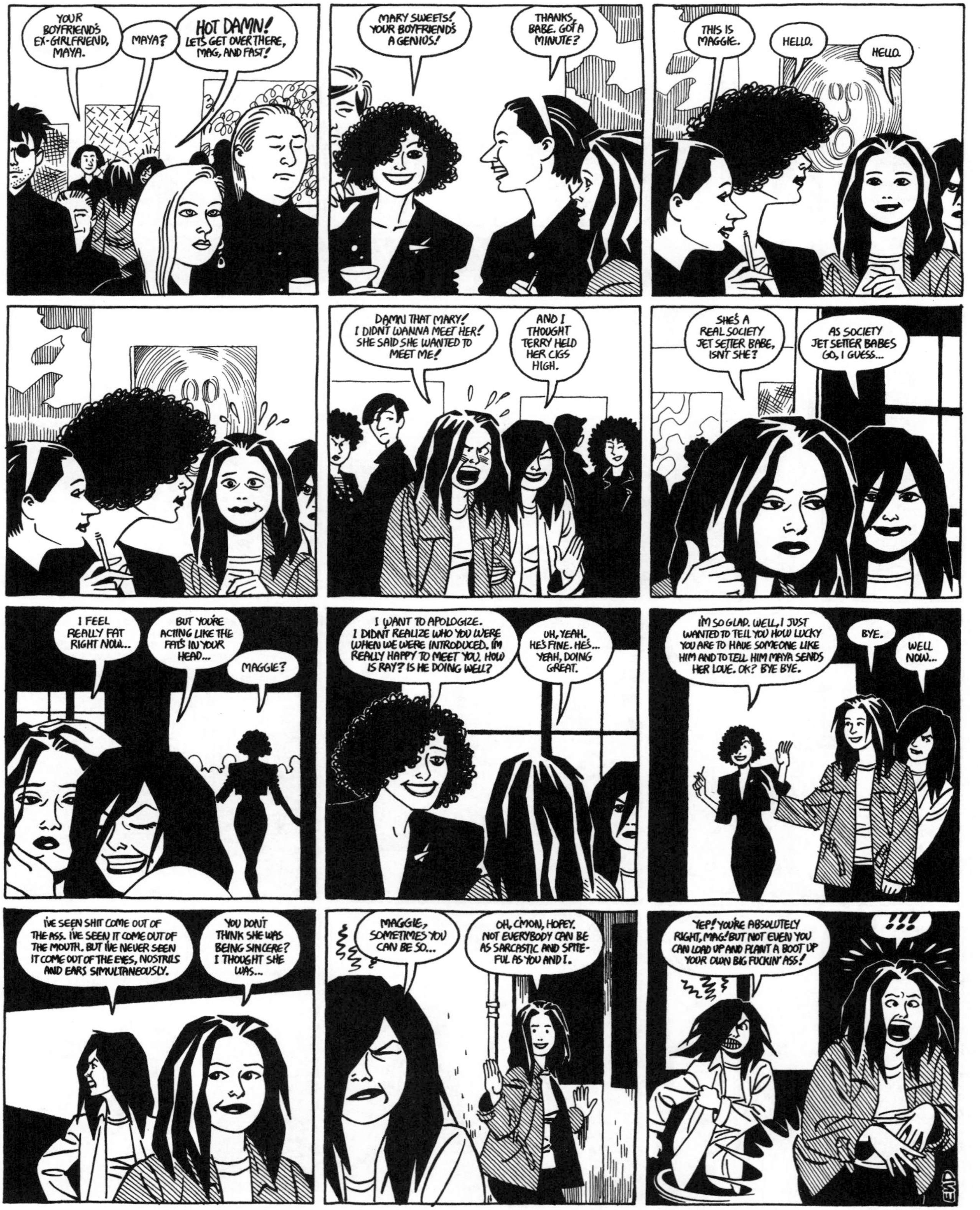
YOUR BOYFRIEND'S EX-GIRLFRIEND, MAYA.
MAYA?
HOT DAMN! LET'S GET OVER THERE, MAG, AND FAST!
MARY SWEETS! YOUR BOYFRIEND'S A GENIUS!
THANKS, BABE. GOT A MINUTE?
THIS IS MAGGIE.
HELLO.
HELLO.
DAMN THAT MARY! I DIDN'T WANNA MEET HER! SHE SAID SHE WANTED TO MEET ME!
AND I THOUGHT TERRY HELD HER CIGS HIGH.
SHE'S A REAL SOCIETY JET SETTER BABE, ISN'T SHE?
AS SOCIETY JET SETTER BABES GO, I GUESS...
I FEEL REALLY FAT RIGHT NOW...
BUT YOU'RE ACTING LIKE THE FAT'S IN YOUR HEAD...
MAGGIE?
I WANT TO APOLOGIZE. I DIDN'T REALIZE WHO YOU WERE WHEN WE WERE INTRODUCED. I'M REALLY HAPPY TO MEET YOU. HOW IS RAY? IS HE DOING WELL?
OH, YEAH. HE'S FINE. HE'S... YEAH, DOING GREAT.
I'M SO GLAD. WELL, I JUST WANTED TO TELL YOU HOW LUCKY YOU ARE TO HAVE SOMEONE LIKE HIM AND TO TELL HIM MAYA SENDS HER LOVE. OK? BYE BYE.
BYE.
WELL NOW...
I'VE SEEN SHIT COME OUT OF THE ASS. I'VE SEEN IT COME OUT OF THE MOUTH. BUT I'VE NEVER SEEN IT COME OUT OF THE EYES, NOSTRILS AND EARS SIMULTANEOUSLY.
YOU DON'T THINK SHE WAS BEING SINCERE? I THOUGHT SHE WAS...
MAGGIE, SOMETIMES YOU CAN BE SO...
OH, C'MON, HOPEY. NOT EVERYBODY CAN BE AS SARCASTIC AND SPITEFUL AS YOU AND I.
YEP! YOU'RE ABSOLUTELY RIGHT, MAG! BUT NOT EVEN YOU CAN LOAD UP AND PLANT A BOOT UP YOUR OWN BIG FUCKIN' ASS!
!!!
END

BELOW MY WINDOW LURKS MY HEAD

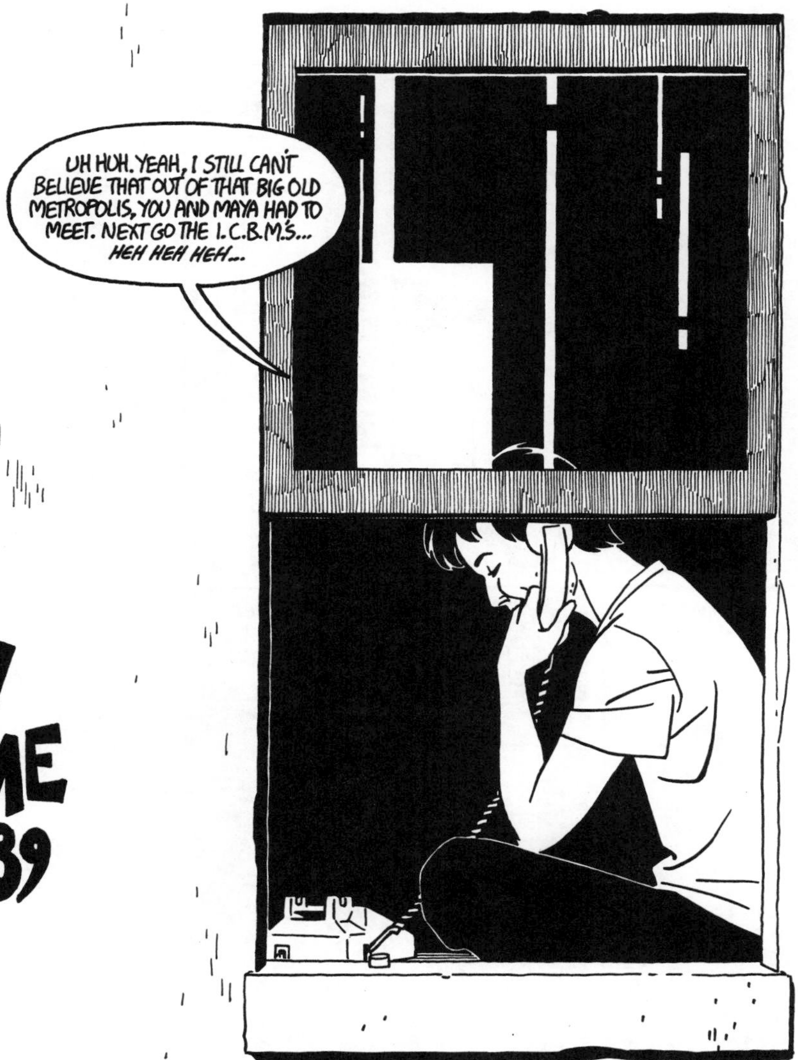
UH HUH. YEAH, I STILL CAN'T BELIEVE THAT OUT OF THAT BIG OLD METROPOLIS, YOU AND MAYA HAD TO MEET. NEXT GO THE I.C.B.M.'S... HEH HEH HEH...

BY XAIME 1989

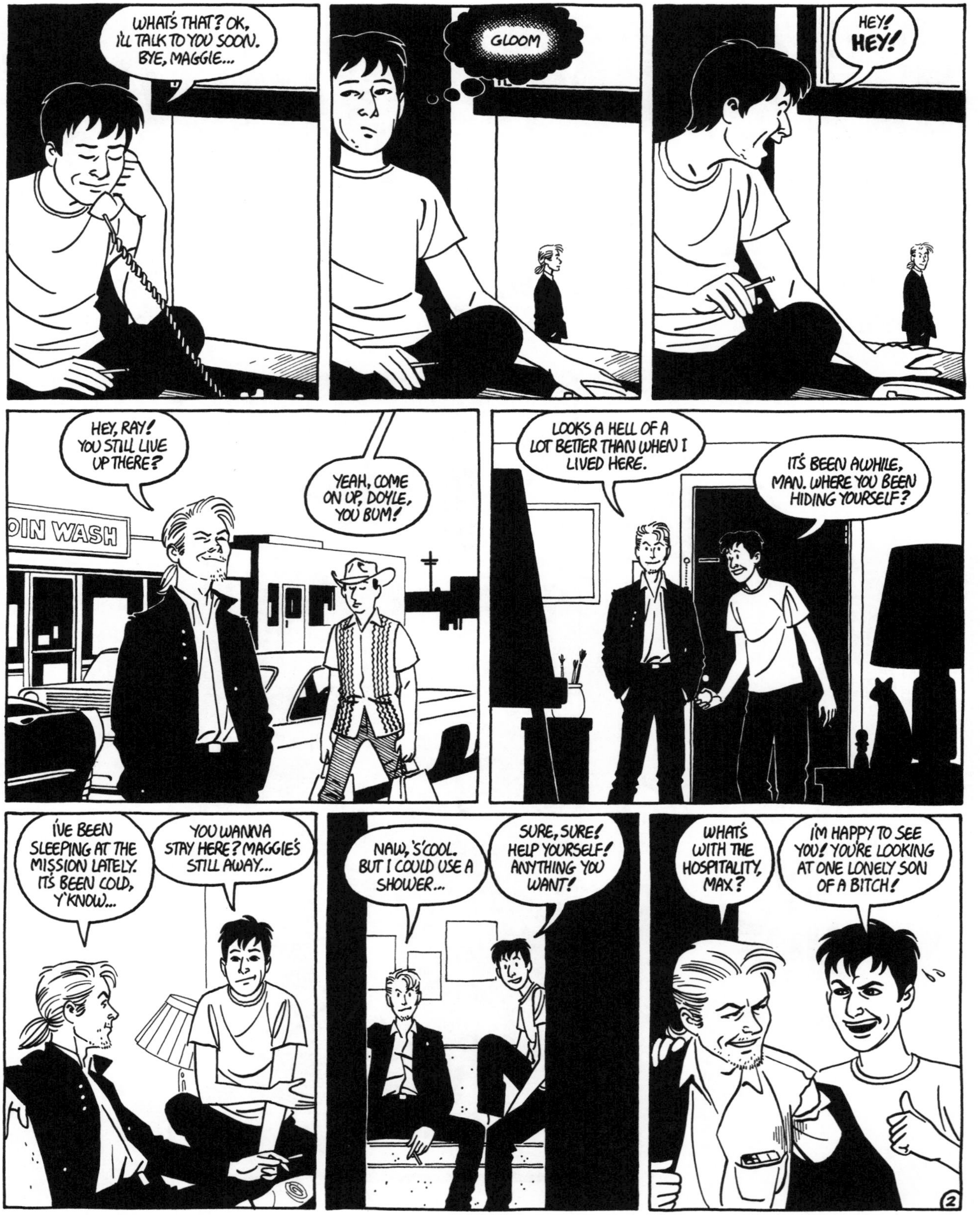
WHAT'S THAT? OK, I'LL TALK TO YOU SOON. BYE, MAGGIE...
GLOOM
HEY! HEY!
HEY, RAY! YOU STILL LIVE UP THERE?
YEAH, COME ON UP, DOYLE, YOU BUM!
OIN WASH
LOOKS A HELL OF A LOT BETTER THAN WHEN I LIVED HERE.
IT'S BEEN AWHILE, MAN. WHERE YOU BEEN HIDING YOURSELF?
I'VE BEEN SLEEPING AT THE MISSION LATELY. IT'S BEEN COLD, Y'KNOW...
YOU WANNA STAY HERE? MAGGIE'S STILL AWAY...
NAW, 'S'COOL. BUT I COULD USE A SHOWER...
SURE, SURE! HELP YOURSELF! ANYTHING YOU WANT!
WHAT'S WITH THE HOSPITALITY, MAX?
I'M HAPPY TO SEE YOU! YOU'RE LOOKING AT ONE LONELY SON OF A BITCH!
2

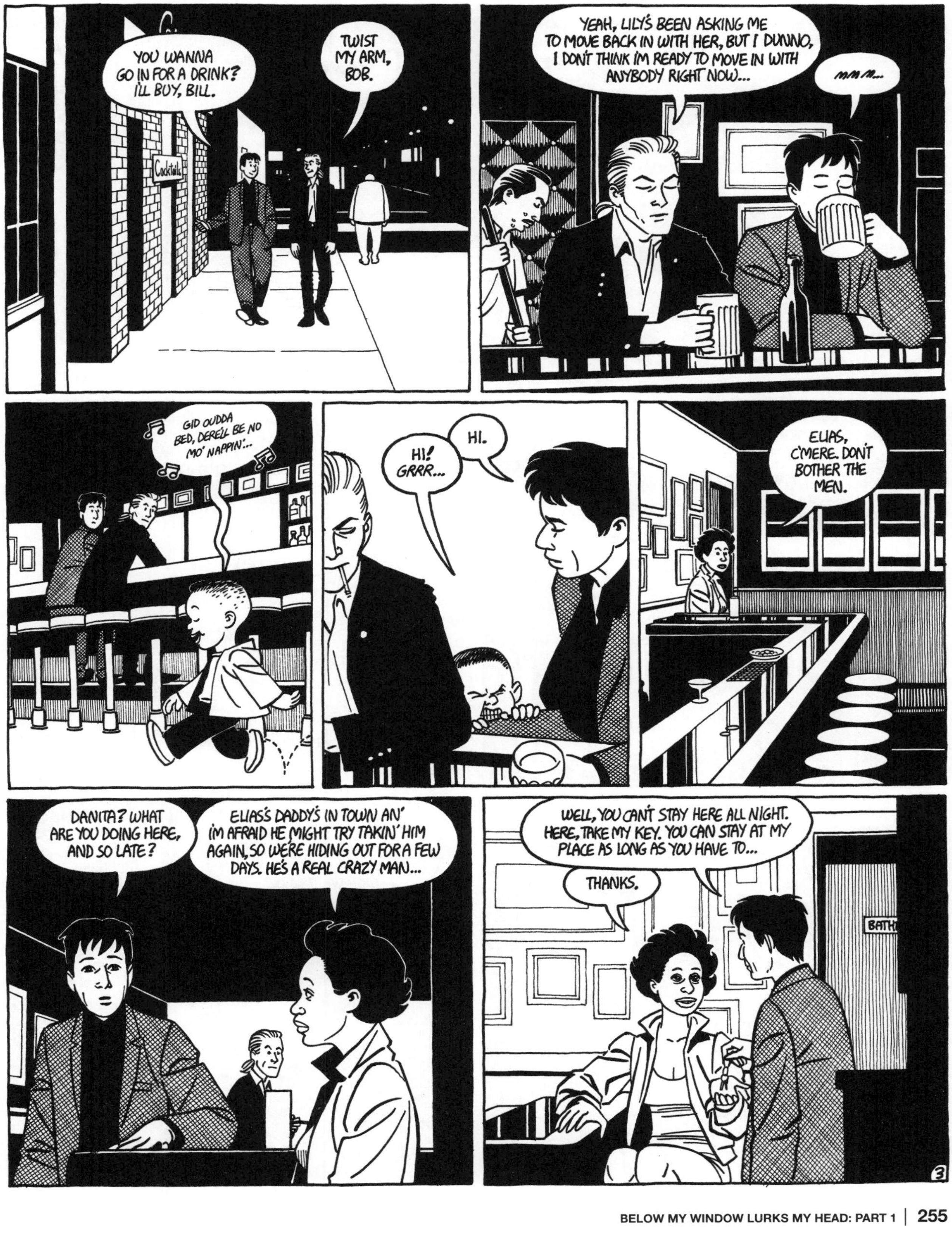
Cocktails
YOU WANNA GO IN FOR A DRINK? I'LL BUY, BILL.
TWIST MY ARM, BOB.
YEAH, LILY'S BEEN ASKING ME TO MOVE BACK IN WITH HER, BUT I DUNNO, I DON'T THINK I'M READY TO MOVE IN WITH ANYBODY RIGHT NOW...
MMM...
GID OUDDA BED, DERE'LL BE NO MO' NAPPIN'...
HI! GRRR...
HI.
ELIAS, C'MERE. DON'T BOTHER THE MEN.
DANITA? WHAT ARE YOU DOING HERE, AND SO LATE?
ELIAS'S DADDY'S IN TOWN AN' I'M AFRAID HE MIGHT TRY TAKIN' HIM AGAIN, SO WE'RE HIDING OUT FOR A FEW DAYS. HE'S A REAL CRAZY MAN...
WELL, YOU CAN'T STAY HERE ALL NIGHT. HERE, TAKE MY KEY. YOU CAN STAY AT MY PLACE AS LONG AS YOU HAVE TO...
THANKS.
BATH
3

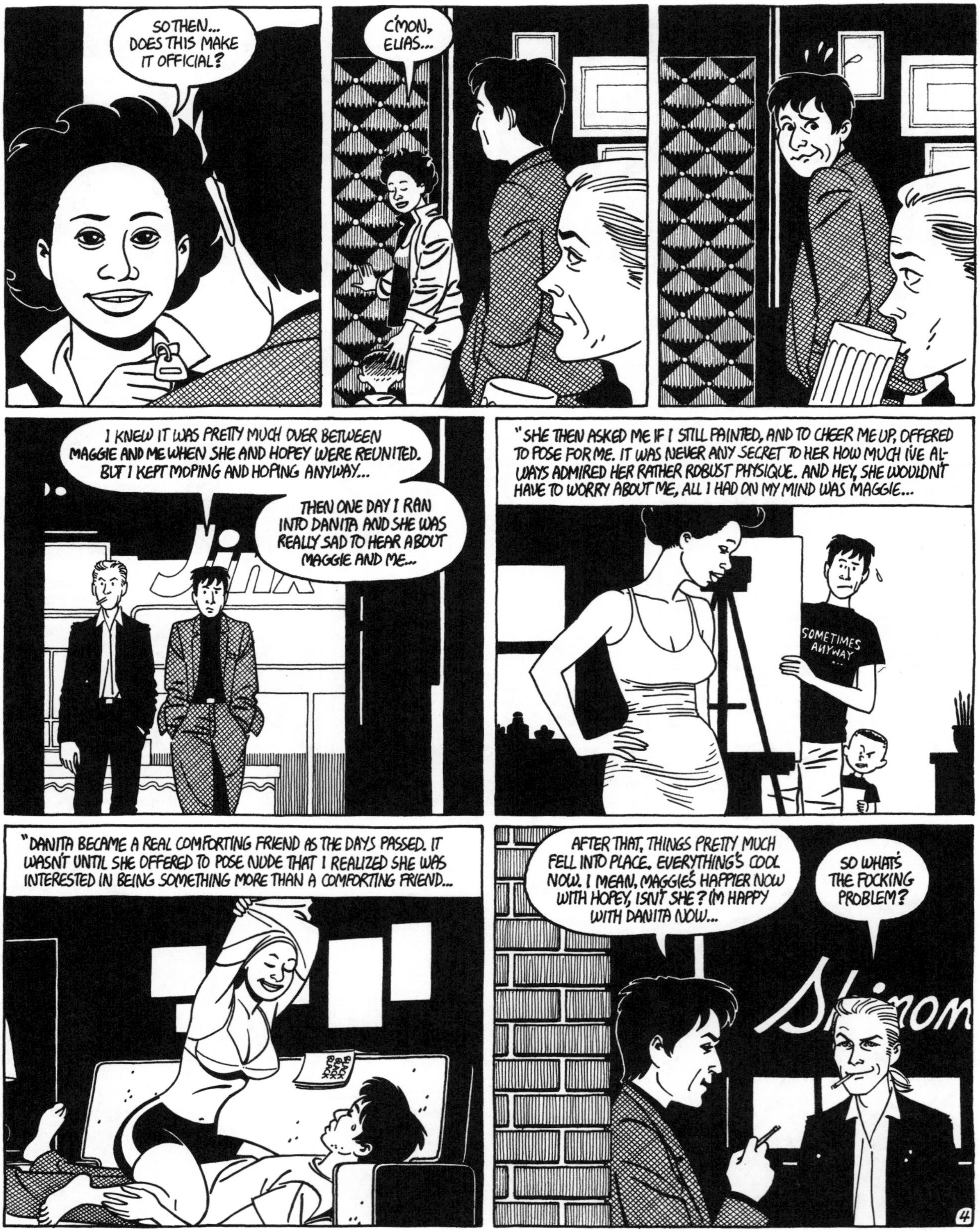
SO THEN... DOES THIS MAKE IT OFFICIAL?
C'MON, ELIAS...
I KNEW IT WAS PRETTY MUCH OVER BETWEEN MAGGIE AND ME WHEN SHE AND HOPEY WERE REUNITED. BUT I KEPT MOPING AND HOPING ANYWAY...
THEN ONE DAY I RAN INTO DANITA AND SHE WAS REALLY SAD TO HEAR ABOUT MAGGIE AND ME...
Jinx
"SHE THEN ASKED ME IF I STILL PAINTED, AND TO CHEER ME UP, OFFERED TO POSE FOR ME. IT WAS NEVER ANY SECRET TO HER HOW MUCH I'VE ALWAYS ADMIRED HER RATHER ROBUST PHYSIQUE. AND HEY, SHE WOULDN'T HAVE TO WORRY ABOUT ME, ALL I HAD ON MY MIND WAS MAGGIE...
SOMETIMES ANYWAY
"DANITA BECAME A REAL COMFORTING FRIEND AS THE DAYS PASSED. IT WASN'T UNTIL SHE OFFERED TO POSE NUDE THAT I REALIZED SHE WAS INTERESTED IN BEING SOMETHING MORE THAN A COMFORTING FRIEND...
BLACK BLACK BLACK
AFTER THAT, THINGS PRETTY MUCH FELL INTO PLACE. EVERYTHING'S COOL NOW. I MEAN, MAGGIE'S HAPPIER NOW WITH HOPEY, ISN'T SHE? I'M HAPPY WITH DANITA NOW...
SO WHAT'S THE FUCKING PROBLEM?
Shimom
4

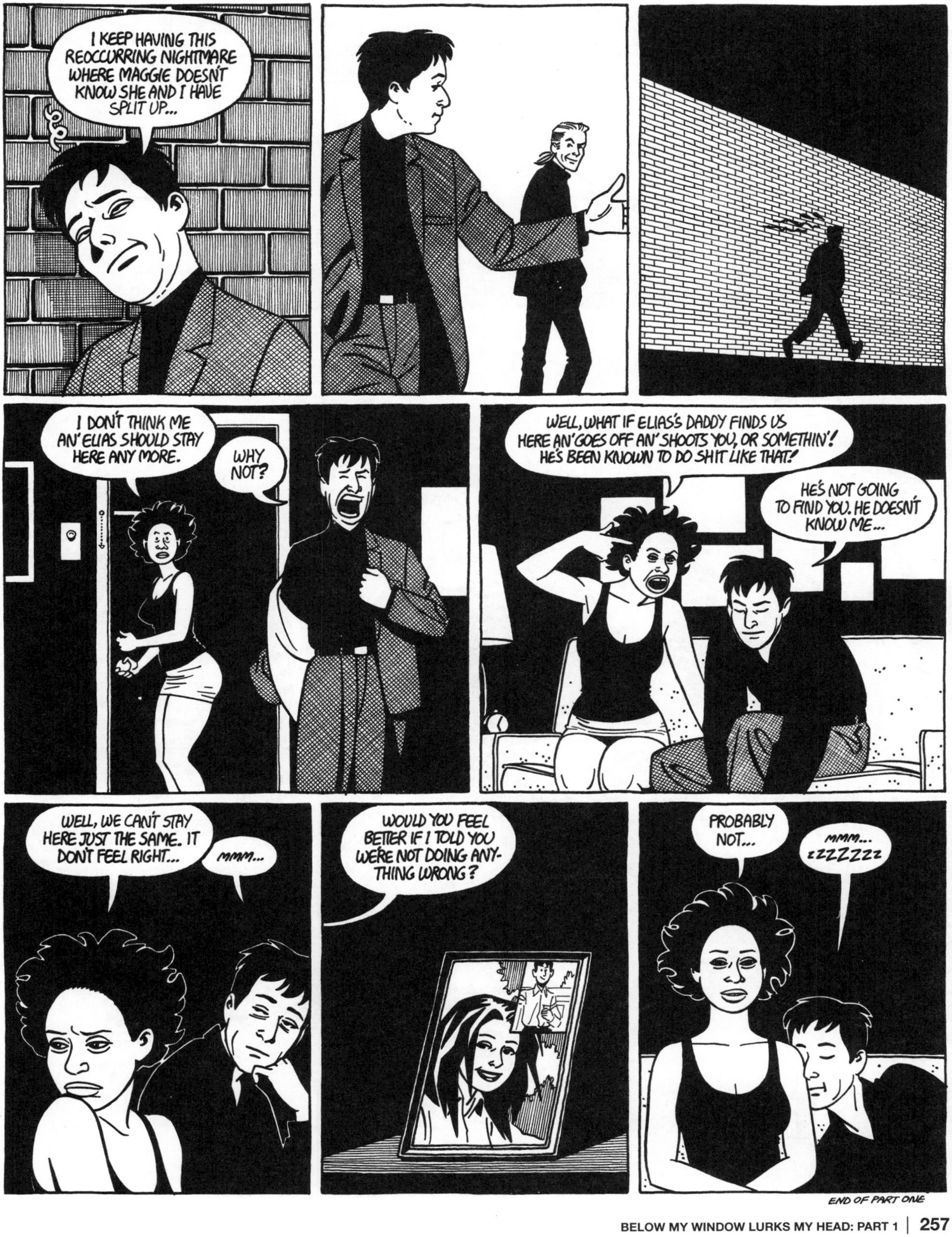
I KEEP HAVING THIS REOCCURRING NIGHTMARE WHERE MAGGIE DOESN'T KNOW SHE AND I HAVE SPLIT UP...
I DON'T THINK ME AN' ELIAS SHOULD STAY HERE ANY MORE.
WHY NOT?
WELL, WHAT IF ELIAS'S DADDY FINDS US HERE AN' GOES OFF AN' SHOOTS YOU, OR SOMETHIN'! HE'S BEEN KNOWN TO DO SHIT LIKE THAT!
HE'S NOT GOING TO FIND YOU. HE DOESN'T KNOW ME...
WELL, WE CAN'T STAY HERE JUST THE SAME. IT DON'T FEEL RIGHT...
MMM...
WOULD YOU FEEL BETTER IF I TOLD YOU WE'RE NOT DOING ANY-THING WRONG?
PROBABLY NOT...
MMM... ZZZZZZZ
END OF PART ONE

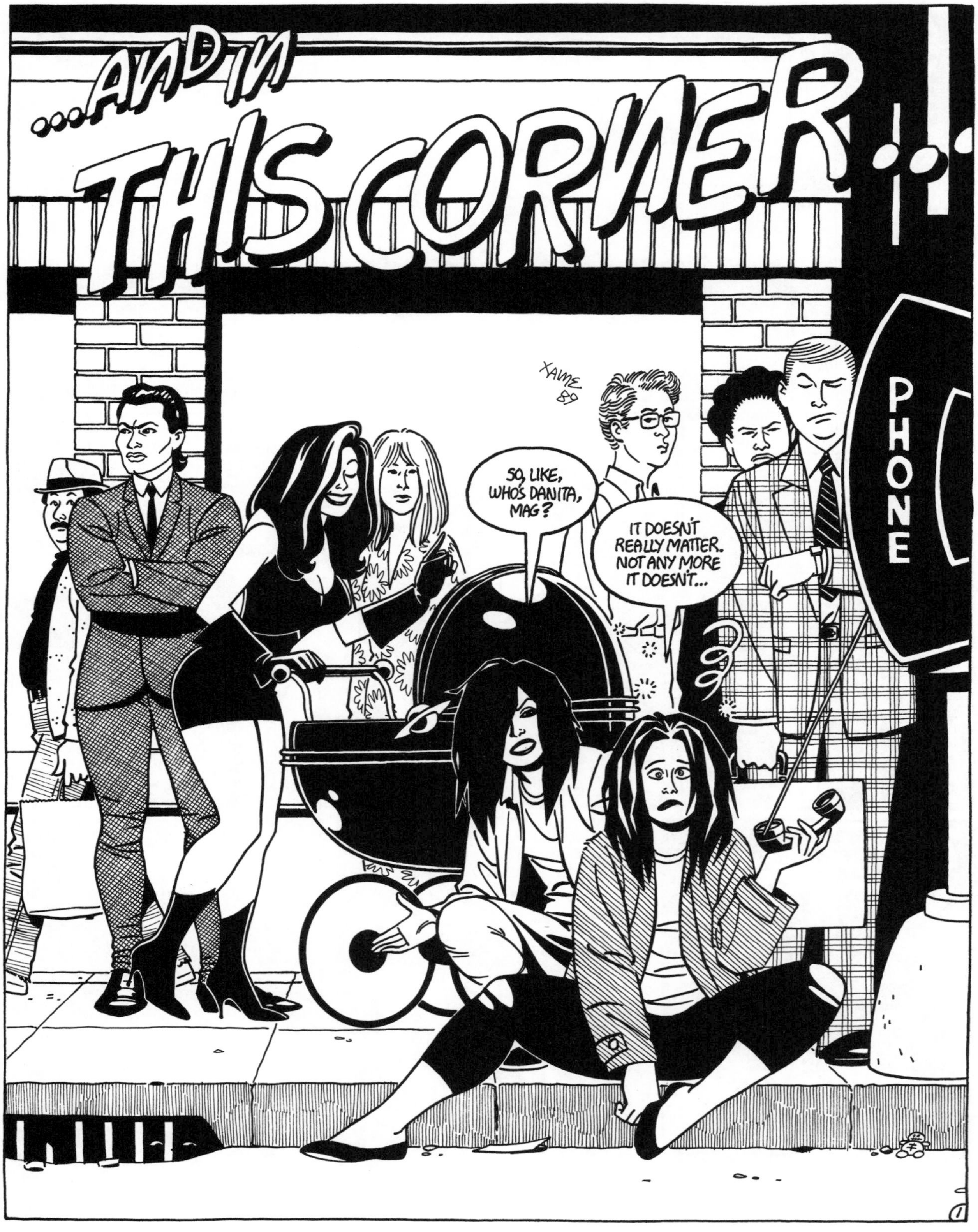
...AND IN THIS CORNER...
XAIME 89
SO, LIKE, WHO'S DANITA, MAG?
IT DOESN'T REALLY MATTER. NOT ANY MORE IT DOESN'T...
PHONE
1

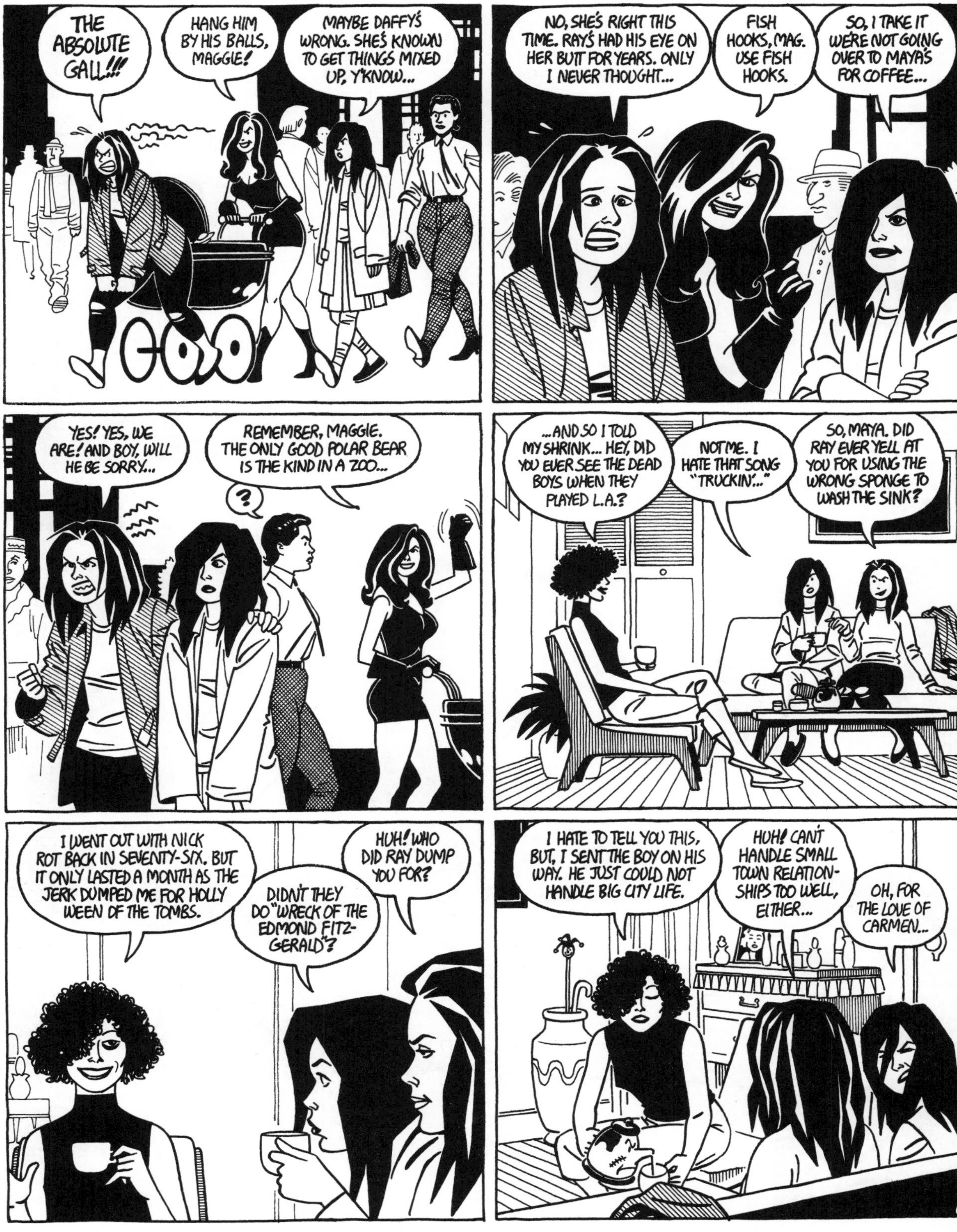
THE ABSOLUTE GALL!!!
HANG HIM BY HIS BALLS, MAGGIE!
MAYBE DAFFY'S WRONG. SHE'S KNOWN TO GET THINGS MIXED UP, Y'KNOW...
NO, SHE'S RIGHT THIS TIME. RAY'S HAD HIS EYE ON HER BUTT FOR YEARS. ONLY I NEVER THOUGHT...
FISH HOOKS, MAG. USE FISH HOOKS.
SO, I TAKE IT WE'RE NOT GOING OVER TO MAYA'S FOR COFFEE...
YES! YES, WE ARE! AND BOY, WILL HE BE SORRY...
REMEMBER, MAGGIE. THE ONLY GOOD POLAR BEAR IS THE KIND IN A ZOO...
?
...AND SO I TOLD MY SHRINK... HEY, DID YOU EVER SEE THE DEAD BOYS WHEN THEY PLAYED L.A.?
NOT ME. I HATE THAT SONG "TRUCKIN'..."
SO, MAYA. DID RAY EVER YELL AT YOU FOR USING THE WRONG SPONGE TO WASH THE SINK?
I WENT OUT WITH NICK ROT BACK IN SEVENTY-SIX. BUT IT ONLY LASTED A MONTH AS THE JERK DUMPED ME FOR HOLLY WEEN OF THE TOMBS.
DIDN'T THEY DO "WRECK OF THE EDMOND FITZ-GERALD"?
HUH! WHO DID RAY DUMP YOU FOR?
I HATE TO TELL YOU THIS, BUT, I SENT THE BOY ON HIS WAY. HE JUST COULD NOT HANDLE BIG CITY LIFE.
HUH! CAN'T HANDLE SMALL TOWN RELATION-SHIPS TOO WELL, EITHER...
OH, FOR THE LOVE OF CARMEN...
2

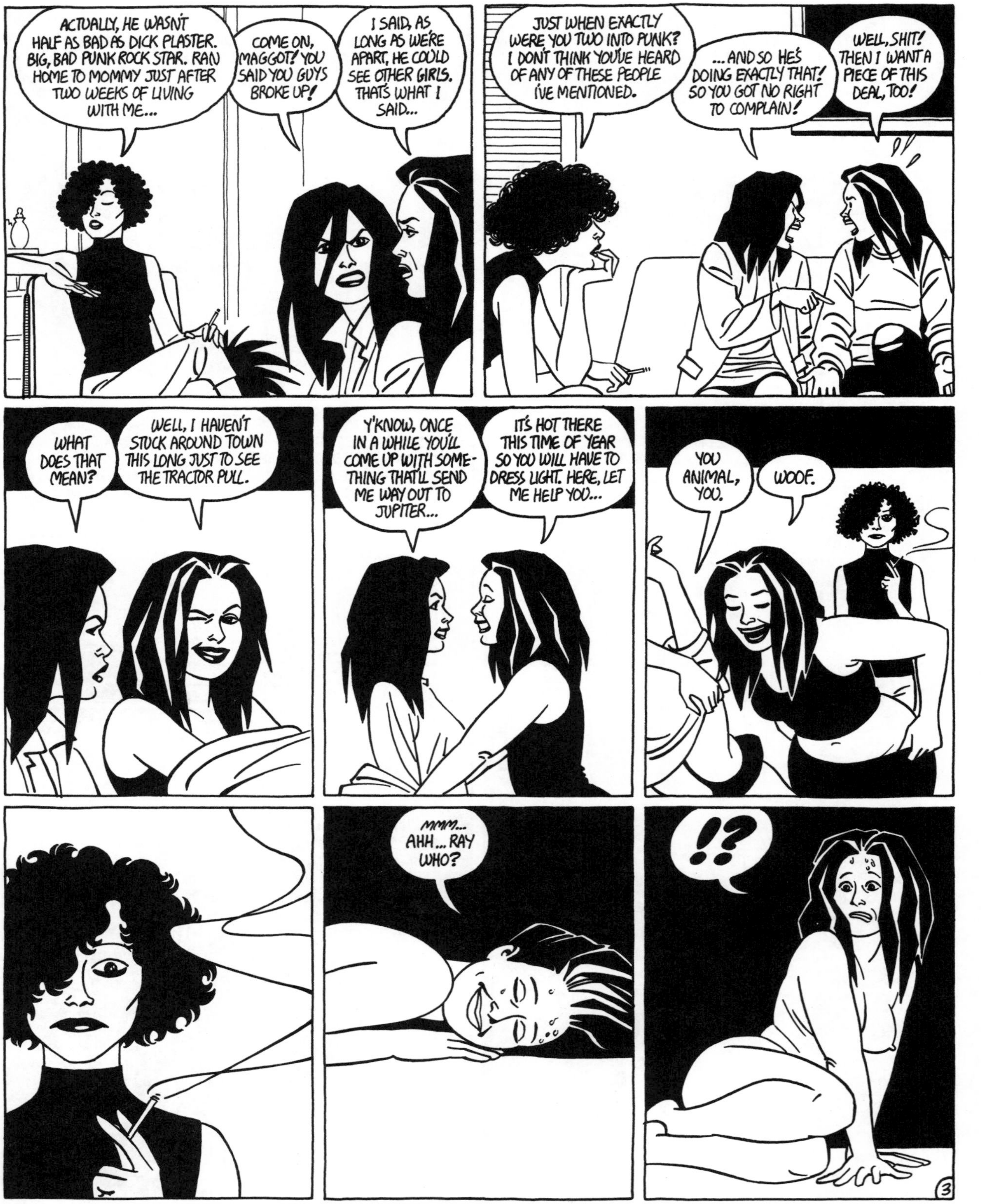
ACTUALLY, HE WASN'T HALF AS BAD AS DICK PLASTER. BIG, BAD PUNK ROCK STAR. RAN HOME TO MOMMY JUST AFTER TWO WEEKS OF LIVING WITH ME...
COME ON, MAGGOT! YOU SAID YOU GUYS BROKE UP!
I SAID, AS LONG AS WE'RE APART, HE COULD SEE OTHER GIRLS. THAT'S WHAT I SAID...
JUST WHEN EXACTLY WERE YOU TWO INTO PUNK? I DON'T THINK YOU'VE HEARD OF ANY OF THESE PEOPLE I'VE MENTIONED.
...AND SO HE'S DOING EXACTLY THAT! SO YOU GOT NO RIGHT TO COMPLAIN!
WELL, SHIT! THEN I WANT A PIECE OF THIS DEAL, TOO!
WHAT DOES THAT MEAN?
WELL, I HAVEN'T STUCK AROUND TOWN THIS LONG JUST TO SEE THE TRACTOR PULL.
Y'KNOW, ONCE IN A WHILE YOU'LL COME UP WITH SOME-THING THAT'LL SEND ME WAY OUT TO JUPITER...
IT'S HOT THERE THIS TIME OF YEAR SO YOU WILL HAVE TO DRESS LIGHT. HERE, LET ME HELP YOU...
YOU ANIMAL, YOU.
WOOF.
MMM... AHH... RAY WHO?
!?
3

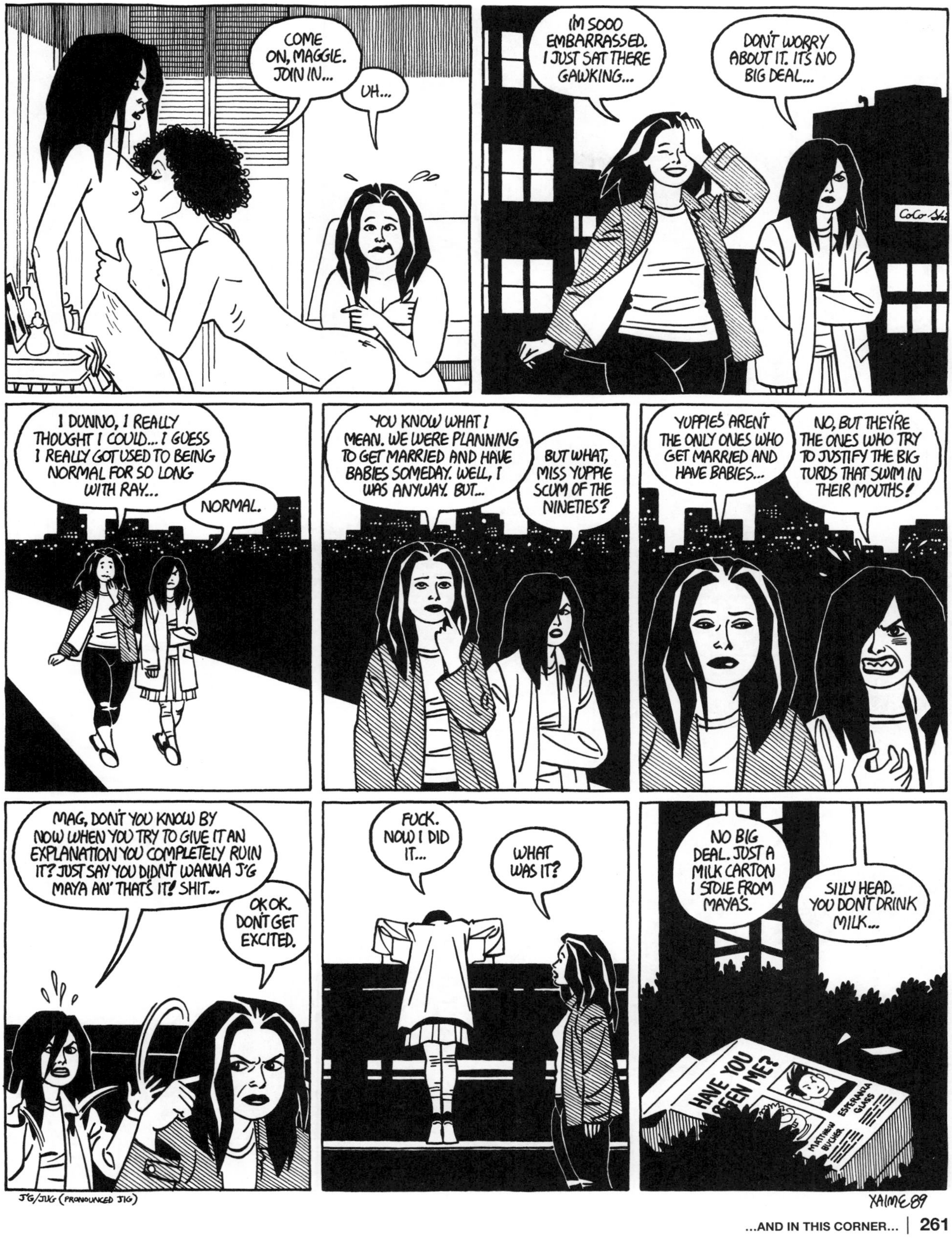
COME ON, MAGGIE. JOIN IN...
UH...
I'M SOOO EMBARRASSED. I JUST SAT THERE GAWKING...
DON'T WORRY ABOUT IT. IT'S NO BIG DEAL...
I DUNNO, I REALLY THOUGHT I COULD... I GUESS I REALLY GOT USED TO BEING NORMAL FOR SO LONG WITH RAY...
NORMAL.
YOU KNOW WHAT I MEAN. WE WERE PLANNING TO GET MARRIED AND HAVE BABIES SOMEDAY. WELL, I WAS ANYWAY. BUT...
BUT WHAT, MISS YUPPIE SCUM OF THE NINETIES?
YUPPIE'S AREN'T THE ONLY ONES WHO GET MARRIED AND HAVE BABIES...
NO, BUT THEY'RE THE ONES WHO TRY TO JUSTIFY THE BIG TURDS THAT SWIM IN THEIR MOUTHS!
MAG, DON'T YOU KNOW BY NOW WHEN YOU TRY TO GIVE IT AN EXPLANATION YOU COMPLETELY RUIN IT? JUST SAY YOU DIDN'T WANNA J'G MAYA AN' THAT'S IT! SHIT...
OK OK. DON'T GET EXCITED.
FUCK. NOW I DID IT...
WHAT WAS IT?
NO BIG DEAL. JUST A MILK CARTON I STOLE FROM MAYA'S.
SILLY HEAD. YOU DON'T DRINK MILK...
HAVE YOU
ESPERANZA GLASS
MATTHEW BUCHER

J'G/JUG (PRONOUNCED JIG)

XAIME 89

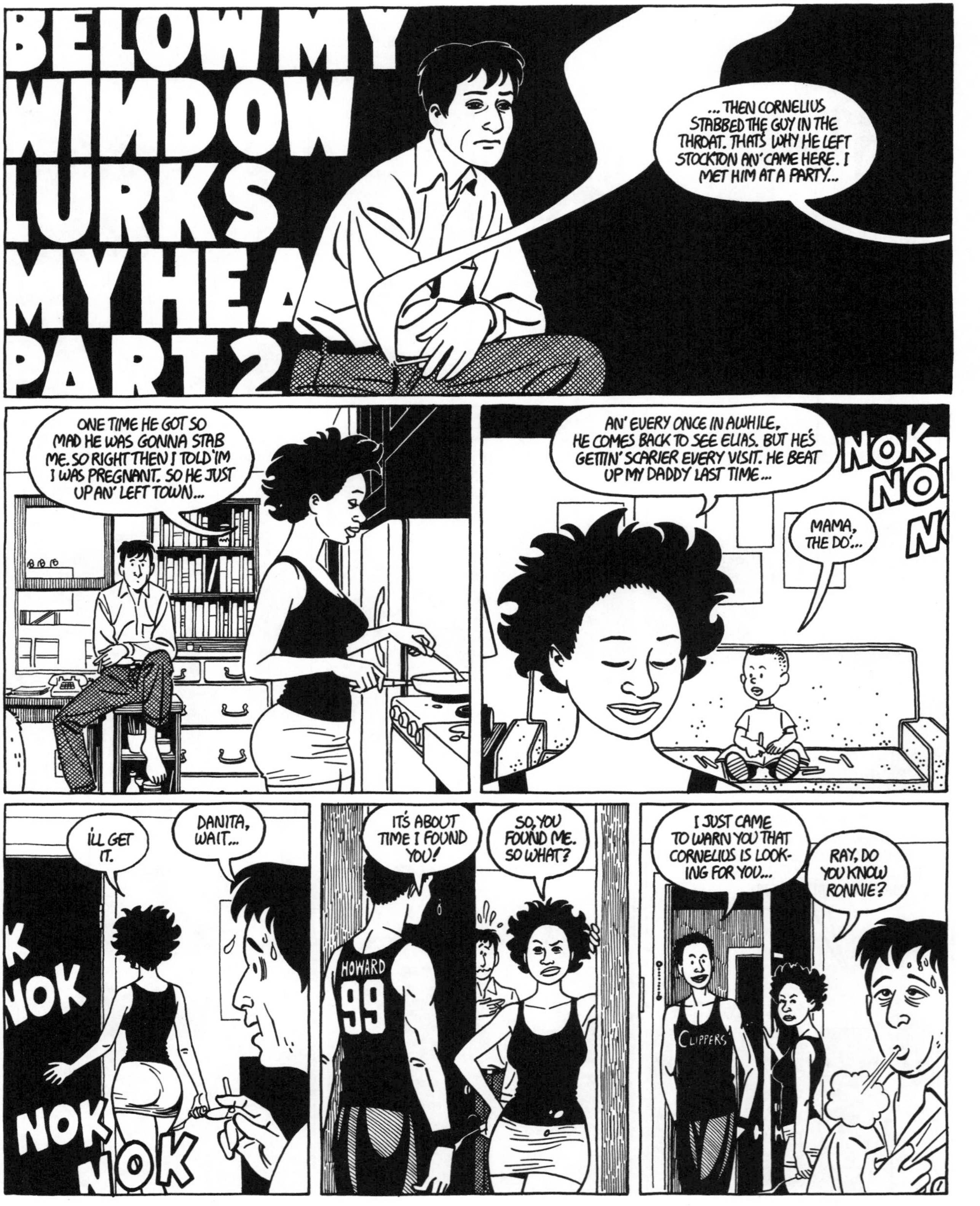
BELOW MY WINDOW LURKS MY HEA
PART 2
... THEN CORNELIUS STABBED THE GUY IN THE THROAT. THAT'S WHY HE LEFT STOCKTON AN' CAME HERE. I MET HIM AT A PARTY...
ONE TIME HE GOT SO MAD HE WAS GONNA STAB ME. SO RIGHT THEN I TOLD 'IM I WAS PREGNANT. SO HE JUST UP AN' LEFT TOWN...
AN' EVERY ONCE IN AWHILE, HE COMES BACK TO SEE ELIAS. BUT HE'S GETTIN' SCARIER EVERY VISIT. HE BEAT UP MY DADDY LAST TIME...
NOK
MAMA, THE DO'...
I'LL GET IT.
DANITA, WAIT...
NOK
NOK NOK
IT'S ABOUT TIME I FOUND YOU!
SO, YOU FOUND ME. SO WHAT?
HOWARD
99
I JUST CAME TO WARN YOU THAT CORNELIUS IS LOOKING FOR YOU...
RAY, DO YOU KNOW RONNIE?
CLIPPERS

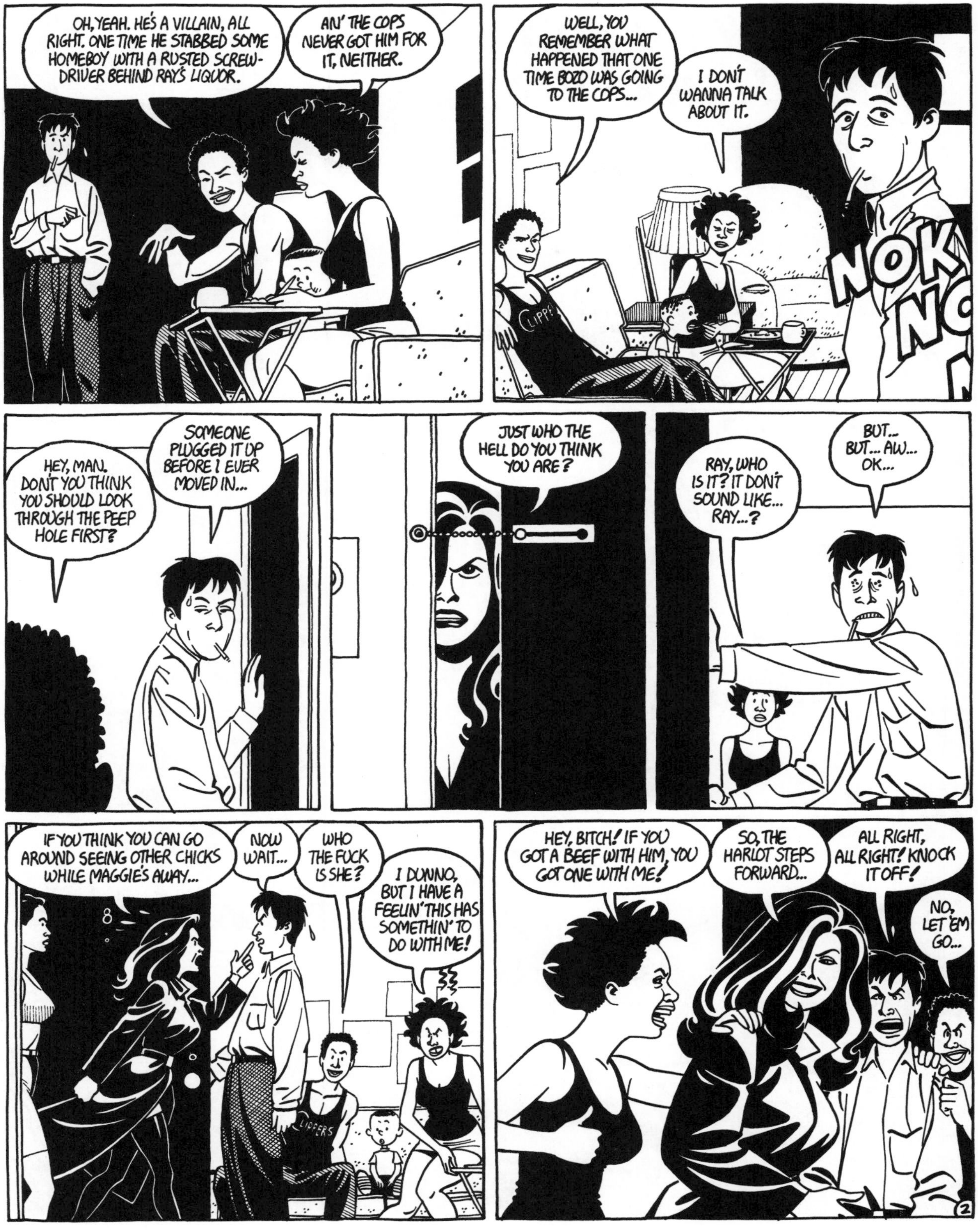
OH, YEAH. HE'S A VILLAIN, ALL RIGHT. ONE TIME HE STABBED SOME HOMEBOY WITH A RUSTED SCREW-DRIVER BEHIND RAY'S LIQUOR.
AN' THE COPS NEVER GOT HIM FOR IT, NEITHER.
WELL, YOU REMEMBER WHAT HAPPENED THAT ONE TIME BOZO WAS GOING TO THE COPS...
I DON'T WANNA TALK ABOUT IT.
NOK
NO
HEY, MAN. DON'T YOU THINK YOU SHOULD LOOK THROUGH THE PEEP HOLE FIRST?
SOMEONE PLUGGED IT UP BEFORE I EVER MOVED IN...
JUST WHO THE HELL DO YOU THINK YOU ARE?
RAY, WHO IS IT? IT DON'T SOUND LIKE... RAY...?
BUT... BUT... AW... OK...
IF YOU THINK YOU CAN GO AROUND SEEING OTHER CHICKS WHILE MAGGIE'S AWAY...
NOW WAIT...
WHO THE FUCK IS SHE?
I DUNNO, BUT I HAVE A FEELIN' THIS HAS SOMETHIN' TO DO WITH ME!
HEY, BITCH! IF YOU GOT A BEEF WITH HIM, YOU GOT ONE WITH ME!
SO, THE HARLOT STEPS FORWARD...
ALL RIGHT, ALL RIGHT! KNOCK IT OFF!
NO, LET 'EM GO...
2

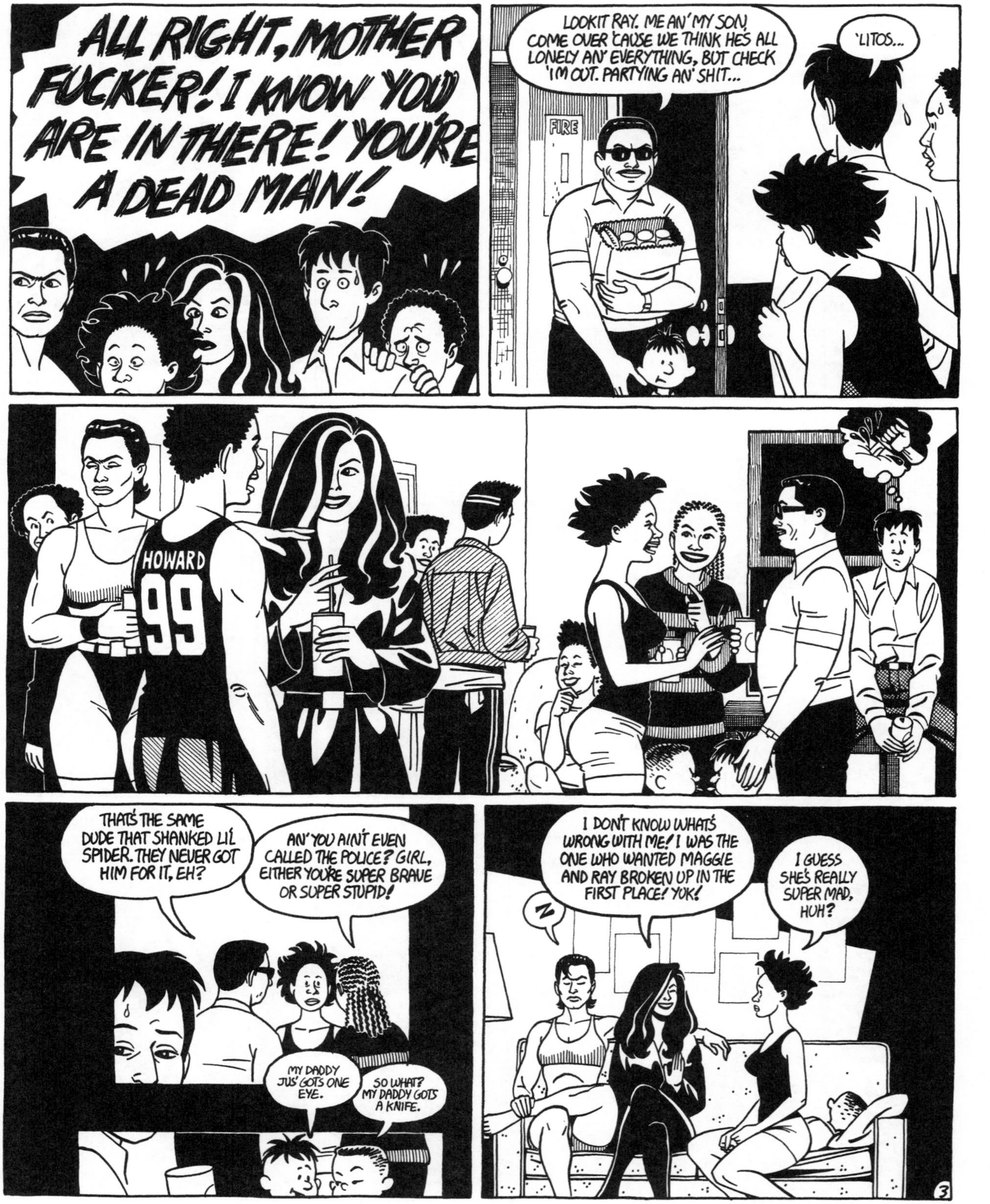
ALL RIGHT, MOTHER FUCKER! I KNOW YOU ARE IN THERE! YOU'RE A DEAD MAN!
LOOKIT RAY. ME AN' MY SON COME OVER 'CAUSE WE THINK HE'S ALL LONELY AN' EVERYTHING, BUT CHECK 'IM OUT. PARTYING AN' SHIT...
FIRE
'LITOS...
HOWARD
99
THAT'S THE SAME DUDE THAT SHANKED LI'L SPIDER. THEY NEVER GOT HIM FOR IT, EH?
AN' YOU AIN'T EVEN CALLED THE POLICE? GIRL, EITHER YOU'RE SUPER BRAVE OR SUPER STUPID!
MY DADDY JUS' GOTS ONE EYE.
SO WHAT? MY DADDY GOTS A KNIFE.
I DON'T KNOW WHAT'S WRONG WITH ME! I WAS THE ONE WHO WANTED MAGGIE AND RAY BROKEN UP IN THE FIRST PLACE! YOK!
Z
I GUESS SHE'S REALLY SUPER MAD, HUH?
3

MAD? NAW, I'LL BET BY NOW SHE'S EVEN FORGOTTEN HIS NAME. HATE TO SAY IT, GUY, BUT YOU'RE JUST NO HOPEY.

ANYWAY, I HOPE YOU TWO HAVE A WONDERFUL, LASTING RELATIONSHIP EVEN THOUGH WHAT'S-HIS-NAME WITH THE KNIFE WILL DO EVERYTHING IN HIS POWER TO TRY AND STOP IT.

JUST KIDDING...

WELL, IT'S LATE, SO WE BETTER GET GOING. ELIAS, LET'S GO. GET YOUR JACKET...

WE GOIN' HOME NOW?

≥ AHEM ≤

BABY, I NEVER WANTED TO GET YOU INVOLVED IN THIS. YOU DON'T WANT ANY PART OF MY TROUBLES.

WHY DON'T YOU LET ME DECIDE ON WHAT I WANT AND DON'T WANT.

HEY, DON'T GET MAD. IT'S NOT LIKE I'M GONNA FORGET YOU OR ANYTHING. I'LL BE AROUND. I PROMISE.

C'MON, ELIAS.

CAN WE GO TO CARLOS'S HOUSE TO-MORROW? HE SAID HIS DADDY GOTS JUST ONE EYE...

④

WHERE THEY AT?

OK, EDWARDS. DON'T MOVE A MUSCLE OR YOU'RE FUCKING DEAD MEAT...

CLICK! CLICK! CLICK!

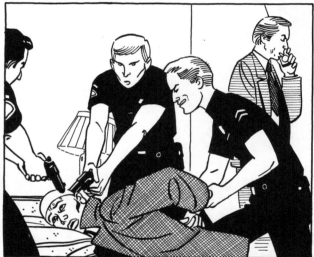

TELL ELIAS HIS DADDY SAID HI.

THE END

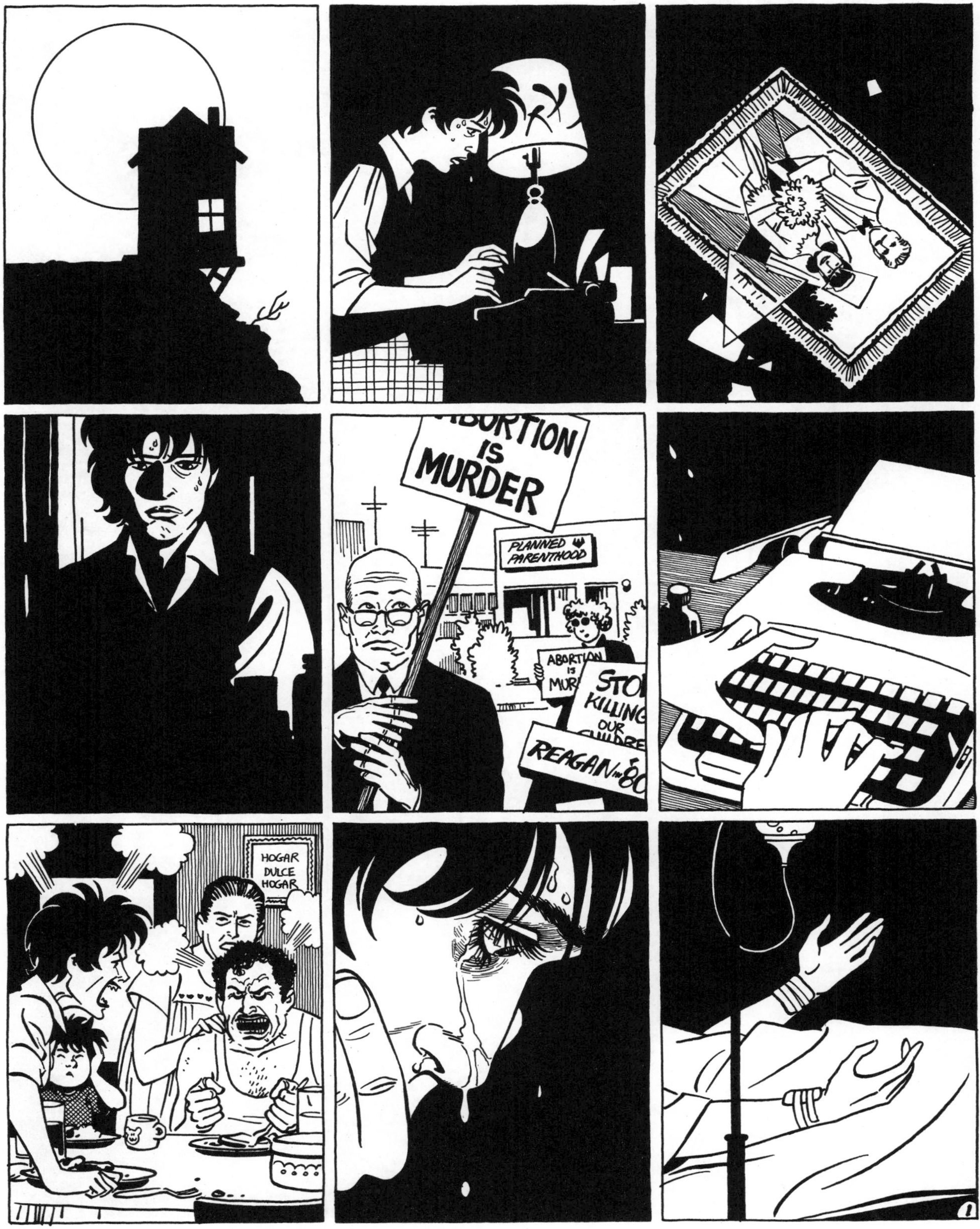
ABORTION IS MURDER
PLANNED PARENTHOOD
ABORTION IS MUR
STO
KILLING OUR
REAGAN
HOGAR DULCE HOGAR

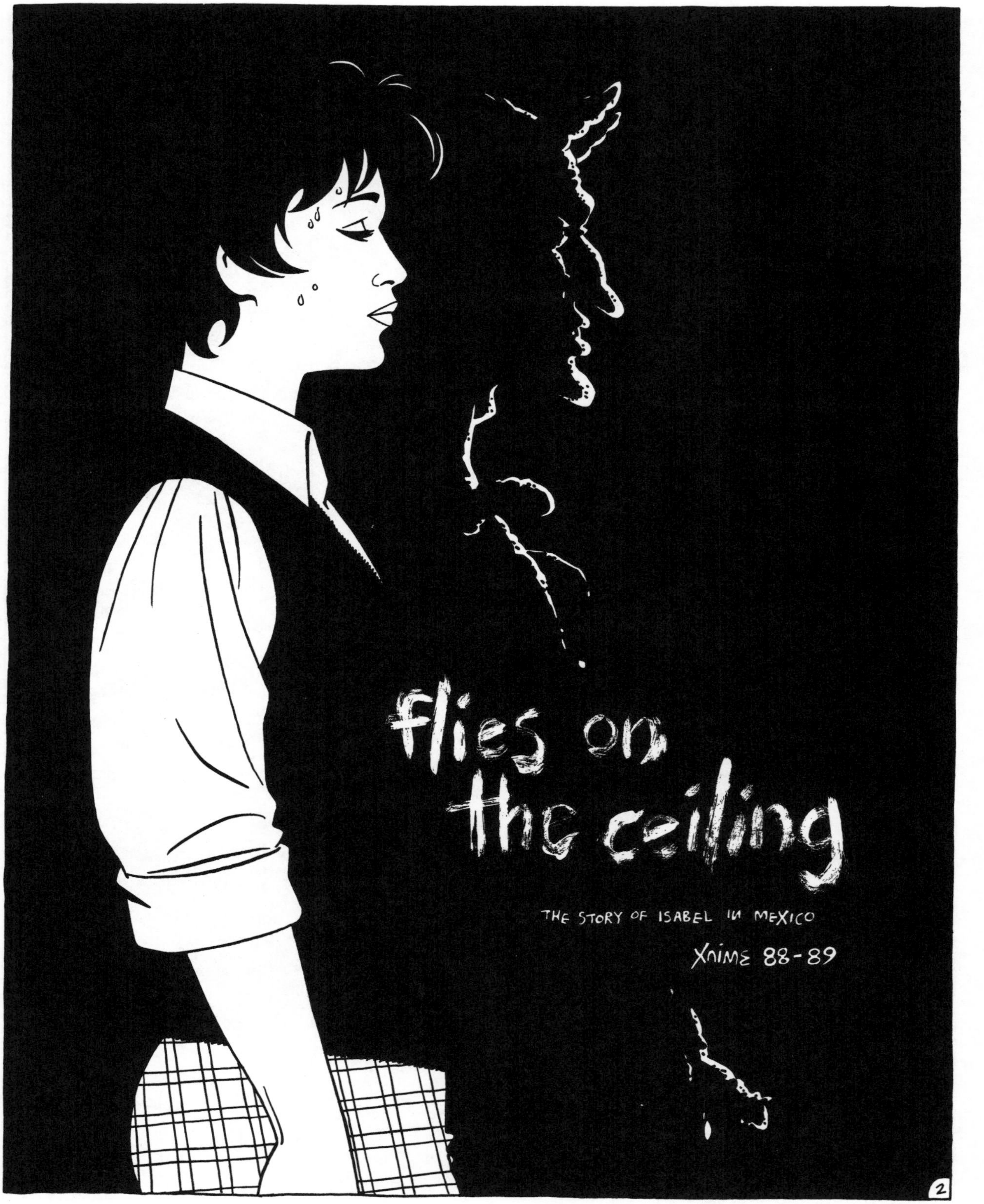
flies on the ceiling
THE STORY OF ISABEL IN MEXICO
Xaime 88-89
2

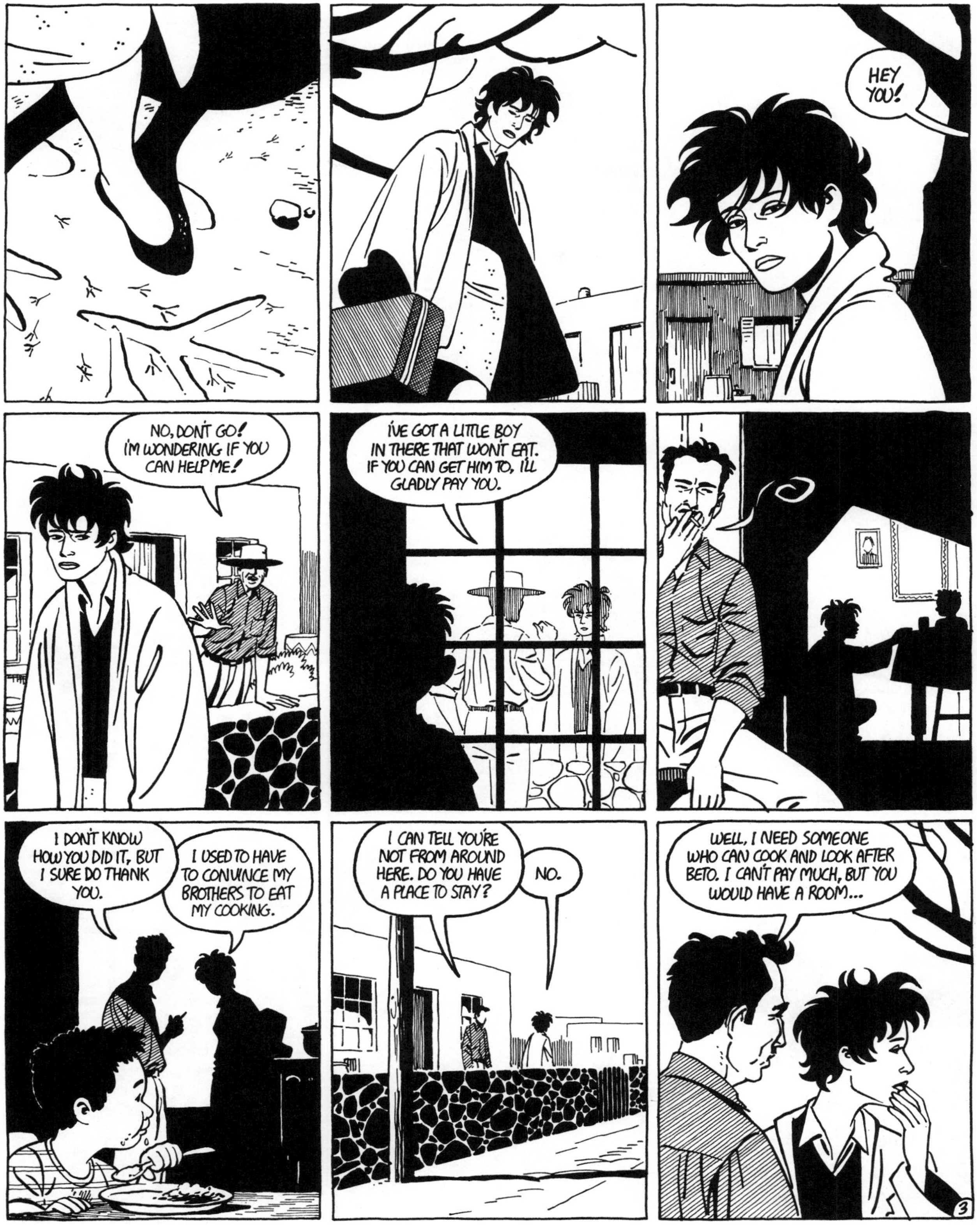
HEY YOU!
NO, DON'T GO! I'M WONDERING IF YOU CAN HELP ME!
I'VE GOT A LITTLE BOY IN THERE THAT WON'T EAT. IF YOU CAN GET HIM TO, I'LL GLADLY PAY YOU.
I DON'T KNOW HOW YOU DID IT, BUT I SURE DO THANK YOU.
I USED TO HAVE TO CONVINCE MY BROTHERS TO EAT MY COOKING.
I CAN TELL YOU'RE NOT FROM AROUND HERE. DO YOU HAVE A PLACE TO STAY?
NO.
WELL, I NEED SOMEONE WHO CAN COOK AND LOOK AFTER BETO. I CAN'T PAY MUCH, BUT YOU WOULD HAVE A ROOM...
3

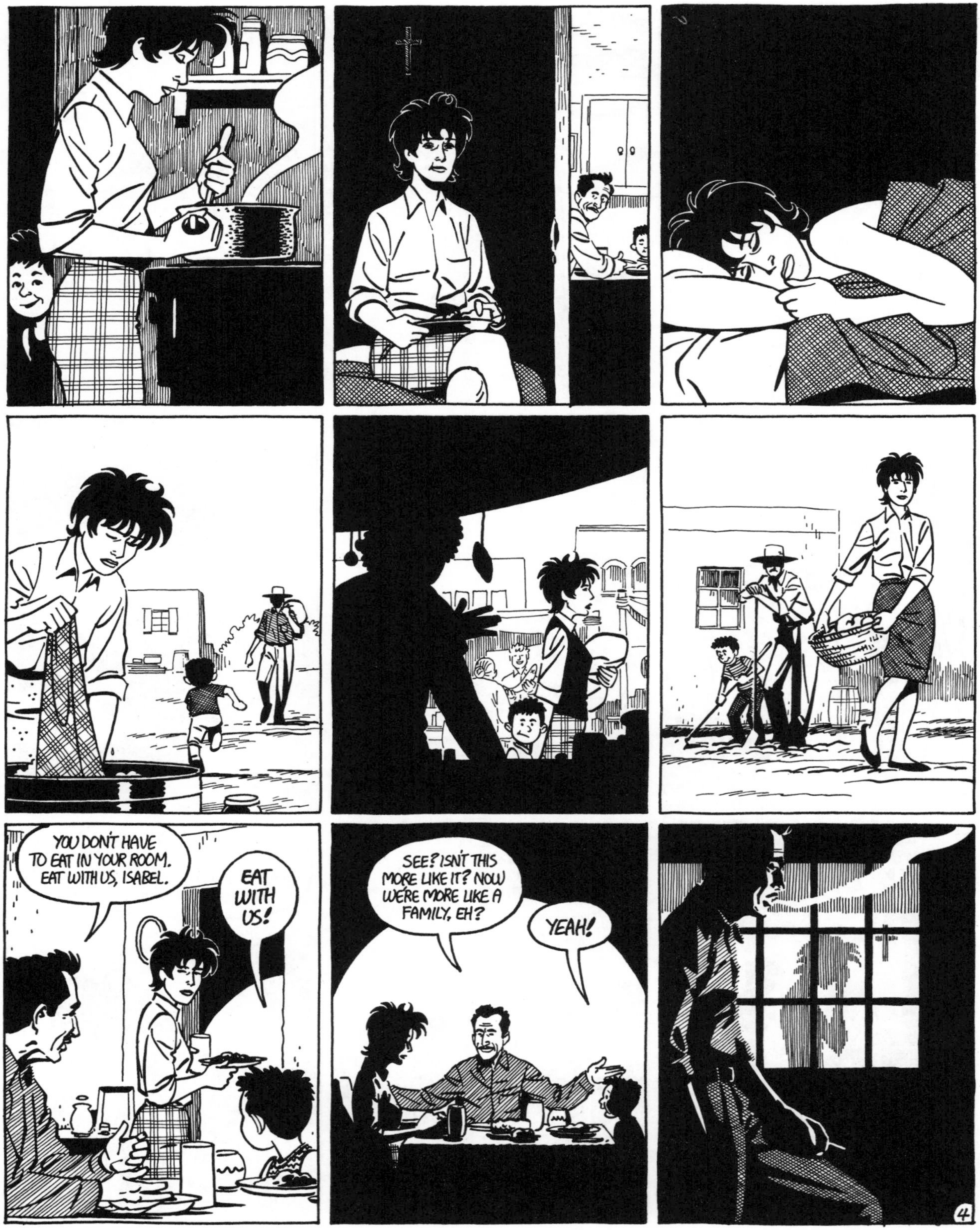
YOU DON'T HAVE TO EAT IN YOUR ROOM. EAT WITH US, ISABEL.
EAT WITH US!
SEE? ISN'T THIS MORE LIKE IT? NOW WE'RE MORE LIKE A FAMILY, EH?
YEAH!
4

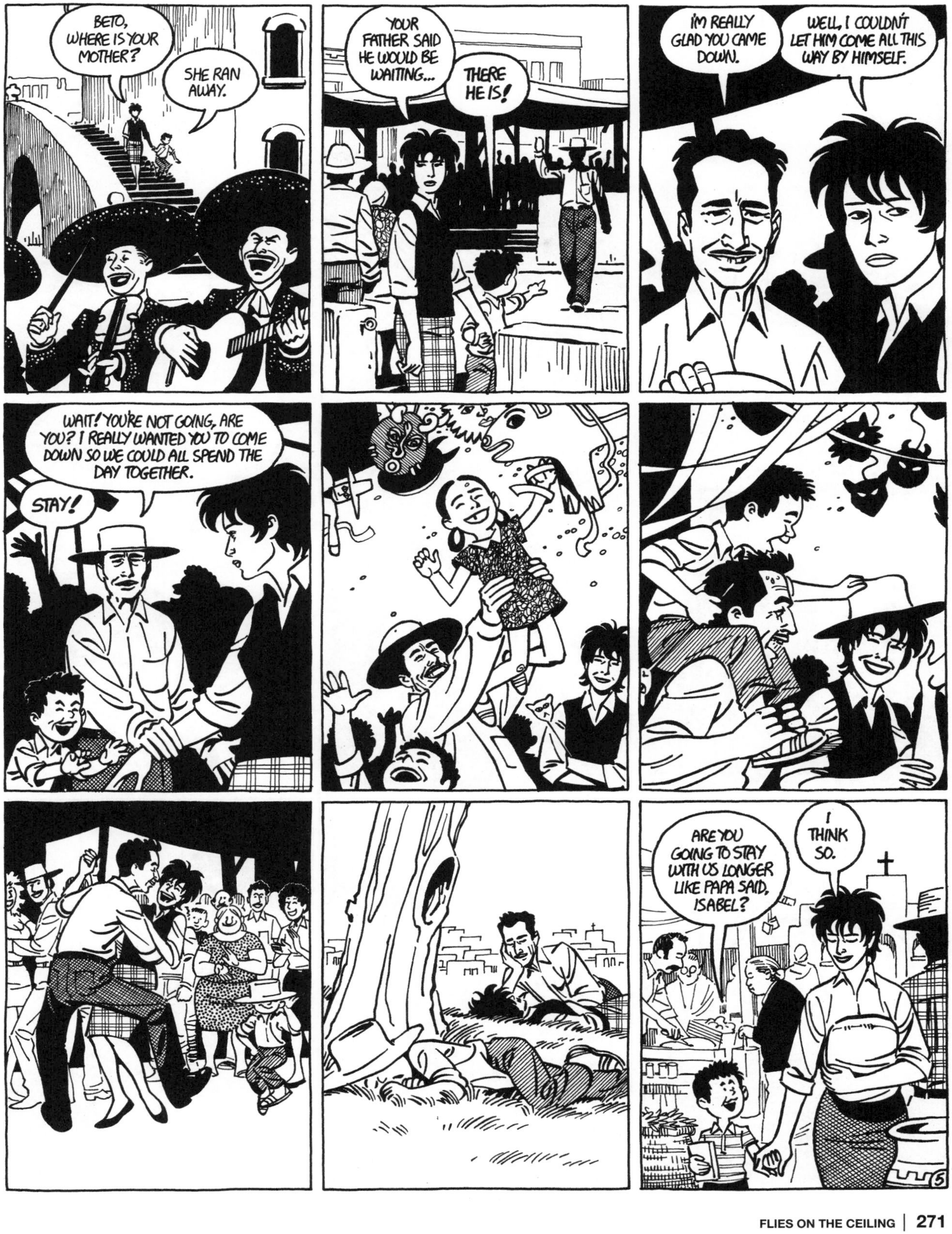
BETO, WHERE IS YOUR MOTHER?
SHE RAN AWAY.
YOUR FATHER SAID HE WOULD BE WAITING...
THERE HE IS!
I'M REALLY GLAD YOU CAME DOWN.
WELL, I COULDN'T LET HIM COME ALL THIS WAY BY HIMSELF.
WAIT! YOU'RE NOT GOING, ARE YOU? I REALLY WANTED YOU TO COME DOWN SO WE COULD ALL SPEND THE DAY TOGETHER.
STAY!
ARE YOU GOING TO STAY WITH US LONGER LIKE PAPA SAID, ISABEL?
I THINK SO.
5

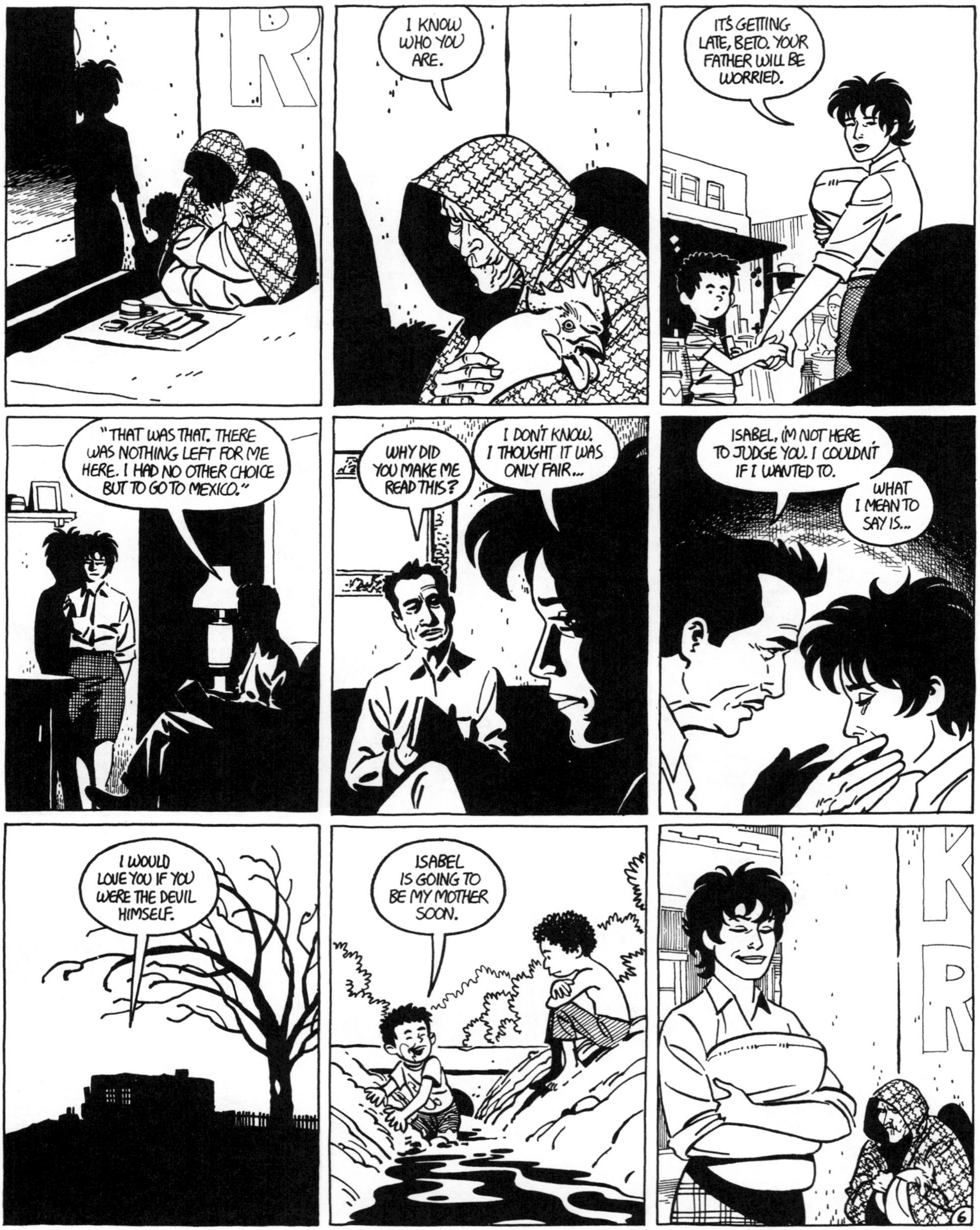
I KNOW WHO YOU ARE.
IT'S GETTING LATE, BETO. YOUR FATHER WILL BE WORRIED.
"THAT WAS THAT. THERE WAS NOTHING LEFT FOR ME HERE. I HAD NO OTHER CHOICE BUT TO GO TO MEXICO."
WHY DID YOU MAKE ME READ THIS?
I DON'T KNOW. I THOUGHT IT WAS ONLY FAIR...
ISABEL, I'M NOT HERE TO JUDGE YOU. I COULDN'T IF I WANTED TO.
WHAT I MEAN TO SAY IS...
I WOULD LOVE YOU IF YOU WERE THE DEVIL HIMSELF.
ISABEL IS GOING TO BE MY MOTHER SOON.
6

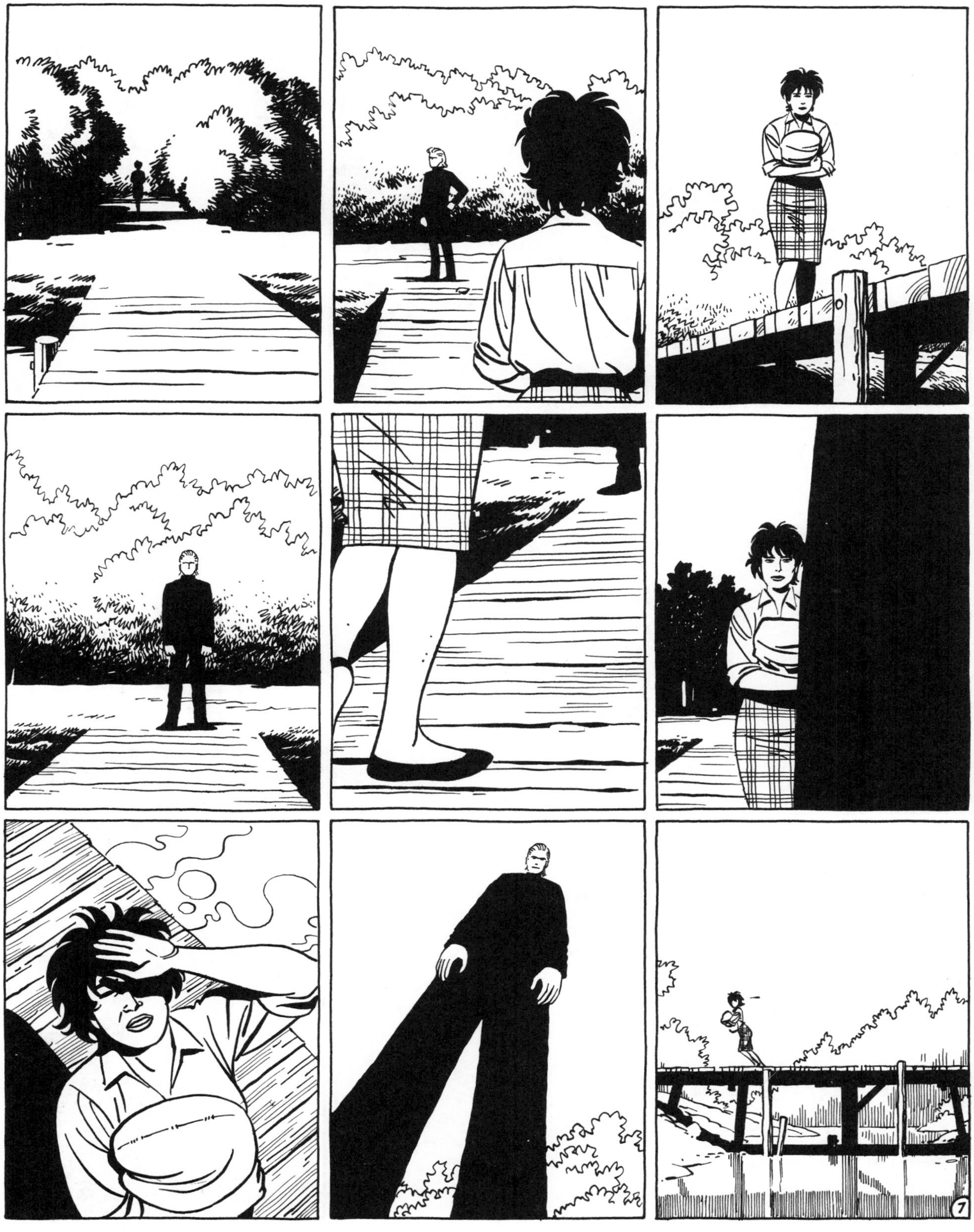
7

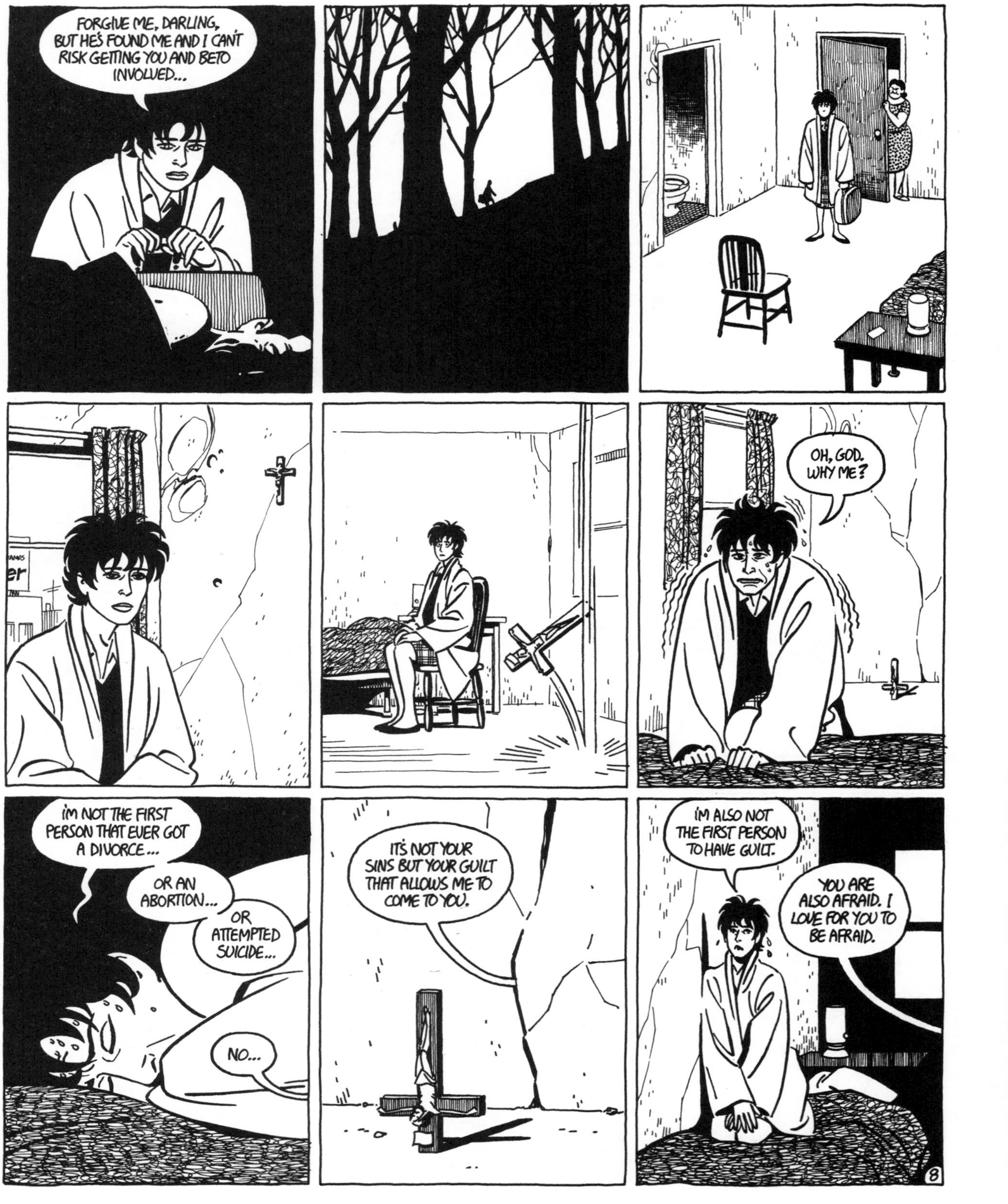
FORGIVE ME, DARLING, BUT HE'S FOUND ME AND I CAN'T RISK GETTING YOU AND BETO INVOLVED...
OH, GOD. WHY ME?
I'M NOT THE FIRST PERSON THAT EVER GOT A DIVORCE...
OR AN ABORTION...
OR ATTEMPTED SUICIDE...
NO...
IT'S NOT YOUR SINS BUT YOUR GUILT THAT ALLOWS ME TO COME TO YOU.
I'M ALSO NOT THE FIRST PERSON TO HAVE GUILT.
YOU ARE ALSO AFRAID. I LOVE FOR YOU TO BE AFRAID.
8

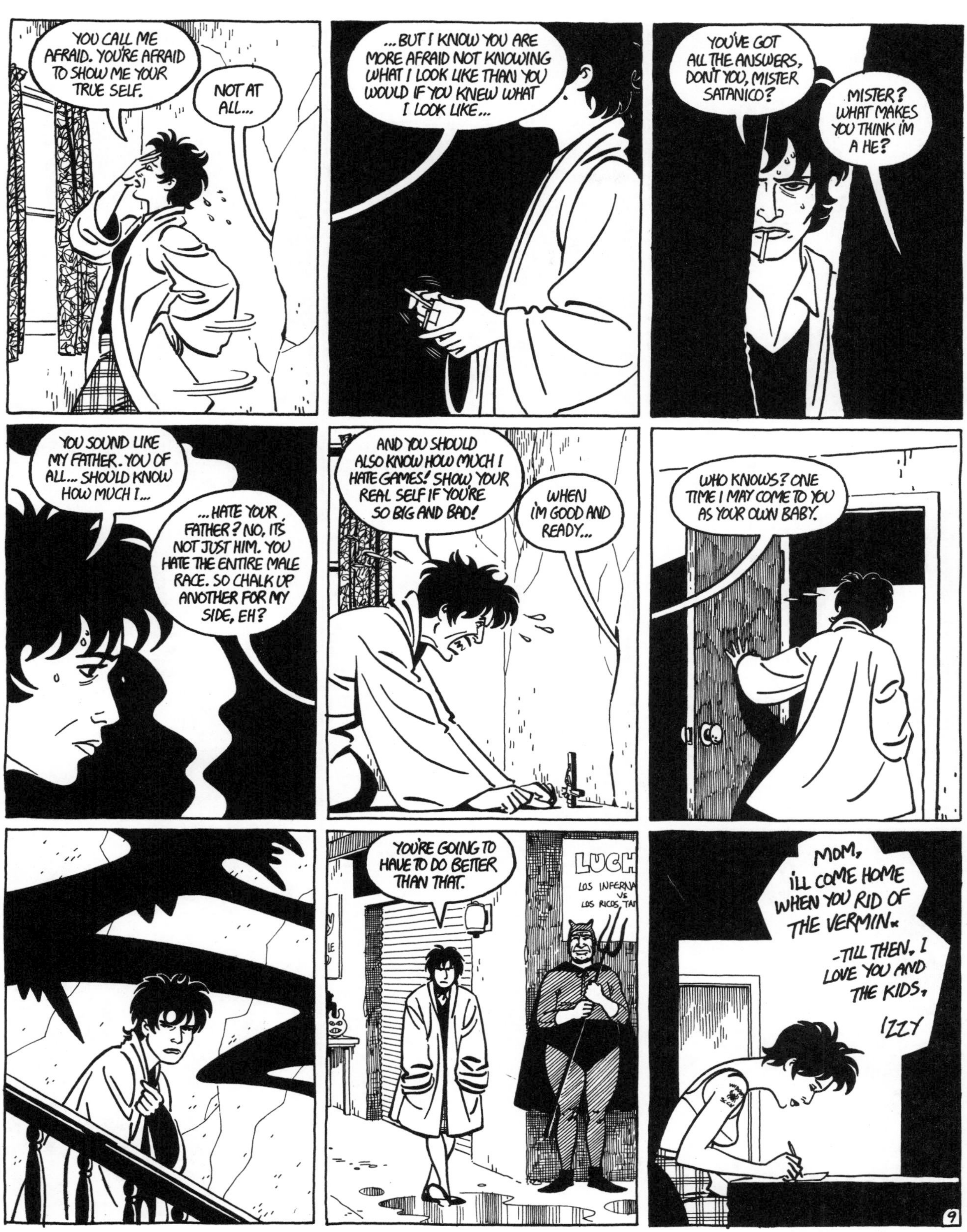

YOU CALL ME AFRAID. YOU'RE AFRAID TO SHOW ME YOUR TRUE SELF.
NOT AT ALL...
...BUT I KNOW YOU ARE MORE AFRAID NOT KNOWING WHAT I LOOK LIKE THAN YOU WOULD IF YOU KNEW WHAT I LOOK LIKE...
YOU'VE GOT ALL THE ANSWERS, DON'T YOU, MISTER SATANICO?
MISTER? WHAT MAKES YOU THINK I'M A HE?
YOU SOUND LIKE MY FATHER. YOU OF ALL... SHOULD KNOW HOW MUCH I...
...HATE YOUR FATHER? NO, IT'S NOT JUST HIM. YOU HATE THE ENTIRE MALE RACE. SO CHALK UP ANOTHER FOR MY SIDE, EH?
AND YOU SHOULD ALSO KNOW HOW MUCH I HATE GAMES! SHOW YOUR REAL SELF IF YOU'RE SO BIG AND BAD!
WHEN I'M GOOD AND READY...
WHO KNOWS? ONE TIME I MAY COME TO YOU AS YOUR OWN BABY.
YOU'RE GOING TO HAVE TO DO BETTER THAN THAT.
MOM, I'LL COME HOME WHEN YOU RID OF THE VERMIN.
-TILL THEN, I LOVE YOU AND THE KIDS,
IZZY
9

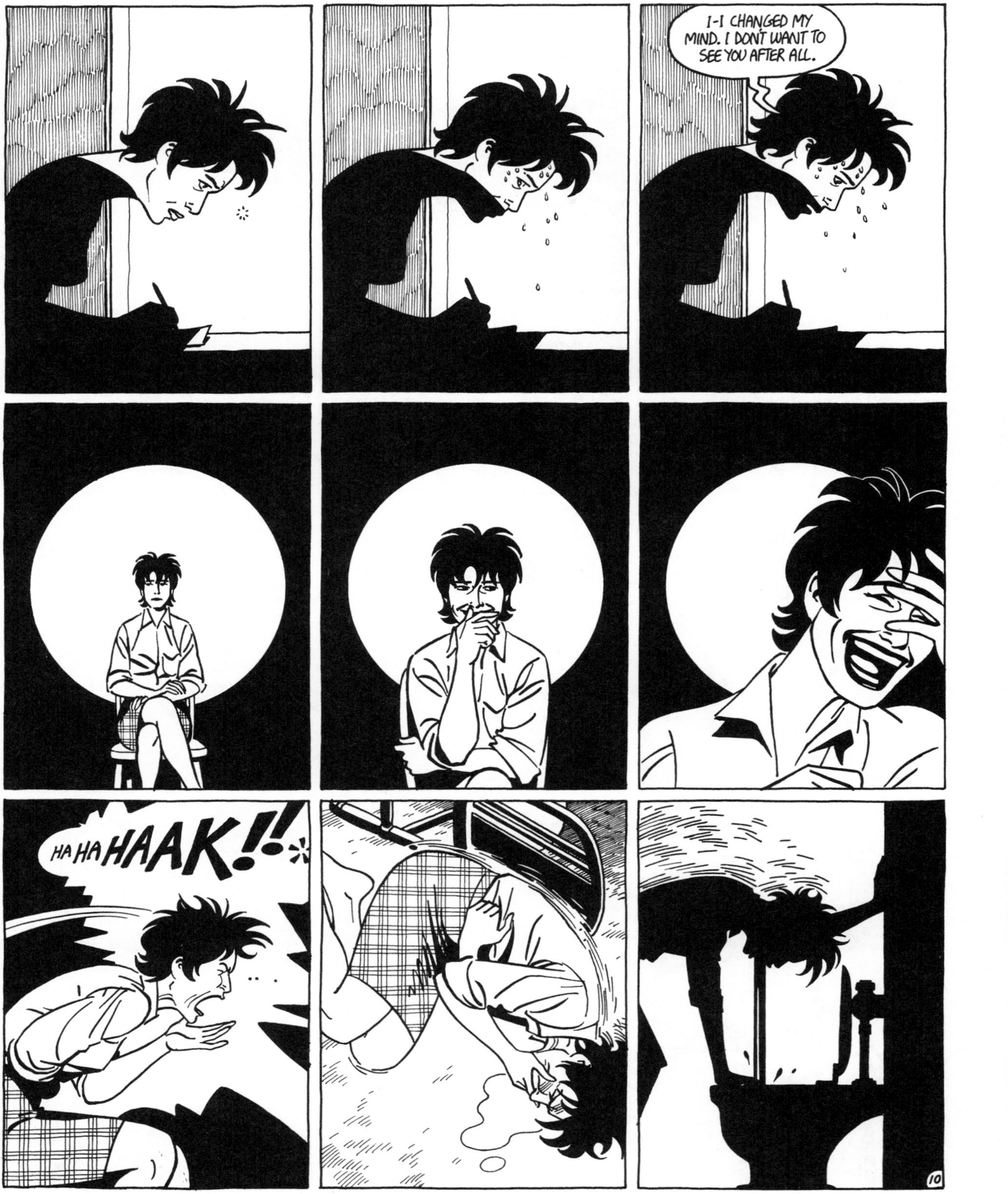
I-I CHANGED MY MIND. I DON'T WANT TO SEE YOU AFTER ALL.
HA HA HAAK!!
10

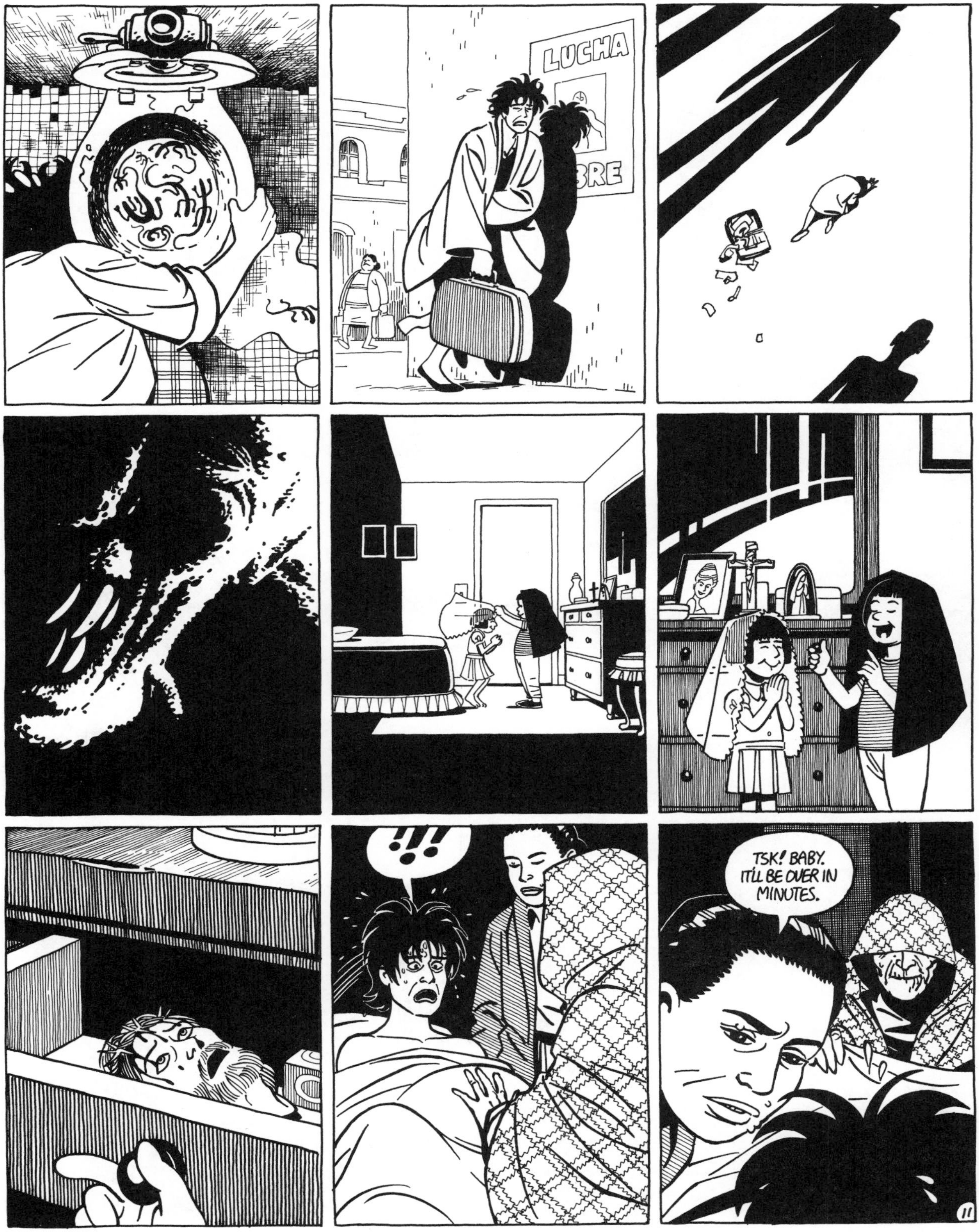
LUCHA
!!!
TSK! BABY. IT'LL BE OVER IN MINUTES.
11

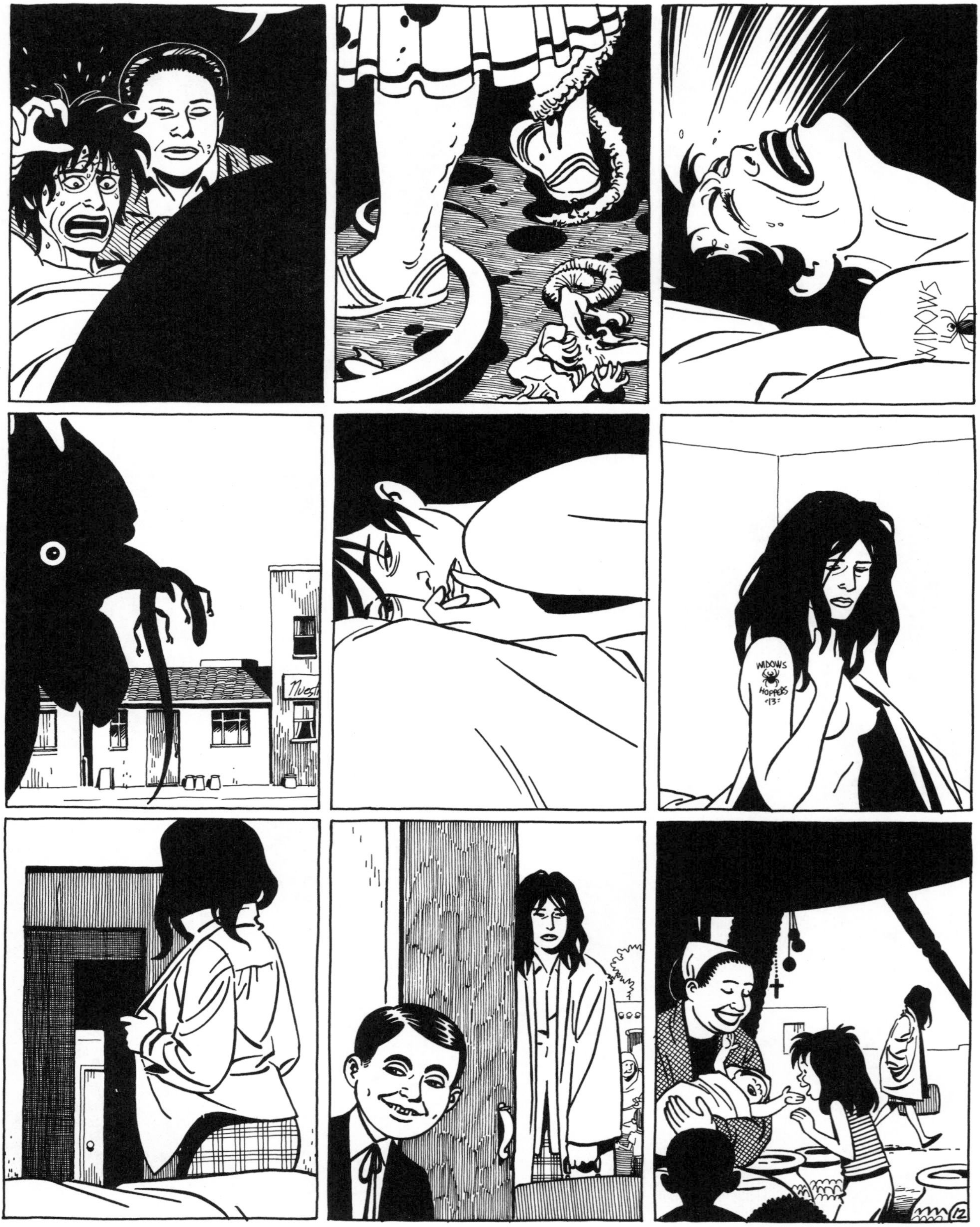
WIDOWS
WIDOWS
HOPPERS
13

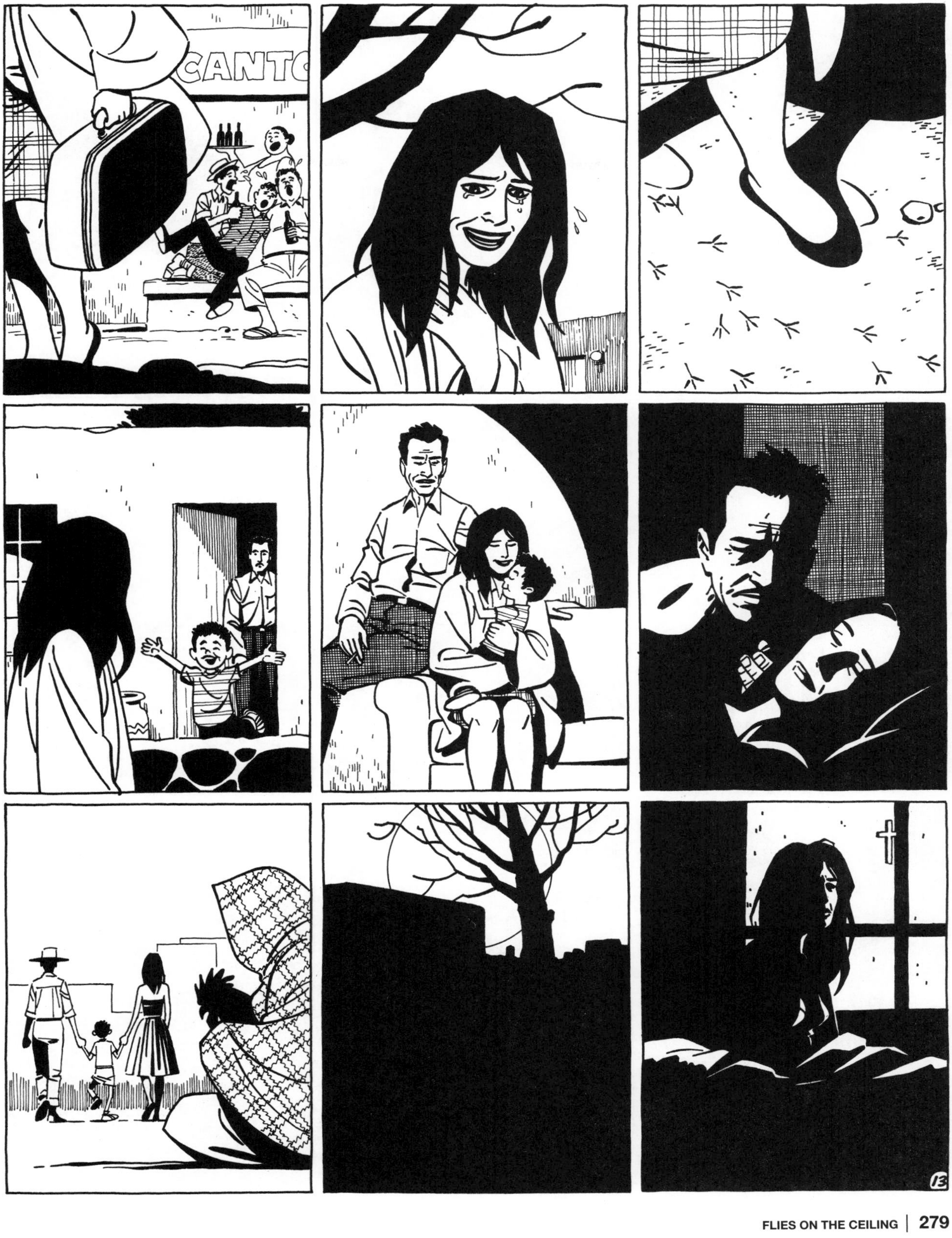
CANTO
13

ISABEL!

I THINK THIS TIME YOU OWE US AN EXPLANATION...

I WAS WRONG. IT'S NOT OVER. IT NEVER IS.

I-ISABEL, I DON'T PRETEND TO UNDERSTAND, BUT IF YOU'LL JUST...

WE...

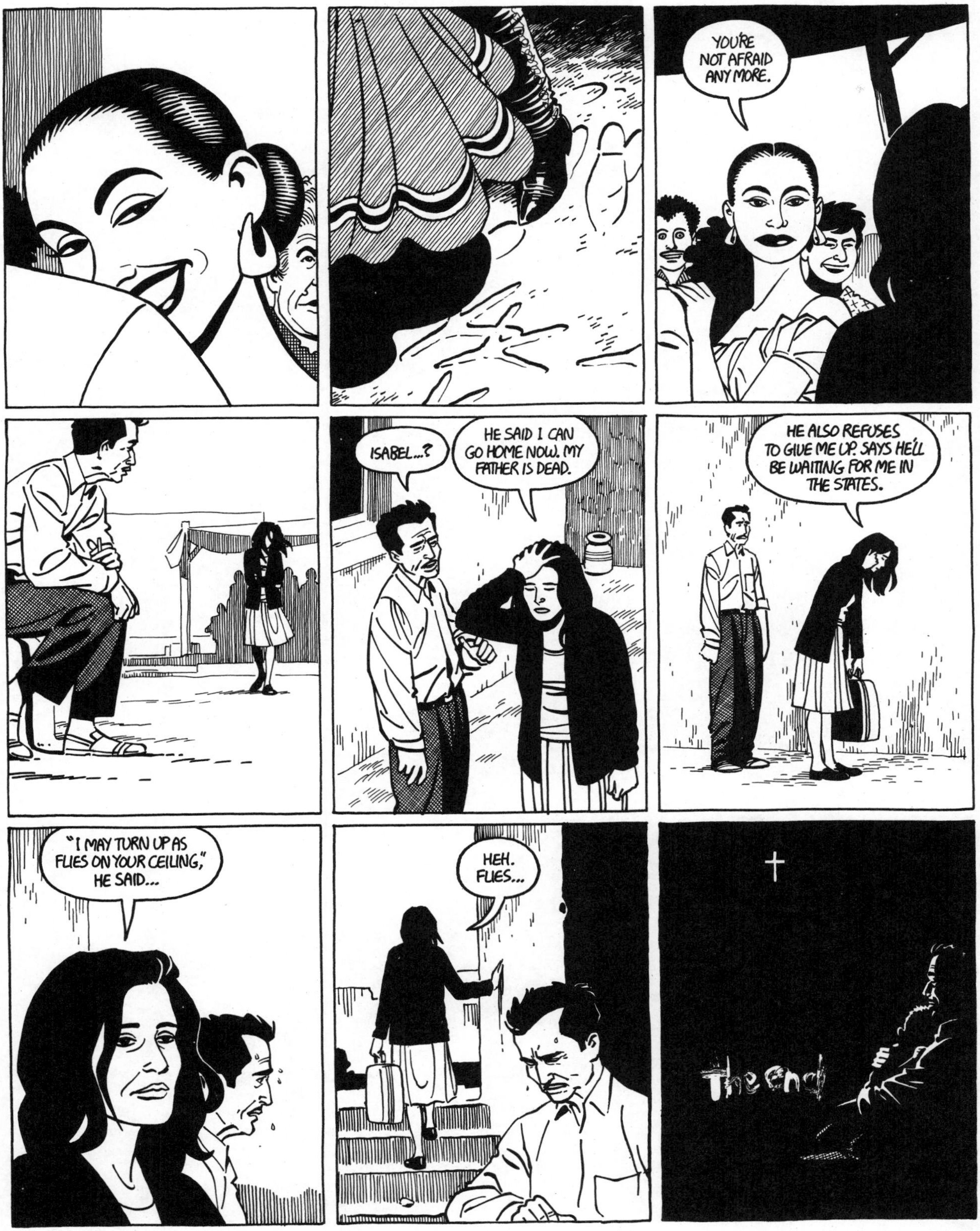
YOU'RE NOT AFRAID ANY MORE.
ISABEL...?
HE SAID I CAN GO HOME NOW. MY FATHER IS DEAD.
HE ALSO REFUSES TO GIVE ME UP. SAYS HE'LL BE WAITING FOR ME IN THE STATES.
"I MAY TURN UP AS FLIES ON YOUR CEILING," HE SAID...
HEH. FLIES...
The end

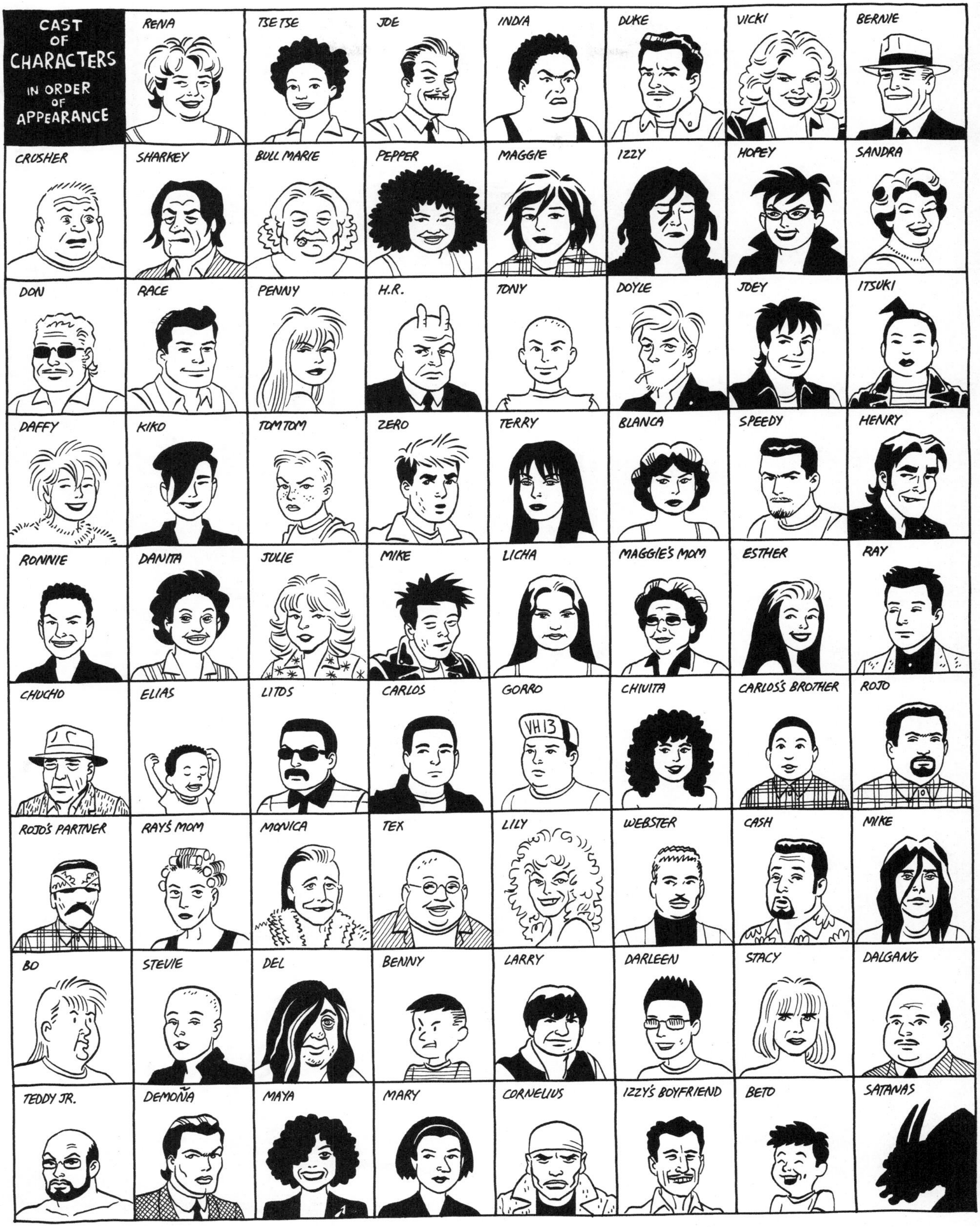

CAST OF CHARACTERS IN ORDER OF APPEARANCE
RENA
TSETSE
JOE
INDIA
DUKE
VICKI
BERNIE
CRUSHER
SHARKEY
BULL MARIE
PEPPER
MAGGIE
IZZY
HOPEY
SANDRA
DON
RACE
PENNY
H.R.
TONY
DOYLE
JOEY
ITSUKI
DAFFY
KIKO
TOMTOM
ZERO
TERRY
BLANCA
SPEEDY
HENRY
RONNIE
DANITA
JULIE
MIKE
LICHA
MAGGIE'S MOM
ESTHER
RAY
CHUCHO
ELIAS
LITOS
CARLOS
GORRO
VH13
CHIVITA
CARLOS'S BROTHER
ROJO
ROJO'S PARTNER
RAY'S MOM
MONICA
TEX
LILY
WEBSTER
CASH
MIKE
BO
STEVIE
DEL
BENNY
LARRY
DARLEEN
STACY
DALGANG
TEDDY JR.
DEMOÑA
MAYA
MARY
CORNELIUS
IZZY'S BOYFRIEND
BETO
SATANAS

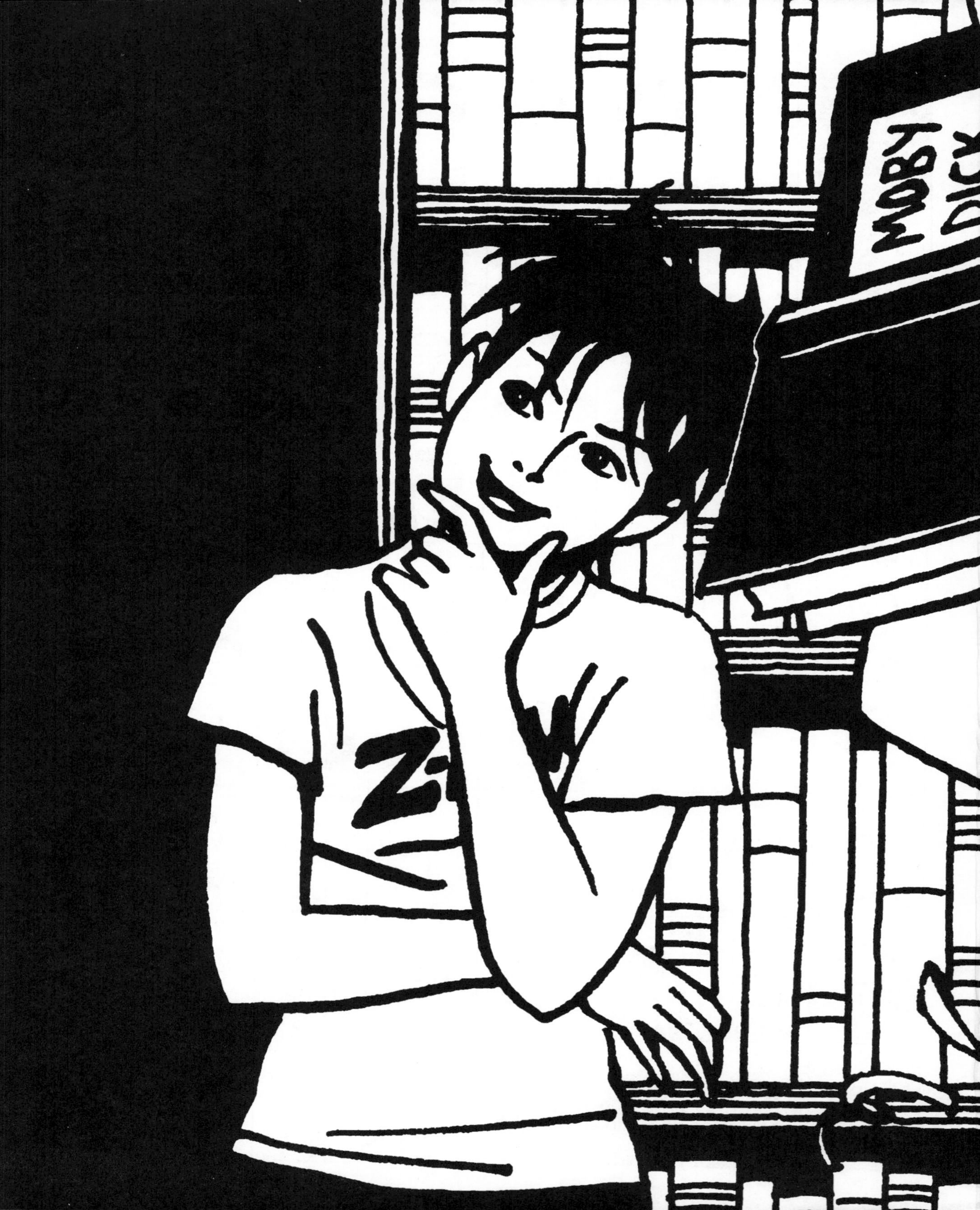
MOBY

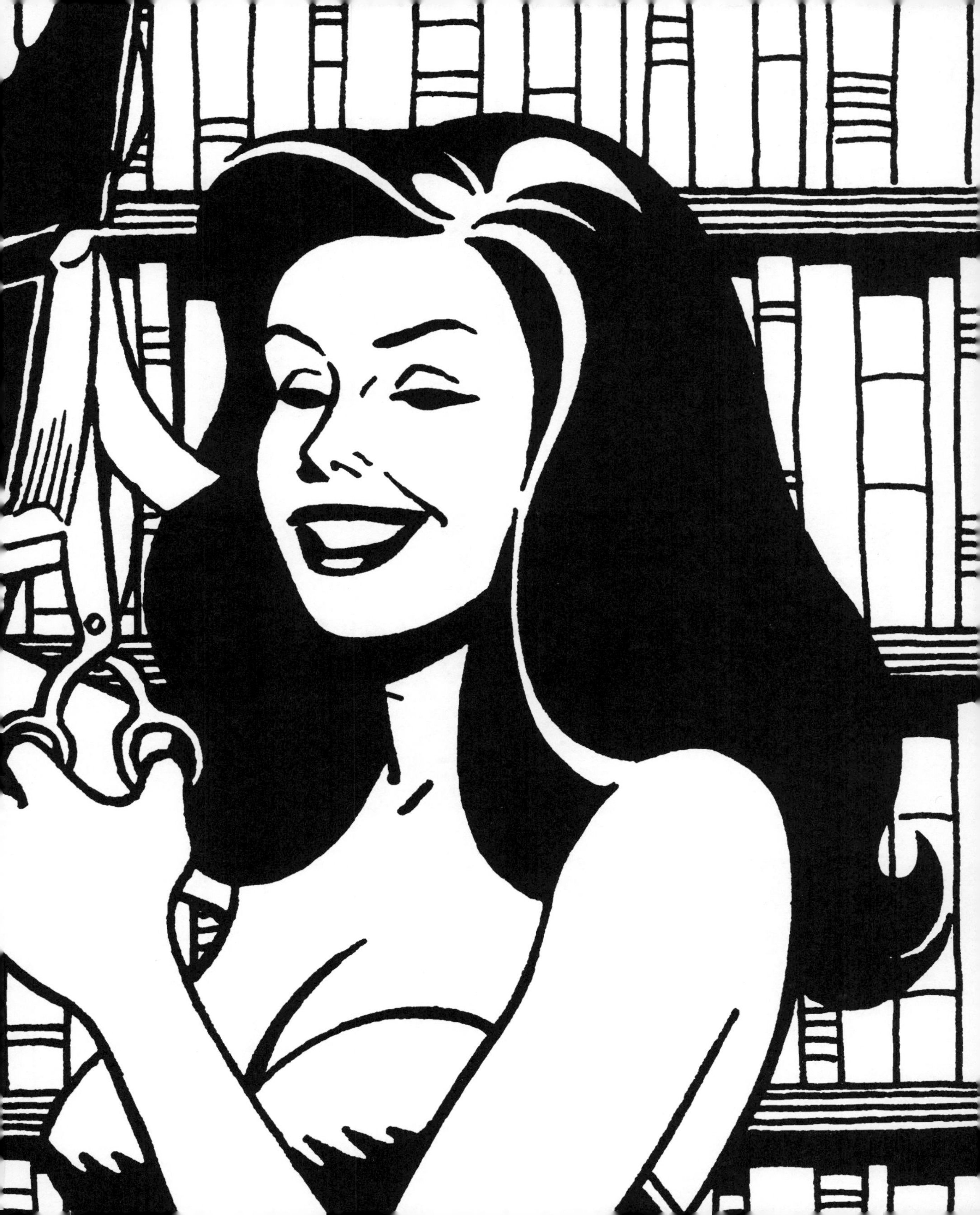

THE COMPLETE LOVE AND ROCKETS LIBRARY

This towering and beloved body of work remains a must-have for any discerning comics lover, and this comprehensive trade paperback series, along with the ongoing *Love and Rockets: The Magazine*, is the place to start.

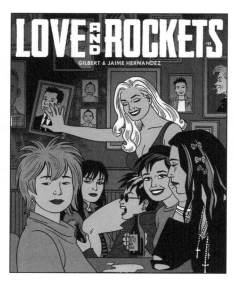

VOL. 1

MAGGIE THE MECHANIC
$18.99 | ISBN 978-1-56097-784-1
The ground zero stories of spunky Maggie, her brash best friend and sometimes lover Hopey, and their friends.

VOL. 2

HEARTBREAK SOUP
$18.99 | ISBN 978-1-56097-783-4
The first half of Gilbert's acclaimed magical-realist tales of Palomar, the Central American hamlet, and its memorable inhabitants.

VOL. 3

THE GIRL FROM H.O.P.P.E.R.S.
$18.99 | ISBN 978-1-56097-851-0
Centered on "The Death of Speedy," one of *L&R*'s peaks, with wrestling action and the love triangle of Maggie, Hopey, and Ray Dominguez.

VOL. 4

HUMAN DIASTROPHISM
$19.99 | ISBN 978-1-56097-848-0
Palomar's idyll is broken by a serial killer, the modern world's intrusions, and a shocking death.

VOL. 5

PERLA LA LOCA
$18.99 | ISBN 978-1-56097-883-1
Jaime drops a narrative bomb on Hopey (and us) in "Wig-wam Bam"; Maggie contends with her inner demons and... marriage?

VOL. 6

BEYOND PALOMAR
$18.99 | ISBN 978-1-56097-882-4
Collects two acclaimed graphic novels: "Poison River" (Luba's life story) and "Love and Rockets X" (an Altman-esque story set in L.A.).

VOL. 7

AMOR Y COHETES
$16.99 | ISBN 978-1-56097-926-5
All of the stand-alone, non-"Locas" and non-"Palomar" stories from the original *Love and Rockets* series (1982–1996).

VOL. 8

PENNY CENTURY
$18.99 | ISBN 978-1-60699-342-2
In "Whoa, Nellie!," Maggie settles in with her pro-wrestler aunt for a while, then it's back to chills and spills with the old gang.

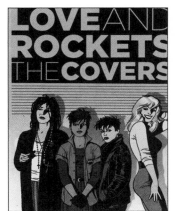

LOVE AND
ROCKETS
THE COVERS

LOVE AND ROCKETS: THE COVERS
$35.00 Hardcover
ISBN 978-1-60699-598-3
A beautiful, oversized art book featuring over 120 iconic comic covers (front & back) from the first 3 decades of *Love and Rockets*, collected for the first time in full color.

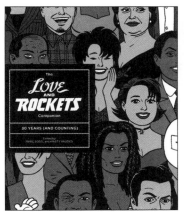

The
Love
AND
ROCKETS
Companion
30 YEARS (AND COUNTING)

THE LOVE AND ROCKETS COMPANION
$29.99 Paperback Original
ISBN 978-1-60699-579-2
An indispensable guide and massive love letter to the award-winning, world-renowned series. Interviews, family trees, timelines, unpublished art, bibliography, and more.

VOL. 9

ESPERANZA

ESPERANZA
$18.99 | ISBN 978-1-60699-449-8
An older and wiser Maggie faces down her demons, Hopey becomes a teacher, and Ray tussles with the volatile Vivian.

VOL. 10

LUBA and HER FAMILY
A LOVE AND ROCKETS BOOK

LUBA AND HER FAMILY
$18.99 | ISBN 978-1-60699-753-6
Luba and her clan move to America, where they become further intertwined with Luba's sisters (bodybuilder Petra and therapist/film star Fritz) and their families. Plus: Venus!

VOL. 11

OFELIA
A LOVE AND ROCKETS BOOK

OFELIA
$19.99 | ISBN 978-1-60699-806-9
Luba's family is settled comfortably in California, but when Ofelia threatens to write a book about Luba, past memories, secrets, resentments, and pain resurface.

VOL. 12

COMICS DEMENTIA
A LOVE AND ROCKETS BOOK

COMICS DEMENTIA
$19.99 | ISBN 978-1-60699-907-3
Collects treasures and rarities from outposts of the *Love and Rockets* galaxy, many of which have been available since their original appearance in comic shops in the 1990s.

VOL. 13

ANGELS and MAGPIES

ANGELS AND MAGPIES
$19.99 | ISBN 978-1-68396-090-4
Collects two of Jaime's best works of the past decade: *God and Science: Return of the Ti-Girls* and *The Love Bunglers*. Plus, "Maggie La Loca," and the little-seen short, "Gold Diggers of 1969"!

VOL. 14

THREE SISTERS

THREE SISTERS
$19.99 | ISBN 978-1-68396-114-7
Collecting material primarily from *Love and Rockets Vol. II* and *Luba's Comics and Stories*, Luba, Petra, and Fritz move on to the next phase of their lives, settling in Los Angeles — showbiz calls!

JAIME HERNANDEZ

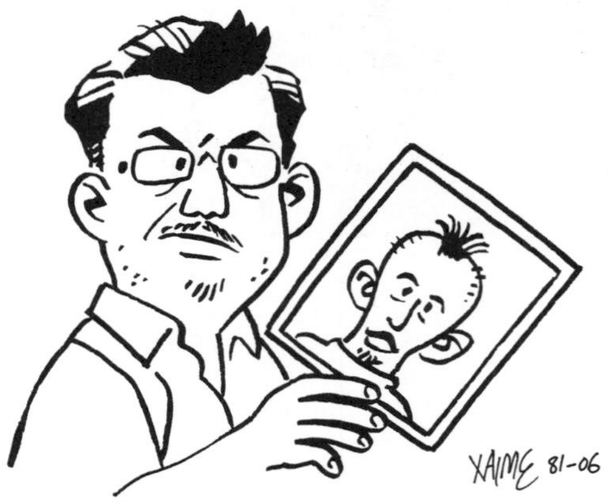
XAIME 81-06

JAIME HERNANDEZ was one of six siblings born and raised in Oxnard, California. His mother passed down a love of comics, which for Jaime became a passion rivaled only by his interest in the burgeoning punk rock scene of 1970s Southern California. Together with his brothers Gilbert and Mario, Jaime cocreated the ongoing comic book series *Love and Rockets* in 1981, which Gilbert and Jaime continue to this day. Jaime's work began as a perfect (if unlikely) synthesis of the anarchistic, do-it-yourself aesthetic of the punk scene and an elegant cartooning style that recalled masters such as Charles M. Schulz and Alex Toth. *Love and Rockets* has since evolved into one of the great bodies of American literary fiction, spanning four decades and countless high-water marks in the medium's history. In 2016, Hernandez won the prestigious *Los Angeles Times* Book Prize for his graphic novel, *The Love Bunglers*. In 2017, he (along with Gilbert) was inducted into the Will Eisner Comic Book Hall of Fame, and, in 2018, he released his first children's book, the Aesop Book Prize-winning *The Dragon Slayer: Folktales from Latin America*. He lives in Altadena, California, with his wife, Meg.